AF871587

# POWERS OF JUDGMENT

This is a book about conscience and moral clarity. It asks how some people keep their judgment steadfast even when many around them are swept away by conspiracy theories, moral panics, and murderous ideologies – or, on a smaller scale, by immersion in a corrupt and corrupting workplace culture. It asks about the surprising fragility of common sense, including moral common sense, and it asks where morality fits into a meaningful human life. Beyond this, the book asks about legal accountability for crimes committed when moral judgment fails on a vast and deadly scale. Hannah Arendt addressed all these questions in a profound and original way. Drawing on her published works, letters, diaries, and notes, David Luban offers clear accounts of Arendt's contributions to moral philosophy and international law, showing how her ideas about judgment and accountability remain crucially important to the moral and legal life of our century.

DAVID LUBAN is Distinguished University Professor at Georgetown University Law Center. He is the author of *Lawyers and Justice: An Ethical Study* (1988), *Legal Modernism* (1994), *Legal Ethics and Human Dignity* (2007), and *Torture, Power, and Law* (2014).

"At this perilous moment in our history, David Luban has delivered a work of exceptional importance. On one level, the book offers an astute and judicious study of Hannah Arendt's moral philosophy, brilliantly illuminating an overlooked dimension of the great thinker's oeuvre. But more distinctively, Luban proves the equal of Arendt, expounding a novel contribution to international legal theory and offering an indispensable guide to preserving our moral bearing and capacity for reasoned judgment in the darkest of times."

Lawrence Douglas, Amherst College

"*Powers of Judgment* compellingly shows how Arendt's reflections on evil, conscience, common sense, responsibility, and judgment can contribute to contemporary debates in moral philosophy and legal theory. David Luban's exemplary clarity and admirable erudition, combined with his humane care for our fractured world, are evident on every page of this magisterial book."

Kei Hiruta, Waseda University

"For decades, David Luban has been the most important moral philosopher working on legal issues of professional responsibility and legal accountability. Hannah Arendt has been his most important interlocutor. In *Powers of Judgment,* Luban brings Arendt alive as he interrogates, elaborates, and critiques her work. This is philosophy as it should be – never merely an exposition, but a dialogue between Luban and Arendt. Through that dialogue, he solves many of the puzzles that have troubled Arendt scholars. Most importantly, Luban brings Arendt into the twenty-first century. He begins and ends with Eichmann's trial in Jerusalem; in between, we get a powerfully illuminating inquiry into the most compelling issues of our day: moral judgment, conscience, evil, guilt, common sense, genocide, and international law."

Paul Kahn, Yale Law School

"There are two reasons to read this fine book. One is the illumination that David Luban provides about an important, but elusive, thinker, Hannah Arendt. The other is the illumination gained from engaging with the ideas of Luban himself, our deepest student of the 'professional responsibility' of lawyers. Both are concerned with the absolutely vital topic of what it means to think for oneself – and to judge others – with regard to the dilemmas created by tolerating or being complicit in what one realizes is political evil, and both should be attended to."

Sanford Levinson, University of Texas Law School and Department of Government

# POWERS OF JUDGMENT

## *Hannah Arendt's Moral and Legal Philosophy*

DAVID LUBAN
*Georgetown University*

CAMBRIDGE
UNIVERSITY PRESS

CAMBRIDGE
UNIVERSITY PRESS

Shaftesbury Road, Cambridge CB2 8EA, United Kingdom

One Liberty Plaza, 20th Floor, New York, NY 10006, USA

477 Williamstown Road, Port Melbourne, VIC 3207, Australia

314–321, 3rd Floor, Plot 3, Splendor Forum, Jasola District Centre, New Delhi – 110025, India

Cambridge University Press is part of Cambridge University Press & Assessment, a department of the University of Cambridge.

We share the University's mission to contribute to society through the pursuit of education, learning and research at the highest international levels of excellence.

www.cambridge.org
Information on this title: www.cambridge.org/9781009647465

DOI: 10.1017/9781009647458

© David Luban 2026

This publication is in copyright. Subject to statutory exception and to the provisions of relevant collective licensing agreements, no reproduction of any part may take place without the written permission of Cambridge University Press & Assessment.

When citing this work, please include a reference to the DOI 10.1017/9781009647458

First published 2026
Cover image: *Hannah Arendt*, Chantal Joffe, 2015. Oil on canvas, 46 x 38 x 2 cm, 18 1/8 x 15 x 3/4 in
© Chantal Joffe. Courtesy the artist and Victoria Miro.

*A catalogue record for this publication is available from the British Library*

*A Cataloging-in-Publication data record for this book is available from the Library of Congress*

ISBN 978-1-009-64746-5 Hardback

Cambridge University Press & Assessment has no responsibility for the persistence or accuracy of URLs for external or third-party internet websites referred to in this publication and does not guarantee that any content on such websites is, or will remain, accurate or appropriate.

For EU product safety concerns, contact us at Calle de José Abascal, 56, 1°, 28003 Madrid, Spain, or email eugpsr@cambridge.org

*In memory of Deborah L. Rhode (1952–2021)*
*Mentor, champion of justice, co-author, advisor, dear friend*

# *Contents*

# *Acknowledgments*

I wrote this book over ten years, and through that time I have been helped by more people than I can count. Special thanks go to Betsy Kuhn, who meticulously edited my first draft, and Arthur Evenchik, who did the same with the second. Their help went far beyond edits: Both pressed me on my arguments and unclarities. Arthur cross-checked quotations from Arendt against their sources and told me when I was misreading her; he spared me several errors. Betsy compiled the bibliography. Kei Hiruta generously read and commented on the second draft of Parts I–IV, and his enthusiasm cheered me immensely. Lawrence Douglas gave me valuable suggestions on the final draft.

Deborah Rhode, my friend of forty years, read the earliest chapters I wrote and guided me at a time when the project was still unformed. This book is dedicated to her memory. I owe a more intangible debt to Jonathan Bordo for his many years of encouragement.

Other friends and colleagues commented on individual chapters. Among them are Bill Blattner, Leora Bilsky, George Ellard, Miriam Galston, Gene Garver, Paul Gudel, Nick Hajdin, Deborah Hellman, Neha Jain, Maximo Langer, Marty Lederman, Elisa Massimino, Tony Kronman, Massimo La Torre, Sandy Levinson, Jim Loeffler, Douglas MacLean, Itamar Mann, Jim Nickel, Moria Paz, Amy Sepinwall, James G. Stewart, Melissa Stewart, Robert Wachbroit, Meredith Williams, and Molly Wilder. Thanks go as well to research assistants Jeremy Etelson, Gabriele Metzger, and David Snower. Special thanks to Allyson Rosenblum, who meticulously read and cite-checked the final draft.

I've had the good fortune of workshopping draft chapters at other universities: Boston University Law School, Cal Western Law School, the University of Florida Law School, Harvard Law School, the Interdisciplinary Center (Israel), New York University's Colloquium on Legal, Political, and Social Philosophy, the University of Pennsylvania's law and philosophy seminar, Princeton's Law and Public Affairs seminar, the University of Toronto, Trent University, University of Virginia Law School, Washington and Lee's international law workshop, Yale University's political theory workshop, and a symposium on an early version of Chapters 12 and 13 at the University of Catanzaro. Thanks go to my commentators at these workshops: Chief Justice (ret.) Aharon Barak, Mitchell Berman, Luís Pereira Coutinho, Moshe Halbertal, Liam Murphy, Clara Picker, Arthur Ripstein, Samuel Scheffler, and Anna Stilz.

I've presented most chapters at my home institution, Georgetown Law. Beyond those workshops, my debt to my Georgetown colleagues, and to our incredible support staff, goes beyond anything I can put in words. Special thanks to Julie O'Sullivan and Mitt Regan, with whom I have spent many hours talking about this book, and to Robin West for her years of encouragement. Law librarians Charles Bjork and Mabel Shaw have provided indispensable support.

My thinking about Arendt as a theorist of international law began in 2010, when Diane Amann, Jaya Ramji-Nogales, and Beth van Schaack invited me to write about her for a symposium on women in international criminal law. The papers were published as a special issue of the *International Criminal Law Review*, in honor of Judge Patricia Wald. The participants' enthusiasm made me recognize how germane Arendt's writing is to the modern project of international criminal justice, and it launched me on the book's final chapters.

Since 2016, I have worked with the Fellowships at Auschwitz for the Study of Professional Ethics (FASPE), which brings together early-career practitioners from six fields for intensive reflection on the ethics of their professions. Done on site in Berlin, Krakow, and Auschwitz, participants study the roles their professions played in the Third Reich. The program offers a stark reminder of how swiftly and insidiously moral judgment can erode, including among highly trained professionals. FASPE's mission harmonizes with themes in this book, and my experiences on its law faculty have shaped my ideas. I am grateful to team members Maya Dobler, Eric Muller, Rebecca Scott, Tim Sperling, Thorsten Wagner, and especially to FASPE's visionary founder, David Goldman.

For twelve years I had the singular honor of serving as Distinguished Chair in Ethics at the Stockdale Center for Ethical Leadership, United States Naval Academy. Special thanks go to the Stockdale Center's directors, Art Athens and Joe Thomas, and especially to Ed Barrett, the Stockdale Center's research director, my co-director in the research seminar, and constant supporter.

Thanks as well to Hilary Gaskin, my editor at Cambridge University Press, whose advice and unflagging support have been essential from the moment I approached her with the project. I am also grateful to senior editorial assistant Abi Sears; to my superb copyeditor Dan Harding; and to the Press's production team, Liz Davey and Hariharan Jayamoorthy. All of them have smoothed the process of bringing the book to print.

As always, my greatest debt is to my wife, Judy Lichtenberg. Judy read my chapters, and she gave me confidence again and again that I could actually finish the book. She patiently put up with my fretting and self-doubts, and her love sustains me in every way.

Along with thank-yous, I must include an apology. The literature on Arendt is vast, and I have read only a fraction of it; early on, I realized that I would have to choose between reading and writing. Undoubtedly, others have anticipated my arguments, both substantive and interpretive. To those I overlooked, I apologize for not having cited and appreciated your work.

*

This book draws on several of my published papers, although my views have changed regarding some of their conclusions.

"Hannah Arendt as a Theorist of International Law" (chapters 14 and 15), *International Criminal Law Review* 11 (2011).
"Arendt on the Crime of Crimes" (chapters 12 and 13), *Ratio Juris* 28 (3) (2015).
"Complicity and Lesser Evils: A Tale of Two Lawyers" (chapter 14), *Georgetown Journal of Legal Ethics* 34(3), (2021).

Material from works by Hannah Arendt are used with the following permissions:

Excerpts from *Responsibility and Judgment* by Hannah Arendt, copyright © 2003 by The Literary Trust of Hannah Arendt and Jerome Kohn. Used by permission of Schocken Books, an imprint of the Knopf Doubleday Publishing Group, a division of Penguin Random House LLC. All rights reserved.
*Denktagebuch 1950–1973* by Hannah Arendt. Copyright © Hannah Arendt Bluecher Literary Trust, New York, 2002, and Piper Verlag GmbH, Munchen/Berlin 2002. Reprinted by permission of Georges Borchardt, Inc., on behalf of the Hannah Arendt Bluecher Literary Trust. All rights reserved.

*Essays in Understanding, 1930–1954* by Hannah Arendt. Copyright © 1994 by Hannah Arendt. Reprinted by permission of Georges Borchardt, inc. on behalf of the Hannah Arendt Bluecher Literary Trust. All rights reserved.

*Within Four Walls: The Correspondence between Hannah Arendt and Heinrich Blücher, 1936–1968*, edited by Lotte Kohler, translated by Peter Constantine. Copyright © 1994 by Hannah Arendt. Reprinted by permission of Georges Borchardt, inc. on behalf of the Hannah Arendt Bluecher Literary Trust. All rights reserved.

*Hannah Arendt Karl Jaspers Correspondence 1926–1929*, edited by Lotte Kohler and Hans Saner. Copyright © R. Piper GmbH & Co. KG, Munchen 1985, © Hannah Arendt Literary Trust, © Hans Saner, English translation copyright © 1992 by Harcourt Brace Jovanovich, Inc., All rights reserved.

*The Human Condition*. Copyright © 1958, University of Chicago Press.

Excerpts from *Eichmann in Jerusalem* by Hannah Arendt, copyright © 1963, 1964 by Hannah Arendt; copyright renewed © 1991, 1992 by Lotte Kohler. Used by permission of Viking Books, an imprint of Penguin Publishing Group, a division of Penguin Random House LLC. All rights reserved.

The cover painting, Chantal Joffe's *Hannah Arendt* (2015)(oil on canvas, 46 x 38 x 2 cm), is used courtesy of the artist and Victoria Miro. © Chantal Joffe.

# *Abbreviations of Frequently Cited Sources*

Most of Arendt's essays cited in this book are reprinted in anthologies, either by her during her lifetime or posthumously by her literary executors. In these cases, I cite the essay by title and the anthology by abbreviation. For example, the essay "Collective Responsibility" is published in *Responsibility and Judgment*, which I abbreviate as *RJ*. I cite the essay as "Collective Responsibility" in *RJ*. I don't use abbreviations for the titles of infrequently cited books and correspondences.

A few essays are cited throughout the text and get their own abbreviations – for example, "Some Questions of Moral Philosophy," in *Responsibility and Judgment*, is SQMP.

Full publication details are given in the first reference to works and in the bibliography. I do not cross-cite to the Critical Edition of Arendt's complete works, because most works were still in preparation as of 2025.

## Books and Anthologies by Hannah Arendt

| | |
|---|---|
| *BPF* | *Between Past and Future: Eight Exercises in Political Thought* |
| *CR* | *Crises of the Republic* |
| *DTB* | *Denktagebuch 1950–1973*. Referred to in the text as "Thought Diary." Entries are listed by notebook number, entry number, date, and page number in the published collection—thus, "*DTB* II.31 (January 1951), 54" is entry number 31 from Notebook II, January 1951, page 54 of the published version. |
| *EJ* | *Eichmann in Jerusalem: A Report on the Banality of Evil* |
| *EU* | *Essays in Understanding 1930–1954* |
| *HC* | *The Human Condition* |
| *JW* | *The Jewish Writings* |
| *Kant Lectures* | *Lectures on Kant's Political Philosophy* |

| | |
|---|---|
| *MDT* | *Men in Dark Times* |
| *OR* | *On Revolution* |
| *OT* | *The Origins of Totalitarianism* (2nd ed.) |
| *PP* | *The Promise of Politics* |
| *RJ* | *Responsibility and Judgment* |
| *T* | *Thinking* (part one of *The Life of the Mind*) |
| *TWB* | *Thinking without a Banister: Essays in Understanding 1953–1975* |
| *W* | *Willing* (part two of *The Life of the Mind*) |

## Frequently Cited Correspondences

| | |
|---|---|
| *BF* | *Between Friends: The Correspondence of Hannah Arendt and Mary McCarthy 1949–1975* |
| *HA-GS* | *The Correspondence of Hannah Arendt and Gershom Scholem* |
| *HA-KJ* | *Hannah Arendt–Karl Jaspers Correspondence 1926–1969* |
| *WFW* | *Within Four Walls: The Correspondence between Hannah Arendt and Heinrich Blücher, 1936–1968* |

## Frequently Cited Essays

| | |
|---|---|
| PRUD | "Personal Responsibility under Dictatorship," in *RJ* |
| SQMP | "Some Questions of Moral Philosophy," in *RJ* |
| TMC | "Thinking and Moral Considerations," in *RJ* |
| TP | "Truth and Politics," in *BPF* |

## Frequently Cited Works by Others

For works of Aristotle, I use the standard Bekker numbers rather than citing page numbers in any specific edition or translation, but when relevant I also cite the translation from which I'm quoting. Similarly, I use the standard Stephanus numbers for Plato's dialogues, and in citing Kant I use the canonical citation form: the volume number from the Prussian Academy edition of Kant's complete works (standardly abbreviated as Ak.) and the page number, separated by a colon. The exception is the *Critique of Pure Reason*, where I use the usual A and B page numbers referring to the two editions; that's because some translations print the A and B references, but not the Ak. references, in the margins.

| | |
|---|---|
| *CJ* | Kant, *Critique of Judgment* |
| *CPR* | Kant, *Critique of Pure Reason* |
| *Eichmann Interrogated* | *Eichmann Interrogated: Transcripts from the Archives of the Israeli Police* |
| Eichmann Trial Proceedings | State of Israel Ministry of Justice, *The Trial of Adolf Eichmann: Record of Proceedings* (6 volumes) |
| *Götzen* | Adolf Eichmann, *Götzen: Die Autobiografie von Adolf Eichmann*. I give double page references to *Götzen*. The first is to the online version, which includes the page numbers in Eichmann's manuscripts. The second is to the 2016 print version. |
| N.E. | Aristotle, *Nicomachaean Ethics* |
| Stangneth | Bettina Stangneth, *Eichmann before Jerusalem: The Unexamined Life of a Mass Murderer* |
| Young-Bruehl | Elizabeth Young-Bruehl, *Hannah Arendt: For Love of the World* |

# *Introduction*
## *Hannah Arendt, the Philosopher of Judgment*

This is a book about conscience and moral clarity. It asks how some people keep their judgment steadfast even when multitudes around them are swept away by conspiracy theories, moral panics, and murderous ideologies – or, on a smaller scale, by immersion in a corrupt and corrupting workplace culture. It asks about the surprising fragility of common sense, including moral common sense. It asks where morality fits into a meaningful human life.

Beyond this, the book asks about legal accountability for crimes committed when moral judgment fails on a vast and deadly scale. How should the law judge perpetrators who commit crimes against humanity, not out of greed or malice but because their leaders and peers tell them it is the right thing to do, and their larger society seems to agree? Who gets to judge, to condemn, and to punish? On what legal and moral basis? What makes some crimes the concern of all humanity? Who speaks for humanity? These questions lie at the heart of international criminal justice.

Hannah Arendt is the most important philosopher to have addressed all these questions. To some readers this will seem obvious; to others, much less so. Arendt had no legal training and wrote very little on law; and her turn to moral philosophy came only in her final years, mostly in manuscripts published after her death. She never developed her views on either subject in a systematic or rigorous way, and her writing never engages with academic literatures.[1] Arendt herself flatly denied that she was a philosopher, "nor do I believe that I have been accepted in the circle of philosophers." This last point is plainly true among moral philosophers trained in the analytic tradition.[2] Her conclusions are often unusual, and some are untenable.

[1] Arendt admits that her failure to engage with her peers is a fault. "Hannah Arendt on Hannah Arendt," in Hannah Arendt, *Thinking without a Banister: Essays in Understanding 1953–1975*, ed. Jerome Kohn (Schocken Books, 2018) (henceforth *TWB*), 464, 472.

[2] "'What Remains? The Language Remains': A Conversation with Günter Gaus," in Hannah Arendt, *Essays in Understanding 1930–1954*, ed. Jerome Kohn (Harcourt Brace, 1994) (henceforth *EU*), 1. Arendt insists that her profession is political theory, not philosophy.

This book nevertheless proceeds from the conviction that Arendt has light to shed on matters of supreme importance to the moral and legal life of our century. To show this, I reconstruct her main lines of thought from scattered texts and letters. Where Arendt's arguments are incomplete, I flesh them out; where they are weak, I investigate whether they can be strengthened. Throughout, I highlight their points of contact with the concerns of (broadly) analytic and postanalytic moral philosophers, and with jurists in today's project of international criminal justice. In some chapters I discuss contemporary events, viewed through an Arendtian lens.

I am not writing principally for Arendt enthusiasts, although I hope they will find the book instructive. My aim is to reach readers who may know little about Arendt beyond her renown as a public intellectual and theorist of totalitarianism – readers who are perhaps skeptical of someone who gets invoked so often as a kind of oracle (a role Arendt would have detested); in short, readers who would like to engage with what she actually argued.

*

When she died of a sudden heart attack in 1975, Arendt had just begun a new book, but she got only as far as its title page, found in her typewriter. The title was *Judging*, and the book would have been the capstone of her three-part *The Life of the Mind*, after *Thinking* and *Willing*.

By "judging," Arendt means sizing up deeds and courses of action without subsuming them under general rules.[3] In her view, the ability to judge right and wrong in cloudy circumstances is our core moral power, more important than reasoning about rules and principles, and more important than casuistry or philosophical argument. Good judgment is crucial for actors deliberating in the moment, but it also matters for historians and jurists who judge actors and their deeds after the fact. Arendt's effort to understand both these powers of judgment, that of the actor and that of the spectator, lies at the heart of her moral philosophy.[4]

Seemingly abstract questions about the powers of judgment had special urgency for Arendt. As a young woman, she witnessed the collapse of moral judgment on a monumental scale in the early months of the Third

[3] Hannah Arendt, "Thinking and Moral Considerations" (henceforth TMC), in Arendt, *Responsibility and Judgment*, ed. Jerome Kohn (Schocken, 2003) (henceforth *RJ*), 188–89; Arendt, "Personal Responsibility under Dictatorship," in *RJ*, 41 (henceforth PRUD); Hannah Arendt, *Thinking* (henceforth *T*) (part one of *The Life of the Mind*, one-volume ed.) (Harcourt Brace, 1971), 69.

[4] Here I differ from a leading analysis of Arendt's moral philosophy, Deirdre Lauren Mahony, *Hannah Arendt's Ethics* (Bloomsbury, 2018). Mahony doubts that judgment plays a significant role in Arendt's ethics, Mahony, *Hannah Arendt's Ethics*, 87, 136.

Reich. In a matter of weeks, erstwhile anti-Nazis decided that Hitler wasn't all that bad. Intellectuals concocted rationalizations for Nazism ("Completely fantastic and interesting and complicated things! Things far beyond the ordinary level!" she recalled bitterly[5]). Stern sentinels of moral rules switched smoothly from Christian or Kantian rules to Nazi rules. They were quick to mold themselves to the new order, and their pliability disgusted her.[6] What she saw up close was "the almost universal breakdown, not of personal responsibility, but of personal *judgment* in the early stages of the Nazi regime."[7] It was a step toward total moral collapse in the decade that followed, not only in Germany but throughout occupied Europe. (Arendt herself fled Germany in the late summer of 1933, after an arrest and eight-day police interrogation.) Stalin's USSR experienced a parallel collapse under the Great Terror, as neighbors denounced neighbors and the Bolshevik faithful treated transparent lies and conspiracy theories as indubitable facts. Never had judgment seemed so fragile; never had it mattered more.

After the war came questions of accountability – for of course the magnitude of the Nazi crimes was known even before the liberation of the camps made them vivid. Personal judgment may have collapsed in the Third Reich, but personal responsibility never went away, much as the perpetrators wished it would. Arendt insisted on this point, and eventually she came to view criminal courts as champions of individual responsibility against evasions and excuses.[8]

From afar Arendt followed the Nuremberg trials, and she was keenly interested in her mentor Karl Jaspers's celebrated lectures on German guilt, published in 1946. The previous year she published her own powerful essay on "organized guilt," which strongly hints at the idea of an international criminal law.[9] Hopes for a new international legal order make brief but striking appearances in her first English book, *The Origins of Totalitarianism.* At the time, though, Arendt had little interest in pursuing legal issues or investigating the role of courts and tribunals. That came later, once she recognized that courts can be institutional embodiments of spectator judgment.[10]

5 Arendt, "'What Remains? The Language Remains'," in *EU*, 11. She adds: "I found that grotesque."

6 Arendt, "Some Questions of Moral Philosophy" (henceforth SQMP), in *RJ*, 138–39.

7 PRUD, 24.

8 Hannah Arendt, *Eichmann in Jerusalem: A Report on the Banality of Evil*, revised ed. (Viking, 1965) (henceforth *EJ*), 8–9, 20, 286, 289; Arendt, "Collective Responsibility," in *RJ*, 148.

9 Karl Jaspers, *The Question of German Guilt*, 2nd ed., trans. E. B. Ashton (Fordham University Press, 2001/1947). Arendt's essay "Organized Guilt and Universal Responsibility," in *EU*, was first published in *Jewish Frontiers* under the title "German Guilt."

10 PRUD, 21–22.

Through the 1950s Arendt likewise showed no interest in moral philosophy. She seemed at times to despise it. A 1951 diary entry complains about the "ghostly lifelessness of morality and moral thought," and even near the end of her life she held that invoking moral principles in everyday matters is usually a fraud (a view I reject).[11] Moral philosophy's "endless comparisons and rational elucidations" are "really like a game."[12]

Her ambivalence toward morality itself (as distinct from moral philosophy) comes from a deeper source: a worry that people whose highest concern is their own purity will sideline themselves from the messy fight against evil. In another diary entry, she calls Kant's categorical imperative "the morality of powerlessness," which abandons "responsibility to the world."[13] It might be said that she mistrusted morality, but for moral reasons. Notably, *The Human Condition* (1958), her philosophical masterpiece, catalogues and analyzes half a dozen basic conditions of our active life – but morality is not one of them.

*

Eventually, though, Arendt did turn to moral and legal philosophy. It was the trial of Adolf Eichmann for crimes of the Holocaust that prompted her investigations into the nature of moral judgment and the foundations of criminal law. Nearly all her writing on the powers of judgment came in the twelve years after she published *Eichmann in Jerusalem: A Report on the Banality of Evil* in 1963 – which itself came twelve years after *Origins*. In that respect, *Eichmann in Jerusalem* marked an inflection point in Arendt's thought – not a break, but an important new direction. For that reason, I begin this book by examining her encounter with the trial, and I return to it at the end.

Today, more than sixty years after his trial, Eichmann is no longer a household name, so perhaps a reminder is in order. Eichmann was an SS lieutenant colonel and self-described "expert" on the "Jewish question." He oversaw the forced emigration of Austrian and Czech Jews during the period when Nazi policy was ethnic cleansing rather than mass murder. After the policy turned to genocide, Eichmann was the man in charge of

11 Hannah Arendt, *Denktagebuch 1950–1973*, ed. Ursula Ludz and Ingeborg Nordmann (Piper, 2002) (henceforth *DTB*), II.31 (January 1951), 54; SQMP, 104. See Chapter 3.

12 Arendt to Heinrich Blücher, April 11, 1952, in *Within Four Walls: The Correspondence between Hannah Arendt and Heinrich Blücher, 1936–1968*, ed. Lotte Kohler, trans. Pete Constantine (Harcourt, 2000) (henceforth *WFW*), 154.

13 *DTB*, Kant-Notebook (April 28–29, 1963), 818. She echoes and elaborates the latter thought in "Collective Responsibility," in *RJ*, 156.

transporting Europe's Jews to death camps, which he did with ruthless efficiency. In 1944, he and his men sent hundreds of thousands of Hungarian Jews to Auschwitz in the space of just four months. Although Eichmann was not a "top Nazi" on the organizational chart, he was the highest-ranking Nazi whose sole responsibility was the destruction of the European Jews, and he played an essential role in the murder of millions. After the war Eichmann hid in Germany for a few years and then escaped to Argentina. There he lived and worked under an alias, and hung out with the Nazi ex-pat community and their sympathizers. In 1960 Israeli agents kidnapped him in Buenos Aires and brought him to Jerusalem to stand trial for genocide against the Jewish people as well as for other crimes. The court rejected his superior orders and "I was only a cog in the machine" defenses. Eichmann was convicted in 1961 and executed on June 1, 1962.

His electrifying trial featured testimony by many Holocaust survivors and received worldwide attention. Arendt covered the trial as a journalist for *The New Yorker*, and she concluded – *very* controversially – that Eichmann was neither a fanatic nor a sadistic, satanic monster. In her estimation, he was an ordinary man, distinguished only by professional ambition and extreme shallowness.[14] In her famous phrase, he represented the *banality of evil*. I explore the Eichmann case and the accuracy of her diagnosis in Chapters 1 and 2. It is the gateway to the investigations that follow.

Arendt argued that perpetrators like Eichmann pose a fundamental challenge to both law and morality. To put someone on trial demands "that human beings be capable of telling right from wrong even when all they have to guide them is their own judgment."[15] Eichmann, however, was "an average, 'normal' person, neither feeble-minded nor indoctrinated nor cynical," who seemingly lacked that ability.[16] He was a mass murderer but personally exceptional only in his shallowness. How can that be? And how can the law condemn someone who committed his crimes "under circumstances that make it well-nigh impossible for him to know or to feel that he is doing wrong," because his government and everyone he looked up to assured him that murdering race enemies is right?[17] What are the implications for lesser and less obvious forms of evil? The Eichmann trial, she concluded, "touches upon one of the central moral questions of all time, namely upon the nature and function of human judgment."[18] These words, from the closing pages of *Eichmann in Jerusalem*, were a promissory

[14] Some distinguished historians disagree, as I discuss in Chapter 2. [15] *EJ*, 294–95.
[16] *EJ*, 26. [17] *EJ*, 276. [18] *EJ*, 294–95.

note. The book itself does not discuss the nature and function of judgment, nor does it offer a theory of evil. Those would come later.

Moral judgment is "an independent human faculty, unsupported by law and public opinion, that judges in full spontaneity every deed and intent anew whenever the occasion arises."[19] One problem lies in understanding how moral judgment so defined is even possible, given that ordinarily we do *not* judge in full spontaneity and unsupported by public opinion. Just the opposite: from childhood on, we cultivate judgment through the company and examples of others, and we take our bearings from the conventional wisdom of those around us – as Arendt recognized and freely acknowledged.[20] How is judgment in Arendt's more demanding sense possible? How are we able to break with conventional wisdom in dark times when, as Arendt liked to say, the chips are down? For Kant, breaking from conventional wisdom – thinking for yourself – is the very definition of enlightenment. Kant blamed the failure to do so on laziness and cowardice.[21] Arendt, living through the collapse of enlightenment in nations neither lazy nor cowardly, diagnosed the failure differently. She offered a paradoxical conjecture: The inability to judge for yourself is somehow connected with the inability to think from the standpoint of others. Her moral philosophy is an effort to make good on that conjecture.

It was her observation of Eichmann that steered her to this insight. The more she pored over his interrogation transcript and trial testimony, the more convinced she became that he was incapable of thinking from the standpoint of others, which in her view is the defining characteristic of both thought and conscience.[22] Could it be, she wondered, that thinking from the standpoint of others is necessary for sound judgment that reaches moral conclusions without deriving them from public opinion, conventional rules, or laws of reason? Thinking of this kind occurs in the back and forth of inner dialogue. Is there a theoretical connection between dialogical thinking and the powers of judgment? She poses the question in her 1971 lecture "Thinking and Moral Considerations," and her answer is a tentative yes. Alongside the banality of evil, this *thinking–judging connection* is central to her moral philosophy. Exploring this connection – and explaining what it has to do with the banality of evil – are the main tasks of Chapters 3, 4, and 5. Arendt herself drew the thinking–judging

[19] PRUD, 41; *T*, 177. [20] *T*, 71.

[21] Kant, "An Answer to the Question: What Is Enlightenment?," Ak. 8:35. Many editions; I use Kant, *Practical Philosophy (The Cambridge Edition of the Works of Immanuel Kant)*, ed. and trans. Mary Gregor (Cambridge University Press, 1996), 17.

[22] *EJ*, 49.

connection in the settings that preoccupied her: "emergency situations," "times of crises when, so to speak, we find ourselves with our back against the wall."[23] When common sense collapses on a mass scale, as in the Third Reich and Stalin's USSR, following the moral rules favored by public opinion is disastrous, and we have nothing to fall back on but our own judgment.

In contrast with the importance she placed on moral judgment in emergencies, Arendt suspected that invoking moral principles in everyday affairs is hypocrisy and fraud – mere moralizing. Apparently, she thought that in daily life conventional morality will settle matters.[24] I disagree. In Chapter 3, I respond that hard moral dilemmas arise in everyday life as well as in emergencies. The stakes may be lower (but not always), and our backs may not be against the wall. But that hardly obviates the need for moral judgment even in mundane matters, for a simple reason: Conventional morality is less determinate than Arendt seems to suppose – it doesn't settle hard questions. Recognizing that moral perplexities are everywhere implies that Arendt's ideas about thought and judgment apply more widely than she herself acknowledged – which, in my view, makes their study especially worthwhile. Arendt's focus in her moral philosophy, as Deirdre Mahony writes, is "ethics after Auschwitz."[25] Mahony is right, but I proceed in the conviction that the philosophy reaches beyond the shadow of Auschwitz. Questions about judgment as a central moral power are obviously not a matter of purely historical interest. They are urgent today, both in public and private life.

*

It's useful to set Arendt's investigation of judgment within the broader context of her work. Her two major pre-Eichmann books, *The Origins of Totalitarianism* and *The Human Condition*, don't discuss judgment at all, at least not under that label. However, a running theme in *Origins* is the collapse of common sense – including moral common sense – in the twentieth-century totalitarian movements, whose members rushed to embrace transparent lies and bizarre conspiracy theories, eventually carrying millions of nonmembers in their train. To be unable to distinguish truth from crackpottery is a sign of skewed judgment or something worse: the willful suspension of judgment, what in Chapter 6 I call *culpable credulousness* – a willingness or even eagerness to be duped. As Arendt

[23] SQMP, 122. [24] SQMP, 104. [25] Mahony, *Hannah Arendt's Ethics*, 1.

put it: "Mass propaganda discovered that its audience was ready at all times to believe the worst, no matter how absurd, and did not particularly object to being deceived because it held every statement to be a lie anyhow."[26] Culpable credulousness becomes especially dangerous when the conspiracy theories tell you that innocent people are out to harm you and your kind. That makes it easy for toxic leaders to repackage ethnic cleansing and murder as justified self-defense.

It is hardly necessary to point out that conspiracy theories and audacious lies continue to blight our politics today. I devote Chapter 6 to examining the collapse of common sense through the lens of *Origins*. I set Arendt's razor-sharp diagnosis side by side with its contemporary manifestations and recent philosophical efforts to analyze them. In *Origins*, though, Arendt doesn't theorize about judgment as such, or explore its connection with common sense.

*The Human Condition* poses a tougher interpretive problem. Not only does the book not discuss judgment; it barely discusses morality. In *The Human Condition*, Arendt recognizes only two moral precepts: the injunction to keep promises and the injunction to forgive wrongdoing. These, Arendt argues, make human action possible by binding us and releasing us. Beyond these precepts, Arendt downplays not only what Bernard Williams (in a similar skeptical spirit) calls "the peculiar institution" that reduces moral life to a system of obligations and permissions; she also neglects the moral emotions that make us human.[27] The richer tapestry of moral life barely makes an appearance in the book, and a few passages suggest an amoralist outlook. I call this absence the Case of the Missing Morality. It's especially jarring because *Origins* focuses relentlessly on radical evil and its assault on human dignity, and its tone of controlled moral fury is impossible to miss. In contrast, the phrase "radical evil" appears just once in *The Human Condition*. It is not a theme of the book, and moral fury is absent.

Yet beyond the Case of the Missing Morality, *The Human Condition* turns out to be rich in ethical content in an older sense. In Chapters 8 and 9, I offer a close reading that unearths an argumentative throughline addressing the question that animates ancient ethics: What is the best life for human beings? Chapter 9 also explains why her neglect of morality leaves Arendt with problems that can't be solved without the fuller appreciation of moral judgment that she sought in her later works.

[26] Hannah Arendt, *The Origins of Totalitarianism*, 2nd ed. (Harcourt, 1976) (henceforth *OT*), 382.
[27] Bernard Williams, *Ethics and the Limits of Philosophy* (Fontana Press/Collins, 1985).

Possibly Arendt was already thinking along those lines: Glimmerings of her theory of judgment appear in a few pages of a manuscript written soon after *The Human Condition* (unpublished in her lifetime).[28] But it was clearly the Eichmann trial that turned Arendt to moral philosophy, where she elaborated the thinking–judging connection and the banality of evil.

*

Unsurprisingly, the Eichmann trial also spurred her thinking about how the law can address atrocity crimes. The epilogue to *Eichmann in Jerusalem* analyzes key legal issues in some depth. Before then, Arendt wrote very little about law, and nothing about criminal law. To be sure, *Origins*, composed in the early postwar period, calls for a "new law on earth" to protect human dignity; but it never details what that law would be. *Origins* also contains a scathing critique of human rights law, and it introduces the fascinating concept of the "right to have rights," which she believes human rights law ignores at its peril. Her critique and the "right to have rights" remain influential in current debates about statelessness and immigration; but their connection with criminal law and accountability is at best indirect. Still, the connection is there, and I draw it out in the final chapters of this book.

Chapter 10 explores Arendt's human rights critique and her conception of human dignity. She rejects the view that human dignity is an inherent property of individual human beings; rather, it is a status we confer on others by recognizing them as our fellows. Arendt calls this stance the "idea of humanity," and making it a reality – what I call the project of *constructing humanity* – is the task of the "new law on earth." Implicit in her reflections is a view of state sovereignty that brings her close to modern formulations that go under the label "sovereignty as responsibility" (as distinct from sovereignty as unfettered control over people and territory). On this conception, sovereigns must shoulder cross-border responsibilities, in an age where mass devastation has become an all-too-real practical threat that no state can manage on its own.

Among those cross-border responsibilities is bringing to justice perpetrators of crimes against humanity – the core mission of international criminal law, and the topic of the book's final chapters.

[28] Hannah Arendt, *The Promise of Politics*, ed. Jerome Kohn (Schocken, 2005) (henceforth *PP*), 104–5, 168–69. The manuscript is titled "Introduction *into* Politics."

For Arendt, "crimes against humanity" is more than a legal label for a specific class of atrocity crimes. Rather, it signifies that the crimes concern all of humanity. She focuses especially on the crimes of the Third Reich, because its entire policy was criminal to the core; and, she argues, orthodox international law is incapable of grasping that a state itself can be criminal. But her ideas readily extend to noncriminal states and nonstate actors who commit core international crimes. Chapter 12 looks closely at Arendt's theory of genocide, contrasting it with the thought of Raphael Lemkin, the lawyer and activist who coined the word "genocide" and helped create the Convention Against Genocide. In law, acts of genocide are crimes committed against individuals because of their identity groups, with the intention to destroy those groups. Chapter 13 explores Arendt's complex theory of group identity and identity politics, a theory I find attractive, although it is fraught with paradoxes and dangers.

In Chapters 14 and 15, I turn to Arendt's legal analysis of the Eichmann trial, where she formulates several of her most important ideas about criminal accountability for "banal" evildoers. She wrote thirty years before the advent of modern international criminal law in the 1990s, and these final chapters investigate how her ideas stand up in the light of three decades' practical experience.

*

Here's a more detailed roadmap. The book consists of five linked but overlapping parts, which explore the themes of judgment, conscience, and accountability from different angles.

Part I (Chapters 1 and 2), "Adolf Eichmann and the Banality of Evil," focuses on Eichmann's trial and Arendt's diagnosis of him. Chapter 1 explains the banality-of-evil thesis and examines the evidence that led Arendt to it. I also set out one of my own theses: that her interest was not only the banal evildoers but also the "righteous few" who keep their moral judgment intact in the face of coercive social pressure, and in whom she found hope for the world. Chapter 2 examines the chief criticisms by historians who think Arendt got Eichmann terribly wrong, and defends her diagnosis of Eichmann. Readers uninterested in the historical question may wish to read only the first and last sections of this chapter: The former sets out the historical issue and my conclusion, while the latter explains Arendt's turn to the moral psychology of judgment.

Part II (Chapters 3–5), "The Moral Philosophy," examines Arendt's unorthodox use of Kant's theory of aesthetic judgment to model moral judgment. Chapter 3 also addresses Arendt's suspicion that appeals to moral principles in everyday matters are usually fraudulent, and it explains why conventional morality itself requires good judgment that can't be reduced to rules – an argument I develop by analogy with common law reasoning.

Chapter 4 introduces and analyzes the thinking–judging connection and what she calls the "Socratic" moral propositions: that it is better to suffer wrong than to do wrong, and that the cost of wrongdoing is being out of tune with yourself. Chapter 5 continues that analysis. It discusses the workings of conscience, sets out Arendt's post-*Eichmann* analysis of the banality of evil, and concludes by examining Eichmann's prison memoir, *Götzen* ("Idols"), to see whether her thoughtlessness theory stands up against his protest that he *did* carry on "a dialogue with my inner 'I' – which also could be called conscience."[29] (My conclusion: It stands up very well indeed.)

Part III (Chapters 6 and 7), "Common Sense and Moral Breakdown," turns to *The Origins of Totalitarianism* to analyze conspiracy theorizing and assaults on truth – with present-day examples very much in mind. Perhaps most importantly, I explain how the collapse of common sense in factual matters undermines moral common sense and the ability to judge right and wrong. I examine Arendt's epistemology of common sense and interweave it with contemporary philosophers' efforts to understand conspiracy theorizing and people's remarkable willingness to believe the unbelievable.

Chapter 7 digs deeper into the concept of common sense and disentangles strands of its intellectual history that Arendt draws on in her epistemology. One danger of conspiracy theorizing is a corrosive skepticism about factual truth itself, and Arendt was especially acute in diagnosing this danger. Skepticism is a traditional philosophical problem as well as a practical political problem, and Arendt occasionally tackled it philosophically. I argue that Arendt proposed a prototype of what today goes by the label "social epistemology," but that in the end she joined the ranks of antiphilosophers who reject the skeptic's question rather than answering it.

Part IV (Chapters 8 and 9), "Arendt before Jerusalem: Ethics in *The Human Condition*," tackles the Case of the Missing Morality through a close reading of *The Human Condition*'s core chapters, reconstructing her argument in a systematic way. On my reading, the chapters examine the capacity of different forms of human activity to make life meaningful, with

29 Adolf Eichmann, *Götzen: Die Autobiografie von Adolf Eichmann*, ed. and annotated by Raphael Ben Nescher (Metropol Verlag, 2016), 581 (450). I give double page references to *Götzen*. The first is to the online version, which includes the page numbers in Eichmann's manuscripts. The second is to the print version.

Arendt's conclusion that only the life of action can overcome the futility inherent in other ways of life. Somewhat misleadingly, Arendt labels this the "Greek solution," which has led critics to accuse her of "Hellenic nostalgia" or even "polis envy"; I show that the accusation misunderstands her point. The real problem with her argument is that it leaves little room for morality, which seems to her like an external constraint on action that threatens to rob it of its capacity to give meaning.[30] This, I show, is a mistake, because morality is far more than a fetter on action. I argue that gaps in her account require the turn to moral philosophy in her final decade.

Part V (Chapters 10–15), "Arendt and International Law," unfolds and explores eight fundamental ideas. First, that defending human dignity in our crisis-ridden world requires a "new law on earth" based on a reconfigured conception of state sovereignty. Second, that human rights law is useless unless it guarantees the right to belong to a political community that will protect your rights. Third, that "the idea of humanity, when purged of all sentimentality, has the very serious consequence that in one form or another men must assume responsibility for all crimes committed by men and that all nations share the onus of evil committed by all others" – the root idea of international criminal law.[31] Fourth, that criminal courts are institutional embodiments of spectator judgment, and their chief mission is portioning out responsibility among perpetrators who dodge it with their "I was only a cog in the machine" defenses. Fifth, that what makes genocide the paradigm of crimes that concern all humanity is its attack on the diversity that defines the "human status." Sixth, that group-based identity must be understood politically and not metaphysically. Seventh, that orthodox international law has a fatal blind spot when a state itself is criminal. In the end, the book circles back to where it began: the case of Eichmann and the banality of evil. It proposes that the thoughtless refusal to judge can itself be a ground of culpability supporting criminal conviction – the eighth fundamental idea growing from Arendt's engagement with spectator judgment embodied in criminal law. I examine these ideas on their own, but also in relation to the institutions of contemporary international criminal justice, as they developed from the 1990s until now.

*

[30] *DTB*, XXI.83 (January 1956), 557–58.

[31] Arendt, "Organized Guilt and Universal Responsibility," in *EU*, 131.

Readers familiar with Arendt's authorship will notice omissions from this book, which does not aim to be a comprehensive study of her thought. Most obviously, I focus on her moral and legal theory and say little about her writing about freedom, constitutionalism, revolution and the "social question," power and violence, Marxism, antisemitism, imperialism, the structure of totalitarian regimes, the nature of politics, or Jewish affairs – in short, the political ideas for which Arendt is best known. This is a deliberate choice, and perhaps a risky one, because it bets that the themes I explore can live on their own outside her broader political theory. Her historical studies of the will (in *Willing*) are tangential to my themes, and I pass over them as well. And, although Chapter 7 discusses Arendt's epistemology, I decided – a bit reluctantly – to omit a follow-up chapter on *The Human Condition*'s interpretation of Descartes and the scientific revolution.

Perhaps more surprising is my neglect of the so-called *Eichmann* controversy. The book was perceived – wrongly – as an attack on the trial and on Israel. As Amos Elon recalls, "Leftists and rightists, young and old, university professors, novelists, columnists, rabbis, Jewish functionaries of all kinds in America, in Israel, and in Europe, Americans, Israelis, and Germans – all were offended by *Eichmann in Jerusalem*."[32] While I address some of the substantive issues that enraged Arendt's critics, the controversy itself was not mainly about substance; as she complained bitterly, it was about a book she hadn't written. It was political more than philosophical, and thus outside the scope and aims of this book.

A final omission concerns Arendt's intellectual roots. She once wrote: "If I can be said to 'have come from anywhere,' it is from the tradition of German philosophy."[33] Although I analyze Arendt's creative use of Kant's aesthetics in her moral theory, I say little else about that tradition, and especially about her intellectual debts to Martin Heidegger. Others have written amply and illuminatingly about Arendt and Heidegger.[34] Instead, I highlight her affinities with analytically trained philosophers I admire,

[32] Amos Elon, "The Case of Hannah Arendt," *New York Review of Books*, November 6, 1997.

[33] Hannah Arendt, "A Letter to Gershom Scholem," July 24, 1963, in Arendt, *The Jewish Writings*, ed. Jerome Kohn and Ron H. Feldman (Schocken Books, 2007) (henceforth *JW*), 466. Aristotle and Augustine were equally important influences.

[34] For example, Seyla Benhabib, *The Reluctant Modernism of Hannah Arendt*, 2nd ed. (Rowman & Littlefield, 2000); Antonia Grunenberg, *Hannah Arendt and Martin Heidegger: History of a Love*, trans. Peg Birmingham, Kristina Lebedeva, and Elizabeth von Witzke Birmingham (Indiana University Press, 2017); Jacques Taminiaux, *The Thracian Maid and the Professional Thinker: Arendt and Heidegger*, ed. and trans. Michael Gendre (SUNY Press, 1997); and Dana Villa, *Arendt and Heidegger: The Fate of the Political* (Princeton University Press, 1996).

both her contemporaries and mine. Admittedly this is an odd choice, because Arendt was almost comically prejudiced against analytic and ordinary language philosophy, about which it is fair to say she knew little and cared less.[35] Yet it shouldn't be surprising that the affinities are there – especially with moral philosophers who lived through the same dark decades that she did, and their students of my own generation. One of my hopes in writing this book is to bring these thought trains into conversation with each other.

Readers will find many textual footnotes throughout this book. Some provide proof texts or additional evidence for assertions in the main text; others contain important asides that connect with the text. They will be of interest to some readers, but the book can be read without them.

*

A personal note about why I wrote this book. I've devoted my career to teaching and studying professional ethics and law. Both subjects are remote from Arendt's interests and sensibility, yet the questions central to my work come straight out of *Eichmann in Jerusalem* and "Thinking and Moral Considerations," which I first read fifty years ago. To borrow a phrase from Oliver Wendell Holmes, Jr.: They hit me where I live.

What becomes of moral responsibility in bureaucratic or organizational settings, where knowledge is fragmented, peer group pressure is powerful, and the individual sense of agency is weak because duties are divided (the so-called problem of many hands)?[36] How can we understand people who do evil thoughtlessly rather than with an evil heart? How can we hold them accountable for doing what everyone in their organization approves? What secret strength keeps some people's moral judgment intact when those

[35] "There is no philosophy in England!" she informed her husband after a visit to that country at the creative zenith of ordinary language philosophy. Arendt to Blücher, November 30, 1955, in *WFW*, 297. Her comments about Oxford philosophy are nasty and dismissive, see *T*, 45, 52, and she earlier suspected that "the new logical movement in philosophy" might have a subterranean connection with totalitarianism, which it most certainly did not. Arendt, "Understanding in Politics," in *EU*, 317. It would be hard to find more resolute foes of totalitarianism than the Vienna Circle and its offspring. Arendt wanted to make the University of Chicago's Committee on Social Thought a haven for "refugees" from analytic philosophy departments. Blake Smith, "Hannah Arendt, Michael Denneny, and the Politics of Protest," *Chronicle of Higher Education*, April 9, 2025.

[36] The phrase was coined by political theorist Dennis F. Thompson. I've discussed these pathologies in "The Legacies of Nuremberg," *Social Research* 54(4) (1987): 779–829, revised and reprinted in David Luban, *Legal Modernism* (University of Michigan Press, 1993), and David Luban, Alan Strudler, and David Wasserman, "Moral Responsibility in the Age of Bureaucracy," *Michigan Law Review* 90 (1992): 2348–92.

around them fail? These are Arendtian questions, but they are mine as well, and my own writing turns to her again and again.

Over the years, though, points of disagreement and doubt surfaced, some minor but others basic. I found myself arguing with Arendt, in both senses of "with"; I came to think of her as half my Virgil and half my sparring partner. A decade ago, I decided it was time to sort out in a systematic way what I've always found inspiring in Arendt and where I think she erred. That mission dictates the nature of the book: part close reading and reconstruction; part critique and fact checking; part friendly amendment; and part my own take on Arendt's topics, especially those that remain urgent today. How much my own take is suffused with Arendt's is for others to judge.

I heard Arendt lecture only once, when I was an undergraduate at the University of Chicago. I hadn't read her work, and I barely knew who she was other than "some famous person." She stood alone on the bare stage of Mandel Hall, in a cyclone of cigarette smoke, and read something about evil, and Socrates, and the death of metaphysics. The lecture went way over my head; I had no idea what she was talking about. Years later, I read "Thinking and Moral Considerations" and thought it was one of her finest essays. It dawned on me that it was the same lecture that I had found so baffling. These two memories, of incomprehension and illumination, stuck with me as I wrote this book. The first reminded me that Arendt is a hard philosopher; it made me determined to unwind her winding arguments and make them as clear as I could. The second reassured me that the effort is worth it.

PART I

# *Adolf Eichmann and the Banality of Evil*

The greatest evil is not now done in those sordid "dens of crime" that Dickens loved to paint. It is not done even in concentration camps and labor camps. In those we see its final result. But it is conceived and ordered (moved, seconded, carried, and minuted) in clean, carpeted, warmed, and well-lighted offices, by quiet men with white collars and cut fingernails and smooth-shaven cheeks who do not need to raise their voice.

C. S. Lewis, *The Screwtape Letters*

They are like chameleons: in a healthy society they look healthy, in a sick one, like ours, they look sick. And they are neither one nor the other. They are mere filler.

Helmuth James von Moltke to Freya von Moltke, November 8, 1941, describing the officials in his office who did not join him in objecting to criminal Nazi orders, *Letters to Freya*, pp. 179–80

The Schmidts obeyed, and marched on Poland.
And there an Anton Schmidt, Feldwebel,
Performed uncommon things, not safe,
Nor glamorous, nor profitable.

Was the expression on his face
"Reposeful and humane good nature"?
Or did he look like any Schmidt,
Of slow and undisclosing features?

I know he had unusual eyes,
Whose power no orders might determine,
Not to mistake the men he saw,
As others did, for gods or vermin.

For five months, till his execution,
Aware that action has its dangers,

He helped the Jews to get away
– Another race at that, and strangers.

He never did mistake for bondage
The military job, the chances,
The limits; he did not submit
To the blackmail of his circumstances.

I see him in the Polish snow,
His muddy wrappings small protection,
Breathing the cold air of his freedom
And treading a distinct direction.

Thom Gunn, "Epitaph for Anton Schmidt," composed after reading Hannah Arendt's *Eichmann in Jerusalem: A Report on the Banality of Evil.*[1]

[1] "Epitaph for Anton Schmidt," from "Misanthropos," in *Collected Poems* by Thom Gunn. Copyright © 1994 by Thom Gunn. Reprinted by permission of Farrar, Straus and Giroux. All Rights Reserved.

CHAPTER I

# *Arendt in Jerusalem*

## 1.1 Judgment as Moral Compass

In May 1960, Israeli agents kidnapped Adolf Eichmann in Argentina and brought him to Jerusalem to stand trial for crimes of the Holocaust. A month later, Hannah Arendt wrote to her friend Mary McCarthy, "I am half toying with the idea to get some magazine to send me to cover the Eichmann trial. Am very tempted. He used to be one of the most intelligent of the lot."[1] Arendt approached William Shawn, editor of *The New Yorker*, who accepted her proposal.[2] As Arendt explained to her friend and mentor, the philosopher Karl Jaspers, "I would never be able to forgive myself if I didn't go and look at this walking disaster face to face in all his bizarre vacuousness."[3]

Readers who know nothing else about Arendt are likely to know the name she gave the "bizarre vacuousness" (*unheimliche Nichtigkeit*) she saw, or thought she saw, when she looked at Eichmann: *the banality of evil.* Many trial observers expected, and wanted, to see a sadistic, fanatical monster glowering at them from the defendant's bulletproof glass booth. Arendt saw an organization man whose motives were not much different from those of organization men everywhere. What made this bizarre is that the SS murder machine was no ordinary organization. What made Eichmann vacuous is that he seemed unable to recognize evil on a monstrous scale.

1 Hannah Arendt to Mary McCarthy, June 20, 1960 in Hannah Arendt, *Between Friends: The Correspondence of Hannah Arendt and Mary McCarthy 1949–1975*, ed. Carol Brightman (Harcourt Brace, 1995) (henceforth *BF*), 81–82.

2 Arendt to McCarthy, October 8, 1960, *BF*, 98–99; cf. Elizabeth Young-Bruehl, *Hannah Arendt: For Love of the World*, 2nd ed. (Yale University Press, 2004), 328. Three years later *Eichmann in Jerusalem: A Report on the Banality of Evil* appeared as a five-part *New Yorker* series as well as in book form. It has sold hundreds of thousands of copies.

3 Arendt to Karl Jaspers, December 2, 1960 in Hannah Arendt and Karl Jaspers, *Hannah Arendt–Karl Jaspers Correspondence 1926–1969*, ed. Lotte Kohler and Hans Saner, trans. Robert Kimber and Rita Kimber (Harcourt Brace, 1992) (henceforth *HA-KJ*), 409–10.

As we will see in this chapter and Chapter 2, the phrase *banality of evil* prompted grave misunderstandings that were part of the furious controversy that raged around *Eichmann in Jerusalem* from the moment of publication. There is no denying that Arendt's powerful phrase is slippery. Its wording suggests that "banality" refers to evil rather than to Eichmann, and "banal" can mean "uninteresting" as well as "shallow," although the latter is what Arendt had in mind. No wonder, then, that one prominent critic complained Arendt was slighting the Holocaust by downplaying its evil.[4]

In fact, nothing could be further from the truth. Arendt called the Holocaust "the unprecedented crime, . . . the crime against humanity – in the sense of a 'crime against the human status', or against the very nature of mankind" – just the opposite of slighting its importance.[5]

As for the wording, Arendt clearly used "banality" to describe Eichmann's personality, not his deeds. When her old friend Gershom Scholem attacked her phrase, Arendt replied, "you have misunderstood the 'banality of evil.' The point isn't to turn evil into something banal or harmless."[6] Other critics got the point but accused her of underrating Eichmann's intelligence and minimizing his role. This too was mistaken, for she insisted that intelligent people can be banal, and she called Eichmann "one of the greatest criminals of that period."[7]

Unfortunately, Arendt failed to define the banality of evil until 1971, when she finally explained that the phrase refers to

> no theory or doctrine but something quite factual, the phenomenon of evil deeds, committed on a gigantic scale, which could not be traced to any

[4] Richard Wolin, "The Banality of Evil: The Demise of a Legend," *Jewish Review of Books* (Fall 2014), attributing to Arendt "the idea that the execution of the Nazis' diabolical plans for an *Endlösung* to the 'Jewish Question' could be considered 'banal.'" Wolin repeats this misreading in "Thoughtlessness Revisited: A Response to Seyla Benhabib," *Jewish Review of Books*, September 30, 2014: "if Eichmann was banal, then the Holocaust itself was banal," a leap of logic that Arendt never came close to suggesting. Twenty years earlier, Wolin condemned Arendt's "famous pronouncement that the evil that the Nazis inflicted on the Jews was, for the man on the witness stand, . . . 'banal.'" Richard Wolin, "Hannah and the Magician," *New Republic*, October 9, 1995. Reprinted, with revisions, in Richard Wolin, *Heidegger's Children* (Princeton University Press, 2001). This too is a misreading: Arendt never attributed to Eichmann the opinion that the Holocaust was banal. Nor, obviously, did Arendt think so. As she told an interviewer, "Why readers who read 'banality of evil' should jump to the conclusion that 'their sufferings are banal' is beyond me." Arendt, "Answers to Questions Posed by Samuel Grafton," in *JW*, 478. She peevishly accuses those who misread her this way of illiteracy.

[5] *EJ*, 268.

[6] Arendt to Scholem, September 14, 1963 in Hannah Arendt and Gershom Scholem, *The Correspondence of Hannah Arendt and Gershom Scholem*, ed. Marie Luise Knott, trans. Anthony David (University of Chicago Press, 2017) (henceforth *HA-GS*), 217.

[7] *EJ*, 288.

> particularity of wickedness, pathology, or ideological conviction in the doer, whose only personal distinction was a perhaps extraordinary shallowness. However monstrous the deeds were, the doer was neither monstrous nor demonic.[8]

Presumably she neglected to define the banality of evil *because* she had no theory or doctrine. To McCarthy, she wrote, "As I see it, there are no 'ideas' in this Report, there are only facts with a few conclusions."[9] Two weeks later, she followed up in another letter to McCarthy:

> My "basic notion" of the ordinariness of Eichmann is much less a notion than a faithful description of a phenomenon. I am sure there can be drawn many conclusions from this phenomenon and the most general I drew is indicated: "banality of evil." I may sometime want to write about this, and then I would write about the nature of evil, but it would have been entirely wrong of me to do it within the framework of the report.[10]

So "banality of evil" is a pre-theoretical general description of a phenomenon. Arendt labels it a conclusion because to claim that a phenomenon falls under a concept *is* a conclusion; she does not mean it is a conclusion based on a theory. Near the end of *Eichmann in Jerusalem*, she calls that conclusion "the lesson that this long course in human wickedness had taught us – the lesson of the fearsome, word-and-thought-defying *banality of evil*."[11] This is the only place in the text where the famous phrase appears, but Arendt fails to explain what lesson she has in mind. If we take her at her word, at the time she wrote *Eichmann in Jerusalem* Arendt had no theory that might articulate the lesson – indeed, she explicitly warns that the lesson is "neither an explanation of the phenomenon nor a theory about it."[12] All she had were observations of a phenomenon she found "word-and-thought defying." In a letter to Rabbi Arthur Hertzberg, Arendt confessed that "the whole truth is that I did not know the answer myself when I wrote the book."[13]

Should we take her at her word, or did she come to Jerusalem theory in hand? After all, her phrase "bizarre vacuousness" to describe Eichmann comes from a letter written months *before* the trial. Furthermore, ideas

8 TMC, 159.

9 She adds: "The only exception to this is the Epilog, which is a discussion of the legal aspect of the case." Arendt to McCarthy, September 20, 1963, *BF*, 148. In Chapters 14 and 15, I discuss the epilogue in some detail.

10 Arendt to McCarthy, October 3, 1963, *BF*, 152. 11 *EJ*, 252. 12 *EJ*, 288.

13 Letter from Hannah Arendt to Arthur Hertzberg, April 8, 1966, quoted in Young-Bruehl, 367.

anticipating the banality of evil crop up in her writings and correspondence as early as 1945, including in *The Origins of Totalitarianism.*[14]

Arendt had done her homework on Eichmann, and "bizarre vacuousness" suggests she went to Jerusalem primed for his banality, in the sense that it did not take her by surprise. (Her first impression of him on Day One of the trial is already disdainful: "a ghost that happens to have a cold. . . . Not even eerie. His only concern, not to lose his composure."[15]) When she wrote to Jaspers about Eichmann's bizarre vacuousness, she was probably reacting to the sensational interview with Eichmann – the "Sassen interview" – published in *Life* magazine just a few days earlier.[16] There Eichmann indeed sounds bizarrely vacuous: He recounts deporting Hungary's Jews to Auschwitz in the same flat way he recalls sharing a grilled bacon and onion snack with a Hungarian colonel, as though he couldn't tell which was more noteworthy.[17]

But there is no reason to doubt her disclaimers of having a theory, because Eichmann in Jerusalem caused her to drop one of her signature ideas, the analysis of "radical evil" in *The Origins of Totalitarianism.*[18] That suggests she was not using Eichmann merely as a stalking horse for a pet theory, nor was she seeing in Eichmann only what she wanted to see.[19]

Arendt's remark to McCarthy – "I may sometime want to write about this, and then I would write about the nature of evil" – in fact anticipated a turn in her thinking provoked by the Eichmann trial, a turn toward what

14 E.g., "Organized Guilt and Universal Responsibility," originally published in 1945 and reprinted in *EU*, 121–31; *OT*, 327, 337–38. She speculates that "the masses of co-ordinated philistines provided much better material and were capable of even greater crimes than so-called professional criminals, provided only that these crimes were well organized and assumed the appearance of routine jobs." *OT*, 337.

15 Letter to Heinrich Blücher, April 15, 1961, *WFW*, 355.

16 Adolf Eichmann, "Eichmann Tells His Own Damning Story," part 1, *Life*, November 28, 1960, 19–24, 101–12. A second installment of the interview appeared a week later: "Eichmann's Own Story: Part II," *Life*, December 5, 1960, 146–61. (Both are available on Google Books; full URLs are in the Bibliography.) These were excerpts from a much longer document. For more on these interviews, see §§2.2 and 2.4.

17 On the Hungarian operation and the bacon and onion snack, "Eichmann Tells His Own Damning Story," 109–10.

18 Arendt to Scholem, July 24, 1963, *JW*, 465; also in *HA-GS*, 209. See also her letter to McCarthy, September 20, 1963, *BF*, 148. I discuss the switch from "radical evil" to "banal evil" in §5.4.

19 At a conference a few months after Eichmann's arrest, but before the trial itself, she remarked that "theoretically, I do not even know the answer to the philosophical question: What is radical evil?" "Challenges to Traditional Ethics: A Response to Michael Polanyi," in *TWB*, 190. She presented this paper in August 1960. Yet it does not mention Eichmann, nor does it hint at anything like the banality of evil. If she already had the banality-of-evil idea in mind, some premonition would surely appear in her paper on "challenges to traditional ethics." If anything, this paper shows that Arendt had not yet jettisoned radical evil in favor of banality of evil.

became a major interest in Arendt's final decade: moral philosophy. The turn is especially striking because in her earlier writing she seldom mentioned moral philosophy, and when she did it was usually with offhand disdain. Why the change? In Arendt's last, incomplete, book, she quotes Kantian language to explain that "after having been struck by a fact that, willy-nilly, 'put me in possession of a concept' (the banality of evil), I could not help raising the *quaestio juris* [legal question] and asking myself 'by what right I possessed and used it.'"[20]

Eventually, Arendt did write about the nature of evil, briefly, in two series of classroom lectures from the mid-1960s, published posthumously under the title "Some Questions of Moral Philosophy." But mostly her final-decade investigation turned out not to be about the nature of evil as such, or at least not directly. Rather, it was an investigation of *judgment* – specifically, of the kind of disastrously bad moral judgment she saw in Eichmann, but also the miraculous moral clarity a few resisters and rescuers maintained even in the darkest moments of the Holocaust.

The latter, for her, was at least as important as the former. As she put it rather dramatically, the fact that under conditions of terror "most people will comply but *some people will not*" is what allows "this planet to remain a fit place for human habitation."[21] She cites a few examples, prompted by testimony at the Eichmann trial about an ordinary German sergeant, Anton Schmid, who over a period of months rescued 250 Jews from destruction, until he was caught and executed. Thom Gunn's poem about Schmid captures in a metonym what Arendt found so thought-provoking: it was Schmid's "unusual eyes" with their power "not to mistake the men he saw for gods or vermin." That perceptual power is the power of moral judgment, and for Arendt as for Gunn it kept Schmid "breathing the cold air of his freedom / And treading a distinct direction."[22] To Arendt, trial testimony about Schmid was "like a sudden burst of light in the midst of impenetrable, unfathomable darkness."[23] What Arendt cared about, more than the Eichmanns of the world, are the Schmids: those who know right

20 *T*, 5. Arendt is quoting from an unpublished manuscript of Kant's, but the Kantian *quaestio juris* – asking by what right we use concepts – is the famous beginning of the Transcendental Deduction in Immanuel Kant, *Critique of Pure Reason*, trans. Norman Kemp Smith (Macmillan and Co., 1929), A84–85, B116–17 (hereafter *CPR*).

21 *EJ*, 233. Her italics. In her lectures on moral philosophy, she makes clear that those who did *not* conform to Nazism are her topic. Arendt, "Basic Moral Propositions," in *RJ*, 278n10.

22 Thom Gunn, "Epitaph for Anton Schmidt" (§11 of "Misanthropos") (1965), in *Collected Poems* (Farrar, Straus & Giroux, 1994), 143–44. Gunn used *Eichmann in Jerusalem* as his source, which is why he and Arendt misspell Schmid's name the same way.

23 *EJ*, 231.

from wrong when others around them have lost their way – in Thom Gunn's words, those who tread a distinct direction.

It is important to dispel a possible misunderstanding. In everyday language practice, "bad judgment" is a mealy-mouthed excuse: "I'm really not a scoundrel. I didn't mean to do wrong. I *merely* had a lapse in judgment." In the lexicon of damage control, bad judgment – *mere* bad judgment – apparently counts as a lesser evil.

That is decidedly not what Arendt means when she talks about bad judgment; for her, there is nothing "mere" about it. Judgment, as Arendt thinks of it, is the ability to tell right from wrong without deducing it from rules.[24] In other words, judgment is what we sometimes call *moral compass*.[25] Functioning properly, our moral compass guides us (fallibly, to be sure) even when nothing visible to the eye offers a clue to the right course. To have persistent bad judgment means to have a defective moral compass. Viewed this way, the excuse "I have a good character, but bad judgment" makes no sense: Defective moral compass *is* defective character. Bad moral judgment, as Arendt understands it, is one of the most serious accusations we can level.

Rightly or wrongly, Arendt was convinced that Eichmann's crimes could not be traced to malice, pathology, or ideology. That seemingly left bad moral judgment as the most plausible alternative. Eichmann's moral compass was disastrously faulty, easily deflected by the local forces of his immediate environment. He exemplified something truly momentous: "an average, 'normal' person, neither feeble-minded nor indoctrinated nor cynical," who nonetheless "could be perfectly incapable of telling right from wrong."[26]

For now, I postpone discussing the implications of this observation, including the problems it poses for legal systems. I also postpone the question whether she got Eichmann right; that comes in Chapter 2. Here I note only that her conjecture, reflected in the definition of "banality of evil" quoted earlier, seems to be that when an average, "normal" person commits extraordinary evil, unprompted by malice, pathology, or ideology, the evil arises from defective moral judgment: the wrongdoer simply fails to recognize (= misjudges) that the conduct is evil. Arendt's decade-long investigation of the human faculty of judgment explores that conjecture and aims to supply a theory to anchor it.

Two important cautions must be emphasized here, to avoid serious misunderstanding. First, to attribute evil deeds to the perpetrator's

[24] TMC, 188–89; PRUD, 27, 41. [25] This is not a term Arendt uses. [26] *EJ*, 26.

defective moral judgment is not to let the evildoer off the hook either morally or legally. Whether defective moral judgment counts as an excuse (akin to a defense of diminished mental capacity) or a ground of blame depends on other theoretical commitments. Arendt's commitments point unequivocally in the direction of blameworthiness; for her, "don't blame me, blame my bad judgment" is absurd. Certainly she never let Eichmann off the hook: Remember that she labeled him "one of the greatest criminals of that period," and she called him and those like him "*hostis generis humani*" – an enemy of all mankind. Contrary to complaints by her critics, she repeatedly and emphatically *rejected* Eichmann's "I was just a cog in a machine" defense, and she endorsed the Jerusalem court's death sentence.[27]

Second, a theory of moral judgment of the kind Arendt hoped to develop will be only a fragment of a theory of evil, because it does not cover the evils that *are* committed from malice, sadism, or fanaticism – in other words, evils arising from something more diabolical (though perhaps no more alarming) than bad moral judgment. She calls the defendants in the Auschwitz trials "monsters" (one is a "ghoul"), about whom she ventures a diagnosis of sadism in a "basically sexual" sense.[28] Elsewhere, she distinguishes the evil of the "'bourgeois' with all the outer aspect of respectability" within the Nazi movement from the perversions and fanaticisms displayed by others among the elite, naming Hitler, Goebbels, Göring, and Streicher.[29] Their evil was anything but banal. And she explicitly contrasts Eichmann's banality with the pride of Lucifer, the resentment and self-loathing of Richard III, the envy of Cain, the weakness of Macbeth, the depraved hatreds of Iago and Claggart, and the covetousness and cupidity we are told is the root of all evil.[30]

What about an alternative diagnosis of Eichmann that also accepts his ordinariness? Perhaps there was nothing wrong with his judgment, but he

27 *EJ*, 288 (greatest criminals), 282 (*hostis generis humani*), 279 (death sentence). Her rejection of the "cog in the machine" is in *EJ*, 289; more elaborately, in PRUD, 29–32; also in "Collective Responsibility," in *RJ*, 148, and in an interview with Joachim Fest published in *The Last Interview and Other Conversations*, 58. Richard Wolin, an unreliable reporter of Arendt's views, wrote: "She insinuated that there was no 'intentionality' to his crimes: Eichmann was merely a cog in a massive bureaucratic machine." Wolin, "Hannah and the Magician." This is close to the opposite of her plainly stated view.

28 Arendt, "Auschwitz on Trial," in *RJ*. Monsters: 251; ghoul: 253; sadism: 252. She describes the sickening details of their crimes with a fury unusual in her writing, but perfectly appropriate to the topic. See 252–56. In this essay, she speculates that these might be "perfectly normal people who in normal life had never come into conflict with the law on such counts" – but only to "wonder about the dream world of many an average citizen who may lack not much more than the opportunity," 252. This essay was published three years after *Eichmann in Jerusalem*.

29 Hannah Arendt, "Organized Guilt and Universal Responsibility," *EU*, 28.

30 *T*, 3–4.

chose to stay in his horrifying job, knowing how evil it was, out of ambition and opportunism, the first cousins to covetousness and cupidity. Before he joined the SS, Eichmann, who never finished high school, was a traveling salesman with middling prospects. His SS job allowed him to make the most of hitherto unsuspected talents for negotiation and organization; and of course he wielded the power of life and death over the Jews, which must have gratified his thirsty ego.[31] If he quit he would have no career, or at least not a career that made him a somebody. He would once again be a mediocrity. (And indeed, in his exile he worked in low-level jobs, the best of which was managing a rabbit farm.) Couldn't it be that he knew full well the evil of what he was doing but lacked the guts to quit, not out of physical fear but merely out of reluctance to accept demotion? Arendt herself remarked on his unusual diligence in advancing his own career.[32]

There is much to be said for this diagnosis, and Chapter 2 takes it up in greater detail. But, taken by itself, it downplays one of the chief characteristics Arendt spotted in Eichmann: a desire to be respectable to the worthies of society. There is no reason to believe Eichmann would have joined the mafia (for example) if that was the only way to get ahead. A successful SS career was appealing precisely because, within the Third Reich, it was a respectable career. Not to have seen through this perverse respectability was itself catastrophically bad moral judgment. And so, even a diagnosis of Eichmann's evil that attributes it to raging ambition has explanatory power only if we can understand how Eichmann's moral judgments about the Nazi hierarchy he inhabited could be so wrong.

To recap the main points so far: Arendt's concept of banality of evil is more than an observation, but less than a theory. It is a summary interpretation of her observations, and Arendt claims that its observational base makes it "something quite factual," "a faithful description of a phenomenon," not a philosophical construction. Theory would come later, and Arendt devoted much of her final decade toward developing that theory. And, as she came to view things, what that theory needed to explain was how some ordinary people can be wholly lacking in elementary judgment – moral compass – while in others it remains intact.

[31] This is precisely the portrait of Eichmann that Bettina Stangneth paints in the opening chapter of *Eichmann before Jerusalem: The Unexamined Life of a Mass Murderer*, trans. Ruth Martin (Alfred Knopf, 2014) (published in German in 2011) (hereafter Stangneth). She demonstrates in detail Eichmann's ambition to advance in the ranks of the SS, his self-aggrandizement and self-promotion, and his vanity.

[32] *EJ*, 287.

Clearly this is a question of far broader moral and philosophical significance than an exclusive focus on Eichmann, the Nazis, and the Holocaust would suggest. We exercise moral judgment in matters great and small, and "banality of evil" might apply in less extraordinary and shattering settings.

In line with this thought, suppose we revise Arendt's definition of the banality of evil quoted earlier: "[T]he phenomenon of evil deeds, *committed on a gigantic scale*, which could not be traced to any particularity of wickedness." Let's drop the italicized phrase, which limits the definition to a handful of mass atrocity cases. That limitation needlessly robs the concept of more general significance. It also implies something false: that the characteristic motivational structure – evil deeds coupled with a lack of commensurably evil motivations – can be found only among mass criminals. A better way to read "evil deeds committed on a gigantic scale" is as an elliptical version of "evil deeds, *even including some* committed on a gigantic scale."

Whatever Arendt intended, "banality of evil" has entered the workaday vocabulary of public discourse to describe lesser wrongdoers. That's no surprise: The phrase seems to perfectly describe a common kind of organizational wrongdoing, be it in corporations or law firms or government agencies. Banality of evil manifests itself whenever the perpetrators are ordinary people acting in accordance with a prevailing organizational culture, without malicious motives and without seeming to grasp how corrupt that culture is and how much evil they are doing by simply doing their job and getting ahead.

To take a present-day example, a commentator applies the label "banality of evil, M.B.A. edition" to consultants implicated in the opioid epidemic.[33] The worldwide consulting firm McKinsey & Company advised pharmaceutical manufacturer Purdue Pharma to aggressively market OxyContin, and McKinsey later recommended paying rebates to distributors when customers overdosed, without cutting back on sales. The ever-helpful consultants scripted a responsibility-ducking sound bite for Purdue executives if they were asked who at the company takes personal responsibility for opioid deaths: "We all feel responsible."

Arendt would surely give a knowing nod: She warned that expressions of collective guilt are a way to duck responsibility, not take it.[34] The sound

[33] Walt Bogdanich and Michael Forsythe, "McKinsey Proposed Paying Pharmacy Companies Rebates for OxyContin Overdoses," *New York Times*, November 28, 2020 (quoting Anand Giridharadas). Giridharadas, the man who called the McKinsey documents "banality of evil, M.B.A. edition" is a former McKinsey consultant.

[34] PRUD, 20–21; "Collective Responsibility," in *RJ*, 147–48.

bite echoes her merciless description of bureaucracy as the rule of Nobody (by which she means Nobody In Particular).[35]

I want to issue an urgent warning: Condemning opioid apparatchiks for banality of evil is not meant to imply that callous profiteering is like the Holocaust, nor that the executives and consultants are Eichmanns. Those would be shocking, silly, and deeply offensive moral equivalences. (Godwin's law decrees that anyone who ventures Nazi analogies in an argument about something else automatically loses.) Let me say it once again, loudly: *No moral equivalence!*

The point is rather that "banality of evil" often seems like the right way to describe perpetrators who appear to be ordinary, nondiabolical people who have somehow lost their moral bearings and who seem clueless about the wrongness of what they've done.

One Arendt critic complains that "the phrase banality of evil has slipped easily into the language, becoming a commonplace, almost a banality itself. Journalists and others freely apply it as an all-purpose explanation."[36] All-purpose explanations explain nothing because they explain everything. That's what makes Arendt's *quaestio juris* of whether we are entitled to the concept "banality of evil" an urgent one, entirely apart from Eichmann.

Recall that Arendt is interested not only in bad moral judgment but in good moral judgment as well. Inquiry into the workings and failings of moral judgment is a central topic of moral philosophy, going back to the Socratic question: "Can virtue be taught?" Arendt's inquiry opens onto several important philosophical issues:

(1) One traditional approach to moral philosophy, which today goes by the name "virtue ethics," analyzes right and wrong, good and evil, in terms of the virtuous or vicious character of the actor. Virtue ethics assumes a kind of congruence between character and act that the banality of evil calls into question. If evil deeds sometimes cannot "be traced to any particularity of wickedness," then the distinction between good and evil must, in some way, swing free of the virtues and vices of the wrongdoer.

Virtue ethics can avoid that result by insisting that good judgment, "practical wisdom," is itself a virtue. Aristotle classified it among the intellectual virtues, under the name *phronēsis*, and in one essay Arendt

[35] *EJ*, 289; Hannah Arendt, "On Violence," in *Crises of the Republic* (Harcourt Brace, 1972) (henceforth *CR*), 178.

[36] Stephen H. Miller, "A Note on the Banality of Evil," *The Wilson Quarterly*, Autumn, 1998.

uses Aristotle's Greek word to denote political judgment.[37] We will see in Chapter 4 that Arendt's view, although different from Aristotle's and quite original, also emphasizes intellectual virtues. Nevertheless, a robust virtue ethics would presumably prefer to assign diabolical deeds, carried out over years, to diabolical vice rather than mere absence of *phronēsis*. So, the banality of evil does pose a puzzle for virtue ethics – call it the *problem of incongruity between person and act*.

(2) Arendt's focus on judgment also raises the question whether reasoning from principles or judging particulars is more basic to moral life – whether, in other words, moral reasoning is principled and top down or particularist and bottom up. On some interpretations, Kant's categorical imperative procedure – about which Arendt had grave doubts – may stand as a paradigm of the former; contemporary moral particularism, which emphasizes the variability of moral reasons among contexts, may stand as a paradigm of the latter.[38] Arendt leans in the latter direction; yet she occasionally argues that action springs from principles, and she explains that principles are criteria of judgment and standards of right and wrong.[39] More basically, she never doubts the ABCs of everyday morality, captured in principles like "thou shalt not murder."

Working out the relationship between principles and particulars, between reasoning and judging, is one of the major theoretical problems implicit in Arendt's diagnosis of Eichmann as an ordinarily intelligent man incapable of distinguishing right from wrong – a man who could calculate but not judge. Call this the *problem of principles and particulars*.

(3) The most basic question is how judgment is supposed to work. "Judgment," understood as noninferential knowledge of particulars, is not merely a philosopher's term of art: Saying that someone has or lacks good judgment is perfectly commonplace. But talk about judgment raises its own *quaestio juris* of what entitles us to invoke a distinct faculty for knowing particulars noninferentially. The sailor's compass is explained by magnetism; what explains moral compass? Call this the *problem of judgment*.

37 Hannah Arendt, "The Crisis in Culture," in *Between Past and Future* (Viking Press, 1961) (hereafter *BPF*), 221. She translates *phronēsis* "insight." So too in Hannah Arendt, *The Human Condition* (University of Chicago Press, 1958) (henceforth *HC*), 226.

38 In saying this, I don't mean to associate Arendt's views with those of contemporary moral particularists.

39 Action springs from principles: "What Is Freedom?," in *BPF* (Viking ed.), 152; principles as criteria of judgment: "Montesquieu's Revision of the Tradition," in *PP*, 65; principles as standards of right and wrong: "On the Nature of Totalitarianism: An Essay in Understanding," in *EU*, 335.

(4) Finally, we might ask what entitles us to suppose there is some moral counterpart to magnetic north – some right direction whose rightness is independent of the observer's subjective convictions. This, of course, is the *problem of moral realism.*

Arendt's *quaestio juris* raises these and other philosophical issues, which are independent of the Eichmann case. It also raises issues in legal theory, which I discuss further down the road – for of course, judgment and judging are central to the law. Arendt rightly remarks that "legal and moral issues are by no means the same, but they have a certain affinity with each other because they both presuppose the power of judgment,"[40] although the differences will bear some scrutiny.

But Eichmann and the banality of evil were the proximate causes of Arendt's inquiry. So, although this is not a book about *Eichmann in Jerusalem*, it must begin there, and I take it up at various points in the argument and return to it in Part V, which discusses Arendt's contributions to the theory of criminal law. Before turning to broader questions, we need to understand what the phenomena were that "banality of evil" describes. What observations generated the concept? What *exactly* did Arendt think she saw in Eichmann?

## 1.2 What Arendt Saw in Jerusalem

Arendt gives us two answers:

1. She saw someone who could not *think*, by which (she immediately explains) she means that he could not think from the standpoint of somebody else.[41]
2. She saw someone who could not *speak* in words of his own. All he could do is mouth clichés, bureaucratese (*Amtssprache*), and phrases that, if they were Eichmann's own, he repeated so often and so literally that they became self-made clichés.[42]

Of course, thinking from the point of view of someone else is not the standard meaning of what it is to think; but in Arendt's philosophy of mind, it is what distinguishes thinking from other cognitive abilities and operations, and her usage is mostly consistent, the exceptions being when she discusses musical and pictorial (i.e., nonverbal) thinking.

To Arendt, (1) and (2) are connected; she argues that Eichmann's inability to speak is a consequence of his inability to think – that is, to

[40] PRUD, 22. [41] *EJ*, 48–49. [42] *EJ*, 48.

think from the point of view of his interlocutor.[43] The inability to think, and the inability to speak that is evidence of it, are the core evidence of Eichmann's banality. From these twin observations, she eventually drew two conclusions:

3. Eichmann lacked a moral personality of his own. He was a *moral chameleon* – my term, not hers – whose convictions came from those around him, and especially from those he looked up to because of their superior social status. (I borrow the phrase from the German resistance martyr Helmuth James von Moltke, describing fellow officials who wouldn't join him in opposing criminal decisions. "They are like chameleons: in a healthy society they look healthy, in a sick one, like ours, they look sick. And they are neither one nor the other. They are mere filler."[44])
4. Because Eichmann could not think from the standpoint of someone genuinely other (most obviously, his victims), nor express his judgments except in clichés, he simply lacked independent judgment, what I have called moral compass. He was stuck with the cues that were handed to him by whatever social world he inhabited.

Other observations than (1) and (2) might also have fed into Arendt's diagnosis of Eichmann's banality. For example: "In court, Eichmann gave the impression of a typical member of the lower middle classes, and this impression was more than borne out by every sentence he spoke or wrote while in prison" – although she immediately adds that the impression is misleading, because in fact Eichmann was "the *déclassé* son of a solid middle class family."[45] Again: "Servatius [Eichmann's lawyer] himself had declared, even prior to the trial, that his client's personality was that of 'a common mailman'" – a judgment Arendt seems to endorse.[46] Again: "Despite all the efforts of the prosecution, everybody could see that this man was not a 'monster,' but it was difficult indeed not to suspect that he was a clown."[47]

Sarcasms like these can make it sound as though Arendt's "banality" diagnosis was little more than snobbish contempt toward an intellectual

[43] *EJ*, 49; Hannah Arendt, *Lectures on Kant's Political Philosophy*, ed. Ronald Beiner (University of Chicago Press, 1989) (hereafter *Kant Lectures*), 74.

[44] Helmuth James von Moltke to Freya von Moltke, November 8, 1941, *Letters to Freya: 1939–1945*, ed. and trans. Beate Ruhm von Oppen (Knopf, 1990), 179–80.

[45] *EJ*, 31.

[46] *EJ*, 145. Arendt notes that the defense team's "feeling of social superiority to Eichmann was more than once in evidence." *EJ*, 145.

[47] *EJ*, 54.

and social inferior. Now, Arendt was by no means immune to elitism and snobbery, and her letters occasionally express cringe-making prejudices and stereotypes. But observations like those I've just quoted are throwaways, and she draws no conclusions from them. Only the two fundamental observations mentioned earlier – about Eichmann's inability to speak and his inability to think (from the standpoint of somebody else) – play a significant role in the conclusions that matter: Eichmann's nature as a moral chameleon and his lack of independent moral judgment.

What was her evidence that Eichmann couldn't think from the standpoint of others? Some examples illustrate what she has in mind. After his arrest, Eichmann was interrogated at length by an Israeli police captain, Avner Less.[48] Eichmann, who spent nearly 300 hours with his interrogator, seemed to bond with him, and at one point found himself complaining to Less about his professional hard luck. As a bureau head, he could never be promoted beyond lieutenant colonel; and when he wanted to transfer to the *Einsatzgruppen*, the killing units in the east, which he regarded as a pathway to promotion, his request was denied.[49] Eichmann complained as though he expected Less to commiserate. Less, unsurprisingly, did not. He was, after all, a German Jew by birth, and – as Eichmann likely knew – his father had been murdered in the Holocaust. Apparently, it never crossed Eichmann's mind that any of that might matter.

A second example concerned Eichmann's solicitude for one of the Jewish leaders he dealt with in Vienna, a man named Berthold Storfer. During the war Eichmann protected Storfer (or so he said), but Storfer tried to escape and was caught and sent to Auschwitz. Somehow, he got a message to Eichmann, who claimed he actually traveled to Auschwitz to gain Storfer's release. When he got there, Eichmann was told that no one could be released from the camp. Next Eichmann tried to get Storfer excused from work, but the camp commandant refused. Finally, Eichmann was able to secure relatively light work for Storfer, "[w]hereupon" (Eichmann recollected) "he was very pleased."[50] Eichmann left feeling happy about this "normal, human encounter. ... It was a great inner joy to me ... that we

48 Excerpts were published in German in 1982 and in English translation a year later. In this book, I use the English version: *Eichmann Interrogated: Transcripts from the Archives of the Israeli Police*, eds. Jochen von Lang with Claus Sibyll, trans. Ralph Manheim (Farrar, Straus & Giroux, 1983) (hereafter *Eichmann Interrogated*).

49 *Eichmann Interrogated*, 82–83, 167.

50 *EJ*, 51.

could speak with each other." Arendt comments acidly: "Six weeks after this normal human encounter, Storfer was dead."[51]

A third example is Eichmann's curious attitude toward his duties in Vienna as the "expert" on forced Jewish emigration, what today we call ethnic cleansing – Eichmann's job before the Nazi policy changed from expelling Jews to murdering them. Under duress, leaders of the Jewish community worked with Eichmann to make the process marginally less arduous for the victims. Eichmann seemed to see the leaders and himself as colleagues in a collective task, "pulling together."[52] In his prison memoir *Götzen* ("Idols"), Eichmann describes his attitude toward the Jewish functionaries as downright "benevolent" (*wohlwollend*), "free of any personal hatred," and marked by a "mutual business-related trust."[53] It was almost as if Eichmann thought they were teammates in the great enterprise of ethnic cleansing. Only if they all worked together could they make Austria *Judenrein*. Historian David Cesarani paints a much darker picture of Eichmann's dealings with the Viennese Jews: They were terrified; Eichmann was stony, cruel, and arrogant.[54]

Arendt might have cited additional examples. During his interrogation, Eichmann exclaims, with outraged horror, that he would have been "a devil" if he had allowed "cases of typhus or any other contagious diseases to be included in a shipment" of Jews to Auschwitz.[55] Apparently it didn't occur to Eichmann that the shipments themselves were diabolical, nor that his interrogator would think so. Historian Deborah Lipstadt offers several other instances drawn from Eichmann's testimony in which he said things that obviously would horrify and infuriate the judges and onlookers –

51 *EJ*, 51. Eichmann's recollection of his encounter with Storfer at Auschwitz is in *Eichmann Interrogated*, 150–51. A recent biographer celebrates Storfer as a rescuer of thousands of Jews, whose reputation was unjustifiably tarnished by his association with Eichmann. Gabriele Anderl, *9096 Leben: Der unbekannte Judenretter Berthold Storfer* (Rotbuch Verlag, 2012).

52 *EJ*, 48. I haven't located the source of her quotation.

53 *Götzen*, 101 (136). Before his capture, Eichmann told Sassen, "I had no difficulty with the Jewish functionaries. ... I just want to say that our collaboration at the Central Office was decently businesslike." "Eichmann's Own Story: Part II: 'To Sum It All Up, I Regret Nothing'," 57. And, referring to Storfer: "The man has always been decent, we worked together ... we both held up our end." *Götzen*, 150. Again, recalling his dealings with one of the leaders of the Hungarian Jewish community: "We were political opponents trying to arrive at a settlement, and we trusted each other perfectly." *Götzen*, 146. As we'll see in Chapter 2, the mutual trust was a figment of Eichmann's imagination.

54 David Cesarani, *Becoming Eichmann: Rethinking the Life, Times, and Trial of a "Desk Murderer"* (Da Capo Press, 2004), 64–71. Raphael Ben Nescher, the editor of *Götzen*, agrees: see the print edition of *Götzen*, 136n152.

55 *Eichmann Interrogated*, 162. Probably he thought it would be diabolical because he knew that those who were not immediately murdered would be put to use as slave laborers.

obviously, that is, had Eichmann been able to hear what he was saying through their ears.[56]

Notice that this inability to think from others' point of view has nothing to do with whether Eichmann was lying. Even if we suspect he was lying about trying to rescue Storfer from Auschwitz, the fact that he would call their last conversation a "normal human encounter" and expect Israeli Jews to agree shows incredible obtuseness. If, as some believe, his trial testimony was from start to finish a calculated misdirection to save his neck, it only reinforces Arendt's conclusion that being clever and calculating is entirely consistent with the inability to think from the standpoint of others. Of course, if his Storfer story was true, he was doubly thoughtless: first by imagining that Storfer in Auschwitz was "very pleased," and second by believing that his Israeli interrogator might sympathize with him because he tried and failed to rescue Storfer.

These examples illustrate quite clearly what Arendt means by Eichmann's inability to think from the point of view of others. Recall, though, that she also connects his inability to think with an inability to *speak*. What most struck her about Eichmann's testimony was his unbearable penchant for slogans, bureaucratic jargon, and expressions he repeated so often and so literally that they became the functional equivalent of clichés. "Officialese is my only language," he apologized at one point.[57] Eichmann recalls the "extraordinary sense of elation" one slogan gave him, and Arendt comments acidly that "you could almost see" the elation whenever a cliché or slogan "popped out of his mouth."[58]

Each period of Eichmann's life had its own phrases to elate him, and it never bothered him if they contradicted each other. During his interrogation, Eichmann explained melodramatically that he would never, ever again take an oath, because it was his loyalty oath to the Führer that led him astray. That included the witness's oath in a courtroom – but then, when the judges gave him the choice of whether or not to testify under oath, he promptly chose the oath.[59] When the Nazi journalist Sassen interviewed him before his capture, Eichmann recalled his end-of-the-war farewell speech to his men in which he declared that he would jump into his grave laughing at the thought of the five million Jews he had shipped to their deaths (a horrifying comment that Arendt, rightly or

[56] Deborah Lipstadt, *The Eichmann Trial* (Schocken, 2011), 110–12, 163–64. [57] *EJ*, 48.
[58] *EJ*, 47, 53.
[59] *EJ*, 54–55. Eichmann's insistence that he would never take an oath, including a witnesses' oath in court, is in *Eichmann Interrogated*, 198. In addition to the contradiction Arendt noticed, Eichmann had earlier told his interrogator that he would swear an oath that he never discussed gassing Jews with the commandant of Auschwitz. *Eichmann Interrogated*, 86.

wrongly, dismisses as "sheer rodomontade").[60] Then, in Israeli custody, he announced, "I shall gladly hang myself in public as a warning example for all anti-Semites on this earth."[61] Arendt remarks with some astonishment: "In his mind, there was no contradiction between 'I shall jump into my grave laughing,' appropriate for the end of the war, and 'I shall gladly hang myself . . . ', which now, under vastly different circumstances, fulfilled exactly the same function of giving him a lift."[62] As we shall see in §1.3, even at his own execution Eichmann sustained himself with uplifting, absurd clichés.

But what does Eichmann's penchant for "elating" clichés have to do with an inability to think from another's point of view? Arendt's idea is this: "No communication was possible with him, not because he lied [although she recognized that quite often he did] but because he was surrounded by the most reliable of all safeguards against the words and the presence of others, and hence against reality as such."[63]

Eichmann, in her diagnosis, was something akin to a solipsist of the present moment. Self-insulated from the reality of others, all he could immediately call on was the stream of his own affects – and that is why, in changed circumstances, contradictory phrases could "fulfill exactly the same function of giving him a lift." Lift trumped logic. Arendt observes that Eichmann's memory of the major events in the war was conspicuously faulty, except when he could associate them with events in his own career that elated him.[64] One of Eichmann's lawyers told an interviewer about Eichmann's astonishing ability to remember meals:

> Even concerning his early SS dinners, in 1934, 1935, he can tell you exactly what soup they had, what meat, and whether the dessert was fruit or cake. But when asked about the deportation of Jews, he says: "One hundred and fifty or two hundred and fifty thousand, I do not recall the exact numbers. It has been too long."[65]

60 *EJ*, 46. This, in fact, was the phrase that gave Eichmann his extraordinary sense of elation. "Eichmann's Own Story: Part II," 150. Arendt's "sheer rodomontade" diagnosis seems to take Eichmann's own explanation at face value: When his Israeli interrogator confronted him with these words from his farewell speech to his men as the Third Reich collapsed, Eichmann stammered out: "That is . . . theater, theater! . . . That was my . . . my, my last speech, my last speech to my men . . . my . . . my summation in the . . . in the . . . how shall I put it . . . in the apocalyptic situation." *Eichmann Interrogated*, 164. Earlier he had also called it "my brief – hmm, how shall I put it? – apocalyptic speech." *Eichmann Interrogated*, 110. Characteristically, Eichmann then denied he ever said it. "That sentence is not at all my style. . . . My men would have taken me for a megalomaniac, because they knew I hadn't killed five million Jews." *Eichmann Interrogated*, 165. Yet the sentence is a direct quote from Eichmann in his interview with Sassen.

61 *EJ*, 53. 62 *EJ*, 53–54. 63 *EJ*, 49. 64 *EJ*, 53, 81–82.

65 Harry Mulisch, *Criminal Case 40/61, the Trial of Adolf Eichmann: An Eyewitness Account*, trans. Robert Naborn (University of Pennsylvania Press, 2005), 52.

Eichmann's memory was little more than the memory of personal milestones, and he could articulate these only through the stock phrases he associated with them at the time. His inability to speak was a symptom of a lack of psychological integrity over time, and Arendt's thesis is that unless an individual can think from the standpoint of somebody else, the individual has no psychological integrity. It is precisely the ability to place ourselves as just one self among many that allows us to differentiate the self from its momentary affects.

Oddly enough, to be one individual, a person must be capable of becoming two, a key point to which I return in Chapter 4. As she argued in a 1971 essay: "For myself, articulating this being-conscious-of-myself, I am inevitably *two-in-one*."[66] Thinking is "the soundless dialogue of the I with itself."[67] The inability to speak with oneself and the inability to speak with others both arise from the fundamental inability to "*think*, namely, . . . think from the standpoint of somebody else."[68]

It is easy to see why Arendt would conclude that Eichmann was a moral chameleon. He drew his convictions from the slogans and opinions of those above and around him. Apart from "an extraordinary diligence in looking out for his personal advancement, he had no motives at all" – by which she evidently means motives arising from deep-seated, thought-out convictions.[69] To switch metaphors, Eichmann's personality was invertebrate, and the convictions of those above and around him, expressed in lowest common denominator slogans and memes, provided the exoskeleton that held it intact. This is *not* the same as thinking from another's point of view. It isn't thinking at all; it's parroting, and then enthusing about the things you parrot. (Whether Arendt got any of this right about Eichmann is deeply contested, and I consider that question in Chapter 2, and again in the postscript to Chapter 5 [§5.6])

"No motives at all" is hyperbole even by Arendt's own account, for she emphasizes that Eichmann took his loyalty oath to the Führer very seriously, and indeed believed his faithfulness to the oath redeemed him as a moral man.[70] But even this motive mirrors a cliché Eichmann got from others – for it happens to be the motto of the SS: "My honor is loyalty."

We need to tread carefully here to avoid caricature. No self-aware being could possibly be as empty as Arendt's sketch of Eichmann depicts him; and self-awareness among us language-users inherently involves inner conversation. A man incapable of talking with himself would be a zombie, not a human. In his prison memoir, Eichmann wrote that in his off hours

[66] TMC, 184. [67] *T*, 74–75. [68] *EJ*, 49. [69] *EJ*, 287. [70] *EJ*, 146–49.

he had always engaged in "a spiritual self-observation, in which my external 'I' carries on a dialogue with my inner 'I' – which also could be called conscience – and then on the basis of this 'conversation' takes a position."[71] This may be a lie, but he could hardly confabulate about internal dialogue if the phenomenon was foreign to him.[72]

So we must not take Arendt literally when she says that Eichmann is *incapable* of inner dialogue. She means that he never questioned the enterprise he was engaged in, or its monstrous premises – and, she claims, not because he believed them in any deep sense. Rather, he took them as givens, and whatever thinking he did took place only within their confines. To return to an earlier example, he congratulates himself on his "normal human conversation" with Storfer in Auschwitz, without considering whether any conversation in Auschwitz could be normal or human, or, more fundamentally, whether Auschwitz should exist. His inner questioning, such as it was, moved within the script provided by his "gods" and their "popes" (as he called the chief Nazi bureaucrats). It was, in that respect, thoughtless. In Chapter 5, we will look closely at Eichmann's weird and revealing descriptions of his own conscience. To anticipate: What Eichmann means by "a dialogue with my inner 'I'" was not a dialogue about right and wrong, but rather about his own feelings and whether they distressed him or reassured him. This is exactly what Arendt suspected: Eichmann cared only about his own elation or desolation.

We should also question whether Eichmann's negotiation skills amounted to genuine human insight. If the answer is yes, it would be evidence that Eichmann was indeed able to think from the point of view of others, casting doubt on Arendt's diagnosis of thoughtlessness. I think the answer is no.

Eichmann boasted that "I loved playing an open hand against all the Jewish political functionaries. ... For me, 'open hand' is a winged word."[73] Eichmann seemed fond of card game metaphors,[74] and the obvious suspicion is that he viewed his negotiations as akin to a card game. Eichmann could read the weaknesses and anticipate the strategic choices of the desperate Jewish leaders, or at least he thought he could. Beyond that poker player's skill, though, he understood nothing.[75] He had only the

71 *Götzen*, 581 (450).

72 Bettina Stangneth is convinced *Götzen* is a pack of lies – a pretense of conscience by an unrepentant Nazi fanatic, in hope of a sentence commutation. Stangneth, 366.

73 Quoted in Stangneth, 265, from the Sassen interviews.

74 *EJ*, 48.

75 This was also the conclusion of one of the psychiatrists, Shlomo Kulcsar, who examined Eichmann after his capture. José Brunner, "Eichmann's Mind: Psychological, Philosophical, and Legal Perspectives," *Theoretical Inquiries in Law* 1(2) (2000), 435–36.

most obtuse insight into their lived situation – the situation of being forced to play senseless card games with death, with a deck stacked against them. I return to this point in Chapter 2, examining in detail one of Eichmann's negotiations where he *mis*understood his Jewish counterpart by seeing in him nothing but another Eichmann.

Recall again Eichmann's conversation with his interrogator, Avner Less. He was trying to lay the foundation for his defense, so we must suppose that his negotiator's radar and manipulation skills were fully activated. Even so, he seemed incapable of hearing how his comments about his career frustrations, or about shipping typhus-infected Jews to Auschwitz, would sound to his interrogator.

## 1.3 Banality and Kitsch

Why call this complex of traits "banality"? Banality is not the most obvious word to describe an inability to speak in one's own words and to think from the standpoint of others. Arendt was convinced that these two failings were crucial to Eichmann's moral psychology. Yet labeling Eichmann "banal" sounds like an aesthetic judgment, not a moral or psychological one.

Perhaps Arendt recalled a 1946 letter from Jaspers, in which he protested attributing any kind of demonic greatness to the Nazis. Jaspers wrote, "we have to see these things in their total banality, in their prosaic triviality, because that's what truly characterizes them. Bacteria can cause epidemics that wipe out entire nations, but they remain bacteria."[76] Jaspers's diagnosis and his word may well have lodged in Arendt's memory. If so, she forgot where it came from. In a letter to Scholem, she wrote: "It's unclear to me why you characterize the phrase 'banality of evil' as a slogan. So far as I know, no one has ever used it before."[77]

I think her word choice is less fortuitous than this suggestion supposes. One fruitful way to connect banality with Eichmann's thoughtlessness and cliché-ridden speech is by focusing on a particular verbal tic of Eichmann's that caught Arendt's attention. Eichmann used the idiom "winged words" (*geflügelte Worte*) – meaning famous sayings that have passed into common speech – to refer to stock phrases and slogans.[78] This misuse of the idiom

[76] Jaspers to Arendt, October 19, 1946, *HA-KJ*, 62.

[77] Arendt to Scholem, July 20, 1963, *HA-GS*, 209.

[78] *EJ*, 48. Arendt called Eichmann's mistake "funny" – but only because "the horrible can be not only ludicrous but outright funny." *Winged Words* was the title of a German equivalent of *Bartlett's Familiar Quotations*, which would have been found in many households. German friends tell me

is, among other sins, an aesthetic misjudgment. To mistake political slogans for literary gems shows – to put it mildly – *bad taste.* It exemplifies bad judgment in the realm of aesthetics rather than morality or politics.

Bad taste of this sort is closely related to kitsch. Slogans are to genuine epigrams as kitsch is to art, and Eichmann's use of "winged words" to describe slogans is itself a kind of linguistic kitsch. Eichmann's own memoir style was notably kitschy, in a faux-literary way. "I came into the world as a human child on 19 March 1906."[79] "How much time fate allows me to live, I do not know."[80] "The voice of my heart, which no man can escape, constantly whispered the search for peace to me."[81] Kitsch is cliché that presents itself as deep and important. This is a point on which aesthetic definitions of kitsch agree. So understood, kitsch is a conspicuous form of banality, so much so that "banal" and "kitschy" are often interchangeable descriptions of artworks. In Eichmann's musings, and his perception of political memes as "winged words," we have textbook manifestations of banality.

The ultimate example of Eichmann's penchant for kitsch and cliché – ultimate in every sense – is his farewell speech at his execution. As Arendt bitingly puts it, Eichmann's "grotesque silliness" stayed with him to the last. "He was in complete command of himself, nay, he was more: he was completely himself."[82] First he announced that he was a *Gottgläubiger*, Nazi-speak for a deist who doesn't believe in the afterlife, and then he continued, "After a short while, gentlemen, *we shall all meet again.*" He concluded with a peroration: "Long live Germany, long live Argentina, long live Austria. *I shall not forget them.*" Arendt comments:

> In the face of death, he had found the cliché used in funeral oratory. Under the gallows, his memory played him the last trick; he was "elated" and he forgot that this was his own funeral.
>
> It was as though in those last minutes he was summing up the lesson that this long course in human wickedness had taught us – the lesson of the fearsome, word-and-thought-defying *banality of evil.*[83]

that "winged words" is no longer part of today's German vocabulary; they are unfamiliar with the idiom.

79 *Götzen,* 18 (77).

80 "Eichmann Tells His Own Damning Story," *Life*, November 28, 1960, 21 (quoting Eichmann from the Sassen interviews).

81 These last two are quoted in Stangneth, 199–200, from Eichmann's 1956 notes.

82 *EJ*, 252.

83 *EJ*, 252, emphasis in original.

Revealingly, this paragraph is the only place that the phrase "banality of evil" appears in *Eichmann in Jerusalem*, and Arendt illustrates it with Eichmann's kitsch at the gallows.

In itself, banality of taste hardly qualifies as banality of *evil.* Who cares if Eichmann had kitschy taste? The bridge between the aesthetic and moral comes when we remember that the kitsch that elated Eichmann was not innocuous mass-produced porcelain Pietàs or Elvis Presley wall hangings. It was Nazi propaganda and SS catchwords: "finance Jewry," "endurance," "hardness!" (as Eichmann explained, "an SS man was expected to be hard on himself and others"). Eichmann described all these as "winged words," and sometimes as "proverbs" (*Sprüche*).[84]

Of course slogans, like rallies, pageantry, and other political kitsch, were a deliberate and much-remarked Nazi propaganda strategy. In Nazi hands, kitsch became an instrument of evil. Official Nazi art was impressively kitschy even by the most exacting standards.[85]

None of this would surprise the last century's major theorists of kitsch: Theodor Adorno, Walter Benjamin, Hermann Broch, and Clement Greenberg.[86] All of them understood kitsch as a moral and political phenomenon, not only an aesthetic one. Kitsch manipulates sentiment and eliminates everything challenging and thought-provoking in art.[87]

84 Finance Jewry (*Finanzjudentum*): *Götzen*, 106 (141). This is a phrase of unusually sinister history: Hitler, in a Reichstag speech of January 30, 1939, said, "If international *Finanzjudentum* in and outside Europe should succeed in once again plunging the nations into a world war, then the result will not be the victory of Jewry, but rather the annihilation of the Jewish race in Europe!" Eichmann quotes this language in *Götzen*, 103 (138–39), but immediately disowns it as foolish (*töricht*). Hardness (*Härte*) and endurance (*Durchhaltevermögen*): *Eichmann Interrogated*, 157. As Eichmann explained, "these maxims (*Sprüche*) – as we called them – of Himmler's, usually made their appearance around the turn of the year. At that time, new winged words always caught on." *Eichmann Interrogated*, 157. (Here I have substituted "winged words" – the literal text – for the translator's "catchwords.")

85 The reader interested in Nazi kitsch may easily view the sculptures of Third Reich luminaries Arno Breker and Josef Thorak, and the paintings of Adolf Ziegler, whose outstandingly kitschy triptych of four Teutonic nudes (*The Four Elements*) hung over Hitler's mantel, was also tasked with purging "degenerate" modern art from the Third Reich.

86 Hermann Broch, "Evil in the Value-System of Art," in *Geist and Zeitgeist: The Spirit in an Unspiritual Age* (Counterpoint, 2003); Clement Greenberg, "Avant-Garde and Kitsch," in *Art and Culture* (Beacon Press, 1961); Theodor W. Adorno, with the assistance of George Simpson, "On Popular Music," *Studies in Philosophy and Social Science* 9(1) (1941): 17–48. All four theorists were friends or acquaintances of Arendt. Arendt edited the volume of Broch's complete works that included his essays on kitsch; she also edited the first English-language anthology of Benjamin's essays. She knew Adorno but detested him.

87 Benjamin had hopes that kitsch might stir up repressed revolutionary energy. But his famous description of fascism as politics made aesthetic marked his horrified recognition that it was Nazi propagandists, not communist revolutionaries, who were successfully using kitsch to mobilize mass political support. See Winfried Menninghaus, "On the 'Vital Significance' of Kitsch: Walter

Arendt agrees, but only up to a point. Unlike Greenberg and Adorno, she has no objection to the mass entertainment industry, and she accuses intellectuals who deny they enjoy the same entertainments as the masses of deluded snobbery.[88] But she fears that when objects of high culture are "rewritten, condensed, digested, reduced to kitsch in reproduction, or in preparation for the movies," the result is "culture . . . being destroyed in order to yield entertainment."[89]

This matters because artworks serve a political purpose that their reduction to kitsch jeopardizes. By its nature, good art poses challenges to its audience that invite discussion with others. Doing so, it creates a miniature society of plural opinions, when we discover through give and take with others that we don't all respond to films and plays and novels in the same way. For Arendt, discussion with others whose opinions differ from ours, including discussion of art and matters of taste, is *the* vital political activity. What bothers her about kitschified versions of high art is their instant emotional availability, which takes away the need for arguing with others about artworks. Here, at least, she agrees with Adorno and Harold Rosenberg: the latter defines kitsch as "art that has a predictable audience, predictable effects, predictable rewards."[90] The kitschification of culture is at once culture destroying and plurality destroying.

Her essay on culture is one of the earliest places where Arendt works out ideas about the close connection between aesthetic judgment and other kinds of judgment.[91] One unorthodox claim she advances there, that Kant's book on aesthetics forms the core of his political philosophy, became central to her later thinking, and we will return to it often in the chapters that follow. It was in the *Critique of Judgment* that Kant set out what he called the three "maxims of common human understanding": to think for oneself, to think from the standpoint of others, and to think consistently.[92] The second, which Kant called the maxim of "enlarged thought," especially caught Arendt's attention – and of course, her diagnosis of Eichmann's thoughtlessness is precisely that he seemed incapable

Benjamin's Politics of 'Bad Taste'," in *Walter Benjamin and the Architecture of Modernity*, eds. Andrew E. Benjamin and Charles Rice (Re.press, 2009), 39–58.

88 Arendt, "The Crisis of Culture," *BPF*, 206. Mysteriously, she praises a snotty diatribe against pop culture by Harold Rosenberg that drips with the kind of snobbery she warns about. Rosenberg, "Pop Culture and Kitsch Criticism," *Dissent* (Winter 1958): 14–19. Arendt calls Rosenberg's smug little essay "brilliantly witty." "The Crisis of Culture," 197. Ugh.

89 Arendt, "The Crisis of Culture," 204.

90 Rosenberg, "Pop Culture and Kitsch Criticism," 17.

91 For a deep and trenchant analysis of this essay, see D. N. Rodowick, *An Education in Judgment: Hannah Arendt and the Humanities* (University of Chicago Press, 2021), chapter 2.

92 Immanuel Kant, *Critique of Judgment*, §40. Ak. 5: 294 (hereafter *CJ*).

of enlarged thought in Kant's sense. Discussing artworks – say, the movie you and your friends have just seen together – not only gets us to notice things we missed, it also gets us to appreciate that other people don't see things the same way we do.

Furthermore, in those animated and highly enjoyable discussions of novels and plays and films, we can never *compel* others to agree with us. Rather, "the judging person – as Kant says quite beautifully – can only 'woo the consent of everyone else' in the hope of coming to an agreement with him eventually."[93] Wooing rather than proving is a kind of persuasion, "the typically political form of people talking with one another . . . where it is not knowledge or truth which is at stake, but rather judgment and decision."[94] Complex art invites multiple interpretations and therefore multiple opinions; wooing the consent of others requires give and take; and the give and take of opinions hones our own judgment.

Kitsch, exiling ambiguities and manipulating all of us to experience the same emotions, reduces that plurality of opinion and erodes human difference. The taste for kitsch is a taste for easy sentiment and uniformly shared pleasures marching in lockstep. It provides the undeniable lift of having others reinforce our own experience, but in doing so it takes away the need to think for ourselves (in violation of Kant's first maxim, to think for yourself, which he labeled the "maxim of unprejudiced thought" and which is his definition of enlightenment); and that lift, or group emotional high, stimulates unthinking conformism.[95] That was the overt aim of the Nuremberg rallies so memorably captured in Leni Riefenstahl's 1935 propaganda documentary *Triumph of the Will.* In that way, the banality of kitsch provides the raw material for the banality of evil.

It matters for Arendt, as it did for Kant, that judgments of taste claim general validity but cannot be proved. As we shall see, she identifies the faculty of moral judgment as the ability to discern right from wrong without appealing to rules or proofs, and in her view aesthetic judgments of beauty are a paradigm example of noninferential judgments that nevertheless lay claim to general validity – one of the cornerstone claims of Kant's aesthetic theory.

The analogy between aesthetic and moral judgment must not be pushed too far. Moral judgment is not the same thing as aesthetic judgment. But

[93] Arendt, "The Crisis in Culture," 222, quoting §19, *CJ*, "*Man wirbt um jedes anderen Bestimmung.*" Ak. 5:237. Arendt repeats this point in *Kant Lectures*, 72.

[94] Arendt, "The Crisis in Culture," 222.

[95] See Arendt's warning about the dangers of mass unanimity in "To Save the Jewish Homeland," in *JW*, 391–92.

Kant's three maxims don't by their terms limit themselves to aesthetic judgment, and in "The Crisis of Culture" it's the maxims that matter. Thinking for yourself, thinking from the point of view of others, and thinking consistently turn out to be intellectual virtues central to moral judgment – or so Arendt hopes to show.

All of which is to say that talking about the banality of evil is not simply the category mistake of judging morality through the lens of aesthetic disdain, which is undoubtedly a common failing among intellectuals. Arendt chose the word because the kind of banality she saw in Eichmann was a symptom of traits that made him a moral chameleon and undermined his moral judgment.

If, that is, she got him right.

CHAPTER 2

# *Did Arendt Get Eichmann Wrong?*

## 2.1 How Much Would It Matter if Arendt Got Eichmann Wrong?

From the beginning, Arendt's portrayal of Eichmann was controversial, and many commentators think Eichmann fooled her into believing he was something other than what he was: a diehard Nazi. Eichmann offered an "I was only a cog in the machine" defense, and while Arendt steadfastly rejects the defense, she seems to think Eichmann believed it. What if it turns out that Eichmann cynically contrived the defense for trial purposes, but in reality he never saw himself as a mere cog in a machine? What if the Eichmann Arendt saw in Jerusalem was a façade adopted purely for the trial? That is the diagnosis of Bettina Stangneth, in her deeply researched *Eichmann before Jerusalem*:

> Hannah Arendt read about Adolf Eichmann in the newspapers for the first time in 1943 at the latest, and eighteen years later she was familiar with all the research on him. . . . She read the transcripts of his hearing and the trial more thoroughly than almost anyone else. And for this very reason, she fell into his trap: Eichmann-in-Jerusalem was little more than a mask. She didn't recognize it.[1]

In their own books on Eichmann, the distinguished historians David Cesarani and Deborah Lipstadt concur that Arendt was deeply mistaken about him.[2] Suppose they are right. (I take up that question in Sections 2.2 and 2.3.) What difference would that make? Obviously, it would immeasurably weaken *Eichmann in Jerusalem* as a reliable piece of Holocaust history. Arendt's trial narrative would remain valuable as a contemporaneous

[1] Stangneth, xxii, xxiii. The "hearing" Stangneth refers to is Eichmann's interrogation by Israeli police captain Avner Less, from which Arendt draws throughout *EJ*. See *Eichmann Interrogated*. In 1943 Arendt read a newspaper story about Theresienstadt that named Eichmann as the "Gestapo Kommissar who terrorized the Jewish community in Prague." Stangneth, 36–37.

[2] Cesarani, 15; Lipstadt, *The Eichmann Trial*.

account by a reporter with "a gift for acute observation."[3] But Arendt's portrait of Eichmann would matter only as a cautionary lesson: Skilled acting can fool even an acute observer.

But *Eichmann in Jerusalem* is not only a historical work. It is also a study in moral psychology, and it was the genesis of the moral and legal philosophy Arendt developed in her final decade, notably in the essays "Thinking and Moral Considerations" and "Some Questions of Moral Philosophy." How would those be affected if Arendt got Eichmann wrong?

One answer is: not at all. Arendt's investigations of moral phenomena in her later works may have been prompted by the Eichmann case, but her arguments don't rest on the case. When she mentions Eichmann, it is only to explain what got her thinking about the themes these works pursue. As with all philosophy, the works stand or fall on the strength of their insights and arguments, not on any single example.

Although that answer is fundamentally right, it isn't entirely satisfying. The philosophy, remember, includes Arendt's effort to answer the Kantian *quaestio juris* of what entitles her to the concept "banality of evil," given that she encountered it as a fact. If the fact is no fact, perhaps there is no *quaestio juris* that needs to be answered.

Of course, even if Eichmann was not the banal evildoer Arendt thought he was, it may well be that others were (and are). But then we would like to know whether those others shared the trait Arendt singled out in Eichmann: the inability to think from the standpoint of others, generating the "moral chameleon" phenomenon and lack of moral judgment. Part of her philosophical proposal is that these phenomena hang together in an intelligible structure; and while that proposal draws on philosophical materials other than the Eichmann case, her diagnosis of Eichmann anchors the argument by keeping it real. Furthermore, the claim that even a high-level active participant in genocide – "one of the greatest criminals of that period"[4] – might be banal has independent interest, because on its face it seems so unlikely. Maybe it seems unlikely because it's wrong.

The discovery that Arendt got Eichmann wrong would be even more damaging to one of her legal conclusions, namely that the ground of his guilt cannot lie in his awareness of wrongdoing (his *mens rea*). Her proposition is "that this new type of criminal, who is in actual fact *hostis generis humani*, commits his crimes under circumstances that make it well-nigh impossible for him to know or to feel that he is doing wrong."[5] Recall that she describes Eichmann as "an average, 'normal' person, neither

[3] Stangneth, xxiii. [4] *EJ*, 288. [5] *EJ*, 276.

feeble-minded nor indoctrinated nor cynical," who nonetheless "could be perfectly incapable of telling right from wrong."[6] If Eichmann *was* indoctrinated or cynical, the challenge to fundamental principles of culpability that his case poses may not be as urgent as she believes.

In sum: If it turns out that Eichmann fooled Arendt, it would make little difference to her philosophical arguments, but it would weaken some of her most striking ancillary conclusions.

With these thoughts in mind, consider four possible readings of *Eichmann in Jerusalem* (which I list from the least to the most sympathetic):

1. Arendt got Eichmann thoroughly wrong, and that invalidates – or, at the very least, fails to confirm – the ideas in the book.
2. Even if her diagnosis of Eichmann was wrong, it is right about enough other perpetrators that the banality of evil remains important. Maybe Eichmann wasn't the "ordinary man" Arendt thought he was; plenty of other *génocidaires* were and are.[7] And not only in Nazi Germany: legal scholar Mark Drumbl has argued in an Arendtian vein that a great many of the perpetrators of the Rwanda genocide were "good citizens" doing what their leaders told them was their patriotic duty.[8] Or, to take a very different example, it is hard to see the Indonesian death squad in Joshua Oppenheimer's astonishing documentary *The Act of Killing* as anything other than the banality of evil brought to life, as they deck themselves in drag and cowboy hats to reenact their 1965 murders. In Arendt's terms, they seem like clowns, not monsters. In line with Arendt's diagnosis of thoughtlessness, their leader Anwar Congo becomes shaken when he reenacts the role of a victim, and the horror of being garroted dawns on him, apparently for the first time. When he next revisits the scene of one of his crimes, he vomits.

6 *EJ*, 26.

7 The allusion is to Christopher Browning, *Ordinary Men: Reserve Police Battalion 101 and the Final Solution in Poland* (HarperCollins, 1992). This second interpretation is a version of what Roger Berkowitz calls the "Yes/No" reading: Yes, Arendt was right about some Nazi murderers; no, she was wrong about Eichmann. Roger Berkowitz, "Yes and No: The Split the Difference Approach to the Banality of Evil," *Amor Mundi* (weekly publication of Hannah Arendt Center for Politics and Humanities), May 31, 2013. Berkowitz believes that the Yes/No reading is contradictory. He believes this, however, only about a stronger version of the Yes/No reading than the one offered here – a version that claims that "she was right in general, but wrong about Eichmann." The version offered here is not that she was right "in general," but rather that her diagnosis fits many evildoers but not Eichmann. There is no contradiction in this version.

8 Mark Drumbl, *Atrocity, Punishment, and International Law* (Cambridge University Press, 2007). For a more skeptical view of Arendt's sociology of mass atrocity, see Mark J. Osiel, *Mass Atrocity, Ordinary Evil, and Hannah Arendt: Criminal Consciousness in Argentina's Dirty War* (Yale University Press, 2001).

3. Arendt got Eichmann largely right. She may have underestimated his vainglory and ambition as well as his Nazi outlook, and gotten some details wrong, but these are mistakes of emphasis in a moral-psychological portrait that is fundamentally sound.

Perhaps the most interesting reading is this:

4. Whether Arendt got Eichmann right is unknowable for a reason she got right. Under her diagnosis, Eichmann was a moral chameleon. In the company of Nazis, including the Nazi ex-pats in Argentina, his colors turned (or relapsed) toward murderous antisemitism and race ideology. He drew his self-recognition from their recognition, and that is why he pumped up his Nazi boasting, including his subjective commitment to what he was saying, when he gave the notorious and damning interviews to SS journalist Willem Sassen in Buenos Aires. But that doesn't imply that Eichmann-in-Argentina was the real Eichmann while Eichmann-in-Jerusalem was an imposter. Both were equally real – or, perhaps more accurately, equally unreal.[9]

I suspect that (2) is correct: Even if Eichmann was not the stereotypical desk criminal, there were and are plenty of desk criminals in the world, committing greater and lesser crimes. But, as noted earlier, one would also want to know whether most display the traits Arendt thought she saw in Eichmann and called "banality of evil." This would be hard to investigate, however, since we have only accidental anecdotes to go on. Of course, if Arendt's conclusions about moral psychology are convincing on independent grounds, they might themselves offer reasons for accepting (2), at least as a working hypothesis.

But I don't think we have to settle for (2). My own assessment combines elements of (3) and (4). For reasons set out in Sections 2.2–2.4, I think Arendt very likely got Eichmann right on her most significant points, notwithstanding errors in emphasis; but at the very least, the historical record is consistent enough with the "moral chameleon" diagnosis to conclude there may be no "true Eichmann" to get right. And that itself would support the concept "banality of evil."

I am not basing these conclusions on new historical discoveries. I base them on the evidence that Cesarani, Lipstadt, and Stangneth themselves present, along with the trial transcript, published excerpts from the Sassen documents, Eichmann's police interrogation, and his prison memoir.

9 Here I am in agreement with Berkowitz, "Yes and No."

## 2.2 The Problem of Interpreting Eichmann

Eichmann may be a riddle, but he was no Sphinx. As Stangneth reveals, Eichmann was logorrheic; he produced reams of memoirs, self-vindications, philosophical pronouncements, even theological forays. In prison, his output sometimes reached eighty pages a day, and he was still scribbling on the day of his execution. His oral style, Stangneth reports, was incessant monologue, and even his German lawyer found his German hard to follow; his written style is convoluted and packed with clumsy, "elevated" metaphors (which I described earlier as kitsch).

His memoirs, interrogation, and testimony remain a riddle because Eichmann was the ultimate unreliable narrator. Before and during the war, he inflated his own importance; in Jerusalem, for obvious reasons, he minimized it. Sometimes he did both at once. Thus, in the Sassen interviews we find Eichmann voicing fanatical dedication to the murder of the Jews, using brutal, undiluted Nazi rhetoric. But then:

> In actual fact, I was a little cog in the machinery that carried out the directives and orders of the German Reich. I am neither a murderer nor a mass-murderer. I am a man of average character, with good qualities and many faults. I was not the "Czar of the Jews," as a Paris newspaper once called me, nor was I responsible for all the good and evil deeds done against them. Where I was implicated in the physical annihilation of the Jews, I admit my participation freely and without pressure. After all, I was the one who transported the Jews to the camps.[10]

Did he call himself a cog because he was already laying the groundwork for a future defense or because he believed it? Were his vicious racial views puffery and Hitler mimicry for the imagined readers of the Nazi publication Sassen had in mind, or did he really see himself as an all-in warrior in a racial death struggle? In Jerusalem, he denied he was an antisemite, and likened his attitude to that of any other soldier who has nothing personal against the enemies he is ordered to kill. Could there possibly be any truth to that? His various versions of his story are replete with factual errors; which ones are lies and which are honest mistakes is sometimes hard to say.[11] And the versions contradict each other.

[10] "Eichmann Tells His Own Damning Story," part 1, 21.

[11] For example, in his interrogation he refers to Benjamin Murmelstein, one of the Jewish leaders in Vienna, as a rabbi in Prague. *Eichmann Interrogated*, 58. Eichmann had no obvious reason to lie; nothing of consequence turned on whether Murmelstein was from Prague or Vienna. Did Eichmann misremember? Misspeak? Or was he deliberately seeding random factual errors into his story to maximize confusion?

As for his lies, they are frequent and mostly obvious, and they were obvious to Arendt as well as to the Jerusalem judges. Others were more subtle and went undetected until Stangneth smoked them out.[12] His prison memoir *Götzen* (*Idols*) laments that he had served false gods whom he later recognized as mere idols – just the opposite of his declarations of Nazi devotion in Argentina.[13] Is *Götzen* a last-ditch fiction to wrest a merciful decree from the Israelis or a genuine change in outlook, and if the latter, when did his outlook change? Were his invocations of Kant at his trial a window into his warped conception of duty, as Arendt thought, or a confession that he always knew he was doing wrong, as per Lipstadt, or an out-and-out lie, as Stangneth argues, or a common Nazi distortion of Kant, as in Michael Wildt's summary of several historians' views?[14]

Or did he, as Arendt would have it, say and write whatever gave him a lift at each moment, indifferent to its truth – changing his chameleon's colors and scattering truth and lies in response to whatever he imagined were his audience's expectations? In Harry Frankfurt's memorable definition, bullshit is speech in which the speaker doesn't care whether it is true or false.[15] Was Eichmann bullshitting as well as lying, and if so, at what points? Might he have been bullshitting himself as well as others?

For that matter, Eichmann's views may have changed over three decades – most people's do – with his latter-day views distorting his memories. Distinguishing truth from falsehood is hard enough; discriminating among falsehoods to sort out deliberate lies from boasting, unconscious memory revisions, errors, changes in view, and sheer bullshit from a known bullshitter is harder still. It is an interpretive and not purely investigative challenge.

For example, Stangneth thinks Eichmann's prison memoir, *Götzen*, was a ruse meant to convince the Israelis that Eichmann had converted to humanitarianism, because according to the Nazi race theory he believed, humanitarianism is the sort of nonsense Jews go for. By contrast, Lipstadt does not find *Götzen* humanitarian at all. Quite the contrary, she sees it as a

[12] For example, when Eichmann was asked who was present at the Sassen conversations, he covered for his Argentinian comrades by giving the names of people who weren't there instead of those who were.

[13] Stangneth notes that *Götzen* "reads like a counterargument" to one of his Argentine memoirs, 232. A comparative study of the two documents is Imtrud Wojak, *Eichmanns Memoiren: Ein kritischer Essay* (Campus Verlag, 2001).

[14] *EJ*, 135–36; Lipstadt, *The Eichmann Trial*, 135; Stangneth, 217–18; Michael Wildt, "Eichmann und der kategorische Imperativ, oder: Gibt es eine nationalsozialististische Moral?," in *Dokumente, Forsschungsstand, Kontroversen*, eds. Norbert Kampe and Peter Klein (Böhlau Verlag, 2013).

[15] Harry G. Frankfurt, *On Bullshit* (Princeton University Press, 2005), 47.

damning piece of evidence against Eichmann.[16] This disagreement between two scrupulous historians (who both think Arendt got Eichmann wrong) illustrates that Eichmann's texts are not self-interpreting.

Compounding the problem, Stangneth and Lipstadt emphasize that those who worked with Eichmann during the war were also unreliable narrators. Even before the war ended, they realized that the more they could distance themselves from Eichmann and pin every crime on him, the better their own chances for postwar rehabilitation, not to mention survival. Their testimony cannot be trusted. Nor can other sources. Sassen had his own agenda of denying the "myth of six million" in order to inspire a Nazi renaissance and a Fourth Reich. Presumably, Eichmann's family had ulterior motives as well, financial and otherwise. (At the time Stangneth wrote, they were still hanging on to one of his Argentina manuscripts until someone met their sale price.)

For an illustration of the difficulty, Eichmann's wife, Vera, recalls that when she arrived in Argentina in 1952 with German news clippings describing her husband as a mass murderer, Eichmann exclaimed, "They've gone mad, I'm not a murderer, I won't stand for it. I'm going to go back to Germany."[17] This excited utterance bolsters Arendt's case that Eichmann could not tell right from wrong. But Vera Eichmann's recollection comes in a 1962 interview she gave to *Paris Match*. There is no way we can know whether Eichmann really thought he was no murderer, nor whether Vera accurately remembered his words ten years later, nor whether she was lying outright about what he said to burnish her husband's image.

## 2.3 How Banal Was Eichmann? (1): Critiques of Arendt

Those who conclude that Arendt got Eichmann wrong point to four issues. First, that Eichmann gulled her into thinking he was stupid when he was anything but. Second, that Arendt bought into his "I was only following orders" defense, when in fact he was an active agent and tireless initiator of anti-Jewish horrors. Third, that Arendt portrayed Eichmann as a petty bureaucrat and "desk murderer," as he misleadingly portrayed himself. Fourth, that Arendt wrongly believed Eichmann when he said he was no antisemite; in reality, he had quaffed deeply from the cup of Nazi eliminationist antisemitism. Even if Arendt drew halfway reasonable

[16] Stangneth, 367; Lipstadt, *The Eichmann Trial*, 164. Lipstadt thinks this because in *Götzen* Eichmann admits that he was following orders that his own conscience told him were wrong.

[17] Stangneth, 121.

conclusions from the information available to her at the time of the trial, half a century of additional research has unearthed a great deal more evidence that Eichmann was a fervent Nazi. The new evidence includes, in particular, the tapes and unabridged transcripts of the Sassen conversations, a large chunk of a 1956 autobiographical manuscript, and a great deal more information about his continuing involvement in Nazi circles during his years in hiding – material that Stangneth uncovered. I consider the first three points in this section, and the final point, which requires lengthier treatment, in the section that follows.

### *2.3.1 Stupidity*

The first criticism, that Arendt thought Eichmann was stupid, is one I earlier called a misunderstanding. But it is so persistent, and seeing its error is so central to understanding Arendt's philosophy, that I take it up again. The source of the error lies in Arendt's crucial description of Eichmann's affliction as an *inability to think*, which may easily be mistaken for charging him with low intellect. Mary McCarthy, who often advised Arendt on English usage, warned her that "thoughtlessness ... doesn't mean what you want it to mean in English."[18] Remember that what Arendt means by thinking is not intellectual horsepower but the ability to think from the standpoint of others, and therefore to engage in inner dialogue and reflection.

McCarthy rightly guessed that Arendt's word choice would mislead her readers, including very distinguished readers. Richard Evans refers to "Arendt's belief that Eichmann was unintelligent." Richard Wolin complains that "[b]y underestimating Eichmann's intellect, Arendt also misjudged the magnitude of his criminality." Tony Judt wrote that "she argues that evil comes from a simple failure to *think*. If this implies that evil is a function of stupidity, then Arendt is merely indulging a tautology of her own making."[19] But the implication is not there, and neither is the tautology.

That this criticism misunderstands Arendt is already clear from *Eichmann in Jerusalem*, where she insisted that Eichmann "was not stupid. It was sheer thoughtlessness – *something by no means identical with*

[18] McCarthy to Arendt, June 9, 1971, *BF*, 296.

[19] Richard J. Evans, "Eichmann before Jerusalem: The Unexamined Life of a Mass Murderer" review, *The Guardian*, October 17, 2014; Wolin, "The Banality of Evil: The Demise of a Legend"; and Tony Judt, "At Home in This Century," *New York Review of Books*, April 6, 1995, 10.

*stupidity* – that predisposed him to become one of the greatest criminals of that period."[20] In subsequent writing she repeats the point that "absence of thought is not stupidity; it can be found in highly intelligent people."[21] This is plain text. Perhaps Arendt's critics overlook it because it seems so counterintuitive: What could inability to think mean if not stupidity?

Wolin points to a 1964 interview in which Arendt spoke of Eichmann's "outrageous stupidity" (or, in Wolin's rendering of *empörende Dummheit*, "revolting stupidity"). But he overlooks her next sentence: "Eichmann was perfectly intelligent, but in this respect [i.e., thinking from another's point of view] he was stupid. It was this stupidity that was so outrageous."[22] He also overlooks that *Eichmann in Jerusalem* asks directly whether Eichmann was afflicted with "outrageous stupidity," using those exact words. And Arendt's answer is no. Rather, "German society of eighty million people had been shielded against reality and factuality by exactly the same means, the same self-deception, lies, *and stupidity* that had now become ingrained in Eichmann's mentality."[23] Obviously, she is not saying that Germans are dopes; she uses "stupidity" in a different sense. But she leaves no doubt about her meaning: Eichmann was an intelligent man who didn't think.

### 2.3.2 *Obedience and Agency*

What about the criticism that Eichmann exhibited a level of agency and initiative that belied his "I was only following orders" defense (which he indeed repeated ad nauseum in both his interrogation and trial)? David Cesarani attributes to Arendt the view that Eichmann engaged in "robot-like obedience to orders."[24] In the same vein, Lipstadt writes that Arendt "saw an automaton who was just passing on information."[25]

Actually not. Arendt's view about Eichmann's obedience to orders is substantially more subtle, more interesting, and above all more important than that, and it emphasizes that obedience can involve high levels of agency and initiative. What prompts her discussion is Eichmann's remarkable claim, in both his police interrogation and the trial, that he had tried to live his life by Kant's principles. He explained that he had read Kant's

[20] *EJ*, 287–88 (emphasis added). [21] *T*, 13.

[22] "Eichmann Was Outrageously Stupid": Interview by Joachim Fest, *Das Thema*, SWR TV, Germany, November 9, 1964, trans. Andrew Brown, in *Hannah Arendt: The Last Interview and Other Conversations* (Melville House: 2013), 48.

[23] *EJ*, 51, 52 (emphasis added). [24] Cesarani, *Becoming Eichmann*, 12.

[25] Lipstadt, *The Eichmann Trial*, 115.

*Critique of Practical Reason*, and astonished the judges even further by quoting the categorical imperative more or less correctly: "I meant by this that the principle of my volition and the principle of my life must be such that it could at any time be raised to be the principle of general legislation, as Kant more or less puts it in his categorical imperative."[26]

Arendt remarks how outrageous it was to invoke Kant in his defense, and guesses that in his own mind Eichmann distorted the categorical imperative to Hans Frank's Nazi version: "Act in such a way that the Führer, if he knew your action, would approve it."[27] In Eichmann's self-proclaimed version of the categorical imperative "for the little man," she explains,

> all that is left of Kant's spirit is the demand that a man do more than obey the law, that he go beyond the mere call of obedience and identify his own will with the principle behind the law – the source from which the law sprang. In Kant's philosophy, that source was practical reason; in Eichmann's household use of him, it was the will of the Führer. Much of the horribly painstaking thoroughness in the execution of the Final Solution ... can be traced to the odd notion, indeed very common in Germany, that to be law-abiding means not merely to obey the laws but to act as though one were the legislator of the laws that one obeys. Hence the conviction that nothing less than going beyond the call of duty will do.[28]

The call of duty requires going beyond the call of duty. If she is right, there is no contradiction between Eichmann's admission that "I did my job with unusual zeal" and his insistence that he was only following orders – specifically, what he believed were the Führer's orders which, as Eichmann pointed out, had the force of law in the Third Reich.[29]

[26] *The Trial of Adolf Eichmann*, vol. 4, Session 105, July 20, 1961, at 1803 (hereafter: Eichmann Trial Proceedings). Eichmann returns to this point in *Götzen*, 140–42 (168–69). He points out that only rarely do orders in wartime correspond to Kant's "moral law within." *Götzen*, 142 (169). He traces his "Kant preference" back to his childhood religious education. *Götzen*, 585 (452).

[27] *EJ*, 136. Arendt says she is quoting from Frank's 1942 *Die Technik des Staates* (1942), 15–16. I have not verified the quotation.

[28] *EJ*, 136–37. Her paraphrase of Eichmann's "categorical imperative for a small man's domestic use" is inaccurate. What Eichmann said was: "True to the law, obedient, a proper personal life, not to come into conflict with the law." Eichmann Trial Proceedings, vol. 4, Session 105, 1803. It does not mention the Führer's will or going beyond the call of duty. This inaccuracy is not important for the argument she makes here. But it is relevant to whether Eichmann hewed to SS morality: Kantian moral regard for other members of one's *Volk* but none at all outside the *Volk* – a kind of "universal particularism," as some writers describe it. Wildt, "Eichmann und der kategorische Imperativ, oder: Gibt es eine nationalsozialistische Moral?," 160 (summarizing views of Aurel Kolnai and Werner Konitzer). Eichmann's "small man" version of the categorical imperative gives no hint of anything as ambitious as "universal particularism."

[29] The quote about zeal is in *Eichmann Interrogated*, 156. For Eichmann's invocation of the Nazi legal maxim *Führerworte haben Gesetzeskraft* – the Führer's words have the force of law – see *Eichmann Interrogated*, 124; *EJ*, 148. The source of this maxim is the constitutional doctrine of the Roman

This conception of obedience as identification of one's will with the superior's is perfectly consistent with active agency and initiative. Indeed, for someone in an executive position, it *demands* active agency and initiative.[30] In this respect, at least, "obedience to orders" differs decisively from the low-level execution of mechanical tasks that was the subject of Stanley Milgram's famous obedience experiments, although those may shed light on the behavior of low-level perpetrators.[31]

Whether or not Arendt is right that this conception of obedience as identification with the superior's will is common in Germany, it is certainly not unique to Germany. It isn't even unusual. Robert Jackall, in his sociological classic about American corporate culture, explains that managers quickly learn the corporate adage that orders should be followed in advance – precisely the model of obedience under discussion. The result is a system where "even the CEO's wishes and whims are taken as commands by close subordinates on the corporate staff, who turn them into policies and directives. . . .'When he sneezes, we all catch colds.'"[32] In one sense, the manager is "just obeying orders": He has his assignments, and his own inclinations are beside the point. But foot-dragging acquiescence, or grudging passive obedience, won't do. Ambitious managers don't merely work to the rule; they aggressively pursue their bosses' ends. That is why "overly conscientious managers are particularly useful at the middle levels

empire: "What the Emperor has determined has the force of a statute" (*quod principi placuit legis habet vigorem*). Barry Nicholas, *An Introduction to Roman Law* (Oxford University Press, 1976), 17n2.

30 See Mark J. Osiel, *Mass Atrocity, Ordinary Evil, and Hannah Arendt: Criminal Consciousness in Argentina's Dirty War* (Yale University Press, 2001), 91–92. Osiel agrees that Arendt never depicted Eichmann as an automaton. He also argues that to navigate the Nazi ecosystem Eichmann must have engaged in thinking and judging in Arendt's sense, but from Nazi rather than Kantian premises – which puts Osiel in fundamental disagreement with Arendt. However, his critique supposes that Arendt is a Kantian in her ethics, which she is not. *T*, 222–23n83. It supposes as well that Eichmann was genuinely committed to Nazi "morality" (the scare-quotes are mine), which is precisely what Arendt doubted – not because he never espoused it, but because his commitment was skin deep.

31 Cesarani complains that "Arendt's assessment possessed almost scientific status thanks to Stanley Milgram's 'research' on the propensity for obedience to orders," Cesarani, *Becoming Eichmann*, 11. In the Milgram experiments, subjects were ordered to administer escalating electric shocks to a man when he got questions wrong in a memory test – ostensibly to test the effect of pain on memory, but actually to study obedience to orders. More than three-fifths of the subjects went all the way to lethal shocks despite the victim's protests and screams. The "victim" was a confederate of the experimenter, and the shocks were fake. Cesarani is doubtless right that many writers conflate Arendt and Milgram – I have made that mistake myself – but it *is* a mistake. I am uncertain why Cesarani uses scare-quotes to refer to "Milgram's 'research.'" It obviously is research. My point is simply that the kind of obedience Milgram studied is not the kind of obedience Arendt ascribes to Eichmann.

32 Robert Jackall, *Moral Mazes: The World of Corporate Managers* (Oxford University Press, 1988), 21–22.

of the structure. Upwardly mobile men and women . . . who find themselves in higher status milieux, seem to have the requisite level of anxiety, and perhaps tightly controlled anger and hostility, that fuels an obsession with detail."[33] (Let me repeat my earlier caution: This comparison is not intended to suggest any moral equivalence between corporate managers and Eichmann. The point is simply that the conception of obedience as active identification with the leader's will is not a quirky one.)

In the Third Reich, the desire to anticipate the Führer's will set off a competition in radicalism among Party elites; in the words of Hitler biographer Volker Ullrich, "his paladins tried to trump one another with ever more extreme demands and measures."[34] Ullrich is referring specifically to the period before the war, and to those higher-ups who had face-to-face access to Hitler, as Eichmann did not. But it seems plausible that some of Eichmann's initiatives grew from parallel motivations with respect to his own superiors' wishes, which he assumed originated with Hitler.[35] One perverse consequence is that functionaries executing the Führer's will may have been emboldening or even shaping that will. Probably, then, Arendt's view that Hitler always had the most radical agenda in his government, and in fact was the sole ultimate decision-maker, is mistaken.[36] She underrates the responsibility of other members of the elite for urging ideas on a Hitler who was more indecisive – and maybe emptier – than Arendt supposed. And she radically underestimates the independent agency of officials up and down the hierarchy of the Third Reich, something well documented by many historians.

These mistakes actually support her diagnosis. The crucial point is that an ambitious manager can launch an initiative and describe it as "just following orders" in the sincere belief that taking the initiative *is* following orders – even if the "orders" are never explicit, merely communicated through generalities, or through winks and nods. This is a moral phenomenon of immense importance in organizational settings. "Gentlemen, the

33 Jackall, *Moral Mazes*, 21. There is evidence of "tightly controlled anger and hostility" in Eichmann; see Lipstadt, *The Eichmann Trial*, 116–17.

34 Volker Ullrich, *Hitler: Ascent, 1889–1939*, trans. Jefferson Chase (Bodley Head, 2016), 578. This is also the view of another Hitler biographer, Ian Kershaw.

35 This is an issue that continues to be debated. Hitler disliked putting orders in writing, and one complication to assigning responsibility for particular decisions lies in the fact that, in the words of Ullrich, "[m]isunderstandings and misinterpretations were an inevitable part of this oral leadership style," which "also opened up considerable room for those around Hitler to exert an influence." Ullrich, *Hitler: Ascent, 1889–1939*, 577–78. In other words, those with personal access to Hitler could shape the very decisions they then implemented. According to one of Hitler's personal aides, Goebbels was especially skilled at this strategy. Ullrich, *Hitler: Ascent, 1889–1939*, 578.

36 E.g., PRUD, 30.

gloves are coming off" – a memo from a US officer to interrogators in Iraq in 2002 – was interpreted by some as an order to torture uncooperative prisoners for information, which perhaps was not its intention (but perhaps was).

None of this denies that Eichmann was also obedient in the more obvious passive sense. Harry Mulisch, who covered the Eichmann trial for a Dutch periodical, noticed that whenever the judges entered the courtroom Eichmann was always the first to stand up; and one of Eichmann's lawyers told Mulisch that "he would jump rope the whole day if they ordered him to jump rope the whole day."[37] When the Israelis captured him, Eichmann requested permission to use the toilet; from behind the closed door he called out "May I begin?" and waited for his captors' go-ahead before moving his bowels.[38] But there is no inconsistency between this jaw-dropping deference and the active agency with which he served Hitler's will during the war.

"May I begin?" does suggest something that may have been truly distinctive about Eichmann's obedience, both in its active and passive varieties: He seemed to worship orders, just because they were orders. This is Mulisch's diagnosis in a chapter titled "The Order As Fate": an order "emerges as something larger than the one giving it and the one receiving it ... as a superhuman power that has to be obeyed."[39] In Eichmann's words, one is to "click one's heels together and say 'Yes, sir,' and simply serve."[40] In *Götzen*, he likens himself to an iron filing caught in a magnetic field – but he also says that he would like to be the magnet bringing the iron filings of his unruly emotions into military formation.[41]

But, to repeat the main point, obedience for a management-level bureaucrat is entirely consistent with demonically active agency and initiative. Eichmann's active agency is something Arendt never denied or doubted.

### 2.3.3 *A Petty Bureaucrat?*

As for the claim that Arendt wrongly believed that Eichmann was no more than a petty bureaucrat, the simple answer is that she suggests nothing of

[37] Mulisch, *Criminal Case 40/61, the Trial of Adolf Eichmann*, 112. Of course, we must take this with a grain of salt. Defense counsel speaking with reporters during a trial will say things consistent with the case they're making in court.

[38] Lipstadt, *The Eichmann Trial*, 17. This anecdote is oddly consonant with a vulgar corporate adage Jackall reports, used by managers to describe "how the power of CEOs ... affects them. ... 'When he says "Go to the bathroom," we all get the shits.'" Jackall, *Moral Mazes*, 22.

[39] Mulisch, *Criminal Case 40/61*, 111.

[40] Quoted in Mulisch, *Criminal Case 40/61*, 110.

[41] *Götzen*, 582–83 (451).

the sort.[42] To be sure, Eichmann described himself this way as part of his defense strategy.[43] But remember that Arendt called him one of the greatest criminals of the period. She reports trial evidence about Eichmann's travels and negotiations, his activism, his visits to murder sites, and his leadership of an "Eichmann Commando" in Hungary – evidence that obviously made his insistence that "all our work was paperwork" absurd.[44] No wonder, then, that she never labels him a mere functionary or petty bureaucrat.

To be sure, in her essay on the Auschwitz trial she calls Eichmann a "desk murderer par excellence," but all she meant was that he was not a direct physical perpetrator like the Auschwitz defendants. Her use of "desk murderer" in that essay cannot mean "petty bureaucrat," for she also calls Hitler and Himmler desk murderers.[45] She *does* insist that Eichmann's role in the Holocaust was not as preeminent as the prosecution asserted, or that his own boasting sometimes made it out to be. But here the facts bear her out. His military rank was lieutenant colonel, and he was fifth in his chain of command: Hitler, Himmler and Göring, Heydrich, Müller, Eichmann.[46] That is high enough to make him far more than a mere accomplice (as he described himself), but not one of the masterminds of the Holocaust. He was upper management but not leadership. What made Eichmann unique was that he was the highest-level Nazi whose sole job was organizing the deportation, and transportation to death camps, of the European Jews. That, not his rank or leadership role, was what made him one of the greatest criminals of the Holocaust.

## 2.4 How Banal Was Eichmann? (2): The Argentina Papers

The final doubt about Arendt's conclusions is that information unknown to Arendt unmistakably reveals Eichmann as a fanatical Nazi. This is the most serious challenge to the banality of evil. Bettina Stangneth, in

42 Even Lipstadt, mostly a careful reporter of Arendt's views, errs on this point, writing, "she declared him a desk-level bureaucrat who showed little initiative and had few talents." *The Eichmann Trial*, 163. Arendt highlighted Eichmann's special talents at organization and negotiation. *EJ*, 45.

43 *Eichmann Interrogated*, 83, 113. 44 *Eichmann Interrogated*, 113.

45 Eichmann as "desk murderer par excellence", Arendt, "Auschwitz on Trial," in *RJ*, 241; Hitler and Himmler as desk murderers, *RJ*, 238.

46 I include Göring, although he was not in the SS chain of command, because it was Göring who commissioned Heydrich to prepare and execute the Final Solution. Letter from Göring to Heydrich, July 31, 1941, www.jewishvirtuallibrary.org/gring-commission-to-heydrich [https://perma.cc/D3RW-M3EN]. However, Göring apparently wrote this letter at Heydrich's prompting. Yaacov Lozowick, *Hitler's Bureaucrats: The Nazi Security Police and the Banality of Evil*, trans. Haim Watzman (Continuum, 2000), 89.

particular, has done a brilliant job of assembling all the scattered evidence into a single picture of an unrepentant and unreconstructed Nazi with exceptional abilities to deceive people.[47]

Stangneth shows, first, that Eichmann planned his initial escape into hiding (in northern Germany) with extraordinary cunning, including planting false information that he had escaped to the Middle East. Second, she shows that he had extensive and continuous involvement with Nazi networks that helped him escape to Argentina, and, further, that during his Argentina years he was a familiar and well-known denizen of Nazi circles who welcomed him, and were themselves welcomed by Argentinian leader Juan Perón.[48] Eichmann was anything but the lonely fugitive. These Nazi circles did more than reminisce about the good old days; they talked German politics and dreamed of resurrecting National Socialism back home. Some hoped to return to Germany, serve what they assumed would be short sentences, and enter electoral politics in coalition with far-right parties – the first step toward a putsch.[49] (The far-right parties were soon outlawed – but stay tuned as the Alternative für Deutschland rises in today's German politics.)

Among this Argentine circle were the Dutch journalist Willem Sassen, an SS man during the war, and Eberhard Fritsch, an Argentinian of German extraction and Nazi enthusiasms, who ran a small publishing house. Fritsch published neo-Nazi books and a newspaper for distribution in Germany – in Stangneth's memorable words, a "pulpy magazine ... with its Nazi ideology (including nightmarish racial theory) and fascist nostalgia – a combination of Alpine kitsch, sentimentality, and Teutonic romanticism, like a lace doily with a swastika pattern."[50] In 1956, Sassen and Fritsch signed a contract with Eichmann to produce a book of memoirs, and to that end Sassen proposed taping and transcribing a series of conversations that would systematically review histories of the war.[51] To prepare for the sessions, Eichmann wrote a manuscript titled *The Others Spoke, Now I Want to Speak!*[52]

The Sassen sessions took place over nearly six months and involved a rotating cast of characters, with as many as six different voices distinguishable on some of the tapes. Eichmann himself reviewed, corrected, and

47 For a detailed and helpful summary of Stangneth's long book, see Tom Teicholz, "The Liar: The Four Personas of Adolf Eichmann," *L.A. Review of Books*, April 18, 2015. Stangneth's research covers multiple subjects: not only Eichmann himself, but also the tangled tale of how he was captured – and, more pointedly, the *Realpolitik* story of why he was not captured sooner – and a detailed saga of the Sassen manuscripts.

48 Stangneth, 121–22.

49 Stangneth, 134–37.

50 On Fritsch, see Stangneth, 235–37; on Sassen, 238–41. The quote is from 111–12.

51 Stangneth, 185–86.

52 Stangneth, 196.

commented on the transcripts. Sassen eventually sold publication rights to *Life* magazine, which published the two excerpts Arendt read. In a tortuous tale Stangneth reconstructs in detail, other versions of the manuscript, some more fragmentary than others, wound up in a variety of hands.

*The Others Spoke* plus the Sassen transcripts plus a few other writings are what Stangneth refers to collectively as the Argentina Papers. The crux of the issue is how to evaluate them. In Jerusalem, Eichmann claimed that the published interviews were fabrications and dismissed the conversations as mere drunken ramblings. Stangneth, who listened to all the tapes, shows that both claims were lies. The discussions were sober, systematic, and serious.[53] The question is whether the Eichmann of the Sassen tapes and the other Argentina Papers was the genuine Eichmann.

Notably, the Argentina Papers include Nazi philosophical musings that directly contradict Eichmann's professed allegiance to Kantian principles. In *The Others Spoke*, he doubts that Kant had "a clear German orientation," and is suspicious of philosophy more generally because it is "international." In reality, every group has its own philosophy, and "the more I listened to the natural world, whether microcosm or macrocosm, the less injustice I found. . . . Everyone was in the right, when seen from his own standpoint." Therefore "what is right, is what aids the people." For him that meant the German people. Waging war against those the German state deemed enemies was thus his moral duty. This was the Nazi Party line, but it was hardly Kant. According to Eichmann, even Socrates, the humanists, and the church preached obedience to the state and its law. "From the tellurian worldview of Copernicus and Galileo to the hyper-galactic worldview of Homo sapiens today: the law creates and expects order."[54]

Whatever Sassen and Fritsch might have thought of Eichmann's hyper-galactic hodgepodge, they were on board with him so long as his conclusions were race war ideology and paeans to power and obedience. But they didn't stay on board for long. Their political project of reviving National Socialism in postwar Germany required unmasking the "myth of six million" as propaganda by the world Jewish conspiracy.[55] Eichmann, to their dismay, would not play along. As it dawned on him where the

[53] In 2020, the tapes were finally released from a German archive and turned over to Israeli producer Kobi Sitt and director Yariv Mozer, whose documentary "The Devil's Confession: The Lost Eichmann Tapes" was broadcast in Israel in 2022. Isabel Kershner, "Nazi Tapes Provide a Chilling Sequel to the Eichmann Trial," *New York Times*, July 4, 2022.

[54] All quotations in this paragraph are from Stangneth, 217–18.

[55] Stangneth, 142, describing the peculiar mix of Jew hatred and paranoia that composed their world view – paranoia in that apparently Sassen and Fritsch actually believed their own propaganda about an all-powerful Jewish conspiracy that had persuaded the world of the Holocaust "myth."

conversations were heading, he decided to set the record straight. In a dramatic set of Concluding Remarks he wrote out in advance (although he inadvertently presented it before the sessions had actually concluded, to the embarrassment of himself and his audience), he let loose. Stangneth quotes the Concluding Remarks in their awful entirety, but an excerpt will have to do here.

> EICHMANN: Before my people bite the dust, the whole world should bite the dust, and then my people. But only then!
>
> I said this. I – and I tell you this as a conclusion to our matters – I, the "cautious bureaucrat," that was me, yes indeed. But I would like to expand on the issue of the "cautious bureaucrat," somewhat to my own detriment. This cautious bureaucrat was attended by a . . . a fanatical warrior, fighting for the freedom of my blood. . . .
>
> No, I have to tell you quite honestly that if of the 10.3 million Jews that Korherr identified, as we now know, we had killed 10.3 million, I would be satisfied, and would say, good, we have destroyed an enemy.[56]

And on in this vein. After that damning confession, Sassen became decidedly cooler toward Eichmann, and a few sessions later the conversations petered out.

The heart of Stangneth's argument is that the Argentina Papers reveal the real Eichmann.[57] They are "conclusive proof" of the mendacity of his Israel writings and testimony; they "allow us to see behind the mirror."[58] When his Israeli interrogator confronted Eichmann with the Sassen documents, he disowned them as "the old song and dance" he had outgrown; but that shows only that Eichmann was trying to save his neck, contrary to Arendt's idea that these "telltale signs of an unregenerate Nazi outlook"[59] (her words, not Stangneth's) were a mere relapse to the clichés of an earlier phase of his life. Stangneth insists they are the true Eichmann.

To be sure, in the voluminous memoir *Götzen* (written after his trial but before the verdict) he insisted that in his innermost self he had never been a Nazi fanatic. "I could not summon up an unconditional inner receptiveness and a fanatical wish for *all* the National Socialist goals, because a heart full of doubt is never able to do that."[60] He says he was not an antisemite. To Stangneth, *Götzen* is more blue smoke. "We can avoid falling into Eichmann's 'Götzen' trap only by keeping a wary eye fixed on the perfidious philosophical swamp of the Argentina Papers."[61]

[56] Stangneth, 303–4. [57] Stangneth, 221. [58] Stangneth, 366, 367. [59] *EJ*, 34.
[60] *Götzen*, 596 (459). On the workings of his "innermost heart," see Stangneth, 581 (450).
[61] Stangneth, 366.

Yet there are difficulties with the conclusion that the Argentina Papers represent the true Eichmann. First of all, as Stangneth herself notes, the Argentina Papers are hardly models of candid self-revelation. Eichmann deliberately injected a "catalog of lies" into *The Others Spoke.* He even minimized his role in exactly the same way he did in Jerusalem. He said he was a little cog in the machine; that he merely passed along evacuation and deportation orders received from above and oversaw compliance; that he had no idea which of the people he deported were actually killed (true but irrelevant); that obedience was a duty; that he was at worst an aider and abettor. These became the pillars of his defense in Jerusalem, both in his interrogation and in the trial itself – and all of them appear in the Argentina Papers as well.[62] He had the temerity to write, "I have not made myself guilty of any crimes, even according to today's laws"[63] – which can only mean denying his role in the mass murders. Weirdly, he expressed the hope that his heart "may even find peace with my former enemy," that is, the Jews – a far cry from the vicious antisemitism of the Concluding Remarks.[64]

Thus, Stangneth cannot think that *all* the Argentina Papers express Eichmann's true convictions, and she does not. In her words, *The Others Spoke* is "a combination of vanity and sporadic bursts of honesty" – and, we must therefore surmise, episodes of dishonesty, both in aggrandizing his responsibility and fending off his culpability.[65] The elements contradict each other, veering between overstatement and understatement, Nazi bluster and denial.

For that matter, Eichmann tried to retract the Concluding Remarks before the Sassen conversations had even ended.[66] The fact is, he lied to former Nazis in Argentina even when he had no ulterior motive, just as he lied in Jerusalem when his motive was all too clear. In the early 1950s, he told a former Nazi that the real number of Jewish victims was half a million maximum.[67] Even to other Nazis he was an unreliable narrator.

It is unsurprising that the Argentina Papers are as slippery as Eichmann's other autobiographies. His motive in producing the Argentina Papers was not simply to speak his mind. Eichmann, Fritsch, and Sassen hoped to make money from their book, which all of them needed, and it was to be tailored to an audience of Nazi sympathizers – a point that Stangneth emphasizes. That audience was "my friends and non-friends," but especially the "large circle of friends, many millions of people, who sympathize with

[62] Stangneth, 200. [63] Stangneth, 202. [64] Stangneth, 200. [65] Stangneth, 210.
[66] Stangneth, 307–8. [67] Stangneth, 108.

the cause."[68] Precisely if Stangneth is right that Eichmann always tailored his utterances to his audience, we should question whether his professions of Nazi faith represent the authentic Eichmann, or even whether – given the contradictions – there is such a thing.[69]

What about Stangneth's diagnosis of Eichmann as a man in the grip of a race war theory, fully worked out as an intellectual system? In her view, "[t]he speed at which Eichmann was able to fill hundreds of pages may have its origin in the monologic structure of his thought."[70] That is entirely plausible – so far, so good. (It also jibes with Arendt's diagnosis of Eichmann's incapacity for dialogical thought.) Stangneth continues: "Eichmann didn't write in order to develop or refine an intellectual construct, his thoughts taking shape as he went; he was laying out a fully formed, rigid train of thought."[71] That is less plausible. Arendt's theory that Eichmann said whatever gave him a lift at the moment is just as likely an explanation.

Stangneth herself notices that sometimes Eichmann "writes himself into a state of euphoria."[72] She observes that his handwriting changed from "tiny and laboriously legible" to "expansive and idiosyncratic. ... The ballpoint pen was clearly flying over the paper."[73] This *could* be the sign of a fully formed train of thought, but it sounds more like the telltale behavior of a man unlocking his word hoard and pouring forth whatever pops into his head, fueled by euphoria and the conviction that it is all brilliant. As Eichmann himself says, "I just started writing what the pen wanted."[74]

Although Stangneth believes Eichmann's philosophical musings are more cogent than the "paradoxical drivel and pseudophilosophy" they seem to be,[75] it is unclear why she thinks so. He cycles through anti-philosophy (philosophy is suspect because it is international) and appeals to philosophical authority (Socrates enjoined obedience to the state), crude relativism (everyone is right from his own standpoint), and cosmic grandeur (the microcosm and macrocosm, the "hyper-galactic worldview of Homo sapiens" – which, if it means anything at all, is the opposite of *Volk*-specific relativism). In *Götzen* he muses that "in distant, distant finitudes, Time will again lose itself in Space."[76] This certainly sounds like drivel and pseudophilosophy. In fact, it sounds like bullshit: words

[68] On the hope to make money: Stangneth, 186; on the target audience, 203.
[69] In "Yes and No," Roger Berkowitz raises similar doubts. [70] Stangneth, 231.
[71] Stangneth, 231. [72] Stangneth, 204. [73] Stangneth, 205. [74] *Götzen*, 7 (63).
[75] Stangneth, 219. [76] *Götzen*, 589–90 (454).

uttered in disregard of truth and coherence, or even of belief that transcends the moment of their utterance. By comparison, Eichmann's exposition of Kant at his trial sounds almost serious:

> If I am subjected to a higher power and a higher force, then my free will as such is eliminated, and then, since I can no longer be master of my free will and volition, I cannot in fact adopt any principles whatsoever which I cannot influence, but, on the contrary, I must, and also may, build obedience to the authorities into this concept, and then the authorities bear the responsibility. In my judgment, that also belongs to it [i.e., to Kant's categorical imperative].[77]

Admittedly, this is neither lucid nor logically consistent. First he acknowledges that by following orders he could not live by Kantian principles or indeed "any principles whatsoever"; then he contradicts himself by claiming that obedience to authority is built into the categorical imperative, in which case obedience *is* a Kantian principle. Inadequate as an argument, the sentence nevertheless sounds like a genuine effort to square the circle and reconcile obedience with morality. Based on content alone, there is no reason to suppose it is less authentically what Eichmann thought than the Argentine musings. If he didn't think it, it would be hard to concoct it on the fly.

Stangneth herself provides ample material for an alternative explanation of the Argentina Papers that is much closer to Arendt's. That explanation focuses not on Eichmann's supposed Nazi fanaticism but rather on his overwhelming drive to exhibit himself as an important person, his "pronounced need for recognition" – which is, in fact, one of Stangneth's main conclusions about Eichmann.[78] Arendt concurs: "Bragging was the vice that was Eichmann's undoing."[79] During his SS days, Eichmann was a relentless self-promoter who kept a file of foreign press clippings about himself and exulted in those that ascribed to him more power and ability than he really had. He did whatever he could to make himself seem more important, including fostering rumors that he was born in Palestine (he wasn't), that he was fluent in Hebrew and Yiddish (he knew a few phrases), and that he was a friend of the Grand Mufti of Jerusalem (they met once). Even his pretensions as an "expert" on Jewish emigration were inflated. His biggest Vienna innovation, a centralized office to handle all the steps of emigration on a kind of conveyor belt, actually came from the Jewish leaders he dragooned; and his Viennese memos to headquarters on emigration law

[77] Eichmann Trial Proceedings, vol. 4, Session 105, July 20, 1962, at 1803. [78] Stangneth, 367.
[79] *EJ*, 46. He had "a great inclination" to "deck himself in borrowed plumes." *EJ*, 44.

and policy were ghostwritten by a rabbi Eichmann impressed into service as a kind of research assistant.[80] Apparently all this self-inflation served him well in the Darwinian struggle for turf within the SS.

Importantly, none of Stangneth's portrait of his SS years turns in any way on Eichmann's ideological commitment, only on his ambition. Here, there is little daylight between her account and Arendt's. Cesarani, too, emphasizes that Eichmann was not a longtime Nazi believer, although he had been drifting toward National Socialist sympathies.[81] He joined the Party relatively late, in a more or less haphazard way after a casual meeting with Kaltenbrunner (before that, he was on the verge of joining a Masonic club).[82] His transfer to the division of Jewish affairs was also happenstance; his first job in the SS was keeping records about the Freemasons. Becoming an "expert" on Jewish affairs turned out to be Eichmann's big professional break; but there is no evidence that he sought the assignment out of ideological conviction – only that he found it a pathway to advancement.

After the war, he chafed under the anonymity of his German life in hiding; apparently that was the principal motive for his move to Argentina.[83] In Perón's Argentina, he no longer had to maintain strict incognito, but the mediocrity of his life still rankled; he yearned to be a somebody once again. To become a somebody in the eyes of his intended audience (the Sassen circle, but also the wider world of Nazis), he had to out-Nazi them and show himself to be the supreme authority on the Final Solution. To attribute his behavior in the Sassen conversations to deep conviction rather than to his situation – an exile showing off to other exiles – risks committing what social psychologists call the "fundamental attribution error" of overfocusing on the person rather than the situation.[84]

The turning point came when he grasped that the Sassen group wanted him to deny the Holocaust. Now the situation had changed. They were asking Eichmann, in effect, to become a nobody once again, for you

80 Conveyor belt: Cesarani, *Becoming Eichmann*, 8 (although later Cesarani seems to attribute it to Eichmann: 66–67). Ghost-writer: so the rabbi, Benjamin Murmelstein, testifies, in his interviews with Claude Lanzmann in Lanzmann's documentary film *The Last of the Unjust* (2013).

81 Cesarani, *Becoming Eichmann*, 30.

82 *EJ*, 32–33; Cesarani, *Becoming Eichmann*, 33. Eichmann's Nazi Party membership number was 889, 895.

83 Stangneth, 73. Stangneth agrees with Arendt that Eichmann was "bored to death" (*EJ*, 236) in his German hideout. Stangneth titles her discussion of this period of his life "Detested Anonymity."

84 Harry Mulisch offers a related but simpler explanation of Eichmann's horrifying Concluding Remarks: "it must also have been bragging among friends." Mulisch adds: "If some day the world press would make public what I have said to my friends, and especially what we have *laughed* about, mankind would also blanch." Mulisch, *Criminal Case 40/61*, 55. Roger Berkowitz offers a similar explanation in "Yes and No." See also Mahony, *Hannah Arendt's Ethics*, 47.

cannot be a supreme authority on something that did not happen.[85] At that point, alarmed by the direction the conversations were taking, he produced his Concluding Remarks, even though they contradicted the comments he made earlier minimizing his responsibilities.

In short: Eichmann's craving for recognition, what Stangneth aptly calls his desire to howl with the wolves once again,[86] suffices to explain his Sassen behavior, and it is entirely consistent with Arendt's diagnosis of Eichmann as a moral chameleon whose main evil motives were careerism and vanity. These may have been extreme in Eichmann; even though Arendt spotted his boasting and his "extraordinary diligence in looking out for his personal advancement," she didn't know the half of it. But these are ordinary, not diabolical or ideological, motives. To commit enormous crimes for everyday motives is very close to what Arendt means by the banality of evil.

There is one other difficulty with Stangneth's conviction that the most vicious portions of the Argentina Papers represent the authentic Eichmann. It requires the corollary that his entire interrogation, as well as his testimony at trial and his final memoir, *Götzen*, were elaborately planned and superbly executed faking it – well-executed enough to fool not only Arendt but other trial observers, too, and even the skeptical Israeli police official, Avner Less, who interrogated Eichmann for 275 hours. Captain Less realized that what Eichmann told him was peppered with lies, but he never suggested that Eichmann's whole persona might be fake.

Undoubtedly Eichmann was doing his level best to save his neck by lying (and Arendt spots many of his lies[87]). But Stangneth depicts Eichmann as something bigger than a simple liar. In her portrayal, he cunningly kept track of what each of his hearers knew and didn't know, and shaped his lies accordingly. Stangneth sees a master manipulator who could maintain an unreal persona through hundreds of hours of professional interrogation and cross-examination. That would have included controlling his demeanor, and even his speech patterns, in a performance worthy of Martin Guerre, the sixteenth-century con man who impersonated a long-lost youth for years and fooled an entire village, including the youth's family.[88] That is how Stangneth describes Eichmann:

85 Stangneth herself notes the built-in contradiction between what his audience wanted to hear and his self-image. Stangneth, 210.

86 Stangneth, 367.

87 E.g., *EJ*, 23, 24, 25, 28, 29, 30, 33, 40, 44, 47, 49, 57 – to take only instances from the beginning of the book.

88 Natalie Zemon Davis, *The Return of Martin Guerre* (Harvard University Press, 1983).

> His ability to inhabit and perfect a role allowed him to keep up this pretense with surprising consistency. ... [He] was practiced in the art of manufacturing and conveying stories with an inner coherence, solely to distract people. ... Like a mirror, he reflected people's fears and expectations. ... Behind all the mirror images lay Eichmann's will to power and desire to control people's thoughts, disguised as diligence.[89]

Of course this is possible; but little in Eichmann's resumé suggests that level of talent. Along with high-level acting and an unflagging ability to keep track of what each of his questioners knew and didn't know, his skills would have had to include insight into others that allowed him to identify their weaknesses and prey on them. And yet, as we saw in §1.2, there is ample evidence of Eichmann's maladroitness in trying to present himself in a sympathetic light – evidence leading Lipstadt to conclude that he was "completely deaf and blind to the identity of those before whom he was testifying," displaying "similar obtuseness" during his interrogation.[90] This was precisely Arendt's diagnosis, and the plentiful evidence of Eichmann's insulation from the reality of his listeners casts doubt on Eichmann as a master manipulator.

Consider a major example Stangneth uses to make her case: Eichmann's "treacherous games with his victims' hopes of finding a way out of their situation, in order to drive them to their deaths without resistance."[91] The reference is to one of Eichmann's most odious Sassen recollections, namely the infamous "Jews for trucks" deal he offered the Hungarian Zionist leader Rudolf Kastner (sometimes spelled Kasztner) in the summer of 1944.

As Eichmann describes it, he told Kastner he would spare the lives of "one million Jews [in return] for 10,000 winterized trucks with trailers." The trucks were to come from the Western Allies, and "[t]hanks to Himmler's directive, I could assure them, on my word of honor, that these trucks would be used only on the Eastern front."[92]

The plan for this farfetched deal had originated with Himmler, not Eichmann, who disapproved.[93] The desperate Kastner kept the negotiations going, and he eventually succeeded in saving 1,700 Jews in return

89 Stangneth, 367. 90 Lipstadt, *The Eichmann Trial*, 111, 112. 91 Stangneth, 365, 367.

92 This from the Sassen documents printed in *Life* magazine: Adolf Eichmann, "To Sum It All Up, I Regret Nothing," *Life*, December 5, 1960, 146.

93 Yehuda Bauer, *Jews for Sale? Nazi–Jewish Negotiations, 1933–1945* (Yale University Press, 1994), 167–68; Robert Mnookin, *Bargaining with the Devil: When to Bargain, When to Fight* (Simon & Schuster, 2010), 280n61. Bauer thinks it is possible that Himmler was serious; *Jews for Sale?*, 170. Perhaps Himmler actually believed Nazi propaganda about Jews as the secret power behind the Allies; or perhaps he hoped to split the Allies, as Kastner's colleague Joel Brand subsequently came to believe. "Allied Rift Called Aim of '44 Nazi Ransom Plan," *New York Times*, May 21, 1964.

for money, in a side deal. (Years later, the side deal led to a notorious trial in Israel on the issue of his supposed collaborationism, soon after which Kastner was murdered.)

But to Sassen, Eichmann did not say he disapproved of Himmler's brainstorm. Instead he boasted that for him the negotiations were nothing more than a ruse designed to get Kastner to keep the Jews dormant while Eichmann deported them. The deal "was really just about 'him [Kastner] continuing to play his role as appeasement councilor [!] with his Jewish community.'"[94]

The Kastner story is an important part of Stangneth's case that Eichmann was a Machiavellian manipulator, skilled at reading other people and deviously bending them to his will. For reasons I now explain, there is reason to doubt this.

The Kastner episode is a story told in many places, including *Eichmann in Jerusalem*, and to this day questions about Kastner's conduct and culpability are unsettled and ferociously debated.[95] Eichmann's own version leaves many things out. But noteworthy is how Eichmann explains his thinking. He describes Kastner as a "fanatical Zionist" who was willing to keep the Hungarian Jews from resisting deportation, in return for Eichmann allowing "a few hundred or a few thousand young Jews to emigrate illegally to Palestine."[96] In Eichmann's eyes, that made Kastner an "idealist," and "there was a very strong similarity between our attitudes in the SS and the viewpoint of these immensely idealistic Zionist leaders who were fighting what might be their last battle. As I told Kastner: 'We, too, are idealists and we, too, had to sacrifice our own blood before we came to power.'"[97]

Does this show insight into Kastner? Stangneth seems to think so, but what stands out is that when he looked at Kastner, all Eichmann saw was another Eichmann. His words support rather than undermine Arendt's diagnosis of Eichmann as a man unable to think from the point of view of others. (Eichmann likewise told one of Kastner's Hungarian Zionist

94 Stangneth, 265. The exclamation mark is Stangneth's.

95 See Bauer, *Jews for Sale?*, 172–95 and more recently, Mnookin, *Bargaining with the Devil*, 53–82; Ladislaus Löb, *Rezso Kasztner – The Daring Rescue of Hungarian Jews: A Survivor's Account* (Pimlico, 2009). For a damning view of Kastner, Paul Bogdanor, *Kasztner's Crime* (Routledge, 2016). On current controversies, see Dan Laor, "Israel Kastner vs. Hannah Szenes: Who Was Really the Hero during the Holocaust?," *Haaretz*, November 9, 2013; Ofer Aderet, "An Israeli Suspected of Nazi Collaboration Was Murdered: What Is Israel Hiding?," *Haaretz*, March 21, 2021.

96 Eichmann, "To Sum It All Up, I Regret Nothing," 146.

97 Eichmann, "To Sum It All Up, I Regret Nothing," 146.

colleagues that the colleague and Eichmann were both idealists. "Idealist" seems to have been one of Eichmann's winged words.[98])

Eichmann boasts that he was merely playing Kastner for his own murderous purposes, but historical accounts suggest that Kastner was playing along, not getting played, and that his game was deeper than exfiltrating a few young Jews to Palestine. Kastner and other leaders of his underground rescue organization, the Va'ada, understood from the start that there was no chance of wheedling ten thousand trucks from the Allies to give to the SS. They were bargaining for time, trying to slow the deportations and rescue at least some Hungarian Jews in the hope that Germany's inevitable surrender would come in time to save the rest.[99] As one writer says of Kastner and his colleague: "While Eichmann deceived, blackmailed and bullied them, they tried to bluff, hoodwink and trick him. They met his lies, broken promises and open threats with subterfuges of their own." He calls Eichmann's and Kastner's strategies a "double bluff."[100]

Arendt herself accepts Eichmann's "idealist" diagnosis of "the strange Mr. Kastner," and her judgment about Kastner is merciless.[101] Curiously, she misses the extent to which Eichmann's depiction of Kastner confirms

[98] Alex Weissberg, *Desperate Mission: Joel Brand's Story as Told by Alex Weissberg*, trans. Constantine FitzGibbon and Andrew Foster-Melliar (Borodino, 2017/1958), 100. Arendt is bitterly sarcastic about Eichmann's and Kastner's "idealism." *EJ*, 42.

[99] Eichmann originally made the "trucks for Jews" offer not to Kastner but to Joel Brand, who along with Kastner was part of the leadership of the Va'ada. Brand reports that after receiving Eichmann's offer he immediately discussed it with Kastner and other Va'ada leaders. They all agreed the trucks were impossible. But Brand persuaded them there would be no need to deliver the trucks, because the Germans would lose the war first. In the meantime, they might be able to drag out negotiations with cash payments, slow deportations, and ransom some Hungarian Jews. Weissberg, *Desperate Mission*, 111–15; Löb, *Rezso Kasztner*, 64–65. They guessed that Himmler and other SS leaders were willing to halt the murders to better position themselves postwar. With Eichmann's blessing, Brand left Hungary to sell the strategy to Zionist leaders in Jerusalem and get them to release funds and open negotiations with the Nazis. But Brand was captured and sidelined by the British; in his absence Kastner took over the Eichmann negotiations. Years later, Brand regretted his part in the deal. "Allied Rift Called Aim of '44 Nazi Ransom Plan," *New York Times*, May 21, 1964.

[100] Löb, *Rezso Kasztner*, 77, 269. Mnookin, a negotiation expert, thinks that is likely but also guesses that Kastner may eventually have talked himself into believing that the deal could work – until Eichmann's mendacity became too unmistakable. Mnookin, *Bargaining with the Devil*, 60. See Löb, *Rezso Kasztner*, 267.

[101] *EJ*, 42, 116–18, 143, 196. Arendt puts the least favorable construction on all his actions. For example, she mentions that Kastner put his own family on the rescue train in a context suggesting favoritism. *EJ*, 143. Other accounts say that he put his family on the train to show suspicious residents that he personally believed it was bound for safety rather than being a trap; whether or not that is true, saving his own family rather than leaving them to die is hardly a sign of moral rot. As another example, by lumping Kastner together with the Jewish Council the Nazis set up, Arendt implies he was a member of that council. He was not.

his own thoughtlessness, in her exact sense of someone incapable of thinking from the point of view of others.

One must of course give great weight to the considered views of a historian like Stangneth, who lived in the unpleasant company of Adolf Eichmann for many years, reading everything, talking to everyone, and pursuing leads from archive to archive. Her ear for which of his tones are authentic and which not is likely to be more reliable than any particulars of the evidence on paper. She is persuaded that the fanatically Nazi portions of the Argentina Papers represent the real Eichmann, while the exculpatory parts, along with his interrogation, his trial testimony, and *Götzen*, do not. Arendt, by contrast, reads his palpable inconsistencies as evidence that none of Eichmann's professed convictions had deep roots.

Stangneth may be right, but this interpretive disagreement has no easy resolution. There is no smoking gun, not even the Concluding Remarks, because the question is which parts of the Eichmann output were the real Eichmann, and we would have to pose that question about the smoking gun as well: real smoke, or blue smoke? To be sure, Stangneth has unearthed a trove of important information that Arendt did not have. Arendt was unaware of how much philosophy Eichmann had read and written; she was unacquainted with most of the Concluding Remarks, the context of the Sassen conversations and much of their content, the details of Eichmann's life in Argentina, the continuity of his Nazi involvements, and the cunning of his postwar escape. She never heard the Sassen tapes, with whatever they reveal aurally about Eichmann's self-presentation.

On the other hand, Arendt was no amateur on Eichmann. As Stangneth forthrightly reminds her readers, Arendt carefully studied the interrogation and the trial transcript. She had at least the *Life* magazine excerpts from the Sassen interviews – which include a few of the most damning paragraphs of the Concluding Remarks[102] – and she saw extracts from *Götzen* that Harry Mulisch showed her. Rereading *Eichmann in Jerusalem*, we can see that Arendt took full notice of Eichmann's boasting, his ambition, his "unregenerate Nazi outlook" in the Sassen interviews, his lying, his skill at negotiation and organization, his arrogance (she cites an instance where he slapped a Jewish leader in the face), his personal visits to death camps and other sites of mass murder, and his relentless zeal in pursuing the Final Solution even in the face of Himmler's cease-and-desist order. (About the latter, she commented that his reluctance to cease and desist bears an unpleasant resemblance to the good soldier who refuses to execute an

[102] See Eichmann, "To Sum It All Up, I Regret Nothing," 150, 161.

illegal order – for Eichmann surmised that continuing the Final Solution was Hitler's will.[103]) Nor did she neglect the magnitude of his deeds; we must not forget that the trial produced overwhelming and hair-raising evidence, to which Arendt was hardly oblivious.

The evidence Arendt relies on most for her "banality" diagnosis lies in the habits of mind and speech Eichmann displays – and these are surely the hardest things to fake over a long period of time, even for a skilled liar. All this seems like enough to support her interpretation, which is in some respects actually not far from Stangneth's and Cesarani's.[104] I provide more evidence of Eichmann's banality in the postscript to Chapter 5 (§5.6), where I analyze his weirdly revealing self-vindication. In what follows, I proceed on the working hypothesis that Arendt had at least a strong case that Stangneth has not refuted.[105]

## 2.5 The Eichmann Trial and Arendt's Turn to Judgment: A Moral and Legal Agenda

I've begun with Arendt at Jerusalem because the Eichmann trial brought to the foreground two striking moral phenomena: the banality of evil and its antithesis – namely, that under conditions of terror "most people will comply but *some people will not.*" Those among the noncompliers who actively resist the terror show immense, almost incomprehensible, courage. But equally important is something less conspicuous: their moral judgment, the fact that they recognize evil even when multitudes around them do not. Moral judgment is the counter-banality phenomenon that Arendt thought hardest about – and that is why her late work is worthy of reflection.

Here's how she posed the issue in the postscript to *Eichmann in Jerusalem*:

> There remains, however, one fundamental problem, which ... touches upon one of the central moral questions of all time, namely upon the

103 *EJ*, 148, 293.

104 Two of Cesarani's reviewers see little difference between his portrayal of Eichmann and Arendt's. I am inclined to agree. Barry Gewen, "The Everyman of Genocide," *New York Times*, May 14, 2006; John Gray, "Eichmann: His Life and Crimes by David Cesarani," *The Independent*, August 19, 2014.

105 A useful article is Rebecca Wittmann, "Eichmann Revisited: The Motivations of a Mass Murderer," *German Studies Review* 35(1) (2012): 135–43 (reviewing several books including Lipstadt's and Stangneth's). Also useful, although marred by its polemical defensiveness of Arendt, is Daniel Maier-Katkin, "The Reception of Arendt's *Eichmann in Jerusalem* in the United States 1963–2011," *Zeitschrift für Politisches Denken/Journal of Political Thinking* 6 (2011).

> nature and function of human judgment. What we have demanded in these trials, where the defendants had committed "legal" crimes, is that human beings be capable of telling right from wrong even when all they have to guide them is their own judgment, which, moreover, happens to be completely at odds with what they must regard as the unanimous opinion of all those around them. . . . Since the whole of respectable society had in one way or another succumbed to Hitler, . . . [t]hose few who were still able to tell right from wrong went really by their own judgments, and they did so freely; there were no rules to be abided by, under which the particular cases with which they were confronted could be subsumed.[106]

The turn to investigating this "central moral question of all time" happened near the midpoint of Arendt's book-writing career in the English language, which began with the publication of *The Origins of Totalitarianism* in 1948 and ended with her death in 1975, leaving behind the incomplete *The Life of the Mind*, which would have concluded with a section on judgment. It seems natural, then, to regard *Eichmann in Jerusalem* as a kind of inflection point in Arendt's thought. Before the Eichmann trial, her books hardly mentioned moral judgment; afterward, moral judgment became a central theme.

In "Thinking and Moral Considerations" she poses a question that arises directly from her astonishment at Eichmann's apparent inability to think: "Is our ability to judge, to tell right from wrong, beautiful from ugly, dependent upon our faculty of thought? Do the inability to think and a disastrous failure of what we commonly call conscience coincide?"[107] At the end of that essay she answers yes, but without offering anything like a full argument. Thinking (she speculates) destroys unexamined opinions, and "this destruction has a liberating effect on another human faculty, the faculty of judgment. . . . It is the faculty to judge *particulars* without subsuming them under those general rules which can be taught and learned until they grow into habits that can be replaced by other habits and rules."[108]

Presumably, making good on the connection between thinking and judging would have been the task of the unwritten capstone of *The Life of the Mind*, and perhaps it would have provided Arendt's answer to the *quaestio juris* raised by the Eichmann trial.

I've called the Eichmann trial an inflection point in her thought: a bend, not a break, for there was no sharp break. Arendt never stopped writing about politics and, as we will see, her political focus strongly influenced her reflections on moral judgment – and not always for the better, I argue.

[106] *EJ*, 294–95. [107] TMC, 160. [108] TMC, 188–89.

On the other side, some of her later ideas about judgment already appear as brief asides in pre-Jerusalem essays. Nevertheless, I think it is fair to describe the Eichmann trial as Arendt's "turn" to moral philosophy.

In *The Human Condition*, Arendt made it clear she did not believe that moral standards come from "some supposedly higher faculty or from experiences outside action's own reach."[109] When the Eichmann trial turned Arendt's attention back to moral matters, she retained her view that moral standards don't come from a "supposedly higher faculty" and don't reflect a realm of objective moral facts. They come from practices of human judgment. It seemed self-evident to her that the major moral problems were three: explaining how a seemingly normal actor like Eichmann could be wholly bereft of the ability to judge right from wrong, while others were not; explaining how others could judge him, even in the absence of transcendent standards of moral judgment; and explaining why those judgments are anything more than subjective beliefs or prejudices. The practice of judgment, above all else, became the moral phenomenon Arendt wished to understand.

The Eichmann trial also caused Arendt to reflect on legal questions. What is the purpose of extraordinary trials of atrocity crimes? What is the appropriate venue for such a trial, and what justifies a venue's jurisdiction? What are the defining characteristics of genocide and crimes against humanity, both legal novelties emerging from World War II, and how should we properly conceptualize them? Finally, what are the grounds for assigning criminal liability to perpetrators like Eichmann, "who is in actual fact *hostis generis humani*," and yet "commits his crimes under circumstances that make it well-nigh impossible for him to know or to feel that he is doing wrong"?[110]

All these questions, those of moral philosophy and those of law, set the agenda for what follows – not only because the questions preoccupied Arendt but also because she was right to be preoccupied by them. Her answers, I argue, are sometimes wrong, even deeply wrong. But her *questions* should matter to us a great deal, as philosophers and as inhabitants of a world where the allure of autocracy is again on the rise.

[109] *HC*, 246. [110] *EJ*, 276.

# PART II

# *The Moral Philosophy*

CHAPTER 3

# *Judgment in Dark Times*

## 3.1 A Heretical Kantian

*Judging* would have been the third part of *The Life of the Mind*, of which the first two parts (published posthumously) are *Thinking* and *Willing*.[1] The titles are a hat-tip to Kant's three critiques, of pure reason, practical reason, and judgment. In an early essay, Arendt calls Kant the secret king of modern philosophy. The titles remind us that philosophically Kant remains, as Robert Brandom quips, the great gray mother of us all.[2]

But Arendt was a heretical Kantian. She drew inspiration from Kant's *Critique of Judgment* in an unorthodox way: She called it the political philosophy Kant never wrote. This is doubly provocative, because she dismisses the political philosophy that Kant did write ("rather boring and pedantic"), and because the *Critique of Judgment* is a book about judgments in aesthetics and in the study of nature, subjects that on their face could hardly be further removed from politics. As we'll see, in her late essays Arendt extends her ideas about the *Critique of Judgment* from politics to morality. As for Kant's ethics, her "chief reservations about Kant's philosophy concern precisely his moral philosophy, that is, the *Critique of Practical Reason*."[3]

Before examining her argument, some background on Kant's theory of judgment will be useful. Its homeland is not Kant's ethics or aesthetics, but rather his epistemology and logic, as set out in the *Critique of Pure Reason*.

[1] Mary McCarthy prepared the manuscripts for publication, and *Thinking* originally appeared in *The New Yorker*. In the postscript to *Willing* Arendt describes *Judging* as the second part of the second volume of *The Life of the Mind*, rather than as a self-standing third volume. A valuable collection of essays on themes in this chapter is *Judgment, Imagination, and Politics*, eds. Ronald Beiner and Jennifer Nedelsky (Rowman & Littlefield, 2001).

[2] "What Is Existential Philosophy?," in *EU*, 168 (secret king). Robert Brandom, *Articulating Reasons: An Introduction to Inferentialism* (Harvard University Press, 2000), 80 (great gray mother of us all). The suggestive parallel is Seyla Benhabib's observation that for feminist thinkers Arendt is "one of our 'early mothers,'" although she "remains the mother who eluded us." Benhabib, *The Reluctant Modernism of Hannah Arendt*, xlvii.

[3] *T*, 222–23n83. Her "rather boring and pedantic" remark is in *Kant Lectures*, 7–8.

In Kant's logic, a judgment (*Urteil*) is simply a proposition – in its most elementary form, a declarative sentence that applies a concept, the predicate, to a grammatical subject. Such elementary judgments can be linked to create more complex compound judgments. Kant tabulates various logical forms compound propositions can take: hypothetical ("if-*p*-then-*q*"), disjunctive ("*p* or *q*"), negative ("not-*p*"), necessary, contingent, and so on.[4] Whatever their form, judgments link together concepts and particulars, and in turn they link to one another through inferences. Crucially, for Kant all empirical knowledge takes propositional form; bare unconceptualized sensations, he famously remarks, are blind, and bare concepts are empty.[5] Kant names the faculty that binds concepts and contents together "the understanding" (*der Verstand*, from *verstehen*, to understand); Arendt translates *Verstand* as "intellect," which makes his meaning clearer. She calls it the faculty of cognition.[6] Kant treats judgments as the basic units of knowledge because (as Brandom puts it) they are the smallest semantic units we can take *responsibility* for: Unlike the bare utterance of a name or a concept, a judgment makes a claim for which, in principle, we can be held answerable. Tendering judgments enrolls us in the Socratic game of giving and taking reasons.[7]

For Kant, empirical knowledge includes rules of experience, encompassing everything from commonsense regularities – objects persist from moment to moment; the sky gets dark after sunset – to profound scientific laws. He regards concepts themselves as rules for sorting things into those that fall under the concept and those that don't. Sorting items of experience under concepts yields judgments about those items – and that is where the faculty of judgment enters the theory. "If understanding in general is to be viewed as the faculty of rules, judgment (*Urteilskraft*) will be the faculty of subsuming under rules; that is, of distinguishing whether something does or does not stand under a given rule."[8] Judgment is a cognitive power irreducible to the "faculty of rules," in the sense that we

[4] *CPR*, A70/B95. [5] *CPR*, A51/B75. [6] *T*, 57.

[7] Brandom, *Articulating Reasons*, 13, 33. Although it is not tied to a specific Kantian text, I find Brandom's interpretation illuminating and satisfying. I can't help but think that Arendt, who was profoundly concerned with responsible and irresponsible speech, would as well – see, for example, *Kant Lectures*, 41. Brandom inherits the interpretation from Wilfrid Sellars, who wrote that "in characterizing an episode or a state as that of *knowing* . . . we are placing it in the logical space of reasons, of justifying and being able to justify what one says." Sellars, "Empiricism and the Philosophy of Mind," in *Science, Perception and Reality* (Routledge & Kegan Paul, 1963), 169. See Brandom, *Articulating Reasons*, 32.

[8] *CPR*, A132/B171. In English, the word "judgment" does double duty, referring both to the capacity or faculty of judgment, and to its verdict or conclusion: the judgment. German has distinct words for the faculty and its product: *Urteilskraft*, the power (or faculty) of judgment, and *das Urteil*, the judgment it renders. Kant's Third Critique bears the title *Kritik der Urteilskraft*, "Critique of the

have no rules for how to judge. For, Kant argues, if judgment were rule-governed, we would need a rule to apply that rule, and another to apply that one, in an infinite regress of rules.[9] Instead, we subsume particulars under rules directly, without the mediation of further rules.

> And thus it appears that, though understanding is capable of being instructed, and of being equipped with rules, judgment is a peculiar talent which can be practiced only, and cannot be taught. It is the specific quality of so-called mother-wit; and its lack no school can make good.[10]

Echoing Kant, Arendt calls judgment "the mysterious endowment of the mind by which the general, always a mental construction, and the particular, always given to sense experience, are brought together." Judgment "is a 'peculiar faculty' ... because no rule is available for the *applications* of the rule" – her compressed restatement of Kant's regress argument.[11]

Elaborating further, Kant remarks that a highly trained person may know all the rules of his calling, "even to the degree that he may become a profound teacher of them, and yet, none the less, may easily stumble in their application" because of poor judgment. "He may comprehend the universal *in abstracto*, and yet not be able to distinguish whether a case *in concreto* comes under it."[12] As Oliver Wendell Holmes, Jr. warned in a famous judicial opinion: "General propositions do not decide concrete cases. The decision will depend on a judgment or intuition more subtle than any articulate major premise."[13] The "articulate major premise" – the rule – cannot yield a conclusion without a minor premise displaying the concrete case as an instance of what the rule regulates. The minor premise is what Holmes calls the "judgment more subtle," and we don't deduce it from some other rule, on pain of finding ourselves in an infinite regress of syllogisms deducing minor premises from rules – syllogisms that themselves have minor premises.[14]

Power of Judgment," although many translations render it "Critique of Judgment" – as I do for convenience.

9 *CPR*, A132/B171–A134/B174. The regress argument is not original to Kant; we find intimations of it in Aristotle's *Nicomachaean Ethics* as well: N.E. 3.3, 1113a 1–3 and N.E. 6.8, 1142a 25–31.

10 *CPR*, A133/B172.

11 *T*, 69. Arendt's "always given to sense experience" is too narrow. Particulars *include* sense experiences, but more abstract entities can also be particulars that are subsumed under concepts. The number 23 is a particular subsumed under the concept "prime number"; a financial transaction may be subsumed under the concept "tax fraud."

12 Kant, *CPR*, A134/B173.

13 Lochner v. New York, 198 U.S. 45, 76 (1905) (Holmes J., dissenting).

14 This regress problem, somewhat different from Kant's, is known today as the paradox of Achilles and the tortoise, after Lewis Carroll's famous and witty logic article "What the Tortoise Said to Achilles," *Mind* 4(14) (1895): 278–80.

In the *Critique of Judgment* Kant draws a further distinction: "[J]udgment is not merely an ability to subsume the particular under the universal (whose concept is given), but also, the other way round, an ability to find the universal for the particular."[15] Kant calls the former *determinate* judgment, while the latter is *reflective* judgment.

The reason for introducing reflective judgment is that particulars "in the wild" don't come with labels; the same particular can be described in more than one way, and before reasoning about it one must judge which concepts describe it best. We do this by reflecting on the item to pick out its most salient features. Hence the label *judgment of reflection* or, more simply, *reflective judgment.* In reflective judgment we move from a concrete particular to a general characterization of it rather than from a general concept to a particular item subsumed under it, as in determinate judgment.

A legal example illustrates the reflective process. A landmark US judicial decision on surrogacy was the 1988 *Baby M* case.[16] The Sterns entered a surrogacy contract with Mary Beth Whitehead; in return for money, she would be inseminated with William Stern's sperm and the Sterns would adopt the baby at birth. After giving birth, Whitehead changed her mind and would not relinquish Baby M. The Sterns sued.

How should a court think about the suit? One possibility is as a straightforward contracts case: Whitehead breached her contract with the Sterns, and one legal remedy would require her to fulfill the contract by relinquishing parental rights to them. But contract isn't the only way to think of the case. It also resembles a custody dispute between a biological father and a biological mother living in separate households, as in divorce. Viewed that way, the prevailing legal standard awards custody based on the best interest of the child. As a third possibility, *Baby M* could be viewed as a baby-selling case. The law prohibits baby selling as contrary to public policy. The surrogacy contract would be void, and the Sterns would lose.

Crucially, before applying the law, the judges must choose the body of law (contract, child custody, baby selling) that they will apply. In an important sense *Baby M* "is" all three things: a breach of contract, a custody battle, and a (failed) money-for-adoption arrangement. The point here is that only after the judges choose the description can they set about applying the law. First comes the reflective judgment by which they examine the particular – the facts of *Baby M* – and choose a legal category to classify it. After picking the category, they can set about the task of

[15] Immanuel Kant, "First Introduction to the Critique of Judgment," Ak. 20:210, trans. Pluhar, 398.

[16] In re Baby M, 109 N.J. 396, 537 A.2d 1227 (N.J. 1988).

applying the rules – the determinate judgment. But the reflective judgment comes first. (In the end, the New Jersey court combined legal regimes: They held that the surrogacy contract was void as a matter of public policy, then awarded custody of Baby M to the Sterns, with visitation rights for Whitehead, based on the best interests of the child. In 2018, New Jersey legalized surrogacy, but not for payment.)

In *Baby M*, three familiar legal regimes fit the facts, each with its own reasonably well-defined rules. But in moral decision making, there might be no predefined regimes or rules, only broad principles with no agreed-on conventions about what kinds of cases are exceptions or how to settle conflicts among rules. In times of unprecedented crisis, there may be no rules at all, or only bad rules. That's how Arendt sees matters, and for her judgment "without banisters" is the all-important moral power in human affairs.[17]

Here she breaks with Kant, for whom the categorical imperative – the moral law – provides the banister (or in Kant's metaphor, the compass). Arendt rejects the categorical imperative on the ground of its supposed rigidity, formalism, and inhumanity, and she argues, rather dismissively, that it is little more than a version of the law of noncontradiction.[18] These are familiar and rather stereotyped objections, and more careful and sympathetic interpreters have shown that Kant's ethics is far more supple than Arendt gives it credit for.[19] The deepest reason for the break, though, is her skepticism that morality speaks to us in the form of imperatives or laws.[20] A legalistic morality "becomes a real source for wrongdoing in all cases where no universal law, not even the imagined law of pure reason, can determine what is right in a particular case."[21]

For Kant, a distinctive feature of aesthetic judgments is precisely that no universal law determines them. In that sense, they aren't judgments of the understanding at all. There is no need to detour through the two-step process of reflection about which general aesthetic principle a particular

17 "Without banisters" comes from Arendt, "On Hannah Arendt," in *Hannah Arendt: The Recovery of the Public World*, ed. Melvyn A. Hill (St. Martin's Press: 1979), 336, republished as "Hannah Arendt on Hannah Arendt," in *TWB*, 473.

18 Rigidity: "On the Nature of Totalitarianism: An Essay in Understanding," in *EU*, 334; formalism: SQMP, 108; inhumanity: Hannah Arendt, *Men in Dark Times* (Harcourt, Brace & World, 1968) (hereafter *MDT*), 27; principle of non-contradiction: "Collective Responsibility," *RJ*, 153; *Kant Lectures*, 37; *Willing* (part two of *The Life of the Mind*, one-volume ed.) (Harcourt Brace, 1971)) (henceforth *W*), 63.

19 See especially Barbara Herman, *The Practice of Moral Judgment* (Harvard University Press, 1993), chapters 4 and 7.

20 I discuss this point in Chapter 5.

21 "On the Nature of Totalitarianism: An Essay in Understanding," in *EU*, 334.

painting or poem or musical composition instantiates, followed by applying that principle to pass determinate judgment on the artwork's merits.[22] That is why Arendt found herself drawn to the critique of aesthetic judgment as a model for morality without banisters. Her view recalls Bernard Williams's observation that routing moral judgment through a universal principle is often "one thought too many."[23] If your spouse is drowning, the argument, "One should, when possible, always rescue a drowning person. My spouse is a drowning person. Therefore, I should rescue my spouse," is one thought too many.[24]

## 3.2 Kant's Aesthetics as a Model for Moral Judgment

We have good evidence about which of the Third Critique's ideas Arendt found so suggestive. In a handful of essays, she broaches some of these ideas, and she discusses others in lecture notes published posthumously.

We saw some of what she had in mind in §1.3: Arendt borrows from the *Critique of Judgment* Kant's three "maxims of common human understanding": to think for yourself, to think consistently, and (especially) to think from the point of view of others.[25] Like Kant himself, she treats these as intellectual and political virtues, outside the context of aesthetics as well as in. Recall that an inability to think from the point of view of others is exactly the vice she placed at the root of Eichmann's banality.

But that's not all. In several essays, Arendt claimed that Kant's theory of aesthetic judgment contains elements that can serve equally well as a theory of political judgment; judgment, she believes, is the most political of our faculties.[26] In her first published essay to identify Kant's theory of aesthetic judgment as a political philosophy, she equates political judgment with *phronēsis*, Aristotle's name for the practical wisdom or insight of a statesman.[27] Importantly, for Aristotle practical judgments are always about particulars, unmediated by generalities.[28]

22 Kant *does* believe that aesthetic judgments are reflective, but the reflection is on the interplay of our own faculties, not on what concept best fits the object. Kant, "First Introduction to the Critique of Judgment," Ak. 20:223–24. For our purposes, I leave this refinement aside.

23 Bernard Williams, "Persons, Character, and Morality," in *Philosophical Papers 1973–1980* (Cambridge University Press, 1981), 18.

24 Arendt makes a similar point: SQMP, 131, citing Nietzsche.

25 *CJ*, §40, Ak. 5: 294.

26 We find this in "Truth and Politics" and the "The Crisis in Culture," both in *Between Past and Future*, but also in a manuscript of the late 1950s, published posthumously: "Introduction *into* Politics," in *PP*, 168–69.

27 "The Crisis in Culture," in *BPF* (Viking ed.), 221.

28 N.E. 6.8 1142a25, N.E. 6.11 1143a27–28.

Then, in her 1965 lectures on moral philosophy, she proposes Kant's aesthetics as a model for *moral* (rather than strictly political) judgment. In effect, the aesthetics becomes a moral philosophy to replace the Kantian ethics she rejects. A main attraction of Kant's aesthetics is its emphasis on particulars rather than principles – case-by-case judgings, rather than applications of moral rules. That is how we judge artworks and beautiful things in nature, and that is how Arendt approaches matters of right and wrong. Another attraction is that we make aesthetic judgments in communities of taste, not in the recesses of individual conscience and deliberation.

On the first point, the argument she offers for the aesthetic judgment/moral judgment analogy is revealing; it emphasizes that the analogy emerged as a response to the moral catastrophe she witnessed in the early years of the Third Reich ("the not very pleasant background of factual experience which gave rise to these considerations"). She transposes Kant's ideas from aesthetics to morality because what she witnessed convinced her that they are not so different:

> I mentioned the total collapse of moral and religious standards among people who to all appearances had always firmly believed in them, and I also mentioned the undeniable fact that the few who managed not be sucked into the whirlwind were by no means the "moralists," people who had always upheld rules of right conduct, but on the contrary very often those who had been convinced, even before the debacle, of the objective non-validity of these standards per se. Hence, theoretically, we find ourselves today in the same situation in which the eighteenth century found itself with respect to mere judgments of taste.[29]

The eighteenth-century aestheticians recognized that the standards of taste cannot be reduced to a set of rules. Artists don't create from a rule book, except in their student exercises on counterpoint or linear perspective; and audiences appreciate or criticize artworks as particulars, not by check-listing them against aesthetic maxims. (This is not to deny that we often classify artworks by their genres.)

Evidently Arendt believed that the same is true of moral judgments. In the passage I just quoted, she pugnaciously observes that it was not the sentinels of rule-based morality who withstood the Nazi assault on decency. They simply traded traditional rules for Nazi rules. What better reason to reject rule-reliant morality? And so, she concludes, we face the same puzzle in ethics that Kant and Hume confronted in art: Without rules, what entitles us to render judgments about right and wrong (or

[29] SQMP, 138–39.

beautiful and unbeautiful) with any claim to validity beyond personal preference?

Much of Kant's aesthetics is specific to the fine arts and irrelevant to moral philosophy. What does interest her is, first of all, Kant's basic insight about what I call the *rational status* of aesthetic judgments. For Kant, even though we cannot prove to someone else that a thing is beautiful, we nevertheless think that judgments of beauty can be right or wrong, not just to me but to anyone who gives the beautiful thing a proper chance. The same applies to negative aesthetic judgments (kitschy, trite, bombastic, sentimental, etc.). And we continue to think these judgments can be right or wrong, even when we recognize that in fact many people won't agree.

Kant points out that this odd situation makes aesthetic judgments quite different from judgments of what we find agreeable (*angenehm*[30]) and disagreeable. You have a sweet tooth; I don't. That's a matter of mere taste, and it never crosses my mind to say that you're wrong. But if you can't see the beauty in a mountain meadow on a bright summer day, or in Michelangelo's *David*, I will disagree as confidently as if you got today's date wrong. And this is not mere arrogance, because I know that I too get aesthetic judgments wrong. When musicians I respect enthuse about an artist who leaves me cold, I recognize that this is probably a flaw or blind spot in me, hopefully a correctable one. (Maybe I came in with rigid, false expectations; maybe the artist is working in a genre that I haven't yet learned to appreciate; maybe I need to listen more carefully, to give the music a chance to grow on me, to understand what the artist is up to.) My working hypothesis is that I got it wrong, not that it's a matter of arbitrary preference.

Furthermore, Kant saw that this difference in rational status between judgments of mere liking ("agreeableness") and judgments of beauty doesn't turn on statistical consensus. Nearly everyone likes chocolate, but chamber music, even great chamber music, bores most people. Nevertheless, liking or disliking chocolate remains a matter of mere agreeableness, and those who don't like chocolate haven't made an aesthetic error. Liking Brahms's Horn Trio involves judgments of beauty, and Brahms lovers will never shake their sense that the large majority of their friends and neighbors snoozing through the Horn Trio or checking their phones are mistaken. Nor should the Brahms lovers back down: The fact that judgments of beauty sound in the registers of right/wrong, apt/inapt,

[30] In this context, Kant's word "agreeable" (*angenehm*) means "enjoyable." I follow Werner Pluhar's translation of the word.

or valid/invalid doesn't represent a category mistake. It represents a fact of aesthetic life to be explained, not rejected. For the moment we reject it, we reject the capacity to love beautiful things for *their* beauty and not only for *our* enjoyment. In other words, we ascribe a kind of objectivity to aesthetic judgments despite their unprovability and despite dissensus.

Kant found this phenomenon surpassingly interesting. How can we label unprovable judgments about disputed matters "right" and "wrong"? Yet we do. Why don't we do the same when it comes to nearly unanimous matters of mere likeableness or agreeableness, like the sweet tooth? The fact is, we don't. What matters to Arendt about Kant's aesthetics is, quite simply, that Kant noticed this peculiar phenomenon about our practices of judgment and puzzled over it. She fastens on Kant's observation because it exactly captures what she takes to be the special character of moral judgments: They can't be proven, people sometimes disagree about them, and yet we insist on the validity of the moral judgments we adhere to.

Second, for Kant aesthetic judgment (indeed, judgment in general) is about particulars. We admire *this* sonnet, with *this* turn of phrase, not sonnets as a genre or poetic turns of phrase in general. Arendt's suspicion of rule-based morality flows in large part from her belief that judgment is always judgment of particulars.

Third, Arendt was deeply impressed with an idea that she attributed to Kant: We learn to make judgments of beauty in communities of judgment. They reflect a *sensus communis* – a common sense – within those communities. Again and again Arendt insists that the critique of aesthetic judgment is the most political of Kant's writings, and it is his comments about the *sensus communis* that she has in mind. Sometimes, as with the pleasure we take in a beautiful sunset, the community includes nearly everyone, and appreciation doesn't need trained observation and repeated viewings. Other times, as with the pleasure we take in chamber music or poetry, the community is a small minority of people, and the love must be cultivated over years through what one writer, echoing Kant, calls a "discipline of taste and feeling."[31] For Kant, crucially, the *sensus communis* is not the lowest common denominator but a community formed through reflection and critical discussion.[32]

[31] This is as good a place as any to acknowledge how much I have absorbed from Charles Wegener's *The Discipline of Taste and Feeling* (University of Chicago Press, 1992). The book title echoes §50 of the *Critique of Judgment*: "Taste, like the power of judgment in general, consists in disciplining (or training) genius."

[32] *CJ*, §40. Kant never refers explicitly to communities of taste, but the idea seems implicit in his claim that taste needs discipline and training; these are not solitary activities, at least at first. I return to this point in Chapter 7.

Consider again a situation in which music loved by people whose taste I respect leaves me cold. I need to listen a few more times, preferably in the company of someone who "gets it" and can point out what I'm missing. For, Kant explains, even though others can't prove judgments of beauty to me, they can "woo" (*umwerben*) my consent.[33] That is the function of good art criticism: to woo our judgment. The good critic gets us to see or hear what we couldn't on our own, by drawing our attention to features we missed, or by putting into words something we sensed inarticulately but passed over. The same is true of negative judgments. A friend points out that a movie I liked cheats with its happy ending. I come to see that the friend is right. I may still admire the movie, but my judgment changes. And that needn't be the end of the story: My friend's critique may bring into focus merits of the movie that I hadn't noticed before that redeem the pat ending.

Kant's metaphor is striking. Wooing means winning someone's affection when their natural diffidence makes them cautious because it isn't love at first sight. Successful wooing transforms the perceptions of the one being courted, so they find something lovable in the suitor that they didn't spot initially. Perceptions can be changed by giving reasons, but one woos by building emotional bonds of affection – a sense of sharing, a community of feeling – and not through reasons alone. The critic woos our judgment in a similar way: offering reasons that change our perception, while at the same time building what Kant calls a *sensus communis*. The difference, of course, is that the critic is wooing our judgment about an artwork, not about the critic themself.

The discipline of taste and feeling deserves comment. One of the pleasures of youth is hearing for the very first time the music you will love for life, and a key step is learning to like it even if it doesn't take at first – in other words, giving it a second or third chance. (Why would you do that? Perhaps because it's famous; or because your good friend insists.) A crucial next step is cultivating new tastes on your own. This is never a solitary enterprise. You learn from recommendations, from listening to the artists who influenced the musicians you already like, from talking to the people sitting next to you at concerts and clubs, from social media. Learning to love jazz turns out to be identical to joining the society of jazz fans and sharing in their *sensus communis*. Accomplished through conversation as well as listening, entering their society is an aesthetic counterpart to entering a political community, and in Arendt's eyes the conversations

[33] *CJ*, §19. Arendt praises Kant's word choice. "The Crisis in Culture," in *BPF*, 222; *Kant Lectures*, 72.

that discipline your taste and feeling are quintessentially political even though they aren't about public affairs or the conditions of freedom. What makes them political is that they strive at persuading others to join an (aesthetic) community.

The decisive point, though, is that your goal in the discipline of taste and feeling is to become an independent judge – an aesthetic self-starter who knows how to expand your own horizons and make up your own mind about what to accept and what to reject. Knowing what to reject is important: If for some reason the community jumps on the bandwagon of new fads, you won't automatically jump with them.

When we move from aesthetics to morality, that independence becomes all-important. This is Aristotle's insight about moral education: It begins with imitation of the noble actions of the virtuous, without understanding the reason. It then proceeds to the formation of independent powers of moral judgment, what Aristotle called *phronēsis*, practical wisdom. Learning from others in order to acquire the intellectual virtue of independent judgment, which we can exercise in defiance of others if need be, is what allows us (in Thom Gunn's words) to breathe the cold air of our freedom and tread a distinct direction.

That we learn to judge in communities of judgment is a crucial point that Arendt thought Kant got right in his aesthetics but wrong in his ethics. An entry from her Thought Diary reads as follows:

> It is most striking that in the *Critique of Practical Reason* and in the other moral writings of Kant there is hardly any mention of the so-called fellow man. It's really all about the self and reason that works in solitude. . . . In the *Critique of Judgment*, on the other hand, the political person has their say.[34]

## 3.3 Political Judgment and Moral Judgment

Arendt's analogy to eighteenth-century aesthetics is crucial, but before exploring it I want to emphasize a basic point: Whereas in her other writings she recruited Kant's aesthetics for the project of *political* philosophy and the analysis of political judgment, "Some Questions of Moral Philosophy" turns from politics to morals. She barely remarks the change, but it is momentous, once we remind ourselves how different political judgment and moral judgment are.[35]

[34] *DTB*, 818, dated "night from 28 to 29 April 1964."

[35] The account in this chapter has points of overlap with Ronald Beiner, *Political Judgment* (University of Chicago Press, 1983), although Beiner's focus is not on moral judgment, which I argue is quite different from political judgment.

Political judgment is success-oriented and power-oriented. It involves sizing up people's strengths and weaknesses, keeping your bullshit detector switched on, reading your audience, knowing your allies, foreseeing unintended consequences, sensing shifts in public opinion, picking the words most likely to persuade others. These are, fundamentally, skills in discerning other people's intentions and feelings. They are indispensable political skills, but none of them has much to do with the ability to tell right from wrong.

In fact, political judgment and moral judgment can steer in opposite directions; Machiavelli taught the prince how *not* to be good. Political judgment means judging how far you can push your agenda without a backlash, and pushing no further, even if morality urges you to push further. It means knowing when to evade and conceal. It means recognizing when to forge alliances and knowing when to drop them. Political judgment sometimes follows the cynical maxim that the whole secret of politics is knowing who hates whom.[36] That too takes judgment, the ability to read people and pinpoint their resentments.

Politics needn't be amoral, and obviously people can and do enter politics with high aspirations and accomplish worthy goals. But moral judgment itself appears tarnished when it operates in politics. It often requires distinguishing between morally bad compromises that nevertheless ought to be accepted because they are the best you can do, and rotten compromises that must never be accepted.[37] It means discerning how dirty you can get your hands without getting them too dirty. This is what passes in politics for placing duty above inclination.

Once we remind ourselves of these truisms, the gulf between political and moral judgment seems large and obvious. Then why did Arendt slide over it? She was acutely aware that "every resisting of evil done in the world necessarily entails some implication in evil" – an overstatement, perhaps, but a clear recognition of the problem of dirty hands.[38] She thinks that in politics moral propositions become "absolutely valid" only when you are politically powerless, which is a backhanded way of saying that whenever we wield political power, moral propositions are only conditionally and secondarily valid.[39] Yet when Arendt draws on Kant's aesthetics to analyze

36 Attributed to the US Republican Party strategist Kevin Phillips.

37 Avishai Margalit, *On Compromise and Rotten Compromises* (Princeton University Press, 2009).

38 "Collective Responsibility," in *RJ*, 152. She calls this a "Christian insight" but seems to accept it as a secular fact of life. In the Kant lectures, she likewise admits that "by resisting evil, you are likely to be involved in evil." *Kant Lectures*, 50.

39 "Collective Responsibility," 156; *DTB*, 818.

moral judgment as distinct from political judgment, she never acknowledges that she has changed the subject from Machiavellianism to morality, and rather dramatically so. Why?

## 3.4 Emergency Ethics: Moral Compass in Times of Moral Collapse

I think the best explanation is that Arendt's interest in moral phenomena was limited to the political crises that had preoccupied her for decades.[40] In her late essays on morality, she explains that what prompted her inquiries was the moral collapse of Germany (and Europe more generally) in the face of Nazism. As a theorist, she was not interested in the full range of moral issues – interpersonal morality, sexual morality, professional ethics, the treatment of animals – or everyday moral choices. For Arendt, the overwhelming moral question was what kind of moral stance individuals must adopt in dark times when they confront radical evil seeping into public life. "Good men," she writes, "become manifest only in emergencies, when they suddenly appear, as if from nowhere, in all social strata."[41]

Do you retreat into private life and cultivate your garden or throw yourself into the fray? Do you make trouble or stay out of trouble? Do you take risks that endanger your friends and family? Do you go along with lesser evils – and, if you do, where do you draw the line between lesser evils and intolerable evils? Do you gradually lose your sense of outrage, the way so many Germans in 1933 and 1934 did by telling one another, "You have to admit that Hitler is doing some good things for Germany"?[42] Do you drop your Jewish friends, perhaps with a mumbled, "You know how it is"? In the ways we respond to dark political times, and perhaps here alone, moral judgments *are* quintessentially political judgments. They are, precisely, moral judgments about political regimes and about how to conduct yourself in political emergencies, when the line between going about your daily business and silent complicity with evil starts to thin, and you can no longer count on the *sensus communis* to get it right.

Moral judgments of this alarming character appear to be the only ones that interested Arendt, at least in her published writings from the 1950s

[40] Deirdre Lauren Mahony rightly considers "ethics after Auschwitz" and the mystifying mass collusion in evil to be the gravitational center of all Arendt's moral philosophy, and essentially the only moral issue that concerned her. Mahony, *Hannah Arendt's Ethics*, 6–17.

[41] *CR*, 65.

[42] See Peter Fritzsche, *Life and Death in the Third Reich* (Harvard University Press, 2008), 31–36, 56–65.

on. Indeed, she announced that "the invocation of allegedly moral principles for matters of everyday conduct is usually a fraud. . . . All the things we have been talking about here [regarding moral judgment] are important only in exceptional circumstances," when the "conventions, the rules and standards by which we usually live, don't show up too well under examination."[43] She was writing for "emergency situations, in times of crises when, so to speak, we find ourselves with our back against the wall."[44]

These unusual claims can puzzle readers of *The Human Condition*, where Arendt writes that moral standards apply *only* to everyday behavior.[45] In fact there is no contradiction, but there is a revealing slippage in terminology between the pre- and post-*Eichmann in Jerusalem* writings, signifying a shift in attitude. *The Human Condition* equates "moral standards" with "customs and standards of behavior solidified through tradition and valid on the ground of agreements."[46] By contrast, the post-*Eichmann* essays concentrate on the moral judgments we make when conventional morality betrays us. Arendt's overall view is consistent: In normal times we judge conventional behavior by conventional standards, but they won't work in "exceptional circumstances." When conventional morality makes a pact with the devil, good people judge on their own, hanging on to elemental decency in defiance of the rules.

Thus, although she never changed her view that conventional standards govern conduct in ordinary circumstances, Arendt did change her terminology. In *The Human Condition*, she uses "moral standards" as a synonym for conventional morality; in the late essays, she uses "morality" as a name for nonconventional moral judgments. The change is not just terminological, however; it reflects her growing emphasis on the importance of judgment without banisters as a distinctively moral power that never loses sight of basic human decency.[47] This is among the most important "turns" in Arendt's thinking that the Eichmann trial induced.

## 3.5 Why Morality Is Not Only for Emergencies

When Arendt calls the invocation of moral principles in everyday matters a fraud, she may not mean that morality doesn't matter, but rather that the

[43] SQMP, 104. [44] SQMP, 122. [45] *HC*, 205. [46] *HC*, 245.

[47] Another example illustrates the change from pre-Eichmann to post-Eichmann. In 1953 she praises the ability "to judge without the set of customary rules which is morality." "Understanding and Politics," in *EU*, 321. In 1971, she calls judging without rules "the ability to tell right from wrong," which "may prevent catastrophes." TMC, 160, 189. Both phrasings favorably contrast judgment with rote rule-following. But the earlier one equates morality with customary rules; the later places judgment without rules at the heart of morality.

"narrow moralists who constantly appeal to high moral principles" are hypocrites. They are "usually the first to adhere to whatever fixed standards they are offered"; and when the standards change, as in the Third Reich, "respectable society, what the French call *les bien-pensants*, is liable to become very non-respectable and even criminal."[48] Perhaps, then, it's the moralists and not the moral principles that are fraudulent in everyday life.

The fact remains that in the later writings as in the earlier, Arendt remains uninterested in everyday moral questions. Perhaps she never quite shook free of her youthful conviction that in mundane matters of right and wrong (mere "behavior"), customs and mores settle the dilemmas of daily life through the straightforward application of rules – "*das Moralische versteht sich von selbst,*" morality is self-evident.[49]

If so, this is a mistake on her part. In small matters as well as large ones, people confront dilemmas that custom won't resolve. These include dilemmas of conflicting loyalties, keeping secrets, ignoring bad behavior rather than calling people on it, dealing with fools and bores, telling small lies, negotiating affairs of the heart with their innumerable hurts and their small and large betrayals, and reconciling professional duty with personal conviction. What makes these issues *dilemmas* is precisely that customs and mores don't dictate the right answer. There is moral depth in small and medium-size matters as well as in grandiose ones. Arendt seems to overlook the moral depth of everyday life.

Let me frame the objection in different terms. Perhaps surprisingly, Sir Walter Scott greatly admired Jane Austen, though her novels could hardly be more different from his swashbuckling historical romances. He wrote in his journal:

> That young lady had a talent for describing the involvements and feelings of characters of ordinary life which is to me the most wonderful I have ever met with. The Big Bow wow strain I can do myself like any other now going but the exquisite touch which renders ordinary common-place things and characters interesting from the truth of the description and the sentiment is denied to me.[50]

Austen lovers would agree. Austen herself, in a letter to her schoolboy nephew, playfully contrasted his "strong, manly, spirited Sketches, full of Variety & Glow," with "the little bit (two Inches wide) of Ivory on which

48 SQMP, 104. 49 PRUD, 22.
50 Sir Walter Scott, *Journal*, March 14, 1826, quoted in Wegener, *The Discipline of Taste and Feeling*, 11.

I work with so fine a Brush."[51] Austen shows us moral depth in everyday life – a depth Arendt's remark about the fraudulence of moral principle in everyday matters denies.

No doubt Arendt would have appreciated Austen's scathing satires of moral philistines, the "narrow moralists" who "adhere to whatever fixed standards they are offered."[52] But she would not have recognized the moral choices faced by Austen heroines as emergencies when one's back is against the wall. Perhaps they aren't; it hardly follows that dilemmas of marriage and money lack depth, or that social conventions settle them. If they did, Austen's novels would have no stories to tell. Limiting moral judgment to emergencies would wrongly restrict moral choice to the "Big Bow wow strain" – fateful choices in four-alarm historical crises. That leaves little room for the moral world of Jane Austen, which is, after all, a significant chunk of *our* moral world, no matter how remote the society her characters inhabit is from ours.

## 3.6 Common Law Moral Reasoning

Oddly, the reason that Arendt is so uninterested in everyday moral concerns is not that she underrates conventional morality but that she overrates it. She erroneously supposes that our existing "rules and standards" settle moral questions except in emergencies. And the curious result is that she sells her own philosophy of moral judgment short. Her emphasis on moral judgment that is not rule application shouldn't be confined to "emergency ethics" when the world is crashing down around us. Taken rightly, it applies to commonplace dilemmas as well.

Now, there is one way in which Arendt is right that conventional morality suffices to settle conventional moral dilemmas: An agent can always reason analogically from "settled" cases to the novel case. What she overlooks is the element of creativity and individual choice and judgment that goes into moral reasoning of this sort. It is anything but the mechanical or formulaic application of rules and principles.

[51] Letter to James Edward Austen-Leigh, December 16–17, 1816, *Letters of Jane Austen*, ed. Deirdre Le Faye (Oxford University Press, 1995), 323 (letter 146).

[52] SQMP, 104; "Philistines": PRUD, 22. On Austen's scathing side, see D. W. Harding's famous 1940 essay "Regulated Hatred: An Aspect of the Work of Jane Austen," in Harding, *Regulated Hatred and Other Essays on Jane Austen*, ed. Monica Lawler (Athlone Press, 2001). Admittedly, in an age where a wife was a legal vassal of her husband, dilemmas of whom to marry may indeed have been life and death emergencies.

The paradigm of what I have in mind is the kind of reasoning engaged in by common law judges applying precedents to novel facts. Put schematically, their reasoning involves three steps. First, the judge canvases the precedents and selects those she deems good law. Next, the judge asks which of the several possible, and possibly competing, precedents provides the best analogy to the new case. Finally, the judge extracts the rule those governing precedents stand for and applies it to the new case.[53]

Three points about this model matter here. First, you need good judgment at every stage. Prior decisions don't come labeled "good law" or "bad law"; the initial judgment of which precedents have gravitational force and which don't requires the judge to critically evaluate the tradition. So too with customs and mores. The judge will never describe what she does as "critically evaluating the tradition" – that is not how judges talk – but every lawyer learns how to recognize which prior cases matter, which are outliers, and why the outliers *are* outliers.

At the second stage, determining which analogy best fits the facts is a paradigmatic act of judgment – a judgment of similitude, one that rules can't capture. I don't mean that *in principle* complex rules can't capture similitude judgments of the form "*X* resembles *A* more than *B*." Someday, maybe tomorrow (or yesterday?), an artificial intelligence (AI) will do so reliably; there is no a priori argument that a machine using complex rules can't do whatever the brain does, and at far greater speed. Perhaps the brain itself uses complex rules of which we are unaware.

But there's a difference between the resources we use in moral judgment and the underlying mechanisms our brain uses. Think of an analogy: I *use* my calculator to multiply large numbers; my calculator *uses* an algorithm to multiply large numbers. But, in the relevant sense of "use," I don't use the calculator's algorithm. Think of my brain as akin to my calculator – as Arendt says, the brain is the tool of the mind.[54] I don't use whatever algorithm (supposing there is one) that my brain uses. Jurists don't use rules to see similarities, even if their brains do.

At the third stage, extracting a rule from prior cases – formulating it broadly or narrowly and identifying its implicit exceptions – likewise requires judgment and choice. Take a simple illustration. In 1900, an Indiana physician refused a call to treat a gravely ill person. No other

[53] Edward H. Levi, *An Introduction to Legal Reasoning* (University of Chicago Press, 1948), 1–5; for a similar but more elaborated account of common law reasoning, Robert B. Brandom, *Reason in Philosophy: Animating Ideas* (Harvard University Press, 2009), 84–88. See also Cass R. Sunstein, "On Analogical Reasoning," *Harvard Law Review* 106(3) (1993): 741–91.

[54] *W*, 56.

doctor was available, the sufferer died, and the estate sued the doctor. Was the physician's nonfeasance a legitimate cause of action?

As the parties argued the case, it devolved into a choice between competing analogies. Is the only physician in town like an innkeeper or common carrier, obliged by settled law to take on all travelers who present themselves? Or is the physician more like a private contractor, free under settled law to turn down a customer for any nondiscriminatory reason or for no reason at all? If the former, plaintiff's suit can proceed to trial; if the latter, the estate has no cause of action. Both analogies have something to be said for them; the judge must judge.[55]

In one sense, the decision is a Kantian determinate judgment that subsumes a particular fact-situation under a pre-given concept (a rule). In the Indiana example, the court subsumed the facts to the rule governing private contractors, and concluded that the doctor was under no obligation to enter into a contract to treat the patient. The rhetoric of judicial opinion-writing aims to make every judgment sound determinate, as though the law and not the judge has decided the case. Every case should sound like an easy case.

But, as in *Baby M*, getting there demands reflective judgment, Kant's term for finding a concept that aptly suits the particular – a creative judgment that moves from particulars to concepts, not a mechanical one that applies concepts to particulars. Here, the court had to choose between the concept of contract and the concept of common carriers. Which best suits the facts? Answering that question calls for reflection, not deduction – and, by today's lights, many of us would think the Indiana court got it dead wrong. Arendt's objections to rule-based or "legalistic" morality identify it exclusively with determinate judgment, which she regards as too mechanical to be interesting. She overlooks the way that moral reasoning modeled on the common law is reflective (therefore fallible), not mechanical.[56] And as in law the advocate's task is wooing the judge to the favored analogy, in moral deliberation our inner voices woo us to a decision.

Second, she describes conventional mores as rules produced by human agreement. But the model of agreement is misleading. It suggests a

55 Hurley v. Eddingfield, 59 N.E. 1058 (Ind. 1901).

56 Kant scholars disagree over whether the reflective process (described in Kant's logic) of comparison of cases, reflection on those comparisons, and abstraction from them – concept-formation – is the same as reflective *judgment*. Compare Béatrice Longuenesse, *Kant and the Capacity to Judge* (Princeton University Press, 1998), 163–66 with Rudolf A. Makkreel, "Reflection, Reflective Judgment, and Aesthetic Exemplarity," in *Aesthetics and Cognition in Kant's Critical Philosophy*, ed. Rebecca Kukla (Cambridge University Press, 2006), 224–30. For present purposes, there is no need to address the issue.

synchronic and reciprocal meeting of minds, but here the process is diachronic and nonreciprocal. The agreement is a one-way street: The judges who created the precedents have no say in whether later judges take them up, ignore them, reject them, limit their scope, maneuver around them, or for that matter misquote them. Earlier decisions constrain but don't confine the judgment of later judges; they are more like proffers that the later jurists can accept as rules of decision, but can also reject or limit or modify. So too with customary morality, bequeathed to us by the past but accepted (or not) by the present. There was no moment of agreement.

Third, and related: The later judge not only absorbs the tradition and applies its "rule" – in doing so, she modifies the body of precedent by adding to it. Applying the rule to a new case changes the rule. Edward Levi identified this as the special character of common law reasoning: "[T]he classification changes as the classification is made. The rules change as the rules are applied."[57] Law is a moving classification scheme. Although he was not writing about law or morality, Ludwig Wittgenstein captures this idea when he writes: "We use judgments as principles of judgment."[58]

I am suggesting that moral reasoning based on conventional rules and standards is more like common law reasoning along the lines just described than it is like deductive reasoning or the application of a mathematical function to a set of numerical inputs. The form of the latter kinds of reasoning asks: Given a rule or function, and given an input, what does the rule yield as output? In moral reasoning, we are not "given" a rule – the rule is taken (not given) through a process of reflection that remakes it in small or large ways.

So, while Arendt is right that moral judgment is not determinate rule application, she is wrong that determinate rule application is the way custom works in thinking through everyday moral dilemmas. And she is therefore exaggerating when she writes that "the invocation of allegedly moral principles for matters of everyday conduct is usually a fraud."

This is not to deny that moralists can be hypocrites, nor that precedents can fail in emergencies – and of course, in life if not in law, there are no books of precedents to consult. Framed in these terms, Arendt's "emergency situations" and "exceptional circumstances" are those that are, literally, "unprecedented" in the sense that the world has changed so abruptly and dramatically that the conventional moral guidelines are misleading. At the beginning of *The Origins of Totalitarianism*, Arendt

57 Edward H. Levi, *An Introduction to Legal Reasoning* (University of Chicago Press, 1948), 3–4.

58 Ludwig Wittgenstein, *On Certainty*, eds. G. E. M. Anscombe and G. H. von Wright, trans. Denis Paul and G. E. M. Anscombe (J. & J. Harper, 1969), §124, 18e.

warns against "deducing the unprecedented from precedents, . . . explaining phenomena by such analogies and generalities that the impact of reality and the shock of experience are no longer felt."[59] Let's suppose (as I do) that she is right about the unprecedented character of twentieth-century totalitarianism and the continent-wide moral collapse it induced. In that case, moral reasoning along the common law pattern I've just described may indeed fail, and fail dramatically. Then judgment "without banisters" becomes essential, as Arendt insisted.[60] It does *not* follow that conventional moral judgment is either mechanical or deductive. It too requires choices made without banisters, because our choices continuously recreate the conventions in the course of applying them.

## 3.7 The Interdependence of Actors and Spectators

In her later writings, and especially in the posthumously published Kant lectures, Arendt draws a sharp distinction between actors and spectators (including among the latter historians, storytellers, and judges in a criminal proceeding like the Eichmann trial). The spectator, judging human affairs at a distance, is disinterested, just like the judge in aesthetic matters (according to Kant); the actor can never be disinterested, for the urgent question "What shall I do?" is fully engaged. Her Kant lectures seem to confine judging to the realm of after-the-fact evaluation at a distance, and to separate it sharply from practical deliberation. Ronald Beiner, who edited Arendt's Kant lectures for publication, believes this is indeed the direction of her later thought, relocating the power of judgment from the life of action to the life of the mind. The result is "a much narrower (and perhaps less rich) concept of judgment."[61]

That would be an unfortunate place for Arendt to end up. If judgment is solely "our faculty for dealing with the past,"[62] it follows that we don't judge when we act and deliberate in the present. Plainly, though, that is *not* Arendt's view. It does, however, raise the interesting question of whether judgment when we act or deliberate is the same intellectual

[59] *OT*, xiv.

[60] Christine Korsgaard defends, on Kantian grounds, an analogous view about when the virtuous person will take the law into her own hands, notwithstanding that justice prohibits it. Christine Korsgaard, "Taking the Law into Our Own Hands: Kant on the Right to Revolution," in *The Constitution of Agency: Essays on Practical Reason and Moral Psychology* (Oxford University Press, 2008), 258–59.

[61] Beiner, "Interpretive Essay," in *Kant Lectures*, 139–40.

[62] *T*, 216.

power, requiring the same intellectual virtues, as the after-the-fact judgment she focuses on in the Kant lectures.

Arendt certainly thought that judges in the postwar Nazi trials were engaged in judgment of exactly the sort that interested her: judging particulars without banisters. As she comments approvingly, "the judges in all these trials really passed judgment solely on the basis of the monstrous deeds. In other words, they judged freely, as it were, and did not really lean on the standards and legal precedents with which they more or less convincingly sought to justify their decisions."[63] Of course, they were passing legal judgment, not moral judgment; but, as Arendt insists, law and morality "have a certain affinity with each other because both presuppose the power of judgment."[64]

What, then, does the free style of ex post judging she applauds have to do with ex ante "actor" judgment, that is, practical judgment about what to do? If actor and spectator judgment turn out to be different in kind – if *deliberation* and *evaluation* are fundamentally different rational practices – then perhaps there really is no unified faculty of judgment. Not that there has to be – but for the sake of clarity it would be good to know.

It's helpful in this regard to compare the views of Stuart Hampshire, in his wonderful 1989 book *Innocence and Experience*, with Arendt's. In conspicuous ways, including a preoccupation with Nazi evil, which Hampshire encountered as an interrogator during the war, he might be the analytic philosopher closest to Arendt (notwithstanding his low opinion of her philosophy[65]). Hampshire, like Arendt, sharply distinguishes two powers of the intellect. One is computational ability in the broad sense that we sometimes call "smartness," and which includes both logical acumen and means–ends rationality. The other is inner dialogue, "the practice of promoting and accepting arguments for and against a proposal," what Arendt calls the two-in-one.[66] Also like Arendt, he strongly identifies practical reason with the latter; as he puts it elsewhere: "In the silent thought of any individual, rationality is best characterized as two-sided reflection."[67] Finally, like Arendt, Hampshire distinguishes the practical judgment of the actor from spectatorial, evaluative judgment.

But, reversing Arendt's stance in her Kant lectures, Hampshire insists on the primacy of the actor's judgment over the spectator's. This comes out forcefully in his critique of David Hume:

63 *EJ*, 294. 64 PRUD, 22. 65 On Hampshire's dim view of Arendt, see Young-Bruehl, 47.

66 Stuart Hampshire, *Innocence and Experience* (Harvard University Press, 1989), 53. Arendt labels these two powers "cognition" (or sometimes "knowing" or "intellect") and "thinking." *T*, 54, 61.

67 Stuart Hampshire, *Justice Is Conflict* (Princeton University Press, 2000), 19.

> Not alone among eighteenth-century moralists, Hume represents moral thought as principally the activity of projecting upon reality adjectives of approval or disapproval, as commentary on, and criticism of, human performances. Once again the model of Newton misled all those who aspired to be the Newton of the moral sciences, observing human nature as Newton had observed the starry heavens above.[68]

When a person looks back on his own life in a mood of retrospection and stock-taking, he considers "all those things that he might have done, and that he nearly did, and that were real possibilities or options for him, stretching back into the past." Should he have chosen differently? Did he deserve his reversals of fortune? Does his history show that he constantly repeated the same bad patterns in his personal relations? Or does he have less to regret than he had thought?[69] In other words, even retrospective judgment requires us to project ourselves back into the choice situations we faced in practice, reconstructing the deliberative point of view in order to pass judgments on our choices.

The same must be true in judging the conduct of others. You cannot evaluate someone else's behavior without understanding what was going on in their mind and what reasons were available to them – what they knew and intended and when they knew and intended it; what field of possibilities they saw; what pressures and constraints they took into account. Evaluation, in other words, demands that we reconstruct the actor's deliberations, and that is true even when we utterly condemn them. (To understand all is *not* to forgive all!) In criminal law, this point translates into familiar doctrinal concepts: the *mens rea* requirement of evaluating knowledge and intention, determining whether the defendant was acting under mistakes of fact or of law, whether she was suffering from diminished mental capacity, was subject to duress, or acted out of perceived necessity.

But I don't think this proves the primacy of actor-judgment, as Hampshire supposes. Rather, it proves the interdependence of ex ante deliberation and ex post evaluation. For, when we deliberate about what to do, one important element is how we will look back on our choice, especially if it misfires; regret analysis is part and parcel of wise deliberation. We may disregard that future viewpoint, or take moral risks for any number of reasons, good as well as bad – but that should be a deliberate choice. Those who are so impetuous that they don't even think about how they will

68 Hampshire, *Innocence and Experience*, 102.

69 Hampshire, *Innocence and Experience*, 100–1. The questions are closely paraphrased from Hampshire's text.

look back on their choices are textbook exemplars of bad judgment – a fact that suggests that anticipating our own retrodictions is a necessary component of *phronēsis*. As Arendt wrote in her Thought Diary: "To think means: Imagine what as your own witness you will have to say after you have acted and the act is now remembered, i.e., appears to you. Make it appear before it has happened, as though it had already happened."[70]

What about estimations of other people's spectator evaluations, future and contemporaneous, as well as our own? Taking them into account is a requirement of good moral deliberation: We control for the inevitable partiality of our own view by imagining the judgments others will pass on our conduct, not only in the future but in the present.[71]

Kant called thinking in this way an "experiment of pure reason" that is morally imperative whenever our actions affect the rights of others. To perform Kant's experiment, ask yourself whether you could publicly divulge the maxims of your actions without defeating your own purposes. If not, Kant explains, your action is unjust.[72] Kant's experiment of reason won't always yield a determinate result, because some wrong actions might not be self-defeating even if they were revealed publicly; but conducting the experiment of reason is an essential part of moral deliberation.

It doesn't follow that evaluation and deliberation are the same mental process. Deliberators needn't perform Kant's experiment of reason or engage in regret analysis, and evaluators can restrict themselves to what Hampshire derisively calls "a bare log-book of events and actions."[73] But wise deliberation and evaluation combine the actor's view with the spectator's. Moral judgment is a single, albeit complex, moral power.

Arendt connects that power to the "enlarged mentality" Kant praises in the *Critique of Judgment*, and she analyzes enlarged mentality as the kind of thinking from the point of view of others that she found so conspicuously absent in Eichmann. The argument of her later moral psychology, in a nutshell, is that the inner two-in-one dialogue that she calls thinking is a necessary condition for enlarged mentality, and enlarging our mentality to embrace multiple perspectives underwrites common sense and cultivates sound judgment. These are the topics of Chapters 4 and 5. To understand judgment we must understand thinking.

70 *DTB*, XXVII.24 (December 1969), 762 (original in English).

71 As Arendt herself insists: *Kant Lectures*, 55.

72 This "transcendental principle of public law" appears in the second appendix to Immanuel Kant, *Toward Perpetual Peace*, Ak. 8:381, Kant, *Practical Philosophy*, 347.

73 Hampshire, *Innocence and Experience*, 101.

CHAPTER 4

# *The Socratic Moral Propositions*
## *Thinking and Judging*

> One morning he was thinking about something which he could not resolve; he would not give it up, but continued thinking from early dawn until noon – there he stood fixed in thought; and at noon attention was drawn to him, and the rumor ran through the wondering crowd that had been standing and thinking about something ever since the break of day. ... There he stood until the following morning; and with the return of light he offered up a prayer to the sun and went his way.
>
> Plato, *Symposium* 220c–d (Benjamin Jowett trans.)

> *SOCRATES*: And do you apply the word "thinking" to the same thing as I do?
>
> *THEAETETUS*: What do you apply it to?
>
> *SOCRATES*: Speech which the mind itself goes through with itself about whatever it's considering. Mind you, I don't claim to know the truth of what I'm telling you. It looks to me as if, when the mind is thinking, it's simply carrying on a discussion, asking itself questions and answering them, and making assertions and denials. And when it has to come to a decision, either slowly or in a sudden rush, and it's no longer divided, but says one single thing, we call that its judgment. So what I call "judging" is speaking, and what I call "judgment" is speech; but speech spoken, not aloud to someone else, but silently to oneself. What do you think?
>
> *THEAETETUS*: I agree..
>
> Plato, *Theaetetus*, 189e–190a (John McDowell trans.)

### 4.1 The Figure of Socrates

Socrates holds center stage in Arendt's moral thought. He is at once a citizen among citizens and a thinker engaged in perpetual conversation with others and with himself. He was living proof that thinking is not the special preserve of professional philosophers. For Arendt, this point is crucial: The universal availability of thinking is what allows us to judge the conduct of others when they thoughtlessly do wrong.[1] Recall that Arendt links Eichmann's banality to his thoughtlessness. Socrates is the anti-Eichmann – not only in the obvious sense that Socrates was not a criminal but also in the deeper sense that his entire way of being was the polar opposite of Eichmann's. Eichmann mouthed clichés; Socrates questioned them. Eichmann was an organization man; Socrates was a gadfly.

And Eichmann as Arendt depicts him was unable or unwilling to think from the point of view of another person, except strategically. His inner life was monophonic; he remembered external events by relating them to milestones in his own career. Socrates' was a life of dialogue, even when he engaged in solitary thought. For, as he tells his young companion Theaetetus, thinking is the mind's silent conversation with itself. Socrates says that we do everything better when we do it with someone else, preferably with one companion at a time.[2] But that companion can be an inner voice as well as a person in the flesh; the mind's conversation with itself is modeled on conversation with another person. Even when lost in thought for a full day and night, Socrates is actively conversing with himself. To Arendt, Socrates' identity "was formed not by oneness but by a constant hither-and-thither of two-in-one; and this movement found its highest form and purest actuality in the dialogue of thought."[3]

In our first epigraph, Socrates stands by himself, fixed in thought and paying no heed to his fellow soldiers. Arendt emphasizes that thinking is an inherently solitary activity, because it requires an undistracted mind. She immediately clarifies that solitary doesn't mean lonely, because the thinker has herself as a companion, unlike the lonely person who feels cut off from everyone.[4] But silent conversation requires stepping back from the world of affairs into the world of our thoughts – it's inherently a "stop and think."[5] Thinking is in that sense nonpolitical or even anti-political.

[1] TMC, 166, 168–69. Properly speaking, I should have said that Socrates the literary figure, not the historical Socrates, holds center stage in Arendt's thought, a point she carefully notes (TMC, 169). Plato's version of Socrates' apology is different from Xenophon's, and both are reconstructions of whatever the historical Socrates actually said. And, of course, later Platonic dialogues such as the *Theaetetus* and *Republic* are wholly Plato's invention. Arendt incorporated much of "Thinking and Moral Considerations" verbatim (or nearly so) into *Thinking*. For simplicity, in most cases I give page-cites only to the essay. Although *Thinking* offers a more elaborate treatment, much of it is specifically about philosophical thinking and the metaphysical traps it sets for philosophers – a worthy topic, but tangential to her treatment of "thinking and moral considerations."

[2] Plato, *Protagoras*, 348c–d; *Gorgias* 474a.

[3] Hannah Arendt, *On Revolution* (Viking Press, 1965) (hereafter *OR*), 98; cf. *DTB* XXII.41 (1958), 590.

[4] *OT*, 476. Arendt says she takes this insight from Epictetus, *Discourses*, bk. 3, ch. 13.

[5] SQMP, 105; TMC, 176.

And yet, Arendt insists, in a political crisis when demagogues whip up the mob, it's the individuals who stop and think who stand the best chance of resisting. "When everybody is swept away unthinkingly by what everybody else does and believes in, those who think are drawn out of hiding because their refusal to join is conspicuous and thereby becomes a kind of action."[6]

The Socrates of Plato's *Apology* is the perfect exemplar of what Arendt is talking about. On trial for his life before a jury of 500 Athenians, Socrates reminds the jurors of a trial seven years earlier where they behaved shamefully, sweeping aside proper procedure in their rage to punish. It was the aftermath of a naval battle, when the Athenians vengefully executed six of their own commanders for failing to rescue survivors whose ships had sunk in a storm. Xenophon reports that the fickle Athenians quickly regretted what they had done. They turned against the prosecutors, who fled Athens for their lives.[7]

Socrates was the only council member to stand up in public and vote against punishing the commanders. The furious prosecutors "were ready to impeach and arrest me, and you urged them with shouts to do so." Socrates adds, "I thought I must run the risk to the end with law and justice on my side, rather than join with you when your wishes were unjust."[8]

In recalling that harrowing moment, Socrates reminds the jurors of their cruel behavior, including their lynch-mob rage against him for voting to acquit. He stands up against the crowd by reminding them about the last time he stood up against the crowd. Any defense lawyer worth their salt would urge Socrates not to go there: Reminding jurors of their past disgrace is suicidal. Of course Socrates knows how risky it is: "[N]o man will save his life who nobly opposes you or any other populace."[9] It nearly happened to him at the commanders' trial, and just a few moments earlier in his own trial he had to plead with the jurors to stop interrupting him with shouts and heckling.[10]

You might think Socrates was looking for martyrdom, but a careful reading of the *Apology* shows that his defense is genuine, and the best explanation of his speech is that he is continuing his lifelong civic mission

[6] TMC, 188; also "Basic Moral Propositions," quoted in *RJ*, 279n12.
[7] Xenophon, *Hellenica* 1.7.35.
[8] Plato, *Apology*, 32a–c. I use the translation by Harold N. Fowler, in *Plato in Twelve Volumes*, vol. 1 (Harvard University Press and William Heinemann, Ltd., 1925). The event was the Battle of Arginusae, 406 BCE, and Socrates was the "obstinate dissentient" who "insisted that he would do nothing except in accordance with the law." Xenophon, *Hellenica* 1.7.7.
[9] *Apology*, 31e–32a. [10] *Apology*, 30c.

of trying to make the Athenians stop and think, despite the personal danger.[11] In her diary, Arendt calls his speech a political defense. She doesn't mean that Socrates calculated politically that it would save his life, but rather that he carried it out in public for the good of the city.[12]

## 4.2 The First Socratic Proposition: Doing Evil or Suffering Evil

Arendt's diary entry doesn't explore the assumptions underlying Socrates' defense. She did so fifteen years later, after the Eichmann trial prompted her to take up questions of moral philosophy.

The *Apology*, like the *Crito*, brings to life the Socratic teaching that it is better to suffer wrong than to do wrong. Arendt calls this the *first Socratic proposition*, articulated in several Platonic dialogues, notably the *Gorgias*:[13]

POLUS : Then you would rather be treated unjustly than to act unjustly?
SOCRATES : I, of course, would wish for neither. But if it were necessary either to act unjustly or to be treated unjustly, I would choose rather to be treated unjustly than to act unjustly.[14]

In Arendt's lectures on basic moral propositions, this Socratic proposition is the most basic of all – basic in the sense that it can't be proven, but it underlies all morality.[15] (Her own updated version, in *Origins*: "[I]t is better to die a victim than to live as a bureaucrat of murder."[16])

Polus is incredulous. How is it better to suffer wrong than to do wrong? We can all think of wrongs a person might suffer that are life-shattering or life-ending: being murdered or raped or tortured, being swindled out of everything you own, being driven from your home, or having similar disasters inflicted on your loved ones. How can it be better to be raped and maimed than to tell a lie or break a promise?[17]

[11] For a careful argument that Socrates' defense was genuine, see C. D. C. Reeve, *Socrates in the* Apology: *An Essay on Plato's* Apology *of Socrates* (Hackett, 1989). I note, however, that there are contrary opinions. Xenophon reports that Socrates was looking to die. I. F. Stone, the investigative journalist turned classicist, agrees, and makes the case that if the historical Socrates had not gone out of his way to antagonize his jurors, he would have been acquitted. A change of just thirty votes out of 500 would have saved him. I. F. Stone, *The Trial of Socrates* (Little Brown, 1988), 181–92. Socrates' speech doesn't contradict his stricture that serious conversation must be one-on-one, because a large part of it consists of him posing questions to his main accuser in a typical Socratic dialogue – a highly unusual (and in this case ineffective) form of oratory. *Apology*, 24d–27e.

[12] *DTB* XV.24 (May 1953), 362. [13] TMC, 181.

[14] *Gorgias*, 469b12–c2. I use the translation by James A. Arieti and Roger M. Barrus (Focus Publishing, 2007). The translators italicize *you* and *I* to register that the pronoun is explicitly in the Greek text rather than implicit in the verb form, which indicates that Plato means to place special emphasis on it. See p. viii. I've removed their italics.

[15] SQMP, 72, 86; "Collective Responsibility" in *RJ*, 157. [16] *OT*, 452. [17] *Gorgias*, 473c.

Sometimes Socrates answers that virtue is itself happiness and vice misery. Given that premise, a virtuous person suffering injustice is by definition happier than an unjust person.[18] Yet that response is too obviously conclusory. Only a few paragraphs later, Socrates acknowledges the plain truth that the victim of injustice, too, is wretched – misfortunes, including poor health and, indeed, being the victim of injustice, can wreck our happiness.[19] For that matter (although Plato does not discuss it), suffering traumatic injustices can damage our personalities and make us less capable of virtue – the phenomenon known today as moral injury. So even someone committed to the Socratic view that virtue is essential to happiness should acknowledge that being the victim of injustice can destroy our well-being if it damages the capacity for virtue.

Nor is it obvious that committing an occasional injustice rules out being a virtuous person overall. Human judgment, motivation, and character are not infallible right-making machines, and even the most admirable people have lapses, some heedless but others not.[20] It follows that committing an out-of-character injustice need not make one an unjust person. So, one premise of Socrates' argument for the first Socratic proposition – that doing something unjust makes one an unjust person – is doubtful.

In short, if "better" means "better for my well-being," the first Socratic proposition seems patently false. It can hold only if we read "better" as (what we now call) "morally better." In that case, the Socratic proposition reads: "It is morally better to suffer wrong than to do wrong." This near-tautology is not so much a substantive moral principle as an implicit definition of morality. Morality is precisely the domain of life in which doing right matters more than self-interest.

"Morality" is not a Greek philosophical word: Plato and Aristotle speak of "the good" and "the fine," and of "virtue," but never of a separate domain of "the moral." The Socratic proposition exposes a well-known ambiguity in the word "good." The word can describe excellence at some craft – a common Platonic and Aristotelian analogy. Aristotle's typical examples are a good doctor, a good general, and a good physical trainer.[21] The doctor is good at restoring health, the general at winning wars, the

[18] *Gorgias*, 470e6–11; Reeve, *Socrates in the* Apology, 126–30. This is a contested interpretive issue. For useful discussion, including references to relevant passages in the dialogues, see Reeve, *Socrates in the* Apology, 133–39.

[19] *Gorgias*, 473d. For other examples in the Dialogues, see Reeve, *Socrates in the* Apology, 140–42.

[20] Plato denies this, through two controversial doctrines in the *Protagorus*, the denial of weakness of the will (*akrasia*) and the assertion that nobody does wrong voluntarily. I do not discuss these here.

[21] N.E. I.6, 1096a33–34.

trainer at building athletes' strength and speed. Aristotle understood virtues as traits like courage and moderation that are good for achieving overall human flourishing (*eudaimonia*), and in the first book of the *Nicomachaean Ethics*, this functional sense of "good" is the only one he examines. But of course, action that leads to one's own ruin destroys flourishing, and it can hardly be thought of as good in the functional sense.[22]

But we easily recognize a second, moralized, meaning of the word "good" and its cognates. In the finale of Dickens's *A Tale of Two Cities*, Sydney Carton substitutes himself for a condemned, innocent man, and he reflects as he goes to the guillotine in Darnay's place, "It is a far, far better thing that I do than I have ever done." In the purely functional meaning, taking Darnay's place in the tumbril is the most disastrous thing Carton has ever done. Yet we understand perfectly well what Carton means and why he thinks it. Call his act altruism, or benevolence, or love, or heroism, or redemption. Whatever the name, Carton's "better thing that I do" employs an alternative, nonfunctional meaning of "better": what for convenience I am calling the moral meaning. That is the meaning the Socratic proposition registers.

Arendt never discusses these different senses of "good."[23] However, she imagines how foreign the Socratic proposition must have sounded to a Greek audience.[24] She diagnosed classical Greek culture as fatally flawed by a hypercompetitive spirit that eventually ripped it apart.[25] In a culture whose citizens put a premium on "ceaselessly showing oneself to be the

[22] On this point: Philippa Foot, "Moral Beliefs" in *Proceedings of the Aristotelian Society* 59 (1958–59): 101–4.

[23] The one place she explicitly writes about goodness is a quirky gloss on the Gospels. In *The Human Condition*, she approvingly discusses Jesus's injunction that good works must remain hidden; they must be done "for nothing but goodness' sake." These lead her to remark on the "curious negative quality of goodness, the lack of outward phenomenal manifestation." *HC*, 74–75; *PP*, 137. However, I doubt she intends these remarks as anything like an analysis of moral goodness. The passages from Matthew 6 she quotes refer specifically to alms-giving, and, read in context, Jesus is not warning against doing good deeds openly, only against the hypocrisy of doing them openly in order to win applause. Jesus never suggests that the Good Samaritan would be less good if there were bystanders on the road to Jericho watching him bind the injured man's wounds. I presume Arendt would not think otherwise. Elsewhere, she glosses Jesus's "Let not thy left hand know what thy right hand does" as "no doing good is possible if while doing so I am even aware of it" (SQMP, 117) and "if I wish to do good I must not think about what I am doing" (SQMP, 123). Thinking about the goodness of what you are doing threatens to make your good deed a mere means of patting yourself on the back. It doesn't have to, though. When Sydney Carton reflects that substituting himself for Darnay is a far better thing than he has ever done, it may be a reflection on his wastrel earlier life, or a way of reassuring himself that he has not made a terrible mistake, to keep up his courage. He is not saying "hurray for me!"

[24] TMC, 182. [25] Arendt, "Socrates," in *PP*, 16.

best of all," goodness and virtue mostly meant having the right stuff to win, not righteousness.[26] Socrates' adversaries Callicles (in the *Gorgias*) and Thrasymachus (in the *Republic*) are steeped in that outlook, and indeed one natural way to read their exchanges with Socrates is as a debate between the outlook of competitive success and an outlook that values righteousness even at the cost of failure.[27]

Neither Callicles nor Thrasymachus ever concedes the argument; instead, they get frustrated and angry with Socrates and drop out of the conversations, still fuming. It's easy to see why: They and Socrates are talking past each other. When Socrates says it is better to suffer wrong than to commit it, he implicitly means what today we would (anachronistically) call "morally better," while his adversaries barely acknowledge moral virtue distinct from the virtues that make us successful (the right stuff). What looks like a clash of arguments turns out to be a clash of fundamental outlooks.

Arendt regards the Socratic proposition as a basic moral proposition because it can't be proven. Now we can see why: It defines the domain of morality, or, put in different terms, it offers an implicit definition of "morally better."[28]

## 4.3 The Second Socratic Proposition: The Dissonant Lyre

Arendt approaches the Socratic proposition through her emphasis on thinking as inner dialogue, and of the self as a two-in-one. For Arendt, the two-in-one explains the Socratic proposition that it is better to suffer murder than to commit it. Nobody wants to live with a murderer; to murder means that one lives with a murderer perpetually and inescapably.[29] Arendt illustrates with a literary example: the scene in *Richard III* when the shades of Richard's victims haunt his dreams. Richard wakes in terror.

26 *PP*, 16. This is a view championed by A. W. H. Adkins, *Merit and Responsibility: A Study of Greek Values* (Oxford University Press, 1960), but it is by no means undisputed. Adkins is one of Bernard Williams's targets in his superb *Shame and Necessity* (University of California Press, 1993), 81.

27 Thrasymachus's outlook should not be confused with egoism: Success for the warrior is success at defending his own people, and Thrasymachus's definition of justice as rewarding your friends and punishing your enemies supposes that you want to reward your friends.

28 Here I find myself in disagreement with Mahony, who interprets Arendt's claim that the first Socratic proposition is "basic" as an assertion that all moral philosophers would accept it (which, as Mahony points out, is untrue). *Hannah Arendt's Ethics*, 150–51. I take it to mean that it is an unprovable implicit definition of morality, understood as the acceptance of claims on us more powerful than those of self-interest and rewarding your friends.

29 SQMP, 91; TMC, 185.

What do I fear? Myself? There's none else by.
Richard loves Richard, that is, I am I.
Is there a murderer here? No. Yes, I am.
Then fly! What, from myself? Great reason why:
Lest I revenge. What, myself upon myself?
Alack, I love myself. Wherefore? For any good
That I myself have done unto myself?
O, no, alas, I rather hate myself
For hateful deeds committed by myself.
I am a villain. Yet I lie; I am not.
Fool, of thyself speak well. Fool, do not flatter.[30]

Milton's Satan has a similar moment, when "horror and doubt distract / his troubled thoughts"; he laments, "Me miserable! which way shall I fly / infinite wrath and infinite despair? / Which way I fly is Hell, myself am Hell."[31]

Socrates' imagery is less fevered. He compares his self to a lyre, and asserts that he would far prefer that his lyre be out of tune and the chorus he leads be discordant than that he – being one – should be out of tune with himself.[32] For Arendt, the lyre analogy represents a second basic Socratic proposition: that wrongdoing damages the perpetrator's own self. She puts special emphasis on "being one": oneness makes the discords inescapable, a kind of moral tinnitus that never goes away.

We can better understand Socrates' lyre analogy and the conclusion Arendt draws from it by looking at the way Aristotle elaborates the same point. For Aristotle, like Socrates, suffering injustice is less bad than doing injustice, even though "it might be coincidentally a greater evil."[33] Aristotle offers an analogy: Doctors know that pleurisy is worse than stumbling, even if once in a while stumbling has a worse outcome. Educators of the soul know that the unjust person is in worse shape than the just person, even if sometimes hewing to justice will make you a victim of injustice. And for Aristotle, this is no small thing, because justice is the paramount virtue, the "complete virtue to the highest degree."[34] Aristotle is not contradicting his identification of goodness with flourishing: His

30 Richard III, Act 5, sc. 3, ll. 194–204. 31 *Paradise Lost*, bk. IV, ll. 18, 73–75.

32 *Gorgias* 482b–c. Arendt discusses the lyre metaphor in SQMP, 90, and TMC, 181–87. I note, however, that her treatment of the metaphor as a moral proposition is a creative misreading. In context, Socrates uses the metaphor to discuss inconsistency in argument, not qualms of conscience.

33 N.E. V.11, 1138a32–1138b2. Irwin trans. 85. Arendt forgets this passage when she writes that the only non-Platonic passage in Greek literature that states the first Socratic proposition is Democritus's "More unfortunate than the wronged one is the wrong doer." TMC, 183.

34 N.E. V.1, 1129b27–35, Irwin trans. 68–69.

pleurisy analogy is an argument that for the most part being virtuous will help you flourish, even if in some circumstances it brings you to grief. Aristotle would have no problem with admiring Sidney Carton's self-sacrifice, or calling it noble or good.

Aristotle also shares the Socratic moral psychology of inner concord and discord: Decent people are in harmony with themselves, while base people are not. In a vicious person's soul, "each part pulls in a different direction, as though they were tearing him apart."[35] Memories of misdeeds torment the vicious, except when they forget themselves in the company of others; that's why the vicious can't bear to be alone. The vicious "shun themselves"; by contrast, the good are friends with themselves "insofar as someone is two or more parts."[36] Thus, Aristotle too invokes the two-in-one, the self and the murderer that one lives with when one is a murderer. Both the Socratic propositions are Aristotelian as well.

I will have more to say about the Socratic propositions later in this chapter (§4.6) and in Chapter 5 (§§5.1 and 5.2). Before that, however, it's time to ask where the faculty of moral judgment enters the picture. Chapter 3 explained why Arendt believed that moral judgment of particular cases, not reasoning from principles, lies at the core of moral life. I argued further that the account of moral judgment she models on Kant's theory of aesthetic judgment is even more powerful than she believed, because it applies to everyday affairs and not merely to the big bow wow of moral emergencies; I suggested that her skeptical views about morality in everyday life are misplaced.

Now it's time to connect that account of judging with the analysis of thinking as inner dialogue. After examining this thinking–judging connection, I look more closely at the nature of inner dialogue, the two-in-one. Putting these pieces together gives us the core of Arendt's moral psychology. In Chapter 5, these theoretical detours lead us back to the Socratic propositions and, ultimately, to Adolf Eichmann and the banality of evil.

## 4.4 The Thinking–Judging Connection

At the beginning of "Thinking and Moral Considerations," Arendt poses a question: "Is our ability to judge, to tell right from wrong, beautiful from ugly, dependent upon our faculty of thought?"[37] Her answer at the end of the essay is yes. Socratic thinking draws out our unexamined opinions and

[35] N.E. IX.6, 1167b5–10; IX.4, 1166b20–22. Arendt recalls this passage in *T*, 189.

[36] N.E. IX.4, 1166a30–35, 1166b15.

[37] TMC, 160.

demolishes them; this demolition has a "liberating effect" on the faculty of judgment. By this, I take it that Arendt means we are thrown back on our own powers of judgment when we don't let our prejudices (our pre-judgments) do our judging for us. That's why she calls judging "the by-product of the liberating effect of thinking."[38]

By itself, though, this doesn't show that the ability to judge *depends* on thinking, and we all know that sometimes the opposite can be true: Overthinking and second-guessing often lead to worse choices than our intuitive snap judgments. Not all unexamined opinions are wrong, after all, and the vast mass of our commonsense beliefs are truisms we have no reason to question. No doubt thoughtlessness, in the sense of mindlessly going along with the crowd, is a recipe for bad judgment. But nothing guarantees that it works the other way around – that our judgment, "liberated" by thinking, will be sound or reliable. Arendt knew this painfully well from the case of Heidegger, whom she regarded as a great thinker with terrible judgment. So Arendt's quick answer at the end of the essay doesn't stand up.

What her more careful arguments in "Thinking and Moral Considerations" and "Some Questions of Moral Philosophy" actually assert is a less direct connection between thinking and judging. As we saw in Chapter 1, one of the chief ideas she takes from Kant is his maxim of "enlarged thought," the injunction to think from the standpoint of everyone else, which Kant believes helps us distinguish between "subjective and private conditions and objective ones" and attain a "general standpoint." Kant explains: "Now we do this as follows: we compare our judgment not so much with the actual as rather with the merely possible judgments of others, and [thus] put ourselves in the position of everyone else, merely by abstracting from the limitations that [may] happen to attach to our own judging."[39]

Kant believes that cultivating this habit of imaginatively placing ourselves in the position of others helps us develop the power to judge, and Arendt agrees.[40] The goal, Kant tells us in his *Anthropology*, is a healthy

[38] TMC, 188–89.

[39] *CJ*, §40. Ak. 5: 294–95, Pluher trans. 160. Of course, "everyone" is an exaggeration. As Ronald Beiner helpfully notes, Arendt was careful to translate Kant's *allgemein* as "general" rather than the more common translation as "universal": she recognized that we are restricted to "members of the public realm where the objects of judgment appear." Arendt, "The Concept of Culture," in *BPF*, 221. See Beiner's note 155, in *Kant Lectures*, 163.

[40] SQMP, 140–41; *Kant Lectures*, 43 (asserting that the faculty that makes enlarged mentality possible is imagination).

human understanding that "looks at the object from many angles and produces the correct result without being aware of the acts occurring within the mind during this process." Kant names this ability "logical tact."[41]

It's a nice name. The analogy seems to be this: Just as tactful people know when *not* to blurt out whatever pops into their head (out of consideration for others), logically tactful people know when not to get carried away by runaway trains of reasoning – the kind of thing we often call "taking it to its logical extreme" – out of consideration for other ways of viewing matters that might temper our judgment and tether it to the world we inhabit in common. (We revisit Kant's "logical tact" arguments in Chapter 7, which discusses the concept of common sense.) For Arendt, the antithesis of logical tact is the ideological reasoning of totalitarian movements, which claims to deduce every event from inevitable laws of nature or history.[42] Logical tact is the intellectual virtue that tames the vices of mad consistency and pigheadedness.

It's worth spotlighting two other points about Kant's idea. First, a healthy human understanding views things from multiple angles "without being aware of the acts occurring within the mind during this process." How do we get to that happy state? Typically, complex mental processes become automatic only with repetition and practice, and that dynamic is implicit in Kant's description. It's exactly the kind of discipline of judgment we examined in Chapter 3. Both Kant and Arendt believe that we practice enlarging our thought by reflecting on concrete examples.[43] Whether or not they are right about the importance of examples (I think they are), the significant point is that judgment becomes automatic through disciplined repetition.

A corollary is that a person with practiced, developed moral judgment – what we might call *moral tact*, in parallel with Kant's logical tact – will often reach conclusions directly and immediately, with no need for wrenching deliberation or wrestling with their conscience. That is exactly how Arendt describes the righteous few who were never tempted to join in the Nazi crimes. They didn't ponder or agonize or weigh lesser evils. "Nothing of the sort. . . . In other words, they did not feel an obligation

[41] Kant, *Anthropology from a Pragmatic Point of View*, trans. Victor Lyle Dowdell (Southern Illinois University Press, 1978), 24, §6, Ak. 7:140.

[42] Arendt, "On the Nature of Totalitarianism," in *EU*, 355–56. See Chapter 6.

[43] SQMP, 143–45, explicating Kant's statement that examples are the go-cart (*Gängelwagen*) of judgment. *CPR*, B174. A go-cart here refers to an infant's walker, used to train the legs until the child can walk on their own.

but acted according to something which was self-evident to them even though it was no longer self-evident to those around them."[44] Subsequent studies of resisters, rescuer, and more contemporary altruists confirm her observation, at least in some cases.[45]

Second, looking at things from multiple angles does more than shake us loose from our prejudices – the liberating function Arendt highlights in "Thinking and Moral Considerations." As Arendt says, that is a negative or "destructive" process. But viewing matters from multiple angles has a positive function as well. It opens us to new ideas and new modes of perception and understanding. Together, the negative and positive functions of enlarged thought help explain why it cultivates judgment.

Where does thinking come in? Remember that for Arendt, thinking in its most relevant sense means "the soundless dialogue of the I with itself."[46] So understood, being able to think is the precondition of being able to imaginatively adopt the point of view of other people. If you can't or won't do the former, you can't do the latter.

This *thinking–judging connection* is the heart of Arendt's argument that the ability to judge depends on the faculty of thought.[47] It combines two propositions:

(1) The capacity and willingness to engage in inner dialogue is a precondition for thinking from others' point of view ("enlarged thought"); and
(2) enlarged thought helps hone the power of judgment.

The first proposition sets out a necessary connection between thinking and "enlarged" thinking. The second is an empirical conjecture. It asserts that even though enlarged thought is neither necessary nor sufficient for

44 SQMP, 78, 88; also "Basic Moral Propositions," *RJ*, 278n10.

45 Kristen Renwick Monroe, *The Heart of Altruism: Perceptions of a Common Humanity* (Princeton University Press, 1998); Philip P. Hallie, *Lest Innocent Blood Be Shed: The Story of the Village of Le Chambon and How Goodness Happened There* (Harper, 1994); Eyal Press, *Beautiful Souls: The Courage and Conscience of Ordinary People in Extraordinary Times* (Farrar, Straus and Giroux, 2012). Wesley Autrey, the New York City "Subway Samaritan" who sheltered a man who fell on the tracks with his own body as the train rolled over them, said "I don't feel like I did something spectacular. I just saw somebody who needed help. I did what I felt was right." Cara Buckley, "Man Is Rescued by Stranger on Subway Tracks," *New York Times*, January 3, 2007.

46 *T*, 74–75.

47 Here, I differ with Mahony about the significance of thinking in Arendt's moral philosophy. Mahony suggests two possible interpretations: that thinking will itself give us moral knowledge of good and evil, or that "the person whose inner life is characterized by this kind of broad, open, dialogic thought, will not entertain notions of evil actions." Mahony, *Hannah Arendt's Ethics*, 104. I am suggesting a third, less direct interpretation: that thinking helps cultivate moral judgment.

good judgment, it helps. Specifically, it helps us get beyond our own narrow outlook, open ourselves to unfamiliar points of view, and align our judgment with that of others who are similarly engaged in the effort of honest judgment.[48] Or rather, it does so provided we are willing to think for ourselves – Kant's first maxim of "common human understanding." As an empirical conjecture, I regard it as unproven, probably hard to test in any rigorous way, but intuitively plausible.

Arendt may have believed a third conjecture as well:

(3) Not only does enlarged thought help hone the power of judgment, sound judgment in human affairs *requires* looking at matters from multiple angles, whether consciously or – as Kant maintained – unconsciously.[49]

Only with this conjecture can judgment truly be said to *depend* on the faculty of thought, as Arendt maintains. Where proposition (2) holds that enlarged thought is a pathway to good judgment, proposition (3) holds that enlarged thought is the *only* pathway to good judgment. We can think of (2) and (3) as weak and strong versions of the thinking–judging connection.

Obviously, (3) is even more speculative than (2): We don't actually know what goes on in the minds of people blessed with good judgment. Speculative or not, (3) has a ring of plausibility, more so at any rate than throwing up our hands and regarding good judgment as a mysterious primitive superpower that some people have and some people don't.

As I hope is clear, the thinking–judging connection does not assert that thinking *guarantees* good judgment.[50] Nor is it even that *enlarged* thinking guarantees good judgment; "guarantees" is way too strong. In any case, good judgment is not infallible judgment. In moral life, there are never guarantees of getting it right. But the thinking–judging connection goes further than Arendt's proposition that examining our unexamined opinions "liberates" judgment from our prejudices, as if liberation – thinking for yourself, Kant's first maxim – is as far as we need to go. It is only the first step. Cultivating judgment requires the next step as well: enlarging one's thought to take in the standpoints of others, Kant's second maxim. The thinking–judging connection sets out a program or discipline for

[48] SQMP, 141.

[49] As we will see in Chapter 7, looking at things from multiple perspectives is key to Arendt's account of empirical knowledge. *HC*, 57; *T*, 50.

[50] Arendt agrees: *T*, 5.

cultivating judgment about human affairs by expanding our outlook – a program that requires us to exercise both of Kant's maxims.

## 4.5 Enlarged Thought as Sympathy: Kant, Arendt, Smith

Notice that Kant tells us to compare our judgment, not with the actual, but with the possible judgments of others. Enlarged thinking, Arendt explains, does not require taking on the *feelings* of the other. She offers an example. People who have lived their lives in abject poverty may be "dulled to the outrage of their condition," so that empathically taking on their feelings would make you equally numb to injustice. To think from their position is to imagine what *you* would judge in their position, namely that their poverty is an outrage – even if they themselves don't feel it.[51] Feeling what the other feels is what we ordinarily call *empathy*; imaginatively projecting ourselves into their position is *sympathy*. Both Kant and Arendt are calling for sympathy, not empathy.[52]

This same argument lies at the heart of Adam Smith's sympathy-based theory of moral sentiments, and Smith explains it more clearly than either Kant or Arendt.

> Sympathy, therefore, does not arise so much from the view of the passion, as from that of the situation which excites it. We sometimes feel for another, a passion of which he himself seems to be altogether incapable; because, when we put ourselves in his case, that passion arises in our breast from the imagination, though it does not in his from the reality.[53]

Smith illustrates with the case of someone who has "lost their reason" but is unaware of it:

> The anguish which humanity feels, therefore, at the sight of such an object, cannot be the reflection of any sentiment of the sufferer. The compassion of the spectator must arise altogether from the consideration of what he himself would feel if he was reduced to the same unhappy situation, and, what perhaps is impossible, was at the same time able to regard it with his present reason and judgment.[54]

This is close to what Arendt is getting at. Note, however, Smith's caution: Actually feeling what the person suffering dementia does while at the same time maintaining your present reason and judgment is impossible. Sympathetic projection will never be better than an imaginative leap,

[51] SQMP, 140. [52] *Kant Lectures*, 43 ("enlarged" thinking is not empathy).
[53] Adam Smith, *Theory of the Moral Sentiments* (Liberty Classics, 1976), 51.
[54] Smith, *Theory of the Moral Sentiments*, 52.

and Arendt emphasizes that the power of imagination is crucial to good judgment.[55] Doing it well resembles the good novelist's gift of getting into their characters' lives to make them plausible – and few of us are good novelists. Sympathy is conspicuously fallible.

Not only fallible, one might object, but also unverifiable: We'll never know whether we really got the other person's situation right. That's not quite true, though. We often find out whether we understood another person's situation correctly, because they tell us so, or show us through their conduct. Our sympathetic imagination is trained by encounters. Recall that Kant instructs us to put ourselves in the position of everyone else, which of course is impossible. But putting ourselves in the position of people we encounter, directly or thirdhand through stories about them, and testing our understanding of them whenever we can, is indeed a way of training our moral imagination.

We should beware of drawing an overly sharp distinction between sympathy and empathy. Smith tells us to consider how we would feel if we were in the other person's shoes, but equipped with our own reason and judgment. He doesn't seem to recognize that our own reason and judgment may be loaded with biases that distort our feeling, just as the imagined other person's is distorted in a different way. One hopes that by now this is well understood. A man may not feel the same anxiety walking alone on a deserted nighttime street as a woman, and a man trying to put himself into the woman's situation needs to recognize the nature and source of this difference. Likewise, as the law belatedly came to recognize, a "reasonable woman" being pressured into sex may experience a man's conduct as threatening and coercive even if the fictitious "reasonable man" might not. So too, a white person in a majority-white country may not comprehend the harm caused by a casual racist comment to a member of a demeaned minority group. Properly enlarged thinking therefore requires a healthy measure of empathy to fully grasp the other person's situation. Smith's repeated reference to feeling comes close to recognizing this; and Kant also speaks of shared feelings. Sympathy without empathy can easily delude itself into a false sense of understanding – and when it does, it fails even as sympathy.

## 4.6 Thinking and the Two-in-One

Only a portion of our intellectual life takes the form of what Arendt calls "the soundless dialogue of the I with itself," the "constant hither-and-

[55] SQMP, 139–40; *Kant Lectures*, 79–85.

thither of two-in-one."[56] Obviously we are all capable of concentrated task-oriented thought without answering back, as when we follow out a line of reasoning or do our taxes. As an analytical matter, the back and forth of inner dialogue necessarily incorporates inner monologues – the "forth" as well as the "back." Otherwise, the dialogue would become an uncontrollable explosion of inner voices as each splits into further voices – a chain reaction of inner chatter. Arendt rightly distinguishes "logical operations such as induction, deduction, conclusion for which no more than one 'operator' is required" from "that form of speech which is carried out between me and myself."[57] Both are parts of our mental life, and the two-in-one always incorporates (mono)logical operations, though not necessarily the other way around.

In that sense, the (mono)logical operations have a kind of primacy. Dialogue requires that the conversational partners take responsibility for the logical coherence and factual fidelity of what they say – the monological part – as Arendt recognizes.[58] That is the force of Kant's third maxim of common human understanding, to think consistently. Consistency doesn't mean never changing your mind; it means rigor and honesty, which will *require* you to change your mind if you come to see that your beliefs are mistaken.

Robert Brandom helpfully lays out the monological responsibilities of making assertions, within the Socratic give and take of reasons. Taking responsibility for what we say involves a twofold commitment: We commit ourselves to the "downstream" inferential consequences of each assertion (and thus to withdrawing the assertion if its consequences are untenable) and to the "upstream" assumptions that entitle us to make the assertion (and thus to withdrawing it if we find ourselves unable to stand by those assumptions).[59] The reasoning process involves making the upstream and downstream inferential connections explicit, and then adjusting our web of beliefs accordingly. As Arendt puts it: "All critical examinations must go through a stage of at least hypothetically negating accepted opinions and 'values' by finding out their implications and tacit

[56] *T*, 74–75; *OR* 98. [57] *OR* 98. [58] SQMP, 86.

[59] Robert B. Brandom, *Making It Explicit: Reasoning, Representing, and Discursive Commitment* (Harvard University Press, 1994), 106; see as well the passages indexed as "giving and asking for reasons." For Brandom, articulating the upstream and downstream inferences of a proposition also gives the *semantic meaning* of that proposition. But it is not necessary to accept Brandom's theory of meaning to accept his analysis of giving and asking for reasons.

assumptions."[60] Implications and tacit assumptions are, respectively, the downstream and upstream inferential connections.

This is a dynamic conception of thinking consistently. In a static sense, consistency means not contradicting myself. But I may not realize that I hold contradictory beliefs. My Socratic partner will draw this out of me, by getting me to see which other beliefs my assertion commits me to, either as downstream consequences or upstream assumptions. Once those inferential connections are in plain sight, consistency requires me to modify my beliefs if, on reflection, I find that I can't keep the commitments. Making his conversational partners' inferential commitments explicit is the process Socrates uses to get them to recognize that they don't actually know what they think they know. And it is the process one's "inner Socrates" uses in the soundless dialogue of the "I" with itself.

Of course, one can engage in this dynamic form of consistent thinking without a dialogical partner (an inner Socrates). A solitary mathematician writing up a proof will explore downstream consequences ("if *p* is true, it leads to a contradiction, therefore *p* is false") and upstream assumptions ("I can't prove *p* without assuming *q*, so I must either prove *q*, postulate *q*, or abandon *p*."). So, even monological thinking requires dynamic as well as static consistency.

But it doesn't follow that two-in-one, dialogical thinking can be reduced to monological thinking. Indeed, the moment our mathematician decides to try a fresh approach to a hard problem that's defeated her so far, she has, in effect, engaged in conversation with herself.[61] Today's most advanced AI reasoning models function dialogically, by generating several tentative answers to questions and evaluating those comparatively.

Let's look more closely at the two-in-one of inner dialogue. Although Arendt has little to say about it, inner dialogue has several important features.

First, the partners challenge each other and argue hard with each other, but they aren't trying to win for winning's sake. Even though inner dialogue can resemble adversary legal argument, it differs in that essential way. An adversary advocate does her best to downplay the weaknesses in her case and tries to cast the adversary's argument in the worst light she can. Her goal is to win, and her skill is to make weak arguments look

[60] TMC, 177.

[61] For that matter, it badly misunderstands creative mathematical research (as opposed to writing up results) to think it is monological or computational.

stronger. If her adversary trips up, she does not rush to the adversary's aid. She exploits the error.

Victory is not what the two-in-one is about. After all, it is me arguing with me! The point of the inner back and forth is to help me get to the best judgment I can. In one way, that is true in legal argument as well: Appellate judges will tell you that they make better decisions when they hear strong adversary presentations. But there's a gap between their goal and the advocates' goal, which is to get a decision in their clients' favor. In thinking, there is no client except the thinker, and the dueling inner voices have the same aim. In this sense, as Arendt says, Socratic partners must be friends.[62]

Second, it is instructive to compare Arendt's Socratic version of the two-in-one with the model set out by Stuart Hampshire, introduced in Chapter 3. Hampshire, recall, also distinguishes between the monological (computational) and dialogical powers of intellect. For Hampshire, the paradigm of practical reasoning is dialogical: a person weighing pro and con arguments. His model is close to adjudication, where advocates make arguments before a judge who weighs the competing arguments and reaches a verdict. Its guiding principle is the legal maxim of fairness: *audi alteram partem*, "hear the other side."[63] In effect, this adjudicative model has three inner dramatis personae, not two: The advocates and the judge are what we might call a three-in-one (a trialogue?).

In Socratic dialogue, no judge in robes renders a verdict after hearing both sides. When it is *inner* dialogue, we are entitled to wonder, then, who it is that eventually decides between the competing arguments. Arendt's answer is that of Socrates, quoted as an epigraph to this chapter: When the mind must come to a decision, and it is no longer divided but says one thing, that is its judgment.[64] *No longer divided* explains why Arendt places special emphasis on the phrase "*I who am one*" in Socrates' lyre analogy.[65] The moment of judgment is the moment when two become one.

Yet is that I who am one as harmonious as the lyre analogy suggests? Here, Arendt and Hampshire reach instructively different answers. Arendt invokes the lyre analogy because Socrates, like Aristotle, emphasizes inner harmony as the desired state. Hampshire emphatically does not. Hampshire was a value pluralist who never supposed that we can

62 *TMC*, 185; "Civil Disobedience," in *CR*, 63.

63 Stuart Hampshire, *Justice Is Conflict*, 8. Unlike Arendt, Hampshire enthusiastically backs the legal adversarial model. I have argued that he is mistaken. David Luban, "Book Reviews," review of *Innocence and Experience*, by Stuart Hampshire, *Journal of Philosophy* 88(6) (1991): 318.

64 TMC, 184–85 and SQMP, 91–92 both cite this passage from *Theaetetus*.

65 SQMP, 90.

harmonize the various incommensurable goods we recognize and seek. He titles one of his books *Justice Is Conflict* – borrowing the phrase from the pre-Socratic philosopher Heraclitus.[66] He endorses "Heraclitus' vision" that "ineliminable conflicts . . . [are] the best condition of mankind from the moral point of view."[67] For Hampshire, a conflict-ridden soul is "unavoidable and desirable," and "the tension between contrary forces and impulses, pulling against each other, is perceptible and vivid, and both forces and impulses have been kept at full strength: with the tension of the Heraclitean bow."[68] The bow imagery comes from a famously cryptic fragment of Heraclitus: "People do not understand how what is borne in different directions comes to be in harmony with itself; a framework like a bow or a lyre turns back on itself." Here we find a very different lyre analogy from Socrates': The strings may be in tune, but what holds them in tune is tension. The bow or lyre keeps the strings taut, and the taut strings bend the frame back on itself.[69]

Arendt is also a deep pluralist, insisting throughout her authorship on the uniqueness and originality of plural individuals. Curiously, though, in one important way she was not a value pluralist but a value monist.[70] As we shall see in Chapters 8 and 9, she ranks the life of action, and especially political action, above all others in its capacity to give meaning. On the other hand, she acknowledges that among human perspectives "no common measurement or denominator can be devised."[71] Furthermore, she was perfectly aware that political action will inevitably require moral compromises. That is tantamount to acknowledging that to preserve some goods we must sacrifice others: Goods aren't practically commensurable. And Arendt had deep reservations about the moral purism of a Thoreau, which requires withdrawing from the moral messiness of the world. Like

66 The Heraclitus fragment reads in full: "We must recognize that war is common and conflict (*eris*) is justice, and all things happen according to conflict and necessity." In the standard edition of the pre-Socratic philosophers by Diels and Kranz, this is fragment B80.

67 Hampshire, *Innocence and Experience*, 189.

68 Hampshire, *Justice Is Conflict*, 37, 32, 72 ("we have faction-ridden souls torn between conflicting influences, and we are normally in dispute with ourselves"). See Hampshire, *Innocence and Experience*, 32–34.

69 Heraclitus, fragment 51. I take this reading from Jane McIntosh Snyder, "The *Harmonia* of Bow and Lyre in Heraclitus Fragment 51 (DK)," *Phronesis* 29(1) (1984): 91–95.

70 A point well discussed in Kei Hiruta's excellent *Hannah Arendt and Isaiah Berlin* (Princeton University Press, 2021), 78. I note that Arendt disliked the philosophical term "value," which she thought has become polluted by its economic meaning, where value means market value. *HC*, 164–66. In that sense the concept of a value implies fungibility with other values "whenever people changed their minds about them." SQMP, 51. Of course there is no need to identify value with market value, or to see values as fungible or commensurable.

71 *HC*, 57.

Hampshire's, her version of political morality is closer to Machiavelli than to Thoreau.[72]

So perhaps what Arendt takes – or ought to take – from the second Socratic proposition is not that we should seek perfect harmony, but only that we should shun the gravest and most destructive disharmony, when the tension in the strings snaps the bow or the lyre in half – when, as Aristotle puts it, the tension in the souls of the vicious tears them apart. And in the end Hampshire does not really disagree: Some evils are so profound that they must never be accepted, even by a Machiavellian.[73]

A final point about the two-in-one is a small but significant tension between the Socratic giving and taking of reasons and Arendt's conception: Hers is less rationalistic. Except when he deliberately resorts to myths or parables, Socrates intends his arguments to be reasoned demonstrations. But Arendt notices that most Socratic dialogues end aporetically, without ever reaching a definitive conclusion. The judgments that thinking reaches can be undone by further thinking, like Penelope's web in the *Odyssey*, woven each day and unraveled each night.[74] That won't do when circumstances demand a decision. In murky settings where incommensurable values collide, Arendt tells us that persuasion consists of wooing rather than proving. As I observed in Chapter 3, suitors don't woo with reasons alone. In the terminology of Aristotelian rhetoric, persuasion requires *ethos* and *pathos* as well as *logos*. That will be as true when the conversational partner is oneself as someone else, because we learn the art of inner dialogue from conversation with others.

72 Arendt, "Civil Disobedience," *CR*, 60–62. She may well have misunderstood Thoreau. Laura Dassow Walls argues that Thoreau based his refusal to pay taxes not on withdrawal from the political community but on his duty as a citizen to speak out. Taxes, as a sign of citizenship, are the proper point of protest. Laura Dassow Walls, *Henry David Thoreau: A Life* (University of Chicago Press, 2017), 248–54. My thanks to Arthur Evenchik for pointing this out to me.

73 Hampshire, *Innocence and Experience*, 66–78.

74 TMC, 166; *T*, 88.

# CHAPTER 5

# *Conscience and the Banality of Evil*

## 5.1 From Consciousness to Conscience

When inner conversation concerns the morality of our own conduct, we call our interlocutor *conscience*.[1] A traditional version of conscience holds it to be the voice of God or of reason (the *lumen naturale*, "natural light"). Arendt is deeply skeptical of conscience so understood, where the voice is not a conversational partner but "an authority that is above and beyond all merely human laws and rules."[2] On this authoritarian view of conscience, the voice of God or reason commands and condemns, but it doesn't converse. It speaks in the imperative mood and brooks no reply.

Not so for Arendt. Genuine morality, Arendt insisted, does *not* come in the form of imperatives, and she criticized Kant's "self-misunderstanding" when he describes morality as a categorical imperative rather than as a proposition.[3] "Reason can only tell the will: this is good, in accordance with reason; if you wish to attain it you ought to act accordingly. Which in Kant's terminology would be a kind of hypothetical imperative, or no imperative at all."[4]

1 "Morality" is here intended as a generic term, not a commitment to any specific moral vocabulary. Right/wrong, good/bad (or good/evil), honorable/dishonorable, praiseworthy/shameful, worthy/unworthy, prudent/reckless, brave/cowardly, kind/cruel – any of these and many more specific terms of approbation or condemnation can be matters of conscience.

2 *T*, 215; "Civil Disobedience," in *CR*, 65–67; "Collective Responsibility," in *RJ*, 152–53. Arendt attributes this view to the influence of Christian philosophy. Perhaps so, but an authoritarian conception of divine command theory predates Christian philosophy, going back at least as far as the early interpreters of the Hebrew Bible, which of course is chock full of divine commands. Christine Hayes, *What's Divine about Divine Law? Early Perspectives* (Princeton University Press, 2015), 253–62.

3 SQMP, 69.

4 SQMP, 71; "Concern with Politics," in *EU*, 441. Arendt's view here is remarkably similar to that of Philippa Foot, in "Morality as a System of Hypothetical Imperatives," *Philosophical Review* 81(3) (1972): 305–16 – remarkable because so far as I know Arendt and Foot had no engagement with each other's work. Arendt's view also overlaps with that of G. E. M. Anscombe's influential "Modern Moral Philosophy," *Philosophy* 33(124) (1958): 1–19, which argues that secular talk of moral imperatives, moral laws, and moral

She contrasts the traditional view of conscience as a divine or rational imperative with the "strictly secular conscience," which comes from "knowing, and speaking, with myself" – in other words, from the inner dialogue that constitutes thinking.[5] This is the version she favors. "Conscience" and "consciousness" both derive from the same Latin root, *conscientia* (con-scientia): to know-with.[6] The etymology itself recognizes that conscience and consciousness take the form of an inner conversation, a division of the self into distinct voices, the self that is acting or about to act, and what Bernard Williams calls the "internalized other" who witnesses and responds – and not just any internalized other, but someone I respect, someone whose response matters to me. The internalized other may be my own better self, but it could also be somebody else – Williams's example is Sophocles' Ajax, whose internalized other is not an echo chamber of himself but the imagined voice of his father, ashamed of what Ajax has done in his madness.[7] The internalized other is, nevertheless, a concretized projection and reminder of one's own ethical ideals.

What makes the two-in-one of conscience distinctive is that our "internalized other" is not merely discussing matters with us. The internalized other reproaches our wrongdoings, gazes on us with indignation or contempt at misdeeds we have done or are about to do, and calls us to account.[8] In lecture notes, Arendt describes four "ever-recurring moments" of secular conscience, suggesting a sequence:

> My conscience is (a) witness; (b) my faculty of judging, i.e., of telling right from wrong; (c) what sits in judgment in myself over myself; and (d) a voice in myself, as against the biblical voice of God from without.[9]

As two-in-one, I witness my own deeds (past or future) through the eyes of the internalized other, conscience. My conscience judges them to be right or wrong, and in doing so it sits in judgment. The voice of conscience

obligations should be jettisoned, because it is a vestigial remainder from an era that believed in a divine legislator, and makes no sense without that belief.

5 "Civil Disobedience," *CR*, 67.

6 *T*, 190 Arendt adds that "consciousness" translates the Greek *syneidenai* – "to know with myself," in her unidiomatic rendering. *T*, 74. Elsewhere she clarifies that "knowing together with myself" means knowing something and being aware that I know it. *RJ*, 280n14. C. S. Lewis, in his philological analysis of "conscience" and "consciousness," explains that one idiomatic use of *syn-oida* and its Latin cognate *con-scio* is sharing a secret with someone else, or even conspiring with them. In the latter sense, "knowing with someone" means being privy to their guilty secret, and "knowing with myself" means being aware of my own guilty secret – hence, having a guilty conscience. C. S. Lewis, "Conscience and Conscious," in *Studies in Words*, 2nd ed. (Cambridge University Press, 1967), 181–213.

7 Williams, *Shame and Necessity*, 82–85. I borrow the phrase "echo chamber" from Williams, *Shame and Necessity*, 84.

8 TMC, 185; SQMP, 145–46; "Socrates," in *PP*, 22–23.

9 *RJ*, 280n14.

proclaims that judgment. It is, crucially, a voice "in myself over myself," in Arendt's well-chosen phrase, not a divine voice from without.

The internalized other witnesses, judges, and speaks. How does the first person in the dialogue respond to the condemnation of conscience? Philosophers commonly distinguish two moral emotions we experience when a respected other rightly takes us to task: *shame* and *guilt*. We are *ashamed* when we imagine a respected other gazing on our failure and inadequacy; we are *guilty* when we imagine their righteous anger at what we have done. As Williams explains the difference: "The psychological model for each emotion involves an internalized figure. In the case of shame this is . . . a watcher or witness. In the case of guilt, the internalized figure is a *victim* or *enforcer*."[10] Importantly, it can be both. "In a moment of cowardice, we let someone down; we feel guilty because we have let them down, ashamed because we have contemptibly fallen short of what we might have hoped for ourselves."[11]

Couched in these terms, how should we think about the second Socratic proposition? Is it about shame, or guilt, or something else? Recall that as Arendt frames the proposition, nobody wants to live with a murderer, and to murder means that one lives with a murderer perpetually and inescapably. Here, the ruling emotion seems to be neither guilt nor shame, but *fear* – fear of the murderer within.[12]

But putting it that way takes the metaphor too literally. A murderous roommate might actually kill me – an excellent reason to be afraid. The intangible murderer within will not kill me. The real danger is that the murderer within will be a perpetual source of horror when, like King Richard and Lady Macbeth, I realize that I am the murderer whose bloodstained hands can never be cleansed. Horror, not fear, is the ruling emotion, as Emily Dickinson understood:

[10] Williams, *Shame and Necessity*, 219. Williams explores these subtleties in *Shame and Necessity*, 82–93, 219–23.

[11] Williams, *Shame and Necessity*, 92.

[12] One complication in these metaphors is discerning which of these internalized figures is which – that is, which is the ego (the "I") and which is the alter ego (the "you") in the internal confrontation. In Williams's example, and Arendt's schematic analysis of conscience, the Internalized Other is the alter ego, witnessing the perpetrator's misdeed and responding with anger or contempt; the perpetrator is the ego who reacts with shame or guilt. By contrast, the second Socratic proposition's imagery is of an "innocent" ego living with a perpetrator as alter ego – a role reversal from Williams's metaphor of the Internalized Other. I am ignoring this complication because I believe nothing essential turns on it – ultimately, both ego and alter are aspects of the same person switching back and forth between vantage points. "Fool, of thyself speak well. Fool, do not flatter."

Ourself, behind ourself, concealed –
Should startle most –
Assassin, hid in our Apartment
Be Horror's least – [13]

Both shame and guilt are wrapped up in this horror. The internalized other is all the things Williams names: a watcher, a witness, an enforcer, and the voice of a victim. These correspond, if only roughly, with Arendt's witness, judge, and voice.

## 5.2 Why the Second Socratic Proposition Is Not Self-Centered

Recall that for Arendt, the second Socratic proposition motivates the first. The reason Socrates would rather be the victim of injustice than its perpetrator (first proposition) is that if he were the perpetrator, he could not live with himself (second proposition). In a few places, Arendt criticizes this motivational structure as a form of self-centeredness – not material self-interest, but a kind of psychological selfishness that puts my desire for a harmonious self ahead of concern for the public world. She raises the criticism in the context of political crises and how we respond to them – withdraw or engage?[14] (Hence the reference to the public world.) But even in matters of interpersonal morality, when the public world is not at stake, we might object to treating the second Socratic proposition as the heart of morality. The objection is that

(A) I couldn't live with myself if I treated someone unjustly

is a pale, self-centered, substitute for

(B) Treating someone unjustly is wrong.

That's because the moral issue is about injustice, not about who I could or could not live with. It's not about me! Not only is (A) self-centered, it

[13] Emily Dickinson, "One Need Not Be a Chamber – to Be Haunted," number 407 in *The Poems of Emily Dickinson: Variorum Edition*, ed. R. W. Franklin (Belknap of Harvard University Press, 1998), 430–32.

[14] *CR*, 62–65; SQMP, 79. In "Collective Responsibility," in *RJ*, 153, Arendt writes: "In the center of moral considerations of human conduct stands the self; in the center of political considerations of conduct stands the world." Albeit on different grounds than the argument offered here, Mahony also criticizes "the idea of living with oneself as a kind of ultimate moral standard." *Hannah Arendt's Ethics*, 159–64; the quoted language on page 160. For Mahony, the flaw in Arendt's idea is that evildoers in fact don't necessarily experience painful disharmony, contradicting "Arendt's insistence that no one will want to live together with a wrongdoer." *Hannah Arendt's Ethics*, 163. As we will see in §5.3, Arendt fully understood that evildoers don't necessarily experience disharmony – and her investigation of that fact is central to how she understood evil and the banality of evil.

threatens to make moral standards entirely subjective, because individuals decide for themselves who they could or could not live with. The subjective character of moral standards is, in fact, a consequence Arendt draws from the second Socratic proposition, and one that should cause concern.[15]

On closer examination, though, Arendt's self-centeredness critique of the second Socratic proposition overlooks something vital: The reason Socrates couldn't live with himself if he acted unjustly is his judgment that acting unjustly is *wrong*. Proposition (A) may explain Socrates' psychological motivation for acting on his moral judgment (B), and "I couldn't live with myself if I did that" may also be the psychological alarm bell that prompts him to recognize that an act is unjust and wrong. But (A) is not a *substitute* for the moral judgment (B) or an analysis of (B), and it certainly isn't a proof of (B).

In the *Apology* Socrates describes his inner prompt as the voice of his *daimon* (a middle-tier divinity), which warns him against wrongdoing.[16] But it is not the *daimon*'s divine authority that makes it wrongdoing. The *Euthyphro* argument holds that the gods love pious actions because they are pious; actions are not pious merely because the gods love them. The same holds if we substitute justice for piety in the *Euthyphro* argument. It follows that Socrates' *daimon* forbids unjust actions because they are unjust; it isn't the *daimon*'s prohibition that makes them unjust. Recast in contemporary language, the *Euthyphro* argument stands for the proposition that piety and impiety, justice and injustice, right and wrong are independent of anyone's will, including divine will, and therefore they are anything but subjective.

Arendt's self-centeredness critique of proposition (A) – the second Socratic proposition – supposes otherwise: that the reason moral agents judge that injustice is wrong is solely that they couldn't live with themselves if they treated someone unjustly. I suggest it is the other way around. The recognition that we couldn't live with ourselves if we did an unjust act doesn't come from nowhere. And it doesn't come solely from idiosyncratic personal standards that we've set for ourselves. It rests, crucially, on our judgment that the act is wrong.[17]

[15] *CR* 60; SQMP, 110–11. On this point, see Mahony, *Hannah Arendt's Ethics*, 143–51. She notes insightfully that Arendt was ambivalent about the reality of moral standards – sometimes dismissive of the realist position, sometimes attracted to it, but at bottom never for a moment doubting the difference between good and evil – an insight about Arendt that I endorse in my discussion of the Case of the Missing Morality at the end of Chapter 9.

[16] *Apology*, 31c–d.

[17] Although I use the term "act," injustice might also be a culpable omission.

Recall Bernard Williams's observation that when we fail morally we feel both shame and guilt – shame at failing to live up to our own standards (represented by the internalized other) and guilt at the wrong we have done. Choosing the standards we hold ourselves to may be up to us, but it doesn't follow that our judgment of right and wrong is up to us. As we saw in Chapter 3, Arendt draws on Kant's aesthetics precisely to deny that the unprovability of moral judgments implies that they are sheerly subjective.

Arendt's misstep here partly accounts for her wariness about morality and disdain for moral philosophy. In effect, she argues that morality, as represented in the second Socratic proposition, is a kind of selfishness that values one's own purity above all else – to the detriment of engagement with the public world. Repair of the world demands engagement and not conscientious withdrawal. The problem with her selfishness critique is that it considers only half the story: the shame half, where what matters is how I appear in the eyes of the internalized other. She neglects the other half: the moral judgments that the internalized other passes. Admittedly, "I couldn't live with myself if I acted unjustly" sounds as if the only thing I care about is me – but only superficially. To see this, notice that "I couldn't live with myself if I failed to fight injustice" may well explain the resisters, the Anton Schmids and Helmuth James von Moltkes, of the world. This, too, would be an instance of the second Socratic proposition.

## 5.3 Indifference and Banality of Evil

Of course, not everyone lives as two-in-one, and no one does all the time. King Richard's comic counterpart is the Second Murderer. Hired by Richard to assassinate Clarence, the Second Murderer feels "certain dregs of conscience" that almost make him back out. He resolves that if conscience comes again, "I'll not meddle with it" because "it fills a man with obstacles."[18] After Richard wakes from his nightmare, he pushes conscience away as "but a word that cowards use."[19]

At least he had a conscience to push away. Perhaps real-life tyrants don't. A character in a Julian Barnes novel muses that Shakespeare's Richard had bad dreams; not so the modern tyrant (Stalin, in Barnes's historical novel). "Penetrate beneath the modern tyrant's skin, go down layer after layer, and you will find that the texture does not change, that

[18] *Richard III*, act 1, sc. 4, ll. 139–45. [19] *Richard III*, act 5, sc. 3, ll. 327.

granite encloses yet more granite; and there is no cave of conscience to be found."[20]

Suppose that is right. Then is all this hand-wringing about the terrible pangs of conscience mere wishful thinking? Perhaps so in the case of the Stalins and Hitlers and other nonbanal evildoers, with their souls of granite. They don't mind living with a murderer within – they may even revel in it. Arendt likens them to Duke Bluebeard, the serial wife-murderer in the French folktale.

But Bluebeards with souls of granite are not Arendt's concern; they are straightforwardly evil. She writes that "the likelihood that someone would come and tell us that . . . any company will be good enough for him is, I fear, by far greater" than the improbable likelihood that an ordinary person actively prefers the company of Bluebeard.[21]

*Indifference*, she therefore argues, poses the greatest moral and political danger of our time. Indifferent actors – those who don't meddle with conscience – can commit atrocious wrongs without any active malice, self-interest, or defiance. To which she adds: "Therein lies the horror and, at the same time, the banality of evil."[22]

One pathway to indifference is refusing to judge at all.[23] It isn't the only pathway, though: Not all indifferent wrongdoers have refused to judge. Some see wrong for what it is but don't care. They recognize that they are doing wrong, and that they will have to live with it. But living with it doesn't seem all that bad to them, and forgetting about it isn't all that hard.[24]

Indifference of this sort is not banality of evil, though. It's simply evil, or at least moral callousness. Banality of evil as Arendt depicts it in *Eichmann in Jerusalem* is different: refusal to judge that comes from failure to think, and which provides an excuse for failure to think. Arendt accuses Eichmann of both. I discussed his thoughtlessness in Chapters 1 and 2, and I return to it at the end of this chapter. But equally damning is his unwillingness to judge.

Here, the revelatory moment was the 1942 Wannsee conference, when the department chiefs of the Nazi bureaucracy met to plan the Final

[20] Julian Barnes, *The Noise of Time* (Knopf, 2016), 179. The novel is based on the life of Dmitri Shostakovich, who is the one doing the musing.

[21] SQMP, 146.

[22] SQMP, 146. Including self-interest in this list is a bit careless, however. Arendt herself spotted Eichmann's careerist ambitions, which certainly count as understandable human motives. *EJ*, 287. What she thinks is not "humanly understandable" is his failure to recognize the horror of the career he had chosen to pursue.

[23] SQMP, 146.

[24] SQMP, 124; "Collective Responsibility," in *RJ*, 157.

Solution and grab pieces of the action for themselves. Eichmann participated in a minor role. Arendt quotes his recollection: "'At that moment, I sensed a kind of Pontius Pilate feeling, for I felt free of all guilt.' *Who was he to judge?*"[25] She comments acidly: "Well, he was neither the first nor the last to be ruined by modesty."[26] She titles the chapter "The Wannsee Conference, or Pontius Pilate." To Arendt, the refusal to judge represents one of the most distressing phenomena of our time, and she returns to it in the postscript to *Eichmann in Jerusalem*, and more venomously in "Personal Responsibility under Dictatorship."[27] The Pontius Pilate feeling marks the abdication of responsibility.

Refusing to judge doesn't necessarily imply thoughtlessness. An indecisive person can think endlessly but never reach a final judgment, most likely defaulting to whichever choice comes easiest. But it's thoughtlessness that made Eichmann an empty vessel into which the prevailing gods and idols could pour whatever poison they wished, which he abstained from judging for himself.

Arendt calls Eichmann's affliction an inability to think, but "inability" is careless language. It sounds too deterministic. As Mary McCarthy complained, "it seems to me that what you are saying is that an Eichmann lacks an inherent human quality: the capacity for thought, consciousness – conscience. But then isn't he a monster simply?" In McCarthy's view: "One cannot help feeling that this mental oblivion is *chosen*, by the heart or the moral will."[28] Her critique is spot on, but *chosen* is also the wrong word. It errs in the opposite direction: Where "inability" is too deterministic, "chosen" is too voluntaristic.

A better diagnosis is this: Thoughtlessness is habit-forming, and breaking habits is hard. Eichmann habituated himself to not thinking. Eichmann's thoughtlessness may have begun as mere moral laziness, neither chosen (McCarthy) nor placed in him by nature (Arendt). Thinking from other people's point of view takes effort. It's so much easier to take your cues from the gods and the Important People around you. But eventually moral lassitude hardens into second nature. "What people then get used to is not so much the content of the rules, a close

[25] *EJ*, 114. Arendt's italics. She is quoting from Eichmann Trial Proceedings, vol. 4, Session 79, June 26, 1961, at 1423. Eichmann's role was to prepare statistical material for Heydrich to use in his speech, to send out the invitations to the conference, and to write up the minutes. Eichmann Trial Proceedings, vol. 4, Session 79, June 26, 1961, 1422–23 (Sessions 78–79); Eichmann Trial Proceedings, vol. 1, Session 11, April 21, 1961, at 146.

[26] *EJ*, 114. [27] *EJ*, 295–97; PRUD, in *RJ*, 18–22; also SQMP, 59.

[28] Mary McCarthy to Arendt, June 9, 1971, *BF*, 296–97.

examination of which would always lead them into perplexity, as the possession of rules under which to subsume particulars. In other words, they get used to never making up their minds," by which Arendt means making up their minds on their own.[29]

The diagnosis was familiar to her. As she wrote in her doctoral dissertation (paraphrasing St. Augustine): "The inclination to sin springs more from habit than from passion itself, because the world man has founded in covetousness is consolidated in habit."[30]

## 5.4 The Virtuous Circle of Thinking and Judging

In the final pages of her moral philosophy lectures, Arendt seemingly changes the subject from the perils of not thinking to the perils of not judging. Which of these two dimensions of moral laziness does she identify with banality of evil? The answer, I believe, is both, because they work in tandem.

In Chapter 4, we examined the proposition that enlarged thinking – thinking from the point of view of others – helps us cultivate good judgment, along with the stronger proposition that cultivating good judgment requires enlarged thinking. I called these the weak and strong versions of the thinking–judging connection. In both, the directional arrow goes from thinking to judging. I now suggest that the arrow goes the other way as well: Recognizing that we've reached a moral crossroads requires a judgment call that impels us to think.

Recall that Arendt insists that thinking always involves a "stop and think" – "the interruption of all other activities."[31] Obviously, we go through most of our daily lives without stopping to think about every little decision. Otherwise, as she reminds us, we would be paralyzed; even Socrates did not spend every moment of every day immobilized in thought.[32] What matters, both intellectually and morally, is recognizing – judging – that something seems awry. In the moments when "everybody is swept away unthinkingly by what everybody else does and believes in,"[33] we are on our own. Nothing warns us to stop and think but our own good judgment that something is amiss – our moral and logical tact. Abdicating judgment makes it impossible to recognize when we must stop and think.

[29] TMC, 178.

[30] Hannah Arendt, *Love and Saint Augustine*, trans. E. B. Ashton, eds. Joanna Vecchiarelli Scott and Judith Chelius Stark (University of Chicago Press, 1995), 84. Written in 1928, Arendt was revising the dissertation for publication just before the Eichmann trial.

[31] SQMP, 105. Emphasis removed, TMC, 176. [32] TMC, 176.

[33] TMC, 188; also "Basic Moral Propositions," in *RJ*, 279n12.

While thinking cultivates judgment, judgments trigger thinking. Although Arendt never explicitly describes this bidirectional relationship of thinking and judging, I suspect it was what she had in mind when she identifies the banality of evil with the lethal combination of thoughtlessness and abdication of judgment.

Let me illustrate with an example far removed from Eichmann and the Nazi crimes. A few years ago, an anti-corruption organization sent an investigator (pseudonym: "Ralph Kayser") with a hidden video camera to the offices of sixteen New York business lawyers. He pretended to be the legal representative of a foreign official who wanted to move millions of dollars of bribes into the United States to buy luxury goods. Shockingly, almost all the lawyers were happy to discuss how they could set up dummy corporations and offshore bank accounts to move the money and disguise its true ownership. Some were enthusiastic.

Only one lawyer, Jeffrey Hermann, said no. The hidden-cam video makes his "stop and think" vivid. He hears Kayser's proposition, and replies, "I have some real questions about that." This is his moment of recognition that something is amiss – the "stop and think!" moment. After a brief back and forth about a legalism, Hermann looks down and rocks his head from side to side for a few ticks of the clock. You can see him thinking. Then he looks up and says firmly, "It's not for me." Pressed by Kayser, he repeats, "This ain't for me. My standards are higher."[34]

What about the other lawyers? For better or worse, lawyers are trained not to pass moral judgment on clients and would-be clients. Anonymous shell corporations are a legal way for wealthy people to conceal what they own. Some clients are legitimate; some are sleazy; some are both. Some transactions are legal; some cross the line into money laundering. In the gray zone of great wealth and legal artifices to conceal it, it takes good judgment to recognize how sleazy is too sleazy. Hermann had it; the others evidently did not.

Arendt's thinking–judging connection is a conjecture that the Socratic practice of thinking cultivates judgment. But this example illustrates that it goes the other way as well: The better our judgment, the better our chances of knowing when to stop and think. In this way, the practice of thinking and the practice of judging form a virtuous circle.

*

[34] The videos were shown in an exposé on the television program *60 Minutes*, titled "Anonymous, Inc." and readily available on the internet. The transcript is in Steve Kroft, "Anonymous, Inc.," CBS News, January 31, 2016, www.cbsnews.com/news/anonymous-inc-60-minutes-steve-kroft-investigation/ [https://perma.cc/34FZ-VV9Z].

The reflections in her lectures on moral philosophy are the closest Arendt comes to theorizing banality of evil and answering the *quaestio juris* of what entitles her to the concept. They are not a worked-out theory, as she freely admits near the end of "Some Questions of Moral Philosophy."[35] But the connections Arendt draws between thoughtlessness, indifference, and moral judgment take us a long way toward understanding the evil that she witnessed in Jerusalem. Banality of evil is moral laziness consolidated in habit.

## 5.5 Radical Evil and Banal Evil: The Scholem Letter

One interpretive loose end remains to be addressed. As I mentioned in Chapter 1, Arendt claimed that the Eichmann trial caused her to abandon her earlier understanding of "radical evil" in favor of banality of evil. In a published exchange of letters about the *Eichmann* book, Gershom Scholem scolds Arendt for doing so. Banality of evil is merely a "slogan," as compared with the earlier concept "which your previous analysis testified to so elegantly and knowledgeably."[36] To which Arendt replies:

> You are quite right: I changed my mind and do no longer speak of "radical evil." . . . It is indeed my opinion now that evil is never "radical," that it is only extreme, and that it possesses neither depth nor any demonic dimension. It can overgrow and lay waste the whole world precisely because it spreads like a fungus on the surface. It is "thought-defying," as I said, because thought tries to reach some depth, to go to the roots, and the moment it concerns itself with evil, it is frustrated because there is nothing. That is its "banality." Only the good has depth and can be radical. . . . Eichmann may very well remain the concrete model of what I have to say.[37]

[35] SQMP, 145. [36] Scholem to Arendt, June 23, 1963, *HA-GS*, 205.

[37] Arendt to Scholem, July 24, 1963, *JW*, 470–71. A slightly different version (bearing the earlier date July 20) is in *HA-GS*. That version omits the sentence about the "thought-defying" character of evil; perhaps Arendt added it when the correspondence was published in *Encounter*; I am quoting from the later version. A few months later she writes in a similar vein to McCarthy that banality of evil contrasts with the radical evil discussed in *Origins*, but "this is too difficult a subject to be dealt with here." Arendt to McCarthy, September 20, 1963, *BF*, 148. Readers might detect an echo of Augustine when Arendt writes that evil has no roots and "only the good has depth and can be radical." Augustine argued that to seek for the cause of evil "is like wishing to see darkness or to hear silence," because evil is the absence of good, not a presence in its own right. St. Augustine, *The City of God against the Pagans*, ed. and trans. R. W. Dyson (Cambridge University Press, 1998), bk. XII, ch. 7, 507–8. For Augustine, God "supremely *is*," and "to defect from that which supremely is, . . . is to begin to have an evil will." St. Augustine, *The City of God against the Pagans*, bk. XII, ch. 2, 500–1; ch. 7, 507. I think it more likely that Arendt was cribbing Augustine's language than that she was adopting his Platonic metaphysical theory that existence comes in degrees, and the highest degree of existence is the highest degree of goodness. In fact, Arendt saw her project as dismantling the entire tradition of metaphysics. *T*, 212. On evil as a lack rather than a thing, see *T*, 161, 179.

Unfortunately, this well-known letter is a source of confusion, because she seemingly agrees with Scholem that she has abandoned her theory of radical evil and substituted a novel theory of banal evil. Scholem reads radical evil and banal evil as a conceptual either–or. But radical evil and banal evil don't have to be a conceptual either–or: As we saw in Chapter 1, evil can be radical even if its perpetrator is banal. That was a crucial point on which Arendt's critics misunderstood her. Why, then, does she tell Scholem "you are quite right"?

The answer is that "radical evil" has multiple meanings, and Arendt doesn't disentangle them, either in the letter to Scholem or in her early analysis of radical evil in *The Origins of Totalitarianism.* Once we do so, the confusion disappears.

The phrase can mean *extreme* evil, referring to the magnitude and cruelty of the deeds; or *cold-blooded* evil, referring to the character of the doer; or *deeply rooted* evil, referring to evil's source in human nature – and at various points Arendt uses "radical evil" in all three ways, sliding from one to the other without signaling the shifts. Once we mark the shifts, we can plainly see the points of continuity and discontinuity in her pre- and post-*Eichmann* accounts.

*Extreme evil.* Most people (who haven't read this letter) will naturally suppose that "radical evil" means *extreme* evil – extreme in cruelty, or extreme in scale, or both. In *Origins* Arendt spoke of the death camps and gulags in exactly those terms, using "radical evil" interchangeably with "unforgivable absolute evil."[38] Notice, though, that Arendt's letter to Scholem continues to affirm that evil can be extreme. This is no slip of the pen. Recall her definition of "banality of evil":

> [E]vil deeds, *committed on a gigantic scale,* which could not be traced to any particularity of wickedness, pathology, or ideological conviction in the doer.[39]

Even if Arendt no longer calls such evil "radical," she never denies its extremity. The puzzle, then, is *why* she no longer calls it radical evil, and why she says that she has changed her mind about radical evil.

*Cold-blooded evil.* Alternatively, readers might take "radical evil" to mean *cold-blooded* evil, that is, evil committed either in defiance of morality or out of a deformed and evil nature. (Think of Richard III's "I am

For discussion of Augustine's influence on Arendt, see Stephan Kampowski, *Arendt, Augustine, and the New Beginning* (Eerdmans, 2008).

[38] *OT*, 459. [39] TMC, 159. Emphasis added.

determined to prove a villain" or Satan's "study of revenge, immortal hate" in *Paradise Lost.*) That is how Prosecutor Gideon Hausner depicted Eichmann.[40] When Arendt tells Scholem that she no longer thinks that evil has a "demonic dimension," she hints that she once thought otherwise, and that this is the account of radical evil she has abandoned.

Here the either – or contrast between cold-blooded, demonic evil and banal evil is genuine, but that doesn't make them competing theories of evil. It makes them different species of evil – as Arendt herself well understood. Arendt disagreed with Hausner about Eichmann, but apart from this letter to Scholem she never denied that some evildoers have determined to prove a villain, and that others are "monsters" or "ghouls," as she called the sneering defendants in the Auschwitz trial.[41]

Reading radical evil as cold-blooded evil, her letter to Scholem runs off the rails when she writes that evil is *never* radical. That is false as a matter of fact, and it contradicts her own efforts to distinguish Eichmann's evil from the monstrosity of some of the Nazi murderers, not to mention the nonradical evil done every day for ordinary comprehensible motives.[42] Here, the letter to Scholem exhibits real confusion, if not outright error.

*Deeply rooted evil.* What Arendt mostly has in mind in the Scholem letter is a third meaning of "radical evil," different from both extreme evil and cold-blooded evil. Radical can mean *deeply rooted*, playing on the etymology of "radical" (it comes from *radix*, the Latin word for "root"). When Arendt tells Scholem that evil can't be radical because it has no depth or roots, she clearly has this third sense in mind.

She had a reason for emphasizing this less familiar sense of "radical evil": It is the sense employed by Kant, who first introduced the phrase into moral philosophy – and Kant was both the inspiration and target for her discussion of radical evil in *Origins*. For Kant, evil consists in choosing to follow our natural inclinations when they conflict with the moral law.[43] The inclinations themselves aren't evil, nor does evil arise from an

40 See Eichmann Trial Proceedings, vol. 1, Session 6, April 17, 1961, at 62–63.

41 In *Origins* Arendt recognized that some of the camp personnel were "beasts in human form." *OT*, 454. She also distinguished the "normal philistine" Himmler from the more pathological members of the Nazi leadership. *OT*, 337–38. Arendt was mistaken about Himmler, who was an occultist crackpot, not a normal philistine. But the point is that she always distinguished banal evildoers from other varieties.

42 *T*, 3–4.

43 Kant, *Religion within the Boundaries of Mere Reason*, Ak. 6:32, 6:37. I am using the translation of George Di Giovanni, in the Cambridge Edition of the Works of Kant: Kant, *Religion within the Boundaries of Mere Reason*, in *Religion and Rational Theology*, ed. Allen Wood and George Di Giovanni (Cambridge University Press, 1998), 55, 59.

"absolutely evil will" like Satan's.[44] Rather, evil stems from the fact that we always have competing incentives at work in us: our inclinations and the moral law. Evil consists in inverting their priority – feeling the pull of the moral law, and recognizing that it should prevail over our inclinations, but choosing inclination over duty nevertheless. The propensity to do this is a "perversity of the heart," and what makes it radical is that it is deeply rooted in human nature itself, and can never be "*extirpated* through human forces." It can only be overcome, each time we confront it.[45]

In *Origins*, Arendt argues that Kant's theory misses the mark when it comes to the "unforgivable absolute evil" of the camps. This "could no longer be understood and explained by the evil motives of self-interest, greed, covetousness, resentment, lust for power, and cowardice." Kant may have suspected that absolute evil exists, but "he immediately rationalized it in the concept of a 'perverted ill will' that could be explained by comprehensible motives."[46] Arendt adds that the entire philosophical tradition, not Kant alone, is powerless to understand this kind of "radical evil, previously unknown to us," because of its sheer pointlessness.[47]

She too has no real explanation for this absolute evil, and she suspects that it defies explanation. The closest she comes is this: "There is only one thing that seems to be discernible: we may say that radical evil has emerged in connection with a system in which all men have become equally superfluous." And not only the victims:

> The manipulators of this system believe in their own superfluousness as much as in that of all others, and the totalitarian murderers are all the more dangerous because they do not care if they themselves are alive or dead, if they ever lived or never were born.[48]

These remarks come in a chapter near the end of *Origins* titled "Total Domination," where Arendt elaborately analyzes the camps and gulags as a "ghastly experiment . . . of transforming the human personality into a mere thing." If the experiment in total domination had succeeded, it would have spelled "inexorable doom for human beings."[49] We would be as disposable as rubbish; we would *be* rubbish.

The specter of superfluous human beings haunts *Origins*. As we'll see in greater detail in Chapter 6, it lies at the heart of Arendt's historical analysis of Europe's slide into totalitarianism. Superfluous capital made imperialism economically rational; superfluous (i.e., unemployed) men became the

[44] Kant, *Religion within the Boundaries of Mere Reason*, 6:35, 58.
[45] Kant, *Religion within the Boundaries of Mere Reason*, 6:37, 60. [46] *OT*, 459. [47] *OT*, 443.
[48] *OT*, 459. [49] *OT*, 438, 443.

army of adventurers who followed the money to Africa and invented bureaucratic racial domination and genocide; the Great War taught an entire generation of men that their lives were superfluous, disposable by the millions; the collapse of the class system stripped away people's sense of belonging somewhere and made them ripe for recruitment into totalitarian mass movements. The word "superfluous" appears more than ninety times in *Origins*.

Death camps take the logic of superfluous humans to its limit, and the nightmarish chapter on "Total Domination" is one of the most relentless things Arendt ever wrote. But notice something important: When she calls the camp system radical evil "previously unknown to us," she also labels it "unforgivable absolute evil." Here she clearly intends the first sense of radical evil, namely extreme evil, not the third, Kantian, sense of deeply rooted evil. Her critique of Kant is precisely that he finds motivations for evil deeply rooted in human nature, whereas the absolute evil of the camps has *no* humanly comprehensible motives. Her "superfluousness" diagnosis is not an alternative theory of evil's roots in human nature. It is a denial that the evil of the camps has any roots. Superfluousness is not a theory of radical (read: deeply rooted) evil but a description of how radical (read: extreme) evil manifests itself – an image of Hell, as she titled one of her essays. As she wrote to Jaspers in 1951,

> *What radical evil really is I don't know*, but it seems to me it somehow has to do with the following phenomenon: making human beings as human beings superfluous (not using them as means to an end, which leaves their essence as humans untouched and impinges only on their human dignity; rather, making them superfluous as human beings).[50]

Recognizing that *Origins* offers no theory of the roots of evil helps us understand her letter to Scholem. Read carefully, the letter doesn't agree with Scholem that Arendt once held a non-Kantian theory of radical evil that she has now abandoned. She says only that she no longer *speaks* of radical evil. She no longer speaks of it because the Kantian phrase wrongly suggests that evil has roots in the clash between human inclination and the moral law within, whereas the evil she has in mind has no roots and no connection with morality.[51] The Scholem letter never abandons her anti-Kantian argument in *Origins*; it abandons only Kant's phrase, which she

[50] Arendt to Jaspers, March 4, 1951, *HA-KJ*, 166. Emphasis added.

[51] This is another point of agreement with Hampshire, for whom Nazism is absolute evil because rather than being an evil morality, it rejects morality itself.

now finds misleading. And she hasn't backed off a bit from the other sense of radical evil as extreme.

To summarize, the vexing letter to Scholem is careless, in two respects. First, because it suggests that she agrees with Scholem that radical evil and banal evil name competing theories – a conceptual either–or – and she has switched out one for the other. As we've just seen, she does *not* agree with him. Second, both in *Origins* and in the Scholem letter she toggles back and forth among the three meanings of "radical" without flagging the shifts (and perhaps without noticing them).

There nevertheless is one substantive change that the Eichmann trial provoked: As Richard Bernstein points out, in the post-Eichmann writings Arendt no longer spoke of superfluousness, and instead turned to thoughtlessness.[52]

It seems clear that when Arendt wrote in *Origins* that totalitarian murderers "do not care if they themselves are alive or dead, if they ever lived or never were born," she had in mind Stalinism and the Great Terror, with the uncanny confessions of Party men who said they deserved death because the Party line called for it, and whose official theory was that human nature itself could be engineered. This was the Stalinism depicted by Arthur Koestler and George Orwell, where a human being is merely a mass of one million divided by a million and the self is a "grammatical fiction" (as Koestler's protagonist puts it in *Darkness at Noon*, as he prepares to confess to fictitious crimes because "objectively" he has become a class traitor). Whether or not it is historically accurate, it's the nightmare that Arendt portrays in the final sections of *Origins*.

This was patently not Adolf Eichmann. Eichmann never thought he was superfluous. He had no interest in reengineering human nature, and there is no reason to think that if he had discovered he was Jewish he would have shipped himself to Auschwitz. He claimed to have little interest in Nazi ideology, only a misplaced admiration for the Nazi "gods" and their "popes." In Arendt's eyes, his most remarkable trait was his inability to think from another's point of view, and the consequent inability to tell right from wrong – in Williams's terminology, to make his victims the Internal Other.

This is what Arendt now had to confront. Hence the switch from radical evil as human superfluousness to radical evil as banality, a fungus spreading

52 Richard J. Bernstein, *Hannah Arendt and the Jewish Question* (MIT Press, 1996), 137–54. She mentions superfluousness once in *Eichmann in Jerusalem*, when she warns that new technologies may make parts of the labor force "superfluous" (the scare quotes are hers), and nuclear weapons will make it easy to destroy them. *EJ*, 273.

across the surface of the Earth. The point isn't that Arendt abandoned the superfluousness hypothesis, only that she concluded that it was insufficient to explain the kind of evil Eichmann represented. Superfluousness makes a cameo appearance in *Eichmann in Jerusalem*, when Arendt calls him "a leaf in the whirlwind of time . . . blown . . . into the marching columns of the Thousand-Year Reich."[53] But Eichmann's rootlessness doesn't get to the heart of his moral psychology. His thoughtlessness does.

To recap: A superficial reading of Arendt's letter to Scholem makes it seem that she abandoned a theory of radical evil in favor of a new theory that evil is not radical but banal. Perhaps she herself believed this, conflating different senses of the word "radical." What she actually abandoned was Kant's question about the roots of evil, and her conjecture (never more than that) that in totalitarian systems the answer to Kant's question must connect with human superfluousness. Eichmann was a counterexample to the superfluousness conjecture, and reflecting on his case led her to drop the conjecture along with Kant's phrase and his question, in favor of an inquiry into thoughtlessness and banality.

## 5.6 Postscript: Did Eichmann Think?

Which brings us, inevitably, to a question. Did Eichmann think, contrary to Arendt? That would be a decisive objection to her "banality of evil" diagnosis. Did he engage in the two-in-one?

Well, he says he did. Recall from Chapter 1 that in his prison memoir *Götzen* he claims that in his off hours (but only then!) he always engaged in "a spiritual self-observation, in which my external 'I' carries on a dialogue with my inner 'I' – which also could be called conscience."[54] That sounds very much like thinking, in just the sense that Arendt intends.

The trouble was, he explains over and over, that he could never act on his conscience because he was bound to higher powers – powers he once thought were gods but now recognizes as idols. He proudly assures us that even the gods never penetrated his conscience ("after all they were only earthly gods") – but that's because he kept it entirely sealed off, and stubbornly guarded as if by tanks and airplanes.[55] But, for that very reason, his conscience didn't – *couldn't* – influence his actions.

53 *EJ*, 32–33.

54 *Götzen*, 581 (450). See also José Brunner, "Eichmann's Mind: Psychological, Philosophical, and Legal Perspectives," *Theoretical Inquiries in Law* 1(2) (2000): 459.

55 *Götzen*, 33 (88). The metaphor is Eichmann's.

In what sense was he bound to the gods? In a few places, he suggests duress. He couldn't disobey orders: In the SS, the sentence for disobedience was death.[56] Nor could he resign, or so he claims: Only SS generals had permission to request a transfer. For lower-ranked "higher bearers of secrets" who objected to their murder mission, suicide was the only way out.[57] And wartime conditions blocked him from living by the Kantian principles he claimed to believe in: "[O]nly in rare cases do wartime orders correspond with the principle of general legislation, the moral law within me. And then try to talk about ethics with a superior SS general in wartime. He kicks you in the butt!"[58]

Duress is a dishonest excuse, though. There is no evidence that Eichmann *wanted* a way out, or thought about quitting. As we saw in Chapter 2, Eichmann admits that he carried out his duties with "unusual zeal," and when Himmler ordered him to pause the Final Solution, Eichmann disobeyed. Of course that may show only that Eichmann had no conscience, only Jew hatred, and his claims to the contrary are bald-faced lies. Stangneth, recall, thinks that *Götzen* was nothing but a mendacious attempt to get a lighter sentence by claiming to be repentant. She may well be right about *Götzen*.

For present purposes, though, that doesn't matter. Even if Eichmann never actually engaged in self-examination or suffered qualms of conscience, we can learn a lot from his description of his encounters with himself. Even if they are fiction, to write about them he had to imagine them. He has the audacity to suggest an alternative title to his memoir: *Gnothi seauton*, the Delphic Oracle's famous injunction to know thyself.[59] What did he imagine that self to be? To answer this question, the best source is part 3 of *Götzen*, which, Eichmann informs us, "reflects the relationship between the external events at that time and my inner feelings."[60]

There Eichmann labors to explain "what inner 'witch's kitchen' a person can come to in practical life when his own freedom of action is bound by a higher power."[61] The metaphor alludes to a scene in Goethe's *Faust*, where Mephistopheles brings Faust to a witch's kitchen for a potion to make him younger and erotically vital. The imagery hardly needs explaining, although Eichmann likening himself to Dr. Faust is a bit much. In any case, he doesn't pursue the Faust analogy, which might

[56] *Götzen*, 549 (441). [57] *Götzen*, 550–51 (442–43).
[58] *Götzen*, 140–42 (99). He says similar things elsewhere: *Götzen*, 190 (204). [59] *Götzen*, 8 (64).
[60] *Götzen*, 7–8 (63). [61] *Götzen*, 581–82 (450–51).

have led him to the awkward fact that Faust pledged himself to the devil of his own free will.

Arendt would surely have pounced on that latter point. She always responds to the "I was only a cog in a machine" defense with the right question: Why did you make yourself a cog?[62] Eichmann's answer, throughout *Götzen*, is that he discovered too late that he was worshipping idols, not gods. (To which the follow-up question would be: Why did you mistake the Nazi leaders for gods?)

In the "witch's kitchen" reflections he uses a different mechanistic metaphor:

> A sheet of paper; iron filings sprinkled on it.
>
> These little pieces of iron lie criss-cross in a confused mess.
>
> This is how it seems with me when I lack inner peace, when I try in vain to bring order into the contents [lit. "things"] of my inner life.
>
> But if I move my magnet under this sheet of paper, then in the area of the magnetic force field this jumble of iron filings is immediately arranged into a – I would almost like to say – military formation.[63]

His inner turmoil, he wants us to believe, comes from the conflict between his Kantian morality and the terrible things the gods make him do.

Revealingly, his beau ideal is not Socrates' harmonious lyre or anything resembling it. It's a military formation, consisting of feelings lined up under the command of a will Eichmann likens to a magnet. Socrates' lyre is an instrument where every string has its distinct voice, and each is as important as the other strings. It's a good metaphor for an inner conversation among equals. Eichmann's imagery is very different. The self he aspires to is a lone commander at the peak of a hierarchy, disciplining his feelings like unruly soldiers, by the force of his will.

Eichmann's imagery changes again. No longer is he the magnet. Now he is the iron filing: "But what use is all the craving for order if my knowledge cannot be converted into action, if I am not allowed to use this magnet, yes if I am just such an iron filing myself, lined up (*eingeordnet*) by this force field."

62 *EJ*, 289; PRUD, 29–32; "Collective Responsibility," in *RJ*, 148, and in an interview with Joachim Fest published in *The Last Interview and Other Conversations*, 58.

63 *Götzen*, 582 (450). Literally, "militarily oriented order" (*militärische ausgerichteten Ordnung*).

Trapped in a force field, he can't quiet his mental turmoil:

> When stronger forces prevent me from doing what I want, and furthermore, because of state orders, I even have to do things opposed to what my inner will tells me to do; to a will, that according to my emotional perception, originates in the area of ethical beliefs, I still yearn to book (*buchen*) inner calm and equilibrium for myself as an individual, even if only for instinctive egoistic reasons.[64]

The yearning for a quiet conscience is merely instinctive egoism.

Earlier in *Götzen*, Eichmann does raise pertinent moral questions; he isn't oblivious to them.

> And as I sit in judgment of myself, many inner voices say many things to me. – Could I have resigned from my business? Could I have simply refused to continue working?
>
> Would this have been mutiny?
>
> What do you call mutiny against murder?
>
> Mutiny stands *against* flag and oath of service!
>
> What is state-commanded murder and what is the oath?
>
> Does keeping the oath still belong to the realm of ethical values? To the unity of ethics?
>
> Does it at least belong to the *fringe* of morality?
>
> What is morality?
>
> I can no longer believe that morality is part of ethical values![65]

There is nothing wrong with those questions, and genuine thought about them might be the stuff of a modern-day Socratic dialogue.

The trouble is that Eichmann asks them twenty years too late, after his trial and awaiting his verdict – when, at last, "after the overthrow of what was recently valid, I see myself slowly and bit by bit arriving at a picture of the world that satisfies me."[66] They aren't what his conversations between his "external 'I'" and his "inner 'I'" were about during his SS years (assuming he actually had them).

We know that because he tells us so. Specifically, those evening conversations were not dialogues about right and wrong, mutiny and murder, oaths and ethics. Instead, he explains, they were examinations of "one's own attitude, one's own reaction to the events of the day." The goal of the

64 *Götzen*, 582–83 (451). 65 *Götzen*, 553 (444). 66 *Götzen*, 8 (63).

dialogue was not a judgment about his conduct but about his feelings. It results in "a position that I register as 'reassuring' or 'disturbing' to me. And depending on this, my psychological state, I then feel a resonating physical state."[67]

Thus, what ultimately concerns Eichmann is not the world he lives in, or the deeds he does, or the harms he inflicts. His inner voices are not sympathetic representations of other people: Storfer, or Kastner, or the millions he transports to their deaths. The only things that matter are his feelings and the "resonating" physical state that comes with them. Because of the "personality split" between outward obedience and inner misgivings, he "suffered more than he ever wanted to admit or admitted."[68]

Shortly after these reflections, Eichmann dives further into maudlin self-pity, and then blasts off into metaphysical kitsch:

> I've often asked myself, how I was able to get through all this without laying hands on myself, to finally shroud everything with the mercifully covering cloth of a voluntary and wanted ending as a human being.
>
> But by doing so I would have admitted guilt that I didn't yet have. And to the extent that I fled into philosophy, my curiosity, my desire to know, always grew greater than the momentary need that was enveloping me; I then always gained distance from the suffering of everyday life, and my personal worries seemed meaningless to me. And I realized that there was no end for me, and neither was there Nothing. In distant, distant finitudes, Time will again lose itself in Space; but I simultaneously know that new "times" will be ready for me again. And then I know how the bounded narrowness of the moment is leaving me. The day's sorrow flees, only I remain surrounded by the invigorating radiance of suns that protect me forever.[69]

The consolation of philosophy! His "personal worries" (about his disturbing feelings, not about the people he shipped to their deaths each day) evaporate into pop cosmology. His sorrow flees to distant galaxies.

This is not thinking. This is, in the words of a Tony Hoagland poem, "what narcissism means to me."[70]

[67] *Götzen*, 581 (450). [68] *Götzen*, 193 (206). [69] *Götzen*, 589–90 (454).

[70] Tony Hoagland, "What Narcissism Means to Me," in *What Narcissism Means to Me* (Graywolf Press, 2003), 16.

PART III

# *Common Sense and Moral Breakdown*

CHAPTER 6

# *The Flight from Common Sense*

> Totalitarian propaganda can outrageously insult common sense only where common sense has lost its validity.[1]

Chapters 3–5 emphasized that moral questions sometimes require difficult judgment calls. But not all moral questions are close calls. Should I participate in mass murder? Should I inform the secret police that my neighbors criticized the government, knowing they will be arrested and sent to a gulag or even shot? Moral common sense tells us that the answer is no; indeed, moral common sense tells us that these don't even rise to the level of serious questions, because answering yes is unthinkable.

Yet for millions of people in the Third Reich and Stalin's USSR, questions like these *did* seem genuine, and multitudes of ordinary people answered yes. One thing that unnerved Arendt was that to all appearances, these were people who just a few years earlier would have agreed without hesitation that mass murder and denouncing their neighbors transgress bedrock morality. What could account for the abrupt reversal of commonsense morality – or, for that matter, its restoration in Germany after the Third Reich fell? Equally unnerving to her was the scale of the moral collapse as it spread throughout occupied Europe. It was not only commonsense morality but common sense itself that collapsed, as millions of people lapped up the bizarre conspiracy theories, pseudoscientific ideologies, and transparent lies that their leaders invoked to support criminal policies. What could account for it all?

These are hardly antiquarian questions about a vanished past. In our current age of rampant conspiracy theories, authoritarian populism, and shameless assaults on truth, Arendt's investigations seem more relevant than ever. An internet search instantly brings up newspaper and magazine articles with titles such as "Why Hannah Arendt is the Philosopher for

[1] *OT*, 352.

Now," "Why We Should Read Hannah Arendt Now," and "Totalitarianism in the age of Trump: Lessons from Hannah Arendt."[2] Sales of *The Origins of Totalitarianism* increased sixteenfold following the 2016 election of Donald Trump, and even nine years later, *Origins* remains among Amazon's top-selling books on political history.

This chapter delves into Arendt's diagnosis in *Origins* of the collapse of common sense and the collapse of moral judgment that accompanied it. Her historical focus was exclusively European. But because of the remarkable echoes of the past in the present, the examples I draw on are contemporary as well as historical; and one aim of the chapter is to bring Arendt's ideas into conversation with contemporary epistemologists and political psychologists who ask similar questions about how, in her words, common sense can lose its validity.

## 6.1 Outrages against Common Sense

A June 2020 survey found one in four Americans agreeing that "powerful people intentionally planned the coronavirus outbreak."[3] An eighth of Americans younger than thirty thought the culprit was Bill Gates, plotting to create a new world order by implanting mind-control microchips in millions of vaccine recipients.[4] This theory was revisionism of a kind: A decade earlier, the mastermind seeking world domination was not Bill Gates but George Soros, at least according to a fifth of Americans surveyed in 2011. The 2011 survey also found that about one in five respondents were "truthers," convinced that the 9/11 attacks were an inside job, and a quarter were Obama "birthers." Trutherism, birtherism, and Soros domination plots were three of seven popular conspiracy theories studied, and it turns out that roughly half the respondents believed at least one of the seven.[5] In fall 2020, 7 percent in a survey of registered American voters said they believed the elaborate and grotesque mythology of QAnon, the then-prevalent version of which pitted Donald Trump against a gang of child-trafficking, Satan-worshipping, blood-drinking leftist elites. Another

[2] Lyndsey Stonebridge, "Why Hannah Arendt Is the Philosopher for Now," *New Statesman*, March 20, 2019; Anne Applebaum, "Why We Should Read Hannah Arendt Now," *Atlantic*, March 17, 2022; Zoe Williams, "Totalitarianism in the Age of Trump: Lessons from Hannah Arendt," *Guardian*, February 1, 2017.

[3] Katherine Schaeffer, "A Look at the Americans Who Believe There Is Some Truth to the Conspiracy Theory that COVID-19 Was Planned," Pew Research Center FactTank, July 24, 2020.

[4] Rainer Zitelmann, "How Many Americans Believe in Conspiracy Theories?," *Forbes*, June 29, 2020.

[5] J. Eric Oliver and Thomas J. Wood, "Conspiracy Theories and the Paranoid Style(s) of Mass Opinion," *American Journal of Political Science* 58(4) (2014): 956 (table 1), 958.

11 percent were unsure whether they believed it.[6] The satanic gang was said to be protected by the Deep State and financed by Soros. In summer 2020, German QAnon enthusiasts interpreted NATO military exercises as a happy sign that Trump, their superhero savior, would soon invade Germany and free it from Angela Merkel.[7] That same year found tens of millions of Americans believing in election-theft plots that would require superhuman levels of coordination and secrecy among dozens, perhaps hundreds, of otherwise unconnected and unidentified miscreants, with hundreds more covering it up or looking away. Four years later, one out of four surveyed Americans claimed to believe that the FBI instigated the January 6, 2021 attack on Congress.[8] Apparently, education offers no immunization: In a 2024 study, a quarter of respondents *with postgraduate degrees* agreed or strongly agreed that "[s]chool shootings, like those at Sandy Hook, CT and Parkland, FL are false flag attacks perpetrated by the government."[9]

Whatever happened to common sense?

The British philosopher Quassim Cassam observes that "anti-Semitism is the original sin of Conspiracy Theories," and it comes as no surprise that antisemitism, that sturdy stalwart, continues to defy common sense today.[10] It defies common sense when a "progressive" Washington, DC city council member posts a video blaming a snowstorm on weather manipulation by the Rothschilds.[11] It defies common sense when Europeans wildly overestimate the Jewish populations of their own countries even though most say they are unaware of ever having met a Jew.[12] Holocaust agnosticism and ignorance exist worldwide and sadly come as no surprise. Given the passage of time, and notable ignorance of history

6 Civiqs, "QAnon Support: Registered Voters," September 10, 2020–October 11, 2020.

7 Katrin Bennhold, "QAnon Is Thriving in Germany; The Extreme Right Is Delighted," *New York Times*, October 11, 2020.

8 Tom Jackman et al., "A Quarter of Americans Believe FBI Instigated January 6, Post-UMD Poll Finds," *Washington Post*, January 4, 2024.

9 Saverio Roscigno, "The Status Foundations of Conspiracy Beliefs," *Socius: Sociological Research for a Dynamic World* 10 (2024). This is twice as many as respondents with a bachelor's degree or less. Roscigno notes that across all the conspiracy theories he studies, white men are far more likely to agree or strongly agree than female and minority respondents; and the gap is greatest among respondents with graduate degrees. See Paul Rosenberg, "Who Believes the Most "Taboo" Conspiracy Theories? It Might Not Be Who You Think," *Salon*, May 5, 2024.

10 Quassim Cassam, *Conspiracy Theories* (Medford, MA: Polity Press, 2019), 123.

11 Peter Jamison and Valerie Strauss, "D.C. Lawmaker Says Recent Snowfall Caused by 'Rothschilds Controlling the Climate,'" *Washington Post*, March 18, 2018.

12 CNN polled in Austria, France, Germany, Hungary, Poland, Sweden, and Great Britain. Richard Allen Green, "CNN Poll Reveals Depth of Anti-Semitism in Europe," CNN, November 27, 2018.

across all topics, these are not necessarily departures from common sense. After all, a third of surveyed Americans don't know in which century the American Revolution took place.[13] What defies common sense is that 11 percent of young Americans believe that the Jews caused the Holocaust.[14]

None of this would have surprised Hannah Arendt. The loss of common sense is one of the main themes of *The Origins of Totalitarianism*, where the phrase appears more than forty times; the very first page warns that "never have we depended so much on political forces that cannot be trusted to follow the rules of common sense."[15] In her later writings on moral judgment, Arendt returns repeatedly to questions about common sense and its collapse.

The questions are central to our inquiry into moral judgment. The connection between common sense and good judgment may seem obvious; indeed, some dictionaries define common sense as a species of good judgment ("sound and prudent judgment based on a simple perception of the situation or facts"; "sound practical judgment that is independent of specialized knowledge, training, or the like"[16]). However, we must not read these definitions to be saying that commonsense judgment is, by definition, *correct* judgment. It needn't be. This is obvious in science and medicine, where common sense often turns out to be wrong; but it's also obvious in every human endeavor where judgment must be honed by training and experience to produce reliable results. Common sense by itself is no guarantor of truth or reliability.

Even apart from fields where judgment needs specialized training, we sometimes find ourselves confronted by decisions in everyday life in which two people of equal common sense might choose differently; that's what makes these choices hard. And we rightly recognize that some people are better at tough choices than others.

In sum, common sense doesn't guarantee good judgment. What nevertheless seems indisputable is that coming unhinged from common sense

[13] Half believe it came after the Civil War, War of 1812, or the Emancipation Proclamation Allen C. Brownfield, "The Danger Ignorance of History Poses to the Future of a Free Society," American Council of Trustees and Alumni, April 22, 2018.

[14] Harriet Sherwood, "Nearly Two-Thirds of US Young Adults Unaware 6m Jews Killed in the Holocaust," *Guardian*, September 16, 2020. These numbers are not out of line with other countries.

[15] *OT*, vii.

[16] *Merriam-Webster Dictionary Online*, s.v. "common sense," accessed March 22, 2025, www.merriam-webster.com/dictionary/common%20sense [https://perma.cc/W5QF-XNUB]; *Dictionary.com*, s.v. "common sense," accessed March 22, 2025, www.dictionary.com/browse/common%20sense [https://perma.cc/PKJ7-FS7Z].

guarantees bad judgment. That is, although common sense isn't a sufficient condition for sound judgment, it is a minimum necessary condition.

Arendt tackles questions about common sense and its collapse from different angles in *Origins*, *The Human Condition*, the moral philosophy essays of the 1960s, and *The Life of the Mind.* In *Origins*, the loss of common sense is rooted in social disintegration and isolation, resulting in cynicism and a reckless indifference to factual truth that made millions of people patsies for totalitarian propaganda. *The Human Condition* ties the loss of common sense to excessive regard for subjective experience at the expense of the world we inhabit in common, an outlook she traces to Cartesian doubt and developments in the Scientific Revolution.[17] In "Personal Responsibility under Dictatorship" and "Some Questions of Moral Philosophy," she focuses specifically on the collapse of *moral* common sense, epitomized by Germany's frictionless slide from moral decency into crackpot racism and its murderous consequences. And, as we saw in Chapter 3, in her final writings she draws on Kant's discussion of common sense in the *Critique of Judgment.*

This chapter examines *Origins* on the collapse of common sense, and its connection with propaganda. It keeps contemporary events very much in mind. In Chapter 7, we turn to the more rarefied epistemological reflections in *The Human Condition* and the late writings.

Before proceeding, I want to flag one of my chief conclusions in this chapter: that what looks like a collapse of moral common sense may not be the mysterious inversion of values it seems. If a person has the outlandish factual belief that innocuous people are actually enemies who pose a deadly threat, they may try to kill the imaginary enemies – not because they now think murder is virtuous, but because killing in self-defense is not murder. The apparent collapse of moral common sense can sometimes be traced to a collapse of factual common sense.

## 6.2 Conspiracy Theories, Ideology, and Common Sense in *The Origins of Totalitarianism*

The first chapter of *Origins* bears the title "Antisemitism as an Outrage to Common Sense," and it poses its questions straightforwardly. How could the European Jews – a small, unarmed, politically unrepresented, largely self-secluded, minority people – come to be feared and blamed for all the misfortunes in Christendom? How could the peoples of supposedly

[17] *HC*, 280–83.

"modern" Europe come to believe the most incredible conspiracy theories about Jews? How could crackpot racial theories migrate from the fringe of society to the center of a mass murder project of unprecedented scale? All of it defies common sense.

To Arendt, an equivalent outrage to common sense was the "artificially fabricated insanity" of Stalin's USSR, where "one mysterious world conspiracy has followed another in Bolshevik propaganda, starting with the plot of the Trotskyites, followed by the rule of the 300 families, to the sinister imperialist (*i.e.,* global) machinations of the British or American Secret Services" – to which she later added the antisemitic Doctors' Plot that the Kremlin unfurled between editions of *Origins.*[18] The Moscow trials and executions of the Old Bolsheviks, based on their own confessions, are a prime instance of outrages against common sense.

> If, for instance, all the "confessions" of political opponents in the Soviet Union are phrased in the same language and admit the same motives, the consistency-hungry masses will accept the fiction as supreme proof of their truthfulness; whereas common sense tells us that it is precisely their consistency which is out of this world and proves that they are a fabrication.[19]

Here we see one of several political and psychological explanations Arendt offers for the loss of common sense: hunger for a consistent explanation that makes sense of the "fortuitousness that pervades reality," especially injustices (real or perceived), personal calamities, and mass misfortunes like economic crashes.[20] Ideology supplies that need with what psychologists today call a *monological belief system* – "a unitary, closed-off worldview in which beliefs come together in a mutually supportive network."[21] Arendt uses the word "supersense."[22] Such

[18] *OT*, 353 (artificially fabricated insanity), 351 (conspiracies), 35n29 (conspiracy accusations against "Jewish cosmopolitanism"), xxxviii (Doctors' Plot). The Doctors' Plot was an accusation that a group of predominantly Jewish doctors were conspiring to kill leading Soviet officials. An antisemitic media campaign followed. A recent empirical study of contemporary Russian conspiracy theories (drawing on a 1,500-item database the author compiled from Russian sources) suggests that contemporary Russian leadership has not changed in its strategy of using conspiracy theories for political reasons. Scott Radnitz, *Revealing Schemes: The Politics of Conspiracy in Russia and the Post-Soviet Region* (Oxford University Press, 2021); for an overview of the conspiracy theories, Radnitz, *Revealing Schemes*, 44–66.

[19] *OT*, 352. [20] *OT*, 351–52.

[21] Michael J. Wood et al., "Dead and Alive: Beliefs in Contradictory Conspiracy Theories," *Social Psychological and Personality Science* 3(6) (2012): 767. The term comes from Ben Goertzel, *Chaotic Logic: Language, Thought, and Reality from the Perspective of Complex Systems Science* (Plenum, 1994) and Ted Goertzel, "Belief in Conspiracy Theories," *Political Psychology* 15(4) (1994): 740. Both Goertzels define a monological belief system as one that speaks only to itself, a description very much in harmony with Arendt's views about thinking and dialogue.

[22] *OT*, 457–58.

hyperlogical theories of everything are, automatically, more intellectually and emotionally satisfying than Arendt's "fortuitousness that pervades reality," more vulgarly known as "shit happens."[23]

Even those who know better can be locked into the logical dungeon of supersense. In Arthur Koestler's *Darkness at Noon*, Rubashov (a fictionalized Nikolai Bukharin) confesses to unreal crimes because the logic of Bolshevik ideology compels him to confess. That's an explanation not so far from Arendt's. We now know that many victims of the Great Terror confessed not because of "supersense" but because they were tortured; but others who were not tortured do seem to have confessed for Rubashovian reasons. As historian Yuri Slezkine explains the logic: "When it came to crimes against the Party, which stood for the Eternal Law, thoughts were not radically different from words, and words were not radically different from deeds. And when it came to the Party's Inquisition, sins were not radically different from crimes."[24] Hence the confessions from men whose sole sin was having at some point doubted the wisdom of the Party line. Common sense tells us that is no reason to confess to crimes one hasn't committed. But common sense is precisely what ideology displaced.

Conspiracy theories, like ideologies, partake of supersense – and, as Arendt notes, they also resemble the mental constructions of paranoiacs, where everything follows inexorably from a delusional first premise; she adds that the insanity lies not only in the premise but also in the sheer logicality by which every observable fact snaps crisply into place within the theory.[25] Reality is never that logical. It is untidy. Shit happens.

Some might protest that, far from being hyperlogical, conspiracy theorists are supremely illogical. Survey subjects in 2012 who believed Princess Diana is still alive were more likely than average to believe she was murdered. Likewise, people who believed that Osama bin Laden was already dead at the time of his killing were more likely to believe he was still alive.[26] Cassam (understandably) concludes that these people hold contradictory views.[27] That's not quite what the survey shows, though. It finds that assents to the inconsistent theories rise and fall together; but it

[23] See Pete Mandik, "Shit Happens," *Episteme: The Journal of Social Epistemology* 4(2) (2007): 205–18; Cassam, *Conspiracy Theories*, 26, 60 (on the unwillingness of conspiracists to accept that sometimes shit happens).

[24] Yuri Slezkine, *The House of Government: A Saga of the Russian Revolution* (Princeton University Press, 2017), 840–53; the quoted passage is at 844.

[25] *OT*, 457–58.

[26] Wood et al., "Dead and Alive."

[27] Cassam, *Conspiracy Theories*, 45; Cassam, *Vices of the Mind: From the Intellectual to the Political* (Oxford University Press, 2019), 70n28.

doesn't follow that people believe them both at once. The finding can just as easily mean that subjects hold them in the alternative, not the conjunctive, and believe both are better than the Official Story. There is nothing illogical in thinking that both of two inconsistent theories are more likely than a "known" falsehood. Where supersense comes in is a step earlier – in the network of runaway inferences "proving" that the Official Story must be a lie.

Leaders have by no means been immune to supersense. Stalin's ideology proclaimed that collectivized farms would be a socialist triumph. Instead, grain production in Ukraine fell between 1931 and 1932. Since the Party line is infallible (premise), what could explain the failure? Stalin concluded it was intentional sabotage by counterrevolutionary and nationalist peasants.[28] What else could it be? Sabotage calls for ruthless repression, not realistic grain quotas. To meet impossible and punitive quotas, even peasants' seed corn was confiscated, guaranteeing lower outputs at next planting. And that provided further proof of active sabotage.[29]

The result was that millions starved to death in the Holodomor, Stalin's man-made famine in Ukraine. Stalin never personally observed the mass starvation, but local officials did. "Forced to interpret distended bellies as political opposition, they produced the utterly tortured conclusion that the saboteurs hated socialism so much that they intentionally let their families die."[30] Utterly tortured, utterly contrary to common sense – and utterly logical, given the axiom that the Party line can never be wrong.

## 6.3 Moral Common Sense

A crucial point to note is that loss of common sense about factual reality leads to loss of common sense in moral matters. If Ukrainian peasants are starving their own families to death to sabotage socialism, perhaps they deserve to die. If the Jews are a powerful and sneaky alien race locked in a death struggle with the German *Volk*, mass murder is self-defense.[31] Mass

[28] Timothy Snyder, *Bloodlands: Europe between Hitler and Stalin* (Basic Books, 2010), 40–41, 44.

[29] Snyder, *Bloodlands*, 45.

[30] Snyder, *Bloodlands*, 41.

[31] Michael Wildt, "Eichmann und der kategorische Imperativ, oder: Gibt es eine nationalsozialistische Moral?," in *Die Wannsee-Konferenz am 20. Januar 1942: Dokumente, Forschungsstand, Kontroversen*, eds. Norbert Kampe and Peter Klein (Böhlau Verlag, 2013), 157–61. The self-defense of Germany against the Jewish menace was in fact one of the arguments made by SS General Otto Ohlendorf in the *Einsatzgruppen* trial at Nuremberg, to reject the charge of murder "in the sense of the indictment." Ohlendorf commanded *Einsatzgruppe D*, which shot and gassed 90,000 men, women, and children. Asked at his trial why his group murdered children, he explained that the aim was not only security but permanent security: When they grew up, "surely being the children of people who had been killed they would constitute a danger no smaller than that of their parents." Quoted in Richard Rhodes, *Masters of Death: The SS-Einsatzgruppen and the Invention of the*

murders are morally heroic if SS men kill for racial reasons and not for personal gain or gratification.[32] If "Trotskyite vacillations in 1923," owned up to by a Soviet official, led him to attend dinners where the Party line was questioned, he will confess that he is "profoundly guilty" of "counter revolutionary wrecking activities" for failing to report the dinners to the secret police.[33]

It follows that crime is not crime, famine is justice, doubts are treason, racism is virtue, and the shining hallmark of the SS killer is his decency (*Anstand*).[34] Here we see artificially fabricated *moral* insanity, in which commonsense principles are twisted into moral hallucinations. Importantly, these examples don't require a total inversion of values, in which evil is now declared to be good. Self-defense, just punishment, patriotism, solidarity, and doing one's painful duty all belong to commonsense morality. All they need to transform into moral insanity is the half-twist of applying them to factual claims that defy common sense. In Bolshevism and Nazism, the other half-twist was supplied by one genuine transvaluation of values: wholly subsuming the worth of individuals into the worth of the collective (the *Volk* or the class) and defining the sole moral imperative as victory over the collective's enemies.

## 6.4 Supersense

Arendt discusses conspiracy theories, ideology, and totalitarian propaganda together. But it is important to recognize that conspiracy theories and ideologies are by no means the same thing. An ideology is a global worldview that purports to explain events as surface manifestations of larger forces, which explain all the events by a few fundamental principles. For the Nazis, the basic principle was a biological struggle for existence among races; for the Bolsheviks, inexorable historical laws of class

*Holocaust* (Vintage, 2007). The tribunal rejected the argument, and Ohlendorf received a death sentence.

32 Wildt, "Eichmann und der kategorische Imperativ, oder: Gibt es eine nationalsozialistische Moral?," 163–66. This comes from Heinrich Himmler's bone-chilling speech to the SS in Posen (Poznan) on October 4, 1943, discussed as well by Arendt, *EJ*, 105–6.

33 Slezkine, *The House of Government*, 843–44. The quotes are from Aron Gaister's confession. Gaister was a good Party man; at the time of the Holodomor, he praised the success of collectivized agriculture and celebrated "the liquidation of the contradiction between town and village." Slezkine, *The House of Government*, 309. His confession was not extracted through torture, and he begged for a chance to expiate his thought crimes, which he freely admitted were dire. He was shot in 1937.

34 Wildt, "Eichmann und der kategorische Imperativ, oder: Gibt es eine nationalsozialistische Moral?," 163–66. Again, this comes from Himmler's 1943 Posen speech.

conflict.[35] These are the ideologies Arendt focused on. Both drew inspiration from the large-scale philosophies of history of the nineteenth century, which conceptualized history, not as a narrative of events, but as an unfolding process, governed by hidden laws of motion that it is the job of historians to uncover.[36] Ideology of this sort connects the seemingly random dots of *histoire des événements* into a lawlike pattern. In this respect, it sounds like science, and it has the pretension of being science, or at any rate of resting on science. The crucial difference is that whereas the aims of science are explanatory, ideologies are politicized through and through.

Conspiracy theories, by contrast, have little or nothing to do with science. In place of the impersonal, law-governed forces of history, they substitute evil cabals hatching secret plots. Conspiracy theories and ideologies both try to make sense (or supersense) of events as surface manifestations of hidden realities, and both are political; but there the resemblance stops. Many of today's conspiracy theorists are frankly anti-science, because scientists belong to the shadowy elites that conspiracy theorists hate and fear.[37] These conspiracists may appear to be credulous, and in obvious ways they are. Yet, as Brian Keeley observes, they also have an almost nihilistic level of skepticism about anything the authorities, including scientific authorities and experts, say.[38]

In that respect, today's New Conspiracists are close cousins to flat-Earthers, whose ranks are apparently swelling courtesy of the internet and social media.[39] Part of the challenge facing flat-Earthers is explaining why their opinions are widely scorned; and the natural answer is that the scientists must be in on the plot to hide the truth, in cahoots with the media and – inevitably – the government. Imagine the vast scientific betrayals that went into faking those space station photos of Round Earth, not to mention the perfidious cartographers who flood the world

[35] These, Arendt notes, are the two ideologies that "have come out on top and essentially defeated all others." *OT*, 159.

[36] Arendt, "The Concept of History," in *BPF*, 51. I analyze this essay in David Luban, "Hannah Arendt's Theory of Theory," *Social Research* 50(1) (1983): 215–48, revised and reprinted under the title "Hannah Arendt and the Primacy of Narrative," in David Luban, *Legal Modernism* (University of Michigan Press, 1994). The obvious progenitor was Hegel; see *OR*, 45–49.

[37] On the related point that the "new conspiracism" is conspiracy shorn of political theory, see Russell Muirhead and Nancy L. Rosenblum, *A Lot of People Are Saying: The New Conspiracism and the Assault on Democracy* (Princeton University Press, 2019), ch. 1.

[38] Brian L. Keeley, "Of Conspiracy Theories," *Journal of Philosophy* 96(3) (1999): 125–26.

[39] Rob Picheta, "The Flat-earth Conspiracy Is Spreading Around the Globe: Does It Hide a Darker Core?," CNN, November 18, 2019. I take the label "New Conspiracism" from Muirhead and Rosenblum, *A Lot of People Are Saying*.

with globes showing Antarctica rather than the wall of ice that holds the oceans in! – What looks at first glance like a harmless, dotty view about an apolitical natural fact turns out to be deeply political: In the words of a psychologist who studies the flat-Earth subculture, they "view the world through this really dark filter where [they] assume that all authorities and institutions and corporations are just there to exploit you."[40]

The sheer contingency of facts means that facts could have been otherwise – and, as Arendt writes, "this annoying contingency is literally unlimited."[41] That opens a logical space for conspiracy theories: They *could* be true. Because the conspiracy theory could be true, the burden of proof is on you to show it isn't, or so the conspiracist insists. You can't deny that sinister and incredible government conspiracies actually have existed – consider, for example, the CIA's multiyear, multimillion-dollar secret research into mind control, which included dosing unwitting subjects with LSD and other mind-altering drugs.[42] If it could happen then, the conspiracist reasons, why doubt that it is happening now? Invariably, the conspiracist has boatloads of "evidence." Unless you're willing to waste your life fact checking the rubbish heap of minutiae that conspiracists always have at their fingertips, the conspiracists triumph, at least in their own minds.[43]

If conspiracy theories are anti-science, what is their connection to "scientific" totalitarian ideologies? The answer is that conspiracy theories can get along fine without a scientific ideology – as shown by the anti-science "new conspiracism" – but a scientific ideology, which (in Arendt's words) "pretends to have found the key to history or the solution to the riddles of the universe," needs conspiracy theories.[44]

First, as Stalin's devastating diagnosis of the bad Ukrainian harvest illustrates, conspiracy theories are necessary to explain away the inevitable

40 Rachel Brazil, "Fighting Flat-Earth Theory," *Physics World*, July 14, 2020, quoting psychologist Asheley Landrum.

41 "Truth and Politics," in *BPF*, 242 (hereafter TP).

42 The programs, code-named Project Artichoke and MK-ULTRA, came to light during several congressional investigations in the 1970s. See generally Stephen Kinzer, *Poisoner in Chief: Sidney Gottlieb and the CIA Search for Mind Control* (Henry Holt, 2019); Alfred McCoy, *A Question of Torture: CIA Interrogation from the Cold War to the War on Terror* (Holt, 2006).

43 Richard Hofstadter's famous essay on the "paranoid style" in American politics notices the conspiracist's "almost touching concern with factuality" as he "carefully and all but obsessively accumulates 'evidence'" in order to "prove that the unbelievable is the only thing that can be believed." Hofstadter, "The Paranoid Style in American Politics," *Harper's Magazine*, November 1964. There is a great deal of overlap between Hofstadter's essay and Arendt's observations.

44 *OT*, 457. Arendt wrote "pretended"; I've adjusted the tense.

but embarrassing predictive failures of the ideology. Events would have unfolded as the ideology predicted (so the supersense reasoning goes) if it hadn't been for sabotage – which, by the way, the ideology rightly predicted. Conspiracy theories provide convenient, easy-to-understand auxiliary hypotheses patched on to a theory to make it fit errant data. As a historian of Soviet Russia notes:

> For at least a decade Bolshevik authorities had promoted the idea that there were no accidents in the Soviet Union, no incompetence, no random crimes, no freak catastrophes. Industrial accidents, production below plan, theft, murder, and rape were "not coincidental." They all had political meanings; they were all perpetrated by saboteurs, class enemies, and foreign intelligence services.[45]

Conspiracy theories make great auxiliary hypotheses to save the ideology. For, as Keeley points out, to a conspiracist evidence *against* the theory is really evidence *for* it: It shows how desperate the conspirators are to bury the truth. Hitler wrote that proof that the Protocols of the Elders of Zion are a forgery is actually "the surest proof that they are genuine."[46] Of course, conspiracy theories do more than save the ideology. They justify crackdowns and repression if the conspiracists are in power.

Second, to be translated from esoteric theory to user-friendly mass propaganda, ideologies need to be repackaged, dumbed down, and dramatized. In place of scientific Marxism, Soviet propaganda accused 300 families of conspiring to run the world. In place of so-called "scientific" racism, the Nazi movement drew on the Protocols of the Elders of Zion. In Arendt's words: "The object . . . was always . . . to demonstrate a sphere of secret influences of which the visible, traceable, and known historical reality was only the outward façade erected explicitly to fool the people."[47]

There is no contradiction between "low" conspiracy theory and "high" ideology, because conspiracy theories can run comfortably in parallel with the more abstract, academic, and "respectable" ideologies to form a unified propaganda package that appeals to elites and masses alike.

Ludwig Bieberbach, a University of Berlin math professor and ardent Nazi, could publish a "scientific" book about the influence of blood and race on mathematical styles. (After trying and failing to find decent excuses

45 Matt Lenoe, "Did Stalin Kill Kirov and Does It Matter?," *Journal of Modern History* 74(2) (2002): 352.

46 Keeley, "Of Conspiracy Theories," 120. Hitler quoted from *Mein Kampf* in Richard J. Evans, *The Hitler Conspiracies* (Oxford University Press, 2020), 32. The Protocols of the Elders of Zion is a fabricated document describing a purported Jewish plan for world domination.

47 *OT*, 333.

for Bieberbach's theories, a renowned British mathematician commented that he found himself "driven to the more uncharitable conclusion that he really believes them true."[48]) Dr. Mengele's mentor, Otmar von Verschuer, ran a well-funded anthropology, genetics, and race science institute; he lectured to London's Royal Society on twin research (Mengele's specialty at Auschwitz) as late as three months before the war.[49] Meanwhile, street-level racists with no interest in genetics or the difference between "J-type" and "S-type" mathematics could settle for the Protocols of the Elders of Zion.

## 6.5 Arendt's Political Sociology in *Origins*

What explains contempt for the rules of common sense? *Origins* offers several explanations: historical, psychological, and philosophical. My interest is mostly philosophical, but a quick overview of Arendt's historical and psychological diagnoses will provide useful context.

We have already seen one such diagnosis: Arendt roots the loss of common sense in the human need for meaningful explanations, however farfetched, of man-made disasters and injustices that befall us. Trying to make sense of economic crashes and the incomprehensibly pointless carnage of World War I drove many Europeans to embrace supersense at the expense of common sense. But that raises a question: Why now? After all, misfortune and injustice are always with us, and so is the human need to make sense of calamities.

Arendt's answer, in brief, is that nineteenth-century capitalism's production of "superfluous wealth and superfluous men" shredded the traditional European class system and created a mass society of atomized individuals, who no longer understood their place in the world and were therefore ripe for recruitment into mass movements peddling meaning in the form of supersense.[50] Politically, parliamentary democracy – with its give and take rooted in real interests – depended on a system in which parties represented classes; with the "wreckage of classes,"[51] the party system collapsed and the mass movements prevailed.

[48] G. H. Hardy, "The *J*-Type and the *S*-Type among Mathematicians," *Nature* 134 (1934): 250. Bieberbach's book is *Stilarten mathematischen Schaffens* [Styles of Mathematical Creativity] (Akademie der Wissenschaften, 1934).

[49] David G. Marwell, *Mengele: Unmasking the "Angel of Death"* (Norton, 2020), 90; Otmar von Verschuer, "Twin Research from the Time of Galton to the Present Day," *Proceedings of the Royal Society of London, Series B Biological Sciences* 128(850) (1939): 62–81.

[50] *OT*, 200, 225. [51] *OT*, 326.

Let's take a deeper look. Arendt's detailed analysis employs a political sociology of her own devising, a quirky taxonomy of European society in the late nineteenth and early twentieth centuries built around six categories: the mob, the people, the masses, the bourgeoisie, the philistines, and the elite.

### 6.5.1 *The Mob and the People*

The *mob* corresponds roughly with Marx's lumpenproletariat, an underclass of the angry, disaffected, thwarted, cynical, and violent – with one significant difference. For Arendt, the mob is drawn from all classes, because she includes in it the inciters and abettors of mob violence, not just the perpetrators. She introduces the term in her discussion of France's Dreyfus affair, where the tangible, physical mobs attacking Jews and Jewish businesses were egged on by both the military and antisemitic intellectuals. Quoting blood-curdling rhetoric from the supposedly respectable classes, she comments that "[t]he upper classes knew that the mob was flesh of their flesh and blood of their blood."[52]

For Arendt, the mob need not be a literal mob, and the anti-Dreyfusard mob is only an instance of "the human debris that every crisis, following invariably upon each period of industrial growth, eliminated permanently from producing society";[53] it is "the refuse of all classes."[54] From its ranks were drawn, among other things, the adventurers and soldiers of fortune in Europe's African colonies, and much of the underworld. Today, we might well include in the mob armed militias and actual physical mobs like the January 6 stormers of the US capitol, but also armies of internet trolls with their distinctive brand of nihilism and cruel amusements, along with the influencers who egg them on.

Because the mob (in her expanded sense) is drawn from all classes, it can easily be mistaken for *the people*, "which also comprises all strata of society. While the people in all great revolutions fight for true representation, the mob always will shout for the 'strong man,' the 'great leader.' For the mob hates society from which it is excluded."[55] Arendt's scattered comments on the mob resonate strongly with contemporary analyses of populism, where strongman leaders appeal to the mob by assuring them that they alone are the true people, and any political opponents are mortal enemies.[56]

52 *OT*, 107. 53 *OT*, 150. 54 *OT*, 155. 55 *OT*, 107.
56 Jens Werner-Müller, *What Is Populism?* (Penguin, 2015).

### 6.5.2 Masses and Philistines

The *masses* are different from the mob, although Arendt cautions that once totalitarian movements acquired mass followings it was easy to overlook the difference: that is because the mentality of their leaders so closely resembled that of nineteenth-century mob leaders.[57] Arendt defines "masses" as follows:

> The term masses applies only where we deal with people who either because of sheer numbers, or indifference, or a combination of both, cannot be integrated into any organization based on common interest, into political parties or municipal governments or professional organizations or trade unions. Potentially, they exist in every country and form the majority of those large numbers of neutral, politically indifferent people who never join a party and hardly ever go to the polls.[58]

Her key conclusion is that totalitarian movements arise "wherever there are masses who for one reason or another have acquired the appetite for political organization."[59] The psychology of the masses includes "a typical feeling of superfluousness . . . the concomitant of mass unemployment and the population growth of the last 150 years." The fact that millions were suffering the same fate could not prevent anyone from "judging themselves in terms of individual failure or the world in terms of individual injustices," and the psychological, or one might even say spiritual, result was a "self-centered bitterness" that made them ripe for recruitment into a mass movement.[60]

Included among the masses are what she calls *the philistines* – "the bourgeois isolated from his own class, the atomized individual who is produced by the breakdown of the bourgeois class itself."[61] Here she evidently means the downwardly mobile middle classes in times of economic and social crisis:

> The mass man whom Himmler organized for the greatest mass crimes ever committed in history bore the features of the philistine rather than of the mob man, and was the bourgeois who in the midst of the ruins of his world worried about nothing so much as his private security, was ready to sacrifice everything – belief, honor, dignity – on the slightest provocation.[62]

### 6.5.3 The Bourgeoisie

Elsewhere in *Origins* where she speaks of *the bourgeoisie*, Arendt means capitalists, that is, owners of capital, not the middle classes. Arendt accepts

57 *OT*, 313–14. 58 *OT*, 311. 59 *OT*, 311.
60 *OT*, 311 (superfluousness), 315 (bitterness). 61 *OT*, 338. 62 *OT*, 338.

Marx's insight that what makes capitalism distinctive is not acquisitiveness but endless expansion of capital, "the bourgeoisie's empty desire to have money beget money," in which "wealth became a never-ending process of getting wealthier."[63] To this she adds Rosa Luxemburg's insight that this process will require endless expansion and therefore imperialism – which, in Arendt's analysis, contradicts the nation-state principle and presaged the twentieth-century collapse of the system of European nation-states.[64]

Most conspicuously, she draws her picture of the (big) bourgeoisie from a reading of Hobbes – "the true . . . philosopher of the bourgeoisie" and "the only great thinker who ever attempted to derive public good from private interest."[65] Hobbes reduces reason to "Reckoning," and human worth to whatever price the market fetches for one's labor power. Accordingly, the bourgeois state is grounded in self-interest, not law or right. And "[p]ower, according to Hobbes, is the accumulated control that permits the individual to fix prices and regulate supply and demand in such a way that they contribute to his own advantage." This requires the help of "some kind of majority. Therefore, if man is actually driven by nothing but his individual interests, desire for power must be the fundamental passion of man."[66] Hobbes, writes Arendt, is "the great idolator of Success."[67]

I leave to one side the accuracy of Arendt's interpretation of Hobbes. For our purposes, what matters is not whether Arendt got Hobbes right (I doubt it) but what she takes from Hobbes, namely a picture of the bourgeois as a success-worshipping moral hypocrite. Her political critique is that the bourgeois willingness to sacrifice freedom for prosperity and security rests on the fallacy that public good can come from aggregating private interests.[68]

But hers is also a moral critique, and as Arendt explores the political psychology that gave rise to totalitarian movements, the moral critique takes on a central role. For, at the same time as Europe's bourgeoisie wrested power from the aristocracy, it embraced the fiction of its own invincible rectitude, namely the fiction that its moral rules aim solely to protect the innocent pursuit of private interest. Bourgeois morality became a hypocritical overlay of pieties masking something far uglier and more ruthless.

63 *OT*, 137, 145.

64 *OT*, 148 (citing Luxemburg's *The Accumulation of Capital*). On the contradiction between the nation-state principle and imperial expansion, see *OT*, 124–28; on the inner contradiction of the nation-state principle, *OT*, 229–36; on the breakdown of the parliamentary party system, *OT*, 252–66.

65 *OT*, 139, 146. 66 *OT*, 139. 67 *OT*, 144. 68 *OT*, 145–46; 336.

### 6.5.4 The Elite

The unmasking of bourgeois hypocrisy came in an especially toxic form from *the elite*. One of Arendt's themes is the alliance between the elite and the mob, evinced early on in "high society's constantly growing admiration for the underworld, which runs like a red thread through the nineteenth century, its continuous step-by-step retreat on all questions of morality, and its growing taste for the anarchical cynicism of its offspring."[69] Elite cynicism intensified after the cataclysm of World War I. The war's trauma filled the Lost Generation (Arendt calls it the "front generation") with a bitter, brittle nihilism. Today, we might diagnose the syndrome as *moral injury*, a cousin to post-traumatic stress disorder.

The disillusioned, morally injured front generation included not only the demobilized soldiers but also civilian contemporaries who shared their bitterness and "were completely absorbed by the desire to see the ruin of this whole world of fake security, fake culture, and fake life."[70] They were filled with "justified disgust" for the pieties of bourgeois morality. Among literary elites this disgust manifested itself in "their brilliant and witty praise of violence, power, and cruelty."[71] The mob wanted "access to history even at the price of destruction" – and the members of the elite who egged them on "did not object at all to paying a price, the destruction of civilization, for the fun of seeing how those who had been excluded unjustly in the past forced their way into it."[72] They did it for the lulz.

### 6.5.5 The Upshot

What should we make of Arendt's taxonomy? It is not grounded in demographic data, surveys, or psychology experiments; rather, it is a narrative cultural study. An obvious first question is whether her underlying history is reliable. The breadth of her research is remarkable. We should nevertheless expect errors of fact at the granular level – after all, Arendt had no access to Soviet archives, she did not read Russian, her material resources were meager, and there has been a mountain of research in the seven-plus decades since *Origins*. For present purposes, there is no need to sort out small errors of fact, and in any case sorting it out isn't anything I am equipped to undertake.

[69] *OT*, 155. [70] *OT*, 328. [71] *OT*, 328 ("justified disgust"), 330 ("brilliant and witty").
[72] *OT*, 332.

As for the overarching narrative – the macro- rather than micro-history – subsequent decades have generated major disputes between competing interpretations of Nazi Germany and Stalinist Russia. Some are roughly consistent with Arendt, others decidedly not.[73] There are likewise differing accounts of the class composition of the Nazi base, which in any case changed over time. Again, some of these views are consistent with Arendt, others less so.[74] A bigger problem is that her picture of Nazi Germany and the Stalinist USSR is a composite, and some elements are true of one but not the other. Arendt is not careful to sort these out. But, as with the granular micro-history, for our purposes there is no need to enter the fray of competing historical interpretations of the macro-history. Whether or not Arendt was right about *how* millions of people lost their moral and factual common sense, the point is *that* they lost it.

Obviously, Arendt's categories are anything but a neutral descriptive sociology. "Mob" and "philistines" are words of contempt, just as "the people" is a theory-laden republican praise-word. "Bourgeoisie" can be used as a neutral class category, but Arendt leaves no doubt that she associates Europe's nineteenth- and early twentieth-century bourgeoisie with moral rot. Masses, defined as people with no interest in public life, comes closest to a purely descriptive term; but Arendt gives it a largely negative inflection and warns that mass society is ripe for totalitarian recruitment. As for the elites, her disgust at their casual nihilism could hardly be plainer. Hers is a morally loaded, normative sociology, not a social science description. And *Origins* is as much a moral argument as a historical and political analysis.

Her sociology is specific to a unique epoch and place, as Arendt herself emphasizes. Yet readers will have no difficulty finding contemporary analogues to Arendt's categories. For example, Arendt attributes the "revolt

[73] Thus, within Soviet studies, "revisionists" like J. Arch Getty dispute "totalitarian" interpretations of Stalinist terror like that of Arendt and Robert Conquest; Third Reich and Holocaust historians long divided between "functionalists" and "intentionalists" (or a fusion: Richard Bessel, "Functionalists vs. Intentionalists: The Debate Twenty Years on or What Has Happened to Functionalism and Intentionalism?," *German Studies Review* 26(1) [2003]: 15–20). Although they draw on a wealth of information unknown to Arendt, histories through the 1980s and 1990s are not necessarily more reliable, because they are often colored by Cold War polemics and the complicated politics of remembrance, dramatically exemplified in the West German "Historians' Controversy" of the late 1980s and the Goldhagen Affair a decade later.

[74] See the useful literature review by Stephen G. Fritz, "The NSDAP as *Volkspartei*? A Look at the Social Basis of the Nazi Voter," *The History Teacher* 20(3) (1987): 379–99. See also Richard Hamilton, "The Rise of Nazism: A Case Study and Review of Interpretations: Kiel, 1928–33," *German Studies Review* 26(1) (2003): 44–45, 58–59; Peter Baldwin, "Social Interpretations of Nazism: Renewing a Tradition," *Journal of Contemporary History* 25(1) (1990): 7.

of the masses against . . . common sense" to "their loss of social status along with which they lost the whole sector of communal relationships in whose framework common sense makes sense."[75] An entire literature about populism and polarization in the contemporary United States offers variants of the same diagnosis. But there are no one-to-one correspondences between then and now. For present purposes, the question is not whether Arendt's typology exactly applies today, but rather what any of this has to do with the loss of common sense.

A great deal, as it turns out. The punchline of Arendt's story of class wreckage, atomization of masses, and backlash against hypocrisy is a corrosive attitude toward factual truth that she was among the first to pinpoint. In addition to the epigraph to this chapter, consider a few other observations:

> Mass propaganda discovered that its audience was ready at all times to believe the worst, no matter how absurd, and did not particularly object to being deceived because it held every statement to be a lie anyhow.
>
> A mixture of gullibility and cynicism is prevalent in all ranks of totalitarian movements, and the higher the rank the more cynicism weighs down gullibility. The essential conviction shared by all ranks, from fellow-traveler to leader, is that politics is a game of cheating.[76]
>
> [T]he difference between truth and falsehood may cease to be objective and become a mere matter of power and cleverness, of pressure and infinite repetition.[77]
>
> The true goal of totalitarian propaganda is not persuasion but organization.[78]

And this from "Truth and Politics," an essay written in 1967: "[F]actual truth is no more self-evident than opinion, and this may be among the reasons that opinion-holders find it relatively easy to discredit factual truth as just another opinion."[79]

In this environment, propagandists happily exploit the conviction that all opinions are created equal and all oppositional news is fake news. Arendt's observations seem as recognizable, and as devastatingly valid, today as when Arendt wrote them seventy years ago. I was not surprised when a US Marine general, an expert on information warfare, told me that he urges his colleagues and students to study the chapter on propaganda from *The Origins of Totalitarianism.*

75 *OT*, 352. 76 *OT*, 382. 77 *OT*, 333. 78 *OT*, 361. 79 TP, 243.

## 6.6 The Epistemology of Bullshit

Let's focus on two of Arendt's observations – that mass propaganda's audience "was ready at all times to believe the worst, no matter how absurd, and did not particularly object to being deceived because it held every statement to be a lie anyhow," and that their mental state is therefore a "mixture of gullibility and cynicism." That mental state sounds like a contradiction in terms. Gullibility normally means excessive willingness to believe, while cynicism means something close to the opposite.

The solution to the contradiction is to reframe gullibility as the willingness to *accept* anything, without necessarily taking it to be true, either because it comes from a favored partisan source, or because one has cynically devalued truth (or both). A perceptive journalist described the attitude of Donald Trump's followers to his torrent of lies as falling "somewhere between true belief and being in on the joke."[80] That sounds a lot like a mixture of gullibility (true belief) and cynicism (being in on the joke).

Muirhead and Rosenblum describe the gullibility side of this attitude as being willing to settle for "true enough" rather than "true" ("Well, it may not be true, but it's true enough"), adding that the corresponding propositional attitude is neither belief nor disbelief.[81] Conspiracists are willing to settle for "true enough" because whose views you accept and whose you reject has become a matter of tribal identity rather than factual belief. Here one thinks of Arendt's observation (quoted earlier) that the goal of propaganda is not persuasion but organization. Persuasion aims at changing someone's belief; organization aims at recruiting them to a tribe, so that belief and truth no longer matter. Or rather, the only truth that matters is truth about tribal identity. What matters isn't factual reality but the reality of "us," the real people, in contrast to the poisonous subtlety of "them," the enemy within the body politic.

### *6.6.1 Epistemic Malevolence*

Contemporary philosophers have become increasingly interested in epistemic vices – mental attitudes that conduce to falsehood, just as mental

[80] Mark Leibovich, "Trump Has Called His Supporters 'Disgusting': Do They Care?," *New York Times*, October 10, 2020. In the same vein, two years earlier, a professional fact-checker reported that many of the vitriolic emails he received from Trump's supporters say that they like Trump's lying "because it bothers 'elites' like me." Daniel Dale, "It's Easy to Fact-Check Trump's Lies: He Tells the Same Ones All the Time," *Washington Post*, November 16, 2018.

[81] Muirhead and Rosenblum, *A Lot of People Are Saying*, 43.

attitudes and traits like attentiveness and honesty conduce to truth. One such vice is *epistemic malevolence*, an oppositional attitude toward the truth, manifesting itself in active efforts to defeat truth and frustrate truth-seekers.[82] This may seem like just a fancy label for lying, but it is a broader category. Epistemic malevolence also includes information suppression (erasing or stealing public records; bribing, intimidating, or murdering witnesses; no-snitch honor codes like *omertá* and police forces' "blue wall of silence").

In addition, it includes what I will call *epistemic decoy flooding*: the release and circulation of so much fake news, sometimes commingled with truth, that it becomes impossible to sort out truth and falsehood in real time. The analogy is to military tactics such as releasing decoy balloons with the same radar characteristics as missiles to confuse missile detection systems, or surrounding warships with a flotilla of civilian craft. Besides camouflaging the truth, Regina Rini shows that an especially deadly aim of epistemic decoy flooding is discrediting truth as merely one of several spin-doctored narratives. As Rini argues, it actually helps malign actors if some of their fake news is transparently false. "The point is not to implant false beliefs. Rather, the point is to *induce skepticism*. By flooding the channels of public discourse with falsehood, then allowing citizens to know that this has happened, anti-democrats make it reasonable for us to trust no one, least of all our co-citizens."[83] Arendt anticipated Rini's observation when she wrote that "factual truth is no more self-evident than opinion, and this may be among the reasons that opinion-holders find it relatively easy to discredit factual truth as just another opinion."[84]

Of course, suppression and concealment need not count as malevolence in a moral sense – that depends on whether keeping something secret is morally justified or not. Not everyone is entitled to know everything that everyone else knows. In a courtroom setting, suppression includes lawful tactics such as invoking the attorney–client privilege or fighting discovery. While legal suppression tactics can be abused, they also serve legitimate purposes. In such cases, epistemic malevolence need not imply moral

82 The term comes from Jason Baehr, "Epistemic Malevolence," *Metaphilosophy* 41(1/2) (2010): 189–213, reprinted in *Virtue and Vice: Epistemic and Moral*, ed. Heather Battaly (Blackwell, 2010). Cassam's discussion of epistemic malevolence is very useful: *Vices of the Mind*, 88–92.

83 Regina Rini, "Weaponized Skepticism: An Analysis of Social Media Deception as Applied Political Epistemology," in *Political Epistemology*, eds. Elizabeth Edenberg and Michael Hannon (Oxford University Press, 2021), 32, 42–43.

84 TP, 243.

malevolence – but information suppression is, by definition, epistemically malevolent nonetheless.

Lying, suppression, decoy flooding; one of Arendt's keenest observations is that the result is not deceit but rather "a peculiar kind of cynicism – an absolute refusal to believe in the truth of anything, no matter how well this truth may be established."[85] As she put it in an interview, "if everyone always lies to you, the consequence is not that you believe the lies, but that no one believes anything at all anymore."[86] Kant was perhaps the first to argue that a generalized permission to lie would undermine the credibility of all statements.[87] Arendt takes the argument a step further and tells us what it is like to live in that world.

### *6.6.2 Credulous Producers*

It's essential to distinguish between the producers, distributors, and consumers of disinformation, and also to ask the separate question of whether producers and distributors actually believe what they are saying. Epistemic malevolence – the desire to defeat truth and frustrate truth-seekers – is a vice of producers and distributors of propaganda, not consumers. It may seem obvious that producers of fake facts don't believe their own fabrications, but that is not always the whole story. Of course, the forgers who wrote the Protocols of the Elders of Zion knew it was fake, but they may well have believed in a world Jewish conspiracy. This was Josef Goebbels's view. He believed the Protocols were fake; they nevertheless represented "the inner, but not the factual truth."[88] To take a more recent example, Jürgen Elsässer, the editor of a far-right German magazine that vigorously promoted QAnon, "does not believe in a conspiracy of pedophile elites, preferring to look at it as 'allegories.'"[89] But he may believe in whatever liberal elite wickedness these phantasms are allegories for. Ideologists presumably believe their own ideology, and they may regard their factual fabrications as "true enough."

And we must not discount the possibility that producers are taken in by their own productions. As I noted earlier, conspiracists often come equipped with buckets of "evidence" – small, innocent, or not-so-innocent

85 TP, 257. 86 Interview with Roger Errera, *TWB*, 491.

87 Kant, "On a Supposed Right to Lie from Philanthropy," in *Kant: Practical Philosophy*, ed. and trans. Mary J. Gregor (Cambridge University Press, 1996), Ak. 8:427, 612.

88 Quoted from Goebbels's diaries in Evans, *Hitler Conspiracy Theories*, 32. Goebbels is an archetypal distributor as well as producer.

89 Quoted in Bennhold, "QAnon Is Thriving in Germany."

facts that to a suitably attuned mind add up to proof. Their basic inference pattern is that if what they suspect *could* happen, their smatterings of evidence "prove" that it *did* happen. If voting machines could be hacked, they *were* hacked.

The logician A. N. Prior coined the label "runabout inference ticket" to describe a bogus rule of reasoning that can get you from anywhere to anywhere else – and "my conspiracy theory *could* explain my scraps of evidence, therefore it *does* explain it" is a perfect runabout inference ticket.[90] Let's look at an example I mentioned earlier: the theory (*au courant* in the first year of the Covid pandemic) that Bill Gates somehow planned to insert mind-control microchips in millions of people through vaccines. Here is the evidence:

- Gates gave pre-Covid speeches about the need for population control to reduce climate threats. Gates noted that improving health in developing countries is a promising strategy, because better health has been shown to correlate with lowered birth rates. Among the health measures Gates favors are vaccination and women's access to birth control. The ineluctable conclusion, as one conspiracy video (now removed from YouTube for violating community guidelines) warned: "Bill Gates Vaccines are used for depopulation."[91]
- In 2017, Gates gave a speech in Davos warning against nations' unpreparedness for "an epidemic, either naturally caused or intentionally caused." This video drew dire comments, especially in the first year of Covid, when conspiracy theories and disinformation were everywhere. "He has not warned; he has planned." "He dropped the 'intentionally' several times PAY ATTENTION. He is giving us hints." "Really easy to predict the future when you write the script." "Why the hell would you even say intentional if you didn't know anything? That implies evilness or maybe he chooses not to admit. Pure evil." "He's working on injections with a microchip to monitor population."[92]

90 A. N. Prior, "The Runabout Inference-Ticket," *Analysis* 21(2) (1960): 38–39.

91 "Bill Gates Vaccines Are Used for Depopulation," YouTube (November 13, 2017), now removed. The explanation of the odd-sounding correlation between better health and lower birth rates seems to be that with better health for mothers and children, poor parents don't feel the pressure to have additional babies as "insurance."

92 "Bill Gates Has a Warning About Deadly Epidemics", YouTube (January 22, 2017), www.youtube.com/watch?v=jDxb21qIilM [https://perma.cc/YEN3-65EF]. The quotations are from the comments section below the video.

- Then came a February 2020 announcement by the Bill & Melinda Gates Foundation that it would commit $100 million "for the global response to the novel coronavirus," including vaccine research.[93]
- Next: a scientific paper on a novel technology to trace who has or has not received vaccinations, by using quantum dots delivered to skin via "microneedle patches" – research supported by none other than the Gates Foundation.[94]
- The icing on the conspiracy cake was a 2018 patent application by Microsoft researchers for a method to link body activity data to blockchain.[95]

There you have it. Population control via vaccination and contraception. Gates hinting at intentional epidemics – at Davos, no less, known by all to be Ground Zero for international elite conspiracies. Covid vaccine research and a "global" response. Microneedles. Vaccine tracing. Gates Foundation. Microsoft. Blockchain monitoring body activity. It's all there, once you stitch the pieces together on a backcloth of antivaxxing, climate denialism, and political rage. One result was that in April 2020, almost 700,000 people petitioned the Trump White House to investigate the Gates Foundation for medical malpractice and crimes against humanity.[96]

The key point is that whoever launched the conspiracy theory may actually believe it, or sort of believe it, because their forward-leaning epistemic stance equips them with a runabout inference ticket that converts suspicions to certainties, catalyzed by these tantalizing smidgens of "evidence." In just the same way, Stalin and Kaganovich may actually have believed that reactionary peasants were sabotaging the Ukrainian harvest. Peasant hostility to collectivized farming was a known fact, the bad harvest was a known fact, and the infallibility of the Party line provided the inference ticket.

[93] Bill & Melinda Gates Foundation Pressroom, "Bill & Melinda Gates Foundation Dedicates Additional Funding to the Novel Coronavirus Response," *Gates Foundation*, February 5, 2020.

[94] Kevin J. McHugh et al., "Biocompatible Near-Infrared Quantum Dots Delivered to the Skin by Microneedle Patches Record Vaccination," *Science Translational Medicine* 11(523) (2019). The technology was tested on rats, not human beings, and microneedles have nothing to do with microchips.

[95] Dustin Abramson et al., "Cryptocurrency System Using Body Activity Data," https://patents.google.com/patent/WO2020060606A1/en [https://perma.cc/SXY6-NEHN]. On the conspiracy theory, see Marie Huillet, "Ex-CIA Agent Drags Microsoft's Crypto-Patent into Right-Wing Conspiracy," *Cointelegraph.com*, September 10, 2020.

[96] "We Call for Investigations into the 'Bill & Melinda Gates Foundation' for Medical Malpractice and Crimes against Humanity," petition, April 10, 2020.

What we see, therefore, is something surprising: that epistemically malevolent actors can have varying degrees of belief in their own fabrications, ranging from clear-eyed knowledge that the fabrications are lies, to belief that they are "true enough" or allegorically true, to belief (based on runabout inference tickets) that they are true full stop. But, regardless of the purveyors' degree of credence, their fabrications directly aim to defeat factual truth, and that makes their propaganda epistemically malevolent.

### 6.6.3 *Epistemic Insouciance and Culpable Credulousness*

Closely related to epistemic malevolence – and crucial to understanding Arendt's insights – is a different vice, what Cassam calls *epistemic insouciance*: "[A]n indifference or lack of concern with respect to whether their claims are grounded in reality or the evidence. Epistemic insouciance means not really caring much about any of this .... Epistemic insouciance is a particular form of not giving a shit."[97] His prime examples are Brexit campaigners such as Boris Johnson, who in his pre-political career as an EU-baiting journalist was fired twice for lying and "laughed it off when it was shown that his stories bore no relation to reality."[98]

Recall Harry Frankfurt's definition of bullshit as speech in which the speaker doesn't care if it is true or false; I mentioned it in Chapter 2 as a possible diagnosis of Eichmann's philosophical flights of fancy in his hectic final writings. Epistemic insouciance is the vice associated with bullshitting. Whereas epistemic malevolence is willful deceptiveness, the bullshitter's mental state is what criminal lawyers call *recklessness*: conscious disregard of a substantial and unjustifiable risk. In mass propaganda, it is a double risk: the risk of deceiving others, and, as Arendt rightly warns, the risk of devaluing truth itself and inducing a kind of all-consuming cynicism that devours common sense.

Epistemic insouciance comes in many flavors. Its motivation can be political, as with the Brexit campaigners. Some among them might truly have believed the Brexit ideology; others might not have, and simply sought power. Among the epistemically insouciant we also find apolitical grifters who make money off of clicks, and who understand that in the market for clickbait, bullshit sells. Some bullshit purveyors may not recognize the cynicism their decoy flooding produces in their audience; others may recognize it and regard it as regrettable collateral damage in

97 Cassam, *Vices of the Mind*, 79. 98 Cassam, *Vices of the Mind*, 79.

pursuit of political victory. And some may actively seek to sow this kind of cynicism, either for political gain or for nihilistic amusement.

This is supply-side insouciance – that is, the epistemic insouciance of propagandists. But there can also be epistemic insouciance on the demand side, that is, on the part of propaganda's targets. Of course, these are the duped, not the dupers. That doesn't make consumers innocent victims, however, if they are willfully or recklessly gullible rather than innocent and naive. Their stance toward the propaganda is receptive, not guarded – in Arendt's words, they are "ready at all times to believe the worst, no matter how absurd."[99] They have lost their taste for facts and reality.

Arendt's insight is that they could choose a more epistemically vigilant stance, but willfully or recklessly prefer not to. Then, when the propaganda they've accepted turns out to be false, they insulate themselves from responsibility for accepting it, either by grudgingly thinking "it's true enough" or – as Arendt argues – by cynically rationalizing that it's all lies and cheating out there anyway. Instead of feeling betrayed by the liar, they like him because he knows how to play the cheating game, and now they are in on the joke.

Whether their response to propaganda is "it's true enough" or "it's all cheating anyway," the result is a radical devaluation of facts and common sense. Here, the maxim of common sense that epistemic insouciance jettisons is, "Fool me once, shame on you; fool me twice, shame on me." In its place, the motto seems to be, "Fool me once, good for you; fool me twice, fine with me. It's all cheating anyway, and I am on your team."

"It's all cheating anyway" becomes a handy excuse for what I call *culpable credulousness*. Mere gullibility needn't be culpable. It can be a sign of an innocent and trusting nature, a character trait that is more touching than vicious. Culpable credulousness is different. It intentionally devalues factual truth as an excuse for letting oneself be fooled – as long as it's "our side" that is doing the fooling.

Recast in these terms, the epistemic stance Arendt calls "a mixture of gullibility and cynicism" would more properly be called a mixture of culpable credulousness and cynicism. The cynicism is at once the product and the source of the credulousness: It is the product, because credulous individuals allow themselves to be fooled again and again, which would be enough to make anybody cynical. It is the source, because the cynical premise that every statement in the public sphere is a lie excuses the

[99] *OT*, 382. Here, I follow Cassam in using "stance" to denote a chosen attitude toward believings; he distinguishes stances from postures, which are involuntary. Naïve trust seems more like a posture.

consumer who keeps coming back for more. Devaluing truth as an excuse for one's own credulousness is precisely what makes credulousness culpable.

This circular and self-reinforcing process gives meaning to the epigraph to this chapter: "Totalitarian propaganda can outrageously insult common sense only where common sense has lost its validity."[100] Common sense has lost its validity when a large segment of the populace has become so bitter and disaffected that it no longer values holding factual truths in common with others.

## 6.7 Rules of Common Sense

The virtue corresponding to the vice of epistemic insouciance is *epistemic vigilance* (a phrase I borrow from Dan Sperber and his co-authors[101]). Given that by far the greater part of what we know comes from other people, vigilance against being misinformed or misled by them is an indispensable trait. It requires us to evaluate testimony from others along the two dimensions of competence and honesty – asking the questions *is my informant in a position to know that?* and *is my informant trying to fool me?* Experiments show that children already make such discriminations by age four, and likely even earlier.[102] This suggests that just as the indispensable propensity to trust other people as sources of knowledge is hardwired into our cognitive heritage, so is the counterbalancing trait of vigilance. An essential part of vigilance consists of following rules of common sense when someone tells us something that matters to us.

Arendt would certainly agree that there are rules of common sense. Recall that she speaks of "general contempt for even the most obvious rules of common sense," and the first page of *Origins* warns that "never have we depended so much on political forces that cannot be trusted to follow the rules of common sense."

Rules of common sense are not inexorable laws of logic; they are rules of thumb. Perhaps the most famous rule of common sense is Occam's Razor, understood here as the principle that baroque or arcane explanations should be rejected in favor of straightforward ones if the straightforward ones cover the facts. But there are others. We have already seen a few examples. One is the rule *if it's too good to be true, it isn't true*: "If, for

100 *OT*, 352.
101 Dan Sperber et al., "Epistemic Vigilance," *Mind and Language* 25(4) (2010): 359–93.
102 Sperber et al., "Epistemic Vigilance," 371–73.

instance, all the 'confessions' of political opponents in the Soviet Union are phrased in the same language and admit the same motives, ... common sense tells us that it is precisely their consistency which is out of this world and proves they are a fabrication."[103] And if a supposed conspiracy would require flawless coordination and leakproof secrecy by hundreds of otherwise unconnected people, common sense tells us that it didn't happen.

Common sense also looks at the competence and honesty of sources. If informants on politicized media outlets claim to know something they are in no position to know, a rule of common sense instructs us to discount what they say. And if an informant has repeatedly lied in the past and been exposed, don't believe that informant the next time. (Fool me once ....) Holding self-serving assertions to a higher standard of proof than adverse admissions is another rule of common sense. Obviously, this list could easily be expanded. The question is, if epistemic vigilance is hardwired into us, as it seems to be, how can rules of common sense get disabled on a mass scale?

As we've seen, Arendt blames it on a kind of willful cynicism and insouciance brought on by the collapse of traditional society – a political explanation with moral overlay. But there are more innocent nonpolitical explanations as well. An inherent problem is that the everyday mechanisms of vigilance we learn from childhood are geared to face-to-face interactions, and they don't scale up to entire populations. Sperber and his co-authors identify at least four points of mismatch, none of which have directly to do with atomization in mass society:

1. The longer the chain of transmission, the more likely that the facts being transmitted are garbled; and we usually have no idea how long the chain is when a friend passes along a sensational tidbit that the friend learned from someone else. We are likely to treat it as though our trusted friend is the source, rather than recognize it as the final link in a long telephone game.
2. Furthermore, ordinary vigilance about sources doesn't work when the intelligence is passed along merely because "a lot of people are saying ...."
3. The normal human pleasure of spreading interesting news is benign and even indispensable in everyday life. But it also means that fake news often comes to us from multiple, seemingly independent sources

[103] *OT*, 352.

that confirm each other, even though it originated with a single producer.

4. And the conformist pressure to believe what a large group believes – or at least to accept what they accept – is surely just as strong as conformist pressure to behave as the group behaves.[104]

To all these one might add that the conspiracy entrepreneur's enticing invitation to "do your own research!" can actively stimulate a kind of *faux* vigilance, as the consumer delves deeper and deeper into the universe of false or misleading information that web searches will always disclose – accompanied by the same "eureka!" moments of exhilaration experienced by scientists and historians making authentic discoveries.[105]

All this would be true regardless of Arendtian "gullibility and cynicism." All the same, Sperber and his co-authors concur that "empty creeds" can invade whole populations when accepting them defines group identities. They argue that in such cases the acceptance is not strictly speaking epistemic, but what they mean is that acceptance is not the same as belief – which is exactly Arendt's point when she writes that the true goal of propaganda is not persuasion but organization. For that reason, I think Sperber and his co-authors misstate their point when they say that tribalist belief-acceptance is not epistemic. The practice of accepting propositions for purely tribalist reasons defeats truth and knowledge, and that is very much an epistemic vice. And when empty creeds invade whole populations, common sense has, as Arendt puts it, lost its validity.

## 6.8 The Breakdown of Moral Common Sense

To conclude this chapter, I return to the loss of *moral* common sense. Earlier I argued that losing moral common sense does not require a radical transvaluation of values where good is now evil and evil is good – although we'll see shortly that Arendt occasionally and mistakenly spoke this way as a figure of speech. To be sure, Nazi fanatics boasted about "a completely

[104] Sperber et al., "Epistemic Vigilence," 379–82. Rini discusses the same phenomena in "Weaponized Skepticism," 40–41.

[105] Sander van de Cruys et al., "Insight in the Conspiracist's Mind," *Personality and Social Psychology Review* 28(3) (2023). The authors hypothesize "that the need for autonomous epistemic agency and discovery is universal but increases as people experience more uncertainty and/or feel epistemically excluded in society." Van de Cruys et al., "Insight in the Conspiracist's Mind," 302.

new spirit of Germanic coldness," but that kind of blather is not required for the loss of moral common sense.[106]

All that is required is false *factual* beliefs about existential threats to things you hold dear. If you believe that entire races or classes are your deadly enemies, or that refugees are an invading army, or that the very existence of your society is menaced by secret conspiracies, then killing or expelling the enemies will seem like justified self-defense. And even people who aren't convinced about existential threats may acquiesce if the falsehood comes to be the prevailing opinion, promoted by leaders and hyped by their propaganda machine; they will do so on the shoulder-shrugging theory that if there's so much smoke perhaps there really is fire. In short, the collapse of *factual* common sense can topple *moral* common sense by conjuring up fictitious enemies and triggering self-defense. This requires no transvaluation of values, only a supersense interpretation of facts, coupled with the normal belief that deadly threats can justify actions in self-defense that would ordinarily be forbidden.

One of Arendt's keenest insights is that in such a toxic epistemic environment, the rules of thumb we use to identify wrongdoing fail, and in failing bring moral collapse. In *Eichmann in Jerusalem* and elsewhere, Arendt discusses several examples of rules of epistemic vigilance that can override common sense in propaganda-saturated regimes.

The first, and most fundamental, such rule is to look around at what conduct respectable and decent people treat as normal. If respectable people continue to go about their business in the face of the arrest of their neighbors, we may assume that things are not as bad as they seem. This observation is connected with the bystander effect familiar from social psychology: If the other bystanders to a disturbing event seem unperturbed, then we are less likely to be perturbed. And the bystander effect may be reciprocal, until aberration becomes normal.

In any case, it is all too easy to equate the conventional views of the majority with common sense. In normal times, mainstream belief *is* common sense.

But conventions can be fickle and quickly swayed by propaganda. If the reigning ideology is evil, someone trying to calibrate their own moral compass by checking it against the weathervane of mainstream opinion is lost. This is central to Arendt's diagnosis of Eichmann: "His conscience

[106] The quoted phrase comes from a letter written at the start of the war by a young Luftwaffe pilot to an anti-Nazi friend, who was horrified by it. Friedrich Percyval Reck-Malleczewen, *Diary of a Man in Despair*, trans. Paul Rubens (Macmillan, 1970), 89–91.

was indeed set at rest when he saw the zeal and eagerness with which 'good society' everywhere reacted as he did. . . . [H]is conscience spoke with a 'respectable voice,' with the voice of respectable society around him."[107] And it was not Eichmann alone. Even Dr. Josef Mengele, the "angel of death" conducting infamous human experiments at Auschwitz, was not the sadistic monster of legend; he was doing respectable normal science in the academic community of Third Reich genetics and anthropology.[108]

In addition to looking up and looking around at other people, we ask, "Is this an exception to a moral rule, or is it prescribed by the rule itself?" The exceptional status of an act is a second alarm bell warning us that the act is presumptively wrong. It signals *deviance*, and deviance is a name we often give to wrongdoing. But this mechanism fails when the prevailing mores have made exceptions into rules. As Arendt explains, "I am alluding, of course, to what happened in Nazi Germany and, to some extent, also in Stalinist Russia, when suddenly the basic commandments of Western morality were reversed: in one case, 'Thou shalt not kill'; in the other, 'Thou shalt not bear false witness against thy neighbor.'"[109] In the SS, "Thou shalt kill" became the rule, and "Thou shalt not kill" was the deviation.

As I remarked earlier, these striking formulations make it sound as if Arendt is describing a transvaluation of values, but I don't think that is what she is getting at. A better way to understand the phenomenon is to recognize that most rules of conduct have exceptions for emergencies. For example, most would agree that "Thou shalt not kill" has a built-in exception for killing in self-defense against deadly threats. By redefining the factual situation as one of existential struggle against enemies, the totalitarian regimes shifted the boundary of who counts as a mortal threat, and in that way they removed the persecution of innocents from the categories of sin and crime and placed it in the category of legitimate self-defense. Although Arendt frames this as the reversal of rule and exception, it's more accurate to describe it as redrawing the boundary of the rules to expand the category of exceptions. Of course, telling when a state of affairs falls under a rule and when it falls under an exception is a paradigmatic judgment call – and so, the willingness of millions of people to unthinkingly accept the totalitarian leaders' redrawing of the boundaries amounts to a catastrophic failure of moral judgment, just as Arendt says.

107 *EJ*, 126. 108 Marwell, *Mengele: Unmasking the "Angel of Death,"* 115–16.
109 *T*, 177; *EJ*, 150, 290–92.

This is an important point. Recall that Arendt marvels bitterly at how quickly and frictionlessly Germany adopted a criminal morality – adding that it should not reassure us about morality that after the war it was equally easy to turn morality upright again. My suggestion here is that morality never did turn upside down; rather, what turned upside down was a factual assessment of whether the world was now in a state of exception – which, if accepted, becomes a self-fulfilling prophecy. Factuality, not morality, turned upside down.

Either way, Arendt's shrewd point remains: Detecting evil by its deviance no longer becomes a reliable rule, and following it can override moral common sense. Once murder gets repackaged as necessary self-defense, it is a legitimate exception to "Thou shalt not kill." Legitimate exceptions don't count as deviant.

A third hallmark we use to recognize evil is temptation. A person is tempted to stray sexually, to break an inconvenient promise, or to lie their way out of trouble. In all these cases, the person is attracted to forbidden fruit. But the very fact that an ordinary human being is not in the slightest bit tempted to murder innocent people takes away this telltale sign by which someone, ordered to kill by his superiors, recognizes evil.

> Evil in the Third Reich had lost the quality by which most people recognize it – the quality of temptation. Many Germans and many Nazis, probably an overwhelming majority of them, must have been tempted *not* to murder, *not* to rob, *not* to let their neighbors go off to their doom .... But, God knows, they had learned how to resist temptation.[110]

A fourth mechanism is even subtler. The mass murders and enslavements committed by the Third Reich were hedged around with bureaucratic restrictions on who, when, where, and how. Participants could see that "by no means all was permitted" even in the Holocaust.[111] That made it appear that there was nothing nihilistically cruel about mass murder on a vast scale. It lacked the "anything goes" earmark of casting moral restraint to the winds.[112] A good illustration is the strange, revealing story of SS judge Konrad Morgen, analyzed in the illuminating moral biography by Herlinde Pauer-Studer and David Velleman.[113] Morgen was a strict rule-

[110] *EJ*, 150. [111] PRUD, 42.

[112] Not that the Holocaust was heavily regulated in on-the-ground practice. One of the revelations at the trial of Auschwitz personnel that drew Arendt's bitterest anger was how at every moment life and death was up to the whims and passing moods of the guards and officials. They operated in an environment where "anything goes" was the actual rule.

[113] Herlinde Pauer-Studer and David Velleman, *Konrad Morgen: The Conscience of a Nazi Judge* (Palgrave-Macmillan, 2015).

of-law prosecutor in the SS's internal justice system. He zealously prosecuted unauthorized looting, killing, and corruption by SS men in death camps – but failed to notice how anomalous that was in a setting where he was surrounded by murder and looting on an industrial scale.

In sum, Arendt calls our attention to four presumptive rules for telling right from wrong (although she doesn't use that terminology, and doesn't discuss all of them in one place):

1. It's wrong if most respectable people around me say it's wrong and behave as if it's wrong.
2. It's wrong if it deviates from a generally accepted social rule.
3. It's wrong if I feel a temptation toward it, coupled with (or recognized by) the lurking sense that I shouldn't give in because the fruit is forbidden.
4. It's wrong if it is part of an antinomian practice, that is, a practice in which it seems as though all restraint has been cast off and all is permitted.

In criminal regimes, none of these alarm bells rings. Those relying on them would be unable to distinguish the twisted edicts of the regimes from moral common sense. We can generalize from the case of criminal regimes: *Any* powerful social institution that manages to set up a system of conventional morality based on "facts" that defy common sense will make it hard for those within it to tell right from wrong. Mechanically applying the everyday rules of moral common sense to fictitious facts speeds us on our way to Hell.

CHAPTER 7

# *Common Sense and Plurality*

It seems, then, that we must not regard a judgment of taste as *egoistic*; rather, we must regard it necessarily as *pluralistic* by its inner nature.

Kant, *Critique of Judgment*[1]

## 7.1 Lay and Learned Meanings of Common Sense

In *Origins*, Arendt never bothered to define "common sense," which, after all, is not an arcane term. In the dictionary definition quoted in Chapter 6, common sense is sound practical judgment independent of specialized knowledge. Common sense is horse sense. Playing a bit with the words, we might even call this the commonsense meaning of "common sense." It's the meaning we intend when we exhort a friend to "use your common sense!" as they are about to blow their money on a luxury they can't afford, marry someone they hardly know, or imbibe quack remedies because social media tell them to.

But the phrase also had specialized meanings in learned traditions from the ancient world through the eighteenth century, and Arendt draws on these as well. I'll call them the *learned meanings* of "common sense," to distinguish them from the commonsense meaning, the *lay meaning*. Exploring those traditions, and the use Arendt makes of them, will help clarify her conception of common sense.

A warning is in order about the commonsense meaning. As just described, "common sense" is an innocent and useful phrase. But in politics, the phrase also has a long history of abuse that is far from innocent: Common sense is whatever "our side" believes, while our adversaries are the enemies of common sense. Historian Sophia Rosenfeld brilliantly traces the politicized rhetoric of common sense from England's Glorious Revolution to modern times.[2]

1 *CJ*, Ak. 5:278, Pluhar trans., 140.

2 Sophia Rosenfeld, *Common Sense: A Political History* (Harvard University Press, 2011).

In eighteenth-century England, publicists packaged partisan positions as Sound British Common Sense, as against their adversaries' factionalism or corruption.[3] In later times, politicized invocations of "common sense" found a natural home in populism. Common sense is the wisdom of plain people (*us!*), pitted against double-talking, self-dealing elites (*them!*). Populist leaders are the self-anointed voice of common sense. Their aim is to cut off policy debates by "convincing us that simple, kitchen-table solutions formulated by everyday people are necessarily better than complex or specialized or scientific ones" – and that the leaders are the *vox populi* of the only people whose kitchen-table solutions count: their followers.[4]

As we we've seen, it by no means follows from the definition of "common sense" as sound, nonspecialist judgment that kitchen-table wisdom is *right*, nor even that people agree in their kitchen-table judgments. For most of human history, common sense held that the Sun goes around the Earth; more than a quarter of Americans and a third of Europeans reportedly still believe this.[5] And, obviously, a leader saying he is the voice of common sense doesn't make it so. Fallacious or not, the rhetoric is so prevalent that "common sense" as a demagogue's label for his followers' pet prejudices must also be considered an ordinary meaning of the phrase. Obviously, though, it is the opposite of what Arendt means by common sense. Her claim in *Origins* is precisely that twentieth-century mass opinion somehow came unmoored from common sense.

## 7.2 The Learned Meanings from Aristotle to Kant

In its oldest learned meaning, "common sense" names the human capacity that binds together the deliverances of the five special senses into perceptions of objects. This *sensus communis* is what enables us to recognize that the whiteness and sweetness of sugar are properties of the same thing, namely the sugar we are seeing and tasting. The example is Aristotle's, and it was Aristotle who inferred that there must be some capacity (*dynamis*) that assigns the two modally different sensation streams to the same object.[6]

3 Rosenfeld, *Common Sense*, 24–54. 4 Rosenfeld, *Common Sense*, 256.

5 National Science Board, *Science and Engineering Indicators 2018*, Table 7–1, www.nsf.gov/statistics/2018/nsb20181/report/sections/science-and-technology-public-attitudes-and-understanding/public-knowledge-about-s-t [https://perma.cc/EH6J-X7YT].

6 Aristotle, *On the Soul (De Anima)*, 426b9–22 (1 Complete Works 678); *Sense and Sensibilia (De Sensu)*, 449a5–20 (1 Complete Works 712). Aristotle himself does not name this faculty "common sense" (*aisthesis koiné*, translated *sensus communis* in Latin); in fact, he doesn't name it at all, he only describes it. He does talk of "common sensibles" (*koina aisthêta*) like shape, number, and motion

For two millennia, *sensus communis* was a scientific concept, entangled with other concepts of epistemology and psychology. Natural philosophers argued about the properties and bodily location of *sensus communis*, and they speculated about how it relates to other cognitive powers. But what they were arguing and speculating about for those millennia was Aristotle's common power connecting all the senses. Call this the *Aristotelian meaning* of "common sense."[7] In his *Critique of Pure Reason* Kant offers his own elaborate account of how the "manifold" of appearances is "synthesized" by the intellect.[8] In the *Critique* Kant does not use the label "common sense" to name the faculty or faculties that synthesize the manifold of appearances, but he does in his *Anthropology*.[9]

A second strand of learned meaning originates with classical Roman authors who used the term *sensus communis* to describe interpersonal tact and good taste, "a social 'sense' necessary for behavior in public life."[10] A boor who chatters away to a poetry lover while he is trying to read is said by Horace to lack common sense. Although this is a different meaning than Aristotle's, writers in the Renaissance and early modern period saw no inconsistency between them. Medieval writers had argued that Aristotelian common sense, uniting the particular senses, is not a raw perceptual capacity but a form of intelligence. The same can be said of a sense of tact and taste. Both involve a discriminating perception of particulars – a principal difference being that while everyone possesses Aristotelian *sensus communis*, not everyone possesses *sensus communis* on the Roman understanding. The Roman idea of common sense gave rise to eighteenth-century theories of *moral* sense, which are not so different from Arendt's

that are detected by more than one sense, and this is why Latin writers introduced the phrase *sensus communis* to refer to Aristotle's unnamed faculty. Charles H. Kahn, "Sensation and Consciousness in Aristotle's Psychology," *Archiv für Geschichte der Philosophie* 48, nos. 1–3 (1966): 52–54. Arendt maintains (I don't know on what basis) that the phrase *sensus communis* originated with Aquinas. *T*, 50. She cites *Summa Theologica*, pt. 1, q. 1, 3 ad 2.

7 The power common to all senses: *On Sleep*, 455a17 (1 Complete Works 723). A useful history of the learned debates is David Summers, *The Judgment of Sense: Renaissance Naturalism and the Rise of Aesthetics* (Cambridge University Press, 1987), chapter 5.

8 Kant, *CPR*, A77/B103.

9 Kant, *Anthropology from a Pragmatic Point of View*, §10, Ak. 7:145, Dowdell trans., 30. There, he explains that the "significance" of the senses, "which belongs to them specifically in what we call the common sense of human intelligence (*sensus communis*)" is that they are subordinated to the understanding. Even intuitive, off-the-cuff judgments come not from sensation but from "real, though obscure, deliberations of the understanding." If they don't, he warns, they result in "fanaticism (*Schwärmerei*) bordering on insanity." Kant, *Anthropology from a Pragmatic Point of View*, 31.

10 Summers, *The Judgment of Sense*, 105–6; the quotation in the text, and the reference to Horace in the following sentence, are both on 105.

moral judgment of particulars. But in addition, writers in the eighteenth century expanded the Roman concept from good taste in conduct to good taste in art; and the Greek word for sensation, *aisthesis*, became the modern word "aesthetics," the science of sense and imagination as it pertains to taste and beauty.[11]

That sets the stage for Kant, whose aesthetic theory is of paramount importance to Arendt (as we already saw in Chapter 3). For Kant, aesthetic judgments presuppose a common sense (*Gemeinsinn*) that allows us to communicate our feelings to others.[12] However, he also drew an important distinction between two meanings of common sense. "This common [aesthetic] sense is essentially different from the common understanding that is sometimes also called common sense (*sensus communis*); for the latter judges not by feeling but always by concepts."[13] For Kant, judging by concepts denotes factual judgment, and so common understanding concerns matters of fact rather than matters of taste.

For Kant, then, there are two capacities that go by the ambiguous label "common sense": the common understanding, which judges particulars by subsuming them under concepts to form factual propositions, and the common sense that underwrites judgments of taste. In short: common sense about facts and a common sense of beauty. About the latter, he emphasizes that judgments of taste are made within communities of judgment – as the epigraph to this chapter puts it, they are pluralistic, not egoistic. This idea is crucial for Arendt's analysis of moral judgment, which she models on aesthetic judgment.

Kant says that common understanding, the bare ability to make factual judgments, is "the very least we are entitled to expect from anyone who lays claim to the name of human being."[14] That doesn't mean he thinks everyone is blessed with common sense in the lay meaning, however: Horse sense is well above the floor of common understanding, and it is not common.[15] To be sure, horse sense doesn't require specialized training

[11] The term "aesthetics" for what had previously gone by the name "poetics" comes from the eighteenth-century theorist Alexander Gottlieb Baumgarten, who included in his "science of sensible cognition" not only "the logic of the lower capacities of cognition" but also "the theory of the liberal arts" and "the art of thinking beautifully." Alexander Gottlieb Baumgarten, *Aesthetica* (1750), §1.

[12] Kant, Critique of Aesthetic Judgment, in *CJ*, §21, 5:238–39, Pluhar trans., 87–88.

[13] *CJ*, §20, Ak. 5:238, Pluhar trans., 87. The parenthetical Latin is in Kant's original, and he includes it to make clear that "common understanding" refers to Aristotelian common sense.

[14] *CJ*, §40, Ak. 5:293. Pluhar trans. 160.

[15] Kant, *Anthropology from a Pragmatic Point of View*, §6, Ak. 7:139, Dowdell trans. 23. "Horse sense" is Dowdell's apt translation of Kant's term for the lay meaning of common sense: *gesunder Menschenverstand* (healthy human understanding), for which Kant also uses the French *bon sens*,

(indeed, Kant warns that too much cultivation can damage it); but unlike the basic ability to use concepts, not everyone has it in full measure.

Harkening back to the Roman meaning of *sensus communis* as social tact, recall from Chapter 4 that Kant's *Anthropology* calls horse sense "logical tact." As for how it works, he explains that someone with logical tact "looks at the object from many angles and produces the correct result without being aware of the acts occurring within the mind during this process."[16] The similarity of this explanation to Kant's definition of "enlarged thinking," which we've already discussed, should be clear: Logical tact *is* the good judgment that enlarged thinking – thinking from the point of view of others – is meant to cultivate.

Kant, it seems, thinks that common sense about factual matters ranges from the barest ability to think conceptually – common understanding, possessed by all humans capable of speech – to the kind of horse sense that only those with good judgment or "logical tact" possess. And they possess it intuitively, although the intuition is not a primitive perception, but rather comes from an unconscious habit of looking at matters from multiple angles.

Elsewhere, Kant warns against invoking common sense as an "oracle" that substitutes for rational judgment. That "is but an appeal to the opinion of the multitude, of whose applause the philosopher is ashamed, while the popular charlatan (*Witzling*) glories and boasts in it."[17] This passage confirms that Kant does not equate common sense with mass opinion. Everyone can make factual judgments; not everyone has logical tact.

which has the same idiomatic meaning. Notice the difference between "common understanding" (in the Third Critique) and "*healthy* human understanding" (in the *Anthropology*). The difference, we can infer, is that only some people have the latter (not everyone's judgment is healthy), while everyone has the former. Everyone makes factual judgments of some sort or other; not everyone has healthy horse sense. Kant said similar things in the First Critique about the "natural power of judgment" or "mother-wit": Some people have it, some people don't. *CPR*, A132/B171–A134/B174.

16 *Anthropology*, §6, Ak. 7:140, Dowdell trans. 24. I have slightly altered Dowdell's translation.

17 Kant, *Prolegomena to Any Future Metaphysics*, trans. Lewis White Beck (Bobbs-Merrill, 1950), Ak. 4:258. Here, "common sense" is *gemeiner Menschenverstand*, rather than *Gemeinsinn* or *gemeiner Verstand* (*CJ*, §20) or *gesunder Menschenverstand* (*Anthropology*). In the German version of *HC*, Arendt translates "common sense" using both *Gemeinsinn* and *gesunder Menschenverstand.* I don't think she intends a rigorous distinction between them, however, because her usage isn't consistent. At one point the terms are explicitly interchangeable. Hannah Arendt, *Vita Activa oder Vom tätigen Leben* (Piper, 1967), 349 (translating *HC*, 275). At another, she uses *Gemeinsinn* for the Aristotelian meaning and *gesunder Menschenverstand* for the lay meaning. Arendt, *Vita Activa oder Vom tätigen Leben*, 284 (translating *HC*, 208–9, where "common sense" does double duty for both). The German version of *Origins* renders "common sense" as "*gesunder Menschenverstand*" throughout; in the sole occurrence of "*Gemeinsinn*," she treats it as a synonym of *gesunder Menschenverstand.* Hannah Arendt, *Elemente und Ursprünge totaler Herrschaft* (Piper, 2023), 59.

What about judgments of taste? In the Third Critique, Kant argues that because we can arrive at and communicate shared judgments about beauty, we must assume that everyone has roughly the same capacities of imagination and understanding, as well as the capacity to reflect on their interplay. That is because judgments of beauty are grounded in a harmony between the imagination and understanding, experienced as the pleasure we take in beautiful things.[18] The capacity to reflect on the interplay of imagination and understanding is analogous to Aristotelian common sense, the capacity to combine the deliverances of the senses; perhaps that is why Kant calls it *sensus communis*.[19]

But those capacities need to be trained.[20] Although Kant never says so explicitly, Arendt is convinced that Kant believes we cultivate our judgment in the company of others – in other words, that the discipline of taste and feeling cannot be a solitary activity, a conclusion I endorsed in Chapter 3.[21] Thus for Kant (or at any rate Arendt's Kant), the "common" in our common sense of beauty has a double connotation: as the shared aesthetic judgments of a community of taste, and as the common faculties of understanding and imagination that underwrite it. His argument brings the Roman and Aristotelian strands of *sensus communis* together in an explicit way, and I call this third strand of learned meaning, common sense as cultivated collective judgment grounded in shared human capacities, the *Kantian meaning* of common sense. Together, the Aristotelian, Roman, and Kantian meanings are the *learned* meanings – related to, but distinct from, the lay meaning of common sense as horse sense.

To summarize, I've just catalogued five meanings of common sense:

1. The *propagandist's meaning* – "common sense" as a propaganda label for what our side believes, opposed to the sophistries and deceptions of elites who think they know better than ordinary people. Because it

[18] *CJ*, §§20–21; 40 Ak. 5:238–39; 295. On this point, see Samuel A. Stoner, "Kant on Common-Sense and the Unity of Judgments of Taste," *Kant Yearbook* 11(1) (2019): 84–85.

[19] Samuel Stoner argues that Kant's *Gemeinsinn* must refer to this reflective capacity. Stoner, "Kant on Common-Sense and the Unity of Judgments of Taste," 89–92.

[20] *CJ*, §50, Ak. 5:319., Pluhar trans., 188.

[21] Samuel Stoner thinks Arendt got Kant wrong on this point – Kant, on his reading, remains focused on individual psychology, not social interaction. Stoner, "Kant on Common-sense and the Unity of Judgments of Taste," 95n11. I'm not convinced. Stoner is right that Kant never explicitly says that training our taste is a conversational and intersubjective activity. But Kant never rules that interpretation out, and how else could we do it? In Chapter 3 I argued that the cultivation of taste is never a solitary activity. Kant thinks we cultivate our mental powers by exposing ourselves to the humanities. *CJ*, §60, Ak. 5:355. Pluhar trans. 231. It's implausible to imagine humanities education as a solo activity.

is the diametrical opposite of what Arendt means by common sense, I will set it aside.

That leaves:

2. The *lay meaning* – common sense as horse sense.
3. The *Aristotelian meaning* – common sense as the psychological capacity that allows us to combine the sensation streams of the five special senses into a connected experience of physical objects.
4. The *Roman meaning* – common sense as social tact and emotional intelligence – and, by the eighteenth century, moral sense.
5. The *Kantian meaning* – common sense as "logical tact," good judgment cultivated in the company of others and grounded in shared human capacities.

The last three are the learned meanings. They each appear (as does the lay meaning) in the *Oxford English Dictionary*, making their first appearances in the English language between the sixteenth and eighteenth centuries.[22]

Arendt borrows the Aristotelian meaning when she writes of "our common sense which regulates and controls all our other senses";[23] she switches to the Kantian meaning when she writes that "community among men produces a common sense. The validity of common sense grows out of the intercourse with people."[24] And she invokes both meanings when she tells us that common sense is "the sixth sense which we not only all have in common but which fits us into, and thereby makes possible, a common world."[25] What they have to do with each other, and how she ties them together, remain to be seen.

## 7.3 From the Lay Meaning to the Learned

In *Origins*, Arendt is concerned almost exclusively with common sense in its lay meaning, and we have seen how she analyzes its fragility under totalitarianism's assaults on reality. But at one point, in a powerful analysis of loneliness and solitude, she switches to the Aristotelian meaning:

> Even the experience of the materially and sensually given world depends upon my being in contact with other men, upon our *common* sense which

[22] "Common sense," *The Compact Edition of the Oxford English Dictionary* (Oxford University Press, 1971), letter "c," 605.
[23] *OT*, 475–76. [24] SQMP, in *RJ*, 141. [25] "Socrates," in *PP*, 36; *HC*, 275.

> regulates and controls all other senses and without which each of us would be enclosed in his own particularity of sense data which in themselves are unreliable and treacherous. Only because we have common sense, that is only because not one man, but men in the plural inhabit the earth can we trust our immediate sensual experience.[26]

This is the only place in *Origins* where the Aristotelian meaning of "common sense" appears. But it recurs in *The Human Condition* and *The Life of the Mind.*

Let's begin by disentangling this dense paragraph, which for convenience I'll label *P1*. Start with its first sentence. In it, Arendt characterizes our common sense as one that regulates and controls all the other senses. This comes straight out of Aristotle, but in order to grasp how closely Arendt's conception follows his, we have to consider two features of Aristotelian common sense that we haven't yet examined. Not only is the common sense the faculty that *unites* the modally different sensation streams but Aristotle also calls it the controlling faculty.[27] For Aristotle, "controlling" doesn't mean it exerts an executive function over the special senses, only that it integrates the incoming sensations into a product available to the other cognitive powers. But for later writers, common sense does have a kind of executive function: The Stoics thought of it as a rational faculty, and called it the soul's "hegemon."[28] This is Kant's view as well, when he writes that the five senses are "like the common people . . . who are happily willing to subordinate themselves to their superior, the understanding, as long as they are listened to."[29] (The less said about the analogy's politics, perhaps, the better.)

Aristotle additionally argued that this common sense is what allows us to sense that we are sensing, and in that respect it is something very like self-awareness or consciousness.[30] Medieval writers elaborated this idea,

[26] *OT*, 475–76.

[27] Aristotle, *On Sleep (De Somno et Vigilia)*, ch. 1, 455a20. I use the word "faculty" rather than "sense" because Aristotle explicitly denies that this binding faculty is a sixth sense on a par with the other five. If it were, he argues, there would be an infinite regress of senses. *On the Soul (De Anima)*, bk. 3 ch. 1, 425a13–30. Arendt, on the other hand, does call the *sensus communis* a sixth sense. "Socrates," in *PP*, 36; *T*, 50, 221n62.

[28] Summers, *The Judgment of Sense*, 92.

[29] Kant:, *Anthropology*, §10, Ak. 7:145, Dowdell trans. 30–31.

[30] Or at least wakefulness – Aristotle explains that when we fall asleep the common sense switches off, and the five special senses along with it. Aristotle, *On Sleep (De Somno et Vigilia)*, ch. 1, 455a9–29. Aristotle does not accept a mind–body dualism; for Aristotle consciousness is a state of the body, as Arendt agrees. *T*, 52.

and came close to identifying common sense with the ego.[31] And for Kant, the ability to sense the interplay of our own faculties belongs to the *sensus communis*.[32] Arendt doesn't delve into these arguments, but they form the background to her claim that the common sense regulates and controls the five special senses.

Arendt says that without "our *common* sense," each of us would be enclosed in "his own particularity of sense data." The phrasing suggests that particularity means "particular to each individual"; but it must also mean "particular to each of the five senses," because she is explaining what would befall us without the Aristotelian common sense: We would be "enclosed" in a world of sounds, smells, tactile sensations, tastes, and sights that don't connect with each other. Arendt's suggestion here, signaled by using the philosophical term "sense data," is that such disconnected sense streams could not give us a world of external objects.[33]

Sense data by themselves are "unreliable and treacherous." Arendt doesn't say why, but presumably it is for two reasons. First, because each sense is fallible and the other senses can (sometimes) correct misperceptions and illusions. Aristotle's example is that when our fingers are crossed, an object passing between them feels like two objects, but our sense of sight corrects this perceptual illusion.[34] Second, the difference in mode among the sensations ensures that we don't mistakenly identify the objects of the world solely with sounds, smells, and the like. Probably Arendt accepted Aristotle's identification of the common sense with reflexive awareness that our sensations are sensations *of* something, without which they would lose their connection with external reality and remain mere sense data.[35]

31 Summers, *The Judgment of Sense*, 96. He attributes this line of argument to Avicenna and Averroes, the leading Aristotelians in the Arab world and highly influential in Europe. So does Rosenfeld, *Common Sense*, 19.

32 "First Introduction to the *Critique of Judgment*," Ak. 20:223–24, Pluwer trans. 412. Jennifer Kirchmeyer Dobe argues persuasively that in the Third Critique the *sensus communis* is the same as the power of reflective judgment. Dobe, "Kant's Common Sense and the Strategy for a Deduction," *Journal of Aesthetics and Art Criticism* 68(1) (2010): 47–60; see also Stoner, "Kant on Common-sense and the Unity of Judgments of Taste."

33 Whether Arendt accepted some version of the sense data theory, or merely borrows its terminology, is unclear. She explicitly rejects the idea that sense data can be detached from the objects of sensation, except in special cases like pain or tickling where our focus is on our own body. *HC*, 114–15. She thinks that the theory that sense data can be detached from objects "is the origin of all specifically modern philosophy," and she disowns it. *HC*, 114.

34 *De Somno et vigilia*, ch. 2, 460b20.

35 *T*, 50. On page 46, in a nod to the theory of intentionality, she writes that "no subjective act is ever without an object."

So far, so good. Arendt is restating in her own terms the Aristotelian meaning of "common sense": the faculty uniting the deliverances of the special senses and assigning the unified deliverances to objects. Cognitive scientists continue to study it today, although the words "faculty" and "common sense" have long vanished from their professional vocabulary. Although today's psychological study of perception is utterly different from Aristotle's and that of the Middle Ages and Renaissance, the leading questions remain the same: What cognitive mechanism binds sensations together and assigns them to discrete objects? What unifies these objects into a single experience? Today these questions are studied by brain scientists under the label "the binding problems." Arendt uses the classical terminology and rightly recognizes the problem's epistemological importance.

But notice that in the first sentence of *P1* she also invokes the Kantian branch of the learned meaning: Common sense comes from "my being in contact with other men." Her argument seems to be that just as the five senses correct and supplement each other to give us knowledge of the external world, other human beings correct and supplement each individual's experience, and without them individual experience would be unreliable and treacherous. She implies as much in *The Human Condition*, in a passage I label *P2*:

> [*P2*] [E]verybody sees and hears from a different position. . . . Only where things can be seen by many in a variety of aspects without changing their identity, so that those who are gathered around them know they see sameness in utter diversity, can worldly reality truly and reliably appear.[36]

And for this to be so, she thinks it is crucial that everybody's perceptual faculties are roughly the same (of course she is not denying individual variation). So, Arendt concludes, the necessary conditions for human experience of a shared external reality include common sense in *both* the Aristotelian and Kantian learned meanings: (1) a capacity that unites the deliverances of the five senses, which is (2) a capacity possessed by us all and cultivated in the company of others who see things from other vantage points. In the paragraph following *P2*, she clarifies that she is speaking specifically of the conditions of knowledge – what it takes for "worldly reality" to "truly and reliably appear" – and not endorsing the idealist thesis that human cognition in any way constitutes that reality: "[R]eality is not guaranteed by the 'common nature' of all men, but rather by the fact

[36] *HC*, 57. She makes the same point in *Thinking*, 50.

that, differences of position and the resulting variety of perspectives notwithstanding, everybody is always concerned with the same object."[37]

Of course, some animals have keener senses than ours, but only other humans can describe perceptible objects in language, and the common perceptual vocabulary we use depends on most of us possessing the same portfolio of senses with roughly similar capabilities. Without that common vocabulary, which evolves from the language game of informing other people and being informed by them, we couldn't even describe our sensations, to others or to ourselves.[38] Her crucial conclusion is that recognizing the existence of other human vantage points on the same object is a necessary condition for recognizing its status as a part of worldly reality.

This is, in fact, very close to how Kant, in the Third Critique, defines the *sensus communis* that underwrites judgment:

> [We] take *sensus communis* to mean the idea of a sense shared [by all of us], i.e., a power to judge that in reflecting takes account (a priori), in our thought, of everyone else's way of representing things, in order to . . . escape the illusion that arises from the ease of mistaking subjective and private conditions for objective ones, an illusion that would have a prejudicial influence on the judgment.[39]

Recall that viewing things from multiple standpoints is precisely what Kant elsewhere calls logical tact.

Although her remarks on these topics are few and far between, I think Arendt sketches an attractive overall picture of perceptual knowledge. "The reality of what I perceive is guaranteed by its worldly context, which includes others who perceive as I do, on the one hand, and by the working

[37] *HC*, 57–58. In her Kant lectures, Arendt quotes a letter from Kant to his friend Marcus Herz, where he writes that the mind should "view the object afresh from every side, and so to enlarge its point of view from a microscopic to a general outlook that it adopts in turn every conceivable standpoint, verifying the observations of each by means of all the others." Kant to Herz, February 21, 1772, quoted by Arendt in *Kant Lectures*, 42.

[38] As Wittgenstein has it in *Philosophical Investigations* (a book Arendt read with bemusement and perhaps admiration), there is no such thing as a private language. Ludwig Wittgenstein, *Philosophical Investigations*, trans. G. E. M. Anscombe, 3rd ed. (Pearson, 1973), §§243–71. Arendt's argument harmonizes as well with one of Wilfrid Sellars's most important philosophical discoveries: that our cautious vocabulary for registering bare sensation – "it seems red to me" rather than "it is red" – is parasitic on the vocabulary of unqualified assertion. For short, "seems" talk is parasitic on "is" talk. And that is because both are part of the intersubjective language game of giving and taking reasons. Sellars, "Empiricism and the Philosophy of Mind." Arendt's version of this argument: "Although everything that appears is perceived in the mode of it-seems-to-me, . . . appearance as such carries with it a prior indication of *realness*." *T*, 49.

[39] *CJ*, §40, Ak. 5:157–58. I slightly amend the translation by Werner S. Pluhar in the Hackett edition. Pluhar trans. 160.

together of my five senses on the other."[40] The objectivity of experience is anchored, that is, both from within and from without – from the neuropsychological mechanisms that synthesize sensations and assign them to objects ("Aristotelian" common sense), and from speech that communicates the perspectives of others, whose perceptual faculties and vocabulary we share in common, but who see things from different angles. The anchoring from without is crucial, because it introduces a social, intersubjective condition on knowing, and in this way it differs greatly from epistemology that focuses exclusively on the powers of the individual mind. We know the external world through give and take with others, and that is true even of perceptual knowledge. Hence the final sentence in *P1*: "Only because we have common sense, that is only because not one man, but men in the plural inhabit the earth can we trust our immediate sensual experience." Arendt hints at a kind of social epistemology *avant la lettre*, although she never pursues the topic.

Elsewhere, Arendt expands the idea beyond perceptual knowledge and the simple model of people gathered around a table examining it from different angles. She writes that common sense is "our mental organ for perceiving, understanding, and dealing with reality and factuality."[41] Not just perceiving, but *understanding* reality and factuality. For Arendt, the human activity crucial for securing *all* factual knowledge, perceptual or not, is the give and take of opinion, *doxa*, with others whose perspectives differ from our own but who are our equals in capacity.[42]

And, if others are absent, we do our best to take account of their positions "in our thought" (as Kant says). Kant explains that "we do this as follows: we compare our judgment not so much with the actual as rather with the merely possible judgments of others."[43] This is the key to cultivating good judgment, and it is precisely what she thought Eichmann lacked.

By no means coincidentally, the public give and take of opinions is Arendt's model of politics and freedom as well as of knowledge; and politics, like knowledge, requires a plurality of human beings who are at once equal and different.[44] She once wrote: "If philosophers ... were ever to arrive at a true political philosophy, they would have to make the plurality of man, out of which arises the whole realm of human affairs – in its grandeur and misery – the object of their *thaumazein* [wonderment]."[45] Human plurality turns out to be central to Arendt's philosophy,

40 *T*, 50. 41 *CR*, 110. 42 This is a major theme in TP and "Socrates," in *PP*.

43 *CJ*, §40, Ak. 5:237. Pluhar trans., 160. Arendt echoes Kant's distinction. SQMP, 140–41.

44 *HC*, 175–76. 45 "Socrates," in *PP*, 38.

and we should recall that in *Eichmann in Jerusalem* she calls genocide – the most radical attack on human plurality ever devised – not merely a crime against its victims but a crime against the human status itself.[46] I return to this theme in Chapter 12, where I examine Arendt's analysis of the crime of genocide.

## 7.4 Beyond Skepticism and Realism

These arguments and ideas tie the learned meanings of common sense together. They undergird some of Arendt's most passionately held convictions about love of the world (*amor mundi*): that we inhabit a world in common; that we can come to doubt it by excessive preoccupation with our own subjectivity; and that our sense of attachment to the world we hold in common demands constant care – a duty to the world that is also a duty to each other.

Our predicament is that (in Arendt's words) "factual truth is no more self-evident than opinion, and this may be among the reasons that opinion-holders find it relatively easy to discredit factual truth as just another opinion."[47] That predicament seems to raise the skeptical question of whether "facts, independent of opinion and interpretation, exist at all."[48]

Realistically, we should recognize that *no* philosophical argument is going to answer the skeptical question of whether facts, independent of opinion and interpretation, exist at all – once we grant the initial premise that factual knowledge must rest on indubitable rather than fallible foundations to count as knowledge. As Arendt recognized, "for this trouble there is no remedy."[49] So she does not even try. She offers, "as an excuse for not pursuing this issue any further," an anecdote about Clemenceau, who when asked how future historians will settle the controversy over who started World War I, replied: "That I don't know. But I know for certain that they will not say Belgium invaded Germany."[50]

Her example is a poor one: When it comes to wars – and culture wars, and infowars – shameless denialism is the rule, not the exception. In February 2025, US President Donald Trump said publicly that Ukraine started the war with Russia. Empirical studies of conspiracy

[46] *EJ*, 268–69; also 279. [47] TP, 243. [48] TP, 238.

[49] TP, 257. For a searching examination of why skepticism follows from the premise that knowledge requires indubitable foundations, see Michael Williams, *Groundless Belief: An Essay on the Possibility of Epistemology*, 2nd ed. (Princeton University Press, 1999).

[50] TP, 239.

theories confirm that anyone can say anything, no matter how preposterous, and count on 15 percent of the public to accept it once it is disseminated by popular but epistemically malevolent influencers.

In fact, though, Arendt's project was never to refute the philosophical skeptic or the relativist about facts, but rather to question their questions. The skeptic starts with subjective experiences, Humean impressions and ideas, and asks how we get from them to objective knowledge – from appearance to reality. The skeptic says we can't. Arendt, like Hume's adversary Thomas Reid, starts at the opposite end, taking for granted "the capacity of human senses for an adequate experience of the world,"[51] which to Reid (and, later, G. E. Moore) is more certain than any argument that denies it.[52] Her question is how we came to lose confidence in common sense and find it less reliable than our subjective experiences.

In the long final chapter of *The Human Condition*, she attributes the loss of confidence to the scientific revolution, which teaches us that the manifest image of the world is far different from its underlying reality. In the manifest image, the Sun goes around the Earth; in the scientific image, the Earth goes around the Sun (and both are perturbations of an immaterial quantum flux).[53] Arendt argues that this realization pushes us toward the "nightmares" of Cartesian doubt – not because Cartesian philosophy was so influential, but because Descartes drew out the skeptical implications of the great divide between the manifest and scientific images.[54] I won't pursue her interpretation of Descartes. Here, I simply register that Arendt's project is not refuting skepticism. Rather, it is diagnosing its causes, and demonstrating the political consequences of "the specifically modern suspicion toward man's truth-receiving capacities" – namely, "the feeling of suspicion, outrage, and despair" that drives multitudes of people to what we today call the "post-truth" world.[55]

Oddly enough, changing the subject in this way places her in the vicinity of the later Wittgenstein, who called philosophical perplexities sicknesses of the understanding, and who famously wrote that his aim in

[51] *HC*, 114.

[52] Thomas Reid, *An Inquiry into the Human Mind on the Principles of Common Sense*, in Thomas Reid, *Inquiry and Essays*, ed. Ronald E. Beanblossom and Keith Lehrer (Hackett, 1983), 52–55, 84–87; G. E. Moore, "A Defence of Common Sense" and "A Proof of the External World," in *Philosophical Papers* (Macmillan, 1959).

[53] I borrow the "manifest image" and "scientific image" terminology from Wilfrid Sellars, "Philosophy and the Scientific Image of Man," in *Science, Perception and Reality* (Routledge & Kegan Paul, 1963), 25–26.

[54] *HC*, 277.

[55] *HC*, 297–98, 267.

philosophy is to show the fly the way out of the fly bottle.[56] Among the last things Wittgenstein wrote were reflections on Moore's defense of common sense, and how to escape the philosophical fly bottle into which both philosophical skepticism and philosophical anti-skepticism lead.[57]

As for Arendt: "I have clearly joined the ranks of those who for some time now have been attempting to dismantle metaphysics, and philosophy with all its categories, as we have known them from their beginning in Greece until today."[58] Arendt's style of thought and expression is worlds apart from Wittgenstein's, but in their own way both belong to the genre of twentieth-century anti-philosophy. Wittgenstein's hope in writing *Philosophical Investigations* was, "in the darkness of this time, to bring light into one brain or another" – a line that surely must have resonated with the author of *Men in Dark Times*, who wrote that "even in the darkest of times we have the right to expect some illumination."[59]

[56] Wittgenstein, *Philosophical Investigations*, §309 (fly bottle). Diseases of the mind: "The philosopher is the man who has to cure himself of many sicknesses of the understanding. . . . If in the midst of life we are in death, so in sanity we are surrounded by madness." *Remarks on the Foundations of Mathematics*, eds. G. H. von Wright, Rush Rhees, and G. E. M. Anscombe, trans. G. E. M. Anscombe, 2nd ed. (MIT Press, 1967), §53, 157.

[57] Wittgenstein's final notes on the subject were composed two days before his death. They were collected and published posthumously as *On Certainty*.

[58] *T*, 212. [59] *Philosophical Investigations*, Preface, viii; *MDT*, 8.

PART IV

# *Arendt before Jerusalem: Ethics in* The Human Condition

CHAPTER 8

# *The Curious Case of the Missing Morality*

## 8.1 Missing Morality

As I noted in the Introduction, before the Eichmann trial Arendt showed little interest in moral philosophy. Reflecting years later, she explained that she grew up in a generation that took basic standards of decency for granted; in her youth, she regarded anyone carping about virtue and character as a Philistine. "We were brought up under the assumption: *Das Moralische versteht sich von selbst,* moral conduct is a matter of course."[1]

She didn't mean that her generation thought people behave decently as a matter of course – the children of the Weimar Republic were hardly so innocent. She meant that her generation took for granted that even wrongdoers know right from wrong.[2] A more literal translation of her German phrase is "what's moral is obvious (or self-evident)." In other words, she and her peers took for granted that bad conduct results, not from moral confusion, but rather from personal weakness or wicked motives of a perfectly comprehensible kind – nothing like the banality of evil that flabbergasted her in Jerusalem. "We had no idea how serious such things were and least of all where they could lead. We did not know much about the nature of these phenomena, and I am afraid we cared even less."[3]

All that changed when Hitler took power and respectable German society swiftly and smoothly embraced a New German Order that turned decency upside down. This must have been shattering; her writing about this period is bitter with a sense of betrayal. Today, "no one in his right mind can any longer claim that moral conduct is a matter of course."[4] She adds that postwar Germany's equally swift and frictionless transition back

[1] PRUD, 22. [2] SQMP, 62. [3] SQMP, 62.

[4] SQMP, 61. Both here and in the previous quotation, she says moral conduct, but she must mean moral standards. Moral conduct has obviously never been a matter of course, and her argument is about the shifting standards of respectability.

to decency is hardly more reassuring. If ordinary Germans could slide from "normality" (Arendt uses scare quotes) to Hitler's criminal morality and then "back again at a moment's notice," how can we take anything about morality for granted?[5]

All this was clear from 1933 on. Why, then, did it take her so long to think and write about moral judgment?[6] The easy answer is that she was preoccupied with other issues: totalitarianism, Marxism in relation to the Western political tradition, and the conformism and consumerism of mass society. These were the topics of her book projects of the 1950s, and they overshadowed the unanswered questions of moral theory. It was only when the Eichmann case rubbed her nose in it that she began serious reflection on what the moral collapse of Europe in the 1930s and 1940s teaches about the nature of moral judgment.

For that matter, she never lost her youthful distaste for preachiness, including the preachiness of moral philosophers. She regarded moralizing as an evasion of reality – and thus an unwitting and very serious threat to politics and to moral judgment. Evidently Arendt thought that moral philosophy is too close to moralizing philosophy.

As often with Arendt, biographical facts tell only half the story, though. It is not simply her immersion in other matters, or her aversion to moralizing, that explains why it took so long for her to reflect on a moral collapse that was already apparent to her in the 1930s. More important than her own story is her own theory.

Before the Eichmann trial, her major theoretical work was *The Human Condition*, published in 1958. It sets out the closest we find in Arendt's writing to a systematic theory of action – a full-blown critique, in Kant's sense of "an examination of its sources and limits," aiming "to clarify our reason, and keep it free from errors."[7] Arendt's topic is not reason, though, but rather our active life, which she labels *vita activa*. Or, in Arendt's terse formulation of her project, "to think what we are doing."[8] The book employs a large conceptual vocabulary that is bread and butter to students of her thought: labor, work, and action, worldliness and plurality, the political and the social, natality and mortality, the web of relationships and the space of appearance. Curiously, though, morality and "the moral" are

[5] SQMP, 54. In fact, the transition back was neither as swift nor as frictionless as Arendt's comment suggests, as she undoubtedly recognized. I don't think her overstatement weakens her point about morality, though.

[6] Actually, a germ of her later work on judgment appears in a manuscript from the 1950s, published posthumously. Arendt, "Introduction *into* Politics," in *PP*, 102–4. But it is brief and undeveloped.

[7] Kant, *Critique of Pure Reason*, trans. Kemp Smith, 59, A11. [8] HC, 5.

not in the working vocabulary of *The Human Condition*. *The Human Condition* recognizes only two authentic moral precepts, the "readiness to forgive and to be forgiven, to make promises and to keep them."[9] These, she explains, are the only moral precepts internal to the concept of action, because they make action possible. All else is merely *mores*, customary standards that change over time.[10] The precepts of forgiving and promise-keeping are, to say the least, a remarkably minimalist moral code. The richer tapestry of morality is nowhere to be found in her theory of action.

In this chapter and Chapter 9, I offer a reading of *The Human Condition* that explains why Arendt ignored morality in her theory of action – what I call "the Case of the Missing Morality." For now, a summary preview will do. In *The Human Condition* Arendt was working through one of the largest of philosophical questions: What makes human life meaningful? Her answer is human action, which in her vocabulary means beginning something new and noteworthy. She didn't believe in an ontology of extra-human moral facts, and she regarded man-made customs and *mores* as fetters on action – essential, no doubt, for everyday living, but antagonistic to action and untrustworthy in times of crisis when political action becomes all-important. She wrote in her Thought Diary that moral rules "in principle come from outside [of action], they can always only restrict, never prescribe, and action will break through and overcome them again and again."[11] Hence her neglect of morality, which threatens to handcuff action and drain life of the meaning action provides. More than that, a morality of constraints – of "do nots" – may keep us from entering the fray against evil. Promise-keeping and forgiving are different: They are enablers of action. The detailed analysis of her argument is the business of this chapter and Chapter 9, and so is my assessment of its strengths and weaknesses; there are plenty of both.

Another entry in her Thought Diary (part of which I quoted in the Introduction) is even more drastic: "Hence the ghostly lifelessness of all morality and all moral thought. Only when life has been killed does morality emerge. But then, in the catastrophe of the heart's devastation and desolation, there is no way out but duty and morality."[12] This may sound like Nietzschean bombast against morality, but Arendt makes clear that she by no means prefers the alternative. "As long as the desert rules, morality is right, and woe unto us if it no longer rules either. The unruled

[9] HC, 245–46. I discuss these in §8.7.
[10] HC, 245.
[11] *DTB*, XXI.83 (January 1956), 557–58.
[12] *DTB*, II.31 (January 1951), 54.

desert is a greater horror than the ruled one."[13] This diary entry exhibits an intense ambivalence about morality. Recall from Chapter 6 that she was horrified by the Lost Generation intellectuals who toyed with immoralism and became front men and useful idiots for political murderers.[14]

Undoubtedly the most jarring aspect of *The Human Condition*'s moral lacuna is that on one reading, Arendt embraces a kind of amoralism about action – notwithstanding her horror at the unruled desert. The book emphasizes the primacy ancient Greek thought gives to the life of action, and Arendt agrees with the Greeks on that crucial point. What, then, are we to conclude when she writes the following?

> Unlike human behavior – which the Greeks, like all civilized people, judged according to "moral standards," taking into account motives and intentions on the one hand and aims and consequences on the other – action can be judged only by the criterion of greatness.[15]

Greatness, she makes clear, can include great evil as well as great good – or neither. The scare quotes around "moral standards" signal skeptical distance, and relegating moral standards to the judgment of "behavior" limits morality's scope. That's because in Arendt's vocabulary "behavior" represents only routine, scripted conduct, while "action" refers to noteworthy and novel deeds.[16] For Arendt, as for Aristotle, the paradigm of action is participation in public life, but as we will see, her category is broader, and includes nonpolitical actions as well. Taking the quoted language at face value would exempt all these actions from judgment by moral standards, motives, or consequences.

Arendt's writing is replete with moral judgments, and there is nothing revisionary in her moral sensibilities. ("*Good* doesn't develop into *bad*, and *bad* doesn't develop into *good*. There I would be *adamant*."[17]) What is lacking is a place for them within *The Human Condition*'s theory.[18]

## 8.2 Morality and the Human Condition

It's important to understand how peculiar *The Human Condition*'s neglect of moral phenomena is. It's as though Arendt chose to ignore a central fact

[13] *DTB*, II.31 (January 1951), 54.

[14] See especially her discussion of the "alliance between the mob and the elite" in *OT*, 337.

[15] *HC*, 205.

[16] See §9.7, on the category of behavior.

[17] "Hannah Arendt on Hannah Arendt," in *TWB*, 464.

[18] In one of the first, and still among the best, book-length studies of Arendt, George Kateb also emphasized the amorality of Arendt's theory of political action and criticized her for it. Kateb feared a slide from amorality to immorality. *Hannah Arendt: Politics, Conscience, Evil* (Rowman & Allanheld, 1983), 33–42.

of the human condition, namely that we feel and think morally and pass moral judgments – not incessantly (that would be awful!), but when circumstances demand. We deliberate about right and wrong, good and bad; and we praise or blame other people in moral terms.

More importantly, we respond to people with moral emotions: resentment, indignation, approbation, gratitude. These *reactive attitudes* toward other people's conduct are moralized through and through. They are surely part of the human condition, intimately tied to human plurality and freedom.[19] We admire kindness and courage, and we condemn cheating and treachery. We condemn people who are cruel to those who love them, we despise naked opportunism, we resent arrogance and laugh at pomposity, we feel shocked and outraged when a friend betrays us.

And we look in the mirror. We feel ashamed of our own faults and flaws, at least when we're able to recognize them. Indeed, it is hard to imagine what recognizing one's own flaws would consist in other than feeling ashamed of them – a point considered earlier, in Chapter 5. Having the capacity to deploy the reactive attitudes toward ourselves is the precondition of conscience.

We moralize in more complex ways as well. We disapprove, for example, of overly self-righteous moral critics even when they are right – a second-order reactive attitude, that is, a reactive attitude toward the reactive attitudes of others. For that matter, we disdain hypocritical critics of overly self-righteous moralizers (e.g., political propagandists who for basely partisan reasons mock the moralizing of "social justice warriors").[20] That's a third-order reactive attitude.

Moral judgments like these, both the simple and the subtle, seem universal and timeless, which is far from what Arendt calls them: "[S]tandards of behavior solidified through tradition and valid on the ground of agreements, both of which change with time."[21] It is not mere social convention that we feel hurt and anger toward treacherous friends. To picture someone wholly lacking such reactive attitudes is to picture someone who is not a human being. The objects of the reactive attitudes

[19] The phrase "reactive attitudes" comes from P. F Strawson's "Freedom and Resentment," *Proceedings of the British Academy*, 48 (1962): 187–211. Strawson argues that when we react emotionally to other people's conduct, we are treating them as responsible agents, not automata, which is a practical if not theoretical commitment to freedom over determinism.

[20] Annette Baier offers a wonderfully acute discussion of these higher-order "postures of the mind" in "Theory and Reflective Practices," in *Postures of the Mind* (University of Minnesota Press, 1985), 207–27.

[21] *HC*, 245.

may shift over time, but the attitudes themselves, and their importance to the human condition, do not.

In some contexts, Arendt understood this perfectly well. When Eric Voegelin complained that in her analysis of totalitarianism she permitted her moral abhorrence to "overshadow the essential," Arendt responded briskly:

> Let us suppose . . . the historian is confronted with excessive poverty in a time of great wealth. . .. The natural human reaction to such conditions is one of anger and indignation because these conditions are against the dignity of man. If I described these conditions without permitting my indignation to interfere, I have lifted this particular phenomenon out of its context in human society and have thereby robbed it of part of its nature, deprived it of one of its important inherent qualities.[22]

In other words, a description that leaches out the reactive attitudes (the "natural human reaction") is a *false* description. Seemingly, *The Human Condition* forgets this insight.

Why, then, does "the moral" remain so peripheral to *The Human Condition*'s treatment of human activity? And how damaging is the omission? Before taking up these questions, however, some scaffolding is necessary. Some readers of this book may be unfamiliar with *The Human Condition*, while others know it well. The remainder of this chapter will introduce its leading ideas. They provide necessary background and vocabulary.

## 8.3 Reading *The Human Condition*

First, a few remarks about the rewards and challenges the book poses to its readers. *The Human Condition* does not fall into any familiar philosophical genre or school of thought. It analyzes the active life – the *vita activa* – as distinct from the life of the mind (the topic of her final, unfinished, book project) – but it is worlds away from analytic philosophy of action, and its idiom is remote from analytic philosophy more generally. It is not exactly "Continental" philosophy either. Although Heidegger influences the book, his name appears nowhere in it.[23] Neither will readers find other mainstays

[22] Arendt, "A Reply to Eric Voegelin," in *EU*, 403.

[23] Arendt herself wrote to Heidegger that the book "owes practically everything to you in every respect," which makes the absence even more striking. Arendt to Heidegger, October 28, 1960, in Hannah Arendt and Martin Heidegger, *Letters: 1925–1975 between Hannah Arendt and Martin Heidegger*, ed. Ursula Ludz, trans. Andrew Shields (Harcourt, 1998), 124.

of Continental philosophy in the index – no Husserl or Sartre, no Gadamer or de Beauvoir or Levinas or Cassirer or Schmitt. Kierkegaard, Hegel, and Nietzsche make only cameo appearances. Marx is Arendt's sparring partner in some of the book, but she ignores latter-day Marxists. Even her mentor, Karl Jaspers, appears only in incidental footnotes.

The writing is nontechnical – reading *The Human Condition* is not like reading Kant or Hegel or Heidegger. Moses Mendelssohn famously complained to Kant that the *Critique of Pure Reason* is a "nerve-juice consuming book." He added pathetically, "I am not entirely without hope that I shall still be able to think my way through it in this life."[24] *The Human Condition* is not a nerve-juice consuming book. But the argument is winding rather than straightforward. It spans a dizzying variety of topics: eternity and immortality, the justification of property and ownership, the nature of exchange markets, the quarrel between the ancients and the moderns, the fallacies of traditional political philosophy, the rise of consumerism and conformism in mass society, the distinction between power and violence, the critique of Marx, Cartesian doubt, the significance of the scientific revolution, and warnings about technology in an atomic age. The breadth of insight is one of the book's rewards; connecting its threads poses a challenge.

A second challenge is this. *The Human Condition* is full of reminders of lost traditions, and Arendt looks attentively, even obsessively, at etymologies and quotations from past thinkers. A special difficulty arises from this continuous engagement with the past, namely figuring out when she is explicating and when she is endorsing. In logician's terms: When is she writing *de dicto*, paraphrasing or explicating the speech of others, and when is she writing *de re*, speaking in her own voice about the things themselves?

The sentence quoted earlier about the Greek view of action illustrates the problem. It asserts that action, unlike behavior, can be judged only by its greatness, not by moral standards. Is this a Greek view being reported, or a Greek view being endorsed? Arendt does not make that clear, but obviously her own stance toward the scope of moral standards turns on it. Superficially, *The Human Condition* extols what Arendt takes to be the Greek conception of politics and action, so much so that critics accused her of "Hellenic nostalgia" and "polis envy."[25] But she emphasizes that the

[24] Letter from Moses Mendelssohn to Kant, April 10, 1783, in *Correspondence (The Cambridge Edition of the Works of Immanuel Kant)*, ed. Arnulf Zweig (Cambridge University Press, 1999), 190–91, Ak. 10:307–8.

[25] Noel O'Sullivan, "Hannah Arendt: Hellenic Nostalgia and Industrial Society," in *Contemporary Political Philosophers*, eds. Anthony de Crespigny and Kenneth Minogue (Dodd-Mead, 1975), 228–51. "Polis envy" was apparently Jean Bethke Elshtain's coinage, see Joanna Vecchiarelli Scott

"agonal spirit" in the Greek concept of action led to the collapse of the polis; and in several places she contrasts Greek ideas about law and politics unfavorably with more familiar Roman notions.[26] A searching interpretation by Roy Tsao concludes that in reality Arendt was a critic, not an advocate, of the Greek conception of politics.[27] (More about this in Chapter 9, where I endorse Tsao's interpretation.)

Near the end of her life, Arendt cautioned readers that she is *not* trying to revive a past tradition. On the contrary, she assumes "that the thread of tradition is broken and that we shall not be able to renew it. . . . What you then are left with is still the past, but a *fragmented* past, which has lost its certainty of evaluation." She quotes Ariel's song from *The Tempest*, about the sea change that transforms sunken bones into coral. "It is with such fragments from the past, after their sea-change, that I have dealt here."[28] In other words, the past she cites in her writing is neither a living past nor even the skeletal remains of a dead past. It is a past transmuted. If this is Arendt's approach in *The Human Condition*, as it is in her final works, we are warned against assuming any simple endorsements of *de dicto* utterances – or even assuming that her paraphrases and inferences would be recognizable by those who penned the dicta.

A final challenge to the reader can't be ignored. Philosophers typically set out their views with supporting arguments, then consider objections and present their responses. That is not Arendt's way. The argument of *The Human Condition* proceeds from insight to insight rather than from premises to conclusions; and Arendt offers her insights without raising and answering objections, or rebutting alternative explanations of her observations. Readers who come to *The Human Condition* from a background in

and Judith Chelius Stark's interpretive essay "Introduction: 'New Beginnings'," in Hannah Arendt, *Love and Saint Augustine*, ed. Joanna Vecchiarelli Scott and Judith Chelius Stark, trans. E. G. Ashton. (University of Chicago Press, 1995), 174.

26 Agonal spirit: *HC*, 41, 194; the "swift decline of the city-state," *HC*, 197. Greece and Rome: *HC*, 59, 63n62, 195. She was even more explicit in her posthumously-published essay on Socrates, written before she composed *The Human Condition*: the agonal spirit "eventually was to bring the Greek city-states to ruin because it made alliances between them well-nigh impossible and poisoned the domestic life of the citizens with envy and mutual hatred (envy was the national vice of ancient Greece)." "Socrates," in *PP*, 16. Margaret Canovan finds other negative statements about the classical Greeks in Arendt's unpublished manuscripts. Canovan, *Hannah Arendt: A Reinterpretation of Her Political Thought* (Cambridge University Press, 1992), 100–1, 135–43.

27 Roy T. Tsao, "Arendt against Athens: Rereading *The Human Condition*," *Political Theory* 30 (2002): 97–123. Tsao argues, among other things, that the "amoralist" view in the sentence under discussion cannot represent Arendt's own view, because it is inconsistent with her theory of action. Tsao, "Arendt against Athens," 113.

28 *T*, 212.

academic philosophy may lose patience with what seems like dogmatism and a lack of rigor.

The book calls for a more sympathetic way of reading. As I hope to show in this chapter and Chapter 9, there is an important ethical through-line knitting together several core chapters of the book: They are an inquiry into how different forms of activity give meaning to human life. Though Arendt's approach is highly original, and takes many detours, the inquiry itself is a traditional one, no different from Aristotle's question in book 1 of the *Nicomachaean Ethics* about what constitutes the highest human good. The reconstruction offered here of Arendt's core argument helps unravel the Case of the Missing Morality, and it helps understand Arendt's post-*Eichmann* turn to moral judgment. And, as a collateral benefit, the reconstruction touches in unexpected ways on themes of perennial interest to philosophers in all traditions, which I highlight as we proceed.

## 8.4 The Human Condition and Human Conditions

I start with the book's title. What does Arendt mean by "the human condition"? The straightforward paraphrase would be "the condition humans find ourselves in," in parallel with, for example, "Hannah's condition." But "Hannah's condition" can refer either to Hannah's internal state (Hannah has a heart condition) or to an external circumstance that affects Hannah's prospects (Hannah is a refugee). In everyday speech the former, internal, sense is common – think of expressions like "the athlete was in top condition," meaning top physical shape. Taken in this internal sense, "the human condition" might refer to human nature; but Arendt takes pains to distinguish them.[29] In her usage "the human condition" means the set of enduring circumstances that condition human life and activity, not human nature or internal conditions.[30] In *Thinking*, she summarizes the title-theme of *The Human Condition*: human beings are "totally conditioned existentially – limited by the time span between birth and death, subject to labor in order to live, motivated to work in order to make themselves at home in the world, and roused to action in order to find their place in the society of their fellow-men."[31]

29 *HC*, 9–11.

30 In one place, however, she employs the former, internal, sense: "the human condition consists in a man's being a conditioned being." *HC*, 147. This comes close to a play on words: "the human condition [= state-description of human beings] is to be conditioned by human conditions [= enduring circumstances in which human beings find themselves]."

31 *T*, 70.

Arendt divides the *vita activa* into three main categories of activity, which she labels labor, work, and action. Roughly, labor consists of the provision of life's necessities, the biological preconditions of living and reproducing. Work is the manufacture of more durable goods. These accumulate over time to produce the artificial environment in which we live (what we might, in a metaphorical nod to St. Augustine, call "the City of Man" – referring, however, not to the civic community but to its man-made physical infrastructure, its waterworks, power grid, housing stock, snowplows; its kitchenware and furniture and artworks; today, its internet and the "internet of things"). Action consists of the significant things we do and say in each other's company – the dramas we enact on the stage set by the physical City of Man.

Each of these three components of the *vita activa* derives from one of the human conditions. Thus, Arendt writes:

> The human condition of labor is life itself.
>
> The human condition of work is worldliness.[32]

And action derives from the human condition of plurality, that is, being one individual living among others of the same kind who all differ from each other. Let's consider these three conditions and forms of activity in order.

"The human condition of labor is life itself" means that labor is necessary to sustain life. Being alive and embodied is the condition that makes labor necessary, for labor makes life possible. "The human condition of work is worldliness" is a parallel construction, to be understood the same way: Worldliness makes work necessary, for work makes worldliness possible.

This latter formula requires some unpacking, because of the unorthodox meaning of "worldliness." The word does not carry its everyday meaning of being wise to the ways of the world; rather, it means belonging to the world. In this context Arendt's usage "world" is a term of art. It refers neither to the social world nor to the external world in its entirety, but specifically to "the man-made home erected on earth," consisting of "things that are used."[33]

[32] *HC*, 7.

[33] *HC*, 134. She evidently takes the word from Heidegger, for her usage is very close to the meaning of "worldhood" introduced in section 18 of *Being and Time*. There Heidegger analyzes "the worldhood of the world" through our relationship with equipment with which we engage. For a close and helpful exegesis, see Robert B. Brandom's "Heidegger's Categories in *Sein und Zeit*," in *Tales of the Mighty Dead: Historical Essays in the Metaphysics of Intentionality* (Harvard University Press, 2002), especially 301–9. Some scholars disagree. Seyla Benhabib examines Heidegger's influence on Arendt's concept of worldhood in *The Reluctant Modernism of Hannah Arendt*, 51–56. Unlike me, Benhabib does not connect worldhood with the Heideggerian analysis of equipment, but rather with human plurality and Heidegger's concept of being-with-others (*Mitsein*). I believe Arendt is thinking of equipment, which is plainly Heidegger's emphasis in ¶

These use objects are, furthermore, related to each other within a system: Twice she tells us that "a heap of unrelated articles" is "a non-world."[34] To illustrate what Arendt has in mind: We build cities that need supplies trucked in; we build highways for the trucks to drive on; we build trucks to drive the highways and supply the cities. Artifacts come in symbiotic sets: No one would make plugs without sockets, and no one would make sockets without plugs. A *world* is a humanly constructed physical and cultural environment, viewed holistically as a system of artifacts with interrelated uses (more accurately: a system of subsystems of artifacts with interrelated uses). It conditions our activities, not only because the City of Man opens new possibilities and forecloses others, but also because it needs to be maintained. Without ceaseless upkeep of the highways and railways, the supply system would fail and city-dwellers would quickly perish. It takes work and labor to maintain the human artifice.[35]

Thus, the claim that "the human condition of work is worldliness" means that constructing a physical home takes work. Worldliness, in the sense of being born into a common world of artifacts and the forms of life they support, is the condition that makes work necessary. Work is precisely the activity of making and maintaining those artifacts.

Finally, the human condition of plurality makes action necessary. For present purposes, we may think of Arendt's paradigm case of action: political speech to persuade one's fellows to join together in a shared enterprise. If we were all identical, recruiting others to my point of view would be unnecessary, for we would all see things the same way.[36] Human

18, and not *Mitsein.* Otherwise, why would Arendt say that worldhood is the human condition of work rather than of action? Action, not work, is the activity she associates with plurality. As further confirmation, she titles one section of *The Human Condition* "The Thing-Character of the World," and explains that "[w]hat consumer goods are for the life of man, use objects are for his world." *HC*, 94. For the same reason, I disagree with George Kateb, who believes that Arendt "uses *world* to mean both a culture (a polis, for example) . . . and more narrowly, the course of political action in the public realm." Kateb, *Hannah Arendt: Politics, Conscience, Evil*, 2. Like Benhabib, Kateb connects "world" and "worldliness" with action, whereas in *HC* Arendt uses the words in connection with work, and specifically with *things.* Admittedly, Arendt is not consistent in her use of "world." In a key passage in *OT*, 458, she clearly uses the word to describe the social and cultural world, just as Benhabib and Kateb suggest. In other places, for example when she speaks of "world alienation" or "love of the world," the word has a more intuitive meaning. But in *HC*, she uses it in the specialized sense described here – a humanly constructed physical environment viewed holistically as symbiotically connected sets of artifacts.

34 *HC*, 9; again at 204. 35 See *HC*, 100.

36 *HC*, 175–76. This argument might be questioned. We can have identical priorities but competing interests. Kant's wry example is a pledge Francis I supposedly made to Emperor Charles V: "What my brother Charles would have . . . that I would also have." They both wanted Milan. *Critique of*

difference makes persuasion necessary, just as human commonality across those differences makes persuasion possible. It is in that way that plurality – with its "twofold character of equality and distinction" – is the human condition of action.[37]

Arendt distinguishes plurality from *otherness*, the ontological individuation of all entities, and *distinctness*, the biological individuation of living beings. "In man, otherness, which he shares with everything that is, and distinctness, which he shares with everything alive, becomes uniqueness, and human plurality is the paradoxical plurality of unique beings"[38] – paradoxical, because it combines equality and difference. Arendt's pluralism runs deep, and it is one of the defining commitments of her philosophy; she describes plurality as "the simultaneous presence of innumerable perspectives and aspects in which the common world presents itself and for which no common measurement or denominator can ever be devised."[39] She adds: "Being seen and being heard by others derive their significance from the fact that everybody sees and hears from a different position. This is the meaning of public life." Conversely, the "unitedness of many into one is basically antipolitical."[40] For that reason she is an adversary of Rousseau's "general will" and of the premises underlying contemporary communitarianism.

Let me summarize. The human condition is, first of all, to exist under the three component conditions that make the three corresponding activity-types necessary. To be alive, in a durable physical environment, among people who are essentially different from (but equal to) one another, makes labor, work, and action necessary. These activities, in turn, transform the world: "men constantly create their own self-made conditions."[41] The latter are contingent, path-dependent, ever-changing specifications of the three fundamental conditions of life, worldliness, and plurality.

## 8.5 The Components of the Active Life

Arendt's distinction between labor and work bears comment, because in everyday life we use the words interchangeably. The laborer leaving home for the day announces, "I'm off to work," and Bruce Springsteen's pick-and-shovel man, desperate for a job, sings, "Stand back, son, and let a man work."[42] Arendt concedes that her distinction is "unusual," and that even

*Practical Reason*, Ak. 5:28; in Kant, *Practical Philosophy (The Cambridge Edition of the Works of Immanuel Kant)*, ed. and trans. Mary J. Gregor (Cambridge University Press, 1996), 161.

37 *HC*, 175. 38 *HC*, 176. 39 *HC*, 57. 40 *HC*, 214. 41 *HC*, 9.

42 Bruce Springsteen, "Shackled and Drawn," a song in the album *Wrecking Ball* (2012).

in antiquity writers overlooked it.[43] For Arendt, though, the labor/work distinction, encoded in many European languages besides English, is fundamental.[44] Labor produces goods for immediate consumption, necessities of the life process; work produces the durable human environment. Labor is ceaseless but evanescent; work produces things built to last. Labor is painful; work is satisfying.

The distinction is nowhere near as crisp as Arendt makes it sound. Borderline cases and problem cases are easy to find; actually, they are everywhere, given that even durable things wear out and have to be replaced, just like the consumption items labor produces.[45] But for the moment let's accept Arendt's distinction and treat it as a potentially useful regimentation of ordinary language.

None of the three categories (labor, work, action) receives a precise definition, and as her argument unfolds, Arendt doesn't give them univocal, stable meanings. Consider the category of labor. In its most basic Arendtian meaning, labor is the onerous activity that produces the biological minimum we need to stay alive – paradigmatically, the food we eat.[46] (In the biblical language that Arendt had in mind, "by the sweat of your brow you will eat.") It is strenuous, ceaseless, exhausting, repetitive, and often painful, and it distracts us from what we still tend to call "higher" pursuits. In short, labor is hard labor. But Arendt introduces another ordinary language referent of the word when she includes the labor of childbirth in her category.[47] Obviously, these meanings are related; it is not a coincidence that our language labels birth pangs "labor." Both are bodily, arduous, and necessary to the perpetuation of human life. But the similarities end there, and the dissimilarities are obvious.

Elsewhere, she emphasizes that labor, unlike work, is done to make a living, not to make an object.[48] In this sense, even the manufacture of durable goods on a Chaplinesque assembly line counts as labor, even though it might count as work if an artisan handcrafted the same objects. The assembly line is a site of labor rather than work because the laborers

43 *HC*, 79–80.

44 *HC*, 48n39, 80n3. Her examples (corresponding to the English "labor" and "work"): *ponein/ergazesthai* (ancient Greek); *laborare/faciri* or *fabricari* (Latin); *arbeiten/werken* (German); *travailler/ouvrer* (French). She might have added *lavoro/operare* (Italian), *trabajar/obrar* or *operar* (Spanish), and *truda/rabota* (Russian).

45 Arendt knows this: *HC*, 138. Her rejoinder – that destruction is "incidental to use [of durable objects] but inherent in consumption" – is unsatisfactory. Destruction is inherent in the consumption of food but not clothing, gasoline but not automobiles. Even so, clothing and automobiles inevitably wear out through use.

46 *HC*, 83. 47 *HC*, 115; also *HC*, 30, 121. 48 *HC*, 46, 83.

are engaged in repetitive activity done out of the necessity of making a living rather than of making a widget. Generalizing further: any job undertaken principally to make a living, as distinct from caring about the task, is labor and not work.[49] Here, her distinction seems to lie in the actor's intention, not in the nature of the product.

In yet another usage, Arendt classifies the taste for endless consumption of throwaway items in contemporary culture as a reflection of the laboring mentality.[50] The similarity lies in the disdain for durability, manifested in consumerism's endless and careless cycle of consume-discard-replace-consume again. Notably, though, this usage detaches labor from biological necessity and associates it with an ideal of boundless abundance. Where Marx famously argued that once laborers are released from necessity they are freed for higher pursuits, Arendt rejoins: "A hundred years after Marx we know the fallacy of this reasoning; the spare time of the *animal laborans* is never spent in anything but consumption, and the more time left to him, the greedier and more craving his appetites." She adds: "That these appetites become more sophisticated, so that consumption is no longer restricted to the necessities but, on the contrary, mainly concentrates on the superfluities of life, does not change the character of this society."[51]

Each of these equivalences picks out one or two salient characteristics that the paradigm case of hard bodily labor in the field or the household shares with something else. But there may be no shared salient characteristics among the various something-elses. The life of idle consumption in a throwaway culture has nothing in common with childbirth. The multiple items Arendt packs into the category of labor bear family resemblances to each other, with no single shared characteristic that can be abstracted into a concept.

Obviously, Arendt knows this. When she lumps categorically different activities together under the heading "labor," she is making a substantive claim, not an analytic classification. To call the life of consumption "labor" and the consumer a laboring animal are normative conclusions, not mere observations. In this example, the unifying point is that labor concerns fleeting and subjective pleasures and pains, while the emphasis in work is on the objects it produces. She warns that conflating work and labor misses an essential distinction between outer and inner, a focus on the external world we create and share versus the subjective focus on pleasure and pain that she diagnoses (rightly or wrongly) as the original sin of consumer society. So too, when she calls the laborer *animal laborans* and the worker *homo faber*, she is doing more than borrowing phrases. She is implying that

[49] *HC*, 126–27; 46. On the assembly line, see *HC*, 145–49. [50] *HC*, 125–26. [51] *HC*, 133.

making durable use objects is distinctively human, while physical activity associated with what she calls "the life process" is not; we share it with all the animals.

Arendt likewise packs definitional instabilities into "work" and "action." Work includes not only handicrafts and toolmaking but also the fine arts, including poetry. The work process requires blueprints or models – mental templates of the finished product. By extension, she argues, Plato's theory of ideas "rested on experiences of *poiesis* or fabrication."[52] Work also involves means–ends thinking, and indeed "the process of making is entirely determined by the categories of means and ends."[53] As a result, *homo faber* turns out to be not only a Platonist in metaphysics but a utilitarian in practical reasoning, and the chapter on work contains a critical discussion of instrumental, means–ends rationality. (More about this in §9.4.)

Later, Arendt argues that political philosophies favoring top-down governance by a ruler seeking to impose order on the unruly *demos* misclassify politics as work, because the tyrant or technocrat (benevolent or not) tries to shape his subjects the way that a sculptor shapes his clay or a physician cures her patients. This is the argument of the crucial section titled "The Traditional Substitution of Making for Acting," which criticizes the very concept of rule, "that is, the notion that men can lawfully and politically live together only when some are entitled to command and the others forced to obey." Denouncing this concept as "an escape from politics altogether,"[54] Arendt offers a startling critique of the entire tradition of political philosophy from Plato and Aristotle on, which assumes that politics essentially concerns who rules and on what basis. Her rejection of that assumption as a category mistake (the conflation of work and action) motivates the radical democracy Arendt hints at in *The Human Condition* and defends at greater length in the final chapter of *On Revolution*.[55] All in all, reviewing her multiple usages of the category of work – from toolmaking to art to metaphysics to practical reasoning to politics – we once again see a family resemblance concept rather than a term with a single, stable definition.

Action is better defined: "To act, in its most general sense, means to take an initiative."[56] But Arendt's elaboration of the concept shifts back and

52 *HC*, 142. 53 *HC*, 143. 54 *HC*, 222.

55 In *The Human Condition* it appears in her discussion of the labor movement, *HC*, 215–17. In *On Revolution* it appears in the final chapter.

56 *HC*, 177.

forth between political and nonpolitical action. The former is her main interest, with a focus especially on persuasive speech-making and the organizing of joint political enterprises. Although she is explicit that action can be nonpolitical as well as political,[57] nonpolitical actions receive lesser treatment in *The Human Condition*, and her elaborate analysis connecting action with "the public realm" is entirely about political action.

Nevertheless, the nonpolitical actions she discusses are crucial ones: market exchange and scientific and technological innovations. She calls the latter "acting into nature," and she has the atomic scientists in mind when she warns against "unchaining elemental processes, which, without the interference of men, would have lain dormant." (Today, her examples might be genomics, AI, and man-made climate change.[58]) Market exchange is action because it takes place in a public agora; scientific and technological advances are action because they initiate processes with large and incalculable collateral consequences. Other nonpolitical conduct falls under the heading of action because it yields the material of stories. Again, we see family resemblance among these usages rather than a single concept. We will look more closely at Arendt's various definitions of action in Chapter 9.[59]

In short, labor, work, and action are conceptual families with varying connections among the family members. The argument of *The Human Condition* is not, therefore, a logical unfolding of the concepts; it is more like a map of connections that run in multiple directions.

## 8.6 Why Distinguish Labor, Work, and Action?

Why draw the distinction between labor, work, and action, with their unstable, expanding and contracting, set of referents? I suggested that Arendt wishes to bind these disparate referents into concept-families to advance normative arguments. As I see it, Arendt advances three central arguments: one about freedom, one about the shared public realm, and one about that most grandiose of philosophical questions – what gives meaning to human life? All are efforts to show the dangerous political consequences of conflating labor with work or work with action. And all

[57] *HC*, 188.

[58] *HC*, 231 (acting into nature and "unchaining elemental processes"). In "Introduction *into* Politics," an unpublished manuscript from the 1950s, she refers to "man's success in exploiting nature to increase his own strength" as the "rape of nature." *PP*, 156–57. On the action-character of market exchange, *HC*, 209.

[59] See §9.5.

depend on interpretations of the ancient world – the world of the Athenian polis and the Roman republic.

### 8.6.1 *Freedom*

In Greek and Roman antiquity there was (she argues) a shared understanding that the three activities are hierarchically ordered: action on top, then work, then labor. Political action, that is, participation in civic affairs, was the highest form of the *vita activa* because it was most closely identified with human freedom. Conversely, labor was the lowest, the form of activity furthest removed from freedom.[60] Notably, the burdens and drudgery of labor were foisted off whenever possible onto the two subjugated classes of the ancient world: slaves and women. Labor is undertaken from dire necessity, and it is so physically demanding and all-consuming that it leaves neither time nor energy for free activity. Work, understood paradigmatically as the craft of skilled artisans, occupies the middle rung between labor and action.

In this Greek and Roman schema, the activities are ranked from highest to lowest on a scale of *freedom*. Arendt agrees, and she warns that the modern world has largely lost or even reversed the ancient valuations, placing labor at the pinnacle of activities, and as a result has lost the taste for freedom in favor of a taste for boundless abundance and consumption.

### 8.6.2 *Publicness*

A second characteristic way Arendt thinks of the three activities is that labor involves bodily maintenance and consumerist pleasure, which focuses it on private and subjective experiences. Work is different: It produces objects in the world we share in common. It is less private than labor, but its end products are detachable from their maker, who may well ply her craft in the solitude of the workshop or studio. Actions alone are performed among other people; action is the quintessentially human–human form of activity, the one in which (as Arendt says repeatedly) actors show each other who they are and what they can do.[61] In this analysis, the activities are ranked from highest to lowest, not on a scale of freedom, but on a scale of *publicness* or, as Arendt often says, worldliness. Considering

60 Famously, in Aristotle's *Politics*, 1254a7–8 (2 Complete Works 1989): "life is action, not production, and therefore the slave is the minister of action."

61 *HC*, 179; *MDT*, viii.

the two analyses together, the ancient hierarchy action–work–labor exemplifies two distinct loves that it is her aim to defend: *love of freedom* and *love of the world.* (*Amor Mundi*, "love of the world," was a title Arendt at one point considered for *The Human Condition*. Here, "world" evidently means something broader than the world of artifacts.)

What happens when the distinctions are blurred or the hierarchy is inverted? Here, Arendt offers two large arguments, one about blurring labor and work and the other about blurring work and action.

When labor and work are blurred – as, she believes, they are blurred by Marx, but also within contemporary consumer society – we lose the sense of a common world. The artisan's interest in the objects he produces gets replaced by the consumption interests of the *animal laborans*, namely his own pleasure and pain. Arendt's fundamental objection to utilitarianism in its classical hedonic form is its elevation of subjective pleasures and pains over connectedness to external reality – a point I take up in greater depth in Chapter 9. Essentially, hers is the same objection to utilitarianism Robert Nozick dramatized with his thought experiment of the "experience machine" that substitutes a pleasure-saturated virtual reality for the far less enjoyable "real" reality. Nozick, of course, thinks this is a trade-off no one should accept.[62] (As the meta-world lurches into existence, we shall see.)

Arendt puts it in different terms that we have already examined. With the loss of the common world and its replacement by subjective experiences and beliefs, we lose common sense, which roots us in shared reality. As we saw in earlier chapters, with the loss of common sense comes the kind of collective gullibility and susceptibility to conspiracy theories that nefarious political actors exploit.[63] An extremely online life can entail the loss of the common world, and we achieve it through using the internet as a kind of experience machine.

Arendt's proposition that phenomena like these arise from the confusion of labor and work is, to say the least, debatable. It sounds abstract and even weird, but it becomes less bizarre if you substitute "treating factual information as entertainment" for "labor" and "caring about a common external world" for "work." Once we realize what kinds of concrete phenomena Arendt is getting at through her admittedly abstract categories of labor and work, her argument becomes plausible and perhaps even compelling.

What about blurring work and action? I've already suggested what Arendt thinks is at stake here: a fundamental error of equating politics

[62] Robert Nozick, *Anarchy, State, and Utopia* (Basic Books, 1974), 42–45. [63] *HC*, 209.

with the question of who rules, rather than understanding it as a joint venture among equals. The consequence is a decline in freedom, understood as free political action among equals. Her most startling conclusion is that the main tradition of political philosophy from Plato and Aristotle on rests on the mistake of analogizing the statesman to the craftsman – for example, to the shipbuilder or the physician (today it would be the technocrat or expert). It seemed clear to Plato that, just as we defer to the skilled physician in matters of health, relying on his expertise instead of making decisions on our own, we defer to the statesman in matters of politics. From this analogy, a hierarchy of ruler over ruled follows, and with it a loss of the kind of freedom experienced in political action undertaken among equals.

### *8.6.3 Meaningfulness*

I have said there is a third macro-argument central to *The Human Condition*, an argument about the quintessentially philosophical question about what gives meaning to life. It is this third line of argument that will help us unravel the Case of the Missing Morality. To give a preview: Arendt's argument purports to show that labor and work are unable to supply meaningfulness on their own terms; but under certain conditions action can do so.

The trouble is that moral rules, viewed as side-constraints on action, seem to come from outside to handcuff the acting self.[64] Morality so understood interferes with our meaning-giving projects, rather than making those projects possible. Arendt was deeply suspicious of any claims of inscrutable higher authority that interferes with free action, and she regarded morality understood as a code of commandments as just such an authoritarian claim. This, I argue, gives rise to the Case of the Missing Morality.

Yet Arendt also understands that this cannot be the whole story. She is not an anything goes amoralist for whom unfettered action is all that matters. That anything does *not* go is abundantly clear from the sarcastic epigraph by Buchenwald survivor David Rousset that she chose for *Origins*: "Normal men do not know that anything is possible." The

[64] Arendt says so explicitly in *DTB*, XXI.83 (January 1956), 557–58. Arendt makes an exception for moral precepts that make action possible, rather than (or in addition to) constraining action. She identifies two such precepts, promise-keeping and forgiving. For the moment, I shall set this complication aside.

implication is that the totalitarian architects of death, and their followers, had lost their grip on what normal men know. Among normal men, after all, *das Moralische versteht sich von selbst* – morality is a matter of course. Put this way, Arendt is anything but an amoralist: Her concern is that moral constraints will cause us to sideline ourselves from the struggle against evil.

Rousset's insight sets her a problem, one that becomes acute at Jerusalem, when she witnesses an apparently normal man for whom, indeed, anything turned out to be possible. It leads her to reconsider morality – to ask whether we can understand the requirements of moral decency as essential to action rather than external to it. Ultimately, it was what led her to an understanding of morality centered on thinking and judgment, not on rules and constraints.

To set up the argument about meaningfulness, which I analyze in Chapter 9, we need two more entries in Arendt's *catalogue raisonée* of human conditions: birth and death, or, as she puts it, natality and mortality.

## 8.7 Unto Us a Child Is Born

We are born and we die. In Arendt's scheme of categories, natality and mortality belong side by side with life, worldliness, plurality, and the earth as fundamental components of the human condition. Because the world is perpetually flooded with newcomers, the human condition of natality implies perpetual change.[65] For Arendt, natality, creativity, human freedom, and action are closely tied together – indeed, the "faculty of action" is "ontologically rooted" in natality, and she likens action to a second birth.[66] In "On Violence," Arendt explains that "without the fact of birth we would not even know what novelty is, all 'action' would be either mere behavior or preservation."[67] For this reason, she calls the human condition of natality "[t]he miracle that saves the world, the realm of human affairs, from its normal, 'natural' ruin." That miracle finds "perhaps its most glorious and most succinct expression in the few words with which the Gospels announced their 'glad tidings': 'A child has been born unto us.'"[68] Or, as she puts the same ideas in "What Is Freedom?": "Because he *is* a beginning, man can begin." She adds that "the sheer capacity to begin . . .

[65] *HC*, 177, 246–47. [66] *HC*, 247 ("ontologically rooted"); *HC*, 176 ("second birth").
[67] *CR*, 179. [68] *HC*, 247. See also *PP*, 113, 126–27.

animates and inspires all human activities and is the hidden source of production of all great and beautiful things."[69]

We can date this insight rather precisely. After hearing a performance in 1952 of Handel's *Messiah* ("The 'Hallelujah Chorus' is ringing in my ears"), Arendt writes to Blücher: "I realized for the first time how marvelous the 'Unto us a child is born' is."[70] She explains in her Thought Diary: "Every new birth is like a guarantee of salvation in the world, like a promise of redemption for those who are no longer beginning." The diary entry is about the *Messiah*, and it begins, "The Hallelujah can only be understood from the text: Unto us a child is born."[71] It would not have escaped her attention that in *Messiah* the exultant chorus "Unto us a child is born" follows immediately on the bass arias "For behold, darkness shall cover the earth" and "The people shall walk in darkness." For Arendt, the phrase "dark times" is loaded with meaning, and the glimmer of hope in dark times lies in natality, the birth of a new generation.

Thus, unlike her teacher Heidegger, for whom, famously, human being is being-toward-death, Arendt emphasizes natality over mortality: "[M]en, though they must die, are not born in order to die but in order to begin."[72] Here she echoes her favorite quotation from St. Augustine: "That there be a beginning, man was created, before whom nobody was."[73] Yet the human condition of mortality also plays an important systematic role in her analysis of human activities. Quite simply, death threatens to make all our activities futile, and all of us face the challenge of overcoming "the futility of individual life" as well as "the natural ruin of time."[74]

As I next argue, the human need to overcome futility drives the argumentative structure of the central chapters on labor, work, and action in *The Human Condition*. Arendt argues that the attempt to derive meaningfulness through labor fails, because meaningfulness requires the kind of durability that only the products of work provide; but work itself turns out to pose problems of meaningfulness that only action can overcome.

With this background in hand, we are in position to pursue Arendt's line of argument prompted by reflection on the human condition of mortality and our quest for meaning.

69 *BPF*, 166, 167. These ideas are, from the point of view of the Abrahamic religions, theologically radical. If only a being that itself has a beginning can initiate something entirely novel, it would follow that an eternal God could never have created the world.

70 Arendt to Blücher, May 18, 1952, in *WFW*, 175.

71 *DTB*, IX.12 (May 1952), 208.

72 *HC*, 246.

73 St. Augustine, *The City of God*, XII, 20, quoted by Arendt in *W*, 18, 108, 158, 217, and *HC*, 177.

74 *HC*, 55, 56. She repeats this thought about the need to overcome futility on pp. 95, 119, 135.

CHAPTER 9

# *The Problem of Futility in* The Human Condition

In the time when Dendid created all things,
he created the sun,
and the sun is born, and dies, and comes again.
He created the moon,
and the moon is born, and dies, and comes again.
He created the stars,
and the stars are born, and die, and come again.
He created man,
and man is born, and dies, and does not come again.[1]

## 9.1 Futility, Eternity, Immortality

Again and again in *The Human Condition*, Arendt asserts that an innate "repugnance to futility," rooted in our mortality, propels human activity.[2] The connection between mortality and futility is a commonplace as ancient as Ecclesiastes. Nothing expresses it better than Macbeth's bitter speech:

Life's but a walking shadow, a poor player
That struts and frets his hour upon the stage
And then is heard no more: it is a tale
Told by an idiot: full of sound and fury,
Signifying nothing.[3]

The human condition of mortality (man struts and frets and then is heard no more) drives us to make life a meaningful tale, one that deserves better than the deadly verdict: *signifying nothing*. In *Thinking*, Arendt remarks on

[1] Old Dinka (Sudanese) Song in Peter Matthiessen, *The Tree Where Man Was Born* (Penguin Classics, 1976), 1, quoting Willard R. Trask, ed., *The Unwritten Song* (Macmillan, 1966), 110.
[2] *HC*, 119. She borrows the phrase from Veblen. Other mentions of futility: *HC*, 56, 95, 121, 135, 197.
[3] Shakespeare, *Macbeth*, act 5, scene 5, lines 23–27.

"the simple fact that nobody can think ... Meaning without thinking futility, vanity, meaninglessness."[4]

To anticipate a bit, the argument of Arendt's chapters on labor, work, and action is propelled by the question of which type of activity can satisfy the human need to signify something rather than nothing. Although she dismisses the so-called question about the meaning of life as an "unanswerable riddle,"[5] it does not follow that questions about the capacities and limitations of labor, work, and action to endow life with meaning are equally unanswerable.

That assumes human activity is the right place to look for meaning, and in *The Human Condition* Arendt first considers two alternatives: the Christian view that seeks meaning in eternity, and the Greek view that seeks it in immortality. The distinction between eternity and immortality, explored in section 3 of *The Human Condition*, is the difference between timelessness and deathlessness – in her words, "timeless being-forever" (eternity) and "deathless life" (immortality).[6]

Arendt steers clear of religious responses to Macbeth's lament. No turn to Heaven, therefore, and no eschatology. She does, however, consider a secularized version of eternity, the practice of contemplation, which played an important role in ancient and medieval thought.[7] But she thinks the turn toward contemplation led to undervaluing the *vita activa*. In *The Human Condition* she never spells out why the turn to eternity is a problem; she makes that clearer only in *Thinking*: "The trouble ... is that by jumping out of the fighting line 'he' [the contemplator] jumps out of this world altogether."[8]

It isn't even clear that a life of eternal contemplation, like the afterlife envisioned by some medieval philosophers, would respond to Macbeth's challenge, because the contemplating self is not a self in the relevant sense.[9]

[4] *T*, 149. [5] *HC*, 171; *T*, 197.

[6] "Timeless being-forever" comes from "The Concept of History," in *BPF*, 230n9; "deathless life" from *HC*, 18.

[7] *HC*, 20–21, 302–4. She cites Duns Scotus for the proposition that the "present which is timeless," the "standing now (*nunc stans*)," serves as a "model or metaphor for divine eternity" (*nunc aeternitas*). *T*, 210 and 238n13.

[8] *T*, 206–12; see especially 207.

[9] For example, Maimonides explains that the body is an obstacle to, rather than a necessary condition for, the kind of eternal contemplation that is the soul's life in the World to Come; and the soul in the World to Come is nothing apart from "the soul being in firm possession of the Idea which is God the Creator." Moses Maimonides, "Helek: Introduction to Mishnah Sanhedrin, Chapter 10," in *A Maimonides Reader*, ed. Isadore Twersky (Berhman House, 1972), 410–12. Between the soul and the mortal self "there is no similarity of any sort." Maimonides, "Helek: Introduction to Mishnah Sanhedrin, Chapter 10," 412. See Moshe Halbertal, *Maimonides: Life and Thought*

As Bernard Williams observes, what makes thinking so attractive and engrossing is that you lose yourself in it, and "losing yourself" is no mere figure of speech. The thinker loses track of time, of place, of self. (Recall Alcibiades's reminiscence of Socrates quoted in the epigraph to Chapter 4.) Arendt, making a similar point, quotes Valéry: *Tantôt je pense, tantôt je suis* (at times I think, at times I am).[10] The intense concentration of all-engrossing thought can't be sustained for long, but for Williams that is a good thing. Eventually you stop thinking and return to yourself – and it's the back and forth between losing yourself and returning to yourself in everyday life that makes contemplative activity meaningful, by ensuring there is a human being it is meaningful *to*. To lose yourself in (for?) eternity would radically and eternally disconnect you from the human person whose self is lost, that is, *you*.[11] In Arendt's words, "experience of the eternal is a kind of death, and the only thing that separates it from real death is that it is not final because no living creature can endure it for any length of time."[12]

If eternity isn't the solution to futility, what about earthly immortality? (In the words of Bob Marley, "If you know what life is worth, you will look for yours on earth.") That, Arendt argues, was the Greek view, at least until the philosophers introduced the distracting concept of eternity.

Arendt explains that the Greeks keenly experienced the painful contrast between the mortality of man and the immortality of the gods. Homer's gods are "human-natured."[13] They look like humans, they talk like humans, and they kvetch and bicker like humans. But they are

(Princeton University Press, 2014), 137–42, especially 140: "this concept of immortality of the soul leaves no room for the distinctiveness of an individual's surviving soul, for the portion of the soul that remains is the collection of metaphysical truths acquired by a person during his life."

10 Arendt, TMC, 165; *T*, 79.

11 Bernard Williams, "The Makropoulos Case: Reflections on the Tedium of Immortality," in *Problems of the Self* (Cambridge University Press, 1973), 96. Aquinas offered a similar argument: "My soul is not me; and so even if [my] soul attained salvation in another life, still neither I nor anybody else would have attained it." Quoted in John Finnis, *Aquinas* (Oxford University Press, 1998), 318n106, from Aquinas's *Commentary on Paul's First Letter to the Corinthians*; Finnis cites parallel passages from *On Being and Essence*, *Commentary on the Sentences of Peter Lombard*, and *Quaestiones de Quodlibet*.

12 HC, 20. Aristotle himself agrees that the contemplative state is one we can enjoy only briefly. *Metaphysics*, bk. 12, ch. 7, 1072b14–16. On the other hand, he believes that contemplation is something we can engage in more continuously than performing any action. N.E., bk. 10, ch. 7, 1177a20–30.

13 *HC*, 18–19. She takes the word from Herodotus, and explains that the word encompasses more than anthropomorphism: The Greek gods were not simply human in shape but in their mental and emotional makeup as well. She also discusses the central significance of immortality to the Greeks in *T*, 134, 138.

incomparably superior to humans, because unlike us, they are immortal. Quite literally, we can't live up to the gods.

It's worse than that. For the Greeks, the reality of lower animals lies in the species, not the individual. A species, endlessly reproducing itself, is immortal. The heavenly bodies, tracing their own circular paths, are also immortal. The gods are immortal. In all the cosmos, only we vanish without a trace, signifying nothing – the same observation as in the beautiful Dinka song in this chapter's epigraph.[14]

As evidence of the importance to the Greeks of immortality, Arendt highlights a passage in Aristotle's *Ethics*, which enjoins us to lead our lives in the way that comes closest to making ourselves immortal.[15] For Aristotle, we do that by exercising our reason, our *noûs*, thinking the same thoughts as the impersonal Aristotelian god.[16] But the contemplative life is emphatically not where Arendt is going. Immediately after quoting Aristotle, and without so much as hinting that the quote appears in his paean to the contemplative life, she remarks that the passage "very properly" appears in his political rather than theological writings – one of Arendt's most creative misreadings.

> For the *polis* was for the Greeks, as the *res publica* was for the Romans, first of all their guarantee against the futility of individual life, the space protected against this futility and reserved for the relative permanence, if not immortality, of mortals.[17]

Set aside for the moment the exalted claim she makes about the polis. I'll return to it later in this chapter. The more general point is that she attributes to the Greeks an entirely this-worldly venue for immortality.

Arendt's commitments lie in this world as well: We should seek meaning within the *vita activa*. What she takes from Aristotle is that, for the Greeks, meaning comes through "immortalizing" ourselves. Here, however, I argue that Arendt and the Greeks part ways. The nearest available human surrogate for immortality is everlasting fame, and Arendt understands that everlasting fame is a delusion. I explain why in §9.6.

14 *HC*, 18–19. Arendt cites Aristotle for the opinion that the reality of animals lies in their species: "The Concept of History," in *BPF*, 229n3, citing *On the Soul*, 415b13, *On Generation and Corruption*, 331a8, and the pseudo-Aristotelian *Economics* 1343b24. In *HC*, 232, she also notes the Greek belief in "the eternal recurrence of all natural things."

15 *HC*, 56. The passage is N.E. 1177b31. See also "The Concept of History," in *BPF*, 46–47 and 230n9.

16 Richard Norman, "Aristotle's Philosopher-God." *Phronesis* 14(1) (1969): 63–74.

17 *HC*, 56. This is a deliberate twisting of Aristotle in a non-Aristotelian direction. In her posthumously published Kant lecture notes, Arendt clearly recognized that what Aristotle meant by "immortalizing" was withdrawal from the active life to the contemplative. *Kant Lectures*, 55.

## 9.2 The Ladder of Human Activities

Let's pursue the Greek view of immortality a bit further. The clearest statement of this view is not Aristotle's but rather Diotima's famous speech on the nature of love, in Plato's *Symposium*. Diotima tells Socrates that "the mortal nature ever seeks, as best it can, to be everlasting and immortal." That is the true basis of the yearning for children, and it explains sexual longing, "the strange state into which all animals are thrown ... when they desire to beget.... Through this device, Socrates, a mortal thing partakes of immortality."

In fact (Diotima goes on), every human ambition, every striving for honor, every risky venture or self-sacrifice, seems inexplicable unless we understand it as "laying up fame immortal for all time to come." The same yearning for immortality through fame motivates poets, craftsmen, and inventors; and a more refined version of the longing to beget impels educators to pass along virtue to the young, and statesmen to lay down regulations for the good of their cities. All "are in love with what is immortal."[18] Wanting children, wanting fame, wanting to pass something along to future generations: all represent the need to defeat death and its futility.[19]

Not that Plato values all these forms of immortality-seeking equally. Diotima tells Socrates that lovers should proceed from loving a single beautiful body to loving all beautiful bodies, and from there to beautiful souls, and ultimately to the form of beauty itself – an ascent from lowest to highest "as on the rungs of a ladder."[20] Someone who ascends the ladder and sees the form of divine beauty becomes the friend of god (*theophilei*) and immortal (*athanato*, deathless).[21] Plato, in other words, links the highest and purest form of love with contemplation of the eternal.

For Arendt, as we've seen, the turn to eternity is a wrong turn; she sticks to the *vita activa* and its this-worldly concerns. She rejects Plato's metaphysics of forms (Ideas), which she elsewhere argues is a philosophical mistake that comes from falsely reifying everyday experiences of thinking and making.[22] But she borrows something like Plato's "ascending the

[18] Plato, *Symposium*. The passages cited are in 207a–209a. I use the translation by Benjamin Jowett, *Symposium* (Bobbs-Merrill, 1956). What I describe as "a more refined version of the longing to beget" refers, literally, to those who want to conceive in their souls more than in their bodies.

[19] Arendt's description of the Greek view on *HC*, 19 pretty faithfully echoes Diotima's speech, although without referencing it.

[20] *Symposium*, 211c. [21] *Symposium*, 211e–212a.

[22] Thinking: *T*, 23; making: *HC*, 142. Metaphysical fallacies: *T*, 211–12.

ladder" procedure in her own crucial argument about the power of labor, work, and action to impart meaning to life:

> We have seen that the *animal laborans* could be redeemed from its predicament of imprisonment in the ever-recurring cycle of the life process, of being forever subject to the necessity of labor and consumption, only through the mobilization of another human capacity, the capacity for making, fabricating, and producing of *homo faber*, who . . . erects a world of durability. . . . We saw furthermore that *homo faber* could be redeemed from his predicament of meaninglessness . . . only through the interrelated faculties of action and speech.[23]

This is Arendt's version of the ladder: labor on the bottom, then work, then action. Each higher rung solves a problem that the lower rung cannot solve – and the problem they solve is providing meaning in the face of Macbeth's skeptical challenge.

Recall from §8.6 that Arendt endorses the ancient hierarchy of action–work–labor on two grounds, a scale of freedom and a scale of publicity or "worldliness." Here we see a third basis for the hierarchy: a hierarchy of meaningfulness. Action is able to impart meaning, and defeat futility, in a way that work cannot, and work is better able to defeat futility than labor.

Why think this? As I see it, Arendt needs to convince the reader of four things. First is that a life of repetitive, incessant, and painful labor is, indeed, an exercise in futility. That seems plausible enough. Second, and more problematic, is that a life of consumerist pleasure, which she also associates with the *animal laborans*, is equally futile. Third is that the resolution of these predicaments lies in the activity of work, as distinct from labor. Fourth, that the life of *homo faber*, the skilled artisan, also faces a "predicament of meaninglessness" that only action can resolve.

## 9.3 Labor, Consumption, and the Subjective Turn

Start with the claim that a life of endless, painful labor just to survive from one day to the next is (at least in secular terms) futile. It offers little or nothing to contradict Macbeth's "signifying nothing" verdict. Perhaps it won't take much to convince ourselves of this, except that, famously, Albert Camus claimed the opposite in his existentialist classic "The Myth of Sisyphus." Camus tells us that even Sisyphus, condemned forever to the repetitive, exhausting, and pointless labor of rolling a rock up a hill

[23] *HC*, 236.

only to have it roll back down, is "superior to his fate" and "stronger than his rock." Recognizing the absurdity of his life allows him to rebel against it inwardly; viewed from a certain point of view everyone's life is absurd, but we can nonetheless create meaning through (inner) rebellion, passion, and embracing destiny as our own free choice. Camus explains that the gods condemned Sisyphus believing "there is no more dreadful punishment than futile and hopeless labor."[24] The defiant Sisyphus proves the gods wrong. Camus ends the essay with a paradox: "One must imagine Sisyphus happy."[25]

Arendt sides with the gods; she could hardly be further from Camus's paradoxes. Camus's metaphysical point is that we are all rolling rocks up hills. Arendt shares the commonplace opinion that there is a qualitative difference among fates, and that a fate like Sisyphus's stinks. In support of this common sense, we might note that Camus never asks himself what Sisyphus would choose if he were offered escape from his punishment back into a conventionally free and pleasant existence. Would he turn down the offer because he is happy pushing his rock? If, as seems far more likely, Sisyphus would gratefully use his get-out-of-jail-free card, then in what sense must we imagine Sisyphus happy pushing the rock? Camus's idea of freedom is inward and Stoic; Arendt's is freedom to act in the world.

Arendt had tremendous respect for Camus; indeed, after visiting him in Paris she gushed that "he is without a doubt the best man they have in France."[26] Nevertheless, in the essays where she discusses Camus, she rejects all the elements of his philosophy. His rebellion is against the human condition itself, and "the heroic gesture has become the characteristic pose of [this] philosophy." She observes that in Camus "the extreme subjectivism of Cartesian philosophy has found here its last and most radical expression." Its consequence is to "deny the possibility of a genuine fellowship between men." Ultimately, she finds the view nihilistic and "world-destroying."[27]

What about Arendt's more problematic second claim: that a life of consumerist pleasure is equally futile? To her it seems obvious that

[24] Albert Camus, "The Myth of Sisyphus," in *The Myth of Sisyphus and Other Essays*, trans. Justin O'Brien (Vintage, 1991), 119.

[25] Camus, "The Myth of Sisyphus," 123.

[26] Arendt to Blücher, May 1, 1952, *WFW*, 164.

[27] Rebellion against the human condition itself: "French Existentialism" and "Concern with Politics in Recent European Thought," both in *EU*, 191–92, 439. Heroic gesture: "What Is Existential Philosophy?," in *EU*, 171. Extreme subjectivism of Cartesian philosophy: "Concern with Politics," 437. Genuine fellowship between men: "French Existentialism," 190. World-destroying: "What Is Existential Philosophy?," 177. Arendt and Camus nevertheless shared commitments to humanism, decentralized democracy, and rebellion, as discussed in Jeffrey C. Isaac, *Arendt, Camus, and Modern Rebellion* (Yale University Press, 1992).

consumerist pleasure is as limited and pointless as its mirror image, painful labor. At times her anti-hedonism can sound almost perverse. "For only the *animal laborans* . . . has ever demanded to be 'happy' or thought that mortal men could be happy."[28] Does she really find the pursuit of happiness so contemptible?

It is easy to misunderstand this attitude as a disdain for physical pleasure. But Arendt has no such disdain, and furthermore she understands quite well that consumerist pleasures don't have to be physical.[29] What matters is the *fleetingness* of consumption, the fact that it doesn't leave durable traces that outlast the consumption itself. That means the rewards of consumption are entirely *subjective*, untethered to a shared world. And because consumer goods must constantly be replenished, a life devoted to consumption is, ultimately, *unfree*. Evanescence, subjectivity, unfreedom: these are the grounds of her claim that the life of ceaseless consumption, even leisurely and pleasurable consumption, is a futile life.

Let's consider these points individually.

*Evanescence.* Of course, there is nothing contemptible about fleeting, subjective pleasures. Happiness "within the moment" is an indispensable part of life, and a life stripped of those moments is terrible to contemplate. Anhedonia, the inability to take pleasure even in pleasurable things, is one of the conspicuous symptoms of depression. Arendt's concern is about the opposite extreme: a definition of the good life that never gets beyond happiness within the moment, and identifies the good life with a sequence of momentary happinesses strung together.

There are legal scholars and contemporary psychologists (including Nobel laureate Daniel Kahneman) who advance precisely this "moment-based" view that identifies well-being with the sum of moment-by-moment pleasures and pains.[30] For those who accept a moment-based theory of well-being, a life consisting of nothing but pleasurable moments

[28] *HC*, 134. See also *HC*, 108.

[29] See *HC*, 56 for a brief discussion of status as a consumer good. When she briefly discusses "the *petit bonheur* of the French people . . . the art of being happy among 'small things,'" her affection is unmistakable. *HC*, 52. She admits that it "may even appear to be the world's last, purely humane corner." *HC*, 52.

[30] See John Bronsteen, Christopher Buccafusco, and Jonathan S. Masur, "Welfare as Happiness," *Georgetown Law Journal* 98(6) (2010): 1585–641; this paper also appears as a chapter in the authors' *Happiness and the Law* (University of Chicago Press, 2014). Bronsteen, Buccafusco, and Masur argue that wellbeing should be defined as "the aggregate of a person's moment-by-moment experiences of positive and negative feeling." "Welfare as Happiness," 1591. They follow Daniel Kahneman, "Experienced Utility and Objective Happiness: A Moment-Based Approach," in *Choices, Values and Frames*, eds. Daniel Kahneman and Amos Tversky (Cambridge University Press, 2000), 673–92.

is, by definition, better than a life in which some moments are more painful.

Arendt thinks defining the best life, or even the most pleasant life, in this way is an illusion. "For mortals," she writes, "the 'easy life of the gods'" – a life of all pleasure and no pain – "would be a lifeless life." Purely as a physical matter, a body that never experiences pain would lose important pleasures as well: without hunger and thirst, the pleasures of eating and drinking would fade to the vanishing point; pleasures without cravings they satisfy might not even be imaginable. "[P]ain and effort are not just symptoms which can be removed without changing life itself; they are rather the modes in which life itself . . . makes itself felt."[31]

Arendt actually combines two different ideas here and in her ensuing discussion. The first is that there are some pleasures in which satisfying a yearning or privation is a constitutive part of the pleasure itself, as relieving thirst is a constitutive part of the pleasure of a cold drink. The second idea is that the intensity of pleasure is comparative, not absolute. We register it by contrast with the surrounding less pleasurable experiences. With no contrast, pleasure and pain flatten out and we would lose "the intensity with which life is felt."[32] We can go even further. Divorced from the context of surrounding experiences, momentary pleasures and pains have indeterminate amplitude: no contrast, no intensity-measure.

It seems likely that at least some intellectual and emotional satisfactions are similarly comparative, in the sense that our experience of them as satisfactions depends on their contrast with surrounding experiences of less satisfaction. If so, it suggests that fleeting moments of satisfaction can only be experienced within a setting where they are conjoined with contrasting moments of lesser satisfaction. In fact, we don't experience moments as moments; rather, singling out moments is an artificial abstraction from larger and more primary units of experience – an act of abstraction accomplished by memory, imagination, and interpretation. For that reason, defining happiness as a maximizing sequence of pleasurable moments is equivalent to defining it through an artificial construct (a plot of pleasure-intensities over time) composed of abstractions, not experiences.

The conspicuous exceptions to the holistic experience of pleasures and pains are momentary sensations of overwhelming intensity – the sudden

[31] Both quotations from *HC*, 120. In her Kant lectures, she attributes this idea to Plato and, indirectly, to Kant: "all pleasure dispels a displeasure, [so] that a life that contained only pleasures would actually lack all pleasure." *Kant Lectures*, 29.

[32] *HC*, 120.

pain of touching a hot stove, for example, or the pleasure of sexual release. These pass a threshold of intensity that makes their quality absolute rather than comparative. Arendt responds that such moments are unrepresentative because "they do not contain the experience of any worldly object. The pain caused by a sword or the tickling caused by a feather indeed tells me nothing whatsoever of the quality or even the worldly existence of a sword or a feather."[33] This helps explain why those moments of intense pain or pleasure don't stick with us. We remember *that* we felt great pain or pleasure, but we don't relive the experience itself – thankfully so in the case of intense pain, perhaps regrettably so in the case of intense pleasure.

These observations raise doubts about the meaningfulness of the happiness research central to the moment-based theory. A prominent version relies on palmtop computer surveys asking subjects every few minutes, hours, or days to rate their happiness at that moment – so-called experience sampling methodology. It then plots the answers to obtain a happiness profile over time.

It follows from the arguments above that, with the exception of the unrepresentative intense pains and pleasures, these moment-by-moment ratings cannot be "pure" reports. They are mediated by context-dependent judgments, and the context they depend on consists of surrounding contrasting experiences. If so, a moment-based approach to evaluating happiness, which simply aggregates the momentary measures, overlooks that the moment-by-moment reports are abstractions and interpretations, not raw data.[34] And a vision of the good life that defines it through the momentary experiences associated with consumption rests on the fallacy that these individual experiences can be meaningful to us on their own, without being embedded in something longer lasting.

What is the longer-lasting something in which momentary pleasures and pains are embedded? Arendt focuses on the activity of work, the fashioning of durable objects that outlast the experience itself. One way to understand this idea is that the natural units of experience are not individual moments of pleasure and pain but temporally extended human projects in which the moments are bound together because they belong to

[33] *HC*, 114. She contrasts such intense experiences, which in her view "prevent our senses from functioning normally," with an everyday experience like eating a bowl of strawberries, where "I taste strawberries, and not the taste itself." *HC*, 114n63 and 115.

[34] Thus I disagree with Bronsteen, Buccafusco, and Masur, who believe that holistic evaluation of momentary experiences "conflates what a person has actually experienced with the judgments the person has made about that experience." "Welfare as Happiness," 1592. On the argument being seconded here, there are no recollectible actual experiences distinct from judgments about them.

a coherent, future-directed activity. Although the terminology of "projects" is not Arendt's, she understands work as inherently such goal-oriented activity. To recognize individual moments of pleasure and pain as abstractions from temporally extended projects, as we should, suggests another problem with moment-based happiness evaluations. Intensity evaluations ("rate your current happiness 1 through 10") are scalar; but the experiences themselves are vectors directed from projects' past to their future.

This is not a new idea; it was common currency among the pragmatists and phenomenologists of the early twentieth century that the project, not the moment, is the natural unit of human experience. As Martha Nussbaum puts it, "among the many available human activities, the activities and relationships that human beings usually value most have, in more or less every case, a temporally extended structure ... we cannot imagine them taking place in an instant without imagining them stripped of much of the human value they have."[35]

*Subjectivity.* Arendt adds another dimension to this idea. In her view, the important point is that the goal of work lies in a durable and publicly accessible object, rather than in the subjective experience of the worker. The problem with moment-based happiness as a source of meaning is not just its fleetingness but its subjectivity as well.

Why is subjectivity a problem? Arendt associates the durability of things with their belonging to a world we hold in common with other people; concomitantly, valuing purely subjective experiences lets go of the public world. Here we might recall Robert Nozick's experience machine thought experiment mentioned in Chapter 8, and the intuition Nozick meant to invoke: that a life of pleasurable experiences is meaningless if the experiences are ersatz. "There is no *actual* contact with any deeper reality, though the experience of it can be simulated." Again, "it is only because we first want to do the actions that we want the experiences of doing them."[36] Connection with public reality that transcends subjective experience matters to us.

Of course these are intuitions, not arguments, but I think knockdown arguments against hedonism and subjectivism are more than we can ask for. Arendt's and Nozick's anti-hedonism may ultimately be more a matter of sensibility than argument. To someone whose honest response to the

[35] Martha C. Nussbaum, *The Therapy of Desire: Theory and Practice in Hellenistic Ethics* (Princeton University Press, 1994), 208–9.
[36] Nozick, *Anarchy, State, and Utopia*, 43.

experience machine is, "Bring it on and plug me in!" there is little to say beyond, "Your world is not my world." By the same token, though, for those whose response to the experience machine thought experiment is the intuition Nozick supposes – that fake reality is *not* valuable even if provides a marvelous subjective experience – no further argument is necessary.

It might be objected that valuing subjective experience is not the same as valuing *pleasure*, nor is there anything fake about subjective experience. Assigning the highest rank to subjective experience is a hallmark of a great deal of twentieth-century thought and literature, and it was neither hedonistic nor indifferent to the distinction between true and false experience. Notably, intense attachment to the subjective is the hallmark of literary modernism – the modernism of Virginia Woolf, James Joyce, and Wallace Stevens:

> I was the world in which I walked, and what I saw
> Or heard or felt came not but from myself;
> And there I found myself more truly and more strange.[37]

"I was the world" is radical subjectivism, but there is nothing hedonistic in Stevens's proclamation. The claim isn't that the world "that came not but from myself" is *pleasant*, nor that we value it on a hedonic scale. The claim is that it is *real* (and really strange). The same goes for Virginia Woolf, for whom "we are the words; we are the music; we are the thing itself": Woolf warns that the thing itself ("this vast mass that we call the world") is painful, experienced as a "blow" with "a power to hurt me."[38]

For Arendt, such attitudes represent a flight from reality, not a turn toward it. The poet must not confuse her articulated subjective experience with this vast mass that we call the world. As we saw in Chapter 8, that confusion undermines common sense, and eventually it endangers both moral judgment and attachment to facts. In a critique of Heidegger, Arendt writes that "a Self, taken in its absolute isolation, is meaningless."[39] She doesn't mean that the inner life is unimportant, only that we must never confuse it with the shared common world, nor identify the common world with our own experience of it. The inner life should remain hidden

37 Wallace Stevens, "Tea at the Palaz of Hoon," in *The Collected Poems of Wallace Stevens* (Vintage Books, 1990), 65. Likewise Stevens, "The Idea of Order at Key West," lines 37–43, 128–30. Arendt's own literary exemplar of the inward turn is a poem of Rilke, "Wunderliches Wort," Denver Lindley translation quoted in "The Concept of History," *BPF*, 44, 229n5.

38 Virginia Woolf, "A Sketch of the Past," in *Moments of Being: A Collection of Autobiographical Writing*, ed. Jeanne Schulkind (Harcourt, Inc., 1985), 72.

39 "What Is Existential Philosophy?," *EU*, 180.

and private "if it is not to lose its depth in a very real, non-subjective sense."[40]

*Freedom.* Lastly, Arendt regards the life of consumption as an *unfree* life. An endless cycle of consumption is like an addiction that leaves us without the freedom to do anything but consume. Recall the diagnosis I quoted earlier: "[T]he spare time of the *animal laborans* is never spent in anything but consumption, and the more time left to him, the greedier and more craving his appetites."[41] As a result, "our whole economy has become a waste economy, in which things must be almost as quickly devoured and discarded as they have appeared in the world, if the process itself is not to come to a sudden catastrophic end."[42]

Now we might protest that it *needn't* be that way. Living in a consumer society does not make us full-time consumers. Nothing prevents us from spending our leisure making durable objects or engaging in public life. And nothing prevents us from striving to lead lives less hectically devoted to acquisition and consumption – as Wordsworth complained, "getting and spending we lay waste our powers." But that is Arendt's point: The protest against assuming that consumer society does nothing but consume backhandedly concedes that consumption alone cannot solve the problem of futility.

## 9.4 Work and Means–Ends Reasoning

Suppose we accept Arendt's argument that a condition necessary to overcome futility is that we live in a shared world of durable things, and that the work process that creates those things is a candidate for something inherently meaningful – it provides satisfactions that neither the life of labor nor of consumption can provide. Creating something durable, be it a physical object like a table, or a song, or a well-wrought academic paper, seems like meaningful activity, and a life devoted to making durable things offers itself as a candidate for a meaningful life. And in many ways it is.

Arendt's concern about it arises from her view that inherent in the activity of *homo faber* is thinking exclusively in terms of means and ends – what is often called instrumental rationality. "What's it *for*?" is the automatic first question we pose to the inventor of an unfamiliar device; the US Constitution grants Congress the power to award patents and copyrights in order to promote the "useful arts," and useful arts are those practiced by *homo faber*.

[40] *HC*, 71. [41] *HC*, 133. [42] *HC*, 134.

Now, not all work aims at utility; a conspicuous exception is artistic work. Arendt recognizes that the fine arts are different from the useful arts, and she devotes a section of *The Human Condition* (§23) to artworks.[43] But among the "useful arts" the predominant question is what the artifact is useful *for*. Here she seems on safe ground in asserting that the predominant mode of thought is instrumental, means–ends thinking.

Arendt's problem with means–ends thinking is simple and familiar (indeed, it comes straight out of Aristotle): If you ask, "What's *X* for?" and get an answer, "It's for *Y*," and then ask, "What's *Y* for?" ("It's for *Z*"), you fall into an infinite regress.[44] The only ways to interrupt the regress are to identify an end to the chain – an "end in itself" – or to break out of means–ends thinking altogether. She regards the "end in itself" version as untenable, and concludes that *homo faber* needs a richer conceptual vocabulary to explain the meaningfulness of the making activity than the instrumental vocabulary internal to work.[45]

Arendt's argument is terse and more than a bit cryptic. An end in itself "is either a tautology applying to all ends or a contradiction in terms."[46] This sentence needs unpacking. It turns on distinguishing two senses of "end," as a goal of action and as the complement of means in the means–end dyad.

The tautology part makes sense of the first meaning of the word "end," as a *goal*. Every end, conceived as the goal toward which our efforts are immediately directed, is *in that respect* an end in itself, even if it's also an intermediate step toward a further end. If an end is defined as a target of purposive activity, all ends are ends in themselves.

What about the claim that in a different sense the concept of an end in itself is a contradiction in terms? Arendt explains that "an end, once it is attained, ceases to be an end and loses its capacity to guide and justify the choice of means, to organize and produce them. It has now become an object among objects."[47] It is "in itself," but it is no longer, properly speaking, an *end*.

Here the idea seems to be that there is a sense of "end" in which "end" and "means" are cognate concepts, defined in terms of each other. An end is the thing for which means must be found; the means are objects and techniques needed to accomplish the end. We distinguish them within the means–ends binary by the fact that the end plays a different functional role

[43] See Patchen Markell, "Arendt's Work: On the Architecture of *The Human Condition*," *College Literature* 38(1) (2011): 15–44.

[44] N.E., bk. I, ch. 2, 1094a18–20. [45] *HC*, 153–55. [46] *HC*, 154. [47] *HC*, 154–55.

from the means. It guides and justifies the choice of means, while the converse is not true. And the functional roles define what it is to be an end or a means – the semantics and pragmatics of the words "means" and "end."

Noting this functional difference does not deny that we often adjust our ends to the means available as well as the other way around. Arendt's argument applies after the mutual adjustment reaches equilibrium. The end, understood as one pole of a means–ends binary, is defined functionally as the goal that guides our organization of means. In this sense, once the end is attained and no longer serves the function of organizing means, it should no longer be called an end.

In short, her argument is that "end" has two senses: the terminus of purposive activity, and the cognate concept to "means" in the means–ends binary. Taken in the first sense, talk of an end in itself is a tautology, because the "in-itself" label simply repeats that an end is a terminus; taken in the second sense, talk of an end in itself is a contradiction in terms, because the "in-itself" label severs the end from the means.[48]

Suppose we accept Arendt's argument and abandon the term "end in itself." So what? Giving up the label needn't stop us from identifying the overall point of a chain of ends and means, what Aristotle called the "final cause" of the activities. Perhaps the terminology doesn't matter.

Here, I take it, Arendt would respond that this is precisely why the terminology matters: The overall point of the chain of means and ends is different in kind from the links of the chain, and identifying it as the final link obscures that difference. The final cause can't be thought of as a means, nor is it an end the way the intermediate links are ends: ends that are simultaneously means to other ends. We need a richer vocabulary to describe it – a vocabulary that includes noninstrumental final causes.

She diagnoses the situation as follows: The inadequacy of instrumental, means–ends vocabulary comes from *homo faber*'s

> innate incapacity to understand the distinction between utility and meaningfulness, which we express linguistically by distinguishing "in order to" and "for the sake of." Thus the ideal of usefulness . . . is actually no longer a matter of utility but of meaning. It is "for the sake of" usefulness in general that *homo faber* judges and does everything in terms of "in order to."[49]

48 Arendt anticipates this argument in her doctoral dissertation, where she points out that Augustine's term "for its own sake" (*propter se ipsum*) contains a contradiction, because *propter* points to something else. *LA*, 33.

49 *HC*, 154.

We don't aim to be useful because usefulness is useful, let alone "useful-in-itself." We aim to be useful for the sake of something else – and Arendt's claim is that that something else is that we find leading a useful life *meaningful.*

Thus Arendt's claim is that instead of asking what usefulness is useful for, we should ask why a life devoted to useful work is meaningful. The answer to that question must lie outside the framework of means and ends – and that is her point. Arendt illustrates with the example of a carpenter, who performs operations with glue and sandpaper *in order to* make a table, but "his whole life as a carpenter is ruled by something quite different, namely an encompassing notion 'for the sake of' which he became a carpenter in the first place."[50] The distinction provides a model for how individual instrumental acts might come to seem meaningful to a person in a noninstrumental way.

I do want to flag a difference between Arendt's conception of "for the sake of" and Aristotle's notion of a final cause, which he too describes as that "for the sake of" which something is done. Arendt's distinction between "in order to" and "for the sake of" doesn't answer Aristotle's question of how to characterize final causes of means–ends chains. To see why, look again at her carpenter example. The carpenter goes to a supply store *in order to* buy sandpaper. He buys sandpaper *in order to* smooth off the wood, and he smooths off the wood *in order to* make a handsome table. So far so good: This is a clear example of a means–ends chain. If we ask him, "What's the table for?" his answer will be something like, "It's a dining room table, which can seat up to sixteen people." Paraphrasing, this means " ... *in order to* seat up to sixteen people," which adds one more link to the means–ends chain. But if you then ask, "What are they sitting around the table for?" the puzzled carpenter might say, "Well, that's up to the customer." It would be natural to say that the carpenter buys and uses sandpaper *in order to* make a table that seats sixteen; but he does so *for the sake of* whatever the customer uses the table for.

However, that is not how Arendt uses "for the sake of." For her, the carpenter makes the table *for the sake of* whatever led him to become a carpenter. Using the distinction Arendt's way, the carpenter does not make

50 "The Concept of History," in *BPF*, 78–79. Though she doesn't say so, her distinction comes straight out of Heidegger. He introduced the distinction between "in order to" and "for the sake of" precisely to differentiate the instrumental purpose of particular acts from the overarching commitments that govern our lives. *Being and Time*, ¶18, 118–22, H. 86–88; ¶41, 236–41; H. 191–95. This is how Arendt uses it as well. Arendt first reflects on "for the sake of" in her dissertation: *LA*, 32–35.

the table for the sake of the customer's ends, but for the sake of his own sense of vocation, which makes the actions meaningful to the carpenter. But the Aristotelian final cause of the actions has to do with the customer's life, not the carpenter's. Furthermore, you can make a table without being a carpenter by vocation. We must carefully distinguish her sense of "for the sake of" – an explanation of what makes work meaningful to the worker – from an explanation of final causes.

## 9.5 Action

In the carpenter example we saw a chain of means and ends, and for each link in the chain there was an intelligible answer to the question, "What's that for?" (or "What is it a means to?"). But we can't ask what the customer is for or what she is a means to! That question is out of order, in fact it is nearly unintelligible. Human beings are not means, but neither are they ends (a human being is not a goal of action unless you are trying to make a baby), let alone ends in themselves. Arendt is quite aware that in saying this, she is rejecting one of Kant's signature ideas, that human beings are ends in themselves. She takes Kant to task for using means–ends terminology when his whole point was to exempt human beings and human action from the category of means and ends.[51]

The reason it's out of order to ask what a human being is for is that human beings are not "for" a purpose; insofar as we are free agents, we set our own purposes. So, one way to enrich the vocabulary of means and ends, and to articulate why constructing a durable human environment is a meaningful thing to do, is to add the concept of *free action* to our philosophical vocabulary. The meaningfulness of work, of fashioning a world of material objects (the physical City of Man), is that it sets the stage for human action. Work produces the scenery for the play, but without the performance itself, building the set is meaningless. That is Arendt's idea: Introducing concepts drawn from the category of action allows us to explain why work is meaningful, in a way that the means–ends vocabulary of work cannot. Let's look closely at what Arendt means by action.

Her concept refers to something narrower than the subject matter of action theory in analytic philosophy, where "action" generally refers to any voluntary muscular motion, like flipping a light switch to turn on the light. Arendt plainly does not think everything we do intentionally is an action – her main point in studying the *vita activa* is to recover distinctions between

[51] *HC*, 155–56.

action and other activities. As for small-scale, everyday muscular motions like turning on the lights, scratching my nose, or lighting a candle, she would think of them as "behavior" or habit, but not action, which requires deliberately initiating a new chain of events. Habitual or mechanical acts don't count.[52] "To act, in its most general sense, means to take an initiative, to begin . . . , to set something into motion."[53]

This is the first definition of action she offers: *action as initiation.* An action initiates a process; it interrupts the regular course of human events (action is like a "second birth," she tells us) setting off a chain of intended and unintended consequences so that "the process he [the actor] starts is never consummated unequivocally in one single deed or event, and . . . its very meaning never discloses itself to the actor but only to the backward glance of the historian who himself does not act."[54]

Her invocation of "the historian" suggests she is thinking only of acts of renown, which would be a narrow concept of action that excludes all but a handful of men and women. It's possible, or even likely, that Arendt accepted a big bow wow, "aristocratic" conception of action: She emphasizes that the Greek historians saw the point of their effort as immortalizing "the great and wonderful actions of the Greeks *and* the barbarians," as she quotes from Herodotus; and she illustrates her conception of freedom by invoking Machiavelli's glory-seeking concept of *virtù*, meaning virtuosity.[55]

But there is no need to restrict her idea in this way, for storytelling is the most democratic of human activities. Any storyteller (*histōr*, in ancient Greek) can count as a historian; grandma or grandpa recounting family lore of no interest outside the family circle would be a historian in Arendt's sense. The defining characteristic of action as initiation is not world-historical magnitude but the fact that others would find the action worthy of recounting. Furthermore, "the hero the story discloses needs no heroic qualities; the word 'hero' originally, that is, in Homer, was no more than a name given to each free man . . . about whom a story could be told."[56] *Action as noteworthiness* is thus Definition #2 of action.[57] In this sense,

52 Arendt spells this out in *W*, 30 and *CR*, 132–33. 53 *HC*, 177.

54 Second birth: *HC*, 176; the quotation: *HC*, 233. Saying that the historian does not act is a mistake, because passing judgment on the past can itself be a form of acting – a crucial point when we consider the process of legal judgment by courts and tribunals.

55 Great deeds: "The Concept of History," *BPF*, 51; see also the section "History and Earthly Immortality" in the same essay. Virtuosity: "What Is Freedom?," in *BPF*, 153.

56 *HC*, 186.

57 "Action as noteworthiness" is a less cumbersome label than "action as the stuff of storytelling," but the latter is more accurate.

routine acts of daily life ("behavior") will ordinarily not count as actions, but little-known deeds by people of no renown may, so long as some set of others finds them noteworthy enough to spin into stories.

Arendt offers a third definition of action as well.[58] In "What Is Freedom?" she insists that a free action cannot be understood in terms either of its motive or its anticipated consequences, alone or together. Rather, its freedom lies in its realization of a "principle."[59] This introduces a new ingredient into the definition of action. She tells us that she borrows her terminology from Montesquieu's analysis of the forms of government. "Principle" is the name Montesquieu gives to commitments that make a government act.[60] By analogy, Arendt thinks a principle is what makes a person act. Of course, this is only an analogy: Montesquieu is talking about principles of government, while Arendt is talking about individual action.

As Arendt explains: "These principles of action should not be mistaken for psychological motives. They are much rather the guiding criteria by which all actions in the public realm are judged beyond the merely negative yardstick of lawfulness, and which inspire the actions of both rulers and ruled."[61] At first glance inspiration and motivation seem very close to each other. The difference is that principles are criteria of judgment, and therefore they are *normative.* A psychological motivation need have no normative import; it is a brute fact about what drives us, not what should drive us. Arendt illustrates with Shakespeare's Richard III, who blames his villainy on his physical deformity. A lifetime of scorn may motivate Richard's villainy, but it is not a principle. By contrast, we might say that Satan in *Paradise Lost* does evil as a matter of principle: His principles, he tells us, are revenge and immortal hate.

Although she doesn't make the connection herself, it seems plausible to identify Arendtian principles with those things "for the sake of" which a person acts.[62] However, not every action is done for the sake of principle. For that reason, I regard Definition #3 – *action as principled conduct* – as more restricted and therefore less fundamental than #1 (action as

58 George Kateb likewise notices that Arendt offers three conceptions of action, although he identifies them differently than I do. *Hannah Arendt: Politics, Conscience, Evil,* 10–14.

59 *BPF,* 150–51.

60 The relevant passages are Montesquieu, *The Spirit of the Laws*, bk. III, ch. 1, 21, and bk. III, ch. 11, 30. Arendt's discussion in "The Concept of Freedom" roughly tracks similar discussions of Montesquieu and principles in essays written before *The Human Condition*: "Montesquieu's Revision of the Tradition," in *PP*, 63–65 (unpublished but written in the early 1950s), and "On the Nature of Totalitarianism: An Essay in Understanding," in *EU*, 331–35, written in 1954.

61 "Montesquieu's Revision of the Tradition," in *PP*, 65.

62 Kateb agrees: *Hannah Arendt: Politics, Conscience, Evil,* 12.

initiation) and #2 (action as noteworthiness). Yet one of her conclusions about principled action – that actions can be judged – is essential to her moral philosophy and her emphasis on legal accountability.

I think action as noteworthiness comes closest to explaining why Arendt looks to human action to solve the problem of futility that she found impossible to solve within the vocabularies of labor and work. Again and again she tells us that by entering the arena of action we show who we are and what we can do.[63] We may not be able to see ourselves, but others can see us and know us. This "revelatory quality of speech and action,"[64] which shows not just *what* we are but *who* we are, need not be the overt purpose of action. It is, when the action consists of entering an athletic competition or a singing contest: The contestants want to show the world who they are by showing what they can do. But actors ordinarily have tangible, practical aims – "in order tos" – when they act, and the self-revelation is a side effect.

Side effect or not, Arendt's view is that action is meaningful because it reveals who we are. Through action, we make our mark on the world; we become the stuff of stories.[65] Importantly, that means that action requires other people, a storyteller and an audience. The meaningfulness *to ourselves* of our lives and activities depends to a surprising extent on the presence of other people. Plurality is the human condition of meaningfulness.

## 9.6 Arendt versus the Greeks: On the Irrelevance of Immortality

Arendt attributes her noteworthiness conception of action to the Greeks, who sought earthly immortality by having their deeds recounted by poets and historians. Certainly we can hear echoes in it of Diotima's theory that everything we do is done for the sake of immortality, at any rate the kind of immortality available to human beings: being remembered.

We may find this a poor substitute for real immortality. As philosopher Jerry Fodor quipped, "What's the good of being immortal if you're dead?"[66] It's hard to disagree; but a strand in recent philosophy has questioned whether personal immortality would actually be desirable. Too many of the things that matter to us – our loves, our virtues, our projects, our accomplishments – are keyed to the phases of our finite life-cycle to survive in recognizable form in an endless life. Truly immortal beings would have to

[63] E.g., *HC*, 179; *MDT*, viii. [64] *HC*, 180. [65] *HC*, 184.

[66] Jerry Fodor, "What Wotan Wants," review of *Finding an Ending: Reflections on Wagner's "Ring"* by Philip Kitcher and Richard Schacht, *London Review of Books* 26(15) (2004): 8–10.

have a motivational structure and set of values so different from ours that they would not even be recognizable. Even though we are doomed to fear death, or to rage against it, and to wish for more (healthy) time on earth, immortality might be unbearable for creatures like us.[67]

If these philosophers are right, we're lucky we don't have the option of personal immortality. But Diotima's argument was not that immortality would be good for us, only that the desire for immortality, rational or not, drives us to seek the next-best thing: perpetuating ourselves in our children, our work, or our deeds. Or, in Arendt's version, "to insert one's self in the world and begin a story of one's own," a story that will enter "the storybook of mankind."[68]

That aim requires a storybook of mankind, which depends on mankind's survival (and not just mankind, but mankind "in my neighborhood" who will inscribe my story in the storybook of mankind). The philosopher Samuel Scheffler proposes that the survival of mankind, which we seldom think about because we take it for granted, matters to the deep structure of our values far more than we might suppose. Scheffler argues the case by reflecting on a thought experiment in which the subject knows that our planet will be wiped out by an asteroid thirty days after the subject's death – the "doomsday scenario."[69] Scheffler concludes, plausibly, that in the doomsday scenario most of our projects and activities – everything from curing cancer to saving up for the kids' education to voting – would become ashes to us. Curiously, an extinction we would not personally experience would matter to us more than our own death, in the sense that knowing the extinction was coming would drain much of the meaning from what we now do in a way that knowing we will die plainly does not.

Many explanations come to mind of why Scheffler's doomsday scenario elicits this reaction; but it seems to me that Diotima's idea that we need a collective afterlife to perpetuate ourselves is among the most plausible.

67 For three importantly different variations on this theme, see Williams, "The Makropoulos Case: Reflections on the Tedium of Immortality," in *Problems of the Self*, 82–100 – the essay that kicked off this discussion; Nussbaum, *The Therapy of Desire*, 225–32, and Samuel Scheffler, *Death and the Afterlife* (Oxford University Press, 2013), 95–100. Nussbaum has subsequently repudiated her version of this argument, in "The Damage of Death: Incomplete Arguments and False Conclusions," in *Death: New Essays on Metaphysics and Bioethics*, ed. James S. Taylor (Oxford University Press, 2013), 36–41. To avoid the obvious concern that living forever might involve descent into endless decrepitude, Williams imagines the fictional case of a woman who is perpetually forty-two years old and healthy, and the other authors assume something similar.

68 The first quote from *HC*, 186; the second from *HC*, 184. In this formulation, she combines action as initiation and action as noteworthiness: What makes an action noteworthy is that it begins something new.

69 Scheffler, *Death and the Afterlife*, lectures I and II.

Scheffler himself observes that "many people seem to feel that not being remembered is what being 'gone' really consists in."[70]

I raise these issues because of their relevance to Arendt's argument. Arendt thought this capacity to grant remembrance was what the Greeks valued in the polis. Her witness in chief is Pericles, who in his Funeral Oration makes two curious boasts: first, that the Athenians had everywhere left "everlasting remembrance of their good and their evil deeds"; second, that because the polis exists, there is no longer any need for poets or historians to memorialize the great deeds of the Athenians.[71] The polis would be the collective afterlife for the Athenians.

*De dicto* or *de re*? Does Arendt agree with Pericles and "the Greeks" about the exalted place of the polis in immortalizing us, and the indifference as to whether we are remembered for good or ill? Some things Arendt says suggest the answer is yes, but I think it is no. The polis she extols is not the city-state viewed as a collective afterlife, but rather the community of our living, breathing peers. Or so I argue in what follows.

Pericles' two boasts are curious for several reasons. As to the first, it is remarkable that Pericles boasts about evil deeds as well as good; apparently, what matters is immortal fame, not the quality of whatever the Athenians are famous for. Arendt claims that Pericles knew full well how foreign this conceit is to everyday moral standards. And not just moral standards: I think Pericles' boast that Athens's evil deeds will be remembered forever is stranger and less coherent than that. Does anyone really want to be remembered forever as a criminal or monster or a freakish tabloid meme? On a lesser scale, would you want the worst thing you ever did in your life preserved forever (an everlasting social media page with undeletable videos of your most shameful and humiliating moments)? That sounds, quite literally, like Hell.

As for the second boast, one wants to know *how* the polis would substitute for the poets and historians. Through national holidays? Naming streets after notables? Public readings from the official state archives? What did Pericles have in mind for how the polis remembers its citizens' deeds, other than the work of poets and historians? Pericles doesn't say, and neither does Arendt. Remembrance doesn't just happen.

It's easy to suppose that she agrees with Pericles that somehow or other the polis will preserve its citizens' stories (but how?). Perhaps the best evidence that she agrees with him is the stunning conclusion of *On Revolution*. On its final page she quotes Sophocles' "famous and

[70] Scheffler, *Death and the Afterlife*, 29–30. [71] Thucydides ii.41, discussed in *HC*, 197, 205–6.

frightening lines" that best of all is never to have been born, second best to die young – surely as powerful a statement of futility as Macbeth's. But, she continues, Sophocles also lets us know "what it was that enabled ordinary men, young and old, to bear life's burden: it was the polis, the space of men's free deeds and living words, which could endow life with splendor."[72]

This finale sounds like an acute case of polis envy, proof that Arendt endorses Pericles' exalted claims for the polis. But that conclusion is hasty and wrong. Notice how she defines the polis: not as a geographical place or a set of laws, nor as a structure of government. It is a space of free deeds and living words. These words echo what Arendt makes clear in *The Human Condition*: "The *polis*, properly speaking, is not the city-state in its physical location; it is the organization of the people as it arises out of acting and speaking together, and its true space lies between people living together for this purpose, no matter where they happen to be."[73]

This defines the polis "properly speaking," and as Roy Tsao points out, it is nearly the opposite of Pericles' bricks-and-mortar-and-laws conception of the polis. As Arendt sums up Pericles' view, the polis is a walled city, with laws designed to ensure that succeeding generations would not "change its identity beyond recognition" (a dead constitution with no space for novel action!) and which, lacking those walls, "could not survive the moment of action and speech itself."[74] Although Arendt's *de re* stance is maddeningly opaque in these pages, I think the best interpretation is Tsao's: that she *rejects* Pericles' boasts in the Funeral Oration. Tsao believes that Arendt saw Pericles' oration as nothing more than "a fantasy wish" that Athens's walls and laws will preserve it forever – a fantasy wish she does not share.[75]

As further evidence that Arendt's *de dicto* summary of Pericles is not her *de re* theory, notice that she introduces Pericles' boast that the polis will guarantee everlasting remembrance with a cautionary note, "if we trust the famous words of Pericles." Of course, we must *not* trust the famous words of Pericles: As Arendt herself points out, at the very moment Pericles boasted that the Athenian polis would guarantee immortal fame to its citizens, it was already doomed.[76] What we remember today is not the Athenian walls, nor the Athenian laws, but Athenian art and democracy –

72 *OR*, 285. 73 *HC*, 198. 74 *HC*, 198.

75 Tsao, "Arendt against Athens," 114. See also *EJ*, 262–63, on why "territory . . . is a political and a legal concept, and not merely a geographical term. It relates not so much, and not primarily, to a piece of land as to the space between individuals in a group."

76 *HC*, 205.

the work of its sculptors, architects, and poets, and the space Athens temporarily created for action. That is what matters for Arendt.

In her final book, Arendt made abundantly clear how little she suffered from Hellenic nostalgia. Quoting Nietzsche's derisive remark that German philosophy wallows in homesickness for the Greek world, to which all bridges are broken except "the rainbow bridge of concepts," Arendt comments: "I did not want to cross the 'rainbow-bridge of concepts,' perhaps because I am not homesick enough."[77] So much for the polis envy theory.

Once we recognize the gulf separating Arendt from "the Greek view" she is describing, we realize as well that the Greek obsession with immortality is not one she shares. An important conclusion follows from her definition of the polis "properly speaking" as "the organization of the people as it arises out of acting and speaking together." Present tense, not future tense: The emphasis here is not on whether distant generations will remember our actions; it is on acting among our contemporaries. For Arendt, evidently, the point of action is *not* earthly immortality.

Of course, she does not deny that being remembered in the future matters to us; obviously it does:

> Experiences and even the stories which grow out of what men do and endure, of happenings and events, sink back into the futility inherent in the living word and the living deed unless they are talked about over and over again. What saves the affairs of mortal men from their inherent futility is nothing but this incessant talk about them.[78]

She writes this in an explanation of why remembrance matters. Contradicting Pericles, she argues that the poets and historians are essential to collective memory, an acknowledgment that collective memory matters.[79] But being remembered in the far future is less central to her account of a meaningful life than being seen, heard, and remembered by our contemporaries. It is acting in the company of our fellows that endows life with splendor, with or without the kind of immortality that Plato and Aristotle believe we need.

Among commentators on Scheffler's doomsday scenario, Susan Wolf comes closest to this point of view. Like Arendt, she believes that "the very idea that things matter relies on a valuing community (of more than one), but that community need not have a future – that it have a past and a

77 *W*, 157–58, quoting Nietzsche, *The Will to Power*, §419. 78 *OR*, 222.

79 *HC*, 173. As we will see in Chapter 14 [§14.8], we should add courts of law that make and authenticate a forensic record to the list of memory makers.

present would be enough."[80] After all, Wolf reminds us, we know that sooner or later the earth will be extinguished, yet that knowledge does not destroy the possibility of leading a meaningful life.

Where have we gotten? Assembling all the material in this chapter, we have an argument that runs something like this. We need meaning in our lives. As self-aware beings who know death, bare existence is not enough. Some people find meaning in religious faith, but Arendt limits her investigation to secular possibilities. One secular counterpart to religious faith is the life of contemplation commended by Plato, Aristotle, and the medieval philosophers – the reasoned contemplation of eternal things. That fails. Other possibilities that fail are the life of pleasure and consumption, and the inward turn to our own subjective experience. These prove to be too evanescent, and too divorced from a common, shared world of durable things, to be truly meaningful. The satisfactions of work come precisely from producing something durable, but the question of why that matters cannot be answered within the means–ends vocabulary associated with work. The answer "for the sake of free action" comes closer to the mark, because the capacity to start something new is inherently meaningful. It turns out, though, that what makes action meaningful is that through action we show who we are: We reveal ourselves to others as unique individuals. Action requires other people as audience and storyteller. It might seem that this matters because we achieve a kind of earthly counterpart to immortality through remembrance by others. One venue for this remembrance is the political community, the polis. But the polis understood as an edifice of walls and laws lacks a mechanism for remembrance. Properly understood, the polis is a community of contemporaries, and action in their company – not the immortality of being remembered in the far future – is what gives life meaning.

## 9.7 The Case of the Missing Morality Resolved

### *9.7.1 Arendt's* Minima Moralia*: Promise-Keeping and Forgiveness*

The central or even exalted place Arendt gives to action has consequences for the Case of the Missing Morality. To see how, it's instructive to examine the only place that Arendt introduces morality into *The Human Condition*: She admits that some moral precepts make action possible, rather than constraining it. "These moral precepts are the only ones that

[80] Wolf, "The Significance of Doomsday," in Scheffler, *Death and the Afterlife*, 124.

are not applied to action from the outside, from some supposedly higher faculty or from experiences outside action's own reach."[81] She identifies just two such precepts: "readiness to forgive and to be forgiven, to make promises and to keep them."[82]

Why these two? The moral code inferred from the practice of promising and promise-keeping – which, if Arendt were legally inclined, she might label with its proper name: contract law – allows actors to combine forces in the face of uncertainty and mistrust. Promise-keeping makes joint endeavors possible, and these are the core endeavors in human action. No promise-keeping, no trust; no trust, no joint action.

Forgiveness has a less obvious, but equally compelling, justification: "Without being forgiven, released from the consequences of what we have done, our capacity to act would, as it were, be confined to one single deed from which we could never recover."[83] Every single mistake would, in effect, doom us to life without moral parole. Using a different but equally suggestive legal metaphor, Arendt's precept of forgiveness is akin to the law of bankruptcy, releasing us from moral debts so we can make a fresh start.

Both of these rationales, for promising as well as forgiving, make sense. But here's the rub: Apart from these precepts of binding and unbinding, which are entirely plausible, Arendt seems to recognize no moral duties intrinsic to action. Of course, there is a conventional morality of "customs and standards of behavior solidified through tradition and valid on the ground of agreements, both of which change with time."[84] But if that is all there is, doesn't she run the danger of a pernicious moral relativism? The swift moral collapse of Germany she saw in 1933 drove home to her that even the most basic principles of human decency are not immune from the fickleness of conventional morality. If there are no moral standards other than the thin morality of promising and forgiving plus the prevailing conventional morality, what would entitle her to call what happened in Germany a moral collapse – as she does? That judgment comes from outside the conventional morality of the Third Reich, and it has nothing to do with promising or forgiving. But it is plainly a moral judgment that Arendt is prepared to make. Isn't there a contradiction between Arendt's neglect of morality in *The Human Condition* and the practice of moral judgment, which she never doubts and which she engages in all the time?

The answer is yes. Earlier, I suggested a diagnosis: Because of the exalted role action plays in her explanation of where meaning comes from in human affairs, Arendt was deeply reluctant to acknowledge external

[81] *HC*, 246. [82] *HC*, 246. [83] *HC*, 237. [84] *HC*, 245.

constraints on action. They seemed to her like a *deus ex machina* – descending from on high, as she says, "from some supposedly higher faculty or from experiences outside action's own reach." The precepts of forgiveness and promising arise from action itself because they make action possible. Extrinsic moral constraints handcuff the actor.

Arendt said this more clearly in a pair of unpublished reflections than in the writing she published. The first is this: "Morality fails as soon as we begin to act"[85] – by which she means that action is novel, unpredictable, and moves by its own imperatives. Action is dangerous, however, to self and to others, and the danger must somehow be cabined.

> Out of this need one invents moral rules and standards. One wants to constrain action. But: Because these rules in principle come from outside, they can always only restrict, never prescribe, and action will break through and overcome them again and again; it will "violate" them.[86]

This is the amoralist strand of her thinking, and our question is whether *The Human Condition* is really committed to it.

### *9.7.2 Amoralism and "Behavior": A Critique*

Let's reconsider a striking claim quoted earlier, which to most readers counts as the clearest proof-text of amoralism in *The Human Condition*: "Unlike human behavior – which the Greeks, like all civilized people, judged according to 'moral standards,' taking into account motives and intentions on the one hand and aims and consequences on the other – action can be judged only by the criterion of greatness."[87] This echoes another unpublished diary entry:

> Morality relates to our "*behavior*," and is therefore a social and not genuinely political concept from the outset. All morality fails, as soon as we begin to *act*, to make a beginning. Morality never foresaw this beginning. All action is amoral, per definitionem [by definition].[88]

*The Human Condition* never says anything as blunt as the final sentence, and we must be cautious about reading too much into a diary entry that Arendt never published. *The Human Condition*'s proposition that action can be judged only by its greatness is Pericles talking, not Arendt, as the context surrounding the quoted sentence makes clear. The part of the quote from *The Human Condition* that obviously *is* Arendt talking consists

85 *DTB*, Heft XXI, [83] (January 1956), 557–58.
86 *DTB*, Heft XXI, [83] (January 1956), 557–58.
87 *HC*, 205.
88 *DTB*, Heft XXI, [83] (March 1955), 520–21.

of the claim that all civilized people judge behavior according to moral standards. In this respect, she is not the amoralist she seems. The oddity is her restriction of morality to "human behavior" rather than action. That, I now argue, is a mistake.

"Behavior" is a residual and underanalyzed category for Arendt: It is not labor, work, or action. Apparently it refers to routine or habitual conduct that doesn't initiate anything new; in the few places she discusses behavior, she equates it with the kind of scripted conformism that she warned was on the rise in American mass society, and which the behavioral sciences of the 1950s promised to predict and control.[89]

There is no good reason to limit the scope of moral judgment to behavior rather than action. When novel action is repeated, copied, and routinized, it loses its novelty and congeals into "behavior," but it's still the same conduct-type. Conversely, conformist behavior doesn't come from nowhere. It originated as novel action on someone's part, which others copied. If, in its guise as behavior, we can judge conduct according to motives, intentions, and consequences, nothing prevents us from tendering the same judgments the first time the conduct occurs, in its guise as action. It follows that any practice of moral judgment capable of judging behavior will always be capable of judging action as well.

Now it may be that Arendt recognized this point; the first diary entry quoted earlier acknowledges that action will "violate" moral rules, which implies that we can indeed pass moral judgment on action. However, she puts "violate" in scare quotes, which suggests that it is only violation from the standpoint of conventional morality, not from the standpoint of action. She also asserts that the need to control the disruptions caused by action will lead to the invention of new moral rules and standards. Perhaps, then, the model she envisions is similar to the evolution of

89 *HC*, 41–43. The second thought diary entry is in German, but she quotes the word "behavior" in English, which makes the American reference clear. The 1950s was a period of hubris in the behavioral sciences, and Arendt was not the only observer who thought that their promise of predicting and controlling human behavior was irredeemably sinister. I note, however, that her argument in *HC* that mass societies are more conformist than smaller ones is a statistical fallacy. She writes that "the more people there are, the more likely they are to behave and the less likely to tolerate non-behavior. Statistically, this will be shown in the leveling out of fluctuation." *HC*, 43. True, as a population gets larger, it exhibits more notable statistical regularities (the mean tends toward the expected value); but from this she seems to conclude that individuals' behavior hews more closely to those regularities, which is a fallacy of division that misses the statistical point completely. Not only is the argument bad, its premise is doubtful. In small, village-sized populations there is closer monitoring of others' conduct, hence more conformism, than in large anonymous cities. A reader of *Middlemarch* is treated to a vivid, scathing, and very realistic look at the conformist pressure in a rural English village.

customary law: Every customary rule originated as a violation of previous rules, before stabilizing into a superseding rule (which will be superseded in turn). On this model, action inherently involves a ceaseless creative destruction in the moral realm.

Calling action "amoral," though, puts it beyond good and evil, and that is a dangerous and fatuous line of thought. It takes away the very standpoint that enables Arendt to judge that the novel standards of the Third Reich amounted to moral collapse, destruction that is the opposite of creative. Perhaps Arendt recognized this problem, which would explain why her published work never says that action is beyond good and evil. Just the opposite.[90]

In addition, the claim that action is amoral would contradict her own theory of what makes action meaningful: the judgment of others. On her account of action, recall, its meaning is indeterminate until others make it into stories and – crucially – judge it.[91] What she seems not to appreciate is that others will judge it *morally*, and not solely by a standard of greatness or even noteworthiness.

The implication is clear: Far from being extrinsic to action, the moral standards spectators use in responding to others' deeds, their "enacted stories," belong to the stories themselves, and therefore to the actions. They are not external standards imposed from on high – they are the standards applied by other individuals, in their role as spectators and judges, who are the actor's peers engaged in a practice of judging that is itself a form of action.

Even though Arendt didn't draw these conclusions in *The Human Condition*, she should have. They are consequences of her systematic theory. And obviously this famously judgmental political theorist never really thought it impossible to pass moral judgment on the conduct around her. She insisted that those who ask, *Who am I to judge?* are guilty of "a quite extraordinary confusion over elementary questions of morality"; their stance is "elaborate nonsense."[92] She certainly never entertained the proposition that her judgments about the Hitler and Stalin regimes rested on nothing but conventional morality, valid solely on the ground of

90 "Hannah Arendt on Hannah Arendt," *TWB*, 464.

91 Arendt says that only the backward glance of the historian can discern the meaning of an action. *HC*, 233. By the time she wrote *Thinking*, she had drawn a clear distinction between the actor and the spectator, and insisted that it is the judging spectator who discerns the meaning in action. *T*, 92, 95, 96.

92 Extraordinary questions: *EJ*, 295; elaborate nonsense: PRUD, 19. She discusses the point at greater length in PRUD, 18–21.

agreements. As we will see in Chapter 10, Arendt was committed to a conception of human dignity that the totalitarian regimes set out to destroy. She simply failed to connect her own moral practice of judgment (and of course it is not hers alone) with the theory in *The Human Condition*.[93] Perceiving that gap had to wait until the Eichmann trial inescapably brought it to the forefront of her attention.

[93] Here I very much agree with Mahony, *Hannah Arendt's Ethics*, 145–46, that Arendt's sensibilities align more with moral realism than relativism or skepticism.

# PART V

# *Arendt and International Law*

CHAPTER 10

# *Statelessness, Human Rights, and Humanity*

Arendt never wrote about most of the textbook subjects in the philosophy of law, and she showed no obvious interest in the everyday workings of legal institutions. Her contributions to legal thought are almost entirely in constitutional theory and international law.[1] I address only the latter in this book. As I hope to show, they dig deep.

Best known is her critique of human rights law in *The Origins of Totalitarianism*, and her much-discussed concept of "the right to have rights." As I argue, both the critique and the concept form part of a larger conception of human dignity and what Arendt calls "the idea of humanity." A few scattered remarks also hint at a revised conception of state sovereignty implicit in the "idea of humanity" – a conception that resembles proposals by contemporary theorists that sovereignty entails cross-border responsibilities. I devote the present chapter to these topics.

Later, the Eichmann trial confronted her with central questions about how (and whether) criminal law can grapple with extraordinary evils; these are the major focus in Chapters 11–15. Her answers turn out to have deep connections with her ideas about statelessness, sovereignty, and human rights – and also with central themes in *The Human Condition* and her moral philosophy.

## 10.1 Statelessness and the Right to Have Rights

Arendt became a refugee when she fled Germany in 1933, and a 1941 Nazi decree stripped her of her nationality; she remained stateless until she became a US citizen a decade later. No doubt personal experience sharpened her focus on the plight of the stateless, a category in which

[1] Her constitutional theorizing appears in *On Revolution* and the essay on civil disobedience in *Crises of the Republic*.

she included de facto as well as de jure statelessness. It encompasses everyone whom no state, including their home state, wants or protects.

De jure statelessness means that a person is not a lawful citizen of any state. De facto statelessness is a broader category. It means that regardless of whether the person possesses legal citizenship, their state won't or can't protect their basic rights. Perhaps they come from a state mired in civil war, or unable to control extreme gang violence, or to feed its people in time of famine. Perhaps the state won't protect women from deadly domestic abuse, or religious minorities from pogroms. Perhaps, as in Arendt's case, the state itself becomes the persecutor. The de facto stateless include refugees, involuntary migrants, and displaced persons – all those who don't enjoy the protection of their rights by any state, regardless of de jure citizenship.[2] Arendt was de facto stateless from the moment she fled Germany, and de jure stateless after the Third Reich stripped away the citizenship of émigré Jews.

But the issue of statelessness was, to say the least, not merely personal to Arendt. In Europe alone, there were tens of millions of refugees and displaced persons between the wars and after World War II – a major humanitarian and political crisis, just as it is today. Arendt saw clearly that human rights did them no good; stateless people, protected by nothing but their human rights, had no protection at all:

> The prolongation of their lives is due to charity and not to right, for no law exists which could force the nations to feed them; their freedom of movement, if they have it at all, gives them no right to residence which even the jailed criminal enjoys as a matter of course; and their freedom of opinion is a fool's freedom, for nothing they think matters anyhow.[3]

Human rights, supposedly signifying universal inclusion in humanity, become instead an emblem of universal exclusion. You only fall back on your human rights, after all, when all other recourses have failed you.[4]

What the stateless lack is a political community that recognizes them as rights-bearers and guarantees their rights. In *Origins*, Arendt calls the right

[2] *OT*, 279–80, 281n28, 286. In my discussion I follow Arendt and use "stateless" as a blanket term that straddles both de jure and de facto statelessness. These include the categories of refugees fleeing persecution, and "survival migrants" who don't meet formal legal criteria for refugee status but who migrate in order to survive, fleeing war or famine. Alexander Betts, *The Wealth of Refugees: How Displaced Persons Can Build Economies* (Oxford University Press, 2021), 37. They also include stateless people who reside in birth countries whose laws deny them citizenship, often on arbitrary and racist grounds contrived to evade antidiscrimination norms. Neha Jain, "Manufacturing Statelessness," *American Journal of International Law* 116(2) (2022): 237–88.

[3] *OT*, 296. [4] *EJ*, 271.

to membership in such a community the "right to have rights," and her point is that without it, no other human rights matter. "Right to have rights" is a cryptic phrase that has provoked considerable interpretive debate.[5] In a 1958 opinion, US Supreme Court Chief Justice Earl Warren interpreted it narrowly as citizenship:

> Citizenship is man's basic right for it is nothing less than the right to have rights. Remove this priceless possession and there remains a stateless person, disgraced and degraded in the eyes of his countrymen. He has no lawful claim to protection from any nation, and no nation may assert rights on his behalf. His very existence is at the sufferance of the state within whose borders he happens to be.[6]

Here, Warren wrote as a dissenter in a deportation case. Writing for the majority that same term, Warren reiterated that "the expatriate has lost the right to have rights" – and he cites a law journal article that credits the phrase to *The Origins of Totalitarianism.*[7]

In an unpublished lecture, Arendt likewise equated the right to have rights with citizenship, and indeed she asserted that citizenship guarantees the right to have rights.[8] Both these points seem careless. As to the first, noncitizens may still enjoy some legal protections. Conversely, and as no one knew better than Arendt, de jure citizenship guarantees a person nothing if their home state persecutes them rather than protects them. In wartime, having a nationality may actually make refugees worse off, if the state to which they flee – the "receiving state" in legal terminology –

5 For a useful summary of the main lines of disagreement, see the editors' introduction and first chapter of Stephanie DeGooyer et al., *The Right to Have Rights* (Verso, 2018). Recent treatments include Melissa Stewart, "'A New Law on Earth': Hannah Arendt and the Vision for a Positive Legal Framework to Guarantee the Right to Have Rights," *Virginia Journal of International Law* 62(1) (2021): 115–79; Alison Kesby, *The Right to Have Rights: Citizenship, Humanity, and International Law* (Oxford University Press, 2012); Ayten Gündoğdu, *Rightlessness in an Age of Rights: Hannah Arendt and the Contemporary Struggles of Migrants* (Oxford University Press, 2015); Peg Birmingham, *Hannah Arendt and Human Rights: The Predicament of Common Responsibility* (Indiana University Press, 2006). Older treatments include Benhabib, *The Reluctant Modernism of Hannah Arendt*, 46, 185; Seyla Benhabib, "'The Right to Have Rights': Hannah Arendt on the Contradictions of the Nation-State," in *The Rights of Others* (Cambridge University Press, 2004), 46–47; Frank Michelman, "Parsing a 'Right to Have Rights'," *Constellations* 3(2) (1996): 200–8.

6 Perez v. Brownell, 356 U.S. 44, 64 (1958)(Warren, CJ, dissenting).

7 Trop v. Dulles, 356 U.S. 86, 102 (1958). The law journal article is "Comment: The Expatriation Act of 1954," *Yale Law Journal* 64(8) (1955): 1166. The interesting fact that Warren was indirectly quoting Arendt was first noted by Stephen J. Whitfield, *Into the Dark: Hannah Arendt and Totalitarianism* (Temple University Press, 1980), 111–12, 285nn47–48; see DeGooyer et al., *The Right to Have Rights*, 10, 126n17.

8 Arendt, "Statelessness," lecture notes, April 22, 1955, Library of Congress, Hannah Arendt Papers: Speeches and Writings File, 1923–1975; Essays and Lectures, www.loc.gov/resource/mss11056dig.052290/?st=pdf&pdfPage=5 [https://perma.cc/S3EY-Q2L4], 4.

treats them as enemy aliens.[9] And in peacetime foreign citizenship may make refugees worse off if it absolves their receiving state of obligations to protect their interests – or, worse, tempts the receiving state to deport them to the home state they fled.[10] All of which is to say that a person can possess de jure citizenship and still be stateless de facto. Since nothing obligates foreign states to protect their rights, and their home ("sending") state won't, the stateless lack the right to have rights, that is, the right to have their rights recognized by law and protected in fact.

Both halves matter. Recognition by law is meaningless if it doesn't bring protection in fact; and protection in fact is unreliable happenstance – charity or luck – if the law will not recognize a person as a subject of rights and responsibilities. Arendt proposes a practical test: You lack the right to have rights if you would benefit from committing a small burglary, because during your trial and imprisonment you would be on the same footing as other burglars, protected from sheer arbitrary police rule. At times it's better to be a criminal than an outlaw.[11] Taken literally, an outlaw is a person outside the law – someone who lacks standing to claim whatever protections the law offers. Arendt observes that "[t]he first essential step on the road to total domination is to kill the juridical person in man."[12] Possessing juridical personality comes closer than de jure citizenship to defining a human being's right to have rights – provided that the receiving state actually protects the rights of juridical persons in its territory, including stateless juridical persons.

None of this is to say that statelessness automatically divests a person of effective legal rights. De facto statelessness comes in degrees, depending on the receiving state's toleration, benign neglect, or lax law enforcement. Refugees and other stateless people can and do own property in their

[9] Mira Siegelberg begins her superb history of modern statelessness with the case of a German businessman in World War I England who sued to be declared stateless so he wouldn't be treated as an enemy alien. His case was far from unique. Mira L. Siegelberg, *Statelessness: A Modern History* (Harvard University Press, 2020), 12–19, 44–45.

[10] Under the 1951 Convention Relating to the Status of Refugees, persons fleeing a country because of a well-founded fear of persecution on the basis of race, religion, nationality, membership in a particular social group, or political opinion are entitled to political asylum. However, many survival refugees don't fit these categories of persecution. Moreover, many countries in the global North are making it harder to get asylum. So, even though the law is more favorable to refugees today than when Arendt wrote, the gap between the law in books and the law in action remains vast.

[11] *OT*, 286.

[12] *OT*, 447. Among her research notes, Arendt copied out extracts from historical sources on the dire and dehumanizing consequences of existing outside all law. Entry "VOGELFREI – Friedlos – Outlawry" and "Excommunication," Library of Congress, Hannah Arendt Papers: Speeches and Writings File, 1923–1975; Excerpts and Notes; Minority Statelessness, www.loc.gov/resource/mss11056dig.053020/?st=pdf&pdfPage=18 [https://perma.cc/R9DB-U7Y9], 26245.

receiving states, open bank accounts, make contracts, run businesses, pay taxes, and participate in other incidents of everyday legal life – only so long as their receiving state allows it, but of course much the same can be said of the state's citizens. Arendt is focusing on one end of the continuum: those whose status is so precarious, and whose civil rights are so little protected by their receiving state, that they have nothing but their human rights standing between them and the abyss. Her point is that once you have entered the limbo where your only rights are human rights, you will not even have your human rights.[13] Even the French Declaration of the Rights of Man insists that "all sovereignty resides essentially in the nation," not in individuals. The sovereignty of the nation-state means that the Rights of Man are useless unless the nation-state gives you the right to assert them and have them protected. Without the right to have rights, you are a ghost.

In this connection, Arendt highlighted the exquisite care the Nazis took to strip Jews of their nationality before deporting them to the camps.[14] Lacking membership in a political community, you are "expelled from humanity," and for that reason she counts deprivation of citizenship as "among the crimes against humanity," adding that "some of the worst recognized crimes in this category have in fact, and not incidentally, been preceded by expatriations."[15] Drawing a line from statelessness to genocide, she was connecting legal and political nonexistence with physical nonexistence, the ultimate exclusion from humanity.

## 10.2 Human Dignity and Rights

Her withering human rights skepticism can make it seem that Arendt has little use for international law and the discourse of human dignity that figures so prominently in postwar human rights instruments. Just the opposite is true. In the wake of the twentieth century's calamities,

[13] *OT*, 299.

[14] *OT*, 280. She is referring to the Eleventh Decree to the Law of Citizenship of the Reich, November 25, 1941 – the decree that rendered her stateless. On the Vichy regime's cooperation, see Richard Weisberg, *Vichy Law and the Holocaust in France* (Routledge, 2013) and Michael R. Marrus and Robert O. Paxton, *Vichy France and the Jews* (Stanford University Press, 1981).

[15] Arendt to Robert M. Hutchins, January 27, 1957, Library of Congress, Hannah Arendt Papers: Correspondence, 1938–1976; Organizations, 1943–1976; Fund for the Republic, 1956–1965, www.loc.gov/resource/mss11056dig.022110/?sp=24&st=pdf&r=-0.235%2C0.497%2C1.469%2C1.469%2C0&pdfPage=25 [https://perma.cc/797Z-23UW ], 12581. Larry May attributes to Arendt the idea that one reason genocide is an especially grave wrong is that it so often forces people to become refugees. May, *Genocide: A Normative Account* (Cambridge University Press, 2010), 69. While he is absolutely right about that causal connection, I believe this gets Arendt's argument backward. Arendt's argument is that statelessness is a waystation toward genocide.

Arendt urged a form of international law that would protect human dignity and promote a cosmopolitan moral community – a community that would do more than warehouse the stateless in camps and wring its hands or shrug its shoulders in the face of atrocity.

She makes this clear from the outset of *Origins*. In the preface she writes that "human dignity needs a new guarantee which can be found only in a new political principle, in a new law on earth, whose validity this time must comprehend the whole of humanity while its power must remain strictly limited, rooted in and controlled by newly defined territorial entities."[16] The dozen places she mentions human dignity in *Origins* all give it fundamental importance. Readers might wonder whether "new law on earth" is a figure of speech; but Arendt clearly has international law in mind: "the idea of humanity ... constitutes the sole regulating idea of international law."[17]

Such talk sounds weirdly utopian coming from an author who dismissively likened human rights organizations to societies for the prevention of cruelty to animals, and who scoffed at the Universal Declaration of Human Rights) (UDHR) (its "lack of reality is rather conspicuous").[18] In 1946, she wrote to Kurt Blumenfeld that "I don't know what human rights really are and nobody else seems to know either."[19]

It's worth remembering, though, that Arendt wrote *Origins* soon after the Nuremberg and Tokyo war crimes trials, and the birth of the United Nations (UN). At that time, it certainly seemed that practical statesmen were trying to imagine a new politics and a reconfigured international law. Legal historians question whether the late 1940s were truly Hour Zero of a new international order, but it seemed possible to Arendt, as it did to many others, that the arc of law might bend toward an idea of humanity that race thinking and tribal nationalism had displaced.

Despite her suspicions about human rights law, Arendt is not a critic who scorns human dignity as sentimental nonsense or theology in disguise. What she does reject is the theory of human dignity as a metaphysical property of individuals, which would endure even if only one human being

[16] *OT*, ix.

[17] *OT*, 157. Read in context, Arendt also maintains that the "idea of humanity" is something we have lost, and what displaced it was modern race doctrines, nationalism, and ideological theories of history.

[18] *OT*, 292; Arendt, "The 'Rights of Man': What Are They?," *Modern Review* 3(1) (Summer 1949): 37.

[19] Arendt to Kurt Blumenfeld, July 17, 1946, in Hannah Arendt and Kurt Blumenfeld, "... *in keinem Besitz verwurzelt": Die Korrespondenz*, eds. Ingeborg Nordmann and Iris Pilling (Rotbuch Verlag, 1995), 41.

remained alive.[20] The individualist conception of human dignity is implicit in traditional theories of the Rights of Man, which define them as rights we possess merely by virtue of being human. For Arendt, by contrast, human dignity is a *relational* property, that is, a status we bestow on one another: Human dignity lies in the relationship between the dignifier and the dignified.[21] It requires "the recognition of my fellow-men or our fellow-nations as subjects, as builders of worlds or cobuilders of a common world."[22]

Perhaps Arendt was reacting to the famous Talmudic dictum that because the first human was created alone, whoever destroys a single soul destroys an entire world. She explains that human beings are never created alone but always in a plurality of others ("male and female created he *them*," she quotes from Genesis 1:27, a reminder that "no human being knows what is MAN in the singular."[23]) As such, we are cobuilders of a common world. But even though she rejects a metaphysically individualist concept of human dignity, Arendt unmistakably writes as someone for whom human dignity matters.

Human dignity, understood as a rank we bestow on each other, is an answer to a philosophical question – a humanized variant of Heidegger's famous, "Why is there anything at all rather than nothing?" Here, the question is, "Why are *we* anything at all rather than nothing?" And the answer is, because we treat one another as something rather than nothing. Doing so is the most rudimentary form of honoring human dignity. In Chapter 9, we saw that Arendt's answer to our confrontation with futility lies in our recognition by others, which inscribes us in "the storybook of mankind."[24] The alternative is to treat other human beings, oneself perhaps included, as superfluous. Recall Arendt's description of the totalitarian system (quoted earlier in §5.4): "The manipulators of this system believe in their own superfluousness as much as in that of all others, and the totalitarian murderers are all the more dangerous because they do not care if they themselves are alive or dead, if they ever lived or never were

[20] *OT*, 297.

[21] *OT*, 301–2. This is the view I defend in David Luban, *Legal Ethics and Human Dignity* (Cambridge University Press, 2007); David Luban, "Human Rights Pragmatism and Human Dignity," in *Philosophical Foundations of Human Rights*, eds. Massimo Renzo et al. (Oxford University Press, 2015), 263–78.

[22] *OT*, 458. The remark comes in her explanation of why totalitarianism must "destroy every trace of what we commonly call human dignity." *OT*, 458; cf. *OT*, 454.

[23] "Hannah Arendt on Hannah Arendt," in *TWB*, 453, emphasis in original. The Talmudic dictum is in Talmud Bavli, Sanhedrin 37a. A similar formulation appears in Qur'an 5:32.

[24] *HC*, 184. In connection with Heidegger's ponderous "why is there anything at all rather than nothing?" (the first sentence of his *Introduction to Metaphysics*), I find Sidney Morgenbesser's response irresistible: if there was nothing, he'd still be complaining.

born."[25] Their mission is to eradicate every trace of human dignity, dissolving it into whatever vast world-historical or biological process their ideology preaches.

Understanding human dignity as a relational property rather than a property of individuals pays dividends, because it gives us a better grasp of Arendt's new law on earth and the right to have rights. A new law on earth is required, she tell us, because "human dignity needs a new guarantee."[26] Human rights law fails to provide stateless people with that guarantee, unless it effectively provides the one right that is a necessary condition for all other rights: the right to recognition by a political body as someone within the scope of its legal rights. The word "recognition" signifies that one is *seen* and *acknowledged* by the polity and its members. One enters the relational space of human dignity. If the new law on earth were to ensure that recognition to everyone, then everyone would have the right to have rights and the dignity it confers. Then we could get started talking about what other protections human dignity requires – and those would be our human rights.

Notably, Article 6 of the UDHR proclaims: "Everyone has the right to recognition everywhere as a person before the law." So far so good. The trouble is that the UDHR is a collection of nonbinding aspirational standards – a declaration, not a hard-law treaty, let alone a hard-law treaty that its parties honor in fact rather than in name only. It exhorts us to recognize everyone as a person before the law, but it imposes no obligation on any state to do so. That is why Arendt complained of the UDHR's "conspicuous lack of reality."

She nevertheless agreed that "[t]he benefits derived from an enumeration of existing rights could be great indeed, and might well belong to those blessings that will come about through the growing interrelatedness of all nations." Maybe – eventually. But in the meantime, the danger is that "in the welter of rights of the most heterogeneous nature and origin, we are only too likely to overlook and neglect the one right without which no other can materialize – the right to belong to a political community."[27] That is the right to have rights. And Arendt surely noticed that this right appears in the UDHR partway down its list, in the minimal form of a right to juridical personality rather than a full-blown right of belonging that carries with it all the protections of law.[28] Worse, it is a right attaching

[25] *OT*, 459. [26] *OT*, ix. [27] Arendt, "The Rights of Man: What Are They?," 37.

[28] The right to recognition before the law also appears in the binding International Covenant on Civil and Political Rights, art. 16. It entered into force in 1976 (a year after Arendt's death), and has 173 states-parties. Although it is binding on its parties, and may represent customary international law, its enforcement mechanism is weak.

only once a refugee has gained admittance to a state. Neither the UDHR nor the 1951 Refugee Convention obligates any state to admit a refugee, and that has not changed since the time Arendt wrote. The UN Human Rights Committee has clarified that the human right to *exit* a country does not include a legal right to enter any other country.[29]

Commentators have puzzled over the first occurrence of the word "right" in "the right to have rights." Is it a synecdoche for the whole body of human rights? Is it a nonlegal moral right grounded in a Kantian conception of the person? Is it a performative political act of demanding rights?[30] On the reading presented here – proposed by legal scholar Melissa Stewart – it seems that Arendt saw it as a positive legal right that does not yet exist but that *could* exist under a new political principle and a new law on earth.[31]

Notice that Arendt calls this right to membership "the one right without which no other can materialize." That makes it a *basic* right in the sense defined by Henry Shue years later: Rights are basic "if enjoyment of them is essential to the enjoyment of all other rights."[32] Shue argues, quite reasonably, that the two most basic rights are those to physical security and subsistence. Rights, in turn, must be "socially guaranteed against standard threats"; that is what makes them rights.[33] Arendt's point is that the right to have rights is no less basic, and indeed logically prior, because without it the state will guarantee nothing. It is the admission ticket to the realm of rights.

[29] Carlos Varela Núñez v. Uruguay, Communication No. 108/1981, U.N. Doc. CCPR/C/OP/2 at 143 (1990) at §9.3. The right to exit is in Article 12(2) of the International Covenant on Civil and Political Rights. For a searching examination of this problem – a human right to exit with no corresponding right of entry anywhere – see Moria Paz, "Toward a Taxonomy of Freedom of Movement Claims: Identifying Rights-Based Pathways for Today's Refugees beyond the 1951 Refugee Convention," *Harvard Journal of International Law* 65(2) (2024): 457–526.

[30] For helpful discussion, see Stephanie DeGooyer, "The Right . . . ," in DeGooyer et al., *The Right to Have Rights*, 21–39.

[31] Stewart, "'A New Law on Earth': Hannah Arendt and the Vision for a Positive Legal Framework to Guarantee the Right to Have Rights." This reading parts ways with Benhabib's interpretation of the right to have rights as a moral right, not a legislated right, as well as the performative theories of Bonnie Honig and Judith Butler. Benhabib, *The Reluctant Modernism of Hannah Arendt*, 185; Bonnie Honig, *Emergency Politics: Paradox, Law, Democracy* (Princeton University Press, 2009), 117; Judith Butler, *Notes Toward a Performative Theory of Assembly* (Harvard University Press, 2015), 49. Butler writes of "Arendt's assertion that even the stateless have 'the right to have rights'." *Notes Toward a Performative Theory of Assembly*, 48. But Arendt's view is that the stateless *lack* the right to have rights: "We became aware of the existence of a right to have rights . . . only when millions of people emerged who had lost and could not regain these rights." *OT*, 296–97.

[32] Henry Shue, *Basic Rights: Subsistence, Affluence, and U.S. Foreign Policy*, 2nd ed. (Princeton University Press, 1996), 19.

[33] Shue, *Basic Rights*, 13.

The right to have rights is the political and legal form that human dignity assumes in its most primordial aspect: being accepted in a polity and recognized as a fellow bearer of rights. Obviously, though, human dignity requires more than bare recognition. You can be recognized as a juridical person and still be treated like dirt. What else human dignity requires cannot be specified through an a priori theory. Rather, we develop our conception of human dignity in a piecemeal way, through the very process of arguing for or against particular human rights. In other words, human dignity is not, as is sometimes said, the *foundation* of human rights – meaning that the rights can be deduced from the concept of human dignity. Rather, our conception of human dignity emerges reciprocally and simultaneously with our recognition of the rights needed to protect it. Human dignity and human rights are two sides of the same coin, where the "dignity" side focuses on human persons and their relationships, and the "rights" side focuses on the political and legal institutions needed to protect those relationships against standard threats. An argument for subsistence or security rights is an argument that human dignity requires security and subsistence. And vice versa: An argument that human dignity is impossible without security and subsistence is an argument for an enforceable basic right to security and subsistence.[34] If human dignity can be secured to workers only if they are able to organize, then the right to organize is a human right, just as the UDHR declares.

Arendt never compiles a list of the rights she thinks the protection of human dignity requires, but they appear piecemeal, and sometimes indirectly, in various writings. They include the negative liberties: freedom of movement, freedom of speech and thought, freedom of the press, freedom of association and assembly, freedom *from* politics (i.e., the right of nonparticipation), the right against enslavement, the right to a fair trial, freedom from arbitrary police power, the right to engage in civil disobedience, and political equality.[35] In other words, the familiar liberal rights, although Arendt denied that she was a liberal.[36]

[34] See Luban, "Human Rights Pragmatism and Human Dignity," 263–78. The idea appears as well in James Griffin, *On Human Rights* (Oxford University Press, 2008), 66.

[35] Civil rights and negative liberties generally: *OR*, 22, 24, 111, 132, 141–42, 220. Freedom of movement: *OR*, 24–25, *PP*, 129. Free speech and thought, *OR*, 272. Free press: *OR*, 326n82 (quoting Rosa Luxemburg approvingly). Freedom of association and assembly: *OR*, 25. Freedom from politics: *OR*, 284, "Collective Responsibility," 154. Slavery as "the primordial crime upon which the fabric of American society rested": *OR*, 66. Right to a fair trial: epilogue to *EJ*. Freedom from arbitrary police power: many passages in *OT*. Civil disobedience: "Civil Disobedience," in *CR*. Political equality: a running theme in *HC* and *OR*.

[36] "Reply to Eric Voegelin," in *EU*, 405. Arendt's antiliberalism was never truly antiliberal, for she never denied the fundamental importance of civil rights and liberties. What she denied was that

Economic rights present a more mixed picture. Arendt supports the right to private property in one's household, and more generally the rights to life, liberty, and property. But she had no libertarian allergy to taxes or business regulation: She denounces the equation of freedom with free enterprise as "a monstrous falsehood," and she argues that protecting large accumulations of wealth as if they were household property is a fallacy. Only the latter deserves protection as a matter of right.[37] She supported trade unions and the labor movement, and she applauded the "extraordinary increase in economic security, social prestige, and political power" it brought to the working class.[38] She therefore supported the right of workers to organize. She called poverty and misery an outrage, which suggests a commitment to at least some safety net economic rights.[39] At the same time, Arendt feared that a full-blown welfare state would subordinate political freedom to insatiable consumerism. In the end, the rights and freedoms she endorses are conventionally liberal, and her list is nowhere near as ambitious as in the human rights treaties now on the books.

But the main point is that Arendt doesn't think of these as pre-political or universal Rights of Man. They are civil rights that protect human dignity within political communities that honor them. Internationally, what human dignity requires is "not a bill with innumerable human rights" but "one internationally guaranteed right to Citizenship" carrying both de facto and de jure protection. (As explained earlier, I think "citizenship" is the wrong word unless it entails de facto protection of rights.) Without this right to have rights, "we shall have more and more people who with respect to their legal status no longer are human, who have no longer a place within humanity."[40]

One other point is worth mentioning. Some human rights theorists equate human dignity with the power of self-legislation and self-direction. James Griffin puts it thus: "What we attach value to, what we regard as giving dignity to human life, is our capacity to choose and to pursue our conception of a worthwhile life." He labels this capacity "normative

freedom lies in private enjoyment of civil rights and liberties rather than participation in public affairs. *OR*, 220. Hiruta's *Hannah Arendt and Isaiah Berlin* is useful on this point.

37 Right to life, liberty, and property, *OR*, 24. Private property in the household: *HC*, 64; "monstrous falsehood": *OR*, 219. Fallacy of equating wealth with property, *HC*, 66–67.

38 *HC*, 215–19; the quotation is on page 216.

39 Poverty and misery as an outrage: SQMP, 140. Poverty in a land of plenty is "against the dignity of man." Arendt, "A Reply to Eric Voegelin," *EU*, 403.

40 Arendt, "Statelessness," lecture notes, 4.

agency," and identifies it with being a bearer of human rights and human dignity.[41] In Griffin's theory, it is normative agency that human rights are supposed to protect.

As we've seen in Chapter 9, Arendt also places great emphasis on human agency, understood as the power to break from the social script to begin something new. Beginning anew is not the same as pursuing our conception of a worthwhile life; but Arendt also emphasizes acting "for the sake of" some conception of what our life is about. In her carpenter example discussed in Chapter 9, "his whole life as a carpenter is ruled by ... an encompassing notion 'for the sake of' which he became a carpenter in the first place."[42] That sounds a lot like pursuing a conception of a worthwhile life. In this respect, she and Griffin are not far apart.

The difference is that Arendt thought the dignity of action lies in its significance not just to oneself but *to others*. "Choosing and pursuing our conception of a worthwhile life" leaves out the others. Recall her complaint about Kant's moral writings: "[T]here is hardly any mention of the so-called fellow man. It's really all about the self and reason that works in solitude."[43] Though she surely agreed that Kantian autonomy (the close cousin of normative agency) matters – it makes us something other than a cog in the machine, beings who can be called to account for our actions – our dignity exists because others whom we dignify will dignify us in our turn. That includes dignifying us by holding us accountable for crimes we commit.

## 10.3 What New Political Principle?

What new political principle did Arendt have in mind for the new law on earth? Very likely she didn't know; at any rate, she never said what it is, only what it isn't. It would not be the prewar state system, which had proven manifestly unfit to address issues of world war, genocide, and mass displacement and statelessness. Nor would it be a world state, "a forbidding nightmare of tyranny" that would bring an end to all political life.[44] That is already clear when she writes that the new principle must be limited and controlled by territorial entities.

However, Arendt never specifies what territorial entities she has in mind, or how these entities would match up with existing states and their

41 Griffin, *On Human Rights*, 44–45. 42 "The Concept of History," in *BPF*, 78–79.
43 *DTB*, 818, dated "night from 28 to 29 April 1964."
44 "Karl Jaspers: Citizen of the World?," *MDT*, 81.

borders. Her phrase "newly defined territorial entities" is ambiguous. It may refer to a redrawn map of states, but it could also refer to a system of territorial entities other than sovereign states. The closest she comes to giving the phrase a definite meaning is her paraphrase of Karl Jaspers's call for "the renunciation of sovereignty for the sake of a world-wide federated political structure."[45] The ancestor of such a scheme is Kant, who claimed that "the law of nations shall be based on a *federalism* of free states," which "are not to be fused into a single state."[46] Arendt presents Jaspers's view sympathetically, so it seems likely that she had a world federation of states in mind, rather than some novel system of nonstate territorial entities. Arendt was a European federalist from her Paris years at least until the 1940s, and in 1943 she thought it likely that the "dream" of a federated Europe would "come true some day."[47]

Reinforcing this thought, Arendt writes in *On Revolution* that "the federal principle, the principle of league and alliance among separate units, arises out of the elementary conditions of action itself," by which she means the conditions that make joint actions possible.[48] Here, though, she is talking about federal structures *within* nations, not *among* nations. Among nations, leagues and alliances have always been military or commercial arrangements – fragile matters of temporary converging interests, not stable structures of governance.

It's hard to know whether world federalism still held the same appeal for Arendt by the time she published *Origins* as it did a decade before. In 1952 she met Henri Frenay, the president of the Union of European Federalists. She was brimful of admiration for him as a man but equally sure he was wasting his time on "this forlorn federalistic five-and-dime joint (*Saftladen*)."[49] Probably this was an efficacy judgment about the Union of European Federalists, rather than opposition in principle to a European federation.

But we know from the final chapter of *On Revolution* that the federalist government Arendt favored was a federation of small units, of councils, townships, and wards. She was skeptical of the US federal scheme of state and national government because both units are too big; and the hero of her chapter is Thomas Jefferson, because he advocated a ward system in

45 *MDT*, 81. 46 Immanuel Kant, "Toward Perpetual Peace," Ak. 8:354.

47 Young-Bruehl, 158, 282–83; Siegelberg, *Statelessness: A Modern History*, 187–88; "The Crisis of Zionism," in *JW*, 334–35.

48 *OR*, 271.

49 Letter to Blücher, May 1, 1952, *WFW*, 164. *Saftladen*: pejorative slang for a dump or dive. Arendt misspells his name "Henry Fresnay."

which small local units would do the governing.[50] Pushing governance down to the most local feasible level is the principle of subsidiarity in Catholic social thought and today's European Union law. Although Arendt never uses the word, subsidiarity follows from her view that politics in its most authentic sense consists in face-to-face debate.

Plainly a federation of small local communities could never be the organizing principle of international politics, and it surely couldn't provide protection for imperiled people in remote places. That kind of protection would require international institutions to complement the local ones. For that, it seems plausible that Arendt hoped for some UN-based organization, something like today's UN Refugee Agency, but with far more robust powers and no legal loopholes allowing states to warehouse or expel the stateless. Arendt can be forgiven for not knowing what such institutions would look like. We are no closer to knowing that today, as evidenced by the 43.7 million refugees and asylum seekers, and as many as ten million de jure stateless people, in 2024.[51]

If I had to guess at Arendt's new political principle of world politics, it would be a federation of federations. Local units would be charged with hands-on governance and protecting the human dignity of their residents, and the umbrella (international) federation would have limited but robust powers to ensure those protections and solve collective action problems. In the case of large territories such as the United States, she seems to have preferred federal states that are themselves federations of smaller units.[52] So perhaps her principle would be a (world) federation of (national) federations of (regional) federations of small local units. But this is entirely a guess: Arendt gives us too little to go on to know for sure, and it seems likely that she had nothing so concrete in mind when she wrote *Origins*.

The fact is that Arendt was never a theorist of institutions and institutional structures. Indeed, it's hard to think of any major political theorist who had as little to say about institutional design as Arendt did. Her political theorizing works at a higher level of abstraction, analyzing what politics is and how it connects to the human condition, both understood in very general terms. We may see this as a theoretical weakness (I do), but Arendt probably did not. One of her strongly held convictions is that it's

[50] *OR*, 238 (skepticism of US federalism), 242, 252–59, 271, 282–83. What she admired in the United States is "not only a government of united states but of united peoples as well." *JW*, 335.

[51] UNHCR Figures at a Glance (2024), www.unhcr.org/en-us/figures-at-a-glance.html [https://perma.cc/D7VV-8QYX]; US Department of State, *Statelessness*, https://2021-2025.state.gov/other-policy-issues/statelessness/ [https://perma.cc/K5HP-NUDQ ].

[52] *OR*, 282.

not philosopher-kings but the actions of free people that create political institutions. Each generation has the capacity to begin anew, and the structures they create are in principle unpredictable and must not be dictated. Philosophers hawking political blueprints would establish "tyrannies of truth," and in *The Human Condition* Arendt tells us that political philosophers from Plato and Aristotle on have erred in this way.[53]

## 10.4 Sovereignty

What about the other half of Jaspers's proposal, the renunciation of sovereignty? Arendt was a skeptic about the nation-state, whose tendency to slide into ethnonationalism and persecution undermines its ability to carry out the legitimate function of the state, namely, "the protection of all inhabitants in its territory no matter what their nationality."[54] This, no doubt, is why she insisted that the "new political principle" would be controlled by *territorial* entities, not ethnically based nation-states. In an interview, she expressed hope for a "council-state . . . to which the principle of sovereignty would be wholly alien" and "power would be constituted horizontally and not vertically."[55]

Notwithstanding this language, she was no sovereignty skeptic so long as sovereignty means freedom of a people from foreign domination (external sovereignty), not when it means license to oppress minorities within the state. Sovereigns, Arendt thought, must refrain from exercising their internal sovereign authority to oppress. But she believed that such benign self-limiting sovereignty can exist only within a comity of nations, and that the European comity, such as it was, collapsed in the twentieth century.[56] If states can no longer be counted on to protect their minority inhabitants as a matter of comity with other states, perhaps the "new law on earth" would limit state sovereignty. It would have to, because "in the realm of human affairs sovereignty and tyranny are the same."[57]

The resulting political principle might take several forms. It might, for example, resemble today's European Union, which requires members to join the European Convention on Human Rights and place themselves under the jurisdiction of the European Court of Human Rights. This is a minimalist interpretation.

53 *HC*, 220–30, and her critique of any "blueprint for the making of political bodies," 227; in the same vein, *OT*, 325. "Tyrannies of truth" comes from TP, 246, and Arendt remarks that "politically speaking" these "are as tyrannical as other forms of despotism."

54 *OT*, 229–36; the quoted language in *OT*, 230.

55 *CR*, 233.

56 *OT*, 278.

57 *OR*, 152.

A more ambitious alternative would be to reimagine sovereignty itself, as something more than exclusive plenary authority over a territory and the people in it (so-called Westphalian sovereignty). In 2001 an international commission proposed that sovereignty "implies a dual responsibility: externally – to respect the sovereignty of other states, and internally, to respect the dignity and basic rights of all the people within the state."[58] The latter responsibility puts a limit on the sovereign's plenary power.

The usual name of this view is "sovereignty as responsibility." From it, the UN derived the so-called responsibility to protect (R2P) doctrine, which assigns states the responsibility of protecting their residents from gross human rights violations, commits the community of states to helping troubled states build capacity to protect those rights, and as a last resort authorizes outside action when states fail to do so.[59]

Critics accuse R2P of being a smokescreen for military aggression and neocolonialism, under the guise of humanitarian intervention. That critique deliberately ignores R2P's main point, which is not about outside military intervention. On the contrary, the main point of R2P is that sovereign states, not outsiders, are responsible for protecting their own inhabitants against gross violations of their human rights. It's perverse and even dishonest to reject this doctrine of sovereign responsibility by equating it with outside military intervention. Military intervention is a rarely used last resort against state irresponsibility.

The UN's version of R2P should be faulted not for permissiveness but for the opposite: its narrow focus on atrocity prevention. A generalized view of sovereignty as responsibility, which some (including me) have advocated, understands sovereignty as responsibility more broadly: Sovereigns are trustees or fiduciaries of all humanity in matters of pressing international concern.[60] Atrocity prevention of course looms large among those matters of international concern. But so does statelessness. So does the nuclear threat, of which Arendt was acutely aware. Today, so do the climate crisis, and the resurgence of strongman politics and brazen kleptocracy.

58 *The Responsibility to Protect: Report of the International Commission on Intervention and State Sovereignty* (December 2001), §1.35.

59 Ban Ki-moon, *Implementing the Responsibility to Protect: Report of the Secretary-General*, January 12, 2009, UNGA A/63/677, §11.

60 Eyal Benvenisti, "Sovereigns as Trustees of Humanity: On the Accountability of States to Foreign Stakeholders," *American Journal of International Law* 107(2) (2013): 295–333; Evan J. Criddle and Evan Fox-Decent, *Fiduciaries of Humanity: How International Law Constitutes Authority* (Oxford University Press, 2016); David Luban, "Responsibility to Humanity and Threats to Peace: An Essay on Sovereignty," *Berkeley Journal of International Law* 38(2) (2020): 185–239.

For reasons I now explain, responsibility to humanity comes close to what Arendt had in mind.

## 10.5 The Idea of Humanity

Start with the "idea of humanity" that "constitutes the sole regulating idea of international law." Arendt first explained what she meant by this term in the 1945 essay "Organized Guilt and Universal Responsibility." For many years, she writes, she has met Germans who declare that they are ashamed of being Germans. "I have often felt tempted to answer that I am ashamed of being human."[61] There is "terror [in] the idea of humanity," once we recognize the human potential for evildoing on a monumental scale. One response to this terror is race thinking, "which denies the very possibility of a common humanity" and evades the responsibilities it implies. But race thinking isn't the only response.

> For the idea of humanity, when purged of all sentimentality, has the very serious consequence that in one form or another men must assume responsibility for all crimes committed by men and that all nations share the onus of evil committed by all others. Shame at being a human being is the purely individual and still non-political expression of this insight.[62]

The first sentence was no throwaway: Arendt repeated it nearly verbatim in *Origins*, where she explains that the shrinking relevance of geographical distances makes shared responsibility imperative.[63] This system of common responsibility across borders follows from "the idea of humanity." It is the heart of sovereignty as responsibility to humanity. As Eyal Benvenisti, who elaborated this conception of sovereignty, explains, in language that echoes Arendt's concerns:

> We live in a shrinking world where interdependence between countries and communities is increasing. These changes also affect – as they should – the concept of sovereignty. In past decades the predominant conception of sovereignty was akin to owning a large estate separated from other properties by rivers or deserts. By contrast, today's reality is more analogous to owning a small apartment in one densely packed high-rise that is home to two hundred separate families.[64]

Humanity, on this conception, is not merely the set of all human beings, nor even the human species taken collectively. A mathematical

61 *EU*, 131. 62 *EU*, 131.
63 *OT*, 235–36. "[W]hether we like it or not, we have really started to live in One World." *OT*, 296.
64 Benvenisti, "Sovereigns as Trustees of Humanity," 295.

set imposes no responsibilities, and species is nothing more than a zoological category. Nor does humanity refer to human kindness or fellow feeling (a linguistic possibility Arendt dismisses sarcastically in *Eichmann in Jerusalem*).[65] Humanity is the fellowship recognized by those committed, for various reasons, to a cross-border project of responsibility. One might call it the project of *constructing humanity*.[66]

International law makes constructing humanity its mission, its "sole regulating ideal." Arendt borrows the concept of a regulating ideal from Kant. Analyzing scientific inquiry, Kant distinguishes between "constitutive" principles that have real-world objectivity and "regulative" principles, like science's goal of completeness and systematicity. Inquiry will never attain the ideal endpoint of comprehending all of nature in a complete system of laws, but that endpoint guides inquiry nevertheless.[67]

The analogy should be clear: Constructing a system of common responsibility across borders is the ideal endpoint of international law. We may never attain it, given the realities of international politics. "The solidarity of mankind may well turn out to be an unbearable burden, and it is not surprising that the common reactions to it are political apathy, isolationist nationalism, or desperate rebellion against all powers that be rather than enthusiasm or a desire for a revival of humanism."[68] Shared responsibility nevertheless remains international law's regulating ideal.

Significantly, where in her 1949 essay on human rights she called the right to have rights "the right to belong to a political community," in *Origins* she calls it "the right of every individual to belong to humanity."[69] The idea of humanity implies "that the right to have rights, or the right of every individual to belong to humanity, should be guaranteed by

[65] *EJ*, 275.

[66] *OT*, 235. Arendt never explicitly connects the idea of humanity with a novel conception of sovereignty; that is my own interpretation of what "a new law on earth" might mean. Revealingly, perhaps, Arendt once wrote of a "Jewish mission in history to achieve *the establishment of mankind*." *OT*, 240 (emphasis added). No doubt she was referring to Isaiah's prophecy, "I shall make you a light for the nations, that My rescue reach the end of the earth." Isaiah 49:6, Robert Alter trans., 786. Of course, Arendt does not mean that the mission of establishing mankind is Jewish in character (that's what a Nazi would have said), or a project entrusted solely to the Jews. What is pertinent for the present argument is the way she phrases the mission: the establishment of mankind. The phrasing makes clear that it has not been accomplished and might never be. It is a normative project.

[67] Kant, *CPR*, A616/B644–A617/B645; A691/B719–A692/B720.

[68] Arendt, "Karl Jaspers: Citizen of the World?," in *MDT*, 83.

[69] "'The Rights of Man': What Are They?," 37; *OT*, 298. On the importance of this difference, see Stewart, "A New Law on Earth," 131, who infers that when Arendt speaks of belonging to a political community, she does not necessarily mean a state.

humanity itself," although again she is far from optimistic.[70] Yet without putting such guarantees into practice, and building them into positive law, the idea of humanity will remain only that: an idea.

This speaks to the problem of statelessness. But in addition, "men must assume responsibility for all crimes committed by men." This is pregnant language. It is the very idea of international criminal law – the only area of international law other than statelessness that Arendt focused on in any detail.[71] It's not a topic that appears in *The Origins of Totalitarianism* or her other books of the 1950s. Her ideas about criminal law grew from the Eichmann trial; they appear in *Eichmann in Jerusalem* and her correspondence with Karl Jaspers about the trial.

And the first question Arendt and Jaspers debate is: Why think the law is the right place to look for shared responsibility for repressing the great crimes?

[70] *OT*, 298.

[71] Plainly, "all crimes" doesn't mean what it literally says; it doesn't include shoplifting or picking pockets. Arendt was thinking of the major crimes that we now regard as international in import – especially the "core" crimes of aggression, genocide, crimes against humanity, and war crimes.

CHAPTER 11

# *The Idea of International Criminal Law*

## 11.1 "We Have No Tools to Hand Except Legal Ones"

As the Nuremberg trials drew to a close, Arendt wrote Jaspers that no punishment a criminal court could mete out would be appropriate (*angemessene*) for the Nazi crimes. The defendants' guilt was beyond criminal guilt, it "oversteps and shatters all legal systems." Göring could be hanged, but strictly speaking his hanging would not be punishment, because guilt beyond criminal guilt is equally beyond criminal punishment. "That is the reason the Nazis in Nuremberg are so smug."[1]

Her view changed by the time of the Eichmann trial. When Arendt told Jaspers she was going to Jerusalem to cover the trial, he scolded her: "The political realm is of an importance that cannot be captured in legal terms (the attempt to do so is Anglo-Saxon and a self-deception ... )."[2] To which Arendt replied, "I even admit that as far as the role of the law is concerned, I have been infected by the Anglo-Saxon influence."

Of course, there is something comical in their fretting whether Arendt has gone over to the Anglo-Saxon team; set that to one side. She continued:

> But quite apart from that, it seems to me to be in the nature of this case that we have no tools to hand except legal ones with which we have to judge and pass sentence on something that cannot even be adequately represented either in legal terms or in political categories. That is precisely what makes the process itself, namely, the trial, so exciting. The question is: Would things be different if we had a law against *hostes humani generis* and not only against murderers and similar criminals?[3]

Notice that in these letters (fourteen years apart) one of her convictions didn't change: that the Nazi crimes transcend the normal categories of

[1] Arendt to Jaspers, August 17, 1946, in *HA-KJ*, 54.
[2] Jaspers to Arendt, December 16, 1960, in *HA-KJ*, 413.
[3] Arendt to Jaspers, December 23, 1960, in *HA-KJ*, 417. I have slightly amended the translation.

both law and politics. But where at the time of the Nuremberg trials Arendt was sure that Nazi policy "oversteps and shatters any and all legal systems," in 1960 "we have no tools to hand except legal ones."

What are those tools? In the letter, Arendt names two. One is the trial process itself (the "grandeur of court proceedings" that turns cogs in the machine back into human beings, as she says elsewhere[4]). We'll examine that idea closely in Chapter 14. The other is a law against *hostes humani generis* – enemies of mankind, a label she attaches to Eichmann in *Eichmann in Jerusalem*. Arendt did not invent the phrase: *hostis generis humani* is the ancient label for pirates, dating back to Cicero. All nations were entitled to prosecute (or kill) pirates, which made piracy the earliest example of what the law now calls a "universal jurisdiction" offense.

The scope of the *hostis humani generis* category expanded over time to encompass other crimes beside piracy. In the eighteenth century Emer de Vattel condemned military aggressors, poisoners, assassins, and arsonists as *les enemis du Genre-humain*; and in the nineteenth century slave traders were declared to be pirates and therefore *hostes humani generis*. Beginning with a landmark US judgment in 1980, the category expanded to include torturers and other atrocity-criminals.[5]

Arendt probably got the idea of including génocidaires among the *hostes humani generis* from an article in *Commentary* by Jacob Robinson, Israel's legal adviser for the Eichmann trial.[6] In the trial itself, Prosecutor Gideon Hausner invoked the phrase to argue that Israel could exercise universal jurisdiction over Eichmann: "There are definitions of *hostis humani generis*. There are definitions of people of whom, in biblical language, it might have been said that they bore the mark of Cain on their foreheads." The Jerusalem court agreed, and its judgment was the first-ever legal holding that a génocidaire is *hostis humani generis*.[7]

For Robinson, Hausner, and the Jerusalem court the significance of the label was to establish universal jurisdiction over Eichmann. For Arendt, the

4 "Collective Responsibility," *RJ*, 148.

5 I trace this history in David Luban, "The Enemy of All Humanity," *Netherlands Journal of Legal Philosophy* 47(2) (2018): 112–37, concurrently published in *The Oxford Handbook of International Criminal Law*, eds. Kevin Jon Heller, Frédéric Megret, Sarah Nouwen, Jens David Ohlin, and Darryl Robinson (Oxford University Press, 2020), 558–82. For more detailed histories, see Daniel Heller-Roazen, *The Enemy of All: Piracy and the Law of Nations* (Zone Books, 2009) and Dan Edelstein, *The Terror of Natural Right: Republicanism, the Cult of Nature, and the French Revolution* (University of Chicago Press, 2009).

6 Jacob Robinson, "Eichmann and the Question of Jurisdiction," *Commentary*, July 1960. To the best of my knowledge, Robinson was the first to apply the *hostis humani generis* label to génocidaires.

7 Eichmann Trial Proceedings, vol. 4, Session 4, April 12, 1961, at 46. Prosecutor v. Eichmann, Trial Judgment, §13.

meaning was substantive, not jurisdictional. She regarded genocide as a crime against humanity, by which she meant a crime that matters, or should matter, to all of humanity, and which all humanity should be willing to prosecute. Remember that "men must assume responsibility for all crimes committed by men." For lawyers, calling genocide a crime against humanity is a legal confusion, because international law distinguishes the two crimes and defines them quite differently. Arendt knew that but evidently didn't care; at any rate, in *Eichmann at Jerusalem* she uses the terms interchangeably:

> It was when the Nazi regime declared that the German people not only were unwilling to have any Jews in Germany but wished to make the entire Jewish people disappear from the face of the earth that the new crime, the crime against humanity – in the sense of a crime "against the human status," or against the very nature of mankind – appeared. Expulsion and genocide, though both are international offenses, must remain distinct; the former is an offense against fellow nations, whereas the latter is an attack upon human diversity as such, that is, upon a characteristic of the "human status" without which the very words "mankind" or "humanity" would be devoid of meaning.[8]

This is a many-layered insight, and I devote Chapter 12 to exploring it. Before that, though, it will be necessary to look at international lawyers' understanding of crimes against humanity and genocide, both at the time Arendt wrote and today. That background will help us understand the relevance of Arendt's thought to international criminal justice today.

## 11.2 The Classical Orthodoxy of International Law

I begin by sketching what I will call the "classical" conception of international law, a state-centered orthodoxy that developed in tandem with the

[8] *EJ*, 268–69. Today, though not when Arendt wrote *Eichmann in Jerusalem*, expulsion is considered a crime against humanity – and rightly so. See the Rome Statute of the International Criminal Court, art. 7(1)(d). It is obviously a crime against the expelled people, and not only against the receiving state, and Arendt should be faulted for uncritically elevating the statist formalism of international law over common sense. Arendt takes the phrase "human status" from François de Menthon, the French prosecutor in the Nuremberg trial of the major war criminals. *EJ*, 257. Menthon used it in his opening statement. The Trial of German Major War Criminals by the International Military Tribunal Sitting at Nuremberg, Germany, vol. 5, 405 (afternoon session of January 17, 1946). Menthon's phrase was *la condition humaine*. Presumably, Arendt followed the official English translation as "human status" to avoid confusion with her own concept of the human condition. Menthon meant something entirely different from Arendt's gloss, namely that human beings are both material and spiritual beings; The Trial of German Major War Criminals, vol. 5, 406–7 (afternoon session of January 17, 1946). He asserted that "the sin against the spirit is the original sin of National Socialism from which all crimes spring." The Trial of German Major War Criminals, vol. 5, 372 (morning session of January 17, 1946). For a critical view of the idea of crimes against humanity as supposedly-universal crime, see Sinja Graf, *The Humanity of Universal Crime: Inclusion, Inequality, and Intervention in International Political Thought* (Oxford: Oxford University Press, 2021).

European state system. The classical orthodoxy was built around a conception of state sovereignty usually called "Westphalian," after the Peace of Westphalia that ended the Thirty Years' War in 1648. The treaty declared that the 300 principalities that made up the Holy Roman Empire "never can or ought to be molested therein by any whomsoever upon any manner of pretence."[9] It granted princes complete control over their territory, religion, and foreign policy.

I call the Westphalian conception "classical" because the post-World War II order, with the UN, the major human rights and humanitarian treaties, and regional human rights regimes, transformed international law. They stripped away sovereigns' right to launch wars at will, or to violate the basic rights of their people – although in other ways they doubled down on statism by enshrining sovereignty and sovereign equality in the UN Charter. Some scholars argue that the transformation was already underway before the war.[10] Others point out that the classical orthodoxy was never a consensus view and was still contested between the world wars.[11] Nevertheless, its main elements define textbook international law today.

In the classical orthodoxy, public international law (the "law of nations") governs the relations of states with each other. Its background is an international system of sovereign states, and the simplest way to think of it is as the legal system of a village with about 200 inhabitants, the so-called international community of states.[12] (Of course, "community" is a euphemism in a rivalrous world.) "Of states" is crucial. States, not human beings, are the citizenry of the international community. From each state's point of view, the internal affairs of other sovereign states are and ought to be a black box, what lawyers call the state's "reserved domain" (*domaine réservé*).[13] This statist orthodoxy has never been uncontested, and

9 Peace Treaty between the Holy Roman Emperor and the King of France and their respective Allies (the Treaty of Münster) (1648), art. 64.

10 Oona A. Hathaway and Scott J. Shapiro, *The Internationalists: How a Radical Plan to Outlaw War Remade the World* (Simon & Schuster, 2018).

11 Siegelberg, *Statelessness: A Modern History* is illuminating on this point.

12 There are 193 member states of the UN, plus two non-member observer states, the Holy See and Palestine. The global village also includes non-UN members such as Taiwan. There were fifty-one original members in the UN, and sixty when Arendt published *Origins*. At the time of the Eichmann trial, the UN had only half the members it has today.

13 The UN Charter calls the reserved domain "matters which are essentially within the domestic jurisdiction of any state." Art. 2, ¶7. And in 1970 the UN General Assembly declared that: "No State or group of States has the right to intervene, directly or indirectly, in the internal or external affairs of any other State." Declaration on Principles of International Law concerning Friendly Relations and Co-operation among States, UNGA Res. 2625, A/RES/2625(XXV).

progressive jurists always argued that individuals too, not only states, are proper subjects of international law; as such, they deserve legal recourse for rights violations without filtering it through their states.[14] But state leaders, foreign ministries, and their lawyers resolutely hew to the statist orthodoxy. (A US State Department legal adviser once remarked to me, "Don't kid yourself – state sovereignty is the only game in town.")

The legal criteria of statehood are a permanent population in a defined territory with a government that has the "capacity to enter into relations with other states."[15] Any state meeting these criteria qualifies as a member of the international community. Traditionally, international law was indifferent to how well or badly the government exercises its control; all that matters is that it *has* control. Democracies and despotisms, kingdoms and kleptocracies, all belong to the club if they control their territory. State responsibility for the rights, dignity, and well-being of its inhabitants was at best a gauzy moral ideal, not a legal requirement. In *Origins*, Arendt took it for granted that a sovereign state's prerogatives are unlimited, including the right to denationalize and expel its own citizens.[16] No doubt this is why she insisted that human dignity needs "a new political principle, in a new law on earth."[17]

International law on the orthodox conception is positivist through and through. States are supreme, and no natural law or higher lawmaker rules over the community of states; thus international law must come from the states themselves. Arendt took it for granted that the sovereign state is "bound by no universal law and acknowledging nothing superior to itself."[18] As the famous 1928 *Lotus* case explains: "The rules of law binding upon States . . . emanate from their own free will as expressed in conventions or by usages generally accepted as expressing principles of law."[19]

Superficially, this sounds like an egalitarian principle, and the UN's Charter reiterates that the organization "is based on the principle of sovereign equality of all its members."[20] For most of the twentieth century, though, colonies and protectorates did not count in the so-called community of states; at the time of *Lotus* the League of Nations had only fifty-five

[14] Siegelberg, *Statelessness: A Modern History*, 109, 155, 163–64.

[15] Montevideo Convention on the Rights and Duties of States (1933), art. 1. But see Frederick Tse-shyang Chen, "The Meaning of 'States' in the Membership Provisions of the United Nations Charter," *Indiana International and Comparative Law Review* 12(1) (2001): 25–51; and, for a comprehensive treatment, James Crawford, *The Creation of States in International Law*, 2nd ed. (Oxford University Press, 2006).

[16] *OT*, 230, 278, 283, 286. [17] *OT*, ix. [18] *OT*, 230.

[19] S.S. Lotus (Fr. v. Turk.), 1927 P.C.I.J. (ser. A) No. 10 (September 7).

[20] UN Charter, art. 2, ¶1.

members, of which just eight were African, Asian, or Middle Eastern. Some states were newly created after World War I, when the victors dismembered the Hapsburg and Ottoman empires; many more states came into existence through post-World War II decolonization. Between the two wars, states were by no means the universal unit of political organization – the reality, as Mira Siegelberg notes, is that "one could find confederacies, federations, protectorates, spheres of influence, suzerainties, and self-governing dominions, all of which flew in the face of the orthodox theory."[21] Nevertheless, statism *was* the orthodox theory. This remains true today even if, for many decades, statism occupied an uneasy halfway point between empire and decolonization.

On the *Lotus* picture, the sole source of international law is state consent: either express consent in the form of conventions, that is, treaties, or implicit consent in the form of customs ("usages") recognized as legally binding. It follows that states are free to do anything they wish, provided it doesn't violate a treaty or customary rule to which they have consented, for there is no higher law or authority to limit them. This "*Lotus* freedom principle" represented the state of international law at the onset of World War II – once again, with the caveat that the club of states excluded much of the world.

Many decades later, three eminent judges looking back on *Lotus* called it "the high water mark of laissez-faire in international relations,"[22] but it's unclear how far the high water has receded. As a legalistic matter, the International Court of Justice (ICJ) has never repudiated *Lotus*, and jurists still cite its authority on occasion. And as a political matter, former colonies in the global South are just as jealous of their Westphalian sovereignty as the so-called great powers (understandably so). Even if today's human rights law limits state freedom, at least in theory, human rights law is itself a creature of treaty and custom. States could, if they wish, withdraw from the treaties or change the customs. That is true even of the *jus cogens*, the peremptory norms of international law like the prohibitions on aggressive war, torture, and genocide that supposedly trump all treaties: even these basic decencies can be replaced by "a subsequent norm of the same character" (whatever that might be).[23] The UN

[21] Siegelberg, *Statelessness: A Modern History*, 93–94. Moria Paz argues that the state-centric orthodoxy only consolidated between the two world wars, beginning at the Paris Peace Conference. Moria Paz, "States and Networks in the Formation of International Law," *American University International Law Review* 26(5) (2011): 1249, 1281–84.

[22] Arrest Warrant of April 11, 2000 (Dem. Rep. Congo v. Belg.), Judgment, I.C.J. Reports 2002, p. 3 (joint separate opinion of Judges Higgins, Buergenthal, and Kooijmans, §51).

[23] Vienna Convention on the Law of Treaties, art. 53.

Charter's principle of sovereign equality of all member states reinforces the orthodoxy's emphasis on sovereignty, although it repudiated the imperialist and colonialist assumption that only the self-anointed "civilized" states count.

## 11.3 "The Paraphernalia of Sovereignty": Acts of State, Immunities, and the Problem of Criminal States

The boundaries of sovereignty's *domaine réservé* have always been fuzzy and subject to reinterpretation as novel issues arise. Today, for example, the question of what kinds of hostile cyber-operations violate other states' sovereignty remains unsettled, and in this context some governments declare that sovereignty is merely a broad principle, not a hard-law rule.[24] Like all legal concepts, the contours of "sovereignty" are defined issue by issue through the process of drawing out legal implications, and those are often precisely the disputed matters that sovereignty is invoked to settle by definitional fiat.

That said, in the classical orthodoxy of international law, one deeply entrenched legal implication of sovereign equality is that states can't call other states to account in their own courts. As a legal maxim puts it, *par in parem non habet imperium*: Equals have no dominion over equals.[25] This medieval principle is the source of sovereign immunity, which to this day protects state officials from being sued or prosecuted in the courts of another state for their state acts, even atrocious criminal acts (what lawyers call violations of the *jus cogens*). The issue of whether there is a *jus cogens* exception to sovereign immunity arose in several twenty-first-century cases before the ICJ and the European Court of Human Rights – and in each of them, the courts found no *jus cogens* exception to the immunity rule.[26] Heads of state and heads of government, who supposedly personify the state (another relic of medieval political theology), are immune from

[24] Michael N. Schmitt, "The Law of Cyber Conflict: *Quo Vadis* 2.0?," in *The Future Law of Armed Conflict*, eds. Matthew C. Waxman and Thomas W. Oakley (Oxford University Press, 2022), 103–22.

[25] The maxim comes from Dante's *De Monarchia* (1313). See Yoram Dinstein, "*Par in parem non habet imperium*," *Israel Law Review* 1 (1966): 409–10.

[26] These decisions include Jurisdictional Immunities of the State (Germany v. Italy: Greece intervening), Judgment, I.C.J. Reports 2012, p. 99 (February 3, 2012); Case concerning the Arrest Warrant of April 11, 2000 (Democratic Republic of the Congo v. Belgium), Judgment, I.C.J. Reports 2002, p. 3 (February 14, 2002); Al-Adsani v. The United Kingdom, 35763/97, ECHR (November 21, 2001); Jones and Others v. UK, 35346/06 and 40528/06, ECHR (January 14, 2014).

prosecution in the courts of another state for all their acts, state or private, no matter how heinous.

Yet even this rule is not an inevitable logical consequence of sovereignty. The twenty-first-century immunity cases reaffirming *par in parem non habet imperium* are best thought of as a conservative backlash against efforts to hold murderous leaders accountable; and they drew powerful dissenting opinions. The UN's International Law Commission has proposed exceptions to the rule of immunity for certain core international crimes.[27] And, in the wake of Russian aggression in Ukraine, some jurists have questioned the personal immunity of heads of state.

Few if any jurists went as far as Arendt in questioning the immunity rule, however, and that fact alone already makes her noteworthy as a theorist of international law. The immunity of state acts from prosecution in another state's courts was one of Eichmann's defenses in Jerusalem.[28] It failed. Arendt observes that "[p]ractically speaking, this argument had already been disposed of at Nuremberg; it stood no chance from the start," because it would have exonerated all the major war criminals including Hitler. "However," she cautions, "an argument that stands no chance on the practical plane has not necessarily been demolished on the theoretical one."[29]

She traces state act immunity back to the doctrine of *raison d'état*, which emerged in the early modern era with the rise of the state. As Arendt explains *raison d'état*, "a government may find itself compelled to commit actions that are generally regarded as crimes in order to assure its own survival and the survival of lawfulness."[30] It is a doctrine of political necessity, "concessions made to the stringencies of *Realpolitik*." Normally, such acts – described in German jurisprudence as *gerichtsfrei* (unbound by law) – are exceptions, hopefully rare ones.[31]

In the Third Reich, however, the exception became the rule. The state policy was criminal through and through; by 1944 *deviation* from genocide was the lawless exception, at least among the executioners of the Final Solution. When Himmler, foreseeing defeat, ordered a halt to genocide, it

[27] *Immunity of State Officials from Foreign Criminal Jurisdiction*, Annual Report of the International Law Commission, 69th Session, UN Doc. A/72/10 (2017), art. 7, 175.

[28] *EJ*, 93; cf. 21.

[29] *EJ*, 290–91. See Prosecutor v. Eichmann, Trial Judgment, §28, which quotes the Nuremberg Tribunal's judgment as well as other sources to reject the act-of-state defense.

[30] *EJ*, 291.

[31] *EJ*, 291. In 1973, she remarked that the American term "national security," which was relatively new at the time, is a rough translation of "*raison d'état*." "Interview with Roger Errera," *TWB*, 493. And indeed, national security has often been invoked to justify US crimes.

was "a concession to necessity imposed by reality."[32] Under such topsy-turvy circumstances, Arendt asks, should the law continue to treat all states as equal, and place all their acts beyond judgment by another state? As with individual abdication of judgment, Arendt is repelled by a juridical construct that forbids courts from judging.

> Does the "*par in parem*" signify no more than the paraphernalia of sovereignty? Or does it also imply a substantive equality or likeness? Can we apply the same principle that is applied to a governmental apparatus in which crime and violence are exceptions and borderline cases to a political order in which crime is legal and the rule?[33]

Clearly Arendt thinks the answer is no, and in this she agrees with the dissenting judges in the modern immunity cases who voted against immunity for core international crimes. But orthodox international law is addicted to the paraphernalia of sovereignty. Judges shrink from the prospect of declaring a state itself to be criminal, and the immunity rule continues to insulate state acts in the courts of other states.

For Arendt, the incapacity of law to grasp state criminality is one way the Holocaust "oversteps and shatters all legal systems." The Jerusalem court was only half right when it wrote: "A state that plans and implements a 'Final Solution' cannot be treated as *par in parem*, but only as a gang of criminals."[34] Arendt agrees that such a state cannot be treated as *par in parem*, but that is because its entire political order is criminal, not because its leaders are gangsters who commandeered the state apparatus.[35] A criminal state is different from a state run by criminals – different, more uncanny, and far more dangerous. It's not simply that some of its state acts are crimes (true of most states, at least occasionally), but that its fundamental policy – what Montesquieu would call its "principle" – is criminal. The Third Reich was a criminal state in that sense. One of Arendt's deepest insights is that the classical orthodoxy, which treats states and their sovereignty as foundational, fails when a state itself is criminal.

Some might object that state criminality as Arendt defines it is so rare that there is little point in destabilizing the *par in parem* rule by introducing a legal category of state criminality. Arendt thought that totalitarian states are criminal, but few states are totalitarian. She recognized only two, Hitler's Germany and Stalin's USSR. But the question she asks – whether

[32] *EJ*, 291. [33] *EJ*, 291–92. [34] Prosecutor v. Eichmann, Trial Judgment, §28.

[35] Arendt, "Auschwitz on Trial," in *RJ*, 231, 242. For a deep historical treatment of state criminality, see Lawrence Douglas, *The Criminal State: War, Atrocity, and the Dream of International Criminal Justice* (Princeton University Press, 2026).

*par in parem* requires substantive equality or likeness – and her implicit "yes" answer, lend themselves to an important generalization: that when states commit core international crimes as a matter of policy they are *to that extent* criminal, and their leaders' crimes should not be regarded as acts of state and immunized from accountability in the courts of other states.[36] That would expand the scope of her argument beyond totalitarian states to any states whose leaders adopt internationally criminal policies and act on them.[37]

## 11.4 Judgment at Nuremberg

It's against the background of statist orthodoxy that the Nuremberg Tribunal (also known as the IMT, the abbreviation of its full name) was so sensational.[38] Its charter stripped away head-of-state and head-of-government immunity (article 7); it stripped away the superior orders and act-of-state defenses (article 8). And it declared that attacks on civilian populations are crimes against humanity, "whether or not in violation of the domestic law of the country where perpetrated," and even if they were committed before the war (article 6) – a clear departure from the Westphalian doctrine that what a sovereign state does to its own people is its own business. (However, the "before the war" clause proved to be too much for the IMT judges to swallow, and they held that Germany's prewar persecution of Jews and Hitler's "euthanasia" programs fell outside its jurisdiction.[39])

Most importantly for Arendt's thinking, the IMT made the crucial choice to hold *individuals* responsible for state crimes. To be sure, article 9 of the Nuremberg Charter empowered the IMT to declare that an

[36] This was, in fact, the opinion of two British Law Lords in the famous *Pinochet* case. Lord Browne-Wilkinson's leading opinion argued that from the moment Chile had become a party to the international Convention Against Torture, Pinochet's state-sponsored tortures could no longer be regarded as acts of state. R. v. Bow Street Metropolitan Stipendiary Magistrate and Others, *ex parte* Pinochet Ugarte, March 24, 1999, [1999] All ER 97, HL.

[37] One example that already exists is the UN General Assembly's definition of aggression, which declares that aggressive war is not merely unlawful but is a state crime. UNGA Resolution 3314 (1974), Annex, art. 5(2).

[38] The full name was "International Military Tribunal for the prosecution and punishment of the major war criminals of the European Axis." The IMT is distinct from the courts that conducted the second round of Nuremberg trials – the Nuremberg Military Tribunals. The Tokyo Tribunal's name was International Military Tribunal for the Far East.

[39] They did so on the legalistic ground that the Charter limited the IMT's jurisdiction to crimes connected with the war. Only the Soviets wanted to prosecute the Nazi leaders for persecuting German Jews before the war. Francine Hirsch, *Soviet Judgment at Nuremberg: A New History of the International Military Tribunal after World War II* (Oxford University Press, 2020), 377–78.

organization to which a defendant belonged (for example, the SS) is a criminal organization; and article 10 allowed national courts to convict individuals for mere membership in a criminal organization. But these articles were anomalies that swiftly disappeared from international criminal law. The IMT judges rejected them as collective guilt doctrines, and neither of them appears in the charter of the Tokyo Tribunal, nor in the Nuremberg Principles that distilled the Nuremberg Charter into customary international law. All subsequent international criminal tribunals have made the same choice: They have jurisdiction only over natural persons, not collectivities.

The reason the framers of the Nuremberg Charter chose exclusively individual responsibility was the entirely realistic fear that defendants would hide behind the state. For Arendt, the prospect of assigning individual responsibility to defendants like Eichmann, who portrayed themselves as mere cogs in a machine, is precisely what drew her to criminal courts as paradigms of spectator judgment: The court focuses on the individual and asks him why he chose to become a cog.[40] In practice, the choice to exclude organizational criminality from international tribunals has drawbacks: It forecloses the possibility of declaring a state itself to be criminal, and it prevents courts from recognizing business corporations as international criminals. From Arendt's standpoint (and mine as well), this need not have been an either–or situation – an individual can be personally responsible for crimes that are, at the same time, state or corporate crimes.[41]

An eye-opening study by historian Francine Hirsch reveals that putting the Nazi leadership on trial was originally a Soviet idea, not (as most Western accounts have it) an American one. So was the groundbreaking idea that planning and launching an aggressive war is a "crime against peace": It originated with the Soviet jurist Aron Trainin – a bitterly ironic fact today in light of naked Russian aggression in Ukraine.[42] Initially Great Britain opposed the tribunal, and believed the Nazi leaders should be shot rather than tried. Some US officials shared this view, but the US came around and eventually seized the leadership role in the trials. At Nuremberg, US Chief Prosecutor Robert Jackson delivered a stirring opening statement: "That four great nations, flushed with victory and

[40] Arendt, "Collective Responsibility," 148. I return to this issue in more detail in Chapter 14.

[41] David Luban, "State Criminality and the Ambition of International Criminal Law," in *Accountability for Collective Wrongdoing*, eds. Tracy Isaacs and Richard Vernon (Cambridge University Press, 2011), 61–91.

[42] Hirsch, *Soviet Judgment at Nuremberg*, 8.

stung with injury, stay the hand of vengeance and voluntarily submit their captive enemies to the judgment of the law, is one of the most significant tributes that Power has ever paid to Reason."[43] Jackson was unfazed that the IMT would be breaking new legal ground. As he explained in language that Arendt quotes approvingly in *Eichmann in Jerusalem*:

> [E]very custom has its origin in some single act, and every agreement has to be initiated by the action of some state. Unless we are prepared to abandon every principle of growth for International Law, we cannot deny that our own day has its right to institute customs and to conclude agreements that will themselves become sources of a newer and strengthened International Law.[44]

All the Nuremberg Charter features I've mentioned were innovations, including the new crimes against peace and against humanity. The conclusion that the Nuremberg Charter's principles represent international law, and not merely victors' law written by four Allies, came in a 1946 UN General Assembly resolution.[45]

The "Nuremberg Moment" was only partly successful in stripping away immunities, however. As the law stands today, immunity-stripping is a feature of international criminal tribunals, but the twenty-first-century judicial decisions mentioned earlier keep immunity intact in national courts – and there is little agreement about what makes a tribunal genuinely "international."

## 11.5 Crimes against Humanity

The Nuremberg innovation that mattered most to Arendt was the introduction of crimes against humanity as a category of international crime. As we have seen, for her the label has substantive meaning. That is not how modern lawyers use the term; from Nuremberg to the present, it is a term of art for a discrete category of international offenses, alongside the other categories of war crimes, genocide, and aggression. These four are often

43 The Trial of German Major War Criminals by the International Military Tribunal Sitting at Nuremberg, Germany, vol. 2, November 21, 1945 (1946).

44 The Trial of German Major War Criminals, vol. 2, November 21, 1945. See *EJ*, 273–74.

45 UN General Assembly Resolution 95(I), *Affirmation of the Principles of International Law Recognized by the Charter of the Nürnberg Tribunal*, A/RES/95(I) (December 11, 1946); UN General Assembly Resolution 177, *Formulation of the Principles Recognized in the Charter of the Nürnberg Tribunal and in the Judgment of the Tribunal*, A/RES/177(II) (November 21, 1947). The principles were codified in 1950. International Law Commission, Principles of International Law Recognized in the Charter of the Nürnberg Tribunal and in the judgment of the Tribunal (1950/2005). However, the General Assembly never voted to adopt the International Law Commission's Nuremberg Principles.

called the "core crimes" in international law. (Sometimes torture is included among the core crimes.) In a broad sense, all the core crimes are "against humanity," which on Arendt's understanding means that they are properly the business of international rather than solely domestic criminal law. But that is not how the legal terminology uses the label.

In the early nineteenth century, "crimes against humanity" was occasionally used in connection with the slave trade and international efforts to suppress it; and the 1860 Republican Party platform in the US presidential election called slave-trading a crime against humanity. This was rhetoric, not yet law, and when slave traders were prosecuted it was not for crimes against humanity.

The same was true later in the century, when Russian jurists used the phrase to denounce the oppression of Christians in the Ottoman Empire.[46] In 1915, Russia proposed trying the perpetrators of the Armenian genocide for crimes against humanity. The proposal was scuttled by US opposition based on the lack of any preexisting law that defined such crimes. (Ironically, and perhaps tellingly, Turkish nationalists during the 1919–22 civil war accused the Western occupiers of a crime against humanity.[47])

Matters rested there until Nuremberg, where the crimes were at last legislated and defined. The charter defined crimes against humanity as

> murder, extermination, enslavement, deportation, and other inhumane acts committed against any civilian population, or persecutions on political, racial or religious grounds.[48]

This became the template for legal definitions in the statutes of all future international tribunals and national criminal codes. Allied occupation law added rape and torture to the list of crimes against humanity. Genocide was not included, but extermination was. Such was the state of the law when Arendt wrote *Eichmann in Jerusalem*. Arendt knew what the Nuremberg Charter said, but she never discussed the particulars of this

46 Peter Holquist, "'Crimes Against Humanity': Genealogy of a Concept (1815–1945)" (unpublished presentation to the research project "Between Restoration and Revolution: National Constitutions and Global Law: An Alternative View on the European Century, 1815–1914," Helsinki University, March 6, 2012).

47 Banu Turnaoğlu, *The Formation of Turkish Republicanism* (Princeton University Press, 2017), 208. The term also appears in some Latin American criminal codes in the 1920s, but I am unaware that they were ever used to prosecute anyone. Harvard Research Project on Criminal Jurisdiction, 29 AJIL 435, 571 (supp. 1935) (citing penal codes of Costa Rica and Venezuela).

48 Nuremberg Charter, art. 6(c). Here I've stripped away jurisdictional language in the definition to focus on the substance of the crime.

legal definition; perhaps she assumed that "extermination" was simply another name for genocide.

The defining features of a crime against humanity in the "lawyers' law" are, first, a list of predicate crimes (murder, extermination, enslavement, deportation, persecution, rape, torture, other inhumane acts); second, a contextual element, namely that they are committed in an organized attack against a civilian population.

Over time, the list of predicate crimes has expanded, and so has the list of classes of people whose persecution counts as a crime against humanity. Where the Nuremberg Charter recognized only six predicate crimes against humanity, the Rome Statute of the International Criminal Court (ICC) adds nine more.[49] Likewise, the Nuremberg Charter recognized only persecution on political, racial, or religious grounds as a crime against humanity. The Rome Statute criminalizes persecution on "political, racial, national, ethnic, cultural, religious, gender, or other grounds that are universally recognized as impermissible under international law."[50]

But the fundamentals remain the same. Predicate crimes are crimes against humanity (in its technical legal sense) when they are part of an organized attack against a civilian population, launched as a matter of policy. The physical perpetrators don't necessarily have a hand in formulating the organization's policy, and they needn't be official members of the attacking organization. What matters is that they commit their criminal acts as part of the organized attack. The point of the latter requirement is to distinguish genuine participants from opportunists piggybacking on large-scale violence to commit private crimes for private reasons. Only the former have committed crimes against humanity.[51]

The contextual elements, not the predicate crimes, are the defining feature of a crime against humanity. This is an important, potentially confusing, legal point. Murder can be a crime against humanity, but, if committed in a different context, murder can instead be a war crime or a crime of genocide. Or it might be an "everyday" domestic law murder that is not an international crime at all.

49 To the Nuremberg Charter's predicate crimes of murder, extermination, enslavement, deportation, persecution, and "other inhumane acts," the Rome Statute adds illegal imprisonment, torture, half a dozen forms of sexual violence, enforced disappearance, and apartheid.

50 Rome Statute, art. 7(1)(h).

51 Massimo Renzo rejects this distinction and argues that any serious violation of basic human rights, including private violence committed for private reasons, should count as a crime against humanity. "Crimes against Humanity and the Limits of International Criminal Law," *Law and Philosophy* 31 (4) (2012): 443–76.

To summarize: The core feature of crimes against humanity as the law defines them is that they are crimes of violence and persecution, committed as part of an attack against civilians, launched by a state or organization as a matter of policy. Arendt would have agreed with the Rome Statute's emphasis on state or organizational policy: that is what makes the state criminal.[52]

But remember that for Arendt, "crimes against humanity" is not simply a legal term of art, a category of crimes grouped together under a suggestive label. She took the name to signify something crucial: that these crimes are an affront to all humanity, not only to the victims and their state. The crucial philosophical question is *why* they concern all of humanity, and therefore deserve to be internationalized. The legal definition gives no hint of an answer; like most statutes, it is not explicit about its underlying motivation (which of course is not to deny that it has one). No doubt that is why Arendt hoped the Eichmann trial would finally unpack the concept and answer the philosophical question.

In earlier publications, Richard Vernon and I have each argued that these crimes' crucial evil – what concerns all humanity – is that political institutions essential to our survival instead turn on us and attack us. Vernon calls this an "inversion" of politics, and I label it "politics gone cancerous." I pointed to "the special danger that governments" – and, I would now add, nonstate organizations like the Islamic State – "which are supposed to protect the people who live in their territory, will instead murder them, enslave them, and persecute them, transforming their homeland from a haven into a killing field." Vernon, in a similar vein, explains that in a crime against humanity, "territoriality is transformed from a refuge to a trap."[53] Human beings are social and political animals, and living in territories with governments is an inescapable part of the human condition. That is why politics gone cancerous concerns all of humanity.

This is not the occasion to defend this view once again; I think it harmonizes with, and perhaps elaborates, Arendt's understanding of politics and crimes against humanity. It also captures the defining feature of the legal definition as an organized attack against a civilian population.

52 *EJ*, 262.

53 David Luban, "A Theory of Crimes against Humanity," *Yale Journal of International Law* 29 (2004): 117; Richard Vernon, "What Is a Crime against Humanity?," *Journal of Political Philosophy* 10 (2002): 241–46. See Richard Vernon, "Crime against Humanity: A Defence of the Subsidiarity View," *Canadian Journal of Law and Jurisprudence* 26(1) (2013): 229–42, which defends the view taken here against important alternative theories of Larry May and Norman Geras.

Arendt herself uses "crimes against humanity" and "genocide" interchangeably. As we will soon see, she has theoretical reasons for doing so. But that is not how lawyers' law defines them, and the jurists who wrote the lawyers' law had their own reasons for distinguishing the crimes. Before examining her analysis, it will help to look at the legal definition of genocide and the concerns that went into its framing.

## 11.6 Genocide

The crime of genocide was defined in a 1951 treaty, known officially as the Convention on the Prevention and Punishment of the Crime of Genocide, and more commonly as the Genocide Convention. The Rome Statute uses the same definition.

Like crimes against humanity, genocide consists of a roster of predicate crimes, plus a contextual element that explains what makes them genocide rather than some other kind of crime. Genocide is "any of the following acts committed with intent to destroy, in whole or in part, a national, ethnical, racial, or religious group, as such" (article 2). It names five acts of genocide:

1. killing members of the group;
2. causing serious bodily or mental harm to members of the group;
3. deliberately inflicting on the group conditions of life calculated to bring about its physical destruction in whole or in part;
4. imposing measures intended to prevent births within the group;
5. forcibly transferring children of the group to another group.

These are the five predicate crimes. Here, the contextual element is the intent of the perpetrator, namely to destroy the group as such.

The definition recognizes four kinds of groups whose intended destruction counts as genocide: national, ethnical, racial, and religious. A reasonable question is: Why only these? Why not political groups (for example)? After all, the definition of persecution as a crime against humanity includes political persecution. You might think that genocide is persecution taken to its highest degree.[54]

The answer is instructive but not uplifting: The states negotiating the Genocide Convention split over the issue of including political groups and cautiously decided against it. Pretty clearly the negotiators were worried that if the Genocide Convention protected political groups, internal

[54] This is the view of Larry May, *Genocide: A Normative Account* (Cambridge University Press, 2010).

conflicts in which government forces slaughter dissidents or rebels would open their governments to genocide accusations.[55]

This is just one indication of how timidly states approached the Genocide Convention, for fear that a broad definition would invite trouble. Not without reason: By late 1947, émigré groups from Ukraine and the Baltic states were accusing the USSR of genocide,[56] and in 1951 American activists filed a petition in the UN titled *We Charge Genocide: The Crime of Government against the Negro People.* The petition documented decades of lynching and police murders of Black Americans.[57] Colonial powers fretted with good reason that their treatment of indigenous peoples might count as genocide.[58]

For the same reason – timidity – the negotiators did not make genocide a universal jurisdiction crime that can be prosecuted by any state. Efforts to include cultural destruction as a predicate crime also failed; among other objectors, US delegates feared that "sporadic outbreaks against the Negro population of the United States" could count as cultural genocide.[59] A measure of state angst is that it took two years for the Genocide Convention to gain the twenty ratifications needed to activate it; and at the time of the Eichmann trial a decade later, only sixty-one states had joined the Genocide Convention, out of ninety-nine UN members.

Today, more than forty states are still holdouts. The United States didn't join the Genocide Convention until 1988, and eleven senators voted no. However, genocide is also an ICC crime, and the ICC has 125 members. Even so, a dozen states today belong neither to the Genocide Convention nor to the ICC; the largest of these double holdouts are Indonesia and Thailand.[60]

[55] However, some states have expanded the listed of protected groups in their own genocide legislation to include genocide against political groups.

[56] Hirsch, *Soviet Judgment at Nuremberg*, 401–4.

[57] William L. Patterson, *We Charge Genocide: The Crime of Government against the Negro People* (Civil Rights Congress, 1951).

[58] The worried states included the UK, France, Canada, New Zealand, and South Africa. Douglas Irvin-Erickson, "The Life and Works of Raphael Lemkin: A Political History of Genocide in Theory and Law" (PhD dissertation, Rutgers University, 2014), 22. At the Convention's drafting the Egyptian and Syrian delegations argued that the new state of Israel was committing genocide. Irvin-Erickson, "The Life and Works of Raphael Lemkin," 313–14. And, as of 2025, South Africa has accused Israel of genocide in Gaza, Nicaragua accuses Germany of complicity in genocide because it supplies Israel with weapons, and Sudan accuses the United Arab Emirates of complicity in genocide because of alleged support for the Rapid Support Forces. All three cases are before the International Court of Justice.

[59] Douglas Irvin-Erickson, *Raphaël Lemkin and the Concept of Genocide* (University of Pennsylvania Press, 2017), 159–60.

[60] The International Court of Justice stated in a nonbinding 1951 advisory opinion that "the principles underlying the Convention are principles which are recognized by civilized nations as

Furthermore, a controversial 2008 decision by the ICJ makes it nearly impossible to prove genocidal intent. The ICJ held that the proof fails unless genocidal intent is the only conclusion that can explain the attackers' conduct.[61] To critics, it seemed that the ICJ was deliberately aiming to spare states the ignominy of being labeled genocide sponsors.

Let's turn to the conceptual difference between the crime against humanity of extermination and the crime of genocide. Why distinguish the crimes at all? The differences turn out to be significant. A crime against humanity involves an organized attack on a civilian population, but it can be a "mixed" population of many ethnicities or religions living together. The law doesn't require that the attackers are targeting members of a distinctive group, nor that they are doing so in order to destroy the group "as such."

Thus a crime against humanity, even the crime of extermination, doesn't focus on identity groups as collective entities. Genocide does. For crimes against humanity, it's the civilian status of the targeted population and the organizational policy to attack them that matter, not the population's identity. "Extermination" consists of a mass killing of civilians; genocide aims to destroy identity groups as such.[62] And predicate acts of genocide include methods other than killing, a signal that the focus of genocide is group identity rather than violence.

It is tempting to think of "civilian populations" as groups distinguished by nationality or ethnicity. That would fuzz up the line between crimes against humanity and genocide (as Arendt did). But except for the crime against humanity of persecution, the statutory text doesn't support or even hint at the group discrimination view, and courts and commentators overwhelmingly reject it. For good reason: Accepting it would exclude some of the worst crimes against humanity in recent years, those motivated by greed or ideology rather than ethnic or racial animus. Sometimes warlords pursuing mineral riches massacre civilians not because of who they are but because they are in the way. That doesn't make the massacres any the less crimes against humanity; it does mean that in the eyes of the law they are not genocide.

binding on States, even without any conventional obligation." Reservations to the Convention on Genocide, Advisory Opinion: I.C.J. Reports 1951, p. 15, at 23.

61 Application of the Convention on the Prevention and Punishment of the Crime of Genocide (Bosnia and Herzegovina v. Serbia and Montenegro), Judgment, I.C.J. Reports 2007, p. 43, §373.

62 ICC Elements of Crimes, Article 7(1)(b), Crime against humanity of extermination, Elements 1 and 2, 243–44.

This explains why genocide as the law defines it can't substitute for crimes against humanity: Doing so would leave out organized massacres that don't target identity groups. What about the other way around? Extermination, defined in law as mass killing of civilians, is a crime against humanity. Is it necessary that the law contain a separate crime of genocide, that is, a crime whose intended victims are not only a mass of individuals but also identity groups as such? Why do groups matter, over and above the individuals who belong to them? These are deep questions, and disagreements over their answers go back to the very inception of modern international criminal law in the "Nuremberg Moment." And, as we shall see, these questions are crucial to understanding Arendt's answer to the question she posed to Karl Jaspers: "Would things be different if we had a law against *hostes humani generis* and not only against murderers and similar criminals?"

We must start, though, not with Arendt but with Raphael Lemkin, the lawyer who coined the word "genocide" and was the first to call it a crime against humanity. Lemkin strongly believed that groups matter as such, and he offered an explanation of why. It isn't Arendt's explanation, and setting them side by side will help us better understand and evaluate hers.

CHAPTER 12

# *The Crime against the Human Status: Lemkin and Arendt*

## 12.1 Lemkin's Word

Genocide is sometimes called "the crime of crimes." Some jurists reject that label because they fear that singling out genocide might downplay other crimes – or, as historian Dirk Moses argues, it might obscure the true source of mass political violence: the illusory quest for permanent security.[1] These are important cautions. But the fact remains that few words pack the punch of the "G-word," and there can be little doubt that in most people's minds genocide is indeed the crime of crimes.

Remarkably, the word *genocide* did not exist until Lemkin coined it in 1944. Lemkin was a Polish Jew and a lawyer, who fled the German invaders at the beginning of World War II – his escape on foot across Poland was harrowing – and wound up in the United States in 1941, the same year Arendt arrived. Most of his friends and relatives were murdered in the Holocaust.

Lemkin knew nine languages, and he understood the power of words. As he struggled to alert the world to "the crime without a name" (Churchill), he knew the name he gave it must be unique and unforgettable. Earlier in his career, Lemkin had labeled the crime *barbarism*, and he urged the League of Nations to outlaw barbarism. But the name never caught on, and his lobbying failed. Lemkin tried again.

This time he succeeded: It's hard to think of another linguistic innovation in law that entered common speech so quickly. *Genos* is the Greek word for "tribe," while *-cide* comes from the Latin for "act of killing." Lemkin formed the word *genocide* to indicate that this crime was not simply the destruction of human beings, even large numbers of human beings. It was the deliberate destruction of entire peoples.

[1] A. Dirk Moses, *The Problems of Genocide: Permanent Security and the Language of Transgression* (Cambridge University Press, 2021).

Writing at the turn of the century, Michael Ignatieff described Lemkin as a forgotten figure.[2] That is hardly true today. Lemkin's singular story is by now well-known, popularized first in Samantha Power's Pulitzer Prize-winning book *A Problem from Hell*, and later in another prize-winning book, Philippe Sands's *East West Street*.[3] An excellent biography and analysis is Douglas Irvin-Erickson's *Raphaël Lemkin and the Concept of Genocide*.[4]

Lemkin's incomplete memoir was published in 2013. We learn that from the time he could read, Lemkin was obsessed with the history of persecutions: "I had the strange and profound conviction that feelings of sympathy for one's fellow man require actual implementation. . . . Thus my basic mission in life was formulated: to create a law among nations to protect national, racial, and religious groups from destruction."[5]

Even before he got to the United States, Lemkin began collecting and analyzing Nazi decrees from occupied Europe. The analysis confirmed his worst fears: The occupations' brutalities were not the ordinary cruelties of war. They aimed quite deliberately at destroying entire peoples. Ignatieff rightly calls Lemkin's effort "scholarship as heroism: a patient, detailed, unprecedented, and unflagging demonstration, decree by decree, of modern despotism's infernal logic."[6]

Lemkin published *Axis Rule in Occupied Europe* in 1944, and in its ninth chapter he unveiled the word "genocide," analyzed its techniques, and showed that international law failed to prohibit many parts of the Nazis' genocidal program. His recommendations were to add genocide to the short list of international crimes, to subject it to universal jurisdiction, and to place an obligation on all states to prosecute perpetrators in their custody, or else extradite them to the state where the genocide took place for prosecution.[7] Here, at least, the similarity to Arendt's "in one form or another men must assume responsibility for all crimes committed by men" is unmistakable.

[2] Michael Ignatieff, "Lemkin's Word," *The New Republic*, February 26, 2001.

[3] Samantha Power, *"A Problem from Hell": America and the Age of Genocide* (Basic Books, 2002); Philippe Sands, *East West Street: On the Origins of "Genocide" and "Crimes against Humanity"* (Vintage, 2016).

[4] Douglas Irvin-Erickson, *Raphaël Lemkin and the Concept of Genocide* (University of Pennsylvania Press, 2017).

[5] Raphael Lemkin, *Totally Unofficial: The Autobiography of Raphael Lemkin*, ed. Donna-Lee Frieze (Yale University Press, 2013), 2.

[6] Ignatieff, "Lemkin's Word."

[7] Raphael Lemkin, *Axis Rule in Occupied Europe: Laws of Occupation, Analysis of Government, Proposals for Redress* (Carnegie Foundation, 1944), 92–94.

Lemkin managed to persuade the Nuremberg prosecutors to include genocide in their indictment of the top Nazis, but genocide didn't make it onto the Nuremberg Charter's list of crimes, and the IMT's judgment never mentions genocide.[8] Disappointed but undeterred, Lemkin launched a lobbying campaign in the new UN to declare genocide an international crime. He had no long-term institutional affiliation, and very little money – he was, as the *New York Times* put it ten years later, "that exceedingly patient and totally unofficial man" (and *Totally Unofficial* became the title of his memoir).[9] His unflagging efforts recruited wide support and resulted, first, in a 1946 General Assembly resolution affirming that genocide is an international crime, then in the 1948 Genocide Convention, and in the ensuing years the uphill fight to gain enough ratifications to activate it. In his final years, Lemkin continued his Sisyphean efforts to persuade the United States to ratify the Genocide Convention. He died in 1959, three decades before US ratification.

The picture of Lemkin as a heroic loner who waged a solo battle and eventually triumphed romanticizes a complex life and an achievement that involved many other actors.[10] He was not a lone prophet: His campaign had the backing of nongovernmental organizations, and of course the political pressure on states to ratify the Genocide Convention came from a much wider coalition. That said, his career and achievements are an example almost without parallel of canny campaigning on slender resources. It was Lemkin who jump-started the movement, recruited supporters, and coordinated their efforts.[11]

As we've seen, the Genocide Convention is a compromised and imperfect document, narrower in crucial respects than Lemkin's original idea.

[8] Lemkin wrote to US Supreme Court Justice Robert Jackson two days after Truman appointed Jackson chief US prosecutor at Nuremberg; Jackson hired Lemkin as a consultant, and library records show that Jackson borrowed a copy of *Axis Rule* and kept it throughout the Nuremberg proceedings. Irvin-Erickson, *Raphaël Lemkin and the Concept of Genocide*, 140; Hilary Earl, "Prosecuting Genocide before the Genocide Convention: Raphael Lemkin and the Nuremberg Trials, 1945–1949," *Journal of Genocide Research* 15(3) (2013): 322–25.

[9] "The Crime of Genocide," *New York Times*, October 20, 1957.

[10] See, for example, James Loeffler, "Becoming Cleopatra: The Forgotten Zionism of Raphael Lemkin," *Journal of Genocide Research* 19(3) (2017): 340–60; James Loeffler, "The First Genocide: Liberal Antisemitism and Jewish Apologetics in the Thought of Raphael Lemkin," *Jewish Quarterly Review* 112(1) (2022): 139–63; Mira L. Siegelberg, "Unofficial Men, Efficient Civil Servants: Raphael Lemkin in the History of International Law," *Journal of Genocide Research* 15(3) (2013): 297–316. A special issue on Lemkin in *Genocide Studies and Prevention: An International Journal* 13(1) (2019) offers contributions that further illuminate and complicate the image of Lemkin.

[11] Irvin-Erickson corrects the romantic misimpression that Lemkin won his victories in the UN single-handedly. *Raphaël Lemkin and the Concept of Genocide*, 162–63.

It doesn't make genocide a universal jurisdiction crime. And, notably, it omits a predicate crime that Lemkin says was crucial to him: "the destruction of the cultural pattern of a group, such as the language, traditions, monuments, archives, libraries, and churches. In brief: the shrines of a nation's soul." Lemkin feared that insisting on a cultural genocide clause would endanger the Genocide Convention, because the other members of the drafting committee opposed it. "So with a heavy heart I decided not to press for it." He consoled himself that at least one remnant of the idea remained, namely the prohibition on transferring children out of the group.[12]

This should remind us of one reason why the crime against humanity of extermination cannot fully capture genocide. Extermination is killing, either directly or by inflicting conditions of life calculated to destroy a target population.[13] These correspond to the first and third predicate crimes in the Genocide Convention. But the Convention criminalizes other modes of physically destroying a group that don't involve killing. Forcibly transferring children out of the group can be done without killing anyone.

It isn't impossible that a cultural understanding of genocide along Lemkin's lines might someday be revived, but it would require a major and unlikely revision in the law. Even so, many people undoubtedly share the intuition that forcibly erasing a national, ethnic, racial, or religious group's culture is a way to destroy the group.[14] In 2021 the US secretary of state declared that China's indoctrination and de-Islamification "Strike Hard" campaign against Muslim ethnic minorities in Xinjiang is genocide, because it aims at "forced assimilation and eventual erasure" of their identities.[15] The intuition is also at the forefront of discussion concerning Russia's 2022 invasion of Ukraine. The Ukrainian National News Agency

[12] Lemkin, *Totally Unofficial*, 172–73. However, in his unpublished later work, Lemkin rejected the proposition that destroying a culture is genocide, unless it results in destroying a nation. Irvin-Erickson, *Raphaël Lemkin and the Concept of Genocide*, 221–23.

[13] ICC Elements of Crimes, Article 7(1)(b)(1), 4.

[14] An example is Lithuania's *Vasiliauskas* case, where the defendant was accused of genocide for killing two Lithuanian partisans at the time of the Soviet takeover. The Lithuanian government called it genocide because the partisans were emblematic of the Lithuanian nation, and the Soviet aim was "to destroy the former Lithuanian way of life and to replace it by a new Soviet order comprised of persons without nationality or ethnicity (*homo sovieticus*)." That replacement would be cultural but not physical genocide. Vasiliauskas v. Lithuania, App. No. 35343/05, 2015 Eur. Ct. H.R. (October 20, 2015), §135. See also Kurt Mundorff, *A Cultural Interpretation of the Genocide Convention* (Routledge, 2020).

[15] US Department of State, Determination of the Secretary of State on Atrocities in Xinjiang, January 19, 2021.

wrote: "Historical monuments are in enemy crosshairs because of their will to destroy the Ukrainian identity. Therefore, the aggressor's actions can be seen as an element of the crime of genocide against the Ukrainian people" – a view expressed as well by Ukraine's Minister of Culture.[16] This clearly refers to cultural, not physical, genocide.

As we will see in §12.2, the emphasis on culture as a paramount value is central to Lemkin's theory of what makes genocide a uniquely terrifying crime. Later in this chapter, we will see that despite the individualism of Arendt's concept of plurality – her emphasis on the uniqueness of each human individual coupled with her alarm at group conformism – she never disagrees that the culture we build in common with others in our group matters immensely, even if it is not as central as Lemkin thought.

Today it's tempting to lump Lemkin together with other jurists, statesmen, and activists in what might broadly be described as the postwar human rights project. That would be a mistake in several ways, because Lemkin and human rights activists were often rivals. One reason is a conceptual difference that we've already begun to explore: Emphasizing groups as such seemingly de-emphasizes individual rights, so human rights activists at the time saw Lemkin's project as a competitor, not an ally – and vice versa.[17]

Their critique is half right. As we'll see shortly, groups ("nations") are at the core of Lemkin's concern. But the critique is also half wrong. Genocide requires the intention to destroy a group, but the law criminalizes *acts* of genocide, not genocidal intent or genocide as a generic phenomenon. The law doesn't even define "a genocide," only acts of genocide.[18] Acts of genocide are perpetrated on individuals, people with names, identities, and human dignity. They are the victims, even if the group as such is the victim behind the victim.

To be sure, in the eyes of the perpetrator, the individual victims' names and actions don't matter. They are killed or injured or robbed of their children because of their group, not because of who they are or what they did. But that makes genocide not only an attack on groups but equally a

[16] Ukrinform, "Army of Vandals and Looters: Russians Targeting Ukrainian Cultural Heritage," December 26, 2022. Euronews, "'It's Cultural Genocide': Ukraine's Culture Minister Trying to Salvage the Country's Artifacts," September 13, 2022.

[17] Siegelberg, "Unofficial Men, Efficient Civil Servants"; Lemkin describes but doesn't explain his friction with human rights groups. *Totally Unofficial*, 170–73.

[18] On this point, see Sangkul Kim, *A Collective Theory of Genocidal Intent* (T.M.C. Asser Press, 2016), 106.

radical assault against individual autonomy and human dignity.[19] Individual victims *do* matter to the law as individuals, and their names (when they are known) will appear in genocide indictments. Thus the Genocide Convention never *substitutes* the group as victim for the individual as victim. The group as victim appears in the defining *mens rea* of intent to destroy the group as such; the individual as victim appears in the predicate acts: not just genocidal acts, but genocidal acts against *these individuals*. In that sense, criminalizing genocide is fully consistent with the individual rights project. Irvin-Erickson explains that Lemkin's aim was to safeguard individuals' right to belong to groups and to express their chosen groups' identities. "Lemkin's argument was very much a communitarian argument, but one that he defended on individualist grounds."[20]

There is a different version of the human rights critique: that focusing the law on groups as such, rather than individuals, reinforces rather than combats the kind of tribalism that gives rise to genocide. As early as 1945, the Austrian economist Leopold Kohr warned Lemkin that he was falling into the trap of biological thinking.[21] Philippe Sands believes that the great human rights lawyer Sir Hersch Lauterpacht, who was responsible for the term "crimes against humanity" in the Nuremberg Charter, feared that emphasizing groups would devalue international human rights for individuals.[22]

If the worry is that criminalizing genocide would pump up the volume of racism and tribalism, it isn't convincing. Would the world really be less racist if the Genocide Convention didn't exist and the word "genocide" had never been coined? Of course not. We mustn't attribute supernatural powers to law. Criminalizing genocide acknowledges genocidal intentions as a fact of life – it doesn't reinforce them.

Perhaps what Lauterpacht and other human rights jurists feared was not that naming genocide as a crime would inflame tribalism, but merely that pushing for a law against genocide would divert UN attention from

19 Berel Lang, *Genocide: The Act as Idea* (University of Pennsylvania Press, 2016), 34–36 is especially good on this point.

20 Irvin-Erickson, *Raphaël Lemkin and the Concept of Genocide*, 13.

21 Sands, *East West Street*, 184–85.

22 Sands, *East West Street*, 110, 324, 327. Historian James Loeffler contends that Sands's contrast is overdrawn (personal communication): Far from being an individualist, Lauterpacht was a lifelong Zionist with a passionate concern for the rights of minority groups. Lauterpacht wrote a brief review of *Axis Rule in Occupied Europe*, which does not voice this criticism. However, the review is not flattering. Lauterpacht ignores Lemkin's proposal to criminalize genocide, and he denies that the book makes a contribution to the law; its value is as a "scholarly historical record." Hersch Lauterpacht, "Review of *Axis Rule in Occupied Europe*," *Cambridge Law Journal* 9(1) (1945): 140.

codifying human rights law. In other words, they may have recognized that juristic and political attention is a scarce resource, and judged that Lemkin's project would suck up too much oxygen. Lemkin's memoir makes clear that he was competing with human rights groups for priority on the UN agenda.

In addition, some friction arose because Lemkin (whom a contemporary described as "a very difficult man, who looked for enemies under every bench"[23]) preferred to work outside bureaucratic channels. But this too was a principled, and not only personal or political, disagreement. As Mira Siegelberg explains, progressive human rights jurists thought Lemkin's focus on protecting groups was a step backward to the regime of minority rights treaties in the 1920s, which failed so conspicuously – a failure Arendt emphasizes in *Origins*. Unlike Arendt, these progressive jurists were pushing for a large-scale, UN-sponsored codification of individual human rights. In their eyes, Lemkin was an anachronism, obsessed with the group-centered nostrums of the prewar era rather than looking forward toward a new age of human rights law. Lemkin, in his turn, thought that soft-law codifications of human rights, such as those produced by the UN's International Law Commission, are no substitute for hard law. And in his eyes, it was the bureaucratized system of UN legal committees and commissions that was the true throwback to the League of Nations era. He dismissed that system as "a cultured cemetery of a dead world."[24] Lemkin preferred to work outside the legal bureaucracy by directly lobbying statesmen and civil society groups – a model for most successful human rights campaigns ever since.

Lemkin is in many ways an inspiring figure – a tenacious and canny strategist, but also a visionary activist with a profound command of history and a sophisticated theory. Sophisticated does not mean right, though, and an examination of his theory reveals some real weaknesses. Identifying these will help us understand Arendt's different view.

## 12.2 Lemkin's Theory: A Critique

The key theoretical question is why groups as such matter in the way that the individuals who compose them matter. In *Axis Rule in Occupied*

[23] Quoted in Siegelberg, "Unofficial Men, Efficient Civil Servants," 300, quoting John Humphrey, who helped draft the UDHR and became the first director of the UN Division of Human Rights.

[24] Lemkin, *Totally Unofficial*, 134. See generally Siegelberg, "Unofficial Men, Official Civil Servants."

*Europe*, Lemkin offers an explanation, which I will call the "world civilization" argument:

> [N]ations are essential elements of the world community. The world represents only so much culture and intellectual vigor as are created by its component national groups. Essentially the idea of a nation signifies constructive cooperation and original contributions, based upon genuine traditions, genuine culture, and a well-developed national psychology. The destruction of a nation, therefore, results in the loss of its future contributions to the world. ... Among the basic features which have marked progress in civilization are the respect for and appreciation of the national characteristics and qualities contributed to world culture by the different nations.[25]

Groups ("nations") should matter to other nations because of their cultural contributions to world civilization. (It's worth observing that the world civilization argument explains why Lemkin saw cultural genocide as a matter of supreme importance.)

This is an attractive argument, but I don't think it succeeds. To see why, let's examine three propositions embedded in it:

*First*, that there is such a thing as "world culture," a kind of common civilization that belongs to all humankind.

*Second*, that the creator of this world civilization is its component national groups, and "the idea of a nation signifies constructive cooperation and original contributions."

*Third*, that there are such things as "a well-developed national psychology" and "national characteristics and qualities."

Each of these is problematic.

*World culture.* If by "world culture" Lemkin means, simply, all the world's disparate cultures taken collectively or additively – like the side-by-side patches on a patchwork quilt – it exists by definition. But very little follows from this. Take one culture away and the result is no less a world culture understood as the set of all remaining cultures.

Lemkin clearly means something more than the side-by-side additive definition of world culture: He means that the cultures interact and enrich each other to form a kind of universal civilization – the "oneness of the world" that inspired his efforts.[26] The image is not a patchwork but a

[25] Lemkin, *Axis Rule*, 91.

[26] Lemkin, *Totally Unofficial*, 68. Irvin-Erickson confirms that Lemkin "conceptualized the entire world as one society," and was attracted to the ideas of the cosmic consciousness movement "that

tapestry. But this is a simplified, idealized picture of the world we live in. It seems plausible only among related cultures with thick mutual interactions, not remote cultures that differ profoundly from each other with little cultural exchange.

Ignatieff writes, "Lemkin remained trapped by the hopeful optimism of a civilization in twilight, just as he was trapped by the illusion that what was Western was universal."[27] This is not fair to Lemkin, whose vast knowledge of non-Western civilizations was a by-product of his in-depth studies of genocide in all eras and all parts of the world. In *Totally Unofficial* he is just as enthralled by Japanese culture as by the cultures of other stopovers on his escape route to America.[28] But Ignatieff is right to this extent: Lemkin's vision of world civilization as a tapestry seems modeled on the much smaller and more interrelated civilization of Europe. It is anything but obvious that this model scales up to encompass the entire world.

*Nations as creators of civilization.* What about the second proposition, that the creator of world civilization is nations? Lemkin puts it thus:

> Our whole cultural heritage is a product of the contributions of all peoples. We can best understand this if we realize how impoverished our culture would be if the so-called inferior peoples doomed by Germany, such as the Jews, had not been permitted to create the Bible or to give birth to an Einstein, a Spinosa [*sic*]; if the Poles had not had the opportunity to give to the world a Copernicus, a Chopin, a Curie, the Czechs a Huss and a Dvorak; the Greeks a Plato and a Socrates; the Russians, a Tolstoy and a Shostakovich.[29]

Of course, Lemkin is not arguing that it's the geniuses that matter – an argument that would devalue cultures that never produced individuals recognized elsewhere as geniuses, while also devaluing all us nongeniuses. I take Lemkin's list as nothing more than a vivid reminder of notable contributions by members of "so-called inferior peoples," to emphasize

sought to locate a unified human consciousness that transcended particular expressions." Irvin-Erickson, *Raphaël Lemkin and the Concept of Genocide*, 241, 15.

[27] Ignatieff, "Lemkin's Word."

[28] Lemkin, *Totally Unofficial*, 88–98. Characteristically, he includes in his glowing appreciation a reminder of Japanese genocide against Christians in the seventeenth century.

[29] Raphael Lemkin, "Genocide: A Modern Crime," *Free World* 4 (April 1945): 39–43. A nearly identical paragraph, missing only the crucial words "so-called inferior" and referring to "nations" rather than "peoples" appears in Raphael Lemkin, "Genocide," *The American Scholar* 15(2) (1946): 228.

that no peoples are inferior.[30] Arendt is rightly indignant at arguments that cultured nations matter more than supposedly less cultured ones or that Einstein matters more than "little Hans Cohn from around the corner, even though he was no genius."[31] Presumably Lemkin would agree.

Even taken at their genius-genuflecting face value, the "genius" examples prove less than Lemkin wants to get from them. Of course, everyone is born into some people or other, and in that sense the Poles "gave" the world a Marie Curie. If that people is destroyed, then its geniuses perish along with everyone else. But it could equally be said that the *French* gave the world a Marie Curie; she studied, lived, and worked in France for half a century. Had the French been annihilated, she would have perished with them. Or it could be said that the *chemists* gave the world a Marie Curie – her discoveries were not written on a blank slate.

Although it is true that if a people is destroyed, its geniuses perish with it, the same would be true if a mixed-nationality group including the genius were killed en masse. And the same would be true if the genius were murdered by a jealous lover. In short, an argument based on the geniuses a nation produces is a protest against killing, not against genocide.

It becomes an argument against genocide only if we also believe that contributions to civilization draw in some essential way on the contributors' national culture. Rather clearly, the influences of national cultures on creative works, as on sports and business practices, range from strong to weak to none. Shostakovich's music is recognizably Russian, just as Chopin's mazurkas and polonaises are Polish. Yet it's hard to see anything distinctively Polish in Copernicus's astronomy or Curie's chemistry – or, for that matter, in Chopin's waltzes. Drawing a line from national culture to individual accomplishments is too crude to ground an argument for the civilizational value of national cultures.

Furthermore, it's a mistake to identify "the idea of a nation" solely with "constructive cooperation" and civilization's triumphs. Cultures have dark sides, and we should never forget Walter Benjamin's reminder that every document of civilization is also a document of barbarism. Injustice and

30 Here I read Lemkin more sympathetically than Dirk Moses, who interprets this paragraph to mean that Lemkin "equated national culture with high culture" and believed that "the value of culture inhered in its elites." Dirk Moses, "Raphael Lemkin, Culture, and the Concept of Genocide," in *The Oxford Handbook of Genocide Studies*, eds. Donald Bloxham and A. Dirk Moses (Oxford University Press, 2010), 29.

31 *EJ*, 96–97, 134. Arendt was not immune to thoughts about national geniuses and peoples' contributions to civilization; she once described Jewish emancipation as "the fostering soil on which Jewish creative genius could grow and contribute its products to the general spiritual life of the Western world." "The Jew as Pariah," in *JW*, 276.

exploitation, militarism, colonialism, and tribalist hatreds are just as much (or just as little) products of national cultures as their poetry and music.

*National traits.* As for "national psychology" and "national qualities," we just shouldn't go there. They are nothing more than crude stereotyping. And stereotypes include negatives as well as positives, which is why appealing to them is a dangerous way to impute value to groups.

In sum, Lemkin's argument that groups are valuable because of their contributions to universal civilization is not strong, because none of its three components is strong.

### *12.2.1 And Yet . . .*

And yet it's clear that Lemkin was on to something important: Our identity groups, be they religious, ethnic, or racial, matter a great deal to most of us, even if we can't say exactly why. And to most people the destruction of their ancestral group, whether by violence or by absorption and assimilation, would count as an additional disaster on top of the loss of individual life.

Is this mere sentimentality? I don't think so. Knowing our origins is a way of interpreting our place in the world; having them extinguished cuts us adrift; having them despised and exterminated is a degradation of ourselves and of our origins. Philosopher Claudia Card captures this idea by arguing that the specific evil genocide inflicts on surviving group members is "social death," the loss of cultural heritage and intergenerational connections, "producing a consequent meaninglessness of one's life and even of its termination" (the latter because of lost rituals and social connections that make dying bearable).[32]

A feature of her argument is that it focuses more on the harm done to genocide survivors than genocide victims. That seems like an odd way to analyze a crime. Criminal laws against homicide are grounded in the wrong done to the homicide victim, not the collateral wrong to their survivors. So Card's argument should not be understood as an analysis of the crime of genocide, but rather as an answer to the question of why our identity groups matter to us. To understand why the group matters to its

[32] Claudia Card, "Genocide and Social Death," *Hypatia: A Journal of Feminist Philosophy* 18(1) (2003): 73. Republished in Claudia Card, *Confronting Evils: Terrorism, Torture, Genocide* (Cambridge University Press, 2010). Larry May finds Card's concept of social death exaggerated, but he agrees with her that the distinctive evil inflicted on survivors of genocide is loss of identity and status. May, *Genocide: A Normative Account*, 84–94.

members, ask what they would lose if it were intentionally destroyed in whole or substantial part, and they survived.

The question is: Why should the group's destruction matter to distant strangers in other groups? As Ignatieff puts it:

> When Claude Lanzmann was filming *Shoah*, he asked a Polish peasant whose fields abutted a death camp what he felt when he saw human ash from the crematoria chimneys raining down on his fields. The peasant replied: "When I cut my finger, I feel it. When you cut your finger, you feel it." The man's reply takes us to the heart of the problem of genocide. . . . Why is a crime committed against Jews or any other human group a crime against those who do not belong to that group?[33]

Lemkin's answer is that we are all part of the same world community, threads in a civilizational tapestry that is the common property of all. We've seen the infirmities of that argument. At this point, it is time to turn back to Arendt's answer to the question of why genocide is a crime against humanity – not in the lawyers' technical sense of a crime committed as part of an organized attack on civilian populations, but in the root conceptual sense of a crime that should matter to all humanity because it assaults the human status itself.[34]

## 12.3 The Human Status: "Diversity as Such"

Arendt's explanation (quoted in Chapter 11) is brief but pregnant. Genocide is "an attack upon human diversity as such, that is, upon a characteristic of 'the human status' without which the very words 'mankind' or 'humanity' would be devoid of meaning."[35] Where Lemkin emphasized human civilizational unity (multifaceted, to be sure, but unity nonetheless), Arendt emphasizes human diversity.

As we saw in Chapter 11, "the idea of humanity" implies a normative project of setting up a practical system of cross-border responsibility. Thus, for Arendt, "crime against humanity" is a term with double significance: It means a crime against the human status for which the responsibility to

[33] Ignatieff, "Lemkin's Word."

[34] For another account of the relationship between Arendt's and Lemkin's thought, see Seyla Benhabib, "International Law and Human Plurality in the Shadow of Totalitarianism: Hannah Arendt and Raphael Lemkin," in *Hannah Arendt and the Law*, eds. Marco Goldoni and Christopher McCorkindale (Hart, 2012), 191–214; published originally in *Constellations* 16(2) (2009): 331–50.

[35] *EJ*, 268–69. Although he neglected to attribute it to Arendt, Michael Ignatieff borrowed this powerful idea years later, when he wrote "Lemkin's Word."

hold perpetrators accountable is an international, and not a merely national, one.

What bothered Arendt about Israel's prosecution of Eichmann was its failure to internationalize the crime of genocide. Israel indicted Eichmann for "crimes against the Jewish people" under a statute modeled on the Genocide Convention – but the statute criminalizes the predicate offenses only when committed against Jews.[36] Arendt objects that "although the crime at issue was committed primarily against the Jews, it is in no way limited to the Jews or the Jewish question."[37] It is a crime against humanity inflicted on the body of the Jewish people.

Her distinction rests on a domestic law analogy. A serious intentional injury is a private wrong against the victim (a tort), but also a public wrong against the state, perpetrated on the body of the victim (a crime). By analogy, Arendt thought the distinctive feature of crimes against humanity and genocide is that they are wrongs inflicted on the bodies of their victims, but they are crimes against humanity.[38]

In her imaginary sentencing speech to Eichmann, Arendt tells him that because of his crime, "no one, that is, no member of the human race, can be expected to want to share the earth with you."[39] That curiously fussy phrase "no one, that is, no member of the human race" indicates that the interested party is *not* only the victims, nor is it the international community of states. It is humanity itself. (For Arendt, the Nazi offense against the community of states was not the murder of the Jews but expelling the Jews onto the territory of other states.[40])

[36] Nazi and Nazi Collaborators (Punishment) Law, 5710-1950. Section 1(b) defines "crimes against the Jewish people" without labeling it genocide. Israel also indicted Eichmann for war crimes and crimes against humanity (using a definition of the latter close to that of the Nuremberg Charter). "Text of the Indictment against Eichmann," *American Jewish Yearbook* 63 (1962): 120–31. Arendt had no objections to these charges, and she undoubtedly approved of the four counts of crimes against humanity perpetrated on non-Jewish victims. Eichmann was convicted on all fifteen counts of the indictment.

[37] Letter from Arendt to Jaspers, February 5, 1961, *HA-KJ*, 423.

[38] *EJ*, 261; she says she borrows the analogy from Telford Taylor. This is not to deny a basic distinction between crime and tort: Criminal law focuses on the wrongfulness of the defendant's conduct, whereas tort law focuses on the wrongfulness of the plaintiff's injury. John C. P. Goldberg and Benjamin C. Zipursky, *Recognizing Wrongs* (Harvard University Press, 2020), 186–88. The difference is incidental to the distinction Arendt is drawing; and in any case, it thins when we consider intentional torts and crimes in which injury to the victim is an element.

[39] *EJ*, 279.

[40] *EJ*, 268. Under today's international law, expulsion too is a crime against humanity; it is the basis of the current (as of 2025) ICC investigation of Myanmar for expelling its Rohingya minority to Bangladesh. It is also known as ethnic cleansing.

Arendt never doubted that Israel had the right to try Eichmann for crimes against the Jewish people, in just the way that half a dozen occupied countries tried Nazi officials for crimes against their nationals.[41] Her critique was not that Israel overstepped, but rather that it did not step far enough. It should have characterized genocide not (only) as a crime against the Jews but (also) as a crime against all humanity.

It is in this legal context that Arendt explains why genocide is a crime against the human status: Genocide against the Jews *or any other identity group* is an attack against human diversity as such, and diversity defines the human status. In this way, Arendt's understanding of genocide differs from Lemkin's, because she does not assume a universal world civilization, either an existing civilization or as a hoped-for goal. If anything, her emphasis on diversity implies the impossibility – perhaps even the undesirability – of a universal world civilization. When Arendt invokes "humanity" as a normative ideal underlying international law, she is talking specifically about universally shared *responsibility*, not the creation of a universal culture.[42] Reverting to my metaphor of the patchwork versus the tapestry, Arendt is a "patchwork" theorist where Lemkin is a "tapestry" theorist – but Arendt insists that protecting the patchwork should matter to all human beings, and protecting it is the responsibility of humanity.

## 12.4 Diversity or Plurality?

There is a lurking philosophical puzzle in her theory of crimes against the human status, however. As we've seen in earlier chapters, Arendt maintains that *plurality* is one of the fundamental human conditions. It is the "law of the earth."[43] Here, she uses a different word, *diversity*. It's tempting to regard these as synonyms, but in this context they are not. In *Eichmann in Jerusalem*, the diversity that she identifies with the "human status" is a diversity of *peoples*, that is, of *groups*. Everywhere else in her writing, plurality refers to the multiplicity of unique *individuals*.[44] Groups aren't the basic human units of her ontology. Individuals are.

Of course, the same can be said of hard-nosed social scientists who insist as a point of metaphysics and methodology that collective behaviors must be explained solely as a function of individual behaviors. But what drives Arendt's individualism is not austerity in method and metaphysics. It's the outstanding value she sees in "manyness." For her, the plurality of unique individuals is a source of wonderment and hope. As we saw in Chapter 8,

[41] *EJ*, 258–59, 263. [42] *OT*, 235. [43] *T*, 187. [44] *HC*, 176 makes this explicit.

she calls the constant influx of new unique individuals – the human condition of natality – "the miracle that saves the world," and "the source of all great and beautiful things."[45] She is talking, very clearly, about the birth of individuals ("unto us a child is born"), not the genesis of social groups. From the plurality of individuals "arises the whole realm of human affairs – in its grandeur and misery," and philosophers who seek a true political philosophy "would have to make the plurality of man ... the object of their *thaumazein*."[46]

For that very reason, Arendt is wary of social groups' tendency to homogenize individual action and opinion. She calls the unitedness of many into one "basically antipolitical," and argues that unanimity of opinion "reduces social relationships to those of an ant heap."[47] She has in mind not only the artificial unanimity that totalitarian regimes impose through terror, but also the conformism and Babbittry she observed in 1950s consumer society. In Hanna Pitkin's apt metaphor, Arendt feared the elevation of the social over the political as "the attack of the blob" – a reference to a 1958 horror movie about a jelly-like mass from outer space that engulfs and digests humans.[48]

Arendt's wariness about social groups heightens our problem of explaining what makes genocide a crime against the human status. National, ethnic, racial, and religious groups – the four protected categories in the Genocide Convention – are quintessentially social groups. Why, then, would Arendt call genocide a crime against the human status?

The simple answer is that despite her anxieties about the blob, Arendt *does* think that social groups matter, and for some of the same reasons that Claudia Card and Larry May raise. It's easy to miss this point, because of her dire warnings in *The Human Condition* about the "rise of the social." Read more carefully, her criticisms are quite specific, and they aren't about the intrinsic worth of social groups. It's true that whenever she contrasts social and political phenomena, "the social" comes in second to "the

45 *HC*, 247; *BPF*, 166, 167; *PP*, 113, 126–27.

46 "Socrates," in *PP*, 38. *Thaumazein* is Plato's and Aristotle's word for the wonder at all things from which philosophy arises. Plato, *Theaetetus*, 155d; Aristotle, *Metaphysics*, 982d.

47 *HC*, 214 (antipolitical); "To Save the Jewish Homeland," in *JW*, 391 (ant heap). For the same reason she rejects Rousseau's concept of a "general will" (in *On Revolution*) and insists that a people consists of "manyness" rather than unity. *OR*, 88.

48 Hanna Fenichel Pitkin, *The Attack of the Blob: Hannah Arendt's Concept of the Social* (University of Chicago Press, 1998). Pitkin's book is a well-taken critique of Arendt's overly sharp social/political distinction and her dim view of the social.

political."[49] "Society" is a realm of necessity rather than freedom, discrimination and economic inequality rather than equal citizenship, and conformism rather than individual action. Her contrasts are questionable, but that isn't the point here. What matters is that in these arguments "the social" isn't a general category but a contrast term, largely defined by its opposites, serving specific dialectical purposes. None of the arguments denies the importance of social groups as such. So, instead of focusing on these contrasts, I suggest we look at the smattering of places in her writing where Arendt explains the positive value of social groups, bringing them out from under the shadow of "the political."

## 12.5 Why Peoples Matter

Arendt provides one clue as to why she thinks group diversity matters, when she writes in *Origins* that "respect for human dignity implies the recognition of my fellow-men or our fellow-nations as builders of worlds or cobuilders of a common world."[50] Both fellow men *and* fellow nations build worlds, in the plural.[51] (For the moment, leave the common world they build to one side – we return to it shortly.) To respect individual human dignity, we must respect its handiwork, the worlds that people build together. Even a people as dispersed as the European Jews shared "all kinds of relationships, based on a common language, religion, a common history, customs, and laws."[52] This is a completely commonsensical explanation of why group diversity, not only individual plurality, is a defining characteristic of the human status: Even if individuals are the basic human units of Arendt's ontology, individuals live together in social groups, and in doing so we jointly create common worlds. This is human creativity par excellence, not a blob that negates it.

So understood, it seems that Arendt might have agreed with Lemkin's proposal to include cultural destruction as a form of genocide, insofar as it

[49] I detail seven different contrasts she draws between social and political phenomena in David Luban, "Arendt on the Crime of Crimes," *Ratio Juris* 28(3) (2015): 307–25.

[50] *OT*, 458.

[51] In interpreting the quoted sentence, I am reading her "ors" as "ands," because I don't think she intends disjunction. I am also reading the sentence distributively: People and nations build worlds; and people and nations build a common world. On the non-distributive reading, people build worlds, nations build a common world. While the sentence can be read the latter way, the distributive reading seems more natural and plausible.

[52] *EJ*, 263. She calls such groupings "political and legal," but on the terms she defines in *The Human Condition* this is wrong: They are social, not political. On this point, see Benhabib's helpful discussion, *The Reluctant Modernism of Hannah Arendt*, 28.

destroys a people's common world. (With one crucial caveat: As we saw in Chapter 11, human dignity matters crucially to Arendt. She would have shed no tears over the demise of cultural practices, even deeply rooted ones, that assault human dignity. Recall that she calls human slavery "the primordial crime upon which the fabric of American society rested."[53] Even though she thought that social discrimination – including racial discrimination – can never be eradicated, Arendt obviously did not view it as a valuable part of the American world.) Arendt herself spent years working for an organization whose mission was retrieving Jewish cultural objects stolen or lost during the war.

As for why these communal relationships matter, Arendt is equally commonsensical. Discussing the plight of someone driven into social isolation, she writes:

> He gets lost – or dies from exhaustion. For only within the framework of a people can a man live as a man among men, without exhausting himself. And only when a people lives and functions in consort with other peoples can it contribute to the establishment upon earth of a commonly conditioned and commonly controlled humanity.[54]

Both these propositions are important. The first acknowledges that nobody can live in utter isolation. Elsewhere, she notes that a life lived solely in the public realm makes you shallow.[55] Neither the solitary nor the wholly public life is fully human. We need background routines against which action, initiative, and individuality display themselves. We find comfort among people who share our slang, our jokes, our cuisine.[56] This contrasts with the perpetual need for alertness and calculation faced by refugees (or even tourists in a foreign land). In "We Refugees," Arendt mourns what she and other "Hitler-persecuted people" lost in exile:

> We lost our home, which means the familiarity of daily life. We lost our occupation, which means the confidence that we are of some use in this world. We lost our language, which means the naturalness of reactions, the simplicity of gestures, the unaffected expression of feelings.[57]

[53] *OR*, 66. [54] "The Jew as Pariah," in *JW*, 297. [55] *HC*, 71.

[56] It might be objected to this interpretation that Arendt viewed the customary and familiar as only the domain of "idle talk" (*HC*, 208), Heidegger's *Gerede*, which both Arendt and Heidegger typically treat with contempt (e.g., *T*, 88). Martin Heidegger, *Being and Time*, trans. John Macquarrie and Edward Robinson (Harper & Row, 1962), ¶35 (H 168–69), 212. Yet Heidegger also argues that without the network of idle talk that establishes linguistic conventions, speech itself would be impossible: *Rede* requires *Gerede*. On this crucial point, see Robert B. Brandom, "Dasein, the Being That Thematizes," in *Tales of the Mighty Dead: Essays on the Metaphysics of Intentionality* (Harvard University Press, 2002), 335–42.

[57] *JW*, 264.

Here Arendt paints a sympathetic picture of communal association, "the social," drawn directly from personal experience.

Second, "only when a people lives and functions in consort with other peoples can it contribute to the establishment upon earth of a commonly conditioned and commonly controlled humanity." Superficially, this proposition sounds very much like Lemkin: It takes for granted that humanity consists of *peoples* as well as *people*; it imagines a world in which peoples live in consort with other peoples; and, above all, it asserts that a consort of peoples will create a "commonly conditioned and commonly controlled humanity," which sounds very much like Lemkin's tapestry of world civilization.

On my reading, however, "commonly conditioned and commonly controlled humanity" refers to a political arrangement, not a shared civilization; and the political arrangement is a *modus vivendi*, a way of getting along, not Lemkin's more ambitious knitting together of peoples and cultures into a multifaceted universal civilization. "Commonly conditioned" reminds us that all peoples share the existential conditions Arendt catalogues in *The Human Condition*: natality, mortality, the earth, life, worldliness, and plurality. Plurality entails that every human being exists in the common condition of being one among many, with the benefits and perils that come with that condition. Every people ("nation") does as well.

"Commonly controlled" is more cryptic. It does not refer to world government, which Arendt thought would be tyranny. Rather, common control must refer to a mutual discipline that peoples acting in consort impose on each other. It is necessary "if the new universal neighborship of all countries is to result in something more promising than a tremendous increase in mutual hatred."[58]

In addition to its attack on human diversity, the universal neighborship of all countries provides an additional reason that genocide is a crime against all humanity: neighborship, plus unprecedented technologies of coordination and mass destruction, plus the unhappy fact that "once a specific crime has appeared for the first time, its reappearance is more likely than its initial emergence could ever have been."[59] Any group, anywhere, can find itself the target of a genocidal attack, and the capacity to execute it is greater today than at any time in the past. In *Origins*, Arendt observed that the shrinking of geographical distances "made idealistic talk about mankind and the dignity of man an affair of the past simply because all these fine and dreamlike notions, with their time-honored traditions,

[58] "Karl Jaspers: Citizen of the World?," in *MDT*, 84. [59] *EJ*, 273.

suddenly assumed a terrifying timeliness." And this provoked a backlash of racism and hatred against the "instinctive feeling that mankind . . . implies a common sharing of responsibility."[60] The current anti-immigrant, anti-asylum eruptions in today's developed countries are a concrete reminder of what Arendt foresaw seventy-five years ago. The paramount task of the new law on Earth must be to control and counter this backlash, and to establish a regime of common responsibility.

These are intensely practical, not philosophical, reasons to call genocide a crime against humanity.[61] The two lines of argument, philosophical and practical, converge. The human conditions of diversity and plurality explain why genocide is a crime against the human status. The practical worries explain why suppressing it must become a universal concern: The capacity to carry out genocidal intent is now far too real.

That is the point of Arendt's imaginary sentencing speech to Eichmann. Arendt tells him why "no member of the human race can be expected to want to share the earth with you." The reason is that "you supported and carried out a policy of not wanting to share the earth with the Jewish people and the people of other nations – as though you and your superiors had any right to determine who should and who should not inhabit the world."[62] What made the Nazis *hostes generis humani* is their assumption of a godlike power to decree which peoples shall live and which shall die. If anything makes genocide more horrific than other crimes against humanity, it's the unique danger that genocidal intent poses, once the capacity to carry it out is there. A warlord committing massacres to steal mineral riches will stop when the locals have been driven away and the minerals are securely in his control. A genocidal leader won't stop, for he aims with single-minded intensity at annihilation.[63]

60 *OT*, 235.

61 Lemkin, too, cited practical as well as philosophical reasons for criminalizing genocide, namely that mass persecutions create mass flight and refugee crises. *Axis Rule in Occupied Europe*, 93; May, *Genocide: A Normative Account*, 228.

62 *EJ*, 279. See Alon Confino, *A World without Jews: The Nazi Imagination from Persecution to Genocide* (Yale University Press, 2014). Arendt's hypothetical sentencing speech resembles Kant's argument in his Doctrine of Justice for world law and cosmopolitan possession of the world: "From the fact that nature has enclosed all nations within a limited boundary . . . it follows that the possession of the land on which an inhabitant of the earth can live can always be conceived only as the possession of a part of a determinate whole, such that every person can be conceived as originally having a right to it." Immanuel Kant, *The Metaphysical Elements of Justice*, John Ladd trans., 2nd ed. (Hackett Publishing, 1999), 160; Ak. 4:353. It is entirely possible that Arendt had Kant's argument in mind when she grounded Eichmann's culpability in the unwillingness to share the Earth with "the Jewish people and the people of a number of other nations." Thanks to Turku Isiksel for drawing my attention to this similarity.

63 I am grateful to Julie O'Sullivan for impressing this crucial point on me.

CHAPTER 13

# *The Promise and Peril of Identity as Politics*

## 13.1 Prologue: Arendt in The Hague

In March 2013, I sat in a courtroom gallery in The Hague, at the International Criminal Tribunal for the former Yugoslavia (ICTY). On the other side of the glass window was Radovan Karadžić, the former president of Republika Srpska, on trial for genocide, war crimes, and crimes against humanity. (He was convicted and is serving a life sentence.) That day Karadžić called a witness, named Mirko Šošić, to testify that ethnic Serbs in Sarajevo had been persecuted by Muslims rather than the other way around. Karadžić hoped to prove that "Sarajevo was militarized and it was brutal towards the Serbs," rather than that "wild Serbs attacked Sarajevo which was a peaceful town."[1]

Šošić is a Bosnian Serb surgeon and professor. He had occasional dealings with Karadžić during the war, getting a medal from Karadžić for providing exemplary medical care. Šošić recalled that the two worked together on medical projects in a "spirit of euphoria"; it was "an intensive collaboration."[2] Šošić later became a cabinet minister in Republika Srpska under the ultranationalist Gojko Kličković.[3] As I listened through headphones, Šošić explained his own political trajectory:

> I remembered a thought which was very clever and it wasn't mine. You see, I didn't feel myself a Serb or a nationalist or anything. I considered myself a member of my family and a surgeon and an internationalist.

[1] Transcript, statement of the accused, March 21, 2013, p. 35765 lines 14–16, www.icty.org/x/cases/karadzic/trans/en/130321ED.htm [https://perma.cc/78DS-DJYC].

[2] Transcript, statement of the accused, p. 35782, line 14. The euphoria came because Karadžić helped Šošić set up a clinic for civilians. To be clear, nobody ever accused Šošić of crimes or complicity.

[3] Kličković himself was accused of war crimes and crimes against humanity in the Bosnian Extraordinary Chamber, but was acquitted for lack of proof beyond a reasonable doubt. On Šošić's dealings with Karadžić, see Transcript, pp. 35771, line 22 to 35772, line 6; 35781, line 24 to 35783, line 12.

> And I found a sentence which said if they insult you and attack you as a Jew, you have to defend yourself as a Jew. That is to say, by analogy, if they attack you and insult you as a Serb, you have to defend yourself as a Serb. *I think that Mrs. Hannah Arendt, a prominent philosopher, said this.*
>
> And I found this to be a logical explanation in a way because you are simply forced to go where you are being pushed, because otherwise you don't belong anywhere.[4]

To put it mildly, I was startled.

The irony is extreme. Arendt's slogan was a call to resist persecution and genocide. Šošić uses it to explain his conversion to a nationalist who, in a "spirit of euphoria," worked shoulder to shoulder with a génocidaire.

Šošić did not misquote Arendt, who told an interviewer: "If one is attacked as a Jew, one must defend oneself as a Jew."[5] The aim of this chapter is to understand what she meant, how it connects with her analysis of genocide, and whether it avoids the perils that Šošić's testimony reveals.

## 13.2 Identity as Political Speech Acts

To begin, it is useful to examine Arendt's own views about identity groups and identity politics. She scorned romantic nationalism, which "holds a nation to be an eternal organic body," and she rejected all related views.[6] The crucial chapters of *Origins* about tribal nationalism and the pan-movements explain how romantic nationalism decayed into racism in the century leading up to the Third Reich. Antisemitism was an almost inevitable corollary.[7]

And Arendt surely would have rejected Lemkin's belief in "national psychology" and "national characteristics and qualities." In 1933, she chided Jaspers for writing about German essence and German character. "What troubled me first of all of course is the term 'German character.' You say yourself how misused it is. For me it is almost identical with misuse."[8]

Her rejection of organic nationalism comes out strikingly in the exchange of letters about *Eichmann in Jerusalem* with Gershom Scholem

[4] Transcript, testimony of Mirko Sosić, March 21, p. 35763 lines 14–23, www.icty.org/x/cases/karadzic/trans/en/130321ED.htm [https://perma.cc/78DS-DJYC], emphasis added. Visited April 2, 2025.

[5] Arendt, "'What Remains? The Language Remains': An Interview with Günter Gaus," in *EU*, 12.

[6] "Zionism Reconsidered," in *JW*, 367.

[7] *OT*, 238–41. See generally chapters 6, 8, and 9 of *Origins*.

[8] Arendt to Jaspers, January 6, 1933, *HA-KJ*, 18. Their exchange on this topic begins with her letter on January 1 and his response on January 3. *HA-KJ*, 15–18.

that we examined in Chapter 5. Scholem was repelled by Arendt's tone as well as her criticisms of the wartime Jewish leadership and the Israelis. He chided her for lack of heart and told her that, as "nothing other than a member of this [Jewish] people," she should have been more circumspect. "There is something in the Jewish language that is completely indefinable, yet fully concrete – what the Jews call *ahavath Israel* or love for the Jewish people."[9] She responded:

> I thought it peculiarly touching when you wrote, "I see you as nothing other than a member of this people." Not only have I never acted as if I was something else, but I have never even felt the temptation to do so. ... Tying in with what I just said, I'll begin with *ahavath Israel* .... How right you are that I have no such love .... I have never in my life "loved" some nation or collective – not the German, French, or American nation, or the working class, or whatever else there might be in this price range of loyalties. The fact is that I love only my friends and am quite incapable of any other sort of love.[10]

Now in fact Arendt's Jewish identification ran deep, and her collected Jewish writings, spanning five decades, run to more than 500 pages. Her connection was not religious. She explained her own religiosity in a letter to Jaspers:

> On the personal level I make my way through life with a kind of (childish? because unquestioned) trust in God (as distinguished from faith, which always thinks it knows and therefore has to cope with doubts and paradoxes). There's nothing much you can make of that, of course, except be happy. All traditional religion as such, whether Jewish or Christian, holds nothing whatsoever for me anymore.[11]

In a rare pronouncement on religion, she describes atheists as "fools who pretended to know what no man can know."[12] Perhaps she thought believers are in the same boat.

Even so, five years earlier, she wrote to Jaspers that "the Jewish question" remained "the focal point of my historical and political thinking." She added that she kept her own name rather than taking her husband's because "I wanted my name to identify me as a Jew."[13] But the letter to

[9] Scholem to Arendt, June 23, 1963, *HA-GS*, 202.
[10] Arendt to Scholem, July 24, 1963, *HA-GS*, 206.
[11] Arendt to Jaspers, March 4, 1951, in *HA-KJ*, 165–66. "Anymore" is tantalizing. [12] *MDT*, 67.
[13] Arendt to Jaspers, *HA-KJ*, January 29, 1946, 29, 31. For an overview of Arendt's relationship to "the Jewish question," see Richard J. Bernstein, *Hannah Arendt and the Jewish Question* (MIT Press, 1996; republished by Polity Press, 2013).

Scholem describes her own Jewishness in remarkably bare-bones terms: It is a natural fact of ancestry ("*physei* and not *nomoi*"), nothing more.[14]

In fact there is no contradiction between Arendt's chilliness about love of a people and her own identity politics. Her views about group-based identity are philosophically subtle. Although she rejects group-based metaphysics, she nevertheless believes that describing our identity in group terms may sometimes be politically necessary.

She explains why in her 1959 speech accepting the city of Hamburg's Lessing Prize. Arendt tells her audience that for years her answer to the question, "Who are you?" was: a Jew. "That answer alone took into account the reality of persecution." To have answered, "I'm a human being," would be "a grotesque and dangerous evasion of reality." She adds:

> When I use the word "Jew" I do not mean to suggest any special kind of human being. . . . Rather, I was only acknowledging a political fact through which my being a member of this group outweighed all other questions of personal identity or rather had decided them in favor of anonymity, of namelessness. Nowadays such an attitude would seem like a pose. . . . Unfortunately, the basically simple principle in question here is one that is particularly hard to understand in times of defamation and persecution: the principle that one can resist only in terms of the identity that is under attack.[15]

This is a fuller explanation of her aphorism quoted in The Hague by Mirko Šošić: "If one is attacked as a Jew, one must defend oneself as a Jew." To which she added: "Not as a German, not as a world citizen, not as an upholder of the Rights of Man, or whatever."[16]

What Arendt is getting at, I think, is a *political* and *speech act* theory of ethnic identity. That is, utterances such as "I am a Jew" are not simply neutral descriptions, nor are they metaphysical statements that group affiliation somehow constitutes individual identity. Rather, they are speech acts of alliance and confrontation.

Had Arendt, an imperiled refugee in France in 1940, responded to the question, "Who are you?" with, "I'm a German" or "I'm a human being," she would have been closeting herself (rather clumsily to be sure). She would have disowned other Jews, and let her questioner off the moral hook. By answering, "I am a Jew," she would compel questioners to show

[14] Arendt to Scholem, July 24, 1963, *HA-GS*, 206.

[15] Hannah Arendt, "On Humanity in Dark Times: Thoughts about Lessing," in *MDT*, 17–18. Also "Hannah Arendt on Hannah Arendt," *TWB*, 470.

[16] Arendt, "'What Remains? The Language Remains': An Interview with Günter Gaus," in *EU*, 12.

their stance toward the Nazi persecution (against it? for it? scared to say? opposed but "it's not my problem"?). She would remind her listeners that in the eyes of the Nazis nothing else about her identity matters. She would rub their noses in reality. She would try to make them think.

Accepting a prize in Hamburg, in 1959, is different. Arendt claims that to step to the podium and announce, "I am a Jew," would be a pose, and surely she is right. It would be cheap victimology, said to make her German audience squirm. In effect, Arendt understands identity ascriptions like "I am a Jew" as speech acts. Different situations define different speech acts performed by the same words.

If this interpretation is right, assertions of group identity don't mark out ontological or moral distinctions. "I am a Jew" can be *true* as a matter of ancestry, *false* as a statement about essence, and politically *indeterminate*, making different normative commitments in different circumstances.

Arendt is clearly onto something. In a contextless way, identity ascriptions can be factually true or false. But utterances are always made in a context, and when it comes to assertions or denials of identity, the contexts are typically political. When they are, identity becomes identity politics.

These anti-essentialist views may seem to contradict an important theme in Arendt's authorship: her passionate critique of assimilation as a kind of Jewish self-negation and her insistence that European Jews must identify themselves as Jews, without closeting or covering.[17] As she often put it: Better to be a pariah than a parvenu.[18] That raises the question: How can she assign as little significance to identity as she does in her letter to Scholem and still insist that assimilation was a mistake? Don't these stances contradict each other?

They do not. In fact, they reinforce each other, for her anti-assimilationism was never based on some theory of essential Jewishness. The reason for not assimilating is that in antisemitic societies, closeting or covering makes organized political resistance impossible. That's the "basically simple principle" that is so hard to understand. Arendt well

17 Covering is Kenji Yoshino's name for turning down the volume on one's own distinctive identity and presenting oneself as blandly mainstream, without actually denying that identity (the latter is closeting, not covering). Yoshino, *Covering: The Hidden Assault on Our Civil Rights* (Random House, 2006). The philosophical wit Sidney Morgenbesser described the stance as *incognito ergo sum*.

18 Arendt introduced the distinction between the Jew as pariah and as parvenu in *Rahel Varnhagen*, and stuck with it in other writings. See, for example, "Original Assimilation: An Epilogue to the One Hundredth Anniversary of Rahel Varnhagen's Death," "The Jew as Pariah: A Hidden Tradition," "We Refugees," and "Herzl and Lazare," all in *JW*, and the section "Between Pariah and Parvenu" in *OT*, 56–68.

understood that covering and closeting are psychologically damaging, but her main concern is political.[19] In "We Refugees" Arendt is scathing about the self-deception of Jewish refugees who desperately insisted that now they were superpatriots of their flight countries (until they had to flee to the next country). After the war, she wrote Jaspers that Jews could return to Europe "only if we are welcome as Jews," not as Frenchmen or Germans.[20]

Her political view of identity helps explain Arendt's tense and ultimately oppositional stance toward Zionism. Before 1929 Arendt was uninvolved in politics or Jewish affairs. That changed as German antisemitism swelled along with Hitler's fortunes. After Hitler came to power in 1933, Arendt agreed to do research on German antisemitism for a Zionist group that feared persecution if its own members were caught doing the research. She was arrested, interrogated, and fled from Germany. In Paris, Arendt worked for Youth Aliyah, a Zionist organization that resettled imperiled Jewish youth in Palestine. Isaiah Berlin recalled that when Kurt Blumenfeld introduced him to Arendt in 1941, she was "a hundred per cent Zionist," so much so that "her fanatical Jewish nationalism ... was, I remember, too much for me" (and Berlin was himself a Zionist).[21]

During the 1930s and early 1940s, she saw nothing wrong with European Jews building a homeland in Palestine, which she assumed would become a secular binational state where Jews and Arabs shared equal political rights. In Arendt's eyes, political creation is the heart of freedom, and she reassured herself that the European Jews were not there to exploit Arab labor.[22] But she broke with the Zionist movement in 1943, after the Biltmore Declaration proclaimed that Palestine should become a "Jewish commonwealth."[23] In a 1944 essay, Arendt criticized the folly of a program that "granted minority rights to the Arab majority," leaving them "the choice between voluntary emigration and second-class citizenship" – an essay that infuriated Zionists, including some of her close

19 "Original Assimilation: An Epilogue to the One Hundredth Anniversary of Rahel Varnhagen's Death," in *JW*, 22–24, zeroes in on the psychological damage.

20 Arendt to Jaspers, January 29, 1946, *HA-KJ*, 31–32.

21 Quoted in Kei Hiruta, *Hannah Arendt and Isaiah Berlin*, 15, from an interview with Berlin and a letter from Berlin to Bernard Crick. As Hiruta makes clear, Berlin had an almost allergic dislike of Arendt.

22 She argues thus in "Peace or Armistice in the Middle East?," *JW*.

23 "Hannah Arendt on Hannah Arendt," in *TWB*, 470. For a critique of Arendt's oppositional stance to Zionism, see Susie Linfield, *The Lion's Den: Zionism and the Left from Hannah Arendt to Noam Chomsky* (Yale University Press, 2019), 1–79. See also Hiruta, *Hannah Arendt and Isaiah Berlin*, 15–19.

friends.[24] By 1951 she called Palestine "a colonized and then conquered territory."[25]

Near the end of her life she remarked that the Zionists were the only political group to which she had ever belonged, "only because of Hitler, of course," but it didn't last; in another interview, she said she had never been a Zionist.[26] We can gloss this seeming contradiction as follows: At a time when Zionism in Europe coincided with organized Jewish resistance to persecution, Arendt was a Zionist. But when the Zionist movement veered toward ethnonationalism, she broke away.

Arendt's political view of identity readily explains why she is willing to accept the group identity-based definition of genocide in the Genocide Convention, even though she rejects essentialism about group identity. If one is attacked as an *X*, one must defend oneself as an *X* – even if *X*-ness is otherwise peripheral to one's sense of self (in Arendt's words, if it is *physei* and not *nomoi*). If an effective way to fight against genocide is criminalizing the physical destruction of identity groups "as such," then group identity as such becomes the most politically salient of all our identities.

This analysis fits in well with a holding by the ICTY: "It is the stigmatization of a group as a distinct national, ethnical or racial unit by the community which allows it to be determined whether a targeted population constitutes a national, ethnical or racial group in the eyes of the alleged perpetrators."[27] If you are attacked as a Jew, you become a Jew.[28]

## 13.3 The Perils of Arendt's Brand of Identity Politics

Even so, it's important to recognize the grave dangers in identity politics of the kind Arendt favors. Let's return to Mirko Šošić. As he tells the story,

[24] Arendt, "Zionism Reconsidered" (October 1944), *JW*, 343, 347. On the ferocious reception of this essay by Zionists, see Grunenberg, *Hannah Arendt and Martin Heidegger: History of a Love*, 181–84. Among them was Scholem, who sent Arendt a scathing critique. Scholem to Arendt, January 28, 1946, in *HA-GS*, 41–46. Years later, Arendt wrote to Scholem that "Jews are all secretly of the opinion that I'm an anti-Semite." Arendt to Scholem, July 29, 1959, in *HA-GS*, 195.

[25] *OT*, 290.

[26] "Hannah Arendt on Hannah Arendt," in *TWB*, 470; Arendt, "'What Remains? The Language Remains'," in *EU*, 5 ("I was not a Zionist").

[27] Prosecutor v. Jelisić, Case No. IT-95-10-T, Judgment, §70 (December 14, 1999). A month earlier, the ICTR's Trial Chamber proposed a more inclusive test. An ethnic group is "one whose members share a common language and culture; or, a group which distinguishes itself, as such (self identification); or, a group identified as such by others, including perpetrators of the crimes (identification by others)." Prosecutor v. Kayishema and Ruzindana, Case No. ICTR-95-1-T, Judgment, §98.

[28] On this point, see Carola Lingaas, "Imagined Identities: Defining the Racial Group in the Crime of Genocide," *Genocide Studies and Prevention: An International Journal* 10(1) (2016): 79–106.

her theory explains the thinking that pushed him into the camp of Karadžić, now serving a life sentence for genocide, war crimes, and crimes against humanity.

Šošić's testimony is not simply a case of the devil's witness quoting Scripture. It is rather, one might say, an unpleasant and unexpected Schmittian intrusion on Arendt's political theme of resisting persecution by embracing the identity being persecuted. Here, resistance to (real or supposed) persecution pushed Šošić not only to ethnic nationalism but also to ethnic enmity – us versus them, friend versus enemy, as the Nazi jurist Carl Schmitt defined the concept of the political.[29] It led Karadžić to genocide.

I think of Schmitt as the anti-Arendt, and not only because of his Nazism and antisemitism. He defines politics as the struggle between enemies, where "friend or enemy?" is always the operative question, and where real, nonmetaphorical killing always lurks in the wings.[30] Arendt, by contrast, understands politics as an arena where speech and persuasion matter more than violence, and where political power comes from "the human ability not just to act but to act in concert."[31] Violence is merely an instrument of political power, not power itself, and Arendt never suggests (as Schmitt does) that politics without mortal enmity is too namby-pamby to be truly political.[32]

Arendt was no pacifist, and she recognized that political action sometimes requires violence, because deadly threats are real. In the 1940s Arendt campaigned for a Jewish army to fight the Nazis alongside the other Allies.[33] This gives concrete meaning to "if one is attacked as a Jew, one must defend oneself as a Jew": It shows that Arendt had military as well as political resistance in mind.[34] Nevertheless, when Arendt spoke of armed resistance, she self-evidently did not mean that anything goes, including "fight genocide with genocide."

But why not? Surely, the answer must be that there are humanitarian limits to what a group can do even to resist its own persecution. It cannot mean destroying the enemy as a people. Those limits must come from

29 Carl Schmitt, *The Concept of the Political*, trans. George Schwab, expanded ed. (University of Chicago Press, 2007). For readers unfamiliar with Carl Schmitt (1888–1985), he was one of Germany's leading jurists before and during the Third Reich. Schmitt was a deep thinker and seductive writer, and recent decades have seen a remarkable Schmitt renaissance, despite his Nazi entanglements and his virulent antisemitism.

30 Schmitt, *The Concept of the Political*, 27, 33, 45.

31 Arendt, "On Violence," in *CR*, 143.

32 "On Violence," 134–55; Schmitt, *The Concept of the Political*, 53.

33 This was the running refrain of Arendt's articles and *Aufbau* columns in 1941–42: *JW*, 136–60.

34 Arendt, "The Jewish Army – The Beginning of Jewish Politics?," in *JW*, 137, says this explicitly.

some commitment to decency and human dignity that transcends Schmitt's friend/enemy distinction. That commitment is an integral part of what Arendt meant by the idea of humanity.

Although neither Arendt nor Schmitt ever published anything about each other, recent archival work has unearthed illuminating marginal comments that Arendt scribbled in her copy of Schmitt's *Nomos of the Earth*, and Schmitt's equally revealing marginal comments in his copy of *Eichmann in Jerusalem.*[35] Notably, Arendt criticizes Schmitt for completely ignoring matters of right and wrong.[36] As for Schmitt, it comes as no surprise that he utterly rejected Arendt's conception of crimes against "the human status" in *Eichmann*.

Predictably, Schmitt was tough on humanitarianism: "[W]hoever invokes humanity wants to cheat."[37] Wars fought in the name of humanity are nothing more than bad-faith efforts to demonize the enemy as an outlaw of humanity and do terrible things to him.[38] Invoking humanity "degrades the enemy into . . . a monster that must not only be defeated but also utterly destroyed."[39] In other words, Schmitt believed that fighting in the name of humanity is itself an invitation to genocide.

Schmitt's claim that invoking humanity degrades the enemy into a monster is precisely what Arendt rejects. As we saw in Chapter 11, Arendt's idea of humanity means that we must never treat evildoers like an alien species.[40] Like it or not, they too belong to humanity – a thought that Arendt calls terrifying. For Schmitt, a political community embracing all of humanity cannot exist – a world without mortal enemies is a world without politics. As if in direct response to Schmitt, Arendt claims that "the idea of humanity, excluding no people and assigning a monopoly of guilt to no one," is "the only guarantee" against genocide.[41]

It might finally be objected that this line of thought contradicts her insistence that in times of persecution, "I am a human being" is a grotesque and dangerous evasion of reality. Isn't that tantamount to saying

35 Anna Jurkevics, "Hannah Arendt Reads Carl Schmitt's *The Nomos of the Earth*: A Dialogue on Law and Geopolitics from the Margins," *European Journal of Political Theory* 16(3) (2017): 345–66; Sinja Graf, "Carl Schmitt Reads Hannah Arendt's *Eichmann in Jerusalem*: Archival Perspectives on Convergence and Divergence," *American Journal of Political Science* 66(4) (2022): 918–31.

36 Jurkevics, "Hannah Arendt Reads Carl Schmitt's *The Nomos of the Earth*: A Dialogue on Law and Geopolitics from the Margins," 350–51 (quoting Arendt's marginalia).

37 Schmitt, *The Concept of the Political*, 54.

38 Schmitt, *The Concept of the Political*, 54

39 Schmitt, *The Concept of the Political*, 36.

40 "Organized Guilt and Universal Responsibility," in *EU*, 131.

41 "Organized Guilt and Universal Responsibility," in *EU*, 131. I endorse this argument in Luban, "On the Humanity of the Enemy of Humanity: A Response to My Critics," *Netherlands Journal of Legal Philosophy* 47(2) (2018): 187–99

that in times of persecution one *must not* adopt the standpoint of humanity?

The answer is no. Arendt's point in her Hamburg speech was that "I am a human being," uttered in times of persecution by one who is persecuted, is closeting rather than resisting. But that's a very particular context. What if the words are uttered by a soldier ordered to massacre civilian prisoners, to explain why he won't obey the order – same context, different role? In that setting, it would be a way of resisting rather than closeting – a way of reminding himself and his platoonmates that it is defenseless fellow humans they are being called on to murder – and thus a speech act of refusal to become an enemy of humanity. Refusing can range from quietly seeking a transfer to another unit, to disobeying orders to kill, to courageous resistance like that of Anton Schmid, the German sergeant who sacrificed his life to rescue Polish Jews, or Rwandans who at their own peril sheltered Tutsis during the 1994 genocide. They were confronting reality, not evading it. And they may well have been saying to themselves and to others, "I am a human being."

I drafted this chapter before Hamas's October 7, 2023 attack on Israeli civilians. This book is not the place to discuss the many legal, factual, and moral disputes about events that are still unfolding in real time as I write in late 2025. Nevertheless, Israel's ferocious military response casts a shadow over Arendt's dictum "if one is attacked as a Jew, one must defend oneself as a Jew." It raises in an acute form the question of whether the dictum has any implied limits on the harm one can inflict on the enemy's civilians. Arendt, I have claimed, would answer yes, even against an adversary that massacred more than a thousand innocent civilians. A response that left Gaza in ruins, turned millions of Gazans into internally displaced persons struggling for food and water, and killed or injured hundreds of thousands seems to many of us to have exceeded humanitarian limits however they are defined. Whether Israel's "Swords of Iron" campaign crossed the high threshold of genocidal intent set by the ICJ matters is a legalistic, almost scholastic, question that matters less than the devastating reality on the ground.[42]

*

[42] In the ICJ, South Africa has accused Israel of genocide because of the magnitude of death and suffering it inflicted on Gazan civilians, accompanied by the genocidal rhetoric of some of its most influential politicians and media figures, including cabinet members. Israel denies that they speak for the government. Recall from Chapter 11 that the ICJ decreed that to label extreme violence against a people "genocide," genocidal intent must be the only possible explanation for the violence.

Recall once again Arendt's justification to Jaspers for attending the Eichmann trial. She thought it might answer the fundamental question: "Would things be different if we had a law against *hostes humani generis* and not only against murderers and similar criminals?"[43] In other words, can a law against genocide make a difference, as Lemkin hoped? It was that question, not mere curiosity, that brought Arendt to Jerusalem. If criminal law of the kind she hoped for existed, and was enforced and honored, it would be a step toward making the idea of humanity into something real, rather than a grotesque evasion of reality.

Were any of her hopes fulfilled? To answer that question, we must turn to her trial report, and carefully examine her assay of what succeeded in the Jerusalem proceedings and judgment – and what did not.

[43] Arendt to Jaspers, December 23, 1960, *HA-KJ*, 417.

## CHAPTER 14

# *Doing Justice*

Recall Arendt's explanation to Karl Jaspers of her hopes for the Eichmann trial: "[W]e have no tools to hand except legal ones with which we have to judge and pass sentence on something that cannot even be adequately represented either in legal terms or in political categories. That is precisely what makes the process itself, namely, the trial, so exciting."[1]

Her cautious optimism about the legal process as a site of judgment raises questions that Arendt well understands, but never fully answers. What are criminal trials for? What about trials for atrocity crimes ("core crimes")? Do they differ in their aims or structures from trials for ordinary domestic law crimes? Are they legitimate? Does it even make sense to try individuals for collective crimes? What is the point of courts jumping into the political maelstrom of mass violence? These questions are the subject of this chapter.

An additional question is whether Arendt's thinking sheds light on the modern practices of international criminal law – and vice versa.[2] Arendt's ideas about atrocity crimes and the courts that try them grew out of her engagement with the Eichmann trial. Some are specific to that trial's unique circumstances: Eichmann's notoriety, the magnitude of his crimes, the mountain of evidence that made the verdict a foregone conclusion, the fact that Eichmann was tried in a domestic court and not an international tribunal, the worldwide audience, and the trial's electrifying effect in Israel,

[1] Arendt to Jaspers, December 23, 1960, in *HA-KJ*, 417. I have slightly amended the translation.

[2] "International criminal law" is a bit of a misnomer, because some of the "core crimes" under international law (aggression, war crimes, crimes against humanity, and genocide) are also crimes under many states' domestic criminal law; and, depending on the circumstances, they can be prosecuted either in domestic courts or international courts. If a state prosecutes a core crime under its domestic version of international law – as Israel did with Eichmann and Germany has done with many war criminals – then strictly speaking this is not *international* criminal law, because neither the law nor the court is international. I am using "international criminal law" in an expanded sense, to include domestic-law counterparts of core international crimes. I also use the term "atrocity crimes" loosely, as a synonym for core crimes, including those that do not inflict violence on human bodies – for example, the war crime of wanton destruction of property, and genocide by forcibly transferring children from the targeted group to another group.

Germany, and elsewhere. No trial for atrocity crimes before or since has been remotely like it in all these ways.

Inevitably, these singularities make some of Arendt's ideas irrelevant to modern international criminal law, which restarted twenty years after her death, after a long Cold War interregnum. Some are wrong turns (or so I argue); and she understandably failed to anticipate issues that only emerged many years later. But others remain as important today as they were when Arendt wrote *Eichmann in Jerusalem* – important enough to make Arendt one of the founding mothers of international criminal law, even if she was no prophet. This chapter aims to show why. That requires a close reading of her arguments, in light of lessons learned from modern practice. What Arendt said in her assessment of the Eichmann trial can also be said of her thinking about it: "Success or failure in dealing with the hitherto unprecedented can lie only in the extent to which this dealing may serve as a valuable precedent on the road to international penal law."[3]

## 14.1 What Are Criminal Trials for?

Our first question is simply stated: What are criminal trials for? To be clear, the question is about trials, not policing, punishments, or prisons – institutions of domestic criminal justice systems in which trials are embedded, which may be unjust even when trials themselves are not.

A commonsense answer includes three elements. First, trials hold people who are responsible for crimes *accountable*. Second, they give the accused a forum to explain and defend themselves. And third, when they work properly, they strive to pass disinterested judgment fairly and impartially.

Accountability means treating (accused) perpetrators as responsible human agents, not as beasts or as cogs in a machine – a point of supreme importance to Arendt. Beasts and cogs cannot be called to account for what they do. Only human beings have the gift and curse of responsibility, and we honor the dignity of our fellow human beings by presuming that they are responsible for their choices. Of course, someone facing trial for a serious crime might say bitterly, "If this is respecting my human dignity, I'd rather you didn't!" That misses the point: The alternative to trial is unlikely to be impunity. More likely it will be indefinite confinement or summary vengeance.

A trial gives defendants an opportunity to respond with their side of the story, rather than dismissing it a priori as not worth hearing. That too is a

[3] *EJ*, 273.

requirement of human dignity.[4] So is impartial judging, which safeguards against false condemnation. Inevitably, courts' judgments will be fallible at best, biased or corrupt at worst. But to the extent that rules of procedure and evidence are fair, and judges and juries strive to be impartial, trials shrink the zone of error, prejudice, and vengefulness. All three purposes, including accountability, ultimately flow from respect for the human dignity of the accused.

Perhaps less obvious, but no less important, is that fair and public trials serve crucial expressive purposes.[5] They honor the human dignity of crime victims by showing that the wrongs done to them matter to their fellow citizens. They reassure the law-abiding majority that commitments to legal protection both *by* the state and *from* the state are not empty promises. They assemble evidence in a single locale, present it live, and then preserve the record and the judgment, so that the event does not sink into oblivion.

Obviously, trials in real life can, and often do, fail at any of these goals, sometimes horribly. And even the fairest system of trials is only as just as the laws it enforces and the punishments it inflicts. But in decent justice systems, the three sets of aims – accountability, expression, and creating a record – run in tandem.[6]

Matters are not so simple, though, when it comes to trials for the core international crimes. These are crimes of a different order from everyday crimes of violence, and they are sometimes tried in bespoke courts under bespoke law. Plucking out individual defendants from collective crimes can look like scapegoating. The trials have political overtones that, as Jaspers warned, cannot be captured in legal categories. And, for that reason, their politically expressive purposes threaten to swamp the fundamental aims of justice – which, as we will see, was Arendt's main concern about the Eichmann trial.

## 14.2 A Defender and Critic of the Eichmann Trial

The epilogue to *Eichmann in Jerusalem* systematically dissects legal issues in the Eichmann trial. Surprisingly, in light of the book's reputation as an

[4] On this point, see Luban, *Legal Ethics and Human Dignity*, 68–73. Arendt recognized this indirectly when she observed that the criminal process is better than being subjected to arbitrary police power and treated as an unperson. *OT*, 286.

[5] For useful discussion, see Robert P. Burns, *A Theory of the Trial* (Princeton University Press, 2001). My own earlier thoughts on the expressive aims of trials are in *Legal Modernism*, 379–84.

[6] I leave to one side the justice or injustice of plea bargains, the most common way that criminal cases in the United States are resolved. The discussion here is about trials.

unsparing critique, most of the epilogue (twenty-two pages out of twenty-seven) defends the trial against accusations of unfairness and illegitimacy. To be sure, Arendt criticized the kidnapping of Eichmann, but she thought even that could be justified as a "desperate, unprecedented, and no-precedent-setting act, necessitated by the unsatisfactory condition of international law." (In fact it was anything but unprecedented.[7])

Only in the final pages of the epilogue does Arendt turn to what she sees as the trial's three failures: "the problem of impaired justice in the court of the victors; a valid definition of the 'crime against humanity'; and a clear recognition of the new criminal who commits this crime."[8] Chapter 13 explored the second of these problems: Israel's failure to recognize the Holocaust as an international crime against the human status itself, rather than a crime only against the Jews. What of the first and third?

The "problem of impaired justice in the court of the victors" sounds superficially like the familiar condemnation of victors' justice as innately unfair, but that is not what Arendt means. In fact, she vigorously defends the Jerusalem court against accusations of bias.[9] The only specific impairment she criticizes is a minor point: the court's refusal to immunize potential defense witnesses who might be arrested and prosecuted for their own entanglement with the Holocaust if they came to Jerusalem to testify. Given the overwhelming evidence, this "serious flaw in the Jerusalem proceedings" had no effect on the outcome, and for good reason Arendt says little about it.[10]

[7] *EJ*, 265. The Jerusalem court cited more than a century of British and US decisions that upheld the legal doctrine of "*male captus, bene detentus*," meaning that a state's authority to prosecute a defendant is not spoiled by an illegal capture. Eichmann Judgment, §§41–50. In US law, this rule is known as the *Ker–Frisbie* doctrine, and the Supreme Court upheld it most recently in 1992. U.S. v. Alvarez-Machain, 504 U.S. 655 (1992). The ICTY also upheld *male captus, bene detentus*: Prosecutor v. Nikolić, Case No. IT-94-2-AR73, Interlocutory Appeal concerning Legality of Arrest (June 5, 2003), §§17–31. Nowadays, our genteel euphemism for the longstanding practice of government kidnapping is "extraordinary rendition."

[8] *EJ*, 274. [9] *EJ*, 259.

[10] She discusses it briefly in *EJ*, 220–21. A far more critical view of the trial's fairness is Stephan Landsman, *Crimes of the Holocaust: The Law Confronts Hard Cases* (University of Pennsylvania Press, 2005), chapter 2. Landsman points out that the defense was underresourced (Eichmann's counsel had only one assistant to help him wade through mountains of documents); that Eichmann was interrogated for hundreds of hours without counsel; that Judge Benjamin Halevy had publicly likened Eichmann to the devil in the Kastner case years before (and therefore should have been disqualified); and that the rules of evidence and procedure were distorted. See especially Landsman, *Crimes of the Holocaust*, 63–67, 91–98. Even so, Landsman agrees with Arendt that Chief Judge Moshe Landau successfully "protected the integrity of the trial," and he agrees that the verdict was just. Landsman, *Crimes of the Holocaust*, 69, 91. The defects Landsman details are what lawyers call "harmless error" – meaning that they did not affect the outcome.

The third issue she mentions – the court's failure to recognize that Eichmann represents a new kind of criminal – refers to the banality of evil, which in her view implies that he lacked conventional *mens rea*. I discuss this vitally important issue in Chapter 15. It's important to see, though, that neither the inadequate definition of crimes against humanity nor her concerns about *mens rea* are accusations that Eichmann was treated unfairly, and neither suggests that the trial was illegitimate.

## 14.3 Who Gets to Try?

A threshold objection to the Eichmann trial – urged by the defense – is that Israeli courts had no rightful jurisdiction over crimes committed in Europe. The murdered European Jews were not Israeli nationals, and for that matter there was no state of Israel at the time of the Holocaust. (Arendt dismisses the latter point as "formalistic" and "out of tune with reality."[11]) Arendt devotes five pages of her epilogue to jurisdictional issues, and she exchanged letters with Jaspers about jurisdiction.[12] The heart of their discussion is the question of how trials can properly express the universal character of a crime. Arendt and Jaspers agreed that the best way to acknowledge that genocide is the concern of all humanity, not only the nation of the victims, was to try the case in an international court. Jaspers believed that *only* an international court could legitimately try such cases, and therefore Israel should not. Arendt disagreed, for the simple reason that no international criminal court existed. Israel had the same right to try Eichmann for crimes against the Jews that half a dozen occupied countries had to try Nazi crimes against their people in the many postwar "successor trials." Her sole complaint is that doing so obscures the universal significance of the crimes – that the Holocaust was a crime against humanity, inflicted on the Jews, not solely a crime against the Jews.[13] (Israel's Prime Minister David Ben-Gurion saw matters quite differently: "Israel does not need the protection of an international court. Only anti-Semites or Jews with an inferiority complex would say that it does."[14])

[11] *EJ*, 260.

[12] Jaspers to Arendt, December 16, 1960, *HA-KJ*, 413; Arendt to Jaspers, December 23, 1960, *HA-KJ*, 416; Arendt to Jaspers, February 5, 1961, *HA-KJ*, 423; Jaspers to Arendt, February 14, 1961, *HA-KJ*, 424.

[13] *EJ*, 259–60, 263.

[14] Tom Segev, *The Seventh Million: The Israelis and the Holocaust*, trans. Haim Watzman (Hill and Wang, 1993), 332, quoting "The Eichmann Case Seen by Ben-Gurion," *New York Times Magazine*, December 18, 1960.

Arendt's analyses of jurisdiction are technical and partly mistaken, and I won't discuss them here.[15] I do want to discuss a more fundamental and less legalistic challenge to the central idea that she and Jaspers share: that the so-called interests of humanity authorize criminal law as a vehicle for discharging humanity's responsibility to protect those interests. More briefly: that "humanity" can and should criminalize core international crimes. Antony Duff, one of the deepest and most significant contemporary criminal law theorists, disagrees, because "humanity" is not the kind of community that has the authority to enact criminal laws.

Duff explains that criminal prosecutions are a political community's way of calling its members to account for violating its laws. Their moral legitimacy rests on the fact that the accused belongs to the political community. Outsiders owe that community no allegiance, and it has no authority to call outsiders to account for crimes that have no connection with its people or territory. Criminal laws, as Joshua Kleinfeld has rightly emphasized, are protections of an existing community's ethical life, a view similar in this respect to Duff's.[16] Duff insists that *only* political communities have rightful authority to enforce the norms of their ethical life with criminal prohibitions. "Humanity" is not a political community; at most it is, in Duff's words, an embryonic *moral* community, empowered to denounce radically evil acts but not to prosecute them. To give moral communities enforcement authority would come close to licensing vigilante justice.[17] Duff's is a jurisdictional challenge at the most basic conceptual level.

Certainly, vigilantes claiming to punish on behalf of humanity are a frightening prospect. At the same time, I think the objection rests on two mistaken assumptions: first, that moral communities can only judge, not act; and second, that the ethical life of a political community (paradigmatically, a state) stops at its borders. As to the first, moral communities are more than scorekeepers of good and evil, and moral judgment is more than commentary. Specifically, *moral* communities legitimately act by working through the channels of existing *political* structures (domestic legal

[15] I do so in "Hannah Arendt as a Theorist of International Criminal Law," *International Criminal Law Review* 11 (2011): 627–30. For another view, see Leora Bilsky, "The Eichmann Trial and the Legacy of Jurisdiction," in *Politics in Dark Times: Encounters With Hannah Arendt*, ed. Seyla Benhabib (Cambridge University Press, 2010), 198–218.

[16] Joshua Kleinfeld, "Reconstructivism: The Place of Criminal Law in Ethical Life," *Harvard Law Review* 129(6) (2016): 1486–565. Kleinfeld's impressive article does not address the issues I'm considering here.

[17] Antony Duff, "Authority and Responsibility in International Criminal Law," in *The Philosophy of International Law*, eds. Samantha Besson and John Tasioulas (Oxford University Press, 2010), 599, 601n41.

systems, the UN, the Rome Statute) to institutionalize their judgments. To say this is to acknowledge that today only states and international organizations created by states have the authority and capacity to set up international tribunals that can provide due process and humane imprisonment of those convicted of core international crimes.[18] An activist moral community acting through states and international institutions is not vigilantism, provided that the institutions provide fair legal process and humane punishments, including periodic review of sentences throughout the duration of imprisonment (which may last decades). And, contrary to the assumption that the ethical life of political communities stops at their borders, there's no reason to think that ethical life is inherently isolationist.

This is not to say that states have the moral or legal authority to enforce *all* the norms of their ethical life outside their own borders through criminal law, only those with a reasonable and widely accepted claim to universal significance. Arendt thought that authority extended to criminalizing genocide, but that lesser persecutions were purely national matters.[19] On this issue, she was a legal conservative who failed to appreciate the capacity of international law to evolve. Today, crimes against humanity include persecution and apartheid, and some modern writers would go further and include any serious violations of human rights. Others have proposed an international crime of "ecocide."[20] But even so, nobody proposes that states or international organizations can make any violation of one state's local norms an international crime in the name of "humanity."

Arendt would agree (as do I) with Duff's powerful argument that the point of criminal law is to call wrongdoers to account before the wronged community.[21] She would agree as well that the moral community of

[18] So I have argued in "Fairness to Rightness: Jurisdiction, Legality, and the Legitimacy of International Criminal Law," in Besson and Tasioulas, *The Philosophy of International Law*, 569–88. Duff's paper was a response to mine, and to my earlier "A Theory of Crimes against Humanity." See also our exchange in a symposium on "the enemy of all humanity": Luban, "The Enemy of All Humanity," 128–37; Antony Duff, "Crimes against Humanity and *Hostes Generis Humani*," *Netherlands Journal of Legal Philosophy* 47(2) (2018): 138–48; David Luban, "On the Humanity of the Enemy of Humanity: A Response to My Critics," *Netherlands Journal of Legal Philosophy* 47(2) (2018): 92–94.

[19] *EJ*, 268. Arendt regards the expulsion of the Jews as an international crime, but only because they would become refugees on other states' territory, not because of the moral evil of ethnic cleansing. *EJ*, 268. Today's law deems both persecution and expulsion crimes against humanity.

[20] Renzo, "Crimes against Humanity and the Limits of International Criminal Law," 452; Haroon Siddique, "Legal Experts Worldwide Draw up "Historic" Definition of Ecocide," *Guardian*, June 22, 2021.

[21] *OT*, 462.

humanity – defined by the shared aim of accountability across borders – is embryonic at best, and it is not a full-fledged political community. But that need not stop it from acting. By pressing for universal jurisdiction and fair international tribunals that are institutionally independent from the states that authorize them, the embryo nourishes itself and grows. That is the point of the normative project that I have called constructing humanity, and that Arendt calls the "new law on earth."

## 14.4 "This Trial Has to Take Place in the Interests of Justice and Nothing Else"

Arendt had a more basic critique of the Eichmann trial, though, a critique that has nothing to do with jurisdiction, fairness, crime definitions, or Eichmann's banality. It was about the expressive purpose of this highly publicized and sensational trial – and, by implication, of other criminal trials as well.

Ben-Gurion wanted the trial for reasons of pedagogy and public diplomacy. It would remind the world of the Holocaust and underline the supposed necessity of the state of Israel as a refuge for imperiled Jews. And it would educate young Israeli Jews, especially those of Middle Eastern descent whose families were untouched by the Holocaust, about the terrible fate of the European Jews and the heroism of the ghetto fighters. Prosecutor Gideon Hausner put it this way in his memoir of the trial:

> In order merely to secure a conviction, it was obviously enough to let the archives speak; a fraction of them would have sufficed to get Eichmann sentenced ten times over. But I knew we needed more than a conviction; we needed a living record of a gigantic human and national disaster.[22]

The living record came in the form of witness testimony, lasting for weeks, from scores of survivors. The trouble was that much of their testimony had no bearing on Eichmann's guilt or innocence. An example will illustrate.[23]

Abba Kovner was a celebrated resistance fighter and one of Israel's best-known poets. Although Kovner's testimony touched on Eichmann at a few points, most of it consisted of stories of the Vilna ghetto and the heroism of its resistance, including the courageous deeds of Anton Schmid, the German sergeant who saved Jews until he was caught and executed. After Kovner concluded his testimony, the court scolded the prosecutor:

[22] Gideon Hausner, *Justice in Jerusalem* (Harper & Row, 1966), 291.

[23] Lawrence Douglas discusses this example along with others in *The Memory of Judgment: Making Law and History in the Trials of the Holocaust* (Yale University Press, 2001), 137–38, 145–49.

> *Presiding Judge*: Mr. Hausner, we have heard shocking things here, in the language of a poet, but I maintain that in many parts of this evidence we have strayed far from the subject of this trial. … It is your task … to eliminate everything that is not relevant to the trial, so as not to place the Court once again – and this is not the first time – in such a situation.[24]

In an ordinary trial, wrenching victim testimony not bearing on the guilt of the defendant would be excluded as prejudicial. Here, the judges tried to control the prosecution but failed. The weeks of victim testimony were eye-opening to many Israelis and, for better or for worse, they dramatically elevated that nation's Holocaust consciousness.[25] But, as commentators remarked, the net result was that Eichmann became peripheral to his own trial.[26]

That was what bothered Arendt. For her, the entire significance of the trial lay in the guilt or innocence of the defendant, nothing more:

> Justice insists on the importance of Adolf Eichmann, son of Karl Adolf Eichmann, the man in the glass booth built for his protection. … On trial are his deeds, not the sufferings of the Jews, not the German people or mankind, not even anti-Semitism and racism. …
>
> It may be argued that all the general questions we involuntarily raise as soon as we begin to speak of these matters – why did it have to be the Germans? why did it have to be the Jews? what is the nature of totalitarian rule? – are far more important than the question of the kind of crime for which a man is being tried, and the nature of the defendant upon whom justice must be pronounced; more important, too, than the question of how well our present system of justice is capable of dealing with this special type of crime and criminal. …
>
> I need scarcely say that I would never have gone to Jerusalem if I had shared these views. I held and hold the opinion that this trial had to take place in the interests of justice and nothing else.[27]

The judges took the same view. At the outset of its judgment, the court lists more than half a dozen general questions that the case raises, but immediately warns that it "cannot allow itself to be enticed into provinces which are outside its sphere." A court's fact-finding is limited to whatever

[24] Eichmann Trial Proceedings, vol. 1, Session 27, May 4, 1961, at 466. Kovner's testimony about Schmid is at 461–62, and it is one of the few places he mentions Eichmann: Schmid told him that Eichmann was the man in charge.

[25] The classic study is Segev, *The Seventh Million: Israelis and the Holocaust.*

[26] Mark J. Osiel, *Mass Atrocity, Collective Memory, and the Law* (Transaction Books, 1997), 60 (citing Segev, and quoting Moshe Halbertal's review of Segev's *The Seventh Million*, in *The New Republic*, October 18, 1993, 43).

[27] *EJ*, 5, 286.

the two sides choose to put in evidence, and that is only a tiny fraction of what would be needed even to try to tackle historical "what-ifs?" or to theorize about antisemitism. "As for questions of principle which are outside the realm of law, no one has made us judges of them."[28]

## 14.5 Rejecting Responsibility? Koskenniemi versus Arendt

To some, however, Arendt's single-minded focus on individual responsibility distorts the reality of mass atrocities. They are intrinsically collective endeavors, deeply embedded in complex histories and clashing group narratives. Martti Koskenniemi, a leading skeptic of international criminal law, spells out the objection in his dazzling and by now classic article "Between Impunity and Show Trials."[29] Writing during the genocide trial of Serbian President Slobodan Milošević, he agrees with Arendt that criminal trials must not be staged for purely didactic purposes, on pain of becoming mere show trials; but he forcefully rejects her focus on individual guilt or innocence. He asks rhetorically whether Arendt should "have the final word," and answers no.[30] Koskenniemi warns that

> the truth is not necessarily served by an individual focus. On the contrary, the meaning of historical events often exceeds the intentions or actions of particular individuals and can be grasped only by attention to structural causes, such as economic or functional necessities, or a broad institutional logic through which the actions by individuals create social effects.[31]

For that reason, "there is no guarantee that a criminal process *a priori* oriented towards individual guilt such as the Milošević trial necessarily enacts a lesson of historical truth."[32] Indeed, it gives defendants a chance to turn the courtroom into a propaganda theater of ethnic grievance, as Milošević did in his trial. Representing himself, Milošević flamboyantly denounced the ICTY as a lackey of its Western masters – a strategy known as the "rupture defense," because it accuses the accuser.[33] He bullied

28 Eichmann Judgment, §§1–2; quoted in *EJ*, 254.

29 Martti Koskenniemi, "Between Impunity and Show Trials," *Max Planck Yearbook of United Nations Law* 6 (2002): 1–35. Reprinted in Martti Koskenniemi, *The Politics of International Law* (Hart Publishing, 2011).

30 Koskenniemi, "Between Impunity and Show Trials," 7.

31 Koskenniemi, "Between Impunity and Show Trials," 13–14.

32 Koskenniemi, "Between Impunity and Show Trials," 15.

33 The term was coined by one of Milošević's legal advisers, the "devil's advocate" Jacques Vergès (1925–2013). Vergès employed the *défense de la rupture* throughout his long career of defending terrorists, Vichy war criminals, Khmer Rouge killers and torturers, and Holocaust deniers. Koskenniemi, "Between Impunity and Show Trials," 26–30. Vergès reveled in this strategy.

witnesses and recast the meaning ("historical truth") of the Balkan Wars as an episode in the Serbs' heroic struggle against centuries of foreign imperialism. On Milošević's telling, his trial was nothing more than the latest front in the West's war against the Serbs. To Koskenniemi, Milošević's antics reveal a danger in criminal trials dealing with political events: Defendants can twist them into battles of meaning against meaning, global historical narrative against global historical narrative, rather than accusation against denial.[34]

All this sounds plausible, and if we accept Koskenniemi's warning, the entire idea of responding to mass atrocities through criminal trials of individuals can seem like a mistake. I disagree, and in this section, I explain why.[35] Doing so helps us understand the importance of Arendt's focus on individual responsibility.

Start with Koskenniemi's argument that the individual focus disserves "historical truth." The phrase is one of his favorites – he uses it eight times in his essay – but to him it refers to "the meaning of historical events" and their structural causes, not to a local narrative of the events themselves. Arendt would surely respond that criminal trials must never be inquiries into the *meaning* of historical events; she endorses the Jerusalem court's caution that it "could not 'allow itself to be enticed into provinces which are outside its sphere.'"[36] The kind of historical truth at which criminal courts aim is fact-finding about specific events, rationally supported by tangible evidence, nothing grander or deeper. Even rupture defenses (which are rare) seldom succeed in derailing fact-finding.[37]

In answer to an interviewer's question, "are you attracted to evil?" Vergès replied: "What distinguishes human beings from animals is the ability to speak on behalf of evil. Crime is a symbol of our freedom." Brita Sandberg and Eric Follath, "Interview with Notorious Lawyer Jacques Vergès: 'There Is No Such Thing as Absolute Evil'," *Spiegel Online*, November 21, 2008. He told reporters: "My law is to be against all laws. My morality is to be against all morality." Robert D. McFadden, "Jacques Vergès, Defender of Terrorists and War Criminals, Is Dead at 88," *New York Times*, August 16, 2013.

34 Koskenniemi, "Between Impunity and Show Trials," 25–32.

35 My arguments here closely resemble those of Lawrence Douglas, "History and Memory in the Courtroom: Reflections on Perpetrator Trials," in *The Nuremberg Trials International Criminal Law Since 1945/Die Nürnberger Prozesse Völkerstrafrecht seit 1945*, eds. Herbert Reginbogin and Christoph Safferling (K. G. Sauer Verlag: 2006): 100–1. Douglas is not writing about Koskenniemi's essay; rather, he responds to the general arguments that the individual focus of perpetrator trials distorted historical truth.

36 *EJ*, 253; the quoted language is from the trial judgment, §2.

37 Only Milošević's death prevented the release of a judgment that would have contained ample evidence of his guilt. We know this from subsequent judgments of other defendants that implicated him in their joint criminal enterprises in Croatia, Bosnia, and Kosovo.

This is not to deny that judicial findings of fact, like the advocates' theories of the case, always have a narrative structure – they are not mere log books of context-free events.[38] But their narratives are local, not global. Nor does it deny that those narratives are interpretations that convey moral judgments. Of course they are. But drawing conclusions about what the events *mean* is a task for historians, philosophers, and poets, not trial judges.

Thus, when Koskenniemi writes that the criminal process does not *necessarily* enact a lesson of historical truth, he actually understates the point: The criminal process *necessarily does not* enact a lesson of historical truth, at least not in the sense of uncovering the meaning or causes of historical events. That isn't the job of trials. To which we might add a crucial point: Historical truth nevertheless needs the kind of factual record that trials provide. Without facts it is not truth at all.

As an alternative to the focus on individual responsibility, Koskenniemi proposes inquiry into "structural causes, such as economic or functional necessities." *Causes* and *necessities* belong to the language of determinism, the antithesis of personal responsibility. This is crucial for Arendt. She remarks that unearthing causal laws is the province of political science; by contrast, putting individuals on trial "forces us to look at all these questions from a different point of view."[39]

> [I]n a courtroom there is no system on trial, no History or historical trend, no ism, anti-Semitism for instance, but a person, and if the defendant happens to be a functionary, he stands accused precisely because even a functionary is still a human being, and it is in this capacity that he stands trial.[40]

In one way, there is no daylight here between Arendt and Koskenniemi, for the latter agrees that criminal trials are "*a priori* oriented towards individual guilt." The disagreement is that he considers this a failing when it concerns mass criminality, a built-in bias against "structural causes," where Arendt praises it as "the great advantage of courtroom procedure."[41]

[38] Burns's *A Theory of the Trial* is especially good on this crucial point.

[39] Arendt, PRUD, 29–30; *EJ*, 289–90. [40] PRUD, 30.

[41] PRUD, 31. Koskenniemi does accept the individual focus for everyday crimes. He explains that his point is not "to settle the epistemological controversy about whether the individual or the contextual (functional, structural) focus provides the better truth, but, rather, that neither can *a priori* override the other." Koskenniemi, "Between Impunity and Show Trials," 15. In everyday crime, the individual focus may be right, but not when it comes to "Nazi criminality" or "*Stasi* collaboration in the GDR." Koskenniemi, "Between Impunity and Show Trials," 15.

Her reason is simple and fundamental: It flushes out the human being from the hideaway of structural causes. It redeems the human as human. When Eichmann pleads that he was merely a cog in a machine, "the court immediately raises the next question: 'And why, if you please, did you become a cog or continue to be a cog under such circumstances?'"[42] If a defendant replies that structural causes made him do it, the court will rightly dismiss the reply as evasive nonsense.

Eichmann never denied his role in the Holocaust, but he did deny his responsibility (recall his "Pontius Pilate feeling" at the Wannsee conference). The responsibility fell "one hundred per cent" on the Nazi gods who set the machinery in motion.[43] Eichmann's metaphors for himself are strikingly mechanistic: He was a cog in the machine, an iron filing in a magnetic field, a shredded tire whose inner tube ("the soul of the tire") has burst, but that still must speed along on "smashed rims – until the driver changes his mind or the car goes to hell."[44] The trial cuts through the metaphors and confronts him with the question of why he *chose* to become a cog or an iron filing or a tire – with emphasis on *chose.* Arendt presses the point:

> If the accused wishes to shift responsibilities, he must again implicate other persons, he must name names, and these persons appear then as possible codefendants, they do not appear as the embodiment of bureaucratic or any other necessity. The Eichmann trial, like all such trials, would have been devoid of all interest if it had not transformed the cog or "referent" of Section IV B4 in the Reich Security Head Office into a man. . . . And even this transformation of a cog into a man does not imply that something like cog-ness . . . was on trial.[45]

As the very word "responsibility" indicates, the defendant owes a response to accusers who call out his conduct – he is, we sometimes say, *answerable* for it.[46] Answerability is the point of the trial. It treats the defendant as a human being, holding him to standards to which we hold ourselves, and demanding answers about what he did and why he did it.[47]

[42] PRUD, 31.

[43] Eichmann Trial Proceedings, vol. 4, Session 95, July 13, 1961, at 1662 (Eichmann's testimony).

[44] *Götzen*, 206 (212). See Brenner, "Eichmann's Mind," 458–60.

[45] PRUD, 31–32.

[46] The German word for responsibility (*Verantwortlichkeit*) has a similar root: It derives from the verb "to answer" (*antworten*).

[47] Here my indebtedness to Antony Duff is apparent. See, for example, R. A. Duff, *Trials and Punishments* (Cambridge University Press, 1986) for a classic statement that the aim of criminal trials is calling accused persons to account before a community of their peers. As earlier noted, however, Duff is far more skeptical than I am that international or foreign tribunals have the

This is why trials do not investigate the "broad institutional logic through which the actions of individuals cause social effects." Atrocity trials are about concrete crimes, murders and rapes and persecutions, not "social effects" or institutional logics. Arendt is rightfully scornful of "the huge outcry the moment anyone fixes specific blame on some particular person instead of blaming all deeds or events on ... some mysterious necessity that works behind the backs of men."[48] Abstractions are the enemy of truthfulness.

So let us be concrete. Consider the case of a Croatian commander convicted of presiding over his subordinate's rape and torture of a woman (identified as Witness A) during her interrogation. "Individuals causing social effects" is a high-altitude euphemism for what the subordinate did to Witness A, namely raping her in front of an audience of forty soldiers, after pressing his knife against her thigh and threatening to cut out her private parts. The ICTY Trial Chamber did not indulge in euphemisms. "Accused B hit Witness A and forced her to perform oral sex on him. He raped her vaginally and anally, and made her lick his penis clean."[49] Later he beat her on the soles of her feet with a baton. Calling her anguish and terror a "social effect" that her rapist "caused" according to a "broad institutional logic" is obfuscation that borders on the obscene.[50]

And, obviously, rape and torture are never "economic or functional necessities." More generally, you can't pin specific atrocities on "structural causes." Structural causes may explain the Balkan Wars, but not the torture of Witness A.[51] In domestic settings, structural racism and poverty may explain why rival gangs exist and why members join them; they do not explain why a gang member shot a rival.

Despite flirting with determinism, Koskenniemi does acknowledge individual motivations for core crimes, namely that "one is participating in a collective venture with a sense of historical mission and a moral purpose ('happiness of mankind') such as 'communism,' for

authority to call offenders to account. Duff criticizes my views on this matter in "Authority and Responsibility in International Criminal Law," in *The Philosophy of International Law*, eds. Besson and Tașioulas, 589–604, and "Crimes against Humanity and *Hostes Generis Humani*," *Netherlands Journal of Legal Philosophy* 47(2): 138–48. I respond in Luban, "On the Humanity of the Enemy of Humanity: A Response to My Critics."

48 PRUD, 19–20.

49 Prosecutor v. Furundžija Trial Judgment, Case No. IT-95-17/1-T, December 10, 1998, §§82, 87.

50 "See how high the seas of language run here!" Ludwig Wittgenstein, *Philosophical Investigations* I.194.

51 For an impressive structural analysis of the Balkan Wars, see Russell Hardin, *One for All: The Logic of Group Conflict* (Princeton University Press, 1995).

instance."[52] Here, again, he is dismissive of trials: "[L]ittle is gained by a retrospective interpretation of the effects of that effort – 85 to 100 million innocent killed – in terms of the evil acts of some number of individuals."[53]

But "little is gained" invites an obvious challenge: Is more gained by *ignoring* the acts of those whose plans and policies set in motion the deaths of millions? Or by foisting responsibility onto the "logic of communism," as Koskenniemi does in his next sentence? Logics don't kill people. People kill people.

Undoubtedly, many perpetrators, then and now, believe their cause has a moral purpose that justifies any means, no matter how cruel. Koskenniemi's observation that both the Bolshevik and Nazi ideologies blend "utopianism and scientism with a revolutionary spirit" is sharp and accurate. Bolshevik true believers had visions of a workers' utopia with no class enemies; the Nazi utopia was a world without Jews.[54] Both movements clothed themselves in the trappings of science, both were driven by bitter and very genuine grievances, and in Koskenniemi's view, "even the worst Nazi nightmares were connected to a project to create a better world."[55]

The defendants' resentments and utopian fantasies may help us understand their conduct; what they cannot do is justify it. To say otherwise is either to accept their ideology or – what Arendt feared even more – to abdicate the very possibility of judgment.[56] Judging is itself a moral responsibility of onlookers. Once you abdicate judgment, you surrender the field to the uncontested judgment of murderers.

Koskenniemi presses the "historical mission" justification even further: He argues that putting individuals on trial for core crimes is in itself intrinsically biased. After all, from the perpetrators' point of view, "criminal law itself will come to seem a part of the world which must be set aside, an aspect of the 'evil' that the ideology seeks to eradicate."[57]

52 Koskenniemi, "Between Impunity and Show Trials," 13–15. He may be overestimating the moral purpose. Jon Elster shrewdly observes that in the mature communist regimes "everybody knew that nobody believed in the tenets of the official ideology, and yet everybody was compelled to talk and behave as if they did." In his view, "the reason why the leaders forced people to make absurd statements in public was not to make them believe what they said but to induce a state of complicity and guilt that undermined their morality and ability to resist." Elster, *Closing the Books: Transitional Justice in Historical Perspective* (Cambridge University Press, 2004), 110.

53 Koskenniemi, "Between Impunity and Show Trials," 15.

54 Alon Confino, *A World without Jews: The Nazi Imagination from Persecution to Genocide*. Ignatieff, "Lemkin's Word," acutely describes genocide as a utopian project.

55 Koskenniemi, "Between Impunity and Show Trials," 8.

56 PRUD, 18–20; *EJ*, 295–98. Arendt calls this way of thinking "elaborate nonsense." PRUD, 19.

57 Koskenniemi, "Between Impunity and Show Trials," 8.

No doubt prophets of violence and their followers will feel deeply aggrieved, or even martyred, if they are hauled before a court. That is hardly a reason not to haul them before a court. Crucially, Koskenniemi never tells us what alternatives he has in mind. Grant them impunity because criminal law is part of the evil they wish to eradicate? That would be tantamount to endorsing their view of criminal law. Lock them away with no trial? Round them up and shoot them, as Churchill proposed for the top Nazis? Or assassinate them, as Israeli agents sometimes did with Nazi war criminals? None of these comes close to a palatable alternative to what a trial has to offer: a forum for the accused to defend themselves and, above all, a place of public accountability for their choices.

This is not to deny that defendants' ideology and the overall political context have their place in criminal trials. The racist ideology of a movement to which a defendant belongs can be probative of genocidal intent; so too, the wider pattern of attacks by a defendant's army or paramilitary organization can help establish that his brutalities were part of an organized attack on a civilian population (the legal definition of crimes against humanity). Always, though, context and ideology need to be tied to the defendants and the choices they made, for which the court holds them to account.

## 14.6 Collective Guilt and Collective Responsibility

Perhaps Koskenniemi's point is that matters are different when the perpetrators number in the thousands, spurred on by cadres on fire with vengefulness or utopian fervor and supported by mass opinion. Mass criminality is a collective phenomenon that obviously cries out for an explanation beyond a coincidence of individual choices. Arendt could hardly disagree; after all, she wrote such an explanation herself. The 500 pages of *The Origins of Totalitarianism* take as their subject the "subterranean forces" that led to totalitarianism and culminated in death camps and gulags.[58] Subterranean forces transcend individual choices, exactly as Koskenniemi says.

What matters, though, is that explanations of collective behavior don't rule out the responsibility of individual members of the collective, and especially their leaders, for the choices they made. Such explanations may

58 *OT*, 120 ("subterranean forces of the nineteenth century"); ix ("subterranean stream of Western history"); xv ("subterranean stream of European history"). She even calls this investigation "the search for historical truth," using the phrase in Koskenniemi's broad way. *OT*, xv.

shed light on individuals' circumstances and their perceived choice sets, but they are not deterministic at the level of individual action.

Obviously, groups acting together can commit crimes no individual could commit on their own. International tribunals have developed elaborate doctrines of "joint criminal enterprise" to cover the main patterns of collective criminality, in which individual members can be held vicariously liable for crimes they didn't physically perpetrate. For example, the ICTY held that prison camp personnel could be convicted of abuses committed outside their presence, provided they held positions of authority, knew about the abuses, and intended "to further the common concerted design to ill-treat inmates."[59] These limitations spare bit players like the camp stenographers and janitors, but the doctrine convicts the commandants and overseers of crimes even if they didn't personally commit them or order them. They are individually guilty of collective crimes. That must not be confused with collective guilt.[60]

Unsurprisingly, given her focus on individual accountability, Arendt has nothing but scorn for the concept of collective guilt. That can create the misimpression that she denies the possibility of joint perpetration.[61] She emphatically does not; at one point, indeed, she goes too far in the opposite direction, endorsing a proposal that death camp personnel should be presumed guilty unless they could prove their innocence.[62]

What she *does* reject is the melodrama of people (Germans, but by no means only Germans) who proclaim, "We are all guilty!" even though they never participated in any crimes. Histrionics like that whitewash the actual

[59] Prosecutor v. Tadić, Case No. IT-94-1-A, Judgment (ICTY, July 15, 1999), §§202–3. Along with the concentration camp pattern, and the pattern of full joint perpetration, the ICTY recognized a third pattern: liability for crimes committed by members of the organization outside the common criminal purpose, but which were "a natural and foreseeable consequence of the effecting of that common purpose." For example, a paramilitary unit might plan to ethnically cleanse a town – itself a crime – without planning to kill anyone. But killings are a "predictable consequence" of the attack, and *Tadić* held that unit leaders are culpable for the killings if they were either reckless or indifferent to the risk. Prosecutor v. Tadić, §204. These three patterns of joint criminal enterprise are standardly abbreviated JCE I (full joint perpetration), JCE II (concentration camps), and JCE III (liability for foreseeable crimes outside the scope of the common criminal purpose). Critics argued that JCE III casts the net of liability too wide – some joked that in JCE III the initials stand for "Just Convict Everyone."

[60] On this point, see also Douglas, "History and Memory in the Courtroom: Reflections on Perpetrator Trials," 101.

[61] Here, the main source is "Collective Responsibility," in *RJ*. The paper was written for a symposium at the annual meeting of the American Philosophical Association, in response to Joel Feinberg, "Collective Responsibility," *Journal of Philosophy* 65(21) (1968): 674–88. Arendt had nasty and condescending things to say about Feinberg's paper in a letter to McCarthy, December 21, 1968, *BF*, 228. Unlike Arendt, I think Feinberg's paper is admirable.

[62] "Auschwitz on Trial," in *RJ*, 243–44.

perpetrators, for an obvious reason: "Where all are guilty, nobody is."[63] Arendt understands that we can *feel* guilty for things "our people" have done, because we feel that their crimes reflect on us. Those feelings – which many of us have experienced ourselves or observed among our friends – are the flip side of solidarity. But she warns against confusing these feelings, however authentic or deep, with genuine guilt. Genuine guilt requires personal participation in the joint criminal enterprise.

One complication: Arendt does accept a notion of collective *responsibility* (as distinct from collective guilt) – but she means political responsibility, not criminal liability.[64] The German citizenry were politically responsible for their state's deeds, done in their name. But only those who played an active role in Nazi crimes, either as principals or accomplices, can be criminally guilty – and that is not collective guilt, but rather individual guilt for participating in a collective crime.

What is collective political responsibility? This obscure notion is best understood as Arendt's reaction to Jaspers's 1946 lectures on *The Question of German Guilt.* (It is often referred to by its German title *Die Schuldfrage*, the "guilt question," and I will call it "*Schuldfrage*" for short.) The *Schuldfrage* distinguishes several dimensions of German guilt for Nazi crimes and analyzes their consequences. Among them are political guilt and criminal guilt, which Jaspers carefully distinguishes from each other.[65] Jaspers's notion of political guilt is not far from Arendt's idea of collective political responsibility: It originates in "the deeds of statesmen and of the citizenry of a state," and it "results in my having to bear the consequences of the deeds of the state whose power governs me and under whose order I live."[66] Concretely, Jaspers urges his German readers to accept the yoke

63 Arendt, "Collective Responsibility," in *RJ*, 147; *W*, 184; *EJ*, 251, 278; PRUD, 28.

64 "Collective Responsibility," 149; *EJ*, 297–98.

65 Karl Jaspers, *The Question of German Guilt*, trans. E. B. Ashton (Dial Press, 1947) (hereafter: *Schuldfrage*). The other two are moral guilt and metaphysical guilt. Metaphysical guilt is the guilt that comes from failing to prevent crimes committed in your presence or with your knowledge, and it derives from the "solidarity among men as human beings that makes each co-responsible for every wrong and every injustice in the world." Jaspers, *Schuldfrage*, 32. The similarity to Arendt's "idea of humanity" (discussed in §10.5) is too striking to be accidental: "[M]en must assume responsibility for all crimes committed by men and . . . all nations share the onus of evil committed by all others." However, Arendt speaks of *responsibility*, while Jaspers speaks of *guilt*; and Arendt treats the idea of humanity as a project to be realized, with nothing metaphysical about it. Arendt's essay on organized guilt and the idea of humanity influenced Jaspers: he quotes from it in *Schuldfrage*, 84. See Jaspers to Arendt, December 2, 1945, in *HA-KJ*, 25 (complimenting Arendt on her essay); Jaspers to Arendt, March 12, 1946, *HA-KJ*, 33 (mentioning that he had quoted her essay in a talk); Jaspers to Arendt, May 8, 1946, in *HA-KJ*, 39 (promising to send her *Schuldfrage* when it is published).

66 Jaspers, *The Question of German Guilt*, 31, 36, 49.

of occupation. What they must not accept is criminal guilt for crimes they didn't participate in.

Arendt agrees with Jaspers that a successor regime assumes responsibility for its predecessors' deeds, for which its people may suffer. Even revolutionary governments are on the hook for the debts of the regime they overthrew.[67] But she insists that this collective responsibility is not the same as collective *guilt*, and in that respect, she thinks Jaspers committed a category mistake. Her admittedly murky distinction between guilt and responsibility becomes clearer in correspondence between her, her husband Heinrich Blücher, and Jaspers.[68]

Blücher hated the *Schuldfrage*. Venting in a 1946 letter to Arendt, he calls it "Christian hypocritical jabbering" that will give the vanquished German people "a way to continue occupying themselves exclusively with themselves." He added that "guilt serves the purpose of extirpating responsibility." Authentic responsibility requires action, not "inner transformation"; it demands "a return from the cossackish way to the republican way, [and] actions of solidarity for those who have been degraded." After that, the Germans can if they wish turn to Jaspers for "individual inner cleansing. . . . Jaspers is seeking the salvation of the German people's soul and his own – no wonder he's talking like some cleric." Simmering down a bit, Blücher says to Arendt, "I hope you can show me that I'm unfair. Of course I am."[69]

Evidently Arendt calmed Blücher down; at any rate, her letter to Jaspers about their *Schuldfrage* conversations is a model of tact:

> Well then, "we" [Arendt and Blücher] are very much in agreement with you in all the major points [!] and very thankful not only for the clarification but also for the implicit explanation of a psychological situation that is very difficult to picture to oneself from a distance [!]. In agreement, but with limitations and additions. Monsieur [Blücher], even more than I, insists that assuming responsibility has to consist of more than an acceptance of defeat and of the consequences following on that. He has been saying for a long time now that such an assumption of responsibility . . . has to be accompanied by a positive political statement of intentions addressed to the victims.[70]

67 "Collective Responsibility," *RJ*, 149–50.

68 An alternative, characteristically insightful, reading is Iris Marion Young, *Responsibility for Justice* (Oxford University Press, 2011), chapter 3 ("Guilt versus Responsibility: A Reading and Partial Critique of Hannah Arendt").

69 Blücher to Arendt, July 15, 1946, in *WFW*, 84–86.

70 Arendt to Jaspers, August 17, 1946, in *HA-KJ*, 52–53.

Her examples of what it might mean to take collective responsibility are: Germany must shut down the internment camps for displaced multitudes including Jews, constitutionally outlaw antisemitism, and offer German citizenship to Jews regardless of their place of birth. Political responsibility demands reparation, not punishment. Crime, on the other hand, makes participants in joint criminal enterprises – but only them – liable to conviction and punishment.[71]

One must ask why the German people shared collective political responsibility for the Hitler regime; it isn't obvious. Not all Germans supported the regime; a great many opposed it. Some became "inner emigrants" who stayed in Germany but inwardly disaffiliated themselves from the regime and its supporters and never participated in its crimes. A few resisted.

Arendt's answer connects closely with the collapse of moral judgment she observed in the early months of the Third Reich, as Germans swiftly embraced Hitlerism. In "Personal Responsibility under Dictatorship," and again in "Some Questions of Moral Philosophy," she confesses that it took her by surprise. It wasn't the Storm Troopers who surprised her; thugs are thugs. Rather, it was the betrayals by people she thought were friends. She dates the betrayal to the Nazi policy of "coordination" (*Gleichschaltung*) by which all the main organizations in government and civil society were placed under Party control – a program executed over the first twenty months of the Third Reich.[72] The civil service was "coordinated" almost immediately, with the 1933 April Law that kicked out the Jews. Then came the rest of civil society, with every organization now placed under Party control.[73] Rank-and-file members of football clubs, amateur choirs, women's organizations, and government offices all faced a moral choice, a gut check: stay or quit? For most, the answer was: stay. Thus began the betrayal, whether they recognized it or not. As mentioned in Chapter 3, confronting that choice lay at the heart of Arendt's "emergency ethics" – but it also explains her view of political responsibility as collective responsibility.

Undoubtedly, some stayed in their civil service jobs because they needed those jobs, an excuse that Arendt treated sympathetically.[74] Even so, staying in your "coordinated" job or club can put you on the slippery slope from "there's no real harm if I stay," to "I might as well give the *Heil*

[71] This was one of Jaspers's points as well. Jaspers, *Schuldfrage*, 51–52. [72] PRUD, 24; SQMP, 54.
[73] Richard J. Evans, *The Third Reich in Power* (Penguin, 2005), 14. See also Fritzsche, *Life and Death in the Third Reich*; Peter Fritzsche, *Hitler's First Hundred Days: When Germans Embraced the Third Reich* (Basic Books, 2020); William Sheridan Allen, *The Nazi Seizure of Power in a Small Town: The Experience of a Single German Town 1930–1935* (New Viewpoints, 1973), 213–26.
[74] Arendt, "'What Remains? The Language Remains'," in *EU*, 11.

*Hitler* salute – it's harmless, and I don't want to stand out," to "staying in my government job is the lesser evil," to "I better not speak up against the policies, or I'll be out of the loop," to "you know, Hitler isn't all that bad."[75]

Arendt's response is blunt: In politics, obedience is support.[76] Suppose that at the moment of "coordination" all the self-identified non- or anti-Nazis had stayed home. Not violently or publicly resisted, which might have landed them in a concentration camp, but simply stayed home. The regime would have collapsed. Power, including the tyrant's power, comes not from the instruments of violence but from the concerted support of many people, including the passive support of averting your eyes and going about your business as if nothing is amiss.[77]

She might have added: Obedience is support because by going about their daily routines, people reinforce in each other the sense that nothing too outrageous is taking place. In politics, when everyone goes about their business, everyone looks like a regime supporter regardless of their unspoken opposition. As Arendt liked to say, in human affairs, appearance is reality.[78] The active and passive support of the regime in its crucial early months, including by "inner emigrants," and their continued support through the war, is the reason why the German people bore collective political responsibility for the crimes of the Third Reich. But, to reiterate: Passive or even active support of the regime is not the same as participation in its crimes. Political responsibility is not criminal responsibility.

So, on Arendt's view: yes to collective political responsibility; yes to individual criminal guilt for collective crimes; no to collective guilt.

## 14.7 Extraordinary Trials Today

When Jaspers complains that the political realm can't be captured in legal terms, he clearly has a point. War crimes, crimes against humanity, genocide, aggression, torture – the core crimes – are never apolitical, and criminal prosecutions of core crimes are radically unlike routine law enforcement. The prosecutions always follow political cataclysms: wars and civil wars, bloody ethnic conflicts, revolutions or regime changes that shake the basic structure of societies. Everyday criminal law is a product and sustainer of state continuity; trials of core crimes follow upheaval and

75 I discuss these issues in greater depth in Luban, "Complicity and Lesser Evils: A Tale of Two Lawyers," *Georgetown Journal of Legal Ethics* 34(3) (2021): 613–64.

76 PRUD, 46–47; *EJ*, 279. 77 PRUD, 47. 78 *T*, 19; *OR*, 94; *HC*, 199.

political rupture. That makes them extraordinary trials (and some modern tribunals have "extraordinary" or "special" in their official names). Their legal frameworks of statutes and rules don't even try to capture their political dimension.

The heavy hand of politics on trials for core crimes is so obvious and so constant that it would be foolish to wish it out of existence by focusing solely on the legal formalities. No atrocity-crime tribunal has ever been born of an immaculate conception. This is true whether the trials are conducted by the national courts of the state where they were committed, by the national courts of another state, or by an international tribunal. Extraordinary trials are often components of *transitional justice* – the whole range of legal issues that arise when a dictatorship collapses or yields power, and a successor (or a military occupier) confronts the crimes of the fallen regime.

Inevitably, those trials are shot through with politics, and whether to stage them or not is itself a political decision. Would criminal trials destabilize fledgling democracies, or would failure to hold old-regime criminals accountable pose a greater threat?[79] When perpetrators and surviving victims must live side by side after the downfall of the old regime, how should we weigh the need for a *modus vivendi* going forward against the demand for justice? Would Jaspers's "foolishly simplistic idea" of a truth commission without criminal punishment suffice?[80] It might. Philosopher Lucy Allais argues persuasively that South Africa's post-apartheid Truth and Reconciliation Commission did a better job of allocating blame and responsibility, and condemning wrongdoing, than a fruitless effort to try and punish thousands of perpetrators could possibly have done.[81]

Arendt had no need to address these political questions, because the Eichmann trial had nothing *directly* to do with transitional justice. It did shine a spotlight on something of which she was bitterly aware: the large number of Nazis still in prominent positions in Germany.[82] Exposing

[79] Post-dictatorship democracies in Argentina, Brazil, and Chile initially granted amnesty to perpetrators from the dictatorship, fearing that to prosecute them would infuriate the military and provoke another coup. When that danger subsided, they removed the amnesties and conducted trials in their own courts.

[80] Jaspers to Arendt, December 16, 1960, *HA-KJ*, 413. He repeats this "utopian suggestion" in his letter of January 3, 1961, *HA-KJ*, 420, and again in his letter of February 14, 1961, where he calls it a "simpleminded fantasy," *HA-KJ*, 424.

[81] Lucy Allais, "Restorative Justice, Retributive Justice, and the South African Truth and Reconciliation Commission," *Philosophy & Public Affairs* 39(4) (2011): 331–63.

[82] *EJ*, 18–19.

them led to domestic German prosecutions of Nazi war criminals, which continued until the last known perpetrators died of old age. In that way, the Eichmann trial contributed indirectly to transitional justice in Germany, its confrontation with its past.[83]

International courts are a large step removed from transitional justice within a single state, but they too navigate in a stormy sea of politics. Purely as a financial matter, tribunals like the ICTY, the International Criminal Tribunal for Rwanda (ICTR), and the ICC cost hundreds of millions of dollars a year, and they must beg for money in every budgeting cycle. It would be naive to imagine that donor states create them with no ulterior motives, nor that they fund them for decades solely out of a disinterested desire to see justice done. By contrast, Israel had a preexisting judicial system, and although the Eichmann trial was expensive, the Jerusalem District Court was not created *ex nihilo*. That is another aspect of modern international criminal law that Arendt never had to consider.

So too, Arendt had no need to address the issue of selective prosecution, for the simple reason that Eichmann was the only suspect Israel had in custody. Not so for the international tribunals. Even when the trials themselves are fair, the choice of whom to prosecute and whom not is deeply political. A notable example was the Allies' decision not to prosecute Emperor Hirohito, because continuity on the Chrysanthemum Throne would smooth the democratic transition in occupied Japan.[84] More recently, Special Court for Sierra Leone (SCSL) prosecutor David Crane revealed that the United States government pressured him not to pursue three important suspects, because they were cooperating with the United States on counterterrorism; the government threatened to withhold funding from the SCSL if Crane went after them.[85]

Selective prosecution is one of the least agreeable legacies of the Nuremberg Tribunal, which had jurisdiction only over Axis war criminals, even though Allied forces committed some of the same crimes. Although Arendt never discussed selective prosecution, she was acutely aware that West Germany was shielding many war criminals, and she was acid about

83 *EJ*, 13–15.

84 Gary J. Bass, *Judgment at Tokyo: World War II on Trial and the Making of Modern Asia* (Picador, 2023). Allied commander Douglas MacArthur and U.S. Prosecutor Joseph Keenan went through extraordinary contortions to avoid charging the emperor.

85 These were Burkina Faso's President Blaise Compaouré, Libyan leader Muammar Gaddafi, and arms merchant Ibrahim Bah. Chris Mahony, "A Political Tool? The Politics of Case Selection at the Special Court for Sierra Leone," in *Evaluating Transitional Justice: Accountability and Peace-Building in Post-Conflict Sierra Leone*, eds. Kirsten Ainley, Rebekka Friedman, and Chris Mahony (Palgrave Macmillan, 2015), 91 (citing author's interviews with Crane).

Prosecutor Hausner's discreet decision not to mention them.[86] One of them was German Chancellor Adenauer's chief of staff, Hans Globke; Israel had political reasons for not embarrassing Adenauer.

Recall that she told Jaspers that "we have no tools to hand except legal ones with which we have to judge and pass sentence on something that cannot even be adequately represented either in legal terms or in political categories."[87] Notice her phrasing: The trial will have to pass judgment on some*thing* (*etwas*), not some*one* – and presumably that something was the Holocaust. Prior to the trial, Arendt may not have recognized that efforts to "represent" the Holocaust during the trial would sideline Eichmann and his crimes. The prosecutor's strategy of putting antisemitism itself on trial disabused her of that idea. She was a purist about the mission of criminal courts: to keep the focus on the defendants and their individual responsibility for the collective crimes in which they are accused of participating. Whatever the pedagogical payoffs of a trial, on her view they are at best a collateral benefit. At worst, using a trial to teach large historical lessons distorts the trial, misses the point, and – what matters most to Arendt – threatens to efface individual responsibility by dissolving the defendants' crimes into the porridge of large-scale historical processes. That, ultimately, is her unease about the weeks of survivor testimony that had no direct bearing on Adolf Eichmann. In her eyes, what rescued the trial was Judge Landau's firm understanding of the court's mission: to pass judgment on Eichmann and his deeds, not on the meaning of the Holocaust or the heroism of the ghetto fighters.

## 14.8 The Multiple Goals of International Criminal Law

Let me make my own view explicit: Arendt is right that the basic aim of the trial is to hold defendants accountable and fairly judge their deeds, but she is very wrong to dismiss the pedagogical and political goals of extraordinary trials. Arendt's complaint that Israel staged the Eichmann trial for ulterior political purposes would matter if those aims were illegitimate, which they mostly were not, or if they interfered with accountability, which they did not. Although Arendt disagreed, the expressive and memory-preserving purposes of trials are inextricable from the decision to try defendants in the name of justice. Gathering the evidence and preserving the record are inseparable from accountability, and

[86] *EJ*, 18–19.

[87] Arendt to Jaspers, December 23, 1960, in *HA-KJ*, 417. I have slightly amended the translation.

condemnation and exoneration are expressive acts. Possibly we take all this for granted in domestic trials for common crimes; they play an outsize role in extraordinary trials.[88]

One expressive aim is asserting that the rule of law matters, by making it matter through fair and public trials; in post-conflict extraordinary trials, this can be a crucial way for a liberal successor government to distinguish itself from a past tyranny.[89] Even more important, though, is creating a repository of historical memory as a bulwark against the inevitable future denialism.[90] Courts do this through their published judgments, but also through their investigations and evidence collection and the public exposition of the trial itself. The 3,000 tons of documents the Allies collected for the Nuremberg trials would otherwise have remained scattered across Europe and likely destroyed by those seeking to bury the truth. An entire generation of Holocaust historians relied on those documents.

To take a more recent example, the Extraordinary Chambers in the Courts of Cambodia (ECCC) was formed in 2004 to try Khmer Rouge leaders for Cambodia's "auto-genocide" of 1975–79. From the point of view of accountability, it was an abject failure. Facing intense political headwinds from a hostile government, it dragged on for sixteen years, and in the end it tried only four cases against a handful of geriatric leaders, resulting in just three convictions. From a pedagogical point of view, though, it was a brilliant success. More than 200,000 Cambodians from all over the country visited the hearings, and even more participated in local discussions organized by the ECCC's outreach program.[91] It made the history less forgettable and less deniable.[92]

88 Here, the most comprehensive treatment is Douglas, *The Memory of Judgment: Making Law and History in the Trials of the Holocaust.*

89 Lawrence Douglas marks the shift from penological to didactic purposes beginning with the Eichmann trial, which he discusses in *The Memory of Judgment*, chapters 4 and 5. Mark Osiel makes a compelling case that holding trials to reinforce liberal values after a repressive government falls is a valid one, but only if the trial enacts those values by scrupulous fairness. Osiel, *Mass Atrocity, Collective Memory, and the Law*, 12, 60–67. The didactic effort was unsuccessful at the time of the Nuremberg Trials, because Germans struggling with postwar hardship paid little attention to them; it succeeded only over the course of years. I have argued that the fairness of trials and punishments is itself sufficient to confer legitimacy on international tribunals. Luban, "Fairness to Rightness: Jurisdiction, Legality, and the Legitimacy of International Criminal Law."

90 A purpose that Arendt rejected. Although making a record of the Holocaust is "the noblest of ulterior purposes," she thought it could "only detract from the law's main business: to weigh the charges brought against the accused, to render judgment, and to mete out due punishment." *EJ*, 253. She obviously has no objection to making a trial record of Eichmann's role in the Holocaust.

91 Beth Van Schaack, "Verdict in Cambodia: Too Little Too Late, but Still Important," *Just Security*, August 9, 2014.

92 In 2003, Cambodia criminalized denialism but two decades later found it necessary to toughen the law. The threat of denialism is perpetual.

Arendt is surely right that the central aim of extraordinary trials is doing justice to accused perpetrators by holding them accountable. It's the yearning for accountability that motivates investigators and witnesses alike, and without that yearning nobody would collect or offer the evidence. Witnesses would have little incentive to come forward and relive their trauma; informants would not risk their lives smuggling documents and photographs out of atrocity zones like Assad's Syria.[93] But in addition to their yearning for justice, it also matters to them that the evidence they gather and the testimony they offer will prevent the history from being lost.

Arendt herself was terrified that history might fall into the abyss of forgetting. But she reassured herself that this is impossible:

> It is true that totalitarian domination tried to establish these holes of oblivion into which all deeds, good and evil, would disappear, but just as the Nazis' feverish attempts, from June, 1942, on, to erase all traces of the massacres – through cremation, through burning in open pits, through the use of explosives and flame-throwers and bone-crushing machinery – were doomed to failure, so all efforts to let their opponents "disappear in silent anonymity" were in vain. The holes of oblivion do not exist. Nothing human is that perfect, and there are simply too many people in the world to make oblivion possible. One man will always be left alive to tell the story.[94]

Probably Arendt understood that that one man (or woman) may be too ashamed, or traumatized, or frightened to tell the story of their own rape and abjection without the prospect that it will lead to justice visited on the perpetrators – the aim that Arendt valued. What she should have recognized is that by coming forth, witnesses seeking justice are at the same time seeking to ensure that history is not buried in holes of oblivion.

To be sure, there are legitimate concerns about some international tribunals' fact-finding, regarding both the credibility of witness testimony and the inferences judges draw from it. Nancy Combs's review of ICTR cases found troubling inconsistencies between pretrial statements and trial testimony by nearly half the prosecution witnesses in the early years – inconsistencies which the judges sometimes glossed over.[95] On the other

[93] Ben Taub, "The Assad Files," *New Yorker*, April 11, 2016, reports on the hair-raising risks informants took to exfiltrate records of Assad regime atrocities from Syria to a repository maintained by the Commission for International Justice and Accountability in an unnamed European city, in hopes of a trial someday. See also Adam Ciralsky, "Documenting Evil: Inside Assad's Hospitals of Horror," *Vanity Fair*, June 11, 2015.

[94] *EJ*, 232–33.

[95] Nancy Armoury Combs, *Fact-Finding without Facts: The Uncertain Evidentiary Foundations of International Criminal Convictions* (Cambridge University Press, 2010), 5; Combs, "Grave Crimes

hand, without the trials, there would be no pretrial statements and trial testimony for anyone to review. Concerns about fact-finding are legitimate, but the question must always be: "Compared with what?" If the alternative is no investigation to collect and preserve evidence in a systematic way, later historians – working with fewer resources, long after malefactors have destroyed documents and silenced witnesses – will face insurmountable obstacles. The desire for justice, which Arendt applauds, and the desire to make a historical record and reinforce the rule of law by conducting fair public trials, turn out to be inseparable.

In addition, the expressive aims of atrocity trials are fundamental to the radical ambition of international criminal justice: a transformation in how ordinary men and women regard extreme political violence. The hope is that through public trials that hold perpetrators to account, future generations might come to agree that magic justificatory words like *raison d'état*, military necessity, holy war, and even "liberation struggle" are often sinister euphemisms for atrocities properly called war crimes, crimes against humanity, genocide, and aggression. Leaders in the dock may howl that the violence they unleashed was for a sacred cause, that they are being persecuted by victor's justice, and that labeling their atrocities "crime" is a travesty. Their cause is too high to be brought low by mere law; the sacred violence they unleashed is beyond good and evil.[96]

Not so. The expressive (or "deflationary") aim of international criminal justice is to demystify sacred violence. It does so in two ways. One is by promulgating conceptual innovations like "crimes against humanity" and "genocide" to replace the old abracadabra. The other is by subjecting the leaders who orchestrate atrocities to the tedium and regularity of legal proceedings, shrinking them from gods to mere mortals.[97] These aims are, by their very nature, political and pedagogical.

and Weak Evidence: A Fact-Finding Evolution in International Criminal Law," *Harvard Journal of International Law* 58(1) (2017): 77. Happily, in the latter study, Combs found significant improvement in the trial chambers' performance over time.

96 I borrow the term "sacred violence" from Paul W. Kahn, *Sacred Violence: Torture, Terror, and Sovereignty* (University of Michigan Press, 2008). Kahn's theme is that the modern state and modern conceptions of nationhood are not mere secularized counterparts of a medieval political theology that invested the sovereign's "body politic" with divinity. Rather, secular nationalism never shed its mystical political theology; in an age of popular sovereignty, it merely transferred divine attributes to "the people." Violence (supposedly) on their behalf is sacred violence.

97 Here I draw on arguments I have made elsewhere. David Luban, "Demystifying Political Violence: Some Bequests of ICTY and ICTR," *AJIL Unbound* 110 (2016): 254–55; David Luban, "After the Honeymoon: Reflections on the Current State of International Criminal Justice," *Journal of International Criminal Justice* 11(3) (2013): 509–11; and Luban, "On the Humanity of the Enemy of Humanity: A Response to My Critics," 189.

In fact, Arendt herself insisted on truth in labeling when she argued that only the category "crime against humanity" (and not solely crime against the Jews) properly expresses that genocide offends against all humanity, not only its victims.[98] Arendt plainly thinks that calling the crime by its rightful name matters. She too thought the law might transform the way we think of murderous attacks on human diversity.[99] And she endorsed the second expressive aim of criminal trials: treating the defendant as an ordinary human being, neither a god who is above the law nor a cog in a machine who is beneath it. As for Prosecutor Hausner's effort to make "a living record of a gigantic human and national disaster," it spoke directly to Arendt's concern about events falling into holes of oblivion.[100] Without Abba Kovner's testimony, how would the selfless heroism of Anton Schmid, which she called "a sudden burst of light in the midst of impenetrable, unfathomable darkness," enter into the storybook of mankind?

In effect, I am arguing that Arendt should have been far more sympathetic to the expressive and history-preserving aims of extraordinary trials than she was, because at bottom they are her own ambitions – a concrete form of her injunction that "men must assume responsibility for all crimes committed by men." They fulfill her hope that courts of law may become sites of judgment and memory.

98 Unsurprisingly, labeling matters to defendants as well; some defendants in the ICTR rejected plea bargains that would have spared them extra years in prison because they would not plead guilty to genocide, only to war crimes.

99 For example, *EJ*, 268–69 (on the importance of treating genocide as a crime against the human status); Arendt to Jaspers, December 23, 1960, in *HA-KJ*, 417 (asking hopefully whether a law against *hostes generis humani* would make a difference).

100 *EJ*, 231.

CHAPTER 15

# *Thoughtlessness as Culpability*

## 15.1 "The Very Foundations of Their Profession": Moral and Legal Common Sense

On Arendt's telling, Eichmann was "an average, 'normal' person, neither feeble-minded nor indoctrinated nor cynical," who was "perfectly incapable of telling right from wrong."[1] The judges who condemned him didn't see him that way: In their eyes, he was a Nazi fanatic whose trial testimony was through-and-through untruthful.[2] (This, we saw in Chapter 2, is also the view of some eminent historians.) Arendt speculates that the judges were too good to imagine that a person could do what Eichmann did without being a Nazi fanatic and rabid antisemite – and perhaps (she adds ominously) they were unable to admit to a phenomenon that poses a basic challenge to "the very foundations of their profession."[3] How can a judge condemn someone for wrongdoing if an average, normal person can't be counted on to tell right from wrong? If normal people can't be counted on to recognize that robbery and murder are wrong – and what counts as robbery or murder – the distinction between "normal" and "deviant" would lose its meaning.

Judgment of right and wrong therefore belongs to *legal* common sense, by which I mean broadly shared awareness of the basic contours of law, even among people with no legal training or even legal literacy. Legal common sense, not police or courts, is the true enforcer of the law, because we don't carry law books in our pockets or our heads, and we don't go through life with lawyers whispering in our ear or police at our elbow. All

[1] *EJ*, 26.

[2] Prosecutor v. Eichmann, Trial Judgment, §§183, 231, 243. The judges found him to be lying about many particulars (e.g., §§70, 106, 116(b), 117, 136, 137, 138, 143, 155(e), 167, 170–80), but also more generally about the depth of his Nazi commitment and his claim to blind obedience (§§180, 223–43).

[3] *EJ*, 26.

enacted law, not only criminal law, floats on a sea of legal common sense.[4] It's common sense that carelessly ruining someone else's property requires us to pay damages, that incorporating a business involves paperwork, that signing a contract binds you to a deal. Even if we don't know the legalisms and loopholes, we know the basics (including that there probably *are* legalisms and loopholes). We learn these by osmosis, simply by coming of age in a law-saturated world. If ordinary people didn't know them, law could hardly function. The criminal law maxim that ignorance of the law is no excuse would be a nightmare out of a Kafka story: Without legal common sense to guide us, it would impose a draconian duty to master an inscrutable penal code. The maxim assumes the existence of legal common sense.

Of course, telling right from wrong is not the same as knowing what is lawful and what is not: Legal systems prohibit things that aren't wrongful, and they fail to prohibit things that are. But all decent legal systems forbid major interpersonal wrongs such as armed robbery, kidnapping, arson, murder, rape, and fraud – acts that criminal lawyers classify as *malum in se*, wrong in themselves. Here, the categories of right/wrong and lawful/unlawful overlap in extension. Recognizing that *malum in se* acts are crimes is the heartland of legal common sense. If that recognition isn't part of legal common sense, nothing is; and if nothing is, governance through law is impossible. For that reason, the existence of normal people who can't tell right from wrong threatens the foundations not only of the judicial profession but of law itself. Arendt has not confused law with morality when she connects knowledge of right and wrong with the very possibility of law. Her speculative remark cuts deep.

All this holds in decent legal systems. But what about indecent legal systems? What if the law itself defies common sense, and a topsy-turvy legal order drags the moral judgment of multitudes down with it? Now we can see what troubles Arendt: In an ordinary regime, murder is *malum in se*, and common sense tells us that the law echoes "Thou shalt not kill." Murder is deviant. But in the Third Reich (or at least among the SS and other killing units), murdering Jews was no longer deviant; it was a core mission of the state. That is why Arendt writes that Eichmann committed

[4] Legal philosopher Lon Fuller likewise argued that "made law" rests on implicit norms of "the limits of legal decency and sanity." Lon L. Fuller, *The Anatomy of Law* (Praeger, 1968), 90; Gerald J. Postema, "Implicit Law," *Law and Philosophy* 13(3) (1994): 373–77. Fuller's lesson is that implicit law constrains made law. My point is different: that without implicit legal common sense, made law cannot govern.

his crimes "under circumstances that make it well-nigh impossible for him to know or to feel that he is doing wrong."[5]

Let's review those circumstances. First of all, by the time of the Final Solution, Germans had had a decade to grow accustomed to antisemitic persecution and ethnic cleansing. The baseline of decency had changed for the worse. Then, when persecution turned to genocide, the bureau chiefs at the Wannsee Conference were entirely on board – not merely unruffled but enthusiastic. As Eichmann testified: "Not only did everybody willingly indicate agreement, ... they outdid and outbid each other, as regards to the demand for a Final Solution to the Jewish Question. ... The leading figures of the Reich at the time had spoken at the Wannsee Conference, the 'Popes' had given their orders."[6]

Additionally, by then it was wartime, with innocent death and suffering everywhere. And Eichmann was a military man, expected to obey orders. As such, he told the court, his duty was "cadaver-like obedience" (*Kadavergehorsam*) – a German idiom for blind obedience – and he pled the superior orders defense.[7] The court responded indignantly that even German military law disallows the superior orders defense when the accused knows the order is criminal.[8]

That raises a crucial question: Did Eichmann know his orders were criminal? The answer is more complicated than it appears.

## 15.2 To Know and Not to Know

Germany never abolished the law against murder, or explicitly created exceptions regarding groups the state wished to murder; at some level, then, Eichmann knew that murder is murder – a point to which I'll return. Murder is murder under military as well as civilian law. At his trial, Eichmann testified that he now considers the murder of the Jews "one

[5] *EJ*, 276. [6] Eichmann Trial Proceedings, vol. 4, Session 79, June 26, 1961, at 1423. See *EJ*, 276.

[7] *EJ*, 135; Eichmann Trial Judgment, §228.

[8] Eichmann Trial Judgment, §220, citing art. 47(2) of the German Military Penal Code of 1872. The exception also appears in a post-World War I German judgment, convicting two obedient naval lieutenants as accessories in the war crime of sinking the lifeboats of a hospital ship. "German War Trials: Judgment in the Case of Lieutenants Dithmar and Boldt, Hospital Ship 'Llandovery Castle,' Second Criminal Senate of the Imperial Court of Justice (July 16, 1921)," *American Journal of International Law* 16(4) (October 1922): 722 (henceforth *Llandovery Castle*). The Nuremberg Charter and Nuremberg Principles abolish the superior orders defense, although they permit it as a mitigating factor in imposing sentences. Subsequent international tribunals, including the ICTY, ICTR, and SCSL, also abolished it, and as a matter of customary international law it does not exist in international tribunals. However, the Rome Statute of the ICC permits the defense unless the accused knows the order was illegal or its illegality was "manifest." Rome Statute, art. 33.

of the most heinous crimes in the history of mankind." But when asked what he thought at the time, he says he knew it was "a monstrous deed"; but he twists and turns to avoid labeling it a crime. For example:

Q. Did you consider it to be a crime?
A. What I said to myself was this: The Head of State has ordered it, and those exercising judicial authority over me are now transmitting it. I escaped into other areas and looked for a cover for myself which gave me some peace of mind at least, and so in this way I was able to shift – no, that is not the right term – to attach this whole thing one hundred per cent to those in judicial authority who happened to be my superiors, to the Head of State – since they gave the orders.[9]

To his pre-trial interrogator, Eichmann quoted the Nazi doctrine that the Führer's words have the force of law. Historians debate whether Hitler indeed ordered the Final Solution, for no written "Führer Order" has ever been found; but as Arendt notes, *Führerworte* included Hitler's oral directives as well.[10] Eichmann was sure the orders came from Hitler, and on this point, at least, there is no reason to suppose he was lying.[11] In that case, it might not matter that the German penal code prohibited murder.

This ambiguity or doublethink about whether genocide against "enemy races" was murder under German law was by no means unique to Eichmann, and it teaches us a great deal about how law works under dictatorship. Nazi jurisprudence was from the very beginning hostile to statutory law when it conflicted with "healthy popular sentiment" as represented by the Party and – what was essentially the same thing – by Hitler's will. As early as 1935, the Nazis amended the penal code to include a general provision that acts could be punished if "the spirit (*Grundgedank*) of a rule of criminal law and healthy popular sentiment" justified punishment.[12] Under this general clause, positive law itself commanded anti-positivist interpretation and enforcement.[13]

[9] Eichmann Trial Proceedings, vol. 4, Session 95, July 13, 1961, at 1661–62. He also says that if he had been ordered to personally supervise or carry out the gassings, he would have killed himself. Eichmann Trial Proceedings, vol. 4, Session 95, July 13, 1961, at 1661.

[10] *EJ*, 148.

[11] *EJ*, 24, 128, 293. Eichmann Trial Proceedings, vol. 4, Session 95, July 13, 1961, at 1662. On Eichmann's belief that the "Führer order" existed, see the trial judgment, §§69, 163.

[12] Gesetz zur Änderung der Strafgesetzbuchs vom 28. Juni 1935, *Reichsgesetzblatt* I, 839.

[13] See the eye-opening analysis of Nazi legal theory in Jens Meierhenrich, *The Remnants of the Rechtsstaat: An Ethnography of Nazi Law* (Oxford University Press, 2018), 95–158. Meierhenrich explains that to some Nazi theorists, the *Gesetzesstaat* (a legal system based on statutory law) is a bloodless substitute for a living *Volk*-oriented *Rechtsstaat*; other Nazi theorists rejected the *Rechtsstaat* ideal altogether, because it was so closely bound up with the liberalism that National

In 1942, Hitler proclaimed an end to judicial independence, and that same day the Reichstag formally authorized him to take any steps he wished "without being bound by existing legal provisions," because "the German people is in a struggle for existence or non-existence."[14] But the decree merely made official what had been true since the dawn of the Third Reich: bottomless scorn for legalism. In Nazi ideology, positive law had to give way to the law of nature itself: the struggle for existence among races.

To implement Hitler's decree, Justice Minister Otto Thierack wrote a circular letter to the German judiciary:

> According to ancient Germanic interpretation of the law, the leader of the nation has always been its supreme judge. When the leader therefore vests another person with the authority of a judge, this means that the latter not only derives his judicial power from the leader, and is responsible to him, but also that leadership and judgeship have related characters.
>
> The judge is therefore also the guardian of national self-preservation. He is the protector of the values of the nation and helps in the annihilation of the unworthy [!]. He regulates those functions of life, which are considered diseases in the body of the nation. . . .
>
> Such a corps of judges will not slavishly cling to the letter of the law. It will not anxiously look for the cover of the law.[15]

Let the last sentence sink in. In normal legal systems, we do not think of the law as a "cover" that anxious judges use to dodge their job. The law *is* their job.

Now, Eichmann was no lawyer or legal theorist, but the Nazis' contempt for statutory law was common knowledge. A striking photograph from 1934 depicts the Prussian minister of justice jovially presiding over a symbolic lynching of the "§" symbol, denoting articles in a legal code (Figure 1).

A crucial point: Contempt for laws that might constrain autocracy is not unique to Hitler's Germany. In all autocracies, the law in action is the prerogative of the dictator, regardless of the law in books. In Ernst

Socialism hated. See also the useful discussion of Nazi criminal law theory in Herlinde Pauer-Studer and J. David Velleman, *Konrad Morgen: The Conscience of a Nazi Judge* (Palgrave Macmillan, 2015), 26–29, 37–39.

14 Hitler, Reichstag speech of April 26, 1942; Beschluß des Großdeutsches Reichstags vom 26. April 1942, *Reichsgesetzblat*. I 1942, p. 248.

15 Otto Thierack, *Richterbriefe* [Judges' Letters] Communications of the Reich Minister of Justice, Issue No. 1, 1 October 1942, in 3 Trials of War Criminals before the Nuernberg Military Tribunals under Control Council Law No. 10 (US Government Printing Office, 1951), 525–26. Thierack committed suicide in 1946.

Figure 1 Prussian Minister of Justice Hanns Kerrl lynching the "§" symbol.
Photo credit: bpk Bildagentur/Art Resources, NY.

Fraenkel's terminology, the "prerogative" state will be superimposed on the "normative" state, and the autocrat's prerogative will trump the formal law and become, in effect, the anti-formal law that defies common sense. The state becomes a dual state – Fraenkel's term again, in his eponymous book analyzing the Nazi legal system.[16] As the judges fall in line, and the subjects get used to it, the anti-formal law *becomes* legal common sense, seeping out from the dictator's inner circle to his political base to the public at large.

[16] Ernst Fraenkel, *The Dual State: A Contribution to the Theory of Dictatorship*, trans. Edward Shils, ed. Jens Meierhenrich, republished ed. (Oxford University Press, 2018); on Fraenkel, see Meierhenrich, *The Remnants of the Rechtsstaat: An Ethnography of Nazi Law*; Douglas Morris, *Legal Sabotage: Ernst Fraenkel in Hitler's Germany* (Cambridge University Press, 2020).

Even in the Third Reich, though, the collapse of legal common sense and moral judgment was never total in the justice system. This is a crucial fact – one that Arendt may have missed. Hitler terminated judicial independence because as late as 1942 some judges "obviously don't understand the imperative of the hour," namely that "Germany must live regardless of formal judicial rulings to the contrary."[17] Thierack criticized specific decisions by judges who still treated Jews as if they deserved the same legal protections as Aryans: "This cannot be sanctioned. The Jew is the enemy of the German people. . . . Not only is he of different but of inferior race. Justice, which must not measure different matters by the same standard, demands that just this racial aspect must be considered in the meting out of punishment."[18] The fact that even in 1942 some judges had to be scolded for going by the book shows that the normative state and the "old" legal common sense were still partially intact.[19]

Further evidence may be found in Himmler's terrifying Posen speech to SS officers, where he warned that the Final Solution must be kept completely secret: "Amongst ourselves, for once, it shall be said quite openly, but all the same we will never speak about it in public. . . . This is an unwritten, and never-to-be-written page of glory."[20] Himmler understood that although Party members had for years blustered about exterminating the Jews, the reality was something that even an unmoored public inured to the rhetoric would regard with horror.

We might say, then, that the answer to the question of whether Eichmann knew his orders were illegal is "he did and he didn't." He did, because he knew that murder is murder, and an order to commit murder must not be obeyed; and he was reared in a culture where "Thou shalt not kill" was part of every child's upbringing. He didn't, because as an SS officer and a "higher bearer of secrets," Eichmann knew the prerogative law, radiating from the dictator's will. He zealously executed the prerogative law even when Himmler ordered him to stop – a fact that his judges found damning, but that Arendt points out bears "a most unpleasant resemblance to that of the often-cited soldier who, acting in a normal legal framework, refuses to carry out orders that run counter to his ordinary experience of lawfulness and hence can be recognized by him as criminal."[21]

17 Hitler, Reichstag speech of April 26, 1942. 18 Thierack, *Richterbriefe*, 533.

19 Meierhenrich, *The Remnants of the* Rechtsstaat.

20 Speech by Himmler before senior SS officers, October 4, 1943, www.yadvashem.org/odot_pdf/Microsoft%20Word%20-%204029.pdf [https://perma.cc/A86M-TPTB].

21 *EJ*, 148.

A persecuting society. Open contempt for formal law, emanating from the highest levels of the state and partly inscribed in the formal law itself. Enthusiastically genocidal "popes." A prerogative law of murder. These are the circumstances that Arendt thought made it well-nigh impossible for Eichmann to know or to feel that he was doing wrong.

Arendt's phrasing shows that she disbelieved Eichmann's testimony that he always knew that the murder of the Jews was a "monstrous deed." Yet, as we have seen, she exaggerates the extent to which law and morality had turned upside down, and "Thou shalt kill" had become the law of the land. They had and they hadn't, because the prerogative state and the normative state coexisted in unresolved tension. This observation will prove important when we turn to the question of Eichmann's *mens rea.*

In an obvious way, choosing which law to obey should not have been difficult. The unrepealed normative law against murder tracks millennia of moral teaching, centuries of positive law, and the legal common sense in which Eichmann grew up. The prerogative law rested on Hitler's will and a Party ideology barely two decades old.

But, as I argued in Chapter 6, Nazi propaganda did not reverse "Thou shalt not kill," as Arendt put it.[22] Instead, it redrew the boundary between murder and justified self-defense by treating crackpot racism about the deadly Jewish menace as indisputable fact that justified the extermination of the Jews. The collapse of *factual* common sense can lead to a collapse of *moral* and *legal* common sense – and Arendt observed that in Germany the erosion began at the dawn of the Third Reich, or more likely sooner. She adds that "this early moral disintegration in German society, hardly perceptible to the outsider, was like a kind of dress rehearsal for its total breakdown, which was to occur during the war years."[23] What should have been an easy choice or no choice at all – the normative law against murder or the prerogative law? – became a judgment call in a society where judgment lay in ruins.

## 15.3 Manifest to Whom?

Let's return to the superior orders defense, which is unavailable if the accused knows the orders are criminal. A second prong of this legal doctrine holds that even when a military member doesn't know the orders are illegal, the defense is unavailable if the orders are "manifestly" illegal. The rule that manifest illegality annuls the superior orders defense was well

22 *T*, 177. 23 PRUD, 24–25.

established in the German-speaking military world. It traces back to the 1855 Austrian military penal code, and a 1915 Austro-Hungarian Military Court decision denied the superior orders defense when obedience is "manifestly (*klar und offenbar*) in conflict not only with criminal law but also with the customs of war of civilized peoples."[24] Although the "manifest illegality test" was not in the letter of the German Military Penal Code, the leading German war crimes case interpreted the code to include it.[25]

Were orders to transport millions to their deaths "manifestly" unlawful? Obviously: In a normal environment murder is *malum in se*, and labeling a crime *malum in se* is not only a moral judgment but also an epistemological judgment that its wrongness is clear. If recognizing the criminality of murder is in the heartland of legal common sense, recognizing the monstrosity of mass murder is surely in the heartland of the heartland.

But it wasn't. In a system where every responsible person in Eichmann's chain of command enthusiastically supported mass murder, and where the resources of the state were conspicuously devoted to it, in what sense was the unlawfulness of mass murder self-evident to soldiers? Israel's "Nazi and Nazi Collaborators Law" declares that manifest unlawfulness is a legal concept that is up to the court to define.[26] But the Jerusalem court's definition relies on perceptual and moral judgment, not on law alone. It cites a precedent condemning Israel's own soldiers for massacring Palestinian civilians, excerpting a passage that deserves to be quoted in full:

> The distinguishing mark of a "manifestly unlawful order" should fly like a black flag above the given order, as a warning reading "Prohibited!". Not mere formal illegality, hidden or half-hidden, not the kind of illegality discernible only to the eyes of legal experts, but a flagrant and manifest breach of the law, certain and necessary illegality appearing on the face of the order itself; the clearly criminal character of the order or of the acts ordered, an illegality clearly visible and repulsive to the heart, provided the eye is not blind and the heart is not stony and corrupt – that is the extent of "manifest illegality" required to release a soldier from the duty of obedience upon him and make him criminally responsible for his acts.[27]

[24] Military Penal Code of the Austro-Hungarian Monarchy, art. 158 (no superior orders defense for "an act or omission in which evidently a crime or offense is to be recognized"). The Austrian case is quoted in Paola Gaeta, "The Defence of Superior Orders: The Statute of the International Criminal Court *versus* Customary International Law," *European Journal of International Law* 10 (1999): 175n5.

[25] *Llandovery Castle*, 722.

[26] Quoted in Eichmann Trial Judgment, §218.

[27] Military Prosecutor v. Melinki, 17 P.M. (1958–59) 90, 213–14 Military Court 3/57 (Israel); quoted in the *Eichmann* trial judgment, §219, and in part in *EJ*, 292–93.

The nettlesome question is this: If the illegality of genocide was so "clearly visible," how could hundreds of thousands of killers not see it? Or, posed in the other direction: If hundreds of thousands of soldiers and their civilian collaborators followed orders to commit genocide, doesn't it follow that there was nothing *manifestly* illegal about the orders? In that case, the superior orders defense should be available to them.

This embarrassment persists in today's international criminal law. The Rome Statute of the ICC dodges it by stipulating that "orders to commit genocide or crimes against humanity are manifestly unlawful."[28] Of course the law can, by fiat, remove the superior orders defense for genocide and crimes against humanity, as it should; but it cannot legislate perception. Arendt is right that the plausibility of such a solution "rests on the assumption that the law expresses only what every man's conscience would tell him anyhow": that these orders are self-evident exceptions to the rule commanding military obedience.[29] If so, intent to commit these acts *is* intent to do what the perpetrator knows is wrong.

But what if the assumption is false? That was a riddle Arendt hoped the Jerusalem court would solve when she explained to Jaspers why she was going to Jerusalem. To her disappointment, it did not.

## 15.4 Guilty Mind

Arendt asserts that "in all modern legal systems ... intent to do wrong is necessary for the commission of a crime."[30] This is not obviously true, and it is not how lawyers usually understand the concept of *mens rea*, the "guilty mind" that accompanies the "bad act" (*actus reus*) as basic elements of a crime.

To be sure, the bad act must be done *intentionally*, meaning that the perpetrator meant to do it. And it must be done *knowingly*, meaning with awareness of the nature of the conduct and circumstances, and (where relevant) its likely consequences.[31] For most crimes, though, there is no third *mens rea* requirement that the perpetrator knows the conduct is illegal or morally wrong, let alone that the perpetrator *intends* to break the law or to do wrong. In other words, there is no requirement of subjective guilt consciousness. Partly, this is for practical reasons: to require

[28] Rome Statute of the ICC, art. 33(2) (titled "Superior orders and prescription of law").

[29] *EJ*, 293, 148. [30] *EJ*, 277.

[31] See, for example, the American Law Institute's Model Penal Code, §2.02(b) and the Rome Statute, art. 30.

guilt consciousness as a third *mens rea* would make it too easy for wrongdoers to evade justice by claiming ignorance of the law. Mostly, though, it is because the legal system cares about the wrongful conduct, not the perpetrator's beliefs about the conduct.

The principal exceptions, where the essential *mens rea* includes knowledge of the law, are crimes where the conduct is innocuous on its face and, in the words of the US Supreme Court, "circumstances which might move one to inquire [about its legality] . . . are completely lacking."[32] These are mostly regulatory violations enforced through criminal penalties (e.g., arcane financial reporting requirements). To convict someone of obscure crimes, prosecutors must prove beyond a reasonable doubt that the accused knew they were breaking the law, in addition to proving that they acted knowingly and intentionally.[33] Fairness requires that criminal law not set traps for the unsuspecting.

Seizing a million people and transporting them to death camps is hardly innocuous conduct, and in a normal setting, it flies the black flag of illegality. But, for the reasons we've been examining, in the SS it was not *deviant* conduct; Eichmann "could see no one, no one at all, who actually was against the Final Solution."[34] The black flag was furled. Here, let us recall three rules of moral common sense discussed earlier in §6.8:

> It's wrong if the respectable people around me say it's wrong and behave as if it's wrong.
> It's wrong if it deviates from a generally accepted social rule.
> It's wrong if it is part of an antinomian practice, that is, a practice in which it seems as though all restraint has been cast off and all is permitted.

None of these warning flags was waving within Eichmann's purview. For that reason, just as with obscure regulatory offenses, the lawyers' act-and-consequence-focused *mens rea* framework seems insufficient. If so, then even if Arendt was mistaken that criminal law *always* requires awareness of wrongdoing, in this context she may well have been right. In §15.8, I suggest an alternative – but for the moment, let's stick with Arendt's

[32] Lambert v. California, 355 U.S. 225, 229 (1957). The case concerned a Los Angeles ordinance requiring convicted felons to register within five days of arrival in the city. The Supreme Court found that applying the ordinance to someone who doesn't know about the registration requirement violates the constitutional right to fair notice.

[33] Cheek v. United States, 498 U.S. 192 (1991) (tax cheating); Ratzlaf v. United States, 510 U.S. 135 (1994) (structuring financial transactions to avoid reporting requirements).

[34] *EJ*, 116.

proposition that intent to do wrong is necessary for the culpability of Eichmann's crimes.

## 15.5 The Defiance Theory of *Mens Rea*

The proposition naturally raises the question of what intent to do wrong (subjective *mens rea*) consists of. The traditional Christian account, originating with St. Augustine, equates intent to do wrong with *defiance* of the lawgiver: Lucifer "refused to be subject to his Creator" and "proudly rejoiced as if in a power peculiar to himself."[35] For Augustine, the sin of Adam and Eve was not that they ate the fruit but that they defied God.[36] Arendt notes that in later Christian theology disobedience became the "mortal sin *par excellence*" and obedience "the very foundation of Christian ethics."[37]

In a compelling essay on *mens rea*, the philosopher Jean Hampton develops a secular version of defiance theory. She begins with a nonmoral, nonlegal analogue: defiance of prudential reason. A youth of her acquaintance stubbornly insisted on building his own cabin in rural Maine even though he knew he was not a competent builder; predictably, it collapsed in the winter storms. Like a petulant toddler, he "would have it" that the material world must bend to his will.[38] By analogy – and here Hampton hews closely to Augustine – "immoral people know the better but do the worse because they believe they can install a new reason-giving authority over their actions that transforms the worse into the better."[39] They would have it so. Likewise for legal culpability: The tax cheat believes that "the authority of the law can be defied, and something else that condones what he wishes can be enthroned in its place."[40] Defiance consists in granting one's own wishes supreme authority. Hampton analyzes the textbook *mens rea* categories (knowledge, purposefulness, recklessness) as species of

35 Augustine, *The City of God*, bk. 11, ch. 13, 467; bk. 14, ch. 11, 605.

36 Augustine, *The City of God*, bk. 14, ch. 12, 607; also ch. 13, 609.

37 She cautions, though, that this doctrine "can hardly be derived from the teaching and preaching of Jesus of Nazareth." *W*, 64–65, 68–69.

38 Jean Hampton, "*Mens Rea*," in Jean Hampton, *The Intrinsic Worth of Persons: Contractarianism in Moral and Political Philosophy*, ed. Daniel Farnham (Cambridge University Press, 2007), 75–79.

39 Hampton, "*Mens Rea*," 91.

40 Hampton, "*Mens Rea*," 102. The "sovereign citizen" movement in some countries is an extreme illustration. Sovereign citizens proclaim that they don't owe taxes because no one but themselves has sovereignty over them.

defiance, and she shows that the textbook justification and excuse defenses are "mental states in which no defiance has occurred."[41]

The problem is that Eichmann as Arendt diagnoses him simply does not fit the defiance theory. *Kadavergehorsam* doesn't remotely resemble defiance, nor does Eichmann's shifting responsibility "one hundred per cent to those in judicial authority who happened to be my superiors, to the Head of State." Recall Jaspers's letter to Arendt, in which he objected to the demonic grandeur picture of Nazi criminals; rather, Jaspers believed, they are as banal as bacteria that can nevertheless wipe out nations.[42] Banal evil and defiant evil are polar opposites.[43]

This is the challenge that banality of evil poses to international criminal law. "Banal" perpetrators recognize evil only when it deviates from prevailing norms; when the prevailing norms are evil, the perpetrators lack subjective *mens rea*. If subjective *mens rea* is truly a requirement of culpability, how can we condemn them?

## 15.6 Long-Forgotten, Barbaric Propositions

In the postwar Nazi trials, Arendt believed, the judges "really passed judgment solely on the basis of the monstrous deeds" rather than the standards and legal precedents they cited ("more or less convincingly") in their opinions.[44] In her eyes, judgment without banisters is a good thing.

But condemnation without *mens rea* is not – and we've seen that in a criminal state such as the Third Reich, *mens rea* arguably includes subjective awareness of wrongdoing, not solely that the conduct was done intentionally and knowingly. That awareness was what Eichmann supposedly lacked, and the doctrine of manifest illegality can't make up for that lack. On this point, Martti Koskenniemi agrees: When "the crimes are aspects of political normality . . . there is no *mens rea*."[45] That makes the crimes strict liability offenses, a legal category of dubious credentials.

In the crucial passage in *Eichmann in Jerusalem* where Arendt addresses the basis of Eichmann's culpability in the absence of subjective guilt consciousness, she writes:

[41] Hampton, "*Mens Rea*," 102.
[42] Jaspers to Arendt, October 19, 1946, *HA-KJ*, 62. Quoted in §1.3.
[43] What I here call "defiant evil" straddles the categories of cold-blooded evil and Kant's "perversity of the heart" discussed in §5.4.
[44] *EJ*, 294. [45] Koskenniemi, "Between Impunity and Show Trials," 8.

> On nothing, perhaps, has civilized jurisprudence prided itself more than on this taking into account of the subjective factor. Where this intent is absent, where, for whatever reasons, even reasons of moral insanity, the ability to distinguish between right and wrong is impaired, we feel no crime has been committed. We refuse, and consider as barbaric, the propositions "that a great crime offends nature, so that the very earth cries out for vengeance; that evil violates a natural harmony which only retribution can restore; that a wronged collectivity owes a duty to the moral order to punish the criminal" (Yosal Rogat). And yet I think it is undeniable that it was precisely on the ground of these long-forgotten propositions that Eichmann was brought to justice to begin with, and that they were, in fact, the supreme justification for the death penalty.[46]

"The very earth cries out for vengeance" echoes God's condemnation of Cain, "your brother's blood cries out from the earth" (Gen. 4:10).[47]

Arendt's doubt that Eichmann had subjective *mens rea* drives her (and us?) toward these "long-forgotten propositions" because failing to punish his deeds is unthinkable.[48] But we "refuse, and consider as barbaric," those very propositions. Heightening the sense of contradiction, Arendt asserts that because Eichmann "played a central role in an enterprise whose open purpose was to eliminate forever certain 'races' from the surface of the earth, he had to be eliminated."[49] But "eliminated" makes his execution sound less like punishment than like killing a rattlesnake or a rabid dog – the way we treat a nonhuman menace.[50] Reinforcing the worry that Arendt proposes treating Nazi perpetrators as something other than a human being who can be called to account, Arendt told Jaspers that "[y]our definition of Nazi policy as a crime ('criminal guilt') strikes me as questionable . . . It may well be essential to hang Göring, but it is totally inadequate."[51] If Nazi policy was something other than crime, Göring's hanging would be something other than punishment. Two decades later, in her moral philosophy lectures, Arendt says that the perpetrators are

46 *EJ*, 277.

47 See Joshua Kleinfeld, "Why the Mind Matters in Criminal Law," *Arizona State Law Journal* 53(2). (2021): 552–55, explaining why in some cultures even unknowing and unintentional violations of sacred norms can be punished. These are the prototype of strict liability offenses.

48 PRUD, 26. 49 *EJ*, 277.

50 Compare this chilling remark by Oliver Wendell Holmes: "The world has produced the rattlesnake as well as me; but I kill it if I get a chance, as also mosquitos, cockroaches, murderers and flies." Letter from Holmes to Lewis Einstein, May 21, 1914, in *The Holmes–Einstein Letters: The Correspondence of Mr. Justice Holmes and Lewis Einstein 1903–1935*, ed. James Peabody (St. Martin's Press, 1964), 92.

51 Arendt to Jaspers, August 17, 1946, in *HA-KJ*, 54.

beyond retribution, deterrence, or rehabilitation – they must simply be destroyed.[52]

And yet Arendt clearly believed that Eichmann was sentenced to be punished, not merely "eliminated," and she said so quite explicitly.[53] Eichmann would not have been "brought to *justice*" if his sentence was not what the judges said it was: "due punishment" for his crimes.[54] Even the "barbaric" propositions she quotes from Yosal Rogat speak of retribution and punishment, not elimination.

Plainly, these are contradictions we need to untangle, assuming they *can* be untangled. Was Eichmann punished or merely eliminated?

## 15.7 Can the Unforgivable Be Punished?

The place to begin is with a puzzling dictum in *The Human Condition* and her moral philosophy lectures: that what cannot be forgiven cannot be punished.[55] I believe it is this conviction, coupled with her view that the Nazi crimes are unforgivable, that lands Arendt in the pickle of both asserting and denying that Eichmann was punished.

The proposition that what can't be forgiven can't be punished appears first in *The Human Condition*'s discussion of forgiveness, which we began to examine in §9.7. As part of her argument, Arendt observes that forgiveness and punishment are not conceptual opposites: The opposite of forgiveness is vengeance, not punishment. Unlike vengeance, punishment and forgiveness are alternative ways to close the books on a misdeed and its cascading consequences. By contrast, vengeance leads to a "chain reaction" of retaliations.[56]

A classic exemplar is Aeschylus's *Oresteia*, which Arendt may well have had in mind. The trilogy chronicles a vendetta spanning generations of a single family. Agamemnon sacrifices his daughter Iphigenia to appease the goddess he offended. His wife, Clytemnestra, kills him in revenge. Then their son, Orestes, kills her to avenge Agamemnon. The Furies pursue Orestes to avenge Clytemnestra. Athena finally ends the chain of vengeance by establishing a court of law to try Orestes, and she persuades the Furies to give up their vocation as avengers and instead become civic

[52] SQMP, 125. Here, she is explicating a stern judgment of Jesus in Luke 17:2, which I discuss in §15.7, raising the question of whether she is speaking *de dicto* or *de re*. She makes it clear on the final page of the moral philosophy lectures that she is speaking *de re*. SQMP, 146. See also PRUD, 26.

[53] *EJ*, 273, 287. [54] Eichmann trial judgment, §2. [55] *HC*, 241; SQMP, 109.

[56] *HC*, 240. We see here that Arendt does not accept Rogat's equation of punishment with vengeance.

guardians – a symbolic transformation of raw revenge to measured retribution under law.

Robert Jackson emphasized this crucial distinction in his opening statement at Nuremberg that I quoted earlier: "That four great nations, flushed with victory and stung with injury, stay the hand of vengeance and voluntarily submit their captive enemies to the judgment of the law, is one of the most significant tributes that Power ever has paid to Reason."[57] He admits that it is "hard to distinguish between the demand for a just and measured retribution, and the unthinking cry for vengeance which arises from the anguish of war. It is our task, so far as humanly possible, to draw the line between the two."[58] Arendt wholeheartedly agrees with Jackson that just retribution is not the same as revenge – in my view, a vital insight.[59]

Having ruled out vengeance as a mode of closure, Arendt turns her attention to forgiveness. Her analysis appears in somewhat curious garb, as a gloss on Jesus's injunction to his followers to forgive trespasses; she cites passages from the Gospels on the "duty to forgive."[60] She insists, though, that the duty to forgive can be understood in a secular sense as well.[61] Recall from our discussion in Chapter 9 why Arendt believes that forgiveness is essential to human action: "Without being forgiven, released from the consequences of what we have done, our capacity to act would, as it were, be confined to one single deed from which we could never recover."[62] This is her secular justification of the duty to forgive.

The scope of the duty requires careful scrutiny, though, because calling forgiveness a secular *duty* seems so plainly mistaken. Wrongdoers have no right to demand forgiveness; it follows that victims have no obligation to forgive. Forgiveness, if it comes, is bestowed out of grace, not duty.

On closer inspection, Arendt does not deny this. She emphasizes that the duty to forgive that Jesus taught is predicated on "for they know not what they do" (Luke 23:34); and she repeats that we must forgive others "for what they have done *unknowingly*."[63] Read in context, all Arendt strictly requires is forgiving trespasses for the unforeseen collateral consequences that action makes inevitable – the mounting calamities that, if unforgiven, would accumulate and choke future action to death.

[57] The Trial of German Major War Criminals, vol. 2, November 21, 1945 (1946) (morning session), 98.

[58] The Trial of German Major War Criminals, vol. 2, 100.

[59] On the distinction, see Luban, "War as Punishment," *Philosophy & Public Affairs* 39(4) (2012): 318–23. Arendt uses the phrase "just retribution" in *HC*, 240.

[60] *HC*, 239. [61] *HC*, 237–38. [62] *HC*, 237. [63] *HC*, 239–40, emphasis added.

Importantly, the duty to forgive does *not* apply to "the extremity of crime and willed evil."[64] Thus the duty to forgive as Arendt conceives of it is not a demand for a blanket moral or legal amnesty. It is narrower than that.

At the same time, Arendt never doubts that we have *permission* to forgive crime and willed evil. In law, crimes can be pardoned and sentences commuted; in interpersonal life, victims can and often do forgive those who have harmed them. Arendt emphasizes that "the act of forgiving can never be predicted"; it is "unconditioned by the act which provoked it."[65] Forgiveness is unpredictable and unconditioned because the victim has a choice whether to offer it.

So far, I think, her analysis makes sense (whether you agree with it or not).[66] However, she next asserts that it is "a structural element in the realm of human affairs, that men are unable to forgive what they cannot punish and that they are unable to punish what has turned out to be unforgivable."[67] This is a leap in logic, because neither clause of this proposition follows from the fact that punishment and forgiveness are alternative ways to close the books on misdeeds – and neither is obvious. After all, instead of claiming that an unforgivable crime cannot be punished, you might reasonably conclude that an unforgivable crime *must* be punished, for the very reason that it can't be forgiven. Arendt herself endorsed Grotius's argument that "punishment is necessary 'to defend the honor or the authority of him who was hurt by the offence so that the failure to punish may not cause his degradation.'"[68] On this "punishment is necessary" line of reasoning, the fact that forgiveness is unavailable doesn't negate the punishment alternative. It requires it.[69]

64 *HC*, 239. 65 *HC*, 241.

66 The ethics of forgiveness is a deep subject. It is a commonplace observation that crime victims often need to forgive their victimizers for the sake of their own serenity, to stop the crime from eating away at them; but forgiving too quickly or easily can show a lack of self-respect. See, for example, Jeffrie G. Murphy, *Getting Even: Forgiveness and Its Limits* (Oxford University Press, 2005); and, in the context of the Holocaust, Simon Wiesenthal, ed., *The Sunflower: On the Possibilities and Limits of Forgiveness*, revised ed. (Schocken, 1998). In *The Sunflower*, Wiesenthal asks whether he, a prisoner in a Nazi concentration camp, should have forgiven a dying and repentant SS man who begged him for forgiveness; the SS man had murdered 300 Jews in a single day. Fifty-three thinkers wrote answers to Wiesenthal's question; only a handful of them thought Wiesenthal should have forgiven the SS man. A crucial issue, which I cannot explore here, is whether anyone other than the victim has standing to forgive. If the answer is no, then murder is always unforgivable – a position held by many of the anti-forgiveness writers in *The Sunflower*.

67 *HC*, 241. 68 *EJ*, 287.

69 However, Arendt can be faulted for assuming that punishment and forgiveness are the only alternatives for obtaining closure. Others include truth commissions (as Jaspers suggested), reparations, reconciliation ceremonies, and what Jon Elster calls "disremembering" past wrongs for the sake of moving forward, as in post-Franco Spain. Elster, *Closing the Books*, 62.

Or rather, it requires it if your aim is to close the books. Apparently, Arendt thinks that the books can never be closed on the camps and gulags, the "ghastly experiment ... of transforming the human personality into a mere thing."[70] As she explains in her moral philosophy lectures, "there appears a distinction between transgressions, such as those we are confronted with daily and with which we know how to come to terms or how to get rid of either through punishment or through forgiveness, and those offenses where all we can say is 'This should never have happened.'"[71] These are the crimes she calls "radical evil."[72] In a scripture Arendt quotes several times, even Jesus says of some sinners, "It were better for him that a millstone were hanged about his neck, and he cast into the sea" (Luke 17:2) – a limit to Christian forgiveness.[73]

Perhaps we can agree that the Nazi crimes are impossible to come to terms with. But we still don't know why their perpetrators can't be punished. In her 1946 letter to Jaspers, quoted earlier, Arendt offers a simpler and more intuitive explanation than the oracular argument in *The Human Condition*: Punishment must fit the crime, and "[f]or these crimes, no punishment is severe enough." She adds: "That is the reason why the Nazis in Nuremberg are so smug."[74] In *Eichmann in Jerusalem*, she clarifies that it's the nature of the crimes (which "violated the order of mankind"), not the sheer numbers of victims, that makes it impossible for the punishment to fit the crime.[75]

The argument proves too much. After all, genocide and crimes against humanity are not the only crimes horrible enough that no morally acceptable punishment can truly fit them. The same can be said of mass shooters, serial rapists, torturers, and sadistic killers. It would be odd, and false, to say that they can't be punished because no punishment can ever fit their crimes – as Arendt herself admits.[76] The solution is to impose the maximum fair sentence the law allows, whatever that may be (allowing for possible mitigations). Whether that should be the death penalty, or life imprisonment, or some shorter term of years is an issue I won't try to address here. Arendt supported the death penalty for Eichmann, although she respectfully acknowledged that many people oppose the death penalty on principle.[77]

70 *OT*, 438. 71 SQMP, 109, 127.

72 *HC*, 241. This is the only place the phrase appears in *The Human Condition*. Written as it was prior to the Eichmann trial and her letter to Scholem discussed in §5.4, I assume that "radical evil" means the same as in *Origins*, where it refers to the "unforgivable absolute evil" of the gulags and death camps. *OT*, 459.

73 *HC*, 241; SQMP, 73–74, 109, 125. 74 Arendt to Jaspers, August 17, 1946, in *HA-KJ*, 54.

75 *EJ*, 272; also 250. 76 *EJ*, 250. 77 *EJ*, 252.

Significantly, Israel has no death penalty except for treason and genocide against the Jewish people – the crime of which Eichmann was convicted.

An important proviso is that the maximum penalty must itself be consistent with human dignity, a value of supreme importance to Arendt. As Hampton explains in an essay on the nature of retribution, respect for victims' equal human dignity demands punishment for crimes that violate it, just as Grotius and Arendt insist. But respect for human dignity likewise imposes humanitarian limits on modes of punishment.[78] Arendt believes that "the law presupposes precisely that we have a common humanity with those whom we accuse and judge and condemn."[79] That rules out the cruelty of the *lex talionis* ("an eye for an eye"), which, in Hampton's words, would degrade the wrongdoer "below the level of human beings generally" – but it does not rule out punishment.[80] And, by the time she wrote *Eichmann in Jerusalem*, Arendt explicitly abandoned her earlier argument that "for these crimes, no punishment is severe enough."[81]

In the end, we should reject Arendt's conclusion that Eichmann's crime is somehow beyond punishment, even if we agree that it is beyond forgiveness, and, indeed, beyond reckoning. That still leaves us the problem with which we began: How can Eichmann be punished if he lacks the subjective *mens rea* required for a crime?

## 15.8 Thoughtlessness as Culpable Ignorance

The answer, I suggest, has been with us all along: Eichmann's *mens rea* is his thoughtlessness coupled with his abdication of judgment. In other words, the guilty "subjective factor" lies in what is *absent* from Eichmann's mental life rather than what is present. Perhaps this seems counterintuitive, or even paradoxical – an assertion that nothing equals something, or that emptiness is fullness.

But we should remind ourselves that the point of the *mens rea* requirement in criminal law is to ground culpability, not to measure minds. The textbook mental states – purpose, intention, knowledge, recklessness, negligence – are surrogates for degrees and forms of blameworthiness. For example, we judge that doing something harmful purposely is worse than doing it negligently: As Holmes quipped, even a dog knows the

78 Jean Hampton, "The Retributive Idea," in Jean Hampton and Jeffrie G. Murphy, *Forgiveness and Mercy* (Cambridge University Press, 1988), 135–38.

79 *EJ*, 251–52. 80 Hampton, "The Retributive Idea," 136. 81 *EJ*, 250.

difference between being tripped over and being kicked. A surgeon may *know* that a triple bypass will cause the patient days of pain. What makes it blameless is that the pain is not her purpose or intention. In these examples, the crucial issue is culpability, not naming states of belief or desire. We name them because they roughly correlate with degrees of blameworthiness, not because they are objects of intrinsic legal interest.

In fact, the terminology of "subjective factors" is misleading, if we identify subjectivity with states of consciousness. *Mens rea* terms like "intention" and "knowledge" need not refer to occurrent mental states, the phrase "guilty mind" to the contrary. I *know* that 7 times 7 is 49 even when I am not doing mental arithmetic, and I can *intend* to go to the grocery store tomorrow without thinking about it today.[82]

The most illuminating analogy in existing law to thoughtlessness as culpability is the doctrine of "willful ignorance" (sometimes called "willful blindness" or "conscious avoidance"[83]). According to this doctrine, someone can be convicted of a crime with "knowingly" as its *mens rea* where they have deliberately screened themselves from guilty knowledge. A textbook example is the drug courier who deliberately avoids knowing what is in the package he has been hired to smuggle across the border, so that he can truthfully plead ignorance if he gets caught – the so-called ostrich defense.[84]

More significant in the context of Nazi crimes is Albert Speer's confession of how he shielded himself from knowledge that Auschwitz was a death and slave labor camp, after a friend warned him never to visit it. "I did not query him, I did not query Himmler, I did not query Hitler, I did not speak with personal friends, I did not investigate – for I did not want to know what was happening there." Speer, at any rate, understood that his ignorance was culpable: "From that moment on, I was inescapably contaminated morally; from fear of discovering something which might have made me turn from my course, I had closed my eyes."[85] (Of course, we will never know whether he really didn't know, nor whether knowing would have made him turn from his course. Speer was an accomplished liar.[86])

82 Ludwig Wittgenstein, *Zettel*, ed. G. E. M. Anscombe and G. H. von Wright, trans. G. E. M. Anscombe (University of California Press, 1967), 10, §44–47. Kenneth Simons, "Rethinking Mental States," *Boston University Law Review* 72(3) (1992): 529–35.

83 The name doesn't matter; one writer has identified fourteen different terms for the doctrine in US criminal law.

84 United States v. Jewell, 532 F.2d 697 (9th Cir. 1976).

85 Albert Speer, *Inside the Third Reich: Memoirs*, trans. Richard and Clara Winston (Simon & Schuster, 1970) 375–76.

86 Dan Van Der Vot, *The Good Nazi: The Life and Lies of Albert Speer* (Houghton Mifflin, 1997).

I bring up the doctrine of willful blindness because it is an example in existing criminal law and ethics where absence of subjective awareness can be just as culpable as its presence. And my claim, by analogy with willful blindness, is that thoughtlessness and abdication of judgment can be just as culpable as consciousness of wrongdoing. In her moral philosophy lectures, Arendt plainly recognized this; thus, her own moral philosophy supplies the missing *mens rea* whose absence she found so disturbing.

I mean these points to be general, but it is worth focusing for the moment on Eichmann in particular. Recall from Chapter 5 Mary McCarthy's objection to Arendt's remark that Eichmann was *incapable* of telling right from wrong; that would indicate "brain failure" for which he could scarcely be held accountable. Rather, "[o]ne cannot help feeling that this mental oblivion is *chosen*, by the heart or the moral will."[87] Although I agreed with McCarthy's objection to determinism, I also said that "chosen" is too strong a word: It suggests a moment of active decision, whereas my diagnosis is long-standing moral lassitude. Eichmann had habituated himself to thoughtlessness and abdication of judgment, the fatal combination McCarthy calls "mental oblivion." It had become second nature. Habits are seldom *chosen*, except in the attenuated sense that they solidify from acts or omissions that are voluntary at first but become less so the longer they are repeated. But neither are they something that just happens to us, as if they are caused by an outside force.

In willful blindness cases we can usefully distinguish two sets of acts: the underlying crime, and the actions or omissions by which perpetrators screen themselves from guilty knowledge.[88] Call the latter *screening actions* or *screening omissions* (like Speer's). Habitual thoughtlessness and refusal to judge were the screening omissions that made it "well-nigh impossible for Eichmann to know or to feel that he was doing wrong."[89] It was not *willful*, because drifting along is not willful. But mental oblivion is culpable nevertheless.

To see the difference, compare the habit-based diagnosis with Eichmann's self-description in *Götzen*, which, if it were truthful, would exhibit willful mental oblivion. He explained that he was in thrall to the

[87] McCarthy to Arendt, June 9, 1971, *BF*, 296–97.

[88] David Luban, "Contrived Ignorance," in *Legal Ethics and Human Dignity*, 222. I take the distinction from Holly Goldman, "Culpable Ignorance," *Philosophical Review* 92(4) (1983): 547. She uses the terms "unwitting wrongful acts" and "benighting acts."

[89] *EJ*, 276. Arendt's "well-nigh impossible" is a welcome hedge from her deterministic claim that he was *incapable* of telling right from wrong.

Nazi "gods," but even they could never penetrate his "inner self," his "soul" that would stand revealed in its final hour:

> I kept this as a private matter, over which only I could and wanted to decide. Here I did not let the gods get close, however much I had otherwise devoted myself to them.
>
> Here the parental upbringing and the inner bond to the values handed down from generation to generation were still too strong to give in to attempts to break in. Here I was stubborn.
>
> Stubborn like the new heavy tanks. . . . Stubborn like the courses of the new bomb squadrons that thundered unwaveringly across the Berlin sky.[90]

Apparently, Eichmann didn't realize how damning this confession is. He kept the gods from invading his conscience by locking it away. But a conscience locked away from the field of action is no conscience at all – and Eichmann's "Here I was stubborn" is a confession that he deliberately sealed off his soul from his conduct. That is not habitual thoughtlessness. That is willful blindness.

I bring up his startling confession in *Götzen* only to contrast its willful blindness with the habit-based diagnosis. Under that diagnosis, there were no definite moments when Eichmann screened himself from guilty knowledge, any more than there is a definite moment when repeated behavior congeals into habit. That makes it a poor fit with the recognized *mens rea* categories (purposely, knowingly, recklessly, negligently) that might be applied to the screening omissions.[91] But even if habitual indifference falls outside the textbook *mens rea* concepts, it fits squarely under the concept of culpable ignorance. And Arendt's discovery of the banality of evil implies that can be just as culpable as willful blindness to evil.

## 15.9 Mistake of Law?

Textbook cases of culpable ignorance involve willful blindness to *facts*. The drug courier doesn't want to know what is in the package, and Speer didn't want to know why his friend warned him never to visit Auschwitz (if you believe him). Eichmann's case was different. He knew the facts. His was culpable ignorance of right and wrong, and culpable ignorance of the law insofar as law and morality coincide, which in the case of mass atrocities they obviously do. The legal scholar Itamar Mann speculates that this might give Eichmann a "mistake of law" defense – a standard defense

[90] *Götzen*, 33 (88).

[91] The same is true of their doctrinal analogues in civil law systems.

when the accused person violates the law because they didn't know about it.[92] The defense exists in today's German and Israeli penal law (although neither codified it until well after Eichmann's trial, so it would have been unavailable to him).[93] In Germany, the defense is available if the mistake of law was "unavoidable"; in Israel, if it is "reasonably inevitable."[94]

That leaves us with the question of what makes a mistake of law unavoidable or reasonably inevitable – in Arendt's words, what makes it well-nigh impossible for someone to know they are doing wrong. Mann's concern is that immersion in a cultural context that is morally remote from the lawgiver's might make the mistake of law unavoidable. Take an extreme example: slavery in the ancient world. Cruelty to slaves was a recognized moral issue, but no well-to-do Roman questioned slavery itself, and even the most humane Roman man of letters would find it unintelligible that today's Rome Statute declares enslavement to be a crime against humanity. Transport Pliny and his slaves to modern Rome or The Hague, and his mistake of law would truly be inevitable.[95] Mann speculates that today's international criminal law may be just as foreign to the culture of some perpetrators, and perhaps that was true of Eichmann as well.[96]

Of course, genocide and crimes against humanity were not part of criminal law when Eichmann committed his crimes, and we've examined the circumstances that weakened his capacity to tell right from wrong. But we have also seen why failing to recognize the criminality of murder was anything but unavoidable. The pre-Nazi moral and legal order was not a foreign culture; he was born into it. Eichmann himself acknowledges the "parental upbringing and the inner bond to the values handed down from generation to generation." Whether or not they were locked away in his soul, as he claimed, they were hardly alien to him. He tells us that until 1937 he remained in a church that taught "Thou shalt not kill."[97] And the

92 Itamar Mann, "Eichmann's Mistake: The Problem of Thoughtlessness in International Criminal Law," *Canadian Journal of Jurisprudence* 33(1) (2020): 150–57. Article 32 of the Rome Statute provides that mistake of law can be a defense, but not against charges of genocide or crimes against humanity.

93 Ulfrid Neumann, "Mistake of Law," *Israel Law Review* 30(1/2) (1996): 207–13. Germany codified the defense in 1977, but it was introduced into German law in a 1952 court decision. Bundesgerichtshof [BGH][Federal Court of Justice], 18-03-1952 (1952) GSSt 2/51 (Lexetius.com/1952, 1). See Annemieke van Verseveld, *Mistake of Law: Excusing Perpetrators of International Crimes* (T.M.C. Asser Press, 2012), 27–33.

94 Germany: StGB [Strafgesetzbuch, Penal Code], §17. Israel, Penal Law 5737–1977, §34S.

95 "No one discussed the morality of buying and selling people. It was not a moral question." Finley Hooper, *Roman Realities* (Wayne State University Press, 1979), 423–24. The Rome example is mine, not Mann's.

96 Mann, "Eichmann's Mistake," 152.

97 *Götzen*, 34–37 (89–91).

laws of the normative state, however deformed they became, never went away. If he mistook the law, it was because his own thoughtlessness and refusal to judge made *Kadavergehorsam* the path of least resistance – especially because he was surrounded by millions of compatriots whose culpable credulousness drew them to accept racist conspiracy theories that defy common sense.

Admittedly, it is hard to believe that moral laziness, the habit of thoughtless deference to ersatz popes and gods, could motivate crimes like Eichmann's. As Arendt writes: "Therein lies the horror and, at the same time, the banality of evil."[98] If, in this chapter, I disagree with her that Eichmann lacked the *mens rea* needed to justify punishment, it is because I disagree that Eichmann's crimes "were not caused by human and humanly understandable motives."[99] Thoughtlessly giving over your judgment to the men in charge is all too human and humanly understandable. It is culpable ignorance of right and wrong.

[98] SQMP, 146. [99] SQMP, 146.

# *Conclusion*
## *Taking Stock*

I began and ended this book with *Eichmann in Jerusalem*, because it was Arendt's encounter with the Eichmann trial that turned her attention to moral philosophy and the theory of criminal law. The trial shook her. To readers like Scholem who found her Olympian, ironic tone infuriating, this was not apparent, but when she tells us that survivor testimony portrayed a world of "impenetrable, unfathomable darkness," it is not an Olympian ironist speaking. And when she calls the banality of evil "word-and-thought defying," we should take her dismay at face value.[1]

The trial drove Arendt to the *quaestio juris* of what entitled her to the concept *banality of evil.* It was not her only question, though. In *Men in Dark Times*, she writes that "even in the darkest of times we have the right to expect some illumination," which "may come less from theories and concepts than from the uncertain, flickering, and often weak light that some men and women, in their lives and works, will kindle under almost all circumstances."[2] The story of Anton Schmid was "like a sudden burst of light" that the courtroom spectators, including Arendt, met with reverential silence. Alongside the banality of evil, Arendt urgently desired to understand the steadfastness of good.

These are questions of moral psychology. Arendt's answers feature the concepts of *thinking*, *judging*, and *common sense*, and the catastrophic consequences of their absence. As for the normative core of her ethics, it lies in bedrock respect for human dignity, a relational concept she roots in the human conditions of plurality and natality.

A central contention of this book is that Arendt's ideas about moral judgment, and the thinking–judging connection, apply across many settings, not only the political emergencies that were her primary concern. "Banality of evil" is not only about Eichmann and his ilk, any more than moral decency is found only in heroes like Anton Schmid who put their

[1] *EJ*, 231, 252. [2] *MDT*, ix.

lives on the line. The need for thinking and judging applies in every setting where the conventional wisdom of those around us can no longer be trusted, because the prevailing culture has morally collapsed. Arendt focused on moral collapse in entire nations, but more local settings can also fall into darkness. It happens every day in businesses, in sports leagues, in law firms, in police forces, in military units, in city governments. It happens in families and social circles. It happens in online bubbles circulating lies, rumors, and conspiracy theories. The need to stop, to think, and to judge appears everywhere, in small matters as well as large.

And yet, as we've seen, Arendt was ambivalent about morality – never doubting moral decency, but always suspicious of "germ-proof moralism."[3] When Arendt says that invoking morality in everyday conduct is usually a fraud, and that morality is only for emergencies, I've argued that she underrates the scope and power of her own moral philosophy. This is one of three wrong turns I identified in Arendt's moral thought, all of them stemming from her allergy to moralizing. The second is her suspicion that morality puts handcuffs on action, and that "all morality fails as soon as we begin to act."[4] Because Arendt views action (in her special sense of the term) as essential to a meaningful human life, this would be a devastating critique if it were valid. But even on Arendt's terms it isn't valid, or so I have argued.[5] Action, she maintains, derives its meaning from the judgment of others: "[O]nly the *spectator*, never the actor, can know and understand whatever offers itself as a spectacle"[6] – and spectators will judge actions *morally*, not only by the criteria of fame, audacity, or "greatness."[7] Recognizing this intrinsic moral dimension of action resolves the curious Case of the Missing Morality. Her diary speculation that "all action is amoral per definitionem" cannot stand.[8]

The third wrong turn is Arendt's worry that concern with morality impels us to keep our hands squeaky clean, even when care for the public world urgently requires us to dirty them. Focusing on the second Socratic proposition, Arendt concludes that moral actors' chief concern is with their own inner harmony – "I couldn't live with myself if I did that." She worries that this desire for inner harmony comes at the expense of care for the world. But morality need not be self-centered. Faced with evil in the public world, some people will say, "I couldn't live with myself if I do

[3] PRUD, 36. [4] *DTB*, XXI.83 (January 1956), 557–58. [5] See §9.7. [6] *T*, 92.
[7] *HC*, 205. [8] *DTB*, Heft XXI, [83] (March 1955), 521.

nothing about it." These are the resisters of evil who allow "this planet to remain a fit place for human habitation."[9]

*

In Chapter 1, I observed that Arendt's inquiry into moral judgment touches on several more general philosophical problems. Here, in summary form, I sketch her answers to the four I identified, with a few further thoughts.

*The problem of incongruity between person and act.* What makes the banality of evil "word-and-thought-defying" is the immense gulf between the mediocrity of the doer and the monstrosity of the deed. Shouldn't monstrous deeds require a monstrous doer? Some philosophers, writing in the Aristotelian tradition, go so far as to define the excellence or contemptibility of deeds in terms of the virtues of the doer: A fine deed is the kind of deed a virtuous person characteristically performs, and a vicious deed is what vicious people characteristically do.[10] Eichmann, and the problem of incongruity he exemplifies, would be a living counterexample to any such definition.

As I noted in Chapter 1, the incongruity lessens if we regard good moral judgment as itself a crucial intellectual virtue that Eichmann lacked. That is Arendt's approach. The banal wrongdoer's disastrous inability to tell right from wrong is, on Arendt's diagnosis, grounded in culpable failure to think and judge for themself. She elaborates thinking through Kant's maxims of common understanding: thinking for yourself rather than going along with the crowd; "enlarged" thinking from the standpoint of others; and thinking consistently.[11] The first maxim requires courage, initiative, and epistemic vigilance; the second, sympathy and imagination; the third, honesty and open-mindedness. These mental activities are available to everyone, but following the maxims is a moral choice that requires an array of supporting virtues. To these, we can add the courage to judge in foggy circumstances and the courage to act on your judgment.

[9] *EJ*, 233, emphasis in original. In her lectures on moral philosophy, she makes clear that those who did *not* conform to Nazism are as much her topic as the Eichmanns of the world. Arendt, "Basic Moral Propositions," in *RJ*, 278n10.

[10] This is Rosalind Hursthouse's approach in her impressive *On Virtue Ethics* (Oxford University Press, 1999), 25–42, 49–62. She explains that by "characteristically" she means "acting in character." Hursthouse, *On Virtue Ethics*, 28.

[11] *CJ*, §40, Ak. 5:294. These are pathways to what Hursthouse calls "worldly wisdom," her account of what Aristotelian *phronēsis* requires. Rosalind Hursthouse, "Practical Wisdom: A Mundane Account," *Proceedings of the Aristotelian Society* 106 (2006): 285–309.

Of course, there is no need to put Arendt into any of the standard boxes of contemporary moral theory, including virtue ethics; certainly she never understood her writing in conventional academic terms.[12] I mention the virtues that support thinking and judging only to answer Arendt's question of what specific qualities distinguish those who manage to keep their moral footing even when those around them do not.

*The problem of principles and particulars.* For Arendt, moral choice turns on the noninferential judgment of particulars, not the application of moral rules. She warns that a morality of rules cultivates obedience, rather than reflection, as a supreme virtue. That can bring disaster when the conventional rules change for the worse, as they did in the Third Reich.[13]

What about general moral principles that aren't spelled out as specific rules?[14] To Arendt, these are "banisters," what we might call rules of thumb – handy summaries of conventional morality that can provide guidance across a broad range of settings, but not across all settings. Understood as rules of thumb, Arendt has no objection to moral principles, provided we recognize that they are starting points for thinking, not end points; that they are not commandments that must be obeyed; and that we must never use general principles to shield ourselves from the realities of a particular case.

Treating principles as rules of thumb recognizes that principles have exceptions, and it takes good judgment to discern whether an action falls under a principle or an exception. Consider, for example, the prohibition on lying. Kant derives it by showing that the contrary maxim, "Lying is permitted whenever it suits me," can't be elevated to a universal principle. If it were, it would defeat itself: A world in which everyone is allowed to lie whenever it suits them would be a world in which nobody could trust others to tell the truth – a world where the advantages of lying would disappear.

But what if we frame the maxim more narrowly, to recognize that it has exceptions? To take Kant's own extreme example, lying to a murderer regarding the whereabouts of his prey seems like the obviously right thing

[12] In *Eichmann in Jerusalem*, she never mentions virtue or the virtues apart from ironic comments about Eichmann's "virtue" of blind obedience, when she describes his self-vindications. Recall that she also rejected Kant's moral philosophy, and she never took utilitarianism seriously. See, for example, *TWB*, 303, *HC*, 172–73, 307–10.

[13] PRUD, 45.

[14] Recall from §9.5 that Arendt borrows from Montesquieu the idea that principles are "guiding criteria" by which actions are judged in the public realm. "Montesquieu's Revision of the Tradition," in *PP*, 65. Here I am using the term somewhat differently, to refer to general moral norms – what Kant calls "maxims" – as distinguished from specific moral rules.

to do, although Kant himself denies it.[15] The maxim "everyone is permitted to lie to deflect murderers from their prey" is not self-defeating. Lying to prevent murder won't undermine the overall practice of truth-telling.

With such counterexamples in mind, some commentators believe that Kant meant his test to apply only to maxims framed in their greatest generality. That's how moral principles should be framed; otherwise, it is too easy to cheat by building custom-tailored casuistic exceptions into them.

But it isn't cheating if exceptional circumstances are defining features of the act-description. In the murder example, condemning the misdirection as a lie without adding that it's a lie to prevent murder is a false and highly misleading abstraction. What distinguishes legitimate exceptions to principles from mere casuistic tricks is whether the exceptional facts are morally salient, as they are in Kant's murder example. Principles are incomplete unless they incorporate salient exceptions – and exceptions can't all be specified in advance. Recognizing them when they arise is a matter of judgment. Even if we reframe the issue as a conflict between the general principles "never lie" and "always save people from murder," we still need to judge which principle matters more.

Recall as well Holmes's dictum that general propositions do not decide concrete cases. The decision requires a "judgment or intuition more subtle than any articulate major premise" to supply the minor premise of the deduction. "More subtle" doesn't mean "harder to see" – it means only that the judgment is not itself a deduction from a major premise. Holmes's point – which is also Arendt's – is that applying principles turns on irreducibly particularist judgments.

In short, a purely principle-based, top-down form of moral reasoning is impossible without irreducible acts of judgment, in the sense Arendt sees as the heart of the moral life: moral perception of the weight and salience of particulars.

*The problem of judgment.* As framed in Chapter 1, a basic question is what entitles us to distinguish a faculty of judgment from other intellectual powers, especially from conceptual thinking (what Arendt calls "intellect" or "cognition"). Chapter 3 endorsed Kant's and Arendt's answer: that whereas conceptual thinking may be rule-governed, judging can't be, "because no rule is available for the *applications* of the rule."[16]

[15] Kant, "On a supposed right to lie from philanthropy," in *Kant: Practical Philosophy*, Ak. 8:426–27, 612–13.

[16] *T*, 69.

This is not to say that "judgment" names a single discrete capability. All taxonomies of human faculties, what Plato called "parts of the soul," are theoretical constructions, not facts of nature. Judging distances, judging poetry, and judging your friends' moods have little in common with each other; and none has much in common with judging which of two competing legal or moral principles matters the most in a dilemma. What makes them all instances of judgment are, first, that they are noninferential; second, that they are acquired through experience; and third, that there is no articulable formula or procedure for how to get any of them right. It's these functional properties that make each of them a power of judgment.

A more basic doubt may occur to readers, however: that Arendt's theory treats good judgment as a kind of magic superpower that generates right answers. To this, Arendt's answer is straightforward: She makes no claim that people with good judgment are infallible, or that their judgments are indubitable. That should be clear from her insistence that moral and political judgments are like Kantian judgments of beauty: Their truth cannot be proven; at best, the agreement of others can be wooed. Judgments are dubitable, and the judge's subjective certainty is never a trump card that silences all doubts. The fact that a judgment is noninferential – in the literal sense that we form it without reasoning our way to it – does not place it outside the space of reasons. Even perceptual judgments can be challenged, to which we can respond by citing reasons ("I was looking right at it and the light was good"). And these can be challenged in turn.

Fallibility means that acting on our judgments always carries moral risk. We must act nevertheless. Doing so exposes us to the spectator judgment of others. But spectator judgment is itself a form of action: Reacting is a species of acting, and judges can be judged. In fact, we often doubt the spectator judgments of others, and we criticize them if we find their verdicts on other people unfair. We declare them rash, or gullible, or biased, or dishonest, or uncharitable, or simply lousy judges. But this is our judgment, and it too can be judged. In the end, we never break out of the practices of judgment to an idealized View from Nowhere. C. S. Peirce famously defined truth as "the opinion which is fated to be ultimately agreed to by all who investigate."[17] Peirce was referring to the physical

[17] Charles S. Peirce, "How to Make Our Ideas Clear," *Popular Science Monthly* 12 (January 1878): 273.

sciences. In human affairs, Arendt believed, no opinion enjoys that happy fate.

*The problem of moral realism.* Does that mean she doubted that moral values are real and moral truths objective? At first one might think so. Arendt rejects a conception of conscience as "an authority that is above and beyond all merely human laws and rules," referring explicitly to the word of God and the light of reason.[18] She insists that ethics rests on conventions, and conventions change. And when she discusses the second Socratic proposition, she flirts with the idea that moral standards are entirely subjective – for reasons I criticized in §5.2.[19]

But Arendt also affirms the power of reason to "tell the will: this is good," even if reason can't command the will to seek the good.[20] That sounds like realism about the good. So does her insistence that "*Good* doesn't develop into *bad*, and *bad* doesn't develop into *good.* There I would be *adamant.*"[21] I agree with Deirdre Mahony that, insofar as Arendt had metaethical sympathies, they were realist.[22] It could hardly be otherwise for a writer who believed there is such a thing as "unforgivable absolute evil."[23] What Arendt objects to is not the reality of the good but the authoritarian claim that morality comes in the form of imperatives from divine authority or laws of reason.

At bottom, though, I think that Arendt is neither a metaethical realist nor an anti-realist. "Philosophical truth, when it enters the marketplace, changes its nature and becomes opinion."[24] Opinions are by nature disputable, and no procedure beyond wooing will settle disagreements. Lacking a procedure that is even remotely capable of settling disagreements, the reality or unreality of moral truths is irrelevant to human affairs.

Jeremy Waldron argues this same point compellingly in "The Irrelevance of Moral Objectivity."[25] Waldron contrasts morality with the natural and physical sciences, which have generally accepted methods for settling disagreements. He admits that there will often be scientific outliers who don't accept mainstream methods or results. Even so, it's undeniable that rigorously tested, replicated, and well-confirmed scientific findings attract general and often universal agreement, both about the findings and the methods of verifying them. By contrast, Waldron writes, "[a]mong

[18] *T*, 215; "Civil Disobedience," in *CR*, 65–67; "Collective Responsibility," in *RJ*, 152–53; *HC*, 246.
[19] SQMP, 110–11. [20] SQMP, 71.
[21] "Hannah Arendt on Hannah Arendt," *TWB*, 464, emphasis in original.
[22] Mahony, *Hannah Arendt's Ethics*, 143–48. [23] *OT*, 459. [24] TP, 238.
[25] Jeremy Waldron, "The Irrelevance of Moral Objectivity," in *Natural Law Theory: Contemporary Essays*, ed. Robert P. George (Oxford University Press, 1992), 172–76.

moralists, there is nothing remotely comparable."[26] People who disagree about the death penalty or abortion "share virtually nothing in the way of an epistemology or a method with which these disagreements might in principle be approached."[27] Lacking any method for securing agreement on contested moral issues, it simply doesn't matter whether moral truths are out there somewhere.

For this reason, the philosopher's certainty as he reenters the cave proclaiming moral truth will seem to its inhabitants like a sheer *ipse dixit*. Arendt goes so far as to call philosophical truth coercive.[28] In this, she would have agreed with Robert Nozick's complaint about philosophers' addiction to talk of "knockdown" arguments: "A philosophical argument is an attempt to get someone to believe something, whether he wants to believe it or not. A successful philosophical argument, a strong argument, *forces* someone to a belief."[29] Nozick objects, and so does Arendt. Coercion is not a method for settling disagreements, only for ending them.

Arendt admits that factual truth will often find itself in the same boat as philosophical truth: It is always open to the skeptic, the denier, and the conspiracy theorist to reject it as nothing more than somebody's opinion. Facts, too, are coercive, and those who feel cornered by the facts will often turn to "alternative" facts.[30] But, she responds hopefully, most lies eventually collapse of their own weight, and impartial institutions like the judiciary, the free press, and the academy can help to uphold factual truth against its deniers.[31]

In Chapter 7, we saw that Arendt was never interested in refuting epistemological skepticism; she was interested in understanding what drives us to it. I think the same is true about moral skepticism; in her view it calls for diagnosis, not refutations that will themselves enter the marketplace in the guise of opinion or coercion.

*

It isn't hard to see connections between Arendt's moral thought and her ideas about international law. Fundamental to both is a commitment to human dignity grounded relationally in "the paradoxical plurality of unique beings."[32] Each of us is a new beginning, born with the capacity to inscribe our actions in the storybook of mankind – a storybook that

26 Waldron, "The Irrelevance of Moral Objectivity," 174 (emphasis removed).
27 Waldron, "The Irrelevance of Moral Objectivity," 174.
28 TP, 239–40, 246.
29 Robert Nozick, *Philosophical Explanations* (Harvard University Press, 1981), 4, emphasis in original. Nozick's objection to coercive philosophy is moral; Arendt's is political.
30 TP, 243.
31 TP, 240–64.
32 *HC*, 176.

would be meaningless without an audience whose attentiveness confers human dignity on the author.[33] Sometimes Arendt uses the metaphor of a drama rather than a storybook, as when she writes: "The spectator, not the actor, holds the clue to the meaning of human affairs."[34] I've argued that one way spectators confer human dignity on the actors is by *judging* them.[35] For that reason, accountability for actions is inherent in the concept of action itself. To be outside the scope of accountability is to be bereft of human dignity.

Accountability may take place in the court of one's own conscience ("Fool, do not flatter!"); it may take place in the judgment of my peers, or of historians and chroniclers. It may take place in a court of law – her focus in *Eichmann in Jerusalem* and mine in the final chapters of this book.

The threat Arendt saw in totalitarianism is the annihilation of plurality in favor of a make-believe unanimity, maintained through ideology and terror. There can be no human dignity if individuals are nothing more than fungible tokens of their race or class, a mass of one million divided by a million. *Origins* called for a "new law on earth" that would guarantee human dignity against this threat, which the old law of sovereign states had failed to do.[36] The new law on earth would replace murderous tribalism with the "idea of humanity," international law's "sole regulating idea."[37] It would secure the right to have rights even for stateless persons. It would focus on sovereign responsibilities, not merely sovereign prerogatives. These would include cross-border responsibilities, which are critically important today, when militaries can annihilate distant populations in a matter of hours, where genocide is anything but unprecedented, and where environmental crises are beyond any state's ability to address on its own.[38]

And it would create international tribunals to call to account the perpetrators of crimes that concern all humanity. Criminal courts, in Arendt's view, are paradigmatic sites of spectator judgment, and in her thought spectator judgment bridges the gap between morality and law. Courts honor human dignity by treating defendants as human beings accountable for their deeds, not as cogs in a machine.

As we saw in Chapter 14, Arendt maintained that doing justice to defendants must be the sole purpose of criminal courts. She rejected all

[33] *HC*, 184. [34] *T*, 96. [35] *T*, 95. [36] *OT*, ix. [37] *OT*, 157.

[38] See Luban, "Responsibility to Humanity and Threats to Peace: An Essay on Sovereignty." Obviously, Arendt had no inkling of the impending climate crisis, but she wrote of the "rape of nature" (*PP*, 157) and of the power of modern technology to unleash "elemental" processes beyond our control (*HC*, 231). She was acutely aware of the threat of nuclear extinction (*PP*, 146–48). Dealing with these threats would be a primary task of the new law on earth.

other purposes – pedagogical and political aims, making a historical record, giving victims their day in court, reinforcing the rule of law by enacting it, or anything else ulterior to passing judgment on the accused. At best, she regarded these as collateral benefits of criminal trials; at worst, they delegitimize the trials. I criticized her purism, because Arendt's own concerns should have led her to embrace the expressive and history-preserving aims of international trials. Here, I think, the tight analogy she saw between criminal accountability and other forms of spectator judgment led her astray. Arendt's purism came from regarding courts as official counterparts of individuals judging the conduct of others, without considering them as complex practical institutions.

Even so, her contributions to the theory of international criminal justice are impressive. She offered a deep analysis of what makes the crime of genocide an attack on the human status itself. She recognized that criminal states explode the assumptions underlying classical international law.[39] Among these assumptions is the *par in parem* justification of sovereign immunity in the courts of other states. As I argued in §11.3, her critique of immunity can readily be extended to noncriminal states when they commit core international crimes as a matter of policy. Although this *jus cogens* exception to immunity is not yet encoded in international law, it should be – and Arendt tells us the reason why. Above all, Arendt recognized that some crimes are matters of international concern, which rightly deserve the title "crimes against humanity" in a literal rather than legal sense.

Arendt also wrestled with question of how Eichmann and his ilk can justly be punished if they lack *mens rea*, because they commit their crimes under circumstances that make it "well-nigh impossible" to recognize that what they are doing is wrong.[40] This is the legal problem posed by the banality of evil, and it haunts the project of international criminal justice to this day. Ultimately, Arendt failed to solve the problem – but her moral philosophy holds the germ of the solution, even if she failed to draw the connection. Thoughtlessly accepting that mass murder is legitimate self-defense is *culpable credulousness*. That, together with the failure to think and the refusal to judge, qualifies as *mens rea*, once we remember that *mens rea* is a measure of culpability, not a gradation of mental states.

The banality of evil poses the question of *mens rea*. The banality of evil answers it.

[39] See Douglas, *The Criminal State*. [40] *EJ*, 276.

# *Epilogue*
## *"The Impact of Reality and the Shock of Experience"*

During the years I was writing this book, its connection with today's crisis-filled world was always on my mind, as readers will surely have noticed. I nevertheless decided not to focus on current events – a strategy I stuck to with a few obvious exceptions. This is a philosophical book about morality and law, not a book on Arendt's contemporary relevance. I trusted, and trust, that readers will draw their own connections as they see fit.

Nor did I want to bind the book to the Third Reich – the focal period for Arendt's reflections on morality – or to the present moment. Arendt warns that historical analogies can dull us to "the impact of reality and the shock of experience."[1] And, after all, Arendt's themes of human judgment, responsibility, and accountability are philosophical perennials; the same is true of the issues explored in Chapters 7, 8, and 9.

Furthermore, one of my conclusions is that Arendt's exclusive focus on "emergency ethics" sells her own ideas short, because they apply throughout our moral life, not only to crises when "the time is out of joint."[2]

But the time *is* out of joint. Many countries, including my own, are witnessing a slide toward autocracy and tribal nationalism that in more than one way echoes the early months of the Third Reich, which Arendt identified as the turning point when Germans' moral judgment began to collapse on a mass scale. To ignore those echoes would be an evasion. Although in Chapter 1 I warned against facile Nazi analogies, what makes those analogies overblown and offensive is the hint of equivalence between today's events and the horrors of the Nazi dictatorship, the war, and the Holocaust. But Arendt's essays on morality focus on the opening months of the Nazi regime, before the dictatorship fully consolidated. Exploring that analogy sharpens rather than dulls the shock of experience – so long as we see the disanalogies as well, and remind ourselves that the descent into horror was not and is not inevitable.

[1] *OT*, xxvi. [2] Arendt quotes this phrase from *Hamlet* in PRUD, 28.

I will focus on my own country. Since taking office on January 20, 2025, Donald Trump has launched a blitzkrieg against liberal values and the institutions sustaining them, aiming to refashion the government on principles of unchecked presidential power and personal fealty to the leader. The program includes systematically dismantling institutional guardrails and attacking countervailing centers of authority: the press, the universities, cultural institutions, the independent bar and judiciary, and the career civil service. We've seen similar strategies in other backsliding democracies.

Whereas the Nazis' April Law purged non-Aryans and political opponents from the civil service, Trump targeted the imaginary menace of "diversity, equity, and inclusion" and the Deep State. J. D. Vance's advice to Trump was: "Fire every single midlevel bureaucrat, every civil servant in the administrative state, replace them with our people."[3] The Nazis called this strategy "coordinating" the civil service, and coordination was central to their consolidation of power. In both regimes, a torrent of lies and conspiracy theories cascaded from their leaders and propagandists, and Trump pronounced on social media that "He who saves his Country does not violate any Law" – the premise that granted Hitler dictatorial power to build a prerogative state.[4] None of this is the hard terror of the SA and Gestapo, although immigrants tackled, shackled, detained and deported might beg to differ. Instead, call it *soft terror*: threats to livelihood and reputation, coupled with more frightening online threats from the mob.[5] Both regimes invoked fake emergencies in order to deploy prerogative executive powers, and both rolled back the civil rights of minorities. Both have an open contempt for law when it thwarts the leader's will.

Now for the disanalogies. Obviously, the United States in 2025 is utterly different from Germany in 1933. We haven't lost a war that killed two million of our men and devastated our economy; nor have we suffered the perceived humiliations of Versailles. We haven't experienced political revolution and street fighting, hyperinflation, or the Great Depression. We are not an ethno-state, nor a one-party state. Our democracy is centuries old,

[3] Andrew Prokop, "J. D. Vance's Radical Plan to Build a Government of Trump Loyalists," *Vox*, July 18, 2024.

[4] Maggie Haberman, Charlie Savage, and Jonathan Swan, "Trump Suggests No Laws Are Broken if He's 'Saving His Country'," *New York Times*, February 15, 2025.

[5] There are intimations of hard terror as well. A Democratic congressman reports that some of his Republican colleagues go along with Trump, not out of fear for their jobs, but because of threats of violence to their families. Elizabeth Bumiller, "'People Are Going Silent': Fearing Retribution, Trump Critics Muzzle Themselves," *New York Times*, March 6, 2025.

whereas Germany knew parliamentary democracy for fewer than fifteen unstable years. The political goals are different, too. Hitler wanted to capture and inflate a powerful bureaucracy rather than capture and decimate it.

Even so, the pattern I've just described lands us in a situation not far from what Arendt witnessed in 1933: a moment of autocratic menace where the future is obscure and individuals face moral choices with nothing but their own judgment to guide them. Many Germans chose to jump on the bandwagon. Some pretended that nothing was amiss. Others refused to participate in "coordination," even if it meant leaving a job or quitting a favorite club – and Arendt clearly thought the latter had made the right choice.[6]

Some universities, law firms, and press organizations have surrendered in the face of presidential threats; others obeyed preemptively, even before the threats. Others resisted. When Trump officials ordered federal prosecutors to drop corruption charges against New York City's mayor in return for political favors, top prosecutors – political conservatives – resigned in protest. One wrote to his superior, "I expect you will eventually find someone who is enough of a fool, or enough of a coward, to file your motion. But it was never going to be me."[7] That was a moral choice. Another, who was neither a fool nor a coward, signed solely to save the jobs of his colleagues.[8] That was a moral choice of a different kind: sacrificing his own integrity to spare his colleagues from the excruciating decision of whether to sacrifice theirs. Matters are never simple when resistance endangers the careers or lives of others.

Officials facing these hard choices must make morally risky judgment calls about how drastic the situation is, how real the practical prospects of resistance on the job are, and where to draw the line. Arendt insisted that obedience is support, and that those who think they are doing lesser evils by staying in their government jobs swiftly forget that lesser evils are evils nevertheless. Her concern about staying on was that it is too easy to normalize the abnormal, taking cues from those around us who may be taking their cues from us, until our willingness to think and judge for ourselves goes numb. Recall Helmuth James von Moltke's bitter description of his compliant fellow officials: "They are like chameleons: in a healthy society they look healthy, in a sick one, like ours, they look sick. And they are neither one nor the other. They are mere filler."[9]

[6] PRUD, 46–47.

[7] Resignation letter of Hagan Scotten, Assistant United States Attorney, February 14, 2025.

[8] Devlin Barrett, Glenn Thrush, and Adam Goldman, "Under Pressure to Drop Charges, Career Prosecutors Weighed Stark Options," *New York Times*, February 14, 2025.

[9] Helmuth James von Moltke to Freya von Moltke, November 8, 1941, *Letters to Freya*, 179–80.

The other side of the dilemma is that lesser evils may be evil, but they are lesser nonetheless. Moltke himself stayed on the job as a lawyer in military intelligence during the war – and by doing so he was able to save lives. The decision whether to stay or resign must be based on a realistic assessment of whether officials are likely to have maneuvering room to mitigate the evils of autocracy. If so, they should stay on the job and resist as best they can; if not, resignation sends up a warning flare that all is not okay. Quite possibly, Arendt would agree, notwithstanding her warning about "lesser evilism." After all, she criticized moralists whose chief concern is keeping their hands clean even at the cost of resisting evil.[10]

The concern about normalization pervades Arendt's reflections in "Personal Responsibility under Dictatorship" and "Some Questions of Moral Philosophy." During the period of coordination in 1933, too many Germans accommodated themselves to a regime they didn't necessarily support. Some fooled themselves into thinking that the leader's most extreme threats were mere bluster. Others, as Arendt wrote contemptuously, were driven by "early eagerness not to miss the train of History." She was especially repelled by "the matter-of-course collaboration from all strata of German society, including the older elites which the Nazis left untouched, and who never identified themselves with the party in power."[11] Meanwhile, the leader's base cheered him on, out of strongman worship, culpable credulousness, and reckless indifference to consequences. The Nazis promised Germans national greatness, and they attracted many waverers by the sheer thrill of high-velocity change driven by a powerful leader. But ultimately Hitler could never have succeeded relying only on his base. He succeeded because politically indifferent citizens were prepared to abdicate judgment and pretend that nothing untoward was going on.[12]

As I write the epilogue in December 2025, all this feels too close, and it makes Arendt's ethics especially urgent. In response, Arendt tells us to pause. To think for ourselves. To think from the point of view of others. To reject lies. To judge. And, in her paraphrase of Hamlet, to "set the time aright," as best we are able.

[10] So I have argued in "Complicity and Lesser Evils: A Tale of Two Lawyers." There, I examine the career of von Moltke, but also the strange case of Bernhard Lösener, a lawyer with Nazi convictions who was the specialist on Jewish matters in the Interior Ministry – but who nevertheless worked within the Ministry to spare Jews from persecution.

[11] PRUD, 24; SQMP, 53.

[12] Fritzsche, *Hitler's First Hundred Days: When Germans Embraced the Third Reich.*

# *Bibliography*

## Works by Hannah Arendt


Arendt, Hannah. "Answers to Questions Posed by Samuel Grafton." In *The Jewish Writings*, edited by Jerome Kohn and Ron H. Feldman. New York: Schocken, 2007.

*Between Past and Future: Eight Exercises in Political Thought*. New York: Viking, 1968.

*Crises of the Republic*. New York: Harcourt Brace, 1972.

*Denktagebuch 1950–1973*. Edited by Ursula Ludz and Ingeborg Nordmann. Munich/Berlin: Piper Verlag, 2002.

*Eichmann in Jerusalem: A Report on the Banality of Evil*. Revised and enlarged ed. New York: Viking, 1965.

*Elemente und Ursprünge totaler Herrschaft*. Munich: Piper Verlag, 2023. (German translation of *The Origins of Totalitarianism*.)

Entry "VOGELFREI – Friedlos – Outlawry" and "Excommunication." Library of Congress, Hannah Arendt Papers: Speeches and Writings File, 1923–1975; Excerpts and Notes; Minority Statelessness. www.loc.gov/resource/mss11056dig.053020/?st=pdf&pdfPage=18, 26245.

*Essays in Understanding 1930–1954*. Edited by Jerome Kohn. New York: Harcourt Brace, 1994.

*Hannah Arendt–Karl Jaspers Correspondence 1926–1969*. Edited by Lotte Kohler and Hans Saner, translated by Robert and Rita Kimber. New York: Mariner Books, 1992.

*Hannah Arendt: The Last Interview and Other Conversations*. Brooklyn, NY: Melville House: 2013.

*The Human Condition*. Chicago: University of Chicago Press, 1958.

*The Jewish Writings*. Edited by Jerome Kohn and Ron H. Feldman. New York: Schocken Books, 2007.

Letter from Arendt to Robert M. Hutchins, January 27, 1957. Library of Congress, Hannah Arendt Papers: Correspondence, 1938–1976; Organizations, 1943–1976; Fund for the Republic, 1956–1965. www.loc.gov/resource/mss11056dig.022110/?sp=24&st=pdf&r=-0.235%2C0.497%2C1.469%2C1.469%2C0&pdfPage=25, 12581.

*Lectures on Kant's Political Philosophy.* Edited by Ronald Beiner. Chicago: University of Chicago Press, 1982.

*The Life of the Mind: One-Volume Edition.* Edited by Mary McCarthy. New York: Harcourt Brace, 1978.

*Love and Saint Augustine.* Edited by Joanna Vecchiarelli Scott and Judith Chelius Stark, translated by E. G. Ashton. Chicago: University of Chicago Press, 1995.

*Men in Dark Times.* New York: Harcourt Brace, 1968.

*The Origins of Totalitarianism.* 2nd ed. with added prefaces. New York: Harcourt, 1951.

*The Promise of Politics.* Edited by Jerome Kohn. New York: Schocken, 2005.

*Rahel Varnhagen: The Life of a Jewish Woman.* Translated by Clara Winston and Richard Winston. New York: NYRB Classics, 2022.

*Responsibility and Judgment.* Edited by Jerome Kohn. New York: Schocken Books, 2003.

*On Revolution.* New York: Viking Press, 1965.

"The 'Rights of Man': What Are They?" *Modern Review* (Summer 1949): 24–37.

"Statelessness" lecture notes. Library of Congress, Hannah Arendt Papers: Speeches and Writings File, 1923–1975; Essays and Lectures, April 22, 1955. www.loc.gov/resource/mss11056dig.052290/?st=pdf&pdfPage=5.

*Thinking.* Part one of *The Life of the Mind.*

*Thinking without a Banister: Essays in Understanding 1953–1975.* Edited by Jerome Kohn. New York: Schocken, 2018.

*Vita Activa oder Vom tätigen Leben.* Munich: Piper Verlag, 1967. (German translation of *The Human Condition.*)

*Willing.* Part two of *The Life of the Mind.*

Arendt, Hannah and Heinrich Blücher. *Within Four Walls: The Correspondence between Hannah Arendt and Heinrich Blücher 1936–1968.* Edited by Lotte Kohler, translated by Peter Constantine. New York: Harcourt, 1996.

Arendt, Hannah and Kurt Blumenfeld. "*... in keinem Besitz verwurzelt": Die Korrespondenz.* Edited by Ingeborg Nordmann and Iris Pilling. Hamburg: Rotbuch Verlag, 1995.

Arendt, Hannah and Martin Heidegger. *Letters 1925–1975.* Edited by Ursula Ludz, translated by Andrew Shields. New York: Harcourt, 2004.

Arendt, Hannah and Karl Jaspers. *Correspondence 1926–1969.* Edited by Lotte Kohler and Hans Saner and translated by Robert Kimber and Rita Kimber. New York: Harcourt Brace, 1992.

Arendt, Hannah and Mary McCarthy. *Between Friends: The Correspondence of Hannah Arendt and Mary McCarthy 1949–1975.* Edited by Carol Brightman. New York: Harcourt Brace, 1995.

Arendt, Hannah and Gershom Scholem. *The Correspondence of Hannah Arendt and Gershom Scholem.* Edited by Luise Knott and translated by Anthony David. Chicago: University of Chicago Press, 2017.

## Other Works.


Abramson, Dustin et al., "Cryptocurrency System Using Body Activity Data." https://patents.google.com/patent/WO2020060606A1/en.

Aderet, Ofer. "An Israeli Suspected of Nazi Collaboration Was Murdered: What Is Israel Hiding?" *Ha'aretz*, March 21, 2021. www.haaretz.com/israel-news/.premium-what-is-israel-hiding-on-murder-of-israeli-suspected-of-nazi-collaboration-1.9635171.

Adkins, A. W. H. *Merit and Responsibility: A Study of Greek Values.* Oxford: Oxford University Press, 1960.

Adorno, Theodor W., with the assistance of George Simpson. "On Popular Music." *Studies in Philosophy and Social Science*, New York: Institute of Social Research, 1941.

Allais, Lucy. "Restorative Justice, Retributive Justice, and the South African Truth and Reconciliation Commission." *Philosophy & Public Affairs* 39(4) (2011): 331–63.

Allen, William Sheridan. *The Nazi Seizure of Power in a Small Town: The Experience of a Single German Town 1930–1935*. New York: New Viewpoints, 1973.

Anderl, Gabriele. *9096 Leben: Der unbekannte Judenretter Berthold Storfer.* Berlin: Rotbuch Verlag, 2012.

Applebaum, Anne. "Why We Should Read Hannah Arendt Now." *The Atlantic*, March 17, 2022. www.theatlantic.com/books/archive/2022/03/arendt-origins-of-totalitarianism-ukraine/627081/.

Aristotle. *The Complete Works of Aristotle: The Revised Oxford Translation* (two volumes). Edited by Jonathan Barnes. Princeton, NJ: Princeton University Press, 1984.

*Nicomachaean Ethics.* Translated by Terence Irwin. Indianapolis: Hackett, 1999.

*Politics.* In *The Complete Works of Aristotle*, volume 2. Translated by B. Jowett.

*On Sleep (De Somno et Vigilia).* In *The Complete Works of Aristotle*, volume 1. Translated by J. I. Beare.

*On the Soul (De Anima).* In *The Complete Works of Aristotle*, volume 1. Translated by J. A. Smith.

*Sense and Sensibilia (De Sensu).* In *The Complete Works of Aristotle*, volume 1. Translated by J. I. Beare.

Augustine. *The City of God against the Pagans.* Edited and translated by R. W. Dyson. Cambridge: Cambridge University Press, 1998.

Baehr, Jason. "Epistemic Malevolence," *Metaphilosophy* 41 (2010): 189–213, reprinted in Heather Battaly, ed., *Virtue and Vice: Epistemic and Moral.* Oxford: Blackwell, 2010.

Baier, Annette. *Postures of the Mind.* Minneapolis: University of Minnesota Press, 1985.

Baldwin, Peter. "Social Interpretations of Nazism: Renewing a Tradition." *Journal of Contemporary History* 25(1) (1990): 5–37.

Barnes, Julian, *The Noise of Time.* New York: Knopf, 2016.
Barrett, Devlin, et al. "Under Pressure to Drop Charges, Career Prosecutors Weighed Stark Options," *New York Times*, February 14, 2025.
Bass, Gary J. *Judgment at Tokyo: World War II on Trial and the Making of Modern Asia.* New York: Picador, 2023.
Bauer, Yehuda. *Jews for Sale? Nazi–Jewish Negotiations, 1933–1945.* New Haven, CT: Yale University Press, 1994.
Beiner, Ronald. *Judgment, Imagination, and Politics*. Lanham, MD: Rowman & Littlefield, 2001.
"Interpretive Essay." In Arendt, *Lectures on Kant's Political Philosophy*, edited by Ronald Beiner. Chicago: University of Chicago Press, 1982.
*Political Judgment.* Chicago: University of Chicago Press, 1983.
Benhabib, Seyla. "International Law and Human Plurality in the Shadow of Totalitarianism: Hannah Arendt and Raphael Lemkin." In *Hannah Arendt and the Law*, edited by Marco Goldoni and Christopher McCorkindale. Oxford: Hart, 2012.
*The Reluctant Modernism of Hannah Arendt.* 2nd ed. Lanham, MD: Rowman & Littlefield, 2000.
Bennhold, Katrin. "QAnon Is Thriving in Germany; The Extreme Right Is Delighted." *New York Times*, October 11, 2020.
Benvenisti, Eyal. "Sovereigns as Trustees of Humanity: On the Accountability of States to Foreign Stakeholders." *American Journal of International Law* 107(2) (2013): 295–333.
Bergsmo, Morten, ed. *Thematic Prosecution of International Sex Crimes.* Beijing: Torkel Opsahl Academic EPublisher, 2012.
Berkowitz, Roger. "Yes and No: The Split the Difference Interpretation of the Banality of Evil." *Amor Mundi* (weekly publication of Hannah Arendt Center for Politics and Humanities), May 31, 2013, https://hac.bard.edu/amor-mundi/yes-and-no-the-split-the-difference-approach-to-the-banality-of-evil-2013-05-31 [https://perma.cc/2U9B-YK7N].
Bernstein, Richard J. *Hannah Arendt and the Jewish Question.* Cambridge: MIT Press, 1996.
Bessel, Richard. "Functionalists vs. Intentionalists: The Debate Twenty Years on or What Has Happened to Functionalism and Intentionalism?" *German Studies Review* 26(1) (2003): 15–20.
Betts, Alexander. *The Wealth of Refugees: How Displaced Persons Can Build Economies.* Oxford: Oxford University Press, 2021.
Bill & Melinda Gates Foundation Pressroom. "Bill & Melinda Gates Foundation Dedicates Additional Funding to the Novel Coronavirus Response." www.gatesfoundation.org/Media-Center/Press-Releases/2020/02/Bill-and-Melinda-Gates-Foundation-Dedicates-Additional-Funding-to-the-Novel-Coronavirus-Response.
Bilsky, Leora. "The Eichmann Trial and the Legacy of Jurisdiction." In *Politics in Dark Times: Encounters with Hannah Arendt*, edited by Seyla Benhabib, with

Roy Tsao and Peter J. Verovšek. Cambridge: Cambridge University Press, 2010.

Bogdanich, Walt and Michael Forsythe. "McKinsey Proposed Paying Pharmacy Companies Rebates for OxyContin Overdoses." *New York Times*, November 28, 2020.

Bogdanor, Paul. *Kasztner's Crime*. New York: Routledge, 2016.

Brandom, Robert. *Articulating Reasons: An Introduction to Inferentialism*. Cambridge, MA: Harvard University Press, 2000.

*Making It Explicit: Reasoning, Representing, and Discursive Commitment*. Cambridge, MA: Harvard University Press, 1994.

*Reason in Philosophy: Animating Ideas*. Cambridge, MA: Harvard University Press, 2009.

*Tales of the Mighty Dead: Historical Essays in the Metaphysics of Intentionality*. Cambridge, MA: Harvard University Press, 2002.

Brazil, Rachel. "Fighting Flat-Earth Theory." *Physics World*, July 14, 2020. https://physicsworld.com/a/fighting-flat-earth-theory/.

Broch, Hermann. *Dichten und Erkennen: Essays I*. Edited and with an introduction by Hannah Arendt, in Broch's *Gesammelte Werke*, volume 6. Zürich: Rein, 1955.

*Geist and Zeitgeist: The Spirit in an Unspiritual Age*. New York: Counterpoint, 2003.

Bronsteen, John, Christopher Buccafusco, and Jonathan S. Masur. "Wellbeing as Happiness." *Georgetown Law Journal* 98 (2010). (Also a chapter in *Happiness and the Law*. Chicago: University of Chicago Press, 2014.).

Brownfield, Allen C. "The Danger Ignorance of History Poses to a Free Society." American Council of Trustees and Alumni, April 22, 2018. www.goacta.org/news-item/the-danger-ignorance-of-history-poses-to-the-future-of-a-free-society/.

Browning, Christopher. *Ordinary Men: Reserve Police Battalion 101 and the Final Solution in Poland*. New York: HarperCollins, 1992.

Brunner, José. "Eichmann's Mind: Psychological, Philosophical, and Legal Perspectives." *Theoretical Inquiries in Law* 1(2) (2000): 429–64.

Buckley, Cara. "Man Is Rescued by Stranger on Subway Tracks." *New York Times*, January 3, 2007.

Bumiller, Elizabeth. "'People Are Going Silent': Fearing Retribution, Trump Critics Muzzle Themselves," *New York Times*, March 6, 2025.

Burns, Robert P. *A Theory of the Trial*. Princeton, NJ: Princeton University Press, 2001.

Butler, Judith. *Notes toward a Performative Theory of Assembly*. Cambridge, MA: Harvard University Press, 2015.

Camus, Albert. "The Myth of Sisyphus." In *The Myth of Sisyphus and Other Essays*, translated by Justin O'Brien. New York: Vintage, 1991.

Canovan, Margaret. *Hannah Arendt: A Reinterpretation of Her Political Thought*. Cambridge: Cambridge University Press, 1992.

Card, Claudia. *Confronting Evils: Terrorism, Torture, Genocide.* Cambridge: Cambridge University Press, 2010.

"Genocide and Social Death." *Hypatia: A Journal of Feminist Philosophy* 18(1) (2003): 63–79.

Carroll, Lewis. "What the Tortoise Said to Achilles." *Mind* 4(14) (1895): 278–80.

Cassam, Quassim. *Conspiracy Theories.* Medford, MA: Polity Press, 2019.

*Vices of the Mind: From the Intellectual to the Political.* Oxford: Oxford University Press, 2019.

Cesarani, David. *Becoming Eichmann: Rethinking the Life, Times, and Trial of a "Desk Murderer."* Cambridge, MA: Da Capo Press: 2004.

Chidester, David. *Authentic Fakes: Religion and American Popular Culture.* Berkeley: University of California Press, 2005.

Ciralsky, Adam. "Documenting Evil: Inside Assad's Hospitals of Horror." *Vanity Fair*, June 11, 2015.

Civiqs, "QAnon Support: Registered Voters," September 10, 2020–October 11, 2020. https://civiqs.com/results/qanon_support?uncertainty=true&annotations=true&zoomIn=tr.

Combs, Nancy Armoury. *Fact-Finding without Facts: The Uncertain Evidentiary Foundations of International Criminal Convictions.* Cambridge and New York: Cambridge University Press, 2010.

"Grave Crimes and Weak Evidence: A Fact-Finding Evolution in International Criminal Law." *Harvard Journal of International Law* 58(1) (2017): 47–125.

Confino, Alon. *A World without Jews: The Nazi Imagination from Persecution to Genocide.* New Haven, CT: Yale University Press, 2014.

Crawford, James. *The Creation of States in International Law.* Oxford: Clarendon Press, 2006.

Criddle, Evan J., and Evan Fox-Decent, *Fiduciaries of Humanity: How International Law Constitutes Authority.* Oxford University Press, 2016.

Dale, Daniel. "It's Easy to Fact-Check Trump's Lies: He Tells the Same Ones All the Time." *Washington Post*, November 16, 2018.

DeGooyer, Stephanie, et al. *The Right to Have Rights.* London: Verso, 2018.

Dinstein, Yoram. "*Par in parem non habet imperium.*" *Israel Law Review* 1 (1966): 407–20.

Dobe, Jennifer Kirchmeyer. "Kant's Common Sense and the Strategy for a Deduction." *Journal of Aesthetics and Art Criticism* 68(1) (2010): 47–60.

Docker, John. "Raphael Lemkin's History of Genocide and Colonialism." Paper for the United States Holocaust Museum, Center for Advanced Holocaust Studies, February 26, 2004. www.ushmm.org/m/pdfs/20040316-docker-lemkin.pdf.

Douglas, Lawrence. *The Criminal State: War, Atrocity and the Dream of International Justice.* Princeton, NJ: Princeton University Press, 2026.

"History and Memory in the Courtroom: Reflections on Perpetrator Trials." In *The Nuremberg Trials International Criminal Law Since 1945/Die Nürnberger Prozesse Völkerstrafrecht seit 1945*, edited by Herbert Reginbogin and Christoph Safferling. Munich: K. G. Sauer Verlarg: 2006.

*The Memory of Judgment: Making Law and History in the Trials of the Holocaust.* New Haven, CT: Yale University Press, 2001.

Drumbl, Mark. *Atrocity, Punishment, and International Law.* Cambridge: Cambridge University Press, 2007.

Duff, R. A. "Authority and Responsibility in International Criminal Law." In *The Philosophy of International Law*, edited by Samantha Besson and John Tasioulas. Oxford: Oxford University Press, 2010.

"Crimes against Humanity and *Hostes Generis Humani.*" *Netherlands Journal of Legal Philosophy* 47(2) (2018): 138–48.

*Trials and Punishments.* Cambridge University Press, 1986.

Earl, Hilary. "Prosecuting Genocide before the Genocide Convention: Raphael Lemkin and the Nuremberg Trials, 1945–1949." *Journal of Genocide Research* 15 (2013): 322–25.

Edelstein, Dan. *The Terror of Natural Right: Republicanism, the Cult of Nature, and the French Revolution.* Chicago: University of Chicago Press, 2009.

Eichmann, Adolf. "Eichmann Tells His Own Damning Story." Part 1, *Life*, November 28, 1960. https://books.google.co.il/books?id=oUoEAAAAMBAJ&printsec=frontcover&source=gbs_ge_summary_r&hl=en#v=onepage&q&f=false.

"Eichmann's Own Story: Part II: 'To Sum It All Up, I Regret Nothing'." *Life*, December 5, 1960. https://books.google.com/books?id=900EAAAAMBAJ&printsec=frontcover&dq=life+5+dec+1960&hl=en&sa=X&ei=8UxeVZ_CDcnAtQXuhIDgBw&ved=0CCcQ6AEwAA#v=onepage&q=life%205%20dec%201960&f=false.

*Götzen: Die Autobiografie von Adolf Eichmann.* Edited and annotated by Raphael Ben Nescher. Berlin: Metropol Verlag, 2016. Online version, www.schoah.org/shoah/eichmann/goetzen.htm.

*Eichmann Interrogated: Transcripts from the Archives of the Israeli Police.* Edited by Jochen von Lang with Claus Sibyll and translated by Ralph Manheim. New York: Farrar, Straus & Giroux, 1983.

Elon, Amos. "The Case of Hannah Arendt." *New York Review of Books*, November 6, 1997.

Elster, Jon. *Closing the Books: Transitional Justice in Historical Perspective.* Cambridge: Cambridge University Press, 2004.

Euronews. "'It's Cultural Genocide': Ukraine's Culture Minister Trying to Salvage the Country's Artifacts." September 13, 2022. www.euronews.com/culture/2022/09/13/its-cultural-genocide-ukraines-culture-minister-trying-to-salvage-the-countrys-artifacts [https://perma.cc/78X2-PHGJ].

Evans, Richard J. *The Hitler Conspiracies.* Oxford: Oxford University Press, 2020.

Review of "Eichmann before Jerusalem: The Unexamined Life of a Mass Murderer." *Guardian*, October 17, 2014.

*The Third Reich in Power.* New York: Penguin, 2005.

Feinberg, Joel. "Collective Responsibility." *Journal of Philosophy* 65(21) (1968): 674–88.

Finnis, John. *Aquinas.* Oxford: Oxford University Press, 1998.

Fodor, Jerry. "What Wotan Wants." (Review of Philip Kitcher and Richard Schacht, *Finding an Ending: Reflections on Wagner's "Ring"*). *London Review of Books* 26(15) (2004): 8–10.

Foot, Philippa. "Moral Beliefs." *Proceedings of the Aristotelian Society*, New Series 59 (1958–59): 83–104.

Fraenkel, Ernst. *The Dual State: A Contribution to the Theory of Dictatorship*. Republished version edited by Jens Meierhenrich and translated by Edward A. Shils. Oxford: Oxford University Press, 2018.

Frankfurt, Harry G. *On Bullshit*. Princeton, NJ: Princeton University Press, 2005.

Fritz, Stephen G. "The NSDAP as *Volkspartei*? A Look at the Social Basis of the Nazi Voter." *The History Teacher* 20 (1987): 379–99.

Fritzsche, Peter. *Hitler's First Hundred Days: When Germans Embraced the Third Reich*. New York: Basic Books, 2020.

*Life and Death in the Third Reich*. Cambridge, MA: Harvard University Press, 2008.

Fuller, Lon L. *The Anatomy of Law*. Westport, CT: Praeger, 1968.

Gaeta, Paola. "The Defence of Superior Orders: The Statute of the International Criminal Court *versus* Customary International Law," *European Journal of International Law* 10 (1999): 172–91.

Gewen, Barry. "The Everyman of Genocide." *New York Times*, May 14, 2006.

Goertzel, Ben. *Chaotic Logic: Language, Thought, and Reality from the Perspective of Complex Systems Science*. New York: Plenum, 1994.

Goertzel, Ted. "Belief in Conspiracy Theories." *Political Psychology* 15(4) (1994): 731–42.

Goldberg, John C. P., and Benjamin C. Zipursky. *Recognizing Wrongs*. Cambridge, MA: Harvard University Press, 2020.

Goldman, Holly. "Culpable Ignorance." *Philosophical Review* 92(4) (1983): 543–71.

Graf, Sinja. "Carl Schmitt Reads Hannah Arendt's Eichmann in Jerusalem: Archival Perspectives on Convergence and Divergence." *American Journal of Political Science* 66(4) (2021): 918–31.

*The Humanity of Universal Crime: Inclusion, Inequality, and Intervention in International Political Thought*. Oxford: Oxford University Press, 2021.

Gray, John. "Eichmann: His Life and Crimes by David Cesarani." *The Independent*, August 20, 2014.

Green, Richard Allen. "CNN Poll Reveals Depth of Anti-Semitism in Europe." CNN, November 2018. https://edition.cnn.com/interactive/2018/11/europe/antisemitism-poll-2018-intl/.

Griffin, James. *On Human Rights*. Oxford: Oxford University Press, 2008.

Gudehus, Christian, et al., eds. "Special Issue: Revisiting the Life and Work of Raphaël Lemkin." *Genocide Studies and Prevention: An International Journal* 13(1) (2019): 1–188.

Gündoğdu, Ayten. *Rightlessness in an Age of Rights: Hannah Arendt and the Contemporary Struggles of Migrants*. Oxford: Oxford University Press, 2015.

Gunn, Thom. "Epitaph for Anton Schmidt" (§11 of "Misanthropos"). In *Collected Poems.* New York: Farrar, Straus & Giroux, 1994.

Guskin, Emily, Chris Alcantara, and Janice Kai Chen. "Exit Polls from the 2024 Presidential Election." *Washington Post*, November 6, 2024.

Haberman, Maggie et al. "Trump Suggests No Laws Are Broken if He's 'Saving His Country'." *New York Times*, February 15, 2025.

Halbertal, Moshe. *Maimonides: Life and Thought.* Princeton, NJ: Princeton University Press, 2014.

Hallie, Philip P. *Lest Innocent Blood Be Shed: The Story of the Village of Le Chambon and How Goodness Happened There.* New York: Harper, 1994.

Hamilton, Richard. "The Rise of Nazism: A Case Study and Review of Interpretations: Kiel, 1928–33." *German Studies Review* 26 (2003): 43–62.

Hampshire, Stuart. *Innocence and Experience.* Cambridge, MA: Harvard University Press, 1989.

*Justice Is Conflict.* Princeton, NJ: Princeton University Press, 2000.

Hampton, Jean. "*Mens Rea.*" In *The Intrinsic Worth of Persons: Contractarianism in Moral and Political Philosophy*, edited by Daniel Farnham. New York: Cambridge University Press, 2007.

"The Retributive Idea." In *Forgiveness and Mercy*, edited by Jean Hampton and Jeffrie R. Murphy. New York: Cambridge University Press, 1986.

Hardin, Russell. *One for All: The Logic of Group Conflict.* Princeton, NJ: Princeton University Press, 1995.

Harding, D. W. "Regulated Hatred: An Aspect of the Work of Jane Austen." In D. W. Harding, *Regulated Hatred and Other Essays on Jane Austen*, edited by Monica Lawler. London: Athlone Press, 2001.

Hardy, G. H. "The *J*-Type and the *S*-Type among Mathematicians." *Nature* 134 (1934): 250.

Harvard Research Project on Criminal Jurisdiction. *American Journal of International Law* 29 (Supp. 1935): 435–651.

Hathaway, Oona A., and Scott J. Shapiro. *The Internationalists: How a Radical Plan to Outlaw War Remade the World.* New York: Simon & Schuster, 2018.

Hausner, Gideon. *Justice in Jerusalem.* New York: Harper & Row, 1966.

Hayes, Christine. *What's Divine about Divine Law? Early Perspectives.* Princeton, NJ: Princeton University Press, 2015.

Heidegger, Martin. *Being and Time.* Translated by John Macquarrie and Edward Robinson. New York: Harper & Row, 1962.

Heller-Roazen, Daniel. *The Enemy of All: Piracy and the Law of Nations.* New York: Zone Books, 2009.

Herman, Barbara. *The Practice of Moral Judgment.* Cambridge, MA: Harvard University Press, 1993.

Himmler, Heinrich. Speech before senior SS officers, October 4, 1943. www.yadvashem.org/odot_pdf/Microsoft%20Word%20-%204029.pdf.

Hirsch, Francine. *Soviet Judgment at Nuremberg: A New History of the International Military Tribunal after World War II.* Oxford: Oxford University Press, 2020.

Hiruta, Kei. *Hannah Arendt and Isaiah Berlin.* Princeton, NJ: Princeton University Press, 2021.

Hoagland, Tony. "What Narcissism Means to Me." In *What Narcissism Means to Me*, edited by Tony Hoagland. Minneapolis, MN: Graywolf Press, 2003.

Hofstadter, Richard. "The Paranoid Style in American Politics." *Harper's Magazine*, November 1964.

Holmes, Oliver Wendell, Jr. *The Holmes–Einstein Letters: The Correspondence of Mr. Justice Holmes and Lewis Einstein 1903–1935.* Edited by James Peabody. New York: St. Martin's Press, 1964.

Holquist, Peter. "'Crimes against Humanity': Genealogy of a Concept (1815–1945)." Unpublished presentation to the research project "Between Restoration and Revolution: National Constitutions and Global Law: an Alternative View on the European Century, 1815–1914." Helsinki University, March 6, 2012.

Honig, Bonnie. *Emergency Politics. Paradox, Law, Democracy.* Princeton, NJ: Princeton University Press, 2009.

Huillet, Marie. "Ex-CIA Agent Drags Microsoft's Crypto-Patent into Right-Wing Conspiracy." *Cointelegraph.com*, September 10, 2020. https://cointelegraph .com/news/ex-cia-agent-drags-microsofts-crypto-patent-into-right-wing-conspiracy.

Hursthouse, Rosalind. "Practical Wisdom: A Mundane Account." *Proceedings of the Aristotelian Society* 106 (2006): 285–309.

*On Virtue Ethics.* Oxford: Oxford University Press, 1999.

Ignatieff, Michael. "Lemkin's Word." *The New Republic*, February 26, 2001.

Irvin-Erickson, Douglas. "The Life and Works of Raphael Lemkin: A Political History of Genocide in Theory and Law." PhD diss., Rutgers University, 2014.

*Raphaël Lemkin and the Concept of Genocide.* Philadelphia: University of Pennsylvania Press, 2017.

Isaac, Jeffrey C. *Arendt, Camus, and Modern Rebellion.* New Haven, CT: Yale University Press, 1994.

Jackall, Robert. *Moral Mazes: The World of Corporate Managers.* New York: Oxford University Press, 1988.

Jackman, Tom et al., "A Quarter of Americans Believe FBI Instigated January 6, Post-UMD Poll Finds." *Washington Post*, January 4, 2024.

Jain, Neha. "Manufacturing Statelessness." *American Journal of International Law* 116(2) (2022): 237–99.

Jamison, Peter, and Valerie Strauss. "D.C. Lawmaker Says Recent Snowfall Caused by 'Rothschilds Controlling the Climate'." *Washington Post*, March 18, 2018.

Jaspers, Karl. *The Question of German Guilt.* Translated by E. B. Ashton. New York: Dial Press, 1947 (originally published in 1945 as *Die Schuldfrage: Von den politischen Haftung Deutschlands*).

Judt, Tony. "At Home in This Century." *New York Review of Books,* April 6, 1995.

Jurkevics, Anna. "Hannah Arendt Reads Carl Schmitt's *The Nomos of the Earth*: A Dialogue on Law and Geopolitics from the Margins." *European Journal of Political Theory* 16(3) (2017): 345–66.

Kahn, Charles H. "Sensation and Consciousness in Aristotle's Psychology." *Archiv für Geschichte der Philosophie* 48(1–3) (1966): 52–54.

Kahn, Paul W. *Sacred Violence: Torture, Terror, and Sovereignty*. Ann Arbor: University of Michigan Press, 2008.

Kahneman, Daniel. "Experienced Utility and Objective Happiness: A Moment-Based Approach." In *Choices, Values and Frames*, edited by Daniel Kahneman and Amos Tversky. Cambridge: Cambridge University Press, 2000.

Kampowski, Stephan. *Arendt, Augustine, and the New Beginning*. Grand Rapids, MI: Eerdmans, 2008.

Kant, Immanuel. *Anthropology from a Pragmatic Point of View*. Translated by Victor Lyle Dowdell. Carbondale: Southern Illinois University Press, 1978.

*Correspondence (The Cambridge Edition of the Works of Immanuel Kant)*. Edited by Arnulf Zweig. Cambridge: Cambridge University Press, 1999.

*Critique of Judgment: Including the First Introduction*. Translated by Werner S. Pluher. Indianapolis: Hackett Publishing, 1987.

*Critique of Practical Reason*. In *Practical Philosophy (The Cambridge Edition of the Works of Immanuel Kant)*, edited and translated by Mary J. Gregor. Cambridge: Cambridge University Press, 1996.

*Critique of Pure Reason*. Translated by Norman Kemp Smith. London: Macmillan, and New York: St. Martin's Press, 1968.

*Kant's Philosophical Correspondence 1759–99*. Edited and translated by Arnulf Zweig. Chicago: University of Chicago Press, 1986.

*Practical Philosophy (The Cambridge Edition of the Works of Immanuel Kant)*. Edited and translated by Mary J. Gregor. Cambridge: Cambridge University Press, 1996.

*Prolegomena to Any Future Metaphysics*. Translated by Lewis White Beck. Indianapolis: Bobbs-Merrill, 1950.

*Religion within the Boundaries of Mere Reason*. In *Religion and Rational Theology (The Cambridge Edition of the Works of Immanuel Kant)*, edited by Allen Wood and George Di Giovanni. Cambridge: Cambridge University Press, 1996.

*Toward Perpetual Peace. In Practical Philosophy (The Cambridge Edition of the Works of Immanuel Kant)*. Edited and Translated by Mary J. Gregor.

Kateb, George. *Hannah Arendt: Politics, Conscience, Evil*. Totowa, NJ: Rowman & Littlefield, 1983.

Keeley, Brian L., "Of Conspiracy Theories." *Journal of Philosophy* 96(3) (1999): 109–26.

Kesby, Alison. *The Right to Have Rights: Citizenship, Humanity, and International Law*. Oxford: Oxford University Press, 2012.

Kim, Sangkul. *A Collective Theory of Genocidal Intent.* The Hague: T.M.C. Asser Press, 2016.

Kinzer, Stephen. *Poisoner in Chief: Sidney Gottlieb and the CIA Search for Mind Control.* New York: Henry Holt, 2019.

Kleinfeld, Joshua. "Reconstructivism: The Place of Criminal Law in Ethical Life." *Harvard Law Review* 129(6) (2016): 1486–565.

"Why the Mind Matters in Criminal Law." *Arizona State Law Journal* 53 (2021): 539–64.

Korsgaard, Christine. "Taking the Law into Our Own Hands: Kant on the Right to Revolution." In *The Constitution of Agency: Essays on Practical Reason and Moral Psychology.* Oxford: Oxford University Press, 2008.

Koskenniemi, Martti. "Between Impunity and Show Trials." *Max Planck Yearbook of United Nations Law* 6 (2002): 1–35.

*The Politics of International Law.* Oxford: Hart Publishing, 2011.

Kroft, Steve. "Anonymous, Inc." *CBS News*, January 31, 2016. www.cbsnews.com/news/anonymous-inc-60-minutes-steve-kroft-investigation/ [https://perma.cc/34FZ-VV9Z].

Landsman, Stephan. *Crimes of the Holocaust: The Law Confronts Hard Cases.* Philadelphia: University of Pennsylvania Press, 2005.

Lang, Berel. *Genocide: The Act as Idea.* Philadelphia: University of Pennsylvania Press, 2016.

Laor, Dan. "Israel Kastner vs. Hannah Szenes: Who Was Really the Hero during the Holocaust?" *Ha'aretz*, November 9, 2013. www.haaretz.com/.premium-who-was-the-real-holocaust-hero-1.5287614.

Lauterpacht, Hersch. "Review of Lemkin, *Axis Rule in Occupied Europe*," *Cambridge Law Journal* 9 (1945): 140.

Leibovich, Mark. "Trump Has Called His Supporters 'Disgusting': Do They Care?" *New York Times*, October 10, 2020.

Lemkin, Raphael. *Axis Rule in Occupied Europe: Laws of Occupation, Analysis of Government, Proposals for Redress.* Washington, DC: Carnegie Foundation, 1944.

"Genocide." *The American Scholar* 15(2) (1946): 227–30, www.preventgenocide.org/lemkin/americanscholar1946.htm [https://perma.cc/E8AZ-5VHS].

"Genocide: A Modern Crime," *Free World* 4 (April 1945), www.preventgenocide.org/lemkin/freeworld1945.htm [https://perma.cc/U8Q4-XQXT].

*Totally Unofficial.* New Haven, CT: Yale University Press, 2013.

Lenoe, Matt. "Did Stalin Kill Kirov and Does It Matter?" *Journal of Modern History* 74(2) (2002): 352–80.

Levi, Edward H. *An Introduction to Legal Reasoning.* Chicago: University of Chicago Press, 1948.

Lewis, C. S. "Conscience and Conscious." In *Studies in Words.* 2nd ed. Cambridge: Cambridge University Press, 1967.

*The Screwtape Letters and Screwtape Proposes a Toast.* London: Geoffrey Bles, 1942.

Lingaas, Carola. "Imagined Identities: Defining the Racial Group in the Crime of Genocide." *Genocide Studies and Prevention: An International Journal* 1(9) (2016): 79–106.

Lipstadt, Deborah E. *The Eichmann Trial.* New York: Schocken, 2011.

Löb, Ladislaus. *Rezso Kasztner – The Daring Rescue of Hungarian Jews: A Survivor's Account.* London: Pimlico, 2009.

Longuenesse, Béatrice. *Kant and the Capacity to Judge.* Princeton, NJ: Princeton University Press, 1998.

Lozowick, Yaacov. *Hitler's Bureaucrats: The Nazi Security Police and the Banality of Evil.* Translated by Haim Watzman. London: Continuum, 2000.

Luban, David. "After the Honeymoon: Reflections on the Current State of International Criminal Justice." *Journal of International Criminal Justice* 11 (2013): 505–15.

"Arendt on the Crime of Crimes." *Ratio Juris* 28(3) (2015): 307–25.

"Complicity and Lesser Evils: A Tale of Two Lawyers." *Georgetown Journal of Legal Ethics* 34(3) (2021): 613–64.

"Demystifying Political Violence: Some Bequests of ICTY and ICTR." *AJIL Unbound* 110 (2016): 251–57.

"The Enemy of All Humanity." *Netherlands Journal of Legal Philosophy* 47(2) (2018): 112–37. www.njlp.nl/tijdschrift/rechtsfilosofieentheorie/2018/2/NJLP_2213-0713_2018_047_002_007. Concurrently published in *The Oxford Handbook of International Criminal Law*, edited by Kevin Jon Heller, Frédéric Mégret, and Sarah Nouwen. Oxford: Oxford University Press, 2020.

"Fairness to Rightness: Jurisdiction, Legality, and the Legitimacy of International Criminal Law." In *The Philosophy of International Law*, edited by Samantha Besson and John Tasioulas. Oxford: Oxford University Press, 2012.

"Hannah Arendt's Theory of Theory." *Social Research* 50(1) (1983): 215–48, revised and reprinted under the title "Hannah Arendt and the Primacy of Narrative," in *Legal Modernism.* edited by David Luban. Ann Arbor: University of Michigan Press, 1994.

"Human Rights Pragmatism and Human Dignity." In *Philosophical Foundations of Human Rights*, edited by Massimo Renzo et al. Oxford: Oxford University Press, 2015.

"On the Humanity of the Enemy of Humanity." *Netherlands Journal of Legal Philosophy* 47(2) (2018): 187–95. www.njlp.nl/tijdschrift/rechtsfiloso fieentheorie/ 2018/2/NJLP_2213–0713_2018_047_002_007.

"The Legacies of Nuremberg," *Social Research* 54(4) (1987): 779–829, revised and reprinted in David Luban, *Legal Modernism*, Ann Arbor: University of Michigan Press, 1994.

*Legal Ethics and Human Dignity.* Cambridge: Cambridge University Press, 2006.

*Legal Modernism.* Ann Arbor: University of Michigan Press, 1994.

"Responsibility to Humanity and Threats to Peace: An Essay on Sovereignty." *Berkeley Journal of International Law* 38 (2020): 185–239.

"Review of Hampshire, *Innocence and Experience.*" *Journal of Philosophy* 88(6) (1991): 317–24.

"State Criminality and the Ambition of International Criminal Law." In *Accountability for Collective Wrongdoing*, edited by Tracy Isaacs and Richard Vernon. Cambridge: Cambridge University Press, 2011.

"A Theory of Crimes against Humanity." *Yale Journal of International Law* 29 (2004): 85–167.

"War as Punishment." *Philosophy & Public Affairs* 39(4) (2011): 299–330.

Luban, David, Alan Strudler, and David Wasserman. "Moral Responsibility in the Age of Bureaucracy." *Michigan Law Review* 90(8) (1992): 2348–92.

Mahony, Chris. "A Political Tool? The Politics of Case Selection at the Special Court for Sierra Leone." In *Evaluating Transitional Justice: Accountability and Peace-Building in post-Conflict Sierra Leone*, edited by Kirsten Ainley, Rebekka Friedman, and Chris Mahony. Houndmills: Palgrave Macmillan, 2015.

Mahony, Deirdre Lauren. *Hannah Arendt's Ethics.* London: Bloomsbury, 2018.

Maier-Katkin, Daniel. "The Reception of Arendt's *Eichmann in Jerusalem* in the United States 1963–2011." *Zeitschrift für Politisches Denken/Journal of Political Thinking* 6 (2011). www.hannaharendt.net/index.php/han/article/view/64/84.

Maimonides, Moses. "Helek: Introduction to Mishnah Sanhedrin, Chapter 10." In *A Maimonides Reader*, edited by Isadore Twersky. New York: Berhman House, 1972.

Makkreel, Rudolf A. "Reflection, Reflective Judgment, and Aesthetic Exemplarity." In *Aesthetics and Cognition in Kant's Critical Philosophy*, edited by Rebecca Kukla. Cambridge: Cambridge University Press, 2006.

Mandik, Pete. "Shit Happens." *Episteme: The Journal of Social Epistemology* 4 (2007): 205–18.

Mann, Itamar. "Eichmann's Mistake: The Problem of Thoughtlessness in International Criminal Law." *Canadian Journal of Jurisprudence* 33(1) (2020): 145–81.

Margalit, Avishai. *On Compromise and Rotten Compromises.* Princeton, NJ: Princeton University Press, 2009.

Markell, Patchen. "Arendt's Work: On the Architecture of *The Human Condition.*" *College Literature* 38/1 (2011): 15–44.

Marrus, Michael R., and Robert O. Paxton. *Vichy France and the Jews.* Palo Alto, CA: Stanford University Press, 1981.

Marwell, David. *Mengele: Unmasking the "Angel of Death."* New York: Norton, 2020.

May, Larry. *Genocide: A Normative Account.* Cambridge: Cambridge University Press, 2010.

McCoy, Alfred. *A Question of Torture: CIA Interrogation from the Cold War to the War on Terror.* New York: Holt, 2006.

McFadden, Robert D. "Jacques Vergès, Defender of Terrorists and War Criminals, Is Dead at 88." *New York Times*, August 16, 2013.

McHugh, Kevin J., et al. "Biocompatible Near-Infrared Quantum Dots Delivered to the Skin by Microneedle Patches Record Vaccination." *Science Translational Medicine* 11(523) (2019). https://stm.sciencemag.org/content/11/523/eaay7162.abstract.

Meierhenrich, Jens. *The Remnants of the Rechtsstaat: An Ethnography of Nazi Law.* Oxford: Oxford University Press, 2018.

Menninghaus, Winfried. "On the 'Vital Significance' of Kitsch: Walter Benjamin's Politics of Bad Taste." In *Walter Benjamin and the Architecture of Modernity*, edited by Andrew E. Benjamin and Charles Rice. Melbourne: Re.press, 2009.

Miller, Stephen H. "A Note on the Banality of Evil." *The Wilson Quarterly* 22(4), Autumn, 1998: 54–59.

Mnookin, Robert. *Bargaining with the Devil: When to Bargain, When to Fight.* New York: Simon & Schuster, 2010.

Moltke, Helmuth James von. *Letters to Freya: 1939–1945*. Translated by Beate Ruhm von Oppen. New York: Alfred Knopf, 1990.

Monroe, Kristen Renwick. *The Heart of Altruism: Perceptions of a Common Humanity.* Princeton, NJ: Princeton University Press, 1998.

Montesquieu. *The Spirit of the Laws.* Edited and translated by Anne M. Cohler, Basia Caroline Miller, and Harold Samuel Stone. Cambridge: Cambridge University Press, 1989.

Moore, G. E. *Philosophical Papers.* New York: Macmillan, 1959.

Morris, Douglas. *Legal Sabotage: Ernst Fraenkel in Hitler's Germany.* Cambridge: Cambridge University Press, 2020.

Moses, A. Dirk. *The Problems of Genocide: Permanent Security and the Language of Transgression.* Cambridge: Cambridge University Press, 2021.

"Raphael Lemkin, Culture, and the Concept of Genocide." In *The Oxford Handbook of Genocide Studies*, edited by Donald Bloxham and A. Dirk Moses. Oxford: Oxford University Press, 2010.

Muirhead, Russell, and Nancy L. Rosenblum. *A Lot of People Are Saying: The New Conspiracism and the Assault on Democracy.* Princeton, NJ: Princeton University Press, 2019.

Mulisch, Harry. *Criminal Case 40/61, the Trial of Adolf Eichmann: An Eyewitness Account.* Translated by Robert Naborn. Philadelphia: University of Pennsylvania Press, 2005.

Mundorff, Kurt. *A Cultural Interpretation of the Genocide Convention.* London: Routledge, 2020.

Neumann, Ulfrid. "Mistake of Law." *Israel Law Review* 30 (1996): 207–13.

*New York Times.* "Allied Rift Called Aim of '44 Nazi Ransom Plan." May 21, 1964.

*New York Times.* "The Crime of Genocide." October 20, 1957.

Norman, Richard. "Aristotle's Philosopher-God." *Phronesis* 14(1) (1969): 63–74.

Nozick, Robert. *Anarchy, State, and Utopia.* New York: Basic Books, 1974.

*Philosophical Explanations.* Cambridge, MA: Harvard University Press, 1981.

Nussbaum, Martha C. "The Damage of Death: Incomplete Arguments and False Conclusions." In *Death: New Essays on Metaphysics and Bioethics*, edited by James S. Taylor. Oxford: Oxford University Press, 2013.

*The Therapy of Desire: Theory and Practice in Hellenistic Ethics.* Princeton, NJ: Princeton University Press, 1994.

Oliver, J. Eric and Thomas J. Wood. "Conspiracy Theories and the Paranoid Style(s) of Mass Opinion." *American Journal of Political Science* 58(4) (2014): 952–66.

Osiel, Mark J. *Mass Atrocity, Collective Memory, and the Law.* Piscataway, NJ: Transaction Books, 1997.

*Mass Atrocity, Ordinary Evil, and Hannah Arendt: Criminal Consciousness in Argentina's Dirty War.* New Haven, CT: Yale University Press, 2001.

O'Sullivan, Noel. "Hannah Arendt: Hellenic Nostalgia and Industrial Society." In *Contemporary Political Philosophers*, edited by Anthony de Crespigny and Kenneth Minogue. New York: Dodd-Mead, 1975.

Patterson, William L. *We Charge Genocide: The Crime of Government against the Negro People.* New York: Civil Rights Congress , 2017.

Pauer-Studer, Herlinde, and David Velleman. *Konrad Morgen: The Conscience of a Nazi Judge.* Basingstoke: Palgrave-Macmillan, 2015.

Paz, Moria. "States and Networks in the Formation of International Law." *American University International Law Review* 26(5) (2011): 1241–313.

"Toward a Taxonomy of Freedom of Movement Claims: Identifying Rights-Based Pathways for Today's Refugees beyond the 1951 Refugee Convention." *Harvard Journal of International Law* 65(2) (2024): 457–526.

Peirce, Charles S. "How to Make Our Ideas Clear." *Popular Science Monthly* 12 (January 1878): 286–302.

Picheta, Rob. "The Flat-Earth Conspiracy Is Spreading Around the Globe: Does It Hide a Darker Core?" CNN, November 18, 2019. www.cnn.com/2019/11/16/us/flat-earth-conference-conspiracy-theories-scli-intl/index.html.

Pitkin, Hanna Fenichel. *The Attack of the Blob: Hannah Arendt's Concept of the Social.* Chicago: University of Chicago Press, 2000.

Plato. *Apology*. In *Plato in Twelve Volumes*, volume 1, edited and translated by Harold N. Fowler. Cambridge, MA: Harvard University Press and William Heinemann Ltd., 1925.

*Gorgias*. Translated by James A.Arieti and Roger M. Barrus. Focus Publishing, 2007.

*Protagoras*. In *Plato in Twelve Volumes*, volume 4, edited and translated by W. R. M.Lamb. Cambridge, MA: Harvard University Press and William Heinemann Ltd., 1952.

*Symposium*. Translated by BenjaminJowett. Indianapolis: Bobbs-Merrill, 1956.

*Theaetetus*. Translated by John McDowell. Oxford: Oxford University Press, 1973.

Postema, Gerald J. "Implicit Law." *Law and Philosophy* 13(3) (1994): 361–87.

Power, Samantha. *"A Problem from Hell": America and the Age of Genocide.* New York: Basic Books, 2002.

Press, Eyal. *Beautiful Souls: The Courage and Conscience of Ordinary People in Extraordinary Times.* New York: Farrar, Straus and Giroux, 2012.

Prevent Genocide International, "The Crime of Genocide in Domestic Laws and Penal Codes." www.preventgenocide.org/law/domestic.

Prior, A. N. "The Runabout Inference-Ticket." *Analysis* 21(2) (1960): 38–39.

Prokop, Andrew . "J. D. Vance's Radical Plan to Build a Government of Trump Loyalists." *Vox*, July 18, 2024. www.vox.com/politics/361455/jd-vance-trump-vice-president-rnc-speech.

Public Policy Polling. *Conspiracy Theory Poll Results*, April 2, 2013. https://web.archive.org/web/20170930093655/www.publicpolicypolling.com/main/2013/04/conspiracy-theory-poll-results-.html.

Radnitz, Scott. *Revealing Schemes: The Politics of Conspiracy in Russia and the Post-Soviet Region.* Oxford: Oxford University Press, 2021.

Reck-Malleczewen, Friedrich Percyval. *Diary of a Man in Despair [Tagebuch eines Verzweifelten].* Translated by Paul Rubens. New York: Macmillan, 1970.

Reeve, C. D. C. *Socrates in the Apology: An Essay on Plato's Apology of Socrates.* Indianapolis: Hackett, 1989.

Reid, Thomas. *An Inquiry into the Human Mind on the Principles of Common Sense.* In *Inquiry and Essays*, edited by Ronald E. Beanblossom and Keith Lehrer. Inidanapolis: Hackett, 1983.

Renzo, Massimo. "Crimes against Humanity and the Limits of International Criminal Law." *Law and Philosophy* 31(4) (2012): 443–76.

Rhodes, Richard. *Masters of Death: The SS-Einsatzgruppen and the Invention of the Holocaust.* New York: Vintage, 2007.

Rini, Regina. "Weaponized Skepticism: An Analysis of Social Media Deception as Applied Political Epistemology." In *Political Epistemology*, edited by Elizabeth Edenberg and Michael Hannon. Oxford: Oxford University Press, 2021.

Robinson, Jacob. "Eichmann and the Question of Jurisdiction." *Commentary*, July 1960. www.commentary.org/articles/jacob-robinson/eichmann-the-question-of-jurisdiction/.

Roscigno, Saverio. "The Status Foundations of Conspiracy Beliefs." *Socius: Sociological Research for a Dynamic World* 10 (2024). https://journals.sagepub.com/doi/full/10.1177/23780231241237654.

Rosenberg, Harold. "Pop Culture and Kitsch Criticism." *Dissent* (Winter 1958): 14–19.

Rosenberg, Paul. "Who Believes the Most 'Taboo' Conspiracy Theories? It Might Not Be Who You Think." *Salon*, May 5, 2024.

Rosenfeld, Sophia. *Common Sense: A Political History.* Cambridge, MA: Harvard University Press, 2011.

Sandberg, Brita and Eric Follath. "Interview with Notorious Lawyer Jacques Vergès: 'There Is No Such Thing as Absolute Evil'." *Spiegel Online*, November 21, 2006. www.spiegel.de/international/world/interview-with-notorious-lawyer-jacques-verges-there-is-no-such-thing-as-absolute-evil-a-591943.html.

Sands, Philippe. *East West Street: On the Origins of "Genocide" and "Crimes against Humanity."* New York: Vintage, 2016.

Schabas, William A. *Genocide in International Law.* Cambridge: Cambridge University Press, 2000.

Schaeffer, Katherine. "A Look at the Americans Who Believe There Is Some Truth to the Conspiracy Theory that COVID-19 Was Planned." Pew Research Center FactTank, July 24, 2020. www.pewresearch.org/fact-tank/2020/07/24/a-look-at-the-americans-who-believe-there-is-some-truth-to-the-conspiracy-theory-that-covid-19-was-planned/.

Scheffler, Samuel. *Death and the Afterlife.* Oxford: Oxford University Press, 2013.

Schmitt, Carl. *The Concept of the Political.* Translated by George Schwab, expanded ed. Chicago: University of Chicago Press, 2007.

Schmitt, Michael N. "The Law of Cyber Conflict: *Quo Vadis* 2.0?" In *The Future Law of Armed Conflict*, edited by Matthew C. Waxman and Thomas W. Oakley. New York: Oxford University Press, 2022.

Scott, Joanna Vecchiarelli, and Judith Chelius Stark. "Introduction: 'New Beginnings'." In Arendt, *Love and Saint Augustine.* Chicago: University of Chicago Press, 1929/1996.

Scott, Sir Walter. *The Journals of Sir Walter Scott*, edited by David Douglas. Project Gutenberg, 2005. www.gutenberg.org/cache/epub/14860/pg14860-images.html#FNanchor_222_222.

Segev, Tom. *The Seventh Million: The Israelis and the Holocaust.* Translated by Haim Watzman. New York: Hill and Wang, 1993.

Sellars, Wilfrid. "Empiricism and the Philosophy of Mind." In Sellars, *Science, Perception and Reality.* London: Routledge & Kegan Paul, 1963.

"Philosophy and the Scientific Image of Man." In Sellars, *Science, Perception and Reality.* London: Routledge & Kegan Paul, 1963.

Sherwood, Harriet. *The Guardian.* "Nearly Two-thirds of US Young Adults Unaware 6m Jews Killed in the Holocaust." September 16, 2020.

Shue, Henry. *Basic Rights: Subsistence, Affluence, and U.S. Foreign Policy.* 2nd ed. Princeton, NJ: Princeton University Press, 1996.

Siddique, Haroon. "Legal Experts Worldwide Draw Up 'Historic' Definition of Ecocide." *Guardian*, June 22, 2021.

Siegelberg, Mira L. *Statelessness: A Modern History.* Cambridge, MA: Harvard University Press, 2020.

"Unofficial Men, Efficient Civil Servants: Raphael Lemkin in the History of International Law." *Journal of Genocide Research* 15(3) (2013): 297–316.

Simons, Kenneth. "Rethinking Mental States." *Boston University Law Review* 72 (1992): 464–554.

Slezkine, Yuri. *The House of Government: A Saga of the Russian Revolution.* Princeton, NJ: Princeton University Press, 2017.

Smith, Adam. *Theory of the Moral Sentiments.* Indianapolis: Liberty Classics, 1976.

Smith, Blake. "Hannah Arendt, Michael Denneny, and the Politics of Protest." *Chronicle of Higher Education*, April 9, 2025.

Snyder, Jane McIntosh. "The *Harmonia* of Bow and Lyre in Heraclitus Fragment 51 (DK)." *Phronesis* 29(1) (1984): 91–95.

Snyder, Timothy. *Bloodlands: Europe between Hitler and Stalin.* New York: Basic Books, 2010.

*On Tyranny.* New York: Penguin Books, 2017.

Speer, Albert. *Inside the Third Reich: Memoirs.* Translated by Richard Winston and Clara Winston. New York: Simon & Schuster, 1970.

Sperber, Dan, et al. "Epistemic Vigilance." *Mind and Language* 25 (2010): 359–93.

Stangneth, Bettina. *Eichmann before Jerusalem: The Unexamined Life of a Mass Murderer.* Translated by Ruth Martin. New York: Alfred Knopf, 2014.

State of Israel Ministry of Justice. *The Trial of Adolf Eichmann: Record of the Proceedings in the District Court of Jerusalem* (6 volumes). Jerusalem: State of Israel Ministry of Justice, 1993.

Stevens, Wallace. "Tea at the Palaz of Hoon." *The Collected Poems of Wallace Stevens.* New York: Vintage Books, 1990.

Stewart, Melissa. "'A New Law on Earth': Hannah Arendt and the Vision for a Positive Legal Framework to Guarantee the Right to Have Rights." *Virginia Journal of International Law* 62(1) (2021): 115–79.

Stone, I. F. *The Trial of Socrates.* Boston: Little Brown, 1988.

Stonebridge, Lyndsey. "Why Hannah Arendt Is the Philosopher for Now." *New Statesman* March 20, 2019. www.newstatesman.com/culture/2019/03/why-hannah-arendt-is-the-philosopher-for-now.

Stoner, Samuel A. "Kant on Common-Sense and the Unity of Judgments of Taste." *Kant Yearbook* 11(1) (2019): 81–99.

Strawson, P. F. "Freedom and Resentment," *Proceedings of the British Academy*, 48 (1962): 187–211.

Summers, David. *The Judgment of Sense: Renaissance Naturalism and the Rise of Aesthetics.* Cambridge: Cambridge University Press, 1987.

Sunstein, Cass R. "On Analogical Reasoning." *Harvard Law Review* 106 (1993): 741–91.

Taminiaux, Jacques. *The Thracian Maid and the Professional Thinker: Arendt and Heidegger.* Translated by Michael Gendre. Albany: SUNY Press, 1997.

Taub, Ben. "The Assad Files." *New Yorker*, April 18, 2016.

Teicholz, Tom. "The Liar: The Four Personas of Adolf Eichmann." *L.A. Review of Books*, April 18, 2015.

Tsao, Roy. "Arendt against Athens: Rereading *The Human Condition.*" *Political Theory* 30 (2002): 97–123.

Turnaoğlu, Banu. *The Formation of Turkish Republicanism.* Princeton, NJ: Princeton University Press, 2017.

Ukrinform. "Army of Vandals and Looters: Russians Targeting Ukrainian Cultural Heritage." December 26, 2022. www.ukrinform.net/rubric-ato/3641428-army-of-vandals-and-looters-russians-targeting-ukrainian-cultural-heritage.html [https://perma.cc/U55U-T76L].

Ullrich, Volker. *Hitler: Ascent, 1889–1939.* Translated by Jefferson Chase. London: Bodley Head, 2016.

UNHCR. *Figures at a Glance*. 2024. www.unhcr.org/en-us/figures-at-a-glance.html.
US Department of State. *Statelessness*. 2021–25. https://2021-2025.state.gov/other-policy-issues/statelessness/.
Van de Cruys, Sander, et al. "Insight in the Conspiracist's Mind." *Personality and Social Psychology Review Online First*, September 30, 2023. https://journals.sagepub.com/doi/10.1177/10888683231203145?lh_aid=3539062&lh_cid=ykcixdqwtl&di=e6774f665ffccddb15d624afa254eb8c.
Van Der Vot, Dan. *The Good Nazi: The Life and Lies of Albert Speer*. New York: Houghton Mifflin, 1997.
Van Schaack, Beth. "Verdict in Cambodia: Too Little Too Late, but Still Important." *Just Security*, August 9, 2014. www.justsecurity.org/13923/verdict-cambodia-late-important.
Van Verseveld, Annamieke. *Mistake of Law: Excusing Perpetrators of International Crimes*. The Hague: T.M.C. Asser Press, 2012.
Vernon, Richard. "Crime against Humanity: A Defence of the Subsidiarity View." *Canadian Journal of Law and Jurisprudence* 26(1) (2013): 229–41.
"What Is a Crime against Humanity?" *Journal of Political Philosophy* 10 (2002): 231–49.
Verschuer, Otmar von. "Twin Research from the Time of Galton to the Present Day," *Proceedings of the Royal Society of London, Series B Biological Sciences* 128 (1939): 62–81.
Villa, Dana R. *Arendt and Heidegger: The Fate of the Political*. Princeton, NJ: Princeton University Press, 1996.
Waldron, Jeremy. "The Irrelevance of Moral Objectivity." In *Natural Law Theory: Contemporary Essays*, edited by Robert P. George. Oxford: Oxford University Press, 1992.
Walls, Laura Dassow. *Henry David Thoreau: A Biography*. Chicago: University of Chicago Press, 2017.
Wegener, Charles. *The Discipline of Taste and Feeling*. Chicago: University of Chicago Press, 1992.
Weisberg, Richard. *Vichy Law and the Holocaust in France*. New York: Routledge, 2013.
Weissberg, Alex. *Desperate Mission: Joel Brand's Story as Told by Alex Weissberg*. Translated by Constantine FitzGibbon and Andrew Foster-Melliar. Chicago: Borodino, 2017/1958.
Werner-Müller, Jens. *What Is Populism?* London: Penguin, 2015.
Wildt, Michael. "Eichmann und der kategorische Imperativ, oder: Gibt es eine nationalsozialististische Moral?" In *Die Wannsee-Konferenz am 20. Januar 1942: Dokumente, Forschungsstand, Kontroversen*, edited by Norbert Kampe and Peter Klein. Vienna and Cologne: Böhlau Verlag, 2013.
Williams, Bernard. *Ethics and the Limits of Philosophy*. London: Fontana Press/Collins, 1985.
*Moral Luck: Philosophical Papers 1973–1980*. Cambridge: Cambridge University Press, 1981.

"Persons, Character, and Morality." In *Philosophical Papers 1973–1980.* Cambridge: Cambridge University Press, 1981.

*Shame and Necessity.* Berkeley: University of California Press, 1993.

"The Makropoulos Case: Reflections on the Tedium of Immortality." In *Problems of the Self.* Cambridge: Cambridge University Press, 1973.

Williams, Michael. *Groundless Belief: An Essay on the Possibility of Epistemology.* 2nd ed. Princeton, NJ: Princeton University Press, 1999.

Wittgenstein, Ludwig. *On Certainty.* Edited by G. E. M. Anscombe and G. H. von Wright and translated by Denis Paul and G. E. M. Anscombe. New York: J. & J. Harper, 1969.

*Philosophical Investigations.* 3rd ed. Translated by G. E. M. Anscombe. London: Pearson, 1973.

*Remarks on the Foundations of Mathematics.* 2nd ed. Edited by G. H. von Wright, Rush Rhees, and G. E. M. Anscombe and translated by G. E. M. Anscombe. Cambridge, MA: MIT Press, 1967.

*Zettel.* Edited by G. E. M. Anscombe and G. H. von Wright and translated by G. E. M. Anscombe. Berkeley: University of California Press, 1967.

Wojak, Imtrud. *Eichmanns Memoiren: Ein kritischer Essay.* Frankfurt: Campus Verlag, 2001.

Wolin, Richard. "The Banality of Evil: The Demise of a Legend." *Jewish Review of Books* (Fall 2014). http://jewishreviewofbooks.com/articles/1106/the-banality-of-evil-the-demise-of-a-legend/.

"Hannah and the Magician." *New Republic,* October 9, 1995.

*Heidegger's Children.* Princeton, NJ: Princeton University Press, 2001.

"Thoughtlessness Revisited: A Response to Seyla Benhabib." *Jewish Review of Books,* September 30, 2014. http://jewishreviewofbooks.com/articles/1287/in-still-not-banal-a-response-to-seyla-benhabib/.

Wood, Michael J., Karen M. Douglas, and Robbie M. Sutton. "Dead and Alive: Beliefs in Contradictory Conspiracy Theories." *Social Psychological and Personality Science* 3(6) (2012): 767–73.

Woolf, Virginia. "A Sketch of the Past." In *Moments of Being: A Collection of Autobiographical Writing,* edited by Jeanne Schulkind. New York: Harcourt, Inc., 1985.

Xenophon, *Hellenica* 1.7.7. Translated by H. G. Dakyns. www.gutenberg.org/files/1174/1174-h/1174-h.htm#link2H_4_0002 [https://perma.cc/HX7R-99GX].

Yoshino, Kenji. *Covering: The Hidden Assault on Our Civil Rights.* New York: Random House, 2006.

Young, Iris Marion. *Responsibility for Justice.* Oxford: Oxford University Press, 2011.

Zitelmann, Rainer. "How Many Americans Believe in Conspiracy Theories?" *Forbes,* June 29, 2020. www.forbes.com/sites/rainerzitelmann/2020/06/29/how-many-americans-believe-in-conspiracy-theories/#3e2fd9855e94.

## Table of Cases

Al-Adsani v. The United Kingdom, 35763/97, ECHR (21 November 2001).
Application of the Convention on the Prevention and Punishment of the Crime of Genocide (Bosnia and Herzegovina v. Serbia and Montenegro), Judgment, I.C.J. Reports 2007, p. 43.
Atty. Gen. v. Eichmann, 36 I.L.R. 18 (Dist. Ct. Isr. 1961). Cited as "Eichmann Trial Judgment."
Bundesgerichtshof [BGH] [Federal Court of Justice], 18-03-1952 (1952) GSSt 2/51 (Lexetius.com/1952, 1).
Carlos Varela Núñez v. Uruguay, Communication No. 108/1981, U.N. Doc. CCPR/C/OP/2 at 143 (1990).
Case concerning the Arrest Warrant of April 11, 2000 (Democratic Republic of the Congo v. Belgium), Judgment, I.C.J. Reports 2002, p. 3 (February 14, 2002).
Cheek v. United States, 498 U.S. 192 (1991).
German War Trials: Judgment in the Case of Lieutenants Dithmar and Boldt, Hospital Ship "Llandovery Castle," Second Criminal Senate of the Imperial Court of Justice (July 16, 1921), reprinted in *American Journal of International Law* 16(4) (1922): 708–24.
Hurley v. Eddingfield, 156 Ind. 416, 59 N.E. 1058 (Ind. 1901).
In re Baby M, 109 N.J. 396, 537 A.2d 1227 (N.J. 1988).
Jones and Others v. UK, ECHR (January 14, 2014).
Jurisdictional Immunities of the State (Germany v. Italy: Greece intervening), Judgment, I.C.J. Reports 2012, p. 99 (February 3, 2012).
Lambert v. California, 355 U.S. 225 (1957).
Military Prosecutor v. Melinki, 17 P.M. (1958–59) 90, 213–14 Military Court 3/57 (Israel).
Military Tribunal No. II, "Transcript of the Opinion and Judgment" (1948). Trial 9 – Einsatzgruppen Case. 4. https://digitalcommons.law.uga.edu/nmt9/4.
Perez v. Brownell, 356 U.S. 44 (1958).
Prosecutor v. Furundžija Trial Judgment, Case No. IT-95-17/1-T, December 10, 1998.
Prosecutor v. Jelisić, Case No. IT-95-10-T, Judgment (December 14, 1999).
Prosecutor v. Kayishema and Ruzindana, Case No. ICTR-95-1-T, Judgment.
Prosecutor v. Nikolić, Case No. IT-94-2-AR73, Interlocutory Appeal Concerning Legality of Arrest (June 5, 2003).
Prosecutor v. Tadić, Case No. IT-94-1-A, Judgment (ICTY, July 15, 1999).
R. v. Bow Street Metropolitan Stipendiary Magistrate and Others, ex parte Pinochet Ugarte, March 24, 1999, [1999] All ER 97, HL.
Ratzlaf v. United States, 510 U.S. 135 (1994).
Reservations to the Convention on Genocide, Advisory Opinion: I.C.J. Reports 1951, p. 15.
S.S. Lotus (Fr. v. Turk.), 1927 P.C.I.J. (ser. A) No. 10 (September 7).
"Text of the Indictment against Eichmann," *American Jewish Yearbook* 63 (1962): 120–31.

The Trial of German Major War Criminals by the International Military Tribunal Sitting at Nuremberg, Germany, November 21, 1945 (1946).
Trop v. Dulles, 356 U.S. 86 (1958).
United States v. Alvarez-Machain, 504 U.S. 655 (1992).
United States v. Jewell, 532 F.2d 697 (9th Cir. 1976).
Vasiliauskas v. Lithuania, App. No. 35343/05, 2015 Eur. Ct. H.R. (October 20, 2015).

## Other Official Sources

Ban Ki-Moon, *Implementing the Responsibility to Protect: Report of the Secretary-General*, 12 January, 2009, UNGA A/63/677, § 11.
Beschluß des Großdeutsches Reichstags vom 26. April 1942, *Reichsgesetzblat.* I 1942, p. 248. https://alex.onb.ac.at/cgi-content/alex?aid=dra&datum=1942&page=349&size=45.
Convention on the Prevention and Punishment of the Crime of Genocide, December 9, 1948, 78 U.N.T.S. 277.
Declaration on Principles of International Law concerning Friendly Relations and Co-operation among States, UNGA Res. 2625, A/RES/2625(XXV).
Determination of the Secretary of State on Atrocities in Xinjiang, U.S. Department of State, January 19, 2021. https://2017–2021.state.gov/determination-of-the-secretary-of-state-on-atrocities-in-xinjiang/ [https://perma.cc/8YMN-MNFH].
Gesetz zur Änderung der Strafgesetzbuchs vom 28. Juni 1935, *Reichsgesetzblatt* I, 839.
Hitler, Reichstag speech of April 26, 1942. www.jewishvirtuallibrary.org/adolf-hitler-speech-to-the-reichstag-assuming-new-power-april-1942.
*Immunity of State officials from foreign criminal jurisdiction*, Annual Report of the International Law Commission, 69th Session, UN Doc. A/72/10 (2017), art. 7, 175. https://legal.un.org/ilc/reports/2017/ [https://perma.cc/9X88-YB5H].
International Convention on Civil and Political Rights, 999 UNTS 171 (entered into force March 23, 1976).
Montevideo Convention on the Rights and Duties of States (1933), 49 LNTS 356.
Nazi and Nazi Collaborators (Punishment) Law, 5710–1950. www.mfa.gov.il/mfa/mfa-archive/1950–1959/pages/nazis%20and%20nazi%20collaborators%20-punishment-%20law-%20571.aspx.
Office of United States Chief of Counsel for Prosecution of Axis Criminality. *Nazi Conspiracy and Aggression*, volume 1. Washington, DC: U.S. Government Printing Office, 1946. https://tile.loc.gov/storage-services/service/ll/llmlp/2011525363_NT_Nazi_Vol-I/2011525363_NT_Nazi_Vol-I.pdf.
Peace Treaty between the Holy Roman Emperor and the King of France and their respective Allies (the Treaty of Münster) (1648). https://avalon.law.yale.edu/17th_century/westphal.asp.

Resignation letter of Hagan Scotten, Assistant United States Attorney, February 14, 2025. www.documentcloud.org/documents/25536245-hagan-scotten-resignation-letter/.

*The Responsibility to Protect: Report of the International Commission on Intervention and State Sovereignty* (ICISS) (December 2001). https://idl-bnc-idrc.dspacedirect.org/bitstream/handle/10625/18432/IDL-18432.pdf?sequence=6&isAllowed=y.

Thierack, Otto. *Richterbriefe* [Judges' Letters] Communications of the Reich Minister of Justice, Issue No. 1, October 1, 1942. In 3 *Trials of War Criminals before the Nuernberg Military Tribunals under Control Council Law No. 10*. Washington: US Government Printing Office, 1951.

UN General Assembly Resolution 95(I), *Affirmation of the Principles of International Law Recognized by the Charter of the Nürnberg Tribunal*, A/RES/95(I) (December 11, 1946).

UN General Assembly Resolution 177, *Formulation of the Principles Recognized in the Charter of the Nürnberg Tribunal and in the Judgment of the Tribunal*, A/RES/177(II) (November 21, 1947). https://undocs.org/en/A/RES/177(II). The principles were codified in 1950. Int'l Law Commission, Principles of International Law Recognized in the Charter of the Nürnberg Tribunal and in the judgment of the Tribunal (1950/2005).

UN General Assembly Resolution 3314, 28th Sess, Supp No 31, vol I, at 142, UN Doc A/9631 (1974).

"We Call for Investigations into the 'Bill & Melinda Gates Foundation' for Medical Malpractice and Crimes against Humanity." Petition, April 10, 2020. https://web.archive.org/web/20231129184504/https://petitions.trumpwhitehouse.archives.gov/petition/we-call-investigations-bill-melinda-gates-foundation-medical-malpractice-crimes-against-humanity.

# Index

Printed by Integrated Books International,
United States of America